The mission believes that one of the prime objectives of a development program should be to bring about a better distribution of income and that this can be achieved by appropriate agricultural policies, together with special efforts in the fields of education, health, housing, and environmental sanitation. The report therefore suggests that, while manufacturing is likely to contribute more to the development of the country than agriculture, the Government must assume even greater responsibilities in the agricultural field than in manufacturing, because of the special problems that agriculture poses, particularly in connection with low-income farmers.

The mission finds that Venezuela's "economic overheads"—transport, electric power and telecommunications—are relatively advanced, although the mission does make recommendations for further progress in these areas.

The mission consisted of twelve members, representing seven different nationalities, and included economists and advisers on industry, agriculture, transport and public utilities, education, public health, housing and urban development. The mission was led by Henry R. Labouisse, former director of the U.N. Relief and Works Agency for Palestine Refugees and now head of the International Cooperation Administration of the United States Government.

THE ECONOMIC DEVELOPMENT OF *Venezuela*

*Report of a Mission Organized by the
International Bank for Reconstruction and Development
at the Request of
the Government of Venezuela*

THE
ECONOMIC
DEVELOPMENT
OF *Venezuela*

PUBLISHED FOR

The International Bank for Reconstruction and Development
BY The Johns Hopkins Press, Baltimore

Henry R. Labouisse,	Chief of Mission
Gerald Alter,	Deputy Chief and Chief Economist
Juan Allwood-Paredes,	Adviser on Public Health
R. H. Baldock,	Adviser on Transportation
Bruce M. Cheek,	Economist
Athanasios Hadjopoulos,	Adviser on Housing and Urban Development
W. J. Jenkins,	Adviser on Industry
Pablo Roca,	Adviser on Education
Robert Sadove,	Economist, Transport and Public Utilities
Shigeharu Takahashi,	Agricultural Economist
G. J. A. Terra,	Adviser on Agricultural Production
Wybold van Warmelo,	Industrial Economist
C. A. Doxiadis,	Consultant on Housing and Urban Development
H. David Davis,	Editor

This is the report of an economic survey mission to Venezuela, which was organized by the International Bank for Reconstruction and Development at the request of the Venezuelan Government. The task which the mission was asked to undertake was set forth as follows in an exchange of letters between the Government and the Bank:

"The primary purpose of the mission would be to make recommendations for a long-term development program with particular reference to public investment. The mission would have the following terms of reference:

a) to examine key sectors and to appraise sources of strength and weakness in the Venezuelan economy;
b) to assess prospective financial resources and financial needs; and
c) in the light of (a) and (b), to recommend investment priorities and development policies and to provide the basis for preparing a well coordinated investment program for a 4- to 5-year period and a plan for financing its execution."

The mission consisted of twelve members representing seven different nationalities. Five members were provided from the staff of the Bank. The United Nations and its Specialized Agencies assisted in the recruitment of other members of the mission. Specialists in public health and education were nominated by the World Health Organization (WHO) and the United Nations Educational, Scientific and Cultural Organization (UNESCO). The International Labour Office (ILO) made available to the mission an industrial economist.

There were two preliminary visits to Venezuela by members of the Bank staff during 1959 to arrange for the preparatory work. The entire mission arrived in Venezuela in September 1959 and remained there until December. After leaving Venezuela, the mission reassembled in January 1960 at the Bank's headquarters in Washington to prepare its report.

While in Venezuela, the mission members traveled extensively throughout the country, visited all the important development projects and had many discussions with ministers and officials of national, state and local governments, with the various autonomous public

vii

agencies, with private bankers, businessmen, farmers and technicians and with representatives of international agencies stationed in Venezuela. During the preparation of the report, the mission was also in frequent contact and consultation with officials of the Venezuelan Government. The mission wishes to express its appreciation for the cooperation extended to it by all of those above mentioned, and it wishes particularly to acknowledge the assistance of the Director and Staff of the Central Office of Coordination and Planning.

Throughout the period of the mission's work, the Venezuelan Government was itself drawing up a four-year development program, covering the years 1960/61 to 1963/64, under the general supervision of the Central Office of Coordination and Planning. In consequence, the mission was called upon to comment on many proposals under consideration by the Government for inclusion in its own four-year program. This proved to be a great advantage to the mission in drawing up its report. In several fields the mission's recommendations are based on an appraisal of the proposals which were under consideration by the Venezuelan Government; in all cases the mission took into consideration, to the extent that they were known, the alternative lines of policy which the Venezuelan officials themselves had under review.

It should be noted here, however, that, while many of the mission's recommendations were discussed with government officials either during the mission's stay in Venezuela or while the report was being drafted, the responsibility for its recommendations rests with the mission alone. Certain of them will be at variance with views expressed or held by government officials, and may well be subject to modification in the light of additional information or of special policy objectives. However, the mission believes that, in line with its terms of reference and on the basis of the data and information available to it, the conclusions and recommendations set forth in the report establish a reasonable framework for the achievement of the general objectives which are outlined in Chapter 2.

The report is divided into three parts. The first part, the general report, sets out the mission's recommendations in general terms and summarizes the mission's recommendations with respect to each of the important sectors of the economy. The second part of the report attempts an analysis of the Venezuelan economy, both in terms of its strengths and weaknesses as demonstrated in the immediate past and in terms of the outlook for petroleum, the most significant sector, in the immediate future. The third part of the report then goes into more detail on each of the sectors individually, dealing with the mission's analysis of the current status of each sector, together with the mission's proposals for development expenditures within each sector and related policy recommendations designed to maximize the effectiveness of such expenditures. The fourth part consists of a series of annexes which contain supplementary information not included in the main body of the report. Finally, a number of statistical tables of general interest are included in an appendix.

In transmitting the report to the Government of Venezuela, the President of the Bank noted that, since the Executive Directors and management customarily do not review the recommendations of missions in detail, the report as transmitted represented the views of the mission rather than positive recommendations of the Bank. The letter of transmittal added, however, that the Bank believed that the findings of the report deserved the most careful consideration and discussion. Similarly, while other international agencies were given an opportunity to comment on the portions of the report of particular interest to them, responsibility for the recommendations of the report, as noted above, is to be regarded as that of the mission alone.

CONTENTS

The Mission v

Preface vii

PART I. THE GENERAL REPORT

1. An Introduction to Venezuela 3
   The Country and the People 3
   The Economy 4
   Political History 6
   The Problems of Transition 8
   The Distribution of Governmental Powers 9
   The Future 10

2. The Development Task 11
   Objectives 11
   The Role of Government 14
   A Word of Caution—Inadequacy of Statistics 16

3. Growth Targets and General Economic Policies 18
   Relation of Long-Term Petroleum Outlook to
      Development Program 18
   Gradual Reduction of Dependence on Petroleum 20
   Government Petroleum Policies 21
   Economic Growth in the Next Four Years............... 26
   Creation of Employment Opportunities and
      Immigration Policy 29
   Protection of Domestic Industry and Agriculture 30
   Development of Mining 32
   Financial Policies in the Transition Period 34

4. A Four-Year Development Program and Its Financing 37
   Financing the Development Program 37
   Program of Investment and Other Selected Development
      Expenditures 41

5. Summary of Sector Programs 47
   Basic Economic Overheads 47
   Roads 47

Railways 49
Ports and Water Transport 49
Airports and Air Transport 50
Electric Power 51
Telecommunications 52
Commodity-Producing Sectors 54
Low-Income Farmers 56
Irrigation 57
Credit 57
Government Business Enterprises 58
Industrial Development Areas 61
Education, Health and Social Services 63
χ Education 63
Environmental Sanitation 65
Housing 66
Hospitals and Health Centers 67
Urban Planning 68

6. Possible Adjustments to the Program 70
The More Favorable Assumption 70
The Less Favorable Assumption 72
The Case of a Substantial Decline 73

PART II. AN ANALYSIS OF THE VENEZUELAN ECONOMY

7. Strengths and Weaknesses 81
Economic Growth in the 1950's 82
The Increase in Production and Incomes 82
The Volume and Composition of Investment 84
The Supply and Source of Savings 86
The Growth and Composition of the Work Force 91
Industrial and Agricultural Production 92
Other Sectors of the Economy 98
Foreign Trade and the Pattern of Domestic Demand 101
Financial Aspects of the Growth Process in the 1950's 103
Balance of Payments and Current Financial Problems 105
Money and Banking 107
Bank Credit and Economic Development 109
Government Finance 110
Distribution of the Benefits of Economic Progress 112

8. The Outlook for Petroleum 115
The World Demand for Oil 115
World Oil Supplies 116

Likely Trends in Oil Prices 120
Venezuela's Position in the World Oil Market 125
Difficulties Facing the Venezuelan Oil Industry 127
Factors Favorable to Venezuela 131
Prospects for Increasing Production 134

PART III. THE SECTOR REPORTS

✗ 9. Agriculture 139
    The Present Situation 139
        Land Resources and Current Use 139
        Farm Size and Income Characteristics 141
        Land Tenure 142
        Prices and Output 143
        Recent Tendencies ...:.............................. 143
        The Dual Nature of the Agricultural Problem 145
    The Low-Income Farmer 146
        The Determinants of Policy 146
        Resettlement of a Capital-Intensive Type 148
        Spontaneous Resettlement 150
        A Proposed Resettlement Program with Emphasis
            on Land 151
        Increasing Productivity Without Relocation 154
        Extension Services for the Small Farmer 156
        Agricultural Credit and Subsidies 157
    Increasing Production on Commercial Farms 159
        Technical Research 159
        Agricultural Extension 161
        Fertilizers 163
        Control of Weeds, Pests and Diseases 164
        Mechanization 165
        Production Credit 166
        Government Activities in the Product Market 170
        Marketing, Processing, Storage and Distribution 176
        Access Roads 178
    Irrigation and Drainage 179
        The Guarico Project 182
        The Majaguas Project 186
        The Bocono-Masparro-Tucupido Project 187
        Small Irrigation Projects 188
        Drainage of the Area South of Lake Maracaibo (Zulia) 188
        Other Drainage 189
        Policy and Expenditures 190
    Summary of Proposed Expenditures 192

10. **Manufacturing** 194
   Present Industrial Conditions 194
      The Record of Recent Growth 194
      Raw Materials as a Cost Factor 198
      Wages, Productivity and Costs 199
      Comparative Levels of Manufacturing Costs 204
   The Protective System 204
      The Encouragement of Domestic Industry 204
      Industrial Promotion Policy 207
      Categories of Industries to be Promoted 209
      The Latin American Common Market 212
   Availability of Capital 213
      Capital for Private Enterprise 213
      Government Financial Support 215
      CVF Industrial Credits 217
      Small Industry Credit Program 218
      Industrial Estates 219
      Foreign Capital 220
      The Income Tax Law 220
   Government Industrial Enterprises 221
      Iron and Steel Plant 221
      The Petrochemical Project 226
      The Chemical Plants 227
      The Refinery 231
      The Gas Pipelines 231
      Dry Dock and Shipyard 232
      Sugar Industry 234
      Salt Industry 234
      The Role of Government Enterprise 235
   Developing an Industrial Labor Force 235
      Apprenticeship Training 236
      A National Productivity Program 237
      Selected Immigration 238
      A National Wage Advisory Board 239
   Administrative Implications 240
      The Role of the Ministry of Development and the CVF ... 240
      Regional Field Offices 242
   Summary of Proposed Expenditures 242

11. **Transport** 244
   Roads 246
      Past Benefits 246
      Establishment of Priorities 247
      The 1960/61-1963/64 Road Program 250
      Construction Costs 253

Relating Road Design to Traffic Levels 254
Highway Maintenance 256
Highway Reconstruction 257
Major Bridge Program 260
Road Transport Organization and Regulation 260
Financing Highway Improvement 261
Railroads 262
Past Performance and Present Situation 262
The Proposed National Railroad Network 264
The Naricual-Matanzas Railroad 265
Civil Aviation 267
Airports 267
Air Transport 269
Water Transport 271
Present Limitations 271
Past Port Investment and Current Capacity 272
Future Port Investment 274
Port Administration 278
Coastal Shipping and Waterways 279
Summary of Mission's Proposed Expenditures 279

12. **Electric Power** 281
The Existing Electric Supply Industry 282
The Extent of Electrification 283
The Growth of the Electric Supply Industry 283
Adequacy of Existing Generating Capacity 284
Potential Shortage Areas 286
Caroni-Macagua Hydro Power 287
Caroni-Guri Project 289
Implications for Caroni-Guri of Future Market Trends 290
Frequency Conversion and the Caroni-Guri Project 293
Tentative Evaluation of Caroni-Guri Project 293
Investment Priorities 294
Government Regulation 299

13. **Telecommunications** 301
Urban Telephone Facilities 302
Past Growth 302
The Financial Problem 304
Utilization of Equipment and Cable Plant 305
Traffic Density and Rate Structure 306
Relief of Congestion in the Caracas Area 307
Telephones in the Rest of the Country 309
Long-Distance Telecommunications 313
Present Difficulties 313
Future Plans 314

Organization and Personnel 317
Summary of Mission's Proposed Expenditures 319

14. Education 320
Primary Education 322
Future Enrollment 322
Buildings and Equipment 325
School Books 328
Supply of Primary School Teachers 329
Rural Schools 331
Intermediate Education 332
Distribution Between Types 332
Industrial Schools 335
Commercial Schools 340
Academic Secondary Schools 344
Higher Education 349
Special Educational Programs 353
Agriculture 353
Handicrafts and Industry 355
Summary of Mission's Proposed Expenditures 356

15. Housing and Urban Planning 358
A Long-Term Policy and Program 358
Housing 360
Present Housing Conditions 360
Housing Construction and Role of Public Sector 363
Housing Targets 366
Role of Government Credit 367
Rural Housing 369
Urban Housing for Low-Income Groups 370
Summary of Proposed Capital Expenditures 374
Urban Planning and Municipal Public Works 375
Regional and Town Planning 375
Caracas Transport 377
National and Local Financial Arrangements 379

16. Health and Environmental Sanitation 380
Health 380
Present Health Conditions 380
Doctors 383
Nurses 386
Technical Auxiliary Personnel 387
The Organization of Health Services 387
Health Service Installations 389
Environmental Sanitation 394
Water Supply and Treatment Plants and Wells 397

Piped Water Distribution Networks 399
Sewage and Disposal Systems and Latrines 399
Administrative and Rate Policies 401
Summary of Proposed Capital Expenditures 403

ANNEXES

    I Economic Projections 407
   II Major Agricultural Commodities 415
  III Livestock Policies 424
   IV The Dairy Industry 428
    V Aspects of Regional Development in Agriculture 432
   VI Forestry 441
  VII Fisheries 444
 VIII Methods of Calculating Benefit-Cost Ratios in
        Highway Construction 446
   IX Evaluation of Proposed Railroad Development 452
    X Cost of Shipping Commodities from Matanzas to
        Other Parts of Venezuela 457

STATISTICAL TABLES

S. 1 Gross Domestic Product at 1957 Market Prices 463
S. 2 Contribution of the Oil Sector to the Gross
        National Product 464
S. 3 Venezuela's Terms of Trade, 1950-1959 464
S. 4 Profits, Investment and Taxes of Oil Industry, 1943-59 ... 465
S. 5 Real Income Growth, 1950-59 466
S. 6 Gross National Product by Major Expenditure
        Components 467
S. 7 Gross Fixed Investment by Sector 469
S. 8 Sources of Financing Investment, 1950 & 1955-59 471
S. 9 Government Revenues 1956/57-1959/60 472
S. 10 Emigration and Immigration 473
S. 11 Estimated Distribution of Work Force 474
S. 12 Mineral Production by Volume 475
S. 13 Production and Import of Selected Agricultural
        Products, 1950 and 1959 475
S. 14 The Balance of Payments, 1950-1959 476
S. 15 Price Movements in Venezuelan & Major Trading
        Partners 478
S. 16 Net Official Gold and Foreign Exchange Reserves 478
S. 17 Liquidity of the Private Sector 479

S. 18 Treasury Receipts, Expenditures & Balances,
1949/50-1959/60 479

S. 19 National Income & Product 480

S. 20 Functional Distribution of Government Expenditures
as Percentage of Total Appropriations, 1954/55-
1959/60 481

S. 21 Measures of the Importance of Petroleum in the
Venezuelan Economy, 1921-1959 482

S. 22 Comparable Earnings of Selected Occupations in
Venezuela and United States Manufacturing Industry .. 483

Index 485

MAPS

facing page

Venezuela iv
Population 6
Petroleum 10
Irrigation 182
Road Traffic Flow 248
Transportation—Western Venezuela 254
Transportation—Eastern Venezuela 254
Electric Power 284
Types of Terrain 440
Rainfall and Topography 440

NOTE: *The maps contained in this report are for illustrative purposes
only and do not imply any legal endorsement on the part of
the mission or the International Bank.*

PART **I** *THE GENERAL REPORT*

CHAPTER 1 *AN INTRODUCTION TO VENEZUELA*

The Country and the People

Venezuela is a country of contrasts. Lying entirely within the tropics, it has both torrid swamps in the Orinoco delta and snow-capped peaks in the Andes rising more than 16,000 feet. Caracas, its capital city, is overcrowded and some other sections of the north and northwest are heavily settled, while about one-half of the national territory, south and east of the great Orinoco River, is largely unexplored and practically uninhabited. Venezuela has a cultured, cosmopolitan society and it can boast of one of the oldest universities in the Western Hemisphere—and yet more than one-third of its citizens are illiterate. It has skyscrapers, superhighways and ultra-modern factories, stores, hotels, hospitals and residential buildings—but it also has innumerable *ranchos,* the temporary shacks which blight its cities and house a very high proportion of the people. The rapid growth of the oil industry has been the basic factor in modern Venezuela's development, yet relatively few people earn their living directly from petroleum exploitation. While Venezuela has an average annual real income level of some US$600 per person,[1] it is estimated that almost half the population lives close to subsistence levels in sharp contrast to the prosperous upper tenth of the nation. Over 25 short years, Venezuela has become this paradox: one of the world's most prosperous "less developed" countries.

Standing on the northern coast of South America, bounded by Colombia, Brazil and British Guiana, Venezuela is strategically situated along the Caribbean Sea and the Atlantic Ocean astride the major sea and air routes linking the northern, central and southern portions of the hemisphere. Its national boundaries enclose a territory of 350,000 square miles, larger than the United Kingdom, France, The Netherlands, Belgium, Luxembourg and Switzerland combined. It is divided into four distinct geographic regions: the Andes Highlands and adjacent coastal areas, stretching from San Cristobal in the southwest on a long arc to the Paria peninsula in the northeast; the Maracaibo basin, composed of hot, humid lowlands bordering Lake Maracaibo; the *llanos,* gently sloping plains, flatlands and valleys, sometimes parched

---

[1] Nominally, GNP is close to US$1,000 per capita, but this must be discounted to take into account Venezuela's higher price level.

and sometimes flooded, extending from the Andes to the Orinoco River in the south and east; and the Guayana Highlands south and east of the Orinoco, a vast area of high plateaus and rolling plains.

With a population of over seven million people, Venezuela is one of the least densely populated countries of the hemisphere—about 17 persons per square mile. Four-fifths of the population is concentrated in the northwest quarter of the country: generally speaking, in the Andes between San Cristobal and Caracas and in the Maracaibo basin (see map facing page 6) . The racial composition of the population is about 65 percent mestizo, 20 percent white, 8 percent Negro and 7 percent Indian. To the outside observer, Venezuela seems to be a society with no great friction between racial groups.

The population is growing rapidly. It rose from 2.4 million in 1900 to 3.8 million in 1941 and just over 5.0 million at the time of the last census in 1950. During the 1940's the rate of population growth was approximately 3 percent a year, but the rate of increase during the 1950's may have exceeded 4 percent a year. The death rate has been reduced by almost one-half in the last 15 years and had fallen to 10 per 1,000 by 1956. The birth rate has remained high (e.g., 47 per 1,000 in 1956) , although there is evidence of a declining rate of increase thereafter. Immigration was also substantial, at least until 1958. While the reported birth and death rates are both open to question, Venezuela's population is estimated to have reached 7.2 million by the end of 1959.

The urban population of Venezuela has been growing at even a more rapid rate than the population as a whole. The largest growth has been in Caracas and its immediate surroundings, where the population has risen from 700,000 in 1950 to possibly more than 1,200,000 in 1960. People living in localities with 2,500 inhabitants or more represented about 70 percent of the total population in 1959, compared with about 50 percent in 1950. Consequently, some 30 percent of the population is thought to be living on farms or in small rural settlements.

The Economy

For over 400 years, the people of Venezuela lived by raising cattle, by producing subsistence crops and by exporting gold, coffee and cocoa. This pattern continued well into the 20th century—until the dawn of the petroleum era in the 1920's, which set the stage for modern Venezuela. Then followed the gradual shift from farms to cities and an increase in the proportion of the population finding employment in factory and service industries. Even so, the standard of living of the great mass of the people remains very low—particularly in the rural areas. Lacking both property and education, it is difficult for the under privileged to improve their conditions of life. The social and political strain of poverty has been accentuated by the rapid growth in population, particularly during the 1950's. However, an urban middle class has been developing rapidly in the past decade.

About 3 percent of Venezuela's national territory is used for cropping agriculture and a further 20 percent for cattle raising. The principal crops include coffee, cotton, sugar, cocoa, rice, tobacco, root vegetables and corn. Much of the agricultural land is found in the valleys of the Andes and on the southern Andean slopes at the edge of the llanos. The llanos themselves provide a vast area for cattle grazing while the southern portion of the Maracaibo basin is becoming a center for dairying. Much of the farm land of Venezuela is necessarily plagued with the problems which beset all tropical areas—weedy growth, erosion and leaching of the soil, and lack of long daylight growing periods for annual crops. In addition, the low levels of technical knowledge have resulted in relatively poor use of the country's soil resources. Nevertheless, there are large areas of fertile land which could profitably be brought under cultivation, given appropriate technical and financial assistance.

Mineral exploration and exploitation have been dominated by the development of oil and iron ore resources. The Maracaibo basin, as a whole, is now the focus of the oil industry, including the large proven reserves found under Lake Maracaibo itself (see map facing page 10). In addition, the northeast region of Venezuela contains several less prolific oil deposits. Important iron ore deposits have been found south of the Orinoco, in the hinterland of Puerto Ordaz. There is also some mining for diamonds, gold, nickel, manganese, asbestos, salt and coal; but the scale of activity in the latter fields is so small that there is no significant contribution to national product or exports. Actually, there is little knowledge of the extent of these mineral resources or of such other possibilities as bauxite. Neither the Government nor private interests has made any great effort as yet to explore and assess the resources of the country systematically, despite indications of the existence of large mineral wealth.

The modern industrial development of Venezuela is taking place primarily in the vicinity of Caracas and along the northern mountainous and coastal strip, although efforts are now being made to attract industry to other areas of the country, particularly to the region of the Guayanas. Commerce and service industries are also centered in the Caracas area.

The people of Venezuela have so far sought to harness their resources largely through the efforts of private enterprise. At one extreme, this has been in the form of a subsistence agriculture which involves perhaps 20 percent of the population and which makes a contribution of some 3-4 percent to national product. At the other extreme are the petroleum and mining operations initiated by large foreign enterprises and which, while employing only 2 percent of the work force, contribute 20 percent of the national product and almost all the foreign exchange earnings accruing to Venezuela. In between, there lies the bulk of economic activity which is almost entirely in the hands of private Venezuelan businessmen engaged in commercial agriculture, manufactures, commerce and other services. The country is, then, one of predominantly private enterprise—more indigenous than foreign.

The absence of general import restrictions and of controls over prices and investment has fostered the growth of this private industry and trade. At the same time, however, the Government plays an important positive role in the economy in two principal ways. First, through tariffs and other protective devices, it makes possible and stimulates the growth of local industry and agriculture, despite the high level of wages and prices in Venezuela. Secondly, through its large revenues based mainly on taxes received from the oil industry, the Government is able to devote substantial resources to providing basic economic overheads, such as transport, power and telecommunications, and to fostering private business activity through public credit—without imposing high taxes on the rest of the economy. In addition, in the last few years, the Government has embarked on several state-owned industrial enterprises. In the adoption and execution of these various economic policies, the Government is inspired by the major objectives of diversifying the economy and thereby lessening the present high degree of dependence on the petroleum sector as the pace-setter for economic growth and the source of government revenues and export earnings.

Political History

Discovered by Columbus on his third voyage in 1498, Venezuela was one of the first colonies in the New World to revolt against Spain. The initial movement leading to independence took place in 1810, but it was not until 1821 that independence was achieved, under the leadership of Simon Bolivar, Venezuela's native son and national hero. Venezuela was a part of the Greater Colombian Federation until 1830, when it adopted a constitution of its own. Venezuela's independent existence

has been characterized by frequent periods of political instability, dictatorship and revolt. The nation's modern era began in 1935 after the death of Juan Vincente Gomez, who had exercised an autocratic, almost feudal rule for 27 years. Venezuela enjoyed brief periods of democracy between 1941 and 1948, but a popularly elected Democratic Action (*Accion Democratica*) Government of President Gallegos was overthrown in 1948. A military junta ruled until late 1952, when Marcos Perez Jimenez, the dominant member of the junta, was designated Provisional President by the Armed Forces.

After ten years of military dictatorship, the Armed Forces, with overwhelming popular support, on January 23, 1958, deposed the Perez Jimenez Government and formed a Junta of Government, composed of three military officers and two civilians, as the Provisional Government of Venezuela. The Junta promptly announced that its primary objective was to establish a lawful and honest democratic regime under which individual liberties would be guaranteed. In the first few hours of its existence the Provisional Government restored civil liberties, removed censorship, released political prisoners and invited exiles to return. It promised that it would transfer power to a constitutional government to be elected by the people of Venezuela by the end of 1958. In the ensuing period of transition to democracy, the established political parties, whose activities had been curtailed severely under the previous regime, were reactivated and new parties were formed. All political parties pledged their support to the Junta and entered into a truce designed to avoid bitter partisan strife that might have resulted in the reestablishment of dictatorship.

The Provisional Government convened free national, state and municipal elections on December 7, 1958, in an atmosphere of public order. Efforts of the political parties to agree on a single presidential candidate having broken down, the three major political parties nominated their own candidates. Admiral Larrazabal, who had been Provisional President in the Junta, resigned in mid-November to accept the candidacy of the Democratic Republican Union (URD), and shortly before the election accepted the candidacy of the Communist Party as well. The Christian Social Party (COPEI) nominated its top leader, Rafael Caldera, and the Democratic Action Party (AD) named Romulo Betancourt, who had been exiled when the AD Government was overthrown by the Armed Forces in 1948.

The elections were accomplished peacefully and honestly, with Romulo Betancourt winning a near majority (49 percent) of votes for the Presidency. The new Government was inaugurated for a five-year period in February 1959. In accordance with a pre-election agreement with the

other major political parties (but excluding the Communist Party) —
an agreement which also specified certain common policy approaches
—opposition party members and independents have been given repre-
sentation in the Cabinet and have been appointed to other key positions.[2]

The Problems of Transition

It is against this background that the current regime is attempting to
deal with the difficult economic and social problems discussed in subsequent paragraphs of this report; and it is trying to do so as a matter of
urgency, having in mind the human and social rehabilitation so long
overdue in the country. The Government came to power on a wave of
popular hope that all the deficiencies of the past would be corrected—
and quickly. At the same time, various political and social forces as yet
unenthusiastic—to say the least—toward the present form of government were waiting to see whether the promise of a better future would
actually be fulfilled.

In this atmosphere, the Government has felt itself obliged to initiate
programs which would be immediately striking in their effect and thus
would vividly demonstrate the break with the past. For example, in
order to cope with a growing unemployment problem, the Government
established the *Programa de Obras Extraordinarias* (POE), under
which many unemployed, unskilled workers were given jobs on emergency projects, mainly in road construction and maintenance; in many
cases, these jobs were of a "make work" character and, from a strictly
economic point of view, of low productivity, but it was probably a wise
policy to provide such jobs to bridge the inevitable transitional gap
before more soundly conceived programs for the longer term could be
devised and put into effect. In other sectors of the economy, other types
of "crash programs" have also been in operation. The Government recognizes that the time has now come for a more considered approach to
economic programing, for a period of consolidation under which long-
term needs, not only short-term effects, should be used as criteria for
guiding policy. While applauding this change in approach, we do not
underestimate the political and social pressures which militate
against it.

Another handicap to be overcome, and one to which we will have
occasion to refer throughout this report, is the deficiency in administra-

---

[2] Since the text of this report was prepared, the URD members of the Cabinet
withdrew from the Government in November 1960.

tive capacity. This deficiency is in part simply the result of relatively limited experience with an advanced economy and the concomitant lack of appropriate education. But it also is in part the result of the country's turbulent history. Democracy, government "by the people," is new, very new, in Venezuela. Many officials in the present administration were either in exile or forced retirement during the ten-year period of the Perez Jimenez dictatorship. With the return to constitutional government, there was naturally an initial period of adjustment during which there was a considerable shifting of senior assignments. The result has been a lack of continuity in the direction of the major agencies within the Government. Fortunately, some degree of administrative stability seems now to be established and, if it can be maintained, the appropriate experience will eventually be built up and so redound to the advantage of the entire economy.

The Distribution of Governmental Powers

The country is divided into 20 states, a federal district, 2 federal territories and federal dependencies which include 72 island possessions in the Caribbean Sea. The national government is composed of separate executive, legislative and judicial branches. The President and members of the Senate and Chamber of Deputies are elected by direct vote for terms of five years. Justices of the Federal Court, the Court of Cassation and other courts and tribunals are elected by the two houses of Congress. State Governors are appointed by the President and are considered agents of the national government. Each state has a Legislative Assembly, whose members are elected by popular vote. Municipal Councils are elected for each district of the states, for the Federal District and for the Federal Territories. The President and his Cabinet Ministers comprise the Council of Ministers.

Despite the federal principles underlying Venezuelan constitutional arrangements, power is very much centralized in the national government located in Caracas. The state and local entities have only limited tax revenues, receiving major portions of their budgets from the national government. Furthermore, the constituent ministries and agencies of the national government are overly centralized: their field offices and operations are heavily dependent on the national offices; they are often kept unaware of broader policy issues; they lack statistical information on their own activities and are often compelled to refer to Caracas for decision on the most minor problems. This over-centralization leads to a burdensome bureaucracy, a lack of flexibility, and therefore to a diminution in administrative efficiency. While this centralization arises in part from the structure of governmental organization, it is also in part the consequence of an attitude prevalent among most senior personnel—both in the government and private sector—regarding the Caracas area as the only place in which to live and work.

The Future

It is not easy to forecast the future of any country. It is particularly difficult to do so for Venezuela, with its tumultuous history, its many paradoxes and contradictions, and its economy based almost entirely on a single commodity. Nor is it the task of the mission to attempt such a forecast. However, there are certain observations we do wish to make.

Venezuela is a richly endowed country. Its geographical position and the variety of its internal geography lend it strength. Its great mineral wealth is already well known, and it may prove to be even greater than yet realized. It has large areas of fertile lands and forests not yet exploited—and some lands not even yet explored. The majestic Orinoco, with its tributaries, offers easy means of transport to Venezuelan and foreign ports and possibilities for opening up new territory. Its hydroelectric and thermal power potential is immense. But these natural assets would amount to little if Venezuela did not have the leadership and the dynamism necessary to put them to effective use.

In the final analysis, the human factor is the one that will determine the country's future. Venezuela has had its share of tribulations—many of its own making—and it is now facing a difficult period of transition. The ability of the country to pass through this period successfully and to build a stable and prosperous future will depend upon the ability and willingness of the Government and of the people to take, frankly and with courage, the measures—many of them discussed in the following chapters of this report—which are open to them to ensure economic growth and financial health. This of course will not be easy. But in her struggle to become a modern industrial nation and a true democracy, Venezuela has indeed enviable assets. She has exceptional resources and she belongs to a continent which, turbulent as it may have been, has so far been spared the storms of major conflicts. It has been said that "Venezuela's history is in the future." To a large extent, the Venezuelan people have this rarest of privileges—to hold their future in their own hands.

VENEZUELA

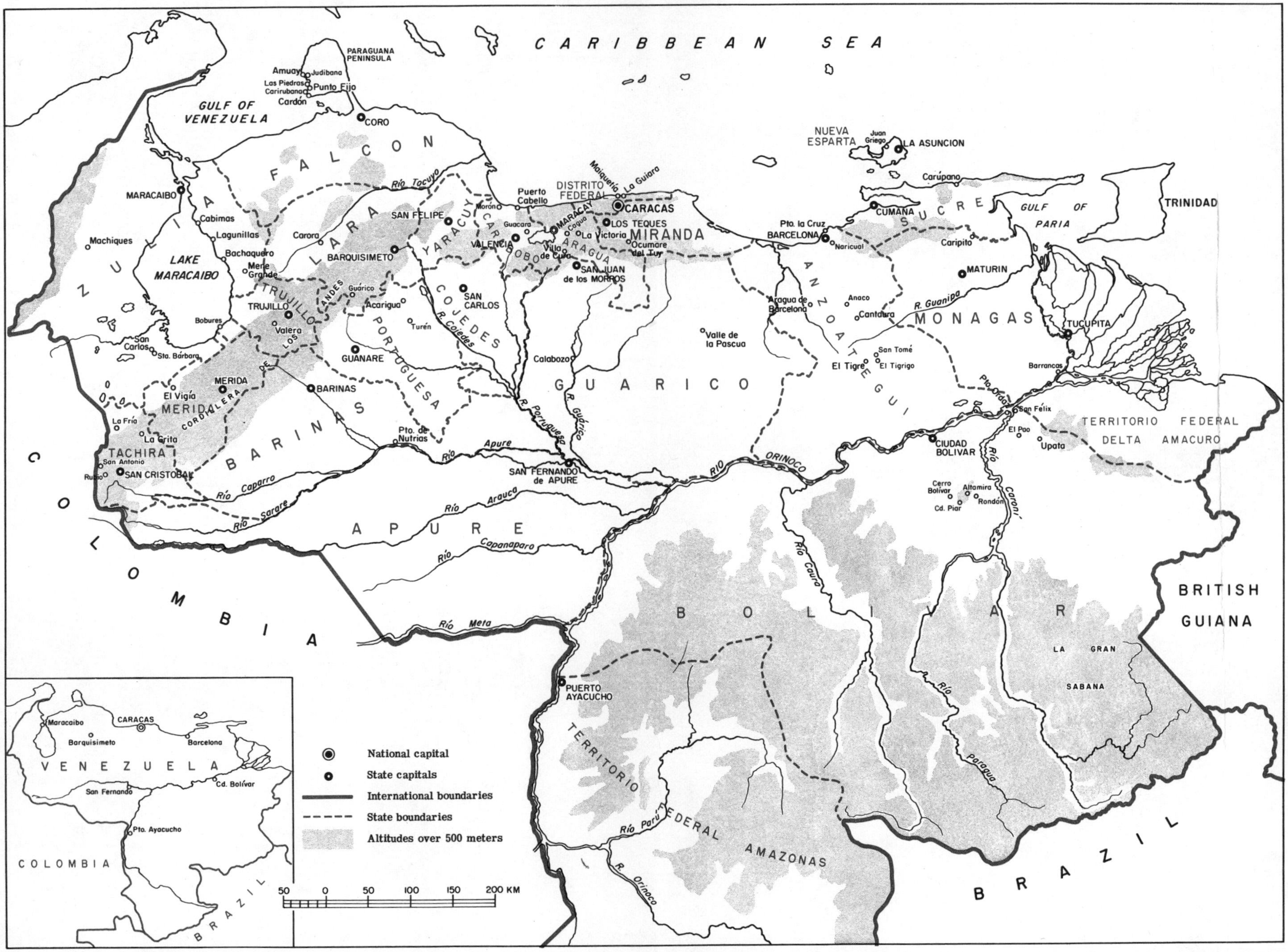
CARIBBEAN SEA
PARAGUANA PENINSULA
Amuay
Judibana
Las Piedras
Carirubana
Punto Fijo
Cardón
GULF OF VENEZUELA
CORO
FALCON
NUEVA ESPARTA
Juan Griego
LA ASUNCION
Carúpano
TRINIDAD
GULF OF PARIA
MARACAIBO
Cabimas
Lagunillas
Machiques
ZULIA
LAKE MARACAIBO
Bachaquero
Mene Grande
Bobures
San Carlos
Sta. Bárbara
Río Tocuyo
Carora
LARA
BARQUISIMETO
SAN FELIPE
YARACUY
Morón
Puerto Cabello
DISTRITO FEDERAL
Maiquetía
La Guiara
CARACAS
LOS TEQUES
MIRANDA
Guacara
MARACAY
Cagua
La Victoria
Ocumare del Tuy
VALENCIA
CARABOBO
ARAGUA
Villa de Cura
SAN JUAN de los MORROS
Pto. la Cruz
BARCELONA
Naricual
CUMANA
SUCRE
Caripito
MATURIN
MONAGAS
R. Guanipa
TUCUPITA
Barrancas
TRUJILLO
Guárico
Acarigua
Turén
ANDES
Valera
LOS
SAN CARLOS
COJEDES
R. Cojedes
PORTUGUESA
GUANARE
Calabozo
Valle de la Pascua
GUARICO
Aragua de Barcelona
Anaco
Cantaura
ANZOATEGUI
San Tomé
El Tigre
El Tigrito
MERIDA
El Vigía
CORDILLERA DE
BARINAS
La Fría
La Grita
TACHIRA
San Antonio
Rubio
SAN CRISTOBAL
Pto. de Nutrias
Río Apure
R. Portuguesa
R. Guárico
SAN FERNANDO de APURE
Río Caparro
Río Sarare
Río Arauca
APURE
Río Capanaparo
Río ORINOCO
Pto. Ordaz
San Félix
El Pao
Upata
CIUDAD BOLIVAR
TERRITORIO FEDERAL DELTA AMACURO
Cerro Bolívar
Cd. Piar
Altamira
Rondón
Río Caroní
Río Caura
BOLIVAR
BRITISH GUIANA
LA GRAN SABANA
Río Paragua
COLOMBIA
Río Meta
PUERTO AYACUCHO
TERRITORIO FEDERAL AMAZONAS
Río Parú
R. Orinoco
BRAZIL
Maracaibo
CARACAS
Barquisimeto
Barcelona
VENEZUELA
San Fernando
Cd. Bolívar
Pto. Ayacucho
COLOMBIA
BRAZIL
National capital
State capitals
International boundaries
State boundaries
Altitudes over 500 meters
50 0 50 100 150 200 KM

POPULATION

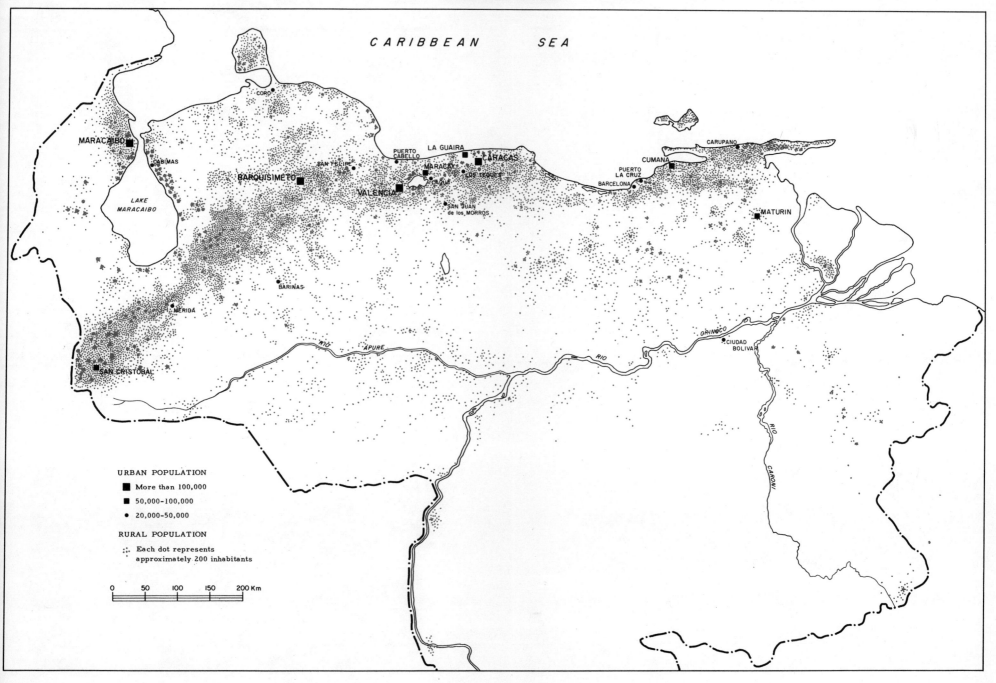

CARIBBEAN SEA

CORO

MARACAIBO

CABIMAS

LAKE
MARACAIBO

BARQUISIMETO

SAN FELIPE

PUERTO
CABELLO

LA GUAIRA

MARACAY

CARACAS

LOS TEQUES

VALENCIA

LA VICTORIA

PUERTO
LA CRUZ

BARCELONA

CUMANA

CARUPANO

SAN JUAN
de los MORROS

MATURIN

BARINAS

MERIDA

ORINOCO

CIUDAD
BOLIVAR

RIO APURE

RIO

SAN CRISTOBAL

RIO CARONI

URBAN POPULATION

■ More than 100,000

■ 50,000–100,000

● 20,000–50,000

RURAL POPULATION

∴ Each dot represents
approximately 200 inhabitants

0   50   100   150   200 Km

PETROLEUM

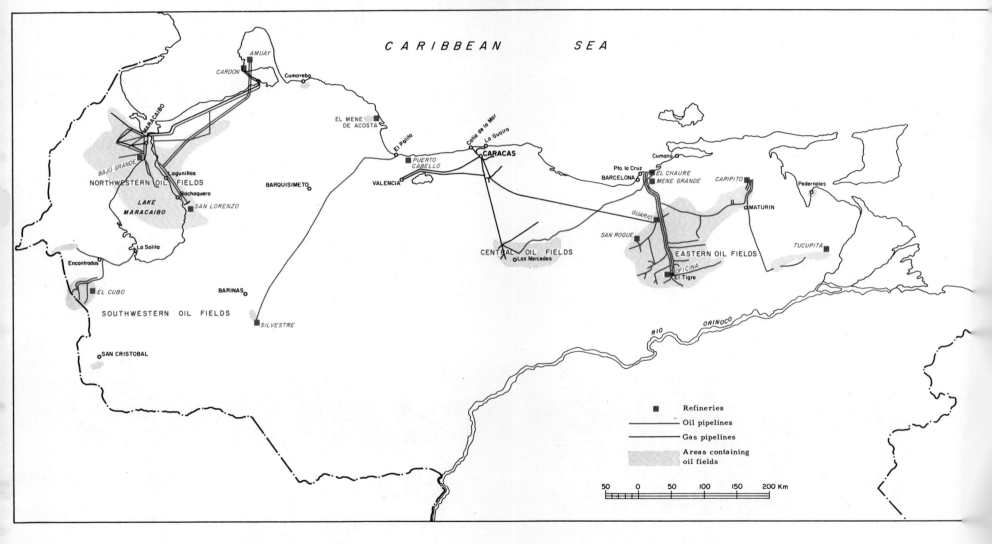

CARIBBEAN SEA

AMUAY
CARDON
Cumarebo
EL MENE DE ACOSTA
El Palito
Catia de la Mar
La Guaira
CARACAS
PUERTO CABELLO
VALENCIA
Cumana
Pto. la Cruz
BARCELONA
EL CHAURE
MENE GRANDE
CARIPITO
Pedernales
MARACAIBO
BAJO GRANDE
NORTHWESTERN OIL FIELDS
Lagunillas
Bachaquero
SAN LORENZO
MATURIN
LAKE MARACAIBO
GUARIO
SAN ROQUE
EASTERN OIL FIELDS
TUCUPITA
CENTRAL OIL FIELDS
Las Mercedes
OFICINA
El Tigre
La Solita
Encontrados
EL CUBO
BARINAS
SOUTHWESTERN OIL FIELDS
SILVESTRE
RIO
ORINOCO
SAN CRISTOBAL
BARQUISIMETO

■ Refineries
—— Oil pipelines
— Gas pipelines
░ Areas containing oil fields

50 0 50 100 150 200 Km

CHAPTER 2 *THE DEVELOPMENT TASK*

Objectives

The principal objectives of the Venezuelan Government in formulating a development program for the four-year period 1960/61-1963/64 are the same as those sought by most governments in their development plans—the building of a strong and broadly based economy, the steady improvement in the living standards of the people and the provision of more and better employment opportunities. The problems which confront the Venezuelan Government in this field, however, are rather different from those of many other countries striving for economic well-being.

For almost 25 years there has been sustained and rapid economic growth in Venezuela, based mainly on government receipts from the exploitation of the country's petroleum resources. Yet, the increases in national income have accrued in large measure to only a small section of the population. A very substantial part of the population still has an extremely low standard of living. With few exceptions, government policy in the past has not been directed to significant modification of the forces leading to the uneven income distribution. The present government is greatly concerned over this situation, but a concerted effort to increase income and to distribute it more evenly has been made more difficult by the check in the growth of the petroleum sector which has occurred since 1957. Indeed, the absence of a substantial growth in oil exports and the decline in total government revenues have already posed severe problems of adjustment for the democratic government installed in 1959. Moreover, these problems have been complicated by the flight of capital abroad, the payment of debts incurred by the previous regime and the necessity to increase expenditures on long overdue social services.

Under these conditions, Venezuela faced in 1960 the need to adopt measures which would not only help sustain the process of economic development, but would also broaden the economic base of the country and diffuse the fruits of economic progress more equitably across the country and between income groups. Through development programs beginning in 1960, the Government is attempting to achieve these basic

11

objectives while at the same time adjusting to a less favorable trading position than that enjoyed in the 1950's.

If the aspirations of the people for greater material welfare and a generally more rewarding life are to be met, and if Venezuela's major problem of relatively low living standards for the great mass of the people is to be progressively resolved, it will be necessary for economic growth to continue at a rate well above the rate of increase in population and labor force. Economic growth substantially in excess of population growth (over 3 percent a year) is unlikely to take place in the next decade unless the petroleum industry in Venezuela remains in a healthy state and thereby continues to contribute very substantial revenues to the Government. One important objective of the development program must therefore be to maintain for Venezuela a strong position in the world oil markets. Despite the considerable uncertainty prevailing as to Venezuela's competitive position, particularly in view of the recently developing sources of petroleum in other parts of the world, it would appear that means are available to the Government and to the oil companies to foster a continuing expansion of output and of government revenues therefrom.

The continued growth of petroleum, at a moderate, even though somewhat slower, rate than in the past ten years, would be a source of considerable strength to the economy in the years ahead—permitting, if not ensuring, the expansion of the Venezuelan economy at an annual rate approaching 5-6 percent. Over the longer term, however, a major objective must be to enable Venezuela to reduce its dependence on petroleum for continued growth. The principal reason for the Government adopting this objective is that petroleum is a nonreproducible natural resource whose exhaustion must be anticipated. In the mission's opinion, a more compelling reason is the fact that alternative low-cost sources of petroleum supply are being developed at a very rapid rate in other parts of the world. There is also the possibility of the development of low-cost alternative sources of energy. Over the long term, these factors might make it difficult to expand Venezuelan petroleum output or, more important, make it difficult for the Venezuelan economy to enjoy larger returns from the industry. In the face of these risks, Venezuela seeks economic diversification even, if necessary, at some cost in terms of current income.

We find that the economic policies and government investment programs in Venezuela which can achieve economic diversification effectively over the longer run are fortunately consistent for the most part with those which will contribute most to income over the medium term.

Most recommendations contained in this report do not require the balancing of probable sacrifices in the near-term against possible long-term gains. The situation would be changed if Venezuela's income from petroleum were expected to decline to a much lower level within the next decade—then many more difficult decisions involving balancing of this type would be required.

If such a pessimistic outlook for Venezuelan petroleum were accepted, the state would be forced to adopt economic policies or programs which would leave little hope for early attainment of the objective of a wider distribution of the benefits of economic expansion. Not only would the rate of economic growth be severely retarded but it would be difficult for the state to continue to allocate adequate sums to education, housing, health and community facilities.

Even if petroleum income continues at a high level, care must be taken in the selection and design of programs geared to distribute more widely the fruits of economic progress. Otherwise, the Government will run the risk of adopting programs which may not foster the rapid growth of the economy in the years immediately ahead and which may prejudice the attainment of the longer-term goal of making the country less dependent upon petroleum. Psychological and human factors will make the selection and design of appropriate programs difficult, for there are strong pressures for governmental action to hasten the process of better income distribution and, in particular, to create more job opportunities to absorb a substantial number of underemployed and unemployed. After many years of dictatorship and restriction on political activity, people are able to express their dissatisfactions and make known their urgent needs. If a democratic system is to endure, the Government must respond in a positive way. At the same time, the Government must interpret these needs and formulate programs which satisfy the demands for immediate and tangible improvement without impairing the bases of future growth and diversification. Income distribution considerations must be given considerable weight, particularly in the design of agricultural, educational, housing and health programs. Nevertheless, other considerations must be taken into account in these sectors. Not only do the various demands on available resources require that the total amount allocated by the state in the interest of "communal consumption" and income redistribution be limited but specific features of individual programs—such as the vocational education program—must be designed in the light of immediate economic objectives. While the stimulation of economic development in many areas outside Caracas makes eminently good sense, care must be taken to avoid the indiscriminate application of government funds to depressed areas of the country just on the basis of immediate need and without regard to the longer-term objectives of expanding and diversifying the economy.

The Role of Government

A development program for Venezuela for the next four years must thus deal with the serious immediate problems confronting the country and seek solutions to those problems which are consistent with longer-term objectives. In formulating policy and in designing specific programs of government expenditures, a delicate balance must be struck between the various objectives, if a rational framework for government action is to be created.

Such a framework can be formulated at different levels of generality. To some, no rational framework exists unless quantitative targets are fixed for "basic" production sectors, their internal consistency rigorously established and national effort is focused on such targets. The mission regards such detailed and interrelated target fixing as unnecessary in view of the powerful growth forces already at work in Venezuela and ill-advised in view of the absence of the tools required to set meaningful quantitative targets. On the other hand, the mission feels that some quantitative projections and tests for consistency are useful even under the limitations imposed by inadequate data. Particular attention must be given to the implications of the petroleum outlook for government finance and the growth of the national product. Furthermore, the financial problems which have plagued the Venezuelan Government in 1959 and 1960 must be considered together with policies capable of dealing with the adjustment problem of 1961. Other essential elements in a development program would include appropriate financial policies, pertinent general economic policies affecting petroleum, manufacturing and agriculture, and a suitable schedule of government expenditures for development, including not only capital expenditures in all the major sectors but also selected development expenditures of a recurring nature, particularly in education, health and agriculture.

The mission has considered alternative development policies and the relative priority of various programs of development expenditures in terms of the objectives stated above. Equally important, however, in determining policy choices are the administrative capacities which can be brought to bear upon particular tasks and the extent to which alternative policies impose a burden upon governmental administration and policy-making machinery. The mission has found that policy choices are severely circumscribed by the limited administrative capacity available in particular fields. This problem of administrative capacity in the Venezuelan Government is an extremely serious one and the mission warmly supports the present efforts of the Venezuelan Government through its Commission on Public Administration to improve administration.[1] As government administration improves and demonstrates its capacities, the policy choices open to the Venezuelan Government will be expanded accordingly.

While feeling compelled to consider policy alternatives and relative priority of various expenditure programs partly in terms of the existing administrative limitations of government, the mission recognizes that certain risks must be taken if progress is to be made toward achieving policy objectives. In such fields as education or housing for lower income groups, there is no real alternative to government action; programs must be pushed vigorously—even perhaps further than existing administrative capacities would otherwise indicate. And conversely, direct government operations are not required in the case of programs involving direct commodity production sectors, particularly in the fields of industry and commercial agriculture, where the private sector has displayed considerable vitality and capacity for growth. In fact, in these fields, where government action may actually inhibit private initiative, government must be particularly careful to select those policy alternatives which do not impose too exacting a burden on the administrative machinery. This applies particularly to the choice of policy instruments. The operation of some types of controls imposes a much greater burden than others—quantitative import controls as compared with tariffs, government ownership and operation of new enterprises as compared with government loans to such enterprises.

For problems specifically involving the commodity-producing sectors, solutions should be found which place considerable reliance on the market mechanism as a device for channeling resources. Government in-

---

[1] Among the administrative reforms which are being suggested are the establishment of a modern and impartial career personnel service which would provide for adequate training, selection and supervision; a strengthened budget system related to sound planning and accounting; the initiation of modern and adequate accounting and pre-audit operations, under the executive branch; the strengthening of the controller's office which should be responsible for review of accounting procedures as well as adequate and expeditious post-audit procedures; and a reorganization of the governmental agencies and procedures in order to assure better executive control and coordination of the work of the ministries and autonomous agencies and in order to avoid the tremendous load of minor decisions and paper work which now accumulates at the top level.

tervention should be limited mainly to activities—tariffs, credit, technical assistance, taxation—which make the market mechanism more responsive to the needs of the economic development program. Some important exceptions had to be made. In agriculture, for example, the mission feels that to improve the status of low-income farmers the Government must assume direct responsibilities for providing resettlement opportunities. Even so, every attempt has been made to design a program which would accomplish this result without continuing government supervision of farm settlements.

In a multitude of specific solutions to specific problems, an economic development program would suggest the scope for private initiative and the role of government intervention. No ideological principles are adopted by the mission to delineate fields where, in its judgment, private or government enterprise should dominate. The mission is convinced that the Government must assume a special responsibility for seeing that basic economic overheads—roads, ports, airports, communications and power—are adequately supplied. This follows not only from the traditional interest of governments in these fields; in Venezuela where so much of the national savings is under government control it is particularly convenient for the Government to assure that adequate capacity is provided in these fields. However, even in the case of economic overhead, no hard and fast rule should be drawn. For example, private electric power companies are effectively supplying major population centers and the Government plans on their continuing to do so—a decision in which the mission fully concurs.

In the mission's judgment, this approach to the roles of government and private sector in economic development has the best prospect of achieving the program's objectives. The mission does not however expect this approach can prevail without serious set-backs. Political forces are such that ideological controversy cannot be avoided, particularly in a newly established democratic society where all controversy has so long been suppressed. The mission hopes, however, that its report will stimulate discussion and will assist the Government in appraising the nature of the development problem of the country and in seeking effective solutions.

A Word of Caution—Inadequacy of Statistics

The statistical and other data available in Venezuela are not all that could be desired. The Government is fully aware of this fact and efforts are being made to overcome the deficiencies. However, a word of caution is necessary about many of the facts and figures upon which the mission's recommendations are based. In almost all aspects of its work, the mission was plagued by problems of securing reliable and consistent information and statistics on current situations and on developments over recent years. All too often data were unavailable or, when obtained, were unreliable or incomplete or in conflict with that from other government sources. Although the mission felt compelled under its terms of reference to arrive at recommendations on the basis of the available information and data, it wishes to emphasize that high priority should be given to improving basic data collection.

CHAPTER 3 *GROWTH TARGETS AND GENERAL ECONOMIC POLICIES*

In formulating a four-year development program for Venezuela, the mission has taken into consideration questions of broad economic policy as well as specific investment proposals. Before we can meaningfully discuss such policy in general, we must first examine the implications of the petroleum outlook, which is discussed in more detail in Chapter 8. We will then make specific suggestions in the field of government petroleum policy and discuss certain general economic policies. Thereafter, we will outline our suggested investment program and the means of financing it (see Chapter 4), summarize our specific recommendations for the various sectors of the economy (see Chapter 5), and, finally, give some indications of possible adjustments in the program (see Chapter 6) in the event that petroleum activity and income varies from our assumptions given in Chapter 8.

Relation of Long-Term Petroleum Outlook to Development Program

The importance of the long-term prospects for petroleum in the formulation of a development program cannot be overstated. This can best be demonstrated by making some assumptions about petroleum for the next 20 years or so, and examining the implications of such assumptions in terms of the growth that would be required in other sectors to achieve given policy objectives, such as a target rate of growth of income. With the cooperation of the Planning Office of the Government, the mission has examined the implications of several such assumptions. While the quantitative results of this exercise have very little value, in view of the great uncertainties surrounding basic assumptions and of the poor statistical basis in Venezuela for most economic projections, such an exercise does make clear the close relationship between the long-term petroleum picture and the formulation of a short-term development program.

In the unlikely event, for example, of a sharp decline in the petro-

18

leum sector and its elimination as an export industry over a 20-year period, the economy would encounter extreme difficulties. In order for per capita income to continue to grow at the same time as petroleum incomes were declining, the economy would have to generate new sources of domestic output and foreign exchange income, tax revenues and domestic savings at a very rapid rate and on a large scale. Neither the private nor the public sector is well equipped to meet such a challenge. Labor skills, management and entrepreneurial abilities in the commodity-producing sectors would have to be developed in great haste, perhaps sometimes without proper regard to orderly planning procedure. Government efforts to solve pressing social problems—in housing, education, health and other social services—would have to be indefinitely postponed. Fortunately, the world petroleum situation (see Chapter 8) does not justify such an outlook and the mission concludes that a decline of this magnitude could only result from extremely misguided government policies which the mission assumes will not be the case.

If the opposite assumption were to eventuate—that petroleum would continue to grow at the rate of 8-9 percent per year for an indefinite period—income targets would be relatively easy to achieve and social welfare considerations could play a very large part in the formulation of government programs. Moreover, if such a petroleum growth could be relied upon for an indefinite period, the country would be under very little compulsion to promote new sources of growth in output, foreign exchange income, tax revenues and savings. Commodity-producing sectors would receive less protection from the Government and the Government would rely on more certain, if less speedy, methods for diversifying the economy.

A third possible assumption would be between the two above extremes—for example, that petroleum would continue to expand for 20 years or so, declining from a rate of growth of about 4 percent a year at the beginning and going down to zero percent only at the end, and would then stabilize at a level perhaps 50 percent above the present. Under this assumption, the growth of income at a rate in excess of population growth cannot be taken for granted but such growth would be much easier to achieve than under the first assumption. While social welfare objectives could be achieved at a somewhat slower rate than under the second assumption, steady progress could be made toward them. Under this third assumption, a crash program of economic diversification would not be called for but, on the other hand, neither would it be prudent to rely exclusively on the very gradual accumulation of skills and experience. New sources of growth in output, foreign exchange, taxes, savings and capital inflow would have to be wisely and actively promoted, even though not at a breakneck pace and on a mammoth scale.

Gradual Reduction of Dependence on Petroleum

Although the mission cannot forecast what will, in fact, happen to petroleum over the long term, we believe that it is most likely the situation will develop somewhere between the extremes of the first and second assumptions mentioned above. How close actuality will approximate to the third assumption no one can foretell. However, one thing is clear: in view of the uncertainty in the long-term outlook, Venezuela should place less reliance than in the past on the petroleum sector as the primary source of growth in the economy. While there would appear to be no great danger that the contribution of the petroleum sector to the economy will go down drastically in the years immediately ahead, it would be imprudent for policy purposes to assume a continued rapid growth for an indefinite period. Accordingly, we believe that the economy must move with "controlled speed" to reduce dependence on the petroleum sector while exploiting for as long as possible the returns to be derived from that sector. The Government must secure for the Venezuelan economy an adequate share of the profits of the petroleum industry while at the same time protecting the continued vitality of the industry for as long as possible.

It would appear most probable that a reduction in dependence on petroleum would be brought about by an increase in the non-petroleum economy at a higher growth rate than the rate of increase in the petroleum sector. As a result, in, say, 1970 or 1980, lower proportions of Venezuela's national product and of its foreign exchange receipts will originate in the petroleum sector. However, it is conceivable that petroleum might grow at such a rapid rate that the present ratios would be maintained. Nevertheless, if the non-petroleum economy should also expand rapidly and in a healthy manner, real—as opposed to numerical —dependence on petroleum might still be considerably reduced. In this latter case, less dependence means the capacity of the economy to sustain the process of economic growth *when* and *if* petroleum no longer supplies a substantial stimulus. This involves the development of other sectors to a fairly substantial absolute level, which necessarily implies a reduction in petroleum's relative importance only if petroleum has been growing more slowly.

The most forceful reason for lessening the dependence on the petroleum sector is the uncertainty as to its long-term future in terms of both availability of reserves and Venezuela's competitive position. Another reason is frequently advanced in favor of a crash program to reduce petroleum's relative importance regardless of the petroleum outlook. It is argued that Venezuela is exposed to considerable short-term instability from external sources so long as such a large part of GNP, and particularly foreign exchange receipts, are derived from this one source. Therefore, it is argued, Venezuela must rapidly either expand other exports or reduce her imports: thus, when oil income falls off temporarily, imports would not have to be reduced as much, and whatever reduction would be necessary would cause less dislocation. While there is something to be said for this argument, its importance is easily overstated. Petroleum prices and volumes have not fluctuated violently in the past and Venezuela's own adjustments to these fluctuations have been fairly smoothly accomplished (see Chapter 7). It is, in fact, difficult to find an export product less subject to violent fluctuation than petroleum, and the establishment in 1960 of the Organization of Petroleum Exporting Countries may reinforce these stabilizing tendencies. In the case of a country dependent on petroleum, it may well be less costly to invest in fairly large international reserves, which can be used to maintain imports, rather than to accept the risks of a crash program of economic diversification.

While the mission does not feel that such a crash program is called for, very substantial efforts looking to economic diversification are nevertheless required. The Venezuelan Government has large resources which will be available to support these efforts so long as the petroleum industry maintains a strong position. Moreover, the process of economic expansion which has been going on in Venezuela has already planted seeds of further diversification (see Chapter 7). The development program would thus not be expected to initiate a process of economic expansion and diversification, but to sustain and deepen one already under way.

Government Petroleum Policies

It is unfortunate for Venezuela that, as the plan period begins, the petroleum industry, which is the basic provider of resources for government investment and of the capacity to import the requirements of the development program, is in a weakened position. This position, which is discussed more fully in Chapter 8, arises primarily from two developments: the great increase in world oil supplies relative to demand, much of the increase being in the form of low cost production; and the decreasing profitability of Venezuelan oil operations compared with other producing areas in the Middle East and North America. As a result of these developments and of certain policy measures of the Government, there has been a gradual weakening in Venezuela's world petroleum position and a general deterioration of confidence in the future of the industry.

In view of these difficulties, the mission believes there is a need for the Government to review its petroleum policies so that Venezuela may strengthen its position in the world oil market through a reduction of costs and an increase of confidence in both the short-run and the long-run prospects of the industry. If Venezuela's oil resources are to contribute most effectively to the desired development and diversification of the economy both during the planning period and in the longer term, some accommodation between the Government and the oil companies could be mutually advantageous. For example, the industry may find that it can assist the Government in meeting its short-term objective of a modest increase in production by utilizing some of the large "shut-in" capacity available in Venezuela at incremental costs which are not substantially greater than those incurred in other producing areas. In addition to aiding the Government, it may well be that there are strategic considerations which might lead the industry to want its Venezuelan sources to share in meeting increasing world demand, particularly in Venezuela's traditional markets. On the other hand, in the absence of some action by the Government to help improve the competitive position of Venezuelan oil, the use of "shut-in" capacity at this time will place the industry in a more unfavorable position in later years than would otherwise be the case. Consequently, it would seem reasonable to expect the Government to meet any such action by the producing companies with measures aimed at improving the industry's competitive position, encouraging an expansion in its activities, and thereby increasing the level of confidence. Accordingly, we now consider in turn government policies with respect to various forms of taxation, the Venezuelan Petroleum Corporation and the granting of further oil concessions.

Taxation:[1] To strengthen the competitive position of the industry, to encourage investment and, above all, to increase the level of confidence, the Government may wish to consider several alternative measures for reducing the burden of taxes. At least three possibilities may be mentioned. In the first place, a reinvestment allowance could be granted whereby income tax would not be levied on the amount of profits equivalent to all (or part of) the *net* investment of a given year. From the industry's point of view, this provision would mean a higher rate of profit[2] and an incentive to expand investment. Benefits to Venezuela would accrue from the increase in its proven oil reserves and in productive capacity, and, more immediately, through the stimulus which new investment and increased business confidence would give to the economy as a whole.

Secondly, the group of prices on which royalty payments are based could be related to Venezuelan prices (posted, actual or a formula involving both), rather than to Texas prices which are no longer closely responsive to competitive pressures in the world oil market. In times of market weakness, this change would give greater flexibility to the cost structure of the industry and avoid a weakening in its competitive position vis-a-vis other sources of supply.[3]

[1] Government revenues from the oil industry are derived from various kinds of taxes:—
   a. Income tax is levied on net profits at a progressive rate, the maximum being 47½ percent if profits exceed Bs 28 million. The major oil companies are subject to the highest tax rate.
   b. A prescribed percent of production—usually one-sixth—is the property of the Government. The companies repurchase this royalty oil at prices which are averages of selected Texan posted prices.
   c. The companies pay import duties on all items except those for which special exemption has been secured, e.g., certain equipment for the construction of refineries has been admitted free of duty.
   d. There are miscellaneous federal and local taxes.
   In addition, the oil companies are subject to a special exchange rate, receiving Bs 3.09 for each US$ brought into the country instead of the general rate of Bs 3.35. This provision does not affect tax and royalty payments as the companies are required in effect to give up the same number of dollars to pay taxes regardless of the exchange rate. However, for dollars converted to bolivars required to purchase local supplies and to pay wages and salaries, the Bs 3.09 rate does constitute a levy on the oil companies.

[2] Other things being equal, it is estimated that a reduction of Bs 100 million in taxes would raise the yield on capital invested by 1 percent a year.

[3] In 1959, there were substantial differences between posted prices in Texas and Venezuela; in addition, the market prices for Venezuelan oil were some 7 percent below Venezuelan list prices. The basing of royalty payments on market prices would have increased industry profits and reduced government revenues by some Bs 75 million.

Thirdly, the special exchange rates for petroleum transactions (Bs 3.07-3.09 to US$1) could be modified or eliminated, all purchases and sales of foreign exchange being conducted at or closer to the present general rates of Bs 3.33-3.35 to US$1. This change would reduce the dollar cost of purchases made by the oil industry within Venezuela (over 40 percent of costs are local), and would increase the attractiveness of any investment undertaking. Venezuela itself would benefit from the stimulus given to local purchases made by the industry, both for current operations and for investment purposes. If all petroleum transactions were to be conducted at the general exchange rates of Bs 3.33-3.35 to US$1, then taking into account the offsetting income tax and royalty effects, the net revenue loss may be estimated at some Bs 40 million a year.

Some reduction in the fiscal burden now placed on the petroleum sector would result, the mission believes, in a net benefit to the Venezuelan economy over a number of years. In considering any such tax incentive devices, the Government would, of course, have to balance its likely revenue and foreign exchange losses directly resulting from such tax incentives against the spur to competitiveness and production which the incentives embody. Indeed, the immediate impact of these incentive measures on the cash position of the Government could be minimized, or wholly offset, by the introduction of a pay-as-you-go tax system whereby the present one-year lag in income tax payments would be eliminated over a number of years. Such a measure could be applied in such a way that it would also create a more regular flow of income from the oil industry to the Treasury in place of the present system of three lump-sum payments each year.

Venezuelan Petroleum Corporation. The Government has recently taken two steps which could greatly affect the longer-run prospects for the development of Venezuela's oil resources. One is the creation of a national petroleum company, and the other is the announcement that no further oil concessions will be granted to private enterprise, an announcement which failed to indicate whether, and on what conditions, private capital would be encouraged to participate in the further development of Venezuelan oil resources. These two measures taken together have raised serious doubts in the minds of Venezuelan and foreign investors concerning the role the private sector will be encouraged to assume in future oil development. In particular—and more immediately—this uncertainty has been partly responsible for the deterioration of the investment climate in Venezuela.

By decree dated April 21, 1960, the Venezuelan Petroleum Corporation was established. The initial capital contributed by the Government was Bs 2.5 million. Some of the proven reserves held by the Government have already been transferred to the Corporation. In addition, it is understood that the small refinery at Moron and the government-owned gas pipelines will be transferred to the new entity. It is stated that the new company's operations will, at least in the early years, be modest, while still active. Moreover, one charter of the Corporation is broadly drawn to allow it to engage in all aspects of the petroleum business—from exploration to marketing. The mission is aware of the reasons why the Venezuelan Government wishes to embark on this new field of endeavor. However, we consider it prudent to suggest that the activities of the company be, in fact, of a very limited nature in the next few years. Any attempt to create a comprehensive operating business would require a very large capital investment. This would impose a heavy demand on the relatively limited investment funds available from the budget at a time when they are urgently needed for other purposes for which alternative sources of funds are scarce—education, health, housing and agricultural reform. Moreover, it is difficult to see how the government company could market petroleum competitively in world markets, particularly in sufficient quantities to offset the losses which would flow from a further slowing down of private company activity in Venezuela, which would surely result from such government action.

On balance, it appears to the mission that Venezuela will derive greater benefits from its oil resources through reasonable tax and other measures applicable to private companies than by attempting to build up a large and competing state enterprise.

Policy on Concessions. The decree establishing the Venezuelan Petroleum Corporation also states the Government's policy that no new concessions will be granted. The principal current concessions were granted in 1943 and expire in 1983: the 1956/57 concessions run until 1996/97.[4] Together these areas contain proven reserves equivalent to about 18 years of output at present rates of production, and they are not yet fully explored.

It is not completely clear what is meant by the announced policy of granting no new concessions. This has been generally understood by the public to mean that private capital is not to be encouraged to engage in

[4] Under the 1943 Hydrocarbons Law, concessions may run for 40 years, and the concessionaire has the right to obtain, once only, a new term which cannot exceed 40 years. To secure this extension, he must enter into an agreement with the Government during the twentieth to thirty-eighth years of the existing concession.

oil operations in areas not now covered by concessions. This interpretation has contributed to the loss of confidence already cited.

The mission is convinced that the future development of the Venezuelan economy would be greatly advanced if the Government were to recognize explicitly the positive role that private capital can continue to play in the development of the oil resources of the country. Whether this is made possible by concessions or by some other form of contractual arrangement is a matter for agreement when market conditions favor an increase in exploration and development. The essential point in the mission's view is that no doctrinaire stand should be taken by the Government in opposition to granting concessions or otherwise encouraging private activity in the oil industry. Over the last 15 years, experience has made it abundantly clear that, on the one hand, through its fiscal policy the Government is well able to regulate the net returns of industry from the exploitation of natural resources and that, on the other, the benefits accruing to the economy from large-scale and efficient private enterprise can indeed be substantial.

Economic Growth in the Next Four Years

In projecting economic growth targets in general, the mission has for working purposes projected a growth in the petroleum sector's contribution to GNP (Gross National Product) of 3.3 percent a year, taking 1959 as the base year (see Annex I, Table A.4). Such a projection is based on the assumption that government petroleum policy is clarified along the lines suggested in the preceding paragraphs and that mutually advantageous accommodations are made between the oil companies and the Government also as suggested above. Given this projection, it is doubtful whether the economy as a whole can continue to move upward at the extraordinarily rapid rate of 8.3 percent a year realized in the past decade. A more realistic estimate would be for an increase in GNP of perhaps 5-6 percent a year on an average over the plan period, and even this rate is by no means guaranteed.

The Venezuelan economy has never grown in the past at a rate substantially in excess of the rate of growth of the petroleum sector. The mission feels, however, that the other commodity-producing sectors, particularly manufacturing and agriculture, have reached a stage in their development where they can now provide part of the stimulus to growth previously provided by the petroleum sector. If these sectors are to provide such a stimulus, carefully planned and effectively administered government programs serving the private sector will be required and competent and independent management of government industrial enterprises will be vital. On the assumption that these and other development policies conducive to a high rate of growth outlined in this report are carried out, the rates of growth by sectors indicated in Table 1 are in prospect. The projected over-all rate of growth of 5.5 percent a year in GDP (Gross Domestic Product), and the implicit estimate of 5.8 percent a year in GNP,[5] are both subject to fairly wide margins of error. They represent a "reasonable guess" of probable developments in the major commodity-producing sectors, in electric power and in government—sectors which together constitute some 55 percent of GDP and 50 percent of GNP.[6] Other sectors of the economy are assumed to grow at more or less the average rate of growth of the directly productive sectors.

The projected growth in manufacturing of 10 percent a year is based on three major considerations: first, the responsiveness of demand for manufactured products to growth of income; second, the relative ease of substituting domestic output for imports which still exists in many lines; third, the assumption that the government steel mill will be in full operation by 1964. On the other hand, it seems difficult to envisage exceeding the 11 percent growth rate of the past in view of the slowdown in petroleum. Even the 10 percent growth in manufacturing will require active governmental promotion of the private sector.

In agriculture, it may be possible to maintain, if not to exceed, the past rate of growth of more than 5 percent. The demand for domestic agricultural products, which is usually considered to be less sensitive to income than that for industrial products, may grow at a faster rate than income growth alone would suggest because of the change in income distribution already in progress and because of the prospects for import substitution. On the supply side, the program of government

---

[5] On the basis of the GDP estimates in Table 1 and the estimated growth of GNP in the oil sector by 3.3 percent a year, growth in GNP is somewhat faster than in GDP. This occurs because the relatively slow-growing oil sector is less important in GNP than in GDP (the latter including and the former excluding profits paid abroad), and so the weighted average of the growth rates of the various sectors contributing to GNP is higher than for GDP.

[6] The reduction in the growth rate compared with that of the past decade may be accounted for in part by a reduction in the rate of domestic savings, which is to be expected with a somewhat better distribution of income, higher income taxes, and an environment less geared to speculative investment undertakings. It is not likely that this lower rate of savings will be offset by the improved composition of investment and other development expenditures recommended below. Greater emphasis on higher priority expenditures will not lead to a reduction in capital-output ratios during the period of the program itself, but is likely to show its main effects on output in subsequent periods.

action proposed in Chapter 9 should lend support to the growth already under way in the commercial sector of agriculture. The programs for

TABLE 1: Actual and Projected Growth in Gross Domestic Product by Sector, 1950-59 & 1959-64

Sector	Average Percentage Annual Growth in GDP		Percentage Contribution to Total Output	
	1950-59 (Actual)	1959-64 (Projected)	1958 & 1959 (Actual)	1964 (Projected)
Oil	7.6	3.5	29.1	26.2
Agriculture	5.5	5.5	6.4	6.4
Mining	40.0	7.0	1.6	1.7
Manufactures	11.4	10.0	11.2	13.7
Power and water	19.2	10.0	1.3	1.6
Construction	8.4		6.6	
Transportation	5.1		4.2	
Commerce	9.8	5.5	15.5	50.4
Services	6.1		14.0	
Housing	9.7		10.1	
Total	8.3	5.5	100.0	100.0

the low-income farmers proposed in that chapter should at least begin to stimulate increased output by the end of the period, although the mission does not expect a very substantial response in the short run.

The anticipated increases of output and income will entail a greater volume of imports than was recorded in 1959. Imported capital goods are essential to industrial and agricultural growth, and rising incomes may be expected to increase the demand for other imported goods, despite tariffs and a growing volume and variety of domestic output in Venezuela. On the basis of assumptions regarding activity in the oil industry and estimates of the level of other exports and of foreign investment, the mission believes that a balance or a moderate deficit on current account would allow an increase of imports (excluding oil company imports) of about 3 percent a year during 1959-64 (see Annex I, Table A.5). The anticipated rates of increase in imports fall short of the estimated growth of 5-6 percent a year in GNP; but it may be expected that, with an intensified policy of import substitution, the growth of imports in the range indicated would be sufficient to meet the needs of increasing investment and consumer demands.

Creation of Employment Opportunities and Immigration Policy

An over-all annual rate of growth of 5-6 percent in GNP will provide a 2-3 percent increase in per capita income.[7] While this is below the growth of the recent past, it will represent a creditable performance. The mission has considered whether growth along the lines indicated in Table 1 will provide adequate employment opportunities in the aggregate. On the basis of very crude estimates given in Annex I, Table A.6, it would appear that the labor force is likely to grow by 80,000-90,000 a year, or by 3.3 percent annually in the next few years. There is some reason to believe that the economy was providing, even at a growth rate of 8-9 percent, barely enough employment opportunities to absorb the rapidly growing labor force (see Chapter 7). With the slow-down in aggregate growth, employment absorption may become a greater problem.

The mission believes it is unlikely that over the next four years the nonagricultural sector will be able to absorb the total increase in the labor force. The agricultural sector, which may now employ something like 35 percent of the labor force, must continue to absorb some of the increase, perhaps as much as 20,000 a year. Partly in recognition of the need to provide employment opportunities on the farm for part— say, one-half or more—of the additions to the labor force originating on farms, the mission has formulated its recommendations on agriculture as outlined in Chapter 9.

In manufacturing it is likely that the projected growth of output will support an increase of employment by about 15,000 a year. This assumes that output per worker will grow much less rapidly than in the past, now that modern factories, with higher output per worker, represent a larger proportion of total manufacturing. It is doubtful that significant additional employment opportunities can be expected from petroleum or mining.

Thus, about 50,000 of the annual increase in the labor force would have to be absorbed by construction, commerce, transport, services and miscellaneous—if the volume of unemployment is not to increase between 1959 and 1964. This would imply a percentage growth of employment in these sectors slightly lower than the percentage growth of output.

Within the limitations imposed by the basic data, this exercise suggests that the projected growth rate of 5-6 percent should go a long way

[7] For estimates of population growth see Annex I, Table A.6.

toward creating adequate employment opportunities. It should be possible with the agricultural settlement program recommended below to limit the movement of rural population to the urban centers, particularly since the Government is cutting back the emergency public works program which accelerated the influx to the cities (see Chapter 7). Moreover, the government investment program recommended here, particularly in housing, environmental sanitation, and education will be on the whole more labor-intensive than in the past and should help absorb those presently engaged in the emergency works program.

In view of the slowdown in economic growth, it does not appear feasible for Venezuela to reinstitute the liberal immigration policy that was maintained for many years. However, the mission is convinced that the complete stoppage of immigration will reduce the rate of growth and mean less, rather than more, employment opportunities. The maintenance of the rate of growth at 5-6 percent a year in the economy as a whole, and the rate of 10 percent a year for the industrial sector particularly, will not be possible unless there is a considerable increase in the number of skilled workers, engineers, teachers, industrial managers, and the like, who are essential to meet the requirements of an expanding economy. Since it will take some time before educational measures, supplemented by actual experience, can exert their influence on the quality of the labor force, immigrants can play a very important role in filling the gap that will exist for some time. This gap is particularly important in the manufacturing sector since it appears that industry will be moving more and more into those activities which require a relatively larger proportion of skilled personnel. The mission therefore recommends that the Government lift its suspension of immigration and prepare a list of occupational groups whose free immigration into the country will be permitted and encouraged.

Protection of Domestic Industry and Agriculture

The mission is convinced that Venezuela must continue substantially to protect domestic agriculture and industry so long as present exchange rates are maintained. Without such protection, agriculture and industry could not have developed to their present levels nor could a high rate of growth in these commodity-producing sectors be maintained in the future. In fact, there are newly developing sectors, particularly in industry, where tariff protection should probably be increased. The mission emphasizes in Chapters 9 and 10 the importance of excluding, as candidates for high protection, those industries which have no prospect of producing competitively, and recommends that the Government's promotional efforts be concentrated on industries with the best prospects for becoming competitive with foreign producers, particularly in export markets. While the Government should adopt a more discriminating approach in this sense, it is worthwhile considering whether a less discriminating approach is not justified insofar as *minimum* and *maximum* protection levels are concerned. If diversification objectives are to be achieved and dependence upon petroleum as a source of future growth is to be reduced, should not virtually all products, except those with a clear natural disadvantage, receive some protection? On the other hand, if the public interest is to be protected against the inefficient or unfavorably situated producer, must not some maximum level of protection be established within which the Government officials are permitted to exercise their discretion?

A minimum level of protection can be regarded as a standard diversification premium to which all producers are entitled, because all are subject to high wages and price levels. In practice almost all present manufacturing enterprises enjoy a higher level of protection than would be provided by such a standard diversification premium. Thus, the premium would in fact confer benefits on new producers who would contribute to diversification. If petroleum were to continue to expand indefinitely or if other export products emerged despite the high domestic cost and price level, the need for the diversification premium in the tariff could of course be questioned. If, however, petroleum declined or stagnated for a considerable period, and other exports did not develop, adjustment of Venezuelan prices and costs to external prices and costs by a change in the exchange rate would probably be necessary. The "standard" diversification premium in the tariff could then be eliminated since it would be incorporated in the exchange rate. Under these circumstances, this change in the exchange rate, if and when it became necessary, would then have the maximum effect in achieving an expansion of exports with minimum disturbance to the economy.

If such a diversification premium were introduced into the present Venezuelan tariff structure, three sectors particularly would be given additional protection: intermediate products, capital goods, and durable consumer goods. As noted above, low tariffs have generally applied to these three sectors. It might be preferable to introduce the minimum diversification premium into the tariff structure in stages, on the grounds that the immediate introduction of such a premium across the board would give too great an upward boost to prices.

The analysis in Chapter 10 suggests that, during the period of the program, intermediate or semi-finished products might be considered the first group on which to try such a policy. If the tariff level in this group were raised generally, increases above the minimum could be carefully studied by the competent agencies of the Government to determine whether special circumstances justify greater protection in particular instances. As noted in Chapter 10, the mission expects that most tariff increases granted for intermediate products could be absorbed by purchasers of these products and that in most cases additional protection need not be granted to the producer of the end product.

The imposition of a ceiling on the extent of protection is designed to protect the public interest against the extremely inefficient or unfavorably situated producer and applies particularly to agriculture. As observed in Chapter 9, it is particularly important to review the whole system of protective tariffs, exonerations and prohibitions applicable to agricultural products. We suggest that the level of protection, whether imposed by tariff alone or in conjunction with other measures, should never permit internal prices to be more than double external prices at present exchange rates, and then only in special cases. Such a ceiling would reduce the area for capricious or uninformed government action. Less reliance on import licensing in the agricultural field—even if it requires an increase in some tariffs (such as on meat) —would accomplish the same result and would widen the area for market adjustments to changing supply and demand conditions.

Development of Mining

The great proven mineral wealth of Venezuela lies in its oil and iron ore. Other minerals are known to exist, but their true worth has yet to be proven. If Venezuela is to take full advantage of its potentialities in the mineral field, the Government must review its own program of mining exploration and geological survey work and must make greater efforts to attract private capital. At least until recently, there has been insufficient governmental effort in developing the necessary basic information on mineral resources; such information would serve to encourage private activity in exploration, and also make it possible for the Government to secure for itself an adequate return. At the same time, the Government has not encouraged private exploration and, in fact, has discouraged it in the case of "reserved" minerals (see Chapter 3).

Mining is essentially a hazardous business more suitable to private venture capital than to government. The return should necessarily be related to the risk involved. In most countries—including industrially advanced ones—where mining has thrived in recent years, this has been encouraged by government tax and other policies. For example, in Canada there is a three-year tax-free period after operations begin and liberal provisions for writing off exploration and development expenses; Ireland and Chile are other governments endeavoring to attract mining venture capital, and in Peru there is a special mining code which has brought many new exploration groups to the country. We suggest that the Venezuelan Government review the measures adopted by these countries in order to determine for itself the most suitable means of encouraging the mining industry.

In addition to providing suitable tax incentives, we suggest that the Government review the policy which in effect reserves to it the right to determine the use of newly discovered deposits, either in specified regions or country-wide, of a list of minerals, including iron ore, bauxite and manganese. The Government asserts that by imposing reservations it can eliminate the opportunists who make claims without having serious intentions of working them. A second purpose of the reservation policy is to ensure the domestic processing of the largest possible quantities of mined minerals. This reservation in its present form serves as a restraint on venture capital and most likely will retard mineral development with its concomitant employment, payrolls and, in due course, royalty and tax payments. Legitimate prospectors might well hesitate to carry out costly survey work if it is considered likely that conditions may be imposed on the exploitation which will make the development unremunerative. The mission believes that this difficulty could be overcome, in part at least, by revision of policy to state clearly in advance of exploration the minimum conditions considered necessary to protect the country's position.

With respect to iron ore, the Government has announced a policy of no further concessions, restricting to a government corporation the exploitation of deposits not previously granted. We understand that it is the intention of the Government to encourage the domestic processing of the largest possible quantities of the ore to be mined, but that only the Government itself will be prepared to sell ore in the export trade. We question that it is in the long-term interests of Venezuela—with such vast deposits already proven and potentially available—to shut the door on private participation in the exploration of new iron ore deposits for export. Iron ore is available in very large volume in many areas of the world, and Venezuela may find that it is advantageous to compete for the world market. It may well be that the granting of concessions to prospective ore users, or the participation of private capital through other contractual arrangements, will be the most effective means of ensuring Venezuela a fair share in those markets. The mission suggests that this question be carefully reviewed, having in mind the potential revenue to the state by way of royalties, taxes, or other contractual payments.

Financial Policies in the Transition Period

Many financial problems face the Government as it inaugurates its four-year development program. The Government is confronted with the task of restoring balance of payments equilibrium in the face of a large and prolonged flight of capital. At the same time, the level of economic activity appears to have fallen below the peak achieved in 1959 and there has been a marked decline in the degree of business confidence. Moreover, the resolution of these problems is made more difficult by the large budget deficit which many fear is inevitable in 1960/61. On the one hand, such a deficit would further strain the balance of payments and disturb business confidence: on the other, elimination of the deficit could further depress levels of business activity. The Government must thus try both to restore equilibrium in the balance of payments and to balance the budget, without unduly interrupting economic growth and without weakening the economic structure of the country.

The solution of these problems will require the careful adjustment of fiscal policy to economic conditions and the progressive elimination of the budget deficit. While this will not be an easy task, there are factors that will aid in its achievement. The loss of gold and foreign exchange reserves in 1958-60 was not produced by excessive imports but by capital outflow. This capital outflow could reach such large proportions for a sustained period only because of excess liquidity, which had been eliminated by mid-1960.

The reduction in liquidity did not immediately eliminate capital flight and in November 1960, the Government felt it was necessary to institute controls over foreign exchange transactions as a temporary measure. The objective was to halt capital flight and thereby avoid devaluation or the further reduction in economic activity that the maintenance of a restrictive monetary policy might have produced.

The mission is hopeful that the imposition of exchange controls for a limited period will reduce capital flight and give to the Government the opportunity to apply policies which will permit the economy to expand. Because of the capital flight in 1960, Venezuela had to reduce its imports by about 25 percent. In the process of limiting capital outflow, a cautious credit policy was followed. This reduced private investment and imports and produced an export surplus to finance the capital outflow. It also led to some reduction in domestic levels of production and employment, although data indicating the extent of the 1960 decline were not available at the time that exchange controls were applied.

Control over external transactions and the reduction of capital outflow should permit some expansion of credit and an increase of imports, both of which would foster an increased level of business activity. Venezuela continues to enjoy a very high level of foreign exchange receipts. On this basis, it should not be too difficult to operate the exchange control system with sufficient efficiency to reduce capital outflow without disrupting the normal flow of imports. However, the over-all volume of money and credit can be permitted to expand only moderately; otherwise the pressure of repressed demand will threaten the efficient operation of the exchange controls and may lead to serious distortions of the economy.

To limit monetary expansion the banking system would have to control credit to both the private and public sectors. If capital flight is halted by exchange controls, a higher level of activity in the private sector should be possible without large-scale borrowing from the banking system. The resulting revival of private investment should then permit the Government to reduce and eventually to eliminate its budgetary deficit without endangering the expansion of economic activity. In fact, if the Government does not bring its budget into balance at that time, it would be difficult to avoid inflation.

Until the end of 1960, government spending was maintained at a very high level. In fact, it was not a slow-down in the public sector, but a reduction in private investment, which produced the apparent decline in economic activity in 1960. While the 1960/61 budget, which contemplated total spending of Bs 5.5 billion, would have involved a substantial reduction in cash expenditures over the previous year, it would not have produced a corresponding reduction in income-generating expenditures because of the decline in net debt payments.[8] Thus, it should be possible, as private investment revives, to bring the total government spending level down to the budget target. The recommendations outlined in the following chapter may assist in this task. Closing the budgetary gap will, however, also require some tax increases. The magnitude

[8] The Ministry of Finance has estimated (see *Memoria, 1959*, Banco Central de Venezuela, p. 314) that gross debt payments in 1960/61 will be Bs 320 million compared with about Bs 900 million in the first six months of 1959/60. Net debt payments will be even less in 1960/61, since disbursements under the foreign credit for the steel mill will accelerate.

of permanent tax increases in 1960/61 may well be adjusted to longer-term revenue requirements (see Chapter 4) ; but some temporary tax increases may also be necessary, particularly if extraordinary external credits cannot be secured in sufficient volume to cover the fiscal gap in the transition period. Government borrowing from the banking system should be severely limited and should be stopped as soon as private investment activity revives. Otherwise, fear of inflation will continue to encourage capital flight and to endanger the whole development program.

The mission is thus hopeful that, if business confidence is restored and economic activity revives, exchange controls can be removed without great delay and that balance on international account can be re-established and maintained at present exchange rates. This judgment would have to be reviewed if the policies outlined in this report designed to rebuild business confidence are not pursued, or if the petroleum situation were to deteriorate.

CHAPTER 4 *A FOUR-YEAR DEVELOPMENT PROGRAM AND ITS FINANCING*

Financing the Development Program

As a first step in formulating fiscal policy recommendations and specific investment proposals, the mission has discussed with Venezuelan officials the probable range of government revenue during the planning period as well as the various claims against that revenue. The mission has made its estimate of total government revenues and has sought to determine the extent of prior claims for current operating expenses, in order to reach a judgment as to the amount of funds which would probably be available for capital investment. The estimates of current expenditures have proved particularly difficult, largely for the reasons set forth in the following paragraphs. However, subject to the appropriate caveats concerning forecasts of this type, the mission has set out in Table 2 its projections of resources for financing the capital investment program.

The mission estimates that tax revenues during the four years of the program will total approximately Bs 21.8 billion, starting at the level of just under Bs 5 billion in 1960/61 and rising to almost Bs 6 billion in 1963/64. This estimate is based on the assumption of present tax rates but a better enforcement of tax laws, a somewhat lower level of petroleum prices than those prevailing in 1959/60, a revival of economic activity and imports in 1961, income growth of 5.8 percent a year and continued growth of imports (see Annex I, Table A.7). The same projection could apply for cash revenues if recommended tax concessions to the petroleum industry were combined with the gradual introduction of current collection of petroleum company income tax liabilities. While national tax revenues relative to GNP would remain at a relatively high level—about 20 percent of GNP—this does not mean that there remains no scope for further tax increases. The tax burden on the non-petroleum sector of the economy is quite moderate.

The Government's current expenditures have increased considerably since 1957/58.[1] They exceeded Bs 3.3 billion in 1958/59 and may have

---

[1] Current expenditures as here defined include the deficit on current account of autonomous enterprises and the whole of the national government's contribution to the budgets of the regional governmental entities.

TABLE 2: Projection of Resources for Financing Development Program, 1960/61-1963/64

(in Bs billion)

1. Current revenues	21.8
2. Current expenditures	14.5-15.0
3. Surplus on current account (1 minus 2)	6.8-7.3
4. Increase in cash balances	0.2
5. Debt repayment	0.7
6. Domestic resources available for financing investment (3 minus 4 minus 5)	5.9-6.4
7. Proceeds of 1959/60 foreign loan	0.2
8. Total resources available (6 plus 7)	6.1-6.6
9. Capital investment program	7.6
10. *Gap* (9 minus 8)	1.0-1.5
Proposed Means ⎱ New external borrowing	0.7
of Financing ⎰ Additional taxation	0.3-0.8

reached Bs 3.4-3.5 billion in 1959/60, having risen from Bs 2.5 billion in 1957/58. The development program we recommend would involve some increase in current expenditures—particularly for education. Current expenditures for education would exceed 1959/60 levels by about Bs 100 million a year on the average during the four years. We also propose new or expanded development programs in agriculture involving substantial current expenditures. However, if the cuts we recommend for milk subsidies and for the administration of existing colonies can be implemented, the over-all increase in current expenditures in agriculture will be negligible; otherwise, current expenditures in agriculture will exceed present levels by at least Bs 40 million a year. In health services a substantial expansion of current activities will be required to administer the new hospitals and clinics coming into operation, even if the modest program of new construction recommended by the mission is accepted. The mission feels, however, that the cost of this expansion of service could be absorbed by the Ministry of Health budget by adoption of certain operating economies to which we refer in Chapter 16. In connection with other programs of a developmental nature, the mission has identified certain opportunities for economizing on current expenditures, for example, in the administration of ports and communications.

The mission is also convinced that budgetary allocations for covering the current operating losses of many of the autonomous and semi-autonomous entities could be reduced and in some cases eliminated by increasing charges and fees to the public and by administrative changes. The mission sees no justification for the low charges imposed by the *Instituto Nacional de Obras Sanitarias* (INOS) for water (see Chapter 16) and, accordingly, we recommend that further investment by INOS be conditional upon the adoption of a reasonable charge to water users. At least Bs 50 million a year could be saved by adopting such a policy. There are a number of other government enterprises now operating at a substantial loss—where the magnitude of the loss is by no means the reflection of a policy decision to subsidize. If the recommendations with respect to the *Linea Aeropostal Venezolana* (LAV) (see Chapter 11) and the operation of the railroads (see Chapter 11) were adopted and if the improvement in the financial administration of the *Banco Obrero* (see Chapter 15) continues, as much as Bs 50 million a year might be saved. In addition, there are opportunities for eliminating operating losses on other government enterprises, such as the government hotels and sugar mills, by sale of these enterprises to the private sector or by reducing the scale of operations.

There thus exist substantial opportunities for reducing government current expenditures in areas of activity falling within the mission's area of investigation. On balance, one would expect that the increases in current expenditures called for in the development program could easily be offset by the reductions recommended above. As the population expands and growth of the economy continues, one would ordinarily expect a 4 percent or 5 percent increase in current expenditures a year. In view of the very substantial growth in current expenditures of the last few years, including the general salary increase, and the opportunities for economies identified by the mission only in the fields covered in the survey, the mission believes that current expenditures need not grow by more than 1-2 percent a year in the next four years. While estimates of current expenditures for the base year, fiscal 1959/60, are not very reliable, we would thus assume total current expenditures during the program period of Bs 14.5 billion to Bs 15 billion. This figure has been adopted for purposes of financial planning.

By deducting current expenditures from projected revenues we estimate that the surplus on current account during the four-year period will amount to Bs 6.8-7.3 billion. Part of these public savings must be used to repay the $200 million loan contracted in early 1960. Also, the Government will probably find it necessary to replenish its cash balances which by June 30, 1960, had been reduced to about Bs 250 million, much of which was frozen in government bank accounts with the

Banco Agricola y Pecuario (BAP) and some of the commercial banks. Assuming Bs 660 million for debt repayments and Bs 200 million for rebuilding cash balances, leaves domestic resources of about Bs 5.9-6.4 billion available for financing investment. To these domestic resources should be added Bs 200 million of the proceeds of the foreign loan which were expected to be unused by June 30, 1960, so that total resources in prospect for financing the capital investment program would be about Bs 6.1-6.6 billion. As the proposed investment program amounts to some Bs 7.6 billion, there would remain a gap of from Bs 1.0 billion to Bs 1.5 billion.

It would not be advisable to rely upon internal borrowing to finance part of this gap, unless private investment activity fails to revive. At the present stage of development, government policy should be such as in effect to reserve private savings for investment in the private sector of the economy. The demand of the private sector for investment funds can be expected to be very large and, once the transition difficulties are overcome, government borrowing from the banking system could have serious inflationary effects.

In view of the magnitude of the high-priority investment program, however, external borrowing for financing part of this gap is justified. The mission suggests that Bs 700 million would not be excessive for the four-year period—this represents less than 10 percent of the total investment program. Borrowing abroad of this amount should also permit the Government to sustain the level of economic activity, particularly during the period of adjustment when the loss in foreign exchange is being brought to a halt. If private investment does not revive quickly in 1961, it may be desirable to maintain a somewhat higher level of total government expenditures than contemplated in the four-year program and to resort to external borrowing on a larger scale. This will have to be determined, however, after the magnitude of external finance available to Venezuela has been more carefully appraised.

On the basis of the above assumptions, tax revenues for the four years might have to be raised by as much as Bs 800 million, an average of Bs 200 million a year. Many excellent proposals for raising revenues have been made in the report of the Commission to Study the Fiscal System of Venezuela.[2] The mission wishes to support in particular the recommendation that gasoline taxes on domestic consumption be increased. An additional Bs 75-100 million a year could be obtained from this source alone.

An additional Bs 100 million a year could be secured from a combi-

[2] Carl S. Shoup and others, *The Fiscal System of Venezuela*, The Johns Hopkins Press, 1959.

nation of additional excise taxes on luxury consumption and an increase in income taxes. The higher-income groups in Venezuela must be willing to bear a greater tax burden. In order to penalize consumption and to encourage savings and investment, some part of these higher taxes could appropriately be levied on consumption rather than income. However, some reduction in private savings may have to be accepted if Venezuela is to develop a more progressive tax system and one which depends less on the external sector. The Venezuelan income tax must be expanded in its coverage and rates must be boosted to secure a more equitable distribution of the fruits of economic progress. Considerably greater reliance on the income tax is feasible in Venezuela because agricultural income, which is usually difficult to tap through the income tax, represents a small part of total income. The establishment of suitable income tax rates would be facilitated if separate rate scales were established for individuals and corporations, as recommended by the Fiscal Commission.[3] The mission also urges that strenuous efforts be applied during the next four years to improve tax collections through better enforcement.

While an increase in the income tax would appear to be essential, taking into account the low tax rates currently in force, the mission does not believe that it is feasible to redistribute the existing tax burden as a whole. It would be possible to reduce the general tax burden on the lower-income groups along the lines suggested by the Fiscal Commission and to offest the effects on revenue by higher income taxes and other tax measures bearing more heavily on the middle- and upper-income groups. However, the reduction of taxation on the lower-income groups presents problems, since about the only significant taxes levied on these groups are customs tariffs and most of these currently have a protective aspect as well.

Program of Investment and Other Selected Development Expenditures

The four-year capital expenditure program of Bs 7.6 billion is designed to sustain a high rate of economic growth, to provide additional employment opportunities, to contribute to the progressive diversification of the economy and to distribute more widely the benefits of economic progress. Capital expenditures by the central government, including credits to agriculture and industry but excluding the central government's contribution to public investment by the regional entities, would be equivalent to about 7 percent of the gross national

[3] *Op. cit.*, p. 15.

product and would continue to place the Venezuelan Government among those able to contribute the highest share of gross national product to investment. Moreover, the capital investment program as such is only part of the development effort. Taking into account total expenditures to be made for education and health, which can be regarded as investment in the human factor, as well as developmental programs of a noncapital nature in industry and agriculture, total developmental expenditures will reach almost Bs 12 billion, the equivalent of government revenues from petroleum. Thus, the program of development is to "sow petroleum" in accordance with the popular slogan.

The national government's capital investment program we recommend is at an average level of Bs 1.9 billion a year, 20 percent below appropriations for capital expenditures in the five-year period 1954/55-1958/59, when they averaged Bs 2.3 billion a year. Capital expenditures in 1959/60 are also likely to have approximated Bs 2.3 billion.[4] A lower level of capital expenditure is necessary because of the reduction in domestic financial resources, as explained above, and also seems justified by the mission's findings on investment requirements in the major sectors. Venezuela has reached a stage in her development where at least a temporary interruption in the upward trend of government capital expenditures appears appropriate. Many of the investments that were undertaken in the past were of low priority and simply by not undertaking projects of this type, substantial savings would be effected. Other investments were of high priority and have already helped to strengthen the economy, but have now created substantial capacity which can be expanded at a slower pace. Thus, in some important areas a decrease in the rate of investment will be appropriate, although our recommended program does provide for substantial increases in certain other sectors.

The annual average of public investment expenditures in the major sectors as recommended by the mission for the four years 1960/61-1963/64 as compared with average annual appropriations during the five years 1954/55-1958/59, would show major reductions in "Basic Economic Overheads" and in the "Miscellaneous" category (see Table 3). Capital expenditures in "Commodity Producing Sectors," particularly credits to the private agricultural and industrial sectors, would increase. Capital expenditures for "Education, Health and Social Services" would remain at about the same total level, with relatively greater emphasis on education, housing and environmental sanitation facilities

---

[4] Appropriations are substantially higher, but they include debt payments.

and less emphasis on new hospital construction and general urban facilities.

While it has not been possible to show a detailed comparison with fiscal year 1959/60, we are able to compare our recommended future investment expenditures with annual average past appropriations over the five-year period 1954/55-1958/59. This appears to us to be the best basis for comparison since the figures for any one year fail to include expenditures financed from special relatively short-term credit operations but include payments on such debts from previous years; by averaging over a period of years, these distortions are kept to a minimum.

The reduction of public investment in transport, telecommunications and power recommended for the next four years is possible primarily because the basic facilities in these sectors necessary for supporting a high rate of economic growth and achieving the other objectives of the program are already in an advanced state. Over one-third of total public investment was concentrated in these fields during the four years 1954/55-1958/59. The basic transport network is in an advanced stage of completion. Most of the main trunk roads are being built to high standards permitting a continued growth of traffic in the future at low cost. The airports are in most instances large and well paved. Most of the ports have substantial excess capacity. The one new railroad is almost completed and the mission has concluded, after an examination of the relative costs of road, water and rail transportation in Venezuela, that construction of additional railroads would not be justified in the years immediately ahead (see Chapter 11). Electric power facilities in the public sector have been greatly expanded, having increased by over 30 percent a year during the last decade. Much of the increased need for electric power in the four years ahead will be met by additions to the capacity of private companies. Similarly in telecommunications, particularly in telephone service, expansion of capacity has been very rapid and, until management and technical capacity are improved so as to secure better utilization of equipment, some slowing down is advisable in this field.

Investment in basic economic overhead facilities can thus be reduced by about 40 percent during the four years 1960/61-1963/64. It is indeed fortunate that economic overheads can be adequately assured by committing what is a relatively modest share—28 percent—of the Government's capital investment. With a slowdown in the growth of the petroleum industry, the momentum of economic advance, including the provision of employment opportunities, will only be maintained if agriculture and manufacturing receive some extraordinary direct stimulus. The decline in basic overhead requirements makes possible a substan-

TABLE 3: Public Investment, 1960/61-1963/64, as Recommended by Mission Compared With Past Appropriations for Public Investment, 1954/55-1958/59

(in annual averages)

	Past Appropriations 1954/55-1958/59		Mission Program 1960/61-1963/64	
	Bs million	%	Bs million	%
Basic Economic Overheads	831[a]	36.6	535	28.2
Transport	675	29.8	428	22.5
Roads and bridges	498	22.0	400	21.0
Railroads	85	3.8	—	—
Ports	34	1.5	16	0.9
Airports	40	1.8	12	0.6
Government airline (LAV)	17	0.8	—	—
Power	97	4.2	64	3.4
Telecommunications	75[b]	3.3	43	2.3
Commodity Producing Sectors	587	26.0	721	38.0
Agriculture	276	12.2	378	19.9
Credit programs	40	1.8	138	7.3
Irrigation and drainage	108	4.8	74	3.9
Settlement	52	2.3	100	5.3
Other	76	3.4	66	3.4
Industry	311	13.8	343	18.1
Credit programs	44	1.9	110	5.9
Steel	101	4.5	200	10.5
Chemical and associated projects	133	5.9	33	1.7
Shipyards and drydocks	33	1.5	—	—
Education, Health and Social Services	459	20.2	447	23.5
Education	61	2.7	104	5.5
Housing	114	4.9	140	7.4
Water and sewage facilities	99	4.4	115	6.0
Hospitals and health centers	60	2.7	26	1.4
Community development	125	5.5	62	3.2
Miscellaneous	392	17.2	197	10.4
Grand Total	2,268	100.0	1,900	100.0

a Excludes CANTV investment financed outside the budget.

b Includes CANTV investment financed outside the budget.

tial increase in capital contributions to direct commodity-producing sectors. In absorbing almost 40 percent of government capital funds, these sectors should contribute during the four-year period to a substantial leap toward achieving a diversified and viable economy, if the confidence of the private sector in the continued expansion of the economy is maintained. The increase in credit facilities to the private industrial and agricultural sectors should contribute to maintaining favorable expectations.

Investment expenditures in education, health and social services will help bring about economic diversification and a better distribution of the benefits of economic progress if some reorientation in expenditures in this field takes place. A large increase in investment in education is essential, in order to ensure that a full six-year primary education becomes available for larger numbers of students and in order to make possible an expansion in secondary education, particularly in vocational fields, at a pace consistent with the growth in the number of primary school graduates. Government investment in housing and in water and sewage facilities would also be increased. The housing program we recommend would be a radical departure from past efforts which provided relatively expensive housing accommodations for a relatively small number of families. Emphasis would now be placed on providing a sufficient number of very modest dwellings to arrest the deterioration in housing accommodation which has occurred. A substantial part of expenditures for the housing program would go to provide water and sewage facilities for low-income family dwellings and would thus supplement the general environmental sanitation program for which a substantial increase is also recommended. Venezuela has reached a stage in the development of public health where major emphasis should be placed on environmental sanitation. In view of the imbalance that has developed between physical health facilities, which have been greatly expanded in recent years, and the personnel necessary to operate such facilities, for which adequate provision is yet to be made, a slowdown in the construction of hospitals and health centers would be possible without any substantial sacrifice in the magnitude and quality of service. Similarly, a cut in expenditures below current levels would appear to be possible for city streets, monuments, and other urban facilities financed by the central government from separate appropriations.

The very large cut recommended in the "Miscellaneous" category from over Bs 390 million a year to less than Bs 200 million a year reflects the following assumptions: first, many projects having a low priority, such as government hotels, telefericos and race tracks, have been completed and the present government has no plans for undertaking further projects of this type; second, government administrative buildings will not have to be constructed on any significant scale during this period; third, buildings necessary for most program purposes which in the data for past years are included in "Miscellaneous" are taken into account in the sector estimates; fourth, no loans or other special financial support to the Federal District will be given; finally, the extraordinary public works plan (POE) will not be continued.

The mission has not made a detailed analysis of requirements in particular fields within the Miscellaneous category and the nearly Bs 200 million allocated in our program for this category is more in the nature of a contingency item, equivalent to about 10 percent of total investment. Miscellaneous governmental building, such as for small administrative centers outside Caracas and for other such buildings, not already included in the particular sector programs, are allowed for here. In addition, the contingency item allows for underestimation of costs in sector programs and additions to sector programs.

In the last chapter we discussed our recommendations concerning government development expenditures, outlining in general our suggestions as to the broad emphasis we believe should be placed on, and between, the various categories and sectors within the economy. In this chapter, we summarize the reasons why we suggest particular expenditures during the four-year period 1960/61-1963/64 within each of the sectors. In the various chapters of Part III of this report (see Chapters 9-16), we discuss these reasons more fully and, in addition, indicate the approach to specific policies in each sector which we believe would be necessary to maximize the effectiveness of the expenditures we suggest.

BASIC ECONOMIC OVERHEADS

Roads

A decline in public investment in the transport field would be fully consistent with the maintenance of a high rate of economic growth and the promotion of economic diversification. Our proposed road program, with investment at an annual rate of Bs 400 million, calls for completion and strengthening of the basic road network as well as the construction of some selected development roads for the promotion of agricultural and industrial expansion. About 21 percent of the total government capital investment program would in fact be allocated to roads, a proportion similar to that allocated in the past. In the judgment of the mission, the investment necessary to complete the basic road network—finishing the interconnection of those areas into which the bulk of present traffic moves and the bulk of future traffic will move —should produce a very high yield in the form of savings in truck transport costs. While most of the investment we propose in the road sector is for the completion of the basic network, including major regional roads, we also include more than Bs 250 million to be spent during the four-year period on roads on which present traffic volume is still very low but where the potentialities for traffic growth are large (see Chapter 11, Table 37). Thus, investment is contemplated for a

new road south of Barinas and for a new road south and west of
Lake Maracaibo because of the agricultural potential of those regions.
Similarly, there are new roads proposed for the San Felix area because
of its industrial potentialities. On the other hand, the mission recommends against about Bs 250 million additional road investment, under
consideration by the Venezuelan Government, on the ground that potential development in the areas concerned does not seem to justify the
proposed expenditure.

The reduction in transport costs resulting from the basic road program now being completed should open up new investment opportunities in both agriculture and industry and should thereby contribute to
sustaining economic growth in the four-year period and thereafter. It
must, however, be recognized that most of the road program would have
a high priority even if diversification were not an explicit objective and
the likelihood of a very substantial rise in imports were great. Lower
costs for internal transport made possible by an integrated network
connected to major ports may in fact stimulate the sale of imported
products as well as domestic products.

As road investment applies more and more to secondary roads, farm
to market roads, and new penetration roads, the potential gains in diversification as such, as well as the risks of misapplying funds, will grow.
The need for more extensive appraisal of the traffic-generating potentialities of particular areas is evident. We suggest, however, that in regions of the country already settled, construction of relatively
low-traffic access roads over and above those provided for in the road
construction program of the Ministry of Public Works cannot wait
upon such appraisals in view of the urgent need to promote domestic
agriculture. The construction of access roads in such areas should be
accelerated as contemplated by the Venezuelan Government, well over
Bs 100 million being earmarked in the mission's agricultural program
for this purpose. In agricultural areas in Barinas-Portuguesa and in the
region south of Lake Maracaibo where the mission contemplates gov-
ernment-stimulated and subsidized settlement for low-income farmers,
construction of access roads, including provision for drainage, is conceived as part of agricultural project costs (see Chapter 9).

The road investment program, including the parts shown under agriculture, will contribute to the wider distribution of the benefits of
economic progress although the program is designed primarily to accelerate development and stimulate diversification by providing lower cost
transportation. The decline in transportation costs which has already
occurred gives promise that the program will achieve its primary
objective.

Railways

Ranking second in importance to highway investment within the transport sector in the past has been the investment in railroads, almost exclusively for the Barquisimeto-Puerto Cabello line. The mission has carefully reviewed all of the information available bearing upon proposals for railroad construction under consideration: first, a new national network of 3,000 km.; second, a first-stage program of 1,400 km.; and, third, a specific rail link between Naricual and Matanzas. It found no justification for the inclusion of any of these three proposals in the four-year program. Such investments would yield little, if any, return for the economy at large. The major highway network is nearing completion. Annual operating savings in a railroad do not appear to be substantial under Venezuelan conditions and the foreign exchange savings that rail operations might produce are not significant. On the assumption that the 1959/60 appropriations will complete rail projects under construction, the mission earmarks nothing for railroad investment in the next four years.

Ports and Water Transport

Investment recommended for ports would average about one-half of the average investment in recent years. The high rate of capital expenditures in the past has raised annual port capacity to 20 percent over the peak load. The current rate of operations is substantially below the peak and it is doubtful if the traffic through the ports will grow more than 3 percent a year in the next five years.

Expenditures on ports for the four-year period contemplated by the mission total Bs 65 million, including Bs 35 million for completion of projects already under way. Some of these projects will simply provide additional excess capacity. The Bs 30 million earmarked for new investment by the mission includes the construction of a new port on the Orinoco River in the vicinity of San Felix, one of the promising areas for industrial expansion. The mission advises against an additional Bs 30 million of new port investment under consideration by the Venezuelan Government on the grounds that it is not needed and would only provide additional surplus capacity. Of course, the port picture will have to be reviewed thoroughly if it should appear later that Venezuela will enjoy a faster growth of imports than now seems probable.

The very substantial investment that has already taken place in port facilities has not produced the returns which could have been expected in terms of low-cost water transportation in a country admirably suited to this means of transport. Effective water transportation is being hindered in Venezuela by poor planning of port facilities, confusion and divided responsibility in the administration of ports, and unduly restrictive customs regulations. Port charges are high, productivity is low and port facilities are poorly utilized, resulting in congestion and delay. Coastal shipping particularly is hampered by the present system and this may hinder the industrially developing region of southeastern Venezuela near San Felix. The mission recommends that the Venezuelan Government take action to eliminate divided responsibility in port administration. Port administration now costs about Bs 70 million a year; the mission believes that substantial sums could be saved if productivity in Venezuelan ports could be brought up to reasonable levels. Even more substantial benefits would be realized by the economy at large by reducing congestion and delay.

Airports and Air Transport

Investment in airports would total about Bs 45 million under the proposed program for the four years, airport facilities having been greatly expanded by the investment of past years. While the mission could not review the airport program under consideration by the Government in any detail, two of the airport expansion projects included therein did not seem to be justified by the traffic levels that can be forecast for the next few years.

Air transport service within Venezuela is generally quite satisfactory and not too expensive. The regular internal passenger service is subject to intense competition, with LAV, the government-owned airline, barely covering its current expenses in its national division. Capacity utilization is poor. It was, however, the international business of LAV that posed the most serious problem at the time of the mission's visit. Not only were operating losses very large, but new equipment was needed if LAV were to continue to compete for international business. New jet planes would have cost very substantial sums, and there was no assurance that LAV would have been able to decrease its operating losses with them. The mission does not include in its program any government contribution to LAV capital investment. It recommends that, unless some profitable arrangement can be made for a joint international service with interests in other countries, LAV's international service should be abandoned.

Electric Power

Investment by the Government in electric power would be reduced from the 1954/55-1958/59 level in both absolute and relative terms under the mission's recommendations. Even so, total capacity in the public sector would be increased from 319,000 kw. in 1959 to about 900,000 kw. in 1964, including the 300,000 kw. of Caroni-Macagua hydro power for which little in the way of additional expenditures must be made. Total public service capacity, including the capacity of the major private companies which are expected to continue to serve the principal population centers, would more than double, increasing from 855,000 kw. in 1959 to over 1,800,000 kw. in 1964.

Major expenditures under the approved program would take place in the thermal plants at Puerto Cabello and Puerto La Cruz and on a transmission line from Macagua to Puerto La Cruz. Expansion in thermal plants at San Lorenzo and Punto Fijo is also included along with funds for an electrification program for the 165 towns in Venezuela with populations above 2,500 that do not now have electricity supply. A substantial sum is also included for improving the distribution network.

The new 150,000 kw. plant at Puerto La Cruz with the related 230,000-volt transmission line to Macagua involves a total investment of about Bs 115 million. While the other parts of the program are related to meeting demands for power clearly in prospect in major consuming areas or in smaller cities not now enjoying central power supply, this project looks to the more distant future and foresees substantial industrial development in eastern Venezuela. Coupled with the Macagua hydro plant on the Caroni River, it will give to the Government the assurance that sufficient capacity will be available in the Barcelona-Puerto La Cruz and San Felix-Puerto Ordaz areas of eastern Venezuela to attract aluminum smelters, gas liquefaction plants and other heavy users of electricity even before a decision is reached on the construction of the Guri hydro project.

It is still too early to judge the merits of the Guri project, which in its first stage would have a minimum capacity of 1,000,000 kw. and an ultimate capacity of 4,000,000 kw. It would involve expenditures for the first stage of Bs 850 million as a minimum, according to preliminary estimates. This includes the cost of a transmission line to the major consuming area in the central region and the cost of cycle conversion in Caracas, both of which would appear to be necessary to ensure anything like reasonably full utilization of capacity. In the judgment of the mission, the amount of power that is implied in the first stage of this project is so great that, even if power-intensive industries like aluminum were established on a large scale, a considerable part of the power would still have to be absorbed in the central area of Venezuela.

If half of the power, say, 500,000 kw., were absorbed by new industrial projects in the San Felix area during the next decade, that would be a great achievement. This would leave 500,000 kw. to be absorbed elsewhere. A decision concerning an investment of the magnitude involved in the Guri project and related investments (Bs 850 million to Bs 1,200 million) must await more precise estimates of costs, a clearer appraisal of—if not actual experience with—industrial possibilities in eastern Venezuela, and a closer examination of the comparative costs of thermal power generation.

Thus, the mission believes that a useful interim program before any decision can be reached on Guri should include the transmission line from the existing hydro facility at Caroni-Macagua to Puerto La Cruz connecting the hydro power with a new 150,000 kw. thermal plant based on natural gas. Together these two facilities will provide more than enough electric capacity in the next few years to service a region where substantial industrial potentialities are now being tested.

The risk that excess capacity may be created seems to be worth taking in this case as a means of stimulating industrial diversification, particularly for the export market. The same cannot be said of some other projects under consideration at the time of the mission's visit, projects which would involve almost Bs 150 million of additional investment beyond that which the mission recommends. Such projects include expansion at Mariposa and the installation of even more capacity at Puerto Cabello than is envisaged in the mission's proposed program.

Telecommunications

The reduction of public investment in telecommunications from a level of more than Bs 75 million a year, including investments by the *Compania Anonima Nacional Telephonos de Venezuela* (CANTV) financed outside the budget, to a level of about Bs 43 million a year is based in part on the fact that in this sector, too, high investment in the past has provided the physical capacity necessary to meet a large part of the future increase in service requirements. Even more important is the fact that, because of inadequate management and lack of qualified technicians, it is likely to take several years before an organization can be built up which will make possible the effective use of additions to equipment over and above the amounts provided for in the mission's recommendations.

Telephone plant capacity is currently very poorly utilized. This is truly anomalous in view of the large unsatisfied demand for telephone service. Moreover, service is poor. While part of the difficulty could not have been avoided in such a rapidly expanding system, the mission concludes that much of the problem could be corrected by better management. System planning has been ineffective, traffic control almost nonexistent, and maintenance of facilities hardly related to operational requirements.

The investment program in the telecommunications field proposed by the mission amounts to about Bs 175 million for the four years and this recommendation is itself conditional upon a reorganization of the system and securing proper management. The program would provide about Bs 100 million for substantial increases in urban telephone capacity. In Caracas it would add lines equivalent to 45 percent of the principal lines now in service. Outside of Caracas, the mission recommends the addition of about 40,000 lines limited to the larger towns and cities; this would more than double principal lines in service outside Caracas in the four years. This represents a scaling down of the urban telephone programs now being considered by the Government, delaying the remaining parts of the program until management has proved itself capable of handling a further expansion. Outside of Caracas a scaled-down program seems to be advisable also because there can be little justification for providing local telephone service in small towns not yet having central electricity, adequate water or a sewage system.

In addition to the urban program, the mission recommends a sizeable expansion in long-distance facilities. Long-distance service is now less well developed than urban service and quality is even worse. The poor service is a positive hindrance to the future development of the country as a whole. Many firms have set up radio communications systems of their own, and the radio spectrum is already overcrowded.

The mission proposes for the long-distance service a step-by-step program adapted to manpower availabilities, market prospects, and management capacities instead of the program now being considered by the Government which would establish a grandiose country-wide network of nearly 1,000 radio channels to be installed within a five-year period. Although the mission was unable to obtain from the Venezuelan Ministry of Communications the type of information that is necessary for outlining a realistic step-by-step program, a preliminary review of the government program now being considered leads to a judgment that no more than Bs 75 million should be earmarked for the long-distance system.

COMMODITY-PRODUCING SECTORS

While government investment in economic overhead facilities—transport, power and communications—would decline almost 40 percent under the mission's recommendations as compared with the 1954/55-1958/59 period, investment proposed for the commodity-producing sectors of agriculture and industry would rise almost 25 percent. The mission's program calls for annual capital expenditures of Bs 378 million and Bs 343 million, respectively, for agriculture and industry. The increase is particularly marked in the case of credit provided by the Government to the private agricultural and industrial sector, which will about triple under the mission's recommendations.

In the judgment of the mission, a substantial increase in the Government's contribution to investment in the commodity-producing fields is fully justified at this stage of the country's economic development. With the slowing down in the growth of petroleum, the momentum of economic advance, including the provision of employment opportunities, will only be maintained at a satisfactory pace if agricultural and manufacturing output receives some extraordinary direct stimulus. Part of the stimulus would be provided by the adoption of the general economic and financial policies recommended above (see Chapter 3). The government expenditure program, particularly capital investment, must also play an important role.

This program is even more important for achieving a diversified and viable economy, an economy which is capable of self-supporting growth even if petroleum should cease to expand at some time in the future. In the field of agriculture particularly, where the benefits of economic progress have yet to penetrate deeply, the economic objectives must also be intertwined with social objectives and a government-sponsored agricultural settlement program must be considered partly at least in these terms.

The capital investment program recommended for agriculture is somewhat larger than the program recommended for industry. In fact, when development expenditures of a noncapital nature are taken into account, total development expenditures on agriculture would be considerably larger than on industry. This does not reflect the relative importance which the mission attaches to these two sectors from the point of view of the future development of the Venezuelan economy. Industry already contributes more than agriculture to the gross national product, and the mission expects that industrial output will expand faster than agricultural output. Despite the greater importance of the manufacturing sector in the economy, the mission feels that government effort, particularly as it is reflected in government expenditures, must be geared as much to agriculture as to industry in the years immediately ahead. The market mechanism, supported by adequate tariff and credit policies and by a general environment conducive to the entry of foreign capital, appears to operate more effectively in the industrial sector than in agriculture. Of great importance here is that foreign capital and know-how are much more inclined to enter the industrial field than the agricultural. In fact, the industrial entrepreneur, whether Venezuelan or foreign, is more sensitive to profit opportunities and is more likely to have, or to know how to acquire, the knowledge necessary for improving productivity.

Much of the existing technical knowledge in agriculture has been developed to fit conditions in the temperate zones and, even when adaptable to tropical regions, tests must be conducted and adaptations to local conditions must be made. The Government must thus undertake substantial programs of agricultural research and extension, both of which have received insufficient attention in the past. While the Government can appropriately provide technical assistance in the industrial field, particularly to the small enterprises, the scale of operations can be smaller. In the agricultural field, moreover, the reluctance of the small farmers to use new methods must be overcome by temporarily subsidizing certain inputs such as fertilizer and improved seeds. Such assistance is also consistent with social objectives since most of the farmers are also extremely poor. The subsidizing of fertilizers is particularly sensible as a temporary measure in view of the excess capacity for fertilizer production that will become available upon completion of the fertilizer factories.

Government programs for research, technical assistance, and subsidies for selected inputs, which are so important for agricultural advance, involve expenditures mainly of a noncapital character. The mission recommendations would call for a substantial increase in these fields, with total current expenditures amounting to over Bs 700 million in the four years. In the industrial sector, on the other hand, technical assistance and industrial extension work, even if augmented considerably, would be unlikely to exceed Bs 15 million.

Low-Income Farmers

Included in the Bs 700 million of noncapital expenditures for agricultural development are substantial sums earmarked particularly for the low-income farmers, who constitute a special social problem. A part of the capital program in agriculture is also geared to the social problem. The problem of raising the income and living level of the subsistence farmer cannot be solved simply by waiting for better education to work its effect. Neither is it practicable under present circumstances to provide adequate job opportunities in urban areas for more than a limited percentage of those wanting to transfer to urban jobs. The Venezuelan subsistence farmer must be given an opportunity to improve his income and living level on the land. In many cases, this calls primarily for extension, subsidy and credit programs which will increase productivity without relocation.

In other cases, a government-sponsored resettlement program will be needed. In contrast with past action of this type, the settlement program suggested by the mission would provide opportunities for resettlement to a large number of families—about 60,000—at a relatively low unit cost. The mission feels that a settlement program costing about Bs 100 million a year could make a substantial contribution to solving the social problem of the low-income farmer, if it takes advantage of the relatively abundant unused good land located not too far from major roads. In dealing with the problem of low-income agriculture there is the danger that emphasis will be placed on establishing model settlements under direct government supervision in which provision of housing and other social amenities becomes the major objective. In this connection, the mission recommends that the agricultural colonies now being operated by the Government be sold to the farmers and that self-supporting local authorities be permitted to assume responsibility for community facilities, the expense for which is now borne by the central government. While the mission agrees that the agricultural settlement program must be judged in large part in terms of the need to distribute the benefits of economic progress, it would be unfortunate if the Government concentrated its efforts on a program which was formulated only in social terms. Venezuela is fortunate in possessing relatively abundant land resources, a much larger proportion of which can be brought under development now that malaria has been virtually eradicated. There need be little conflict in Venezuela between the objective of providing land of better quality to the shifting cultivator now on poor land and the objective of encouraging the commercial farmer to invest in improving his land and increasing productivity.

Irrigation

The mission does not favor an expansion in government investment on irrigation at this time. This is due partly to the fact that good land is still relatively abundant, partly to the fact that a great deal more study is required to determine which areas are most appropriate for irrigation, and partly to the fact that more experience on small projects is needed before Venezuelan farmers can reap full benefits from large-scale undertakings. Serious questions can be raised concerning the Guarico project, to which two-thirds of government funds in the irrigation field have been allocated in the past, and which is still far from complete. The mission suggests that additional study is required before this project is continued. In Guarico and in Majaguas, where another irrigation project is now under construction, it is believed that poor soil conditions may greatly limit the economic yield that can be obtained. While the mission was favorably impressed with soil conditions in the Barinas-Portuguesa area, irrigation is by no means essential here, and the mission would therefore recommend a very cautious approach in executing the Bocono-Masparra project located in this area.

On the other hand, the mission strongly recommends drainage works in the region south of Lake Maracaibo. It also recommends investment in small-scale irrigation projects in favorable areas. There are a number of these which should be undertaken, both because of the economic return they can bring and because they will give the Government and farmers experience with irrigation which may pay big dividends in terms of long-term economic diversification.

Credit

Shorter-term gains in income, as well as longer-term diversification objectives, are at stake in the very substantial increase in credit to the private sector recommended by the mission. The mission suggests that about Bs 140 million and Bs 110 million a year be allocated to expand credit to agriculture and industry respectively during the four-year period. These figures are put forward very tentatively and should be adjusted as experience is gained with the recently expanded credit programs.

The mission suggests however that the credit programs themselves be revised, particularly in agriculture. With respect to the livestock program for which the bulk of the suggested credit is intended, the mission recommends that priority be given to financing sound farm plans designed to meet the fodder and water problem rather than financing simply fencing and imports of foreign breeds. The short-term crop loans made by the *Banco Agricola y Pecuario* (BAP) at low interest rates should be gradually turned over to conventional banks at commercial rates of interest and BAP should shift to medium-term development financing and should initiate a long-term, low-interest mortgage credit program. Another BAP credit program—the recently instituted program of loans to small farmers—should be curtailed to permit proper supervision and the provision of technical assistance, both of which are essential in administering programs of this type.

In the industrial sector, the mission recommends on the same reasoning the adoption of more modest targets with respect to the recently initiated credit program for craft shops and small industrial enterprises. With respect to the loan program for larger enterprises operated now by the *Corporacion Venezolana de Fomento* (CVF), the mission suggests that the purposes of the credit program might be better served if the loan activities were separated from the other activities of the CVF and organized in a separate institution.

Government Business Enterprises

On the basis of the experience Venezuela has had already in trying to establish government industrial enterprises, the mission is convinced that, to the extent that government finance is required in the expansion of the manufacturing sector, it should be associated intimately with private capital and private management capacity. However, the mission is cognizant of the fact that the Government, with the support of all major political parties, is committed to continue the steel mill and chemical factories now being constructed under government ownership.

The investment which the Government is committed to make in completing the steel project is substantial. In fact, when account is taken not only of the contractual payments due on the original contract and its escalator clauses but also of the need to finance spare parts, working capital and initial operating losses, the total is likely to reach almost Bs

800 million, which is more than half of the proposed total contribution by the Government to industrial investment in the program period.

It would appear that, including payments already made, the total capital expenditures on the steel plant per ton of steel product will be substantially higher than they would have ordinarily been in other countries. This is partly due to the variety of products that are to be made, partly to the higher construction costs that prevail in Venezuela, and partly to the peculiar circumstances relating to the negotiation of the original contract. Nevertheless, Venezuela should enjoy some real advantages in the production of steel. The country has easily available good quality iron ore and most of the other needed raw materials. Adequate and relatively cheap power will be available, and the plant is located so as to have ready access to economical transportation for raw materials and finished products. The domestic market for iron and steel products is substantial and growing. There will be a great shortage of supervisory personnel and skilled workers for an undertaking of this type and size, but it should prove possible for the Government to find and bring in foreigners to fill the gaps pending such time as Venezuelans can be fully trained.

On balance, the mission is encouraged to believe that, if first-class management is provided and full government support given, the steel enterprise will be able to supply steel products at a price no higher than Venezuelan customers are paying while earning a reasonable return on the real capital value of the plant. If this is done, the steel plant should make an important contribution to the Venezuelan economy, for virtually all other manufactured products require very substantial protection at present exchange rates. If the enterprise can be established on a paying basis under present conditions for the internal market, there are good reasons to believe that over the longer term Venezuela might become an exporter of steel products. The stakes in the completion and successful operation of the steel plant on the Orinoco are thus high.

The mission is convinced that the most important problem facing the Government at the steel mill is that of providing adequate management, both in the final planning stages and in the first years of operation. In all countries starting up the operation of integrated steel plants for the first time, there is a tendency to minimize the difficulties and to feel that local people, even though they may not have adequate experience, should be able to take over the operation and management from the beginning, with only selected assistance from outside specialists on certain technical aspects. The mission hopes that Venezuela will judge its problem realistically in this respect. In its discussions with Venezuelan officials, the mission has urged the employment of a competent firm, not connected with supply contractors, to review all phases of the project from raw materials through to markets; it has also urged that such a firm be engaged to work with the Iron and Steel Institute in starting up and running the plant, taking full authority and responsibility for financial control, administrative work and mechanical matters. The firm should not only furnish operating guidance directly, but should also provide satisfactory and realistic training for local personnel. This personnel would as a result be in a position more rapidly to take over responsibility for the management and operation of the enterprise.

With respect to the Venezuelan Institute of Petrochemicals, almost all of the investment necessary for completing the projects under construction should have been made by the end of fiscal 1959/60. The mission feels that the cost of the fertilizer and the caustic soda/chlorine factories has been exorbitant—perhaps three or four times more than was necessary to provide facilities of the capacity installed at Moron. It will be necessary to write down the value of these assets. As in the case of the steel mill, the mission recommends that the Government secure the services of an experienced firm to examine the project and to undertake technical and administrative responsibility for operation. If the investment is realistically valued and if efficient management is provided, it seems likely that the caustic soda/chlorine factory can be run at a profit and its products sold below prices now prevailing in Venezuela. The prospects for profitability of the fertilizer plants would appear to be more doubtful, although the program of fertilizer subsidies recommended by the mission should help build up an adequate market.

We recommend that Bs 130 million additional investment be earmarked for completing the fertilizer plants and for financing working capital and initial operating losses. No additional investments in pipelines for transport of natural gas are recommended for the program period. The lines under construction, it is understood, were to have been completed by 1960. While pipelines for transport of gas can be economic if a large enough market is available, or can be developed, the pipeline investments already undertaken have not been based on adequate market analysis nor have arrangements been made to develop the potential market so that the pipelines could be utilized upon their completion. The mission recommends that the Government invite private investors to play a leading part in the development of this market, the cost of which could be substantial. It is provisionally assumed that the Government will not undertake to provide any substantial sums for gas distribution lines in cities to which gas is now available, pending a serious effort to secure private interest in such an investment, and will not during the program period initiate construction of new lines to make gas available to places not now served, pending further experience with and better utilization of pipelines already constructed.

The mission wholeheartedly agrees with the Government's decision to consider no further investment in the chemical field for the time being. While the mission is greatly impressed with the opportunities open to Venezuela in the production of petrochemical products, it is convinced that these opportunities will be properly exploited only if the Government encourages the private sector, including foreign capital, to provide management, risk capital, and the skilled technical and research support which this field requires.

Similarly, the mission is hopeful that private capital can be encouraged to assume responsibility for further investment in the dry docks on which government investment in the past has been substantial. Here, too, experienced management is essential, and the Government's past investment will have to be written down substantially if private investors are to be invited to associate themselves in the enterprise.

In iron and steel, in the chemical and petrochemical field, in the dry dock project, and in the gas pipelines, including urban distribution, the mission is convinced that there are high-priority additional investments in Venezuela which will be undertaken by the private sector if the Government gives concrete and tangible evidence that its own past activity in no way represents a bar to future private activity in these fields. In some cases, the Government may wish to give even more tangible evidence of its desire to promote private investment or may wish to associate itself with private capital in the form of a joint venture. If such ventures should emerge, additional government funds may have to be allocated for the industrial sector. At the moment, it would appear that the contingency reserve contained in the mission program is sufficient to absorb such allocations.

Industrial Development Areas

Government efforts in the promotion of industry can have an important bearing on the geographical distribution of economic activity. From many points of view, including the increasing economic costs involved in the continued expansion of Caracas and the need of other regions to share in the country's economic growth, the development of several major industrial areas would be desirable. While the widespread geographical dispersion of industrial activity would face very serious obstacles at this stage, in view of the advantages to industry in being situated near established markets, it does seem feasible to encourage the location of industrial plants outside Caracas, even if they remain within the section of the country where purchasing power is now concentrated. In this framework, the mission was impressed with the industrial potentials of such areas as Valencia-Maracay, Puerto Cabello-Moron, Barquisimeto, Puerto La Cruz-Barcelona, and Maracaibo. The Government is experimenting with several techniques, including preferential access to credit, to encourage the establishment of plants outside of Caracas, and the mission commends these efforts.

Planning is also going forward looking to the establishment of a larger industrial complex in the Guayanas. Although this region is somewhat removed from presently established consumer markets, the mission was particularly impressed with its long-term possibilities. It is richly endowed. Its iron ore deposits are extensive and of high quality, and other minerals are believed to exist in the area in commercial quantities; its potential for cheap power is very large; it is within easy reach of abundant petroleum and natural gas; and its deep-water port makes it accessible to ocean-going shipping. Iron ore mining has already brought considerable activity to the area. The steel industry, supported by the Macagua hydro plant, is almost a reality. Inquiries have been received from aluminum companies interested in locating an aluminum smelter there. The industries likely to be attracted to the area initially are likely to be, for the most part, those based on the development of power or raw materials—consumer-market oriented industries can be expected to locate elsewhere in the years immediately ahead. However, once the steel mill is established, steel-processing plants of certain types will presumably find it attractive to locate near their source of supply, and, as the market grows, other industries may well find it advantageous to open operations in the area. While it is still too early firmly to judge the potential industrial development of the Guayanas, the mission feels that prospects are sufficiently good to justify the assumption of at least a degree of risks by the Government in investing public funds in certain power and transport projects important for the development of the area. The mission views favorably the attention being given by the Government to studies of this region and hopes that the Government will provide encouragement to private manufacturing and mining enterprises wishing to operate there.

SUMMARY OF SECTOR PROGRAMS 63

EDUCATION, HEALTH AND SOCIAL SERVICES

Investment in education, health and other social services is projected by the mission at the average level of past years but with a substantial reorientation. The reorientation recommended by the mission is in large part consistent with the changes already effected by the Venezuelan authorities, particularly with respect to the very substantial increases in education. The mission would suggest, however, as noted earlier, somewhat lower expenditures on hospitals and health clinics while maintaining expenditures for environmental sanitation at a high level.

Education

The mission is convinced that government expenditures, whether current or capital, to expand and improve the quality of the education of the Venezuelan people rank among the highest priority expenditures the Government can make. Time and time again the mission was impressed with the important limitation on Venezuelan development imposed by the lack of an educated populace. The Venezuelan economy is expanding and should continue to expand at a fairly rapid rate. The Venezuelan economy enjoys a high rate of investment and savings and a growing market is in prospect. Under these circumstances, it is particularly the human factor that limits further growth and diversification.

The education program is perhaps even more important as a means of achieving a wider and more equitable distribution of the benefits of economic progress. Wage and salary differentials in Venezuela are very wide and they reflect to a very considerable extent differences in habits, skills and abilities which education can reduce. While other measures which the mission recommends would also contribute to reducing income differentials, there is no program in the judgment of the mission more important than the education program in this respect, even though the impact will not be felt for some time.

From the strictly economic point of view also, much of the expenditure in education yields a return, although only after a substantial time lag. This is particularly true of primary education. On the other hand, primary education involves less sacrifice in terms of income foregone during the education process, and the income prospects of a person who has completed a primary education are so much better that it is clearly desirable for the nation as a whole to expand its primary education at a rapid rate. The expenditures on primary education must be regarded from this point of view as a means of contributing to long-term growth and diversification, not as a means of stimulating growth in the short term. The program for primary education outlined by the mission does not assume a substantial further increase in the total number of children in primary school. A dramatic increase has already taken place, mainly as a result of large numbers of children of all ages, who had not previously gone to school, entering the first grade during the school years 1958/59 and 1959/60. The short-term objective should now be to retain in primary school a larger proportion than previously of those enrolled and to provide places for a growing proportion of those reaching school age. The high rate of drop-outs is partially correctible by establishing new schools for upper primary grades and improving the quality of education. However, such improvements in retention rates can only be expected to take effect gradually. In addition, first-year intake of new pupils will decline for a few years once the backlog of late starters has been eliminated. Thus, the primary school population, which increased rapidly during 1958-60, will be fairly stable in the next few years.

The intermediate education program should yield somewhat quicker returns, particularly if there is a shift in emphasis to providing more opportunities for vocational education. In view of the fact that the number graduating from the full six years' course at primary school will grow only slowly in the immediate future, the proportion of these graduates who should be encouraged to enter teacher training and vocational courses, at industrial or commercial schools, is very substantial. The same factor—the slow growth of primary school graduates—limits the possible expansion of the academic secondary school program. By providing more secondary schools, however, a larger proportion of those who complete primary school will be encouraged to continue their education.

The need for university-trained personnel is very large in many fields but the present distribution of university enrollment is not well adapted to these needs. The cost of a university education is inordinately high, the quality is poor, teaching is a part-time occupation, eligibility criteria are too low, and the rate of drop-out is high. Budgetary allocations for higher education are now subject to a statutory minimum, 1½ percent of total government receipts, a procedure which does not encourage the universities to earn their increased appropriations by better performance. There is, however, constant pressure to allocate funds to the universities in excess of this minimum, a pressure which the mission recommends should be resisted until the situation is improved.

While the capital expenditure program in the education field would represent almost a doubling of past expenditures and represents almost 6 percent of total capital expenditures, even more important is the high rate of current expenditures envisaged. Total expenditures on education will exceed 11 percent of the total budget, as compared with 4-6 percent in the past. The education program is put forward as a means of strengthening the Venezuelan economy in a fundamental sense. It also meets an immediate social need and will contribute to a better distribution of the benefits of economic progress.

Environmental Sanitation

The other social service programs, while of high priority, do not contribute so significantly to all of the objectives of the development program. The importance of central water supply and sewage disposal systems, housing, hospital and general medical care is obvious. They all provide an important component of a higher living level and their expansion may be regarded as a high priority investment from the point of view of the economy at large. With respect to all of these services, government action as such is necessary for special reasons.

In the case of urban water supply and sewage systems, these services can most economically be organized as monopolies, whether private or public, and in Venezuela the Government has an experienced organization—INOS—set up to provide these services in the larger towns and cities. Moreover, water supply and sewage facilities in an urban community have important public health aspects which by themselves justify the Government in taking a special responsibility. In addition, if the Government is interested in securing a better distribution of the benefits of economic progress, the provision of central water and sewage facilities is a convenient instrument and in many respects preferable to direct income transfers.

The dominant role of gastrointestinal infections in mortality and the high incidence of diarrheal diseases in Venezuela are indicative of the importance of improving environmental sanitation conditions. Although an effective environmental sanitation program requires an educated populace and educational campaigns to make certain that basic sanitary needs are felt by large segments of the population, more adequate sanitary facilities must also be provided. At present and despite the progress of the past decade, almost 50 percent of the urban population is without water service (compared with 27 percent in Colombia, 27 percent in Ecuador and 31 percent in Peru).

The investment program for environmental sanitation envisaged by the mission is more than 15 percent higher than in the past. It would greatly increase the number of households now served by water supply and water treatment plants, water distribution networks and sewers and disposal treatment plants. Not only would the growth of population in urban areas be provided for, but the existing deficit of facilities would be sharply reduced, particularly in the larger cities and towns. In the smaller rural settlements, wells and latrines would be provided for.

Housing

It is clear that housing conditions in Venezuela for the mass of the people are very poor. Any substantial improvement in these conditions over a short period of time would involve such a diversion of investment resources from other productive sectors of the economy as to be inadvisable even if it were practicable. On the other hand, the housing situation cannot be permitted to deteriorate further. There is serious doubt whether the private housing industry would be capable of meeting even a significant part of the needs of the low-income groups. Moreover, there is a serious social, economic and health problem in the cities created by the squatters who build their *ranchos* in densely populated areas. Under these circumstances, the mission has concluded that a government housing program must be continued which would at least arrest the deterioration in housing conditions and perhaps correct some of the existing deficiencies. The Bs 560 million for four years earmarked for this purpose would produce this result if, in addition to providing the housing required in government industrial projects, it were concentrated on very low-cost units. Basically, the mission's program would be to provide developed cleared plots of land with connections to the electricity, water and sewage systems. The structure would either be provided by the occupier on a self-help basis or the Government would provide "core" or unfinished housing, consisting either of small houses built so that they can be increased in size later or of full-size houses the interiors of which are not finished by the builder but by the occupier.

The program would call in most cases for the sale of the units to the owner-occupiers, with long-term credit at concessional rates of interest but with down payments required in all cases. The program envisaged here would be restricted to those earning Bs 12,000 or less, with most of the program serving the 70 percent of the urban population earning less than Bs 10,000. It is thus viewed primarily as a means of benefiting the lower-income groups, while at the same time arresting the deterioration in housing conditions. A substantial part of the cost per unit would be for providing water and sewer facilities in plot development, permitting the dwellers in ranchos to move from their present locations. This program represents a further development of the "minimum services" program recently initiated by the Government. The mission remains in doubt as to whether even a program of the size we contemplate—80,000 units during four years—could be achieved. It may be possible to secure the participation of administrative talent in state and local government but this will require further exploitation. The allocation suggested by the mission for a program of this type would appear to be the maximum which could be executed in view of the administrative limitations.

Hospitals and Health Centers

Administrative and manpower considerations have largely dictated the recommended reduction of the hospital and health center construction program to less than one-half of its former level. The construction of hospitals and health centers in the past few years has greatly outpaced the formation of the trained personnel necessary to operate these facilities. With the exception of certain localities where additional hospital beds must be provided as a top priority, the program envisaged by the mission assumes simply the completion of facilities on which construction has already been initiated. The mission does not question the ultimate need for many of the new hospitals under consideration in Venezuela; we are suggesting however that the construction period be stretched beyond the four years under discussion and that many hospitals be built later on if and when trained personnel become available. The mission therefore recommends a crash program for the training of nurses, dieticians, laboratory technicians and other medical personnel.

Total health expenditures, including current, by the central government are now very substantial, equivalent to 9-10 percent of the national budget. In addition, state and municipal governments also spend substantial funds in this field, as does the Social Security Institute. We feel that the great advances made in Venezuela in the public health field have been made mainly by programs which do not demand active and conscientious participation of the people. In those programs where the sustained collaboration of a well-informed community is required or where success depends on the financial contribution of the beneficiaries, the results have not been too satisfactory. Thus, it appears that many public health efforts may have temporarily outpaced public education and socio-economic development in Venezuela. In the mission's view, governmental health expenditures, which are already very high, should be stabilized for a period, during which time attempts would be made to revise and reorganize the health service in a manner which would permit further advance in a later period.

Urban Planning

The mission believes that much more can be done in the field of municipal public works if the future growth of the cities, towns and other settlements is guided by proper concepts of city and regional planning. To this end, we believe that the various governmental entities concerned should proceed to draw up master plans so that the establishment of new communities and the expansion of existing communities can proceed on a rational and efficient basis. For such community development to be responsive to local needs, local participation is essential.

Expenditures by the central government on municipal public works, other than housing, have averaged Bs 125 million a year in the past and would be cut by half under the program recommended here. In general, the mission feels that such programs should be carried out by state and municipal governments with their own financial resources, including the large general grants currently received from the national government. The larger cities, with very substantial untapped sources of income, should be encouraged to provide finance for city streets, parks, monuments and the like.

The mission feels compelled however to make some exception to this principle in the case of the transportation problem in the metropolitan area of Caracas. The extreme traffic congestion within the capital city interferes seriously with the business of government and financial support by the Government seems to be justified if a proper solution can be found. Proposals are under consideration for the installation of a subway to care for the mass transportation of people into and from the central business district. The cost of the first 30 km. of such a subway, representing only the initial stage of the entire rapid transit project, would be in excess of Bs 600 million. The mission suggests that this project is premature and that, before a subway is seriously considered, efforts first be made to improve traffic movement on the surface streets which will be necessary in any case, and which may eliminate the need for a subway for a long period of time. Improving the traffic movement on the city streets will require, however, the completion of the Cota Mil circumferential autopista to the north of the city, the building of an access-controlled autopista along the route of the Avenida Libertador, and the completion of the east-west autopista. Together with the completion of Caracas area avenues already under construction, the cost of these projects might well reach Bs 250 million. With the adoption of other measures recommended by consultants who have studied the problem, this investment would double the practical capacity of main avenues. Once circumferential avenues are completed, mass transportation could be effectively handled by an improved bus system. Until such an improved surface transportation system has been adequately tested, the construction of a subway system should be deferred.

CHAPTER 6 *POSSIBLE ADJUSTMENTS TO THE PROGRAM*

The basic development program outlined above is based on the assumption that GNP and government revenues originating in the petroleum industry will continue to grow moderately in the next four years. Given the surplus capacity situation now prevailing in the industry, it is possible, although highly unlikely, that petroleum prices will fall substantially and/or that Venezuelan output will be reduced. In either event, it would not be prudent to count on an early return of prices and output to previous levels. It is also possible that petroleum prices could rise from present levels and that Venezuelan output will grow more rapidly than 4 percent per year.

The More Favorable Assumption

Let us consider first the policy implications of the more favorable assumption: that there will be an increase in government revenue resulting from petroleum prices and/or output at higher levels than assumed. Under this assumption the mission would recommend that most government revenues in excess of the Bs 21.8 billion level be used to build up a development and stabilization fund. The fund would be used to finance capital investment if and when sound projects were formulated and made ready for execution, or to fill a gap in government finance if an unfavorable turn in petroleum should later emerge. A part of the excess in revenues could also be used as a substitute for foreign borrowing, although there is something to be said for Venezuela continuing to borrow modest sums and to enjoy greater international liquidity as a result, in order further to establish her credit in the international capital market.

The mission has concluded on the basis of its examination of each of the major sectors that the capital expenditures which make up our recommended program of Bs 7.6 billion are very close to the limit that should be spent during the next four years. If investment were to be increased substantially above this level, the percentage return to the economy at large from additional investment would fall off sharply. Efforts should preferably be devoted to removing the obstacles to the effective employment of additional funds so that the funds could later be spent with greater effect in strengthening the economy.

This does not mean that no increases in investment above the Bs 7.6 billion level would be justified. At the time of the mission's visit, some projects were under examination in Venezuela which might be worthwhile for inclusion in an expanded program. Others might develop during the course of the four years which could not be anticipated by the mission. We feel however that with the possible exception of the Guri hydroelectric project (see Chapter 12), which could be an economic investment only if a large power-intensive industry for the export market were established, it is unlikely that individual projects involving disbursements of any considerable magnitude will emerge. The Caracas subway is another possibility (see Chapter 15), but the appraisals of this project made to date do not convince us that construction of the subway during the next four years should take priority over building up a development fund that could be used later. Similarly, there are large projects in the irrigation field, such as the Bocono-Masparro project (see Chapter 9), on which large funds might be disbursed but which, in the judgment of the mission, could better be built in stages, so that the decision as to the scope and character of the final project can be based on careful study and actual experience.

One of the major limitations in expanding the volume of government investment in the next four years would appear to be the administrative capacity of the government agencies involved in planning and executing major programs. Our proposed programs for education, housing, environmental sanitation, telecommunications and hospitals, appear to be about the maximum that can be planned, executed, and put into use with reasonable efficiency. In the housing field, it would however be possible to devise a credit program, geared to middle-income families and administered by private financing institutions, which could absorb substantial funds. The need for such a program might be less if the economy were to expand more rapidly under the stimulus of a petroleum boom.

In transport, power and heavy construction generally, the absorptive capacity of the agencies responsible for planning and execution of projects is high. But present and prospective physical plant in these sectors is already so large in relation to requirements that there seems to be very limited additional investment that would pass even a minimum test of economic yield. However, some additional highways in new development areas might be worthy of consideration.

This leaves for consideration government capital investment in petroleum, manufacturing and agriculture. For reasons noted in Chapter 3, the mission questions the desirability of expanding a government-owned petroleum enterprise competing with the private companies. In the industrial sector (see Chapter 10), if proper management arrangements are concluded for the operation of the steel mill, it might be feasible to consider some expansion of capacity beyond the 750,000 ingot-ton level, but it would hardly be prudent to go ahead with this until some experience with the initial installation was gained. Moreover, any such expansion would have to be evaluated at that time in terms of existing and potential markets. Some additional allocations might also be made for the credit program for private industry and agriculture, but the situation would have to be re-evaluated, because a more favorable petroleum situation might so affect future expectations that private capital would flow into these sectors with less need for government support. It is also possible that additional allocations could be made for agricultural settlement, primarily by providing somewhat more generous benefits per family.

On balance, the mission suggests that if government revenues were to exceed the Bs 21.8 billion level by about Bs 1 billion, which could occur if prices do not fall and if output expands by 6 percent a year, rather than 4 percent, something in the neighborhood of Bs 750 million should be accumulated in a stabilization and development reserve fund.

In addition to the desirability of building up a development fund for later use, there is also the need to have available substantial international assets to help the economy adjust more smoothly to possible future declines in petroleum exports. The Venezuelan Government's cash balances and the country's gold and foreign exchange reserves were at minimum levels at the beginning of the program period. The mission feels that $700 million to $1,000 million in international assets under the control of the Government and the Central Bank would not be excessive given the current level of imports. These assets could well be partially held in interest-bearing form.

The Less Favorable Assumption

If, on the other hand, there were a shortfall in petroleum revenues, but only a slight one, no substantial change in the program would be necessary. A considerable margin of uncertainty in any case attaches to many of the elements in the program. Nondevelopment expenditures of the Government could be cut by more strenuous economy efforts, taxes could be increased, or external credits might be secured on a larger scale. The best way of making such marginal adjustments would have to be determined on the basis of an appraisal of the economic position at the time the need becomes clear.

If it should become necessary to make marginal reductions in development expenditures for reasons of over-all policy after the program has been in execution for some time, the cuts will have to be made in the light of the progress of construction of projects as well as in the light of relative priorities. Ignoring the former consideration, which might in fact be decisive in practice, the mission suggests the following areas in which some cuts could be made:

	Estimated Savings (in Bs million)
a. A cutback in investment in ports and airports	20
b. Elimination of the Puerto La Cruz power plant and related transmission line	115
c. Elimination of Bocono and Guanare diversion works project	45
d. Reduction in road program	100
e. Elimination of the program for purchase of books and supplies in schools	50
f. Reduction in livestock credit program	70
Total	400

Although other cuts could be made by slowing down education, housing and environmental sanitation, the mission would strongly recommend against them. Moreover, it is the mission's view that very strenuous efforts should be made to avoid even the modest cuts in the program mentioned above. This is particularly the case if the reduction in petroleum earnings were to occur early in the program, before the transition to a balanced budget and foreign exchange situation had been completed. During this period particularly, a modest shortfall in revenues should be offset if necessary by a somewhat higher level of borrowing abroad.

The Case of a Substantial Decline

If the shortfall in petroleum revenues were substantial—say, Bs 400 million[1] a year or more—such questions arise as whether external credits should or could be secured abroad to fill the gap, whether the gap should be covered by deficit financing, whether the development pro-

[1] This could result from a 10 percent reduction in realized petroleum prices from the level assumed by the mission.

gram should be cut back sharply, or whether taxes should be increased and, if so, in what form. The mission recommends that in such an event every effort short of inflationary financing be made to avoid a sharp cut in the program of development expenditures outlined above and would favor increasing tax revenues by means which would simultaneously give a boost to growth and contribute to long-term diversification. Such an increase in tax revenue would be achieved, for example, by the imposition of an import surcharge or exchange tax, or by devaluation.

A substantial cut in the contribution of petroleum to GNP would mean in the first instance a reduction in the GNP and a decline in the share of the total available to the Government. Unless compensatory forces could be set in motion, the decline in government resources would force a reduction in high-priority development expenditures, would create less optimistic expectations on the part of the private sector, and would produce a reduction in real income. The basic objectives of the development program would be placed in jeopardy.

The problem is to design a set of compensatory policies for such a contingency ahead of the event. If those in the private sector recognize that such policies have been formulated and that the Government is prepared to implement them when and if the need arises, they should have greater confidence in the future. Moreover, if the policies formulated to meet such a contingency would effectively stimulate diversification, those in the private sector should be encouraged, even if petroleum did not decline, to make those investments which would contribute to such diversification. Thus, even though the mission does not expect petroleum revenue to decline, the development program should explicitly provide for this possibility.

The least disturbance to the domestic economy in the short term would be produced if the Government simply borrowed abroad the funds necessary to offset the decline in petroleum revenue. The mission doubts, however, whether it would be feasible for Venezuela to secure on reasonable terms external credits to the extent of Bs 400 million or more a year, over and above those envisaged in our program. Moreover, we doubt whether contracting such a volume of external credit would be justified under the circumstances, even if it were practicable. Borrowing at the rate of an additional US$120 million a year or more for several years would soon lead to a large external debt on which the service burden would be quite onerous. The mission does not think the Government should assume such a service burden in order to minimize the short-term disturbance to the economy when other policies would permit the economy to go forward under these adverse circumstances.[2]

The second—and in a sense the "normal"—response to a substantial decline in government revenues would be a cut in government spending. The government sector, which first feels the impact of the decline in petroleum revenue, would absorb the cut and not try to pass on all or part to other sectors. This alternative would not directly interfere with the disposition of private income; it assumes that the full primary adjustment to a lower level of real income should fall on the government sector.

Some reductions could certainly be made in the Government's current expenditures and the basic program outlined by the mission assumes that many of these economies will be made. Any further substantial reduction in current expenditures would require drastic reductions in military expenditures. Assuming that this is not practicable, the program of development expenditures would have to be curtailed if the government sector were to be cut back substantially. Rather than do this, the mission would recommend instead a properly designed program of tax increases, the effect of which would be to reduce private expenditures rather than the high-priority expenditures included in the recommended development program.

It is by no means clear that, if petroleum prices were to decline and the Government simply reduced its expenditures to the extent of the decline in revenues, equilibrium of the budget and of the balance of payments would be achieved at the maximum level of real income. A decline in petroleum would tend to create a pessimistic outlook in the private sector. Private spending would decline, if not stimulated by other governmental policies. The Government, fearing that the decline in private spending would go too far, would be disposed to increase its own expenditures and public pressure in support of this would be strong. In other words, the private sector would be disposed to spend less even as it seeks to avoid a reduction in its income and the Government would be forced to spend more despite the decline in its income. So long as the resulting deficit in the government accounts was offset by this voluntary surplus in the private accounts, no serious financial problem would result, but a serious stagnation and unemployment problem certainly would. The danger is that the Government might feel that it should compensate by larger deficits. Moreover, even after

[2] If a shortfall in petroleum revenues were produced by a temporary drop in prices, additional external borrowing could be justified. However, in view of the petroleum outlook presented in Chapter 8, it would be imprudent to interpret any fall as temporary.

the private sector wanted to increase its spending, the Government might try to continue to maintain its command over real resources by continuing to run a deficit.

The Venezuelan economy is very poorly adapted to the use of such inflationary techniques for compensating for such a decline in petroleum or for financing economic development. A Government deficit might help ease a transition to a lower level of income, particularly if the country has foreign exchange reserves with which to finance the foreign exchange deficit which would emerge. It could not, however, provide any substantial stimulus to private activity without producing a serious disequilibrium in the balance of payments. If the deficit were to continue, controls on imports would be applied and prices would rise. Tax revenues in Venezuela under the present tax structure are almost insensitive to a rise in the domestic price level.[3] The Government's revenues would give it increasingly less command over real resources as prices rose. An inflationary spiral would be hard to avoid, and it is almost certain that the Government would not succeed in maintaining the planned level of real development expenditures. The inflationary spiral would also have effects on private savings and private investment which would be contrary to the aims of the development program. It would most certainly produce capital flight and a balance of payments crisis. Direct import restrictions and exchange controls would have to be applied more and more stringently so long as a change in the exchange system were excluded. Such controls would encounter many practical difficulties and could create serious maladjustments. Venezuela's economic development has benefited greatly from the environment of financial stability which has prevailed and from the absence of widespread direct controls over imports and the balance of payments. It would be worthwhile to go to considerable lengths to preserve the benefits of financial stability.

Thus, neither a reduction in government spending nor adoption of a policy of deficit financing represents a proper response to a substantial decline in the petroleum sector, the former because it requires sacrificing high-priority development expenditures and short-term economic growth, the latter because it would be ineffective in maintaining government command over resources for a sustained period and would

[3] Taxes on the petroleum sector, which constitute 61 percent of total revenues, would in fact decline to the extent that the costs of the petroleum companies increase. Customs duties, which represent another 15 percent of total revenues, would not increase; only income taxes and excise taxes levied on the basis of domestic prices would rise. For a more extensive discussion of the sensitivity of the tax system, see Shoup and others, *op. cit.* Chapter 13.

have unfavorable effects on private savings, investment, and the allocation of resources.

There remains the possibility of an increase in tax rates designed to offset the decline in petroleum. An increase in the petroleum royalty rate or the income tax rate on petroleum might in the short run secure additional foreign exchange and sufficient government revenues to counteract the effect of a decline in petroleum prices. However, this effect is likely to be very short lived, given Venezuela's competitive position described in Chapter 8. Such a tax increase would in fact lead with some lag to a further reduction in petroleum revenues and would make a bad situation even worse. A second alternative in the tax field would be to increase income and excise tax rates, excluding in the first instance any tax increases on imports of goods and services. Bs 400 million a year in additional revenues would add about one-third to the effective tax rate from these sources and would reduce private spending—which is after all one of the purposes of the measure. The danger is however that such a tax increase in the circumstances of an absolute decline in petroleum would aggravate the pessimistic outlook of the private sector and make it even more difficult for the Government to offset the effects of the petroleum decline. Thus, tax measures would have to be devised which would increase government revenues without weakening the petroleum sector, produce more favorable investment expectations and help keep the balance of payments in equilibrium.

In the mission's judgment, economic growth could be maintained at an adequate rate and the foundations for continued growth actually strengthened if, under these circumstances, the Government firmly and promptly took some such action as a devaluation or the imposition of an import surcharge or an exchange tax. Whereas the mission feels that such measures are not necessary under existing circumstances, such measures should certainly be considered if a substantial decline in petroleum revenues were to occur in the program period. Such measures would be relatively simple to introduce and would accomplish three results simultaneously: first, it would effectively transfer command of real resources from the private sector to the Government; second, it would stimulate the rate of economic growth and assure balance of payments equilibrium by changing price-cost relationships in favor of the domestic producers of goods and services who compete with foreign producers; and, third, it would strengthen those commodity-producing and service sectors which need to be expanded in the interest of diversification.

PART **II** *AN ANALYSIS OF*
THE VENEZUELAN ECONOMY

CHAPTER 7 *STRENGTHS AND WEAKNESSES*

In this chapter we examine the recent performance and present condition of the Venezuelan economy, and thereby attempt an assessment of its strengths and weaknesses at the outset of the four-year planning period. We first consider the rapid increase in production achieved during the 1950's and the growth in savings, investment and employment which made such economic development possible. The petroleum sector provided the basic stimulus—as a source of revenues, savings and foreign exchange for the economy as a whole and so as the provider of resources for the even more rapid development achieved in other sectors of the economy as a whole. Most notable was the growth in manufactures which has already begun to broaden the base of the economy. There was also substantial expansion in the production of electric power, in the provision of basic transportation facilities and in a broad range of other industries. However, the record, at least until recently, was not as satisfactory in some sectors of agriculture, nor in the fields of housing and education. Furthermore, an examination of the distribution of the increased production of goods and services among various groups in the economy leads to the conclusion that the benefits of economic progress have been shared very inequitably.

Later in the chapter, the mission deals with the fiscal and monetary aspects of the economy and concentrates on the problems of adjustment which have been facing Venezuela with the less favorable position of its oil industry and the transition from a dictatorship to a democratic form of government.

In the course of the analysis, certain weaknesses become apparent— notably a lack of industrial skills or even of good general levels of education, relatively high costs and prices, a marked inequality of income and wealth, and from one point of view a dependence on oil as a source of revenues and foreign exchange. At the same time, certain basic strengths of the economy emerge: the existence of a modern industrial sector and of commercial agriculture and cattle raising, the provision of extensive public services especially in transportation and power, and a high level of savings and of investment in sectors other than petroleum. These factors are cornerstones for further economic achievement and they have already shown their strength during the adjustment process under way since 1958.

ECONOMIC GROWTH IN THE 1950's

The Increase in Production and Incomes

Dynamic economic growth has been achieved by Venezuela throughout almost all the postwar period. Indeed, following the 1943 decision by the Government and the oil companies to accelerate the development of oil resources, rapid economic expansion wrought a dramatic change in the scale of the economy and in income per head. A relatively small agricultural economy, with a 1943 production of less than Bs 7 billion (1957 prices) and a population of four million was transformed into a petroleum and manufacturing economy of over seven million people producing Bs 26 billion of goods and services a year.

With the high rate of growth in national product and income (8-9 percent a year) there has come a substantial rise in per capita income. Despite the increase of population by more than 4 percent a year, the average annual income per head has also risen at least 4 percent, or by virtually 50 percent during the 1950's.

During the 1950's, the volume of production increased by an average of 8.3 percent a year, the slowest growth being in 1953 and 1958 when petroleum output declined. Yet even in these years, the non-oil sectors achieved quite substantial increases in production. Indeed, perhaps the most significant aspect of this economic growth, apart from the high average rate achieved, was the expansion of the non-oil sectors somewhat more rapidly than the petroleum industry. For the growth in the absolute size and relative importance of other sectors denotes an increasing capacity to generate further expansion in the economy. This growth was particularly apparent in iron ore mining and manufactures, commerce and electric power.[1] Despite the growth of these sectors, however, the oil industry itself is still the dominant sector of the economy, being as large as the four other most rapidly growing sectors combined (see Table 4).

From small beginnings in the early 1920's, the Venezuelan oil industry has grown rapidly, and by 1933 accounted for more than 90 percent of export receipts—a contribution which it has made in each subsequent year. In 1936, the industry created 8 percent of net national

---

[1] Such growth was not always an unmixed blessing; for example, there was also a rapid growth of the construction industry which has led to distortions in the economy as a whole and is currently creating problems of adjustment, as we note elsewhere.

income, which corresponded to only about one-third of the contribution of agriculture. Rapid expansion, particularly from 1943 to 1948, raised the petroleum share in the national product to 20 percent, a proportion exceeding that of manufactures and agriculture combined. This was achieved not only by the rise of production and prices, but also by increasing royalty and income tax rates.

In the last decade the oil industry has doubled its capacity and its proven reserves, and more than doubled its export and its tax payments

TABLE 4: Gross Domestic Product by Major Sectors

(in Bs million at 1957 market prices)

| | | | | | | Indices of Change | | |
| | | | | | | 1959 Output | % of GDP | |
	1950	1955	1957	1958	1959	(1950=100)	1950	1959
Agriculture, livestock and fishing	1,014	1,352	1,507	1,576	1,642	162.0	8.0	6.3
Mining	20	221	383	379	420	2,056.0	0.2	1.6
Petroleum	3,920	5,777	7,472	7,073	7,560	192.8	30.8	29.0
Manufactures	1,150	2,004	2,429	2,607	3,012	261.7	9.0	11.6
Construction	827	1,363	1,581	1,617	1,707	206.2	6.5	6.6
Water & electric power	69	159	238	281	336	487.2	0.5	1.3
Commerce	1,726	2,862	3,933	3,803	4,003	231.7	13.6	15.4
Transportation & communications	699	951	940	1,002	1,090	155.9	5.5	4.2
Rent & interest	1,161	1,752	2,141	2,398	2,664	229.5	9.1	10.2
Services (inc. Govt.)	2,140	2,884	3,224	3,427	3,632	169.7	16.8	13.9
Total	12,728	19,325	23,848	24,164	26,065	205.2	100.0	100.0

Note: For a more detailed annual series for 1950-59, see Statistical Appendix, Table S.1.

Source: Memoria, 1959, Banco Central de Venezuela.

to the Government.[2] This rapid growth has occurred despite three years of market recession and decline in oil output—1949, 1953 and 1958. Indeed, in terms of the contribution of the oil industry to national income as opposed to physical output, there has never been any appre-

[2] In absolute terms, the major increases in oil output and revenues have taken place during the last few years. Half the 40-year output of 13 billion barrels of oil has been produced in the last eight years, and half the Bs 30 billion of government oil revenues (even in constant prices) has been gathered in the last six years.

ciable year-to-year decline. There have been periods of stability in the income accruing to the nation, as in 1948-50 and 1957-59 (see Statistical Appendix, Table S.2). Short-run movements in oil prices and demand, particularly adverse movements, have been less severe than the fluctuations which most other underdeveloped countries have experienced with respect to their principal export commodities.[3] Moreover, oil prices, at least until recently, have easily kept pace with the increases in import prices (see Statistical Appendix, Table S.3).

While the Gross Domestic Product (GDP), which is the value of all production in the country, has broadly fluctuated with variations in the preponderant oil industry, the Gross National Product (GNP), which is the value of output accruing to Venezuela alone (and therefore excludes payments to foreigners—in this case, particularly the foreign oil companies) has to some degree been cushioned from fluctuations in the oil industry by the Government varying the proportion of total oil income which accrues to itself. This is in fact, what happened in 1958 when petroleum output declined. There was a continued growth of income, though at a slower rate (almost 4 percent) than in previous years, and this was made possible in large part by the sharp rise in income taxes which led to a transfer of oil income from profits receivable abroad to government revenues and so to national income (see Statistical Appendix, Table S.5). This transfer more than offset the income-depressing effects of lower output and prices. On the other hand in 1959, further income growth (almost 6 percent) was entirely due to the increased production and incomes generated by the non-oil sectors. These increases outweighed the decline in income from oil and thereby indicated the growing strength and resilience of the other avenues of production.

The Volume and Composition of Investment

Underlying the rapid economic growth achieved during the 1950's has been a high average rate of investment. Venezuela has devoted 30

---

[3] Demand has in fact declined in only three of the last 16 years, and then by only a few percentage points. There was one price fall (5 percent) in 1956, but this was accompanied by a 14 percent increase in export volume. The only significant adjustment which has faced Venezuela is that associated with the 15 percent reduction in market prices between 1957 and 1959. Even so, 1959 output equalled the record level of 1957, and the 1958 tax rise virtually offset the effect on national income which the fall in prices would otherwise have had (see Statistical Appendix, Table S.2). Moreover, the contribution of the oil industry to net export earnings has continued to increase in 1958 and 1959.

percent of its GNP to gross investment, a proportion equalled or exceeded in only a few European countries, notably West Germany and Norway. Moreover, the rate of investment appears to have been fairly consistently maintained (see Statistical Appendix, Table S.6). Of this investment, less than one-quarter has been carried out in the foreign-owned export-oriented petroleum and mining industries. Hence, more than 20 percent of the GNP has been devoted to investment in those sectors of the economy which cater primarily for the domestic market. The most useful results of this high level of investment have been the provision of basic facilities in transportation and power, and the increased capacity of the manufacturing sector.

Dividing investment into government, foreign private and domestic private, we find that the Government has been the principal investor in fixed assets, accounting for over 40 percent of the total (see Statistical Appendix, Table S.7). Moreover, excluding the fields of mining and petroleum where virtually all investment is foreign, the Government appears to have been responsible for almost 60 percent. With its volume of investment averaging 10-12 percent of GNP, the Government has been able to provide large sums for transportation, particularly for highway construction. In addition, the period since 1954 has seen substantial outlays for industry. However, the investment in manufactures was mostly for the steel and petrochemical industries (see Chapter 10) which had made little or no contribution to output by 1959, and these outlays were in any event made at costs well above the real value of investment they represent. Irrigation and colonization have also absorbed large sums, including over Bs 300 million for the Guarico irrigation project which is still to be completed. Almost as important as these industrial and agricultural investments were expenditures for urban development—water, sewers and public housing, particularly in Caracas. Before the change of government in 1958, a large part of government investment was concentrated on the development of the central zone, notably the Federal District. This was especially true in civic improvement and highways. Furthermore, the Government's investment effort was accompanied by waste and lack of planning. As examples of large investments in projects either of low priority or constructed to extravagant standards or both, one may cite the appropriation of over Bs 300 million for twelve luxury hotels and two telefericos, over Bs 100 million for military clubs and housing, and Bs 140 million for the Caracas racetrack.

In the private sector, the most important avenues of investment have, of course, been the foreign-owned mining and oil industries. Private foreign capital has also been significant in the construction industry where, according to the Central Bank, it accounts for about half of investment, and in manufactures and commerce where 15-20 percent of capital has been supplied from abroad. Still, in absolute terms, 90 percent of all foreign funds are in the mining and oil industries. While the Government and foreign investment have therefore been very important, the Venezuelan entrepreneur and capitalist have nevertheless been responsible for large outlays, more or less matching those of the Government, in agriculture, manufactures and electricity. And private Venezuelan interests have predominated in commerce, housing and services. Indeed, as much as two-thirds of private Venezuelan investment has been in these three last-named fields.

The increase in output engendered by this high over-all rate of investment has been influenced by many factors. As limiting factors, we have already referred to the waste and delays entailed in some government programs. Furthermore, there have necessarily been large investments in economic and social overheads and these have resulted in relatively small direct increases in national product. Again, in agriculture, because of poor direction of investment, lack of research and extension services and low levels of efficiency, the response of output to increased investment has been relatively low. On the other hand, in the two dynamic production sectors—petroleum and manufactures— the annual increases in output have been almost as large as the additional investment made each year. For the 1950's as a whole, the ratio of the increase in capital stock to the increase in output in these two sectors has been 1.2:1. And this low ratio has been achieved even though much of the public investment in manufactures has so far been unproductive. The fact that these sectors have been responsible for as much as one-third of all investments made in the 1950's has contributed to the low level of the over-all net capital/output ratio, which was probably little more than 2.5:1.[4] Venezuela's income growth has therefore been favored by a high rate of investment and by the concentration of a large part of new capital outlays in rapidly growing industries with low capital/output ratios.

The Supply and Sources of Savings

The counterpart of the high rate of investment maintained during the 1950's has been an almost equally high rate of domestic savings,

---

[4] The *gross* capital/output ratio for the 1950's was nearer to 3.5:1.

averaging about 29 percent of GNP (see Table 5). It is surprising that so much of the total investment effort of the country has been financed by total domestic savings. Venezuela is known as a country which has enjoyed a very large capital inflow, particularly in the form of petroleum and mining investment. This has certainly been true of gross capital inflow during the latter half of the 1950's. The petroleum companies alone increased their net investment in Venezuela during the decade at an average annual rate of about Bs 400 million, which, however, was concentrated largely in 1956 and 1957 in the form of payments for concessions. As explained below, however, in 1958 and 1959 the country suffered from very large capital exports (including "hot money"), which not only offset the petroleum and other foreign investment in these years but also most of the capital inflow of the previous four years. As a result, for the decade as a whole, domestic savings financed 96 percent of the investment effort. Excluding the depreciation allowances of the petroleum companies, domestic savings financed more than 80 percent of total domestic investment and were equivalent to 25 percent of gross national product. Gross national savings at this level are extraordinarily high for an underdeveloped country and would be sufficient, if invested domestically in an effective manner, to help achieve a substantial rate of growth.

TABLE 5: Sources of Financing Investment, 1950-1959

		Annual Average	
		As % of Total Investment	As % of GNP
Gross Domestic Investment		100	30
Less:	Net foreign capital inflow	4	1
Equals:	Gross domestic savings	96	29
Less:	Depreciation allowances of petroleum companies	14	4
Equals:	Gross national savings	82	25
Of which:	Public sector	31	9
	Private sector	51	16
	Of which: Undistributed profits	20	6
	Depreciation allowances (excluding oil)	4	1
	Other	27	8

Source: Statistical Appendix, Table S.8.

Petroleum company depreciation allowances have risen from Bs 420 million to Bs 900 million in the past decade. So long as the petroleum companies have an incentive to maintain their present productive capacity in the country (see Chapter 8), this source of financing investment will remain available.

The Public Sector. The government sector in Venezuela has been able to maintain a high rate of savings—that is, an excess of current receipts over current expenditures—during the last ten years. Government savings, which have reached a level exceeding Bs 2 billion in each of the three years 1957-1959 (see Table 6), have averaged about 9 percent of gross national product and represented one-third of gross domestic savings. Essential to the maintenance of this high rate of government savings in the past has been the very rapid growth of tax receipts which have been equivalent to almost one-quarter of the gross national product. Tax receipts have continued to rise in the last two years, despite the decline in petroleum prices and earnings, as a result of the 1958 income tax increase and of the one-year lag between tax accruals and actual payments. This rise in revenues has permitted government expenditures on current account to double between 1957 and 1959, without producing a drastic reduction in the savings of the public sector.

TABLE 6: Savings of Public Sector

(in Bs billion)

	1950	1957	1958	1959
Current Income	2.13	4.53	5.07	5.81
Of which: National government	1.92	4.20	4.71	5.43
Current Expenditures	1.38	1.95	3.04	3.73
Of which: Wages and salaries	.88	1.18	1.70	2.17
Deficits of autonomous enterprises	.10	.08	.22	.35
Savings of Public Sector	.75	2.58	2.03	2.08

Source: Rearrangement of data in Tables 19-10, 19-11 and 19-16, *Memoria, 1959,* Banco Central de Venezuela. The Central Bank consolidates autonomous enterprise accounts, whereas only their net position is consolidated here. The Central Bank treats loans to the private sector as current expenditure, but the mission includes these in the capital account. The Central Bank treats receipts from loans, loans repaid, and bonds issued as current income; the mission includes these in the capital account. The 1957 current income excludes Bs 1.2 billion of payments for oil concessions.

Because of the relative ease with which tax receipts could be made to grow in the past, the Venezuelan Government has not been required to exercise any real economy in the administration of the ordinary functions of the Government. It has been able, at least until recently, to have a relatively loose and inefficient government administration and still to reserve substantial funds for financing investment. Moreover, past governments have not paid sufficient attention to many of those functions which are important for economic development and which involve substantial current expenditures. For example, prior to 1958 expenditures for education and training were not accorded a high priority. Now, however, significant increases for these purposes and for expanding programs in other social sectors, general wage and salary increases, staffing problems arising in the administration of a coalition government, and expenditures on the emergency public works program (POE) have raised current expenditures to new highs. In view of past neglect, many of these increases were necessary. However, unless the rise in current expenditures as a whole can be restrained, funds available for financing a development program will inevitably be reduced.

The national government, as distinct from the regional entities, receives over 90 percent of all tax payments made in Venezuela. In addition to covering its own current expenditures with these receipts, it makes very substantial grants to state and municipal governments and to autonomous agencies to help them finance their current expenditures. The States and the Federal District have been particularly dependent on the national government for their revenues, and in recent years the autonomous enterprises have been running large operating losses—over Bs 350 million a year, even without setting aside adequate allowances for depreciation or for return on the capital invested.

The petroleum companies pay almost two-thirds of national tax revenues. While total tax receipts represent an exceptionally large proportion (nearly 25 percent) of gross national product by international standards, non-petroleum taxes are equivalent to about 8 percent of gross national product, which is quite moderate. The two major sources of non-petroleum taxes are the income tax and customs duties; together, they provide about one-quarter of total national tax revenues (see Statistical Appendix, Table S.9). While income taxes on the internal sector have risen substantially—over Bs 600 million is to be collected in 1960/61 compared with Bs 264 million in 1957/58—the tax rates are still low. The income tax revision of December 1958, while it has increased the progressivity of the tax structure and has greatly increased the tax burden on the largest business enterprises, leaves the income tax little more than a token levy on most personal incomes and most business incomes.[5] While these new rates represent about a 50 percent increase over the effective rates previously prevailing, they are, except for the largest business enterprises, which pay a marginal tax rate of 47.5 percent, much below the rates of virtually all countries having income taxes, whatever their level of income per capita.[6]

Customs duties, the other major source of income, are set at a moderate level on goods actually imported. While duties as a whole are very high, many being prohibitive, the average level on goods actually imported is less than 20 percent of the value of imports. This results primarily from the very low rates averaging 5 percent ad valorem equivalent applicable to capital goods and intermediary products, which together account for about 60 percent of total imports.[7] Low duties on these imports are designed to give encouragement to domestic industries. However, duties on durable consumer goods are also relatively low, averaging only about 15 percent of the f.o.b. value, and duties on other luxury goods are likewise relatively low. Duties in these categories of imports have recently been increased, and the Government is considering additional excise taxes on luxury consumption.

The Private Sector. Private savings, excluding the depreciation allowances of petroleum companies, were equivalent to 16 percent of GNP and financed about one-half of total investment during the 1950's. This is a very high rate of private savings, particularly in view of the fact that depreciation allowances in the non-petroleum sector are so low. With the very unequal distribution of income described below which has prevailed over the past decade and with the excellent opportunities for profitable investment that existed, high income groups have been willing in the past to save a very substantial proportion of their incomes either in the form of undistributed profits of business enterprises or directly. Recent changes in income distribution are difficult to pin down, and the annual estimates of private savings are subject to such a wide margin of error that no real evidence exists on recent trends

----

[5] For example, a married person with two children making as much as Bs 25,000 a year in wages or salary pays less than 1.5 percent of his net income in tax. Such a married person earning Bs 100,000 a year in wages or salary pays income taxes equivalent to less than 5 percent of his income, and such an individual earning Bs 1,000,000 a year in busines income pays less than 15 percent.

[6] For a demonstration of this point, see ECLA, *Economic Survey of Latin America, 1955*, p. 147. The comparisons made by ECLA refer to 1955 rates of taxation, but the subsequent rise in Venezuelan tax rates was not sufficient to change Venezuela's comparative position.

[7] Based on a special study of the Ministry of Finance made available to the mission (see Table 8).

in savings (see footnote to Statistical Appendix, Table S.8.) . However, the continuation in the future of the high rate of private savings achieved in the 1950's is not assured, especially if there were to be slower economic growth and a more equitable distribution of income.

The Growth and Composition of the Work Force

During the 1950's, the total population of Venezuela grew from about 5 million to over 7 million at the end of 1959. According to Central Bank estimates, the work force expanded at the same rate, rising from about 1.7 million to almost 2.5 million. The increase of population and work force by an average of 4.2 percent a year has been due in major part to the continued high birth rate and to the sharp decline in death rates occurring since 1945. The high rate of natural increase (nearly 3.5 percent a year) has been supplemented by the large net inflow of migrants which resulted from the postwar policy of encouraging new settlers (see Statistical Appendix, Table S.10) . Moreover, many of these immigrants were adults who made an immediate contribution of technical skills, management ability and capital to various sectors of the economy. The provisional government installed in January 1958 suspended the policy of promoting immigration and the policy is still in abeyance. The slower economic growth and labor absorption achieved in 1958 and 1959, together with the inflow of the rural population to the cities in search of new forms of employment, has not encouraged a return to the previous policy.

It is not clear whether economic growth in Venezuela has created job opportunities at a rate fast enough to absorb the growing labor force. If the Central Bank's estimates of the labor force and employment are accepted—and it is clear that the basic data are fragmentary and unreliable—unemployment averaged 7-8 percent of the labor force in the 1950's and may have risen to 10 percent at the end of the decade (see Table 7) . Whether these figures are accepted or not (and they are a residual series) , there are signs of growing *apparent* unemployment in urban areas. This reflects chronic rural poverty and underemployment and also the measures taken by the provisional government in 1958 under the *Programa de Obras Extraordinarias* (POE) . Under this program, the Government offered wages amounting to Bs 9.50 a day, and then later over Bs 13 a day, a level substantially in excess of day labor rates in rural areas. This accentuated the movement to the cities and made more apparent the underlying problem of maintaining an adequate rate of labor absorption.

TABLE 7: Distribution of Work Force

(in percentages)

Activity	1950	1955	1957	1958	1959
Agriculture	41.3	37.9	36.4	34.8	33.9
Other commodity production[a]	14.9	14.2	13.6	13.1	12.9
Other activities	37.5	39.7	42.6	42.5	42.8
Unemployed	6.3	8.2	7.4	9.6	10.3
Total work force	100.0	100.0	100.0	100.0	100.0
Actual work force (in thousands)	1,706	2,096	2,276	2,371	2,457

[a] Mining, Petroleum and Manufactures.

Source: *Memoria, 1959,* Banco Central de Venezuela.

In absolute terms, each economic sector was employing more labor in 1959 than in 1950, but there were marked differences in the absorptive capacities of the various avenues of employment. This is illustrated in Table 7 which shows estimated changes in the composition of employment.[8] With only a slow growth in farm employment during the decade, there has been a marked reduction in Venezuela's relative dependence on agriculture as a source of employment. In the non-rural commodity-producing sectors, the growth in employment was very small in comparison with the growth in the output of these sectors, or with the increase in the work force as a whole. Non-farm commodity output more than doubled during the 1950's, while estimated employment rose only 25 percent. The large increase in output was therefore related primarily to increased output per man employed. In fact, the increase in employment in these sectors was not sufficient even to maintain the proportion of the work force engaged in commodity-producing activities other than agriculture. It was in a broad range of other industries that most of the new job outlets were created, so that the proportion of the work force in these activities rose during the decade.

Industrial and Agricultural Production

The High Level of Costs and the Protection System. There has been a substantial growth of industrial and agricultural output which has taken place despite the high level of costs and prices. This growth has

[8] A more detailed estimate of the distribution of the work force is given in Statistical Appendix, Table S.11.

been made possible mainly by the protective devices which have been adopted to limit competition from imports.

The high cost condition appears to have existed since the 1930's, and is not related to any postwar inflationary movement. In fact, although Venezuela had the common experience of a marked rise in prices during 1945-51, there was virtual price stability during 1951-58. The high level of prices and costs relative to the U.S., to Western Europe and even more to other underdeveloped countries, was noted by the U.S. Advisory Economic Mission to Venezuela in 1940 and again by the Shoup Commission in 1959.[9] A comparison of these two reports indicates that at both times many Venezuelan prices were a multiple of U.S. prices, though the extent of difference appeared to have lessened somewhat by 1958. It has not been possible for the mission to make its own detailed comparison, but it is believed that prices are, in an over-all sense, some 50 percent above U.S. levels.

A sharp increase in the Venezuelan price level relative to foreign prices occurred in 1934 when the U.S. dollar was devalued and Venezuela did not follow suit. The exchange value of the bolivar rose from Bs 5.27 to US$1 in 1933 to Bs 3.54, equivalent to a 55 percent appreciation. There were relatively minor changes in the dollar value of the bolivar during the next several years, and it was stabilized by the Central Bank at Bs 3.35 to US$1 in 1942. With imports equal to about 15-20 percent of national income in the early 1930's, a fall of more than one-third in the cost of imports constituted a significant price-depressing influence. However, the appreciation of the bolivar was not followed by a fall in the domestic price level relative to the levels prevailing in Venezuela's major trading partners. Rather, the internal price level continued to move upward more or less in line with price changes in the United States during 1935-40. In view of this behavior of prices in the 1930's and the further rise in the 1940's, Venezuela's price, wage and income levels, when converted at the exchange rates prevailing over the last 25 years, appear to be very high.

The causes of this continued high level of prices are to be found primarily in the degree of protection extended to local industry and agriculture, and in the fact that Venezuela's chief source of foreign exchange, the petroleum industry, was in such a favorable position, at least until recently, and it could expand at a rapid rate despite the unfavorable price level within the country. Both of these factors operated

[9] *Report to the Minister of Finance submitted by the American Advisory Economic Mission to Venezuela, 1940; The Fiscal System of Venezuela: A Report, 1959;* also the comparison of Caracas and Quito prices in the *Memoria, 1958,* Banco Central de Venezuela.

in the 1930's to create a high level of internal prices, and then in the 1940's and 1950's to sustain it.[10]

Since World War II, tariffs and other protective measures have continued to help sustain the high level of domestic prices and, as noted above, petroleum continued to expand at a very rapid rate without regard to domestic cost levels. While it is difficult to determine whether the effective level of protection has increased in the last 15 to 20 years, the mission suspects that it has not. Of course, if protection levels had been drastically reduced, the rising demand for imports might have disrupted balance of payments equilibrium despite the rapid growth in export earnings.

The protective system prevailing over the past 25 years has greatly favored the importation of capital goods and semi-processed intermediary goods, as shown in Table 8. High duties are applied to most nondurable consumer goods and to most agricultural raw materials. These duties are in many cases a multiple of import prices or even of domestic wholesale prices (see Chapters 9 and 10). While low tariffs on capital

TABLE 8: Duty Collected as Percentage of Value of Imports, 1957 & 1958

(annual average)

Commodity Group	Value of Imports (f.o.b. in Bs million)	Duty as % of Value
Foodstuffs	128	25.9
Primary materials	74	83.4
Fuels	57	51.9
Consumer goods (exc. durables)	1,108	42.9
Durable consumer goods	343	15.5
Intermediary goods	1,170	9.4
Capital goods	1,607	1.2
Total	4,486	17.4

Source: Ministry of Finance unpublished study of tariff incidence. Imports included in sample reported in the table represented 87 percent of total imports in 1957 and 1958.

[10] It has been argued that low labor productivity, high profit margins and the small size of the market are also important factors in explaining Venezuela's over-all cost level. While these factors may affect the level and growth of income and may explain differences in prices and costs among the various sectors of the economy, they do not qualify as explanatory factors for the general high level of prices and costs stated in foreign currency. Indeed, if these factors were relevant to costs and prices as stated in foreign currency, one would on the contrary expect a *lower* rate of exchange to compensate for them and thus lead to a lower level of prices.

goods and high tariffs on finished products promote domestic agriculture and industry, they also favor the use of capital-intensive methods of production. This substitution of capital for labor operates with particular force in view of the high wage levels prevailing in Venezuela and may in part explain the apparent difficulties experienced in absorbing the rapidly increasing labor force.

In addition to tariffs, quotas and other forms of direct import restrictions are also applied, particularly with respect to agricultural products. As a result, consumer goods prices in particular have been maintained at a high level. This in turn has supported the forces described in Chapter 10 which tend to extend the high wage level prevailing in the petroleum industry to other sectors of the economy. Thus while the protective system is itself a cause of the high level of prices and costs, its extension becomes necessary because of the high level of costs whenever the promotion of new industries for the domestic market is desired.

Manufactures. The principal producing sector, apart from petroleum, is manufacturing industry which now accounts for almost twelve percent of GDP as compared with nine percent in 1950. This sector has two distinct parts: one is a small and slowly declining group of artisan industries; the other is a modern industrial sector which has been expanding some 14 percent a year over the last decade (see Statistical Appendix, Table S.1). This new sector is also one of rapid growth in value added per worker; from official statistics, it appears that both employment and output per man have been increasing some seven percent a year.

Basic to this industrial growth has been the increase in industrial capital from an estimated Bs 1.5 billion in 1950 to Bs 3.7 billion in 1959, with gross investment in the last few years reaching Bs 600-800 million a year. It is only in the past decade that manufactures have attracted capital and entrepreneurial talent on a significant scale in competition with other areas of economic activity. In the earlier years of petroleum boom, commerce, services and construction attracted almost all of the potential capital and entrepreneurial talent. However, the domestic market has recently reached a size where local production of many products is becoming economic. Moreover, while there does not appear to have been a widespread increase in import duties during the 1950's, the government policy of encouraging import substitution has continued to favor the growth of manufactures. The gradual accumulation of managerial and technical experience and the development of greater labor skills were also of some importance, but this process was not greatly supported by government programs during the period. Recently, the Government has been making substantial credit available to the manufacturing sector, although earlier in the 1950's the credits provided were not in significant amounts. Finally, perhaps one of the most important elements in promoting industrial development was Venezuela's general reputation as a booming economy, which attracted immigrants with business and industrial experience and foreign investors. Moreover, government policy had encouraged the inflow of capital and immigrants.

During the 1950's, the value of industrial output increased from Bs 783 million to Bs 2,703 million, and employment rose from 92,000 to 165,000.[11] Even with this rapid growth, the levels of output and employment indicate the small absolute size of the manufacturing sector. Most of this increase occurred in the basic consumer goods industries of food, clothing and woodworking where a marked shift from artisan work to modern industrial production has taken place. There has also been a change in the composition of output, with a growing emphasis on the newer fields of chemicals, rubber, paper and metal manufactures. These newer fields now account for some 20 percent of manufacturing output as compared with 10 percent in 1948.

Much of the country's industrial growth has been at the expense of imports, but the volume of output falls far short of meeting Venezuela's requirements. For example, production in the newer industries rose six or sevenfold in the 1950's but this was not sufficient to prevent a threefold rise in imports of these goods. There is therefore considerable scope for further import substitution, particularly in the production of intermediary and final products in the metal and chemical industries. In these industries, rather than in the processing of agricultural products, Venezuela appears to have some natural resource advantage.

The Government is now attempting to provide a stronger foundation for industrial development by establishing basic steel and chemical facilities in two large state enterprises. However, both undertakings have been slow in getting into operation, and the large investment made since 1956 has yet to contribute significantly to national production.

Mining. In terms of actual production, 90 percent of the mining activity in Venezuela is devoted to the exploitation of the large reserves of high-grade iron ore located in Bolivar State. About half of the proven reserves of one billion tons are located in areas explored and leased by two U.S. companies which presently produce and export some 19 mil-

---

[11] At the same time, artisan production declined from Bs 367 million to Bs 309 million (1957 prices), and artisan employment shrank from 115,000 to 96,000.

lion tons of iron ore a year. With a total investment of about Bs 1.2 billion, the industry has grown rapidly since its first exports were made in 1951, and it now accounts for 5 percent of export earnings, though only 1-2 percent of GDP.

Other mining operations are on a very small scale, with a total value of only Bs 43 million in 1959 as compared with Bs 424 million for iron ore. Minerals produced include diamonds, gold, coal, salt, lime, manganese, nickel and asbestos (see Statistical Appendix, Table S.12). Of these, only nickel and asbestos have shown a large and sustained increase in production during the 1950's. Output of most other minerals has grown slowly or fluctuated. Manganese production, which was never very large, has declined, in large part through lack of continued exploration. In fact, Venezuela's mineral wealth is still largely unknown. Present production cannot be taken to indicate the potential production and export earnings which the mining industry might yield if large-scale exploration and development were undertaken.

Agriculture. Agricultural production grew during the 1950's at an average annual rate of 5.5 percent. However, this expansion was less rapid than that in mining and manufacturing as shown by the decline in the proportion of GDP contributed by agriculture and in the decreasing percentage of the work force so employed (see Tables 4 and 7). Nevertheless, the growth in agricultural output must be considered a notable achievement, especially in a tropical country.

The increase in production was most marked in the livestock and dairy industries, both of which more than doubled their output. Half the increase in the value of farm output was attributable to animal industries, and they now account for one-third of all farm output. The growth of extensive livestock raising on the llanos to meet the growing urban demand for meat also accounts in large part for the increase in output per farmworker. Other major increases in output were recorded in such commercial crops as sugar cane, sesame, Virginia tobacco, cotton and potatoes. On the other hand, there was a failure to achieve such increases in the production of basic food crops, e.g., rice, beans and maize, during the 1950's. Yet Venezuela has both the labor and the fertile land which could be used to increase the output of most agricultural and livestock products.

The changes in production are related to the dual nature of Venezuelan agriculture which consists of a commercial sector and a subsistence sector, each of which supports about 200,000 farm families. The commercial sector has responded to the increasing demand for foodstuffs and agricultural materials in rapidly growing urban areas, and the response has been fostered by a strong protectionist policy and recently by liberal credit policies. On the other hand, the subsistence sector has a comparatively poor record of achievement. The 200,000 peasant farmers, including many shifting cultivators, suffer from many limitations, including their low level of general and technical education, the uneconomic size of plots of 1-2 hectares, and the poor quality of much of the soil.

Over the last ten years, the Government has spent about Bs 2.5 billion on building irrigation and drainage works, establishing colonies and on other agricultural projects. Much could have been achieved if these funds had been used in a program based on careful research into soils and crops. These studies were not made, and several expensive but low-yielding projects were undertaken. Moreover, relatively little attention was given to building up the research and extension services so that existing knowledge could be more widely applied.

One line of policy which has been pursued consistently is that of protecting agriculture from cheaper imports. With the high level of internal costs and the low level of productivity, Venezuelan agriculture has been in a poor competitive position. To encourage a greater degree of self-sufficiency in selected products, the Government has subsidized producers (e.g., milk) and imposed quantitive restrictions on imports (e.g., eggs). With the help of these programs, production of several commercially grown products (e.g., milk, eggs, sugar and meat) increased greatly in the 1950's. But the increased local supplies were often inadequate to meet the increased demand, or even to cater for a substantially higher proportion of the market (see Statistical Appendix, Table S.13). The volume of agricultural imports has therefore increased, and the value of these imports is now some Bs 650 million a year, chiefly for dairy products, wheat and fruits. That is, imports have grown as rapidly as local output, and so no over-all increase in the degree of import substitution has been achieved. Moreover, farm exports, chiefly cacao and coffee, are presently at levels prevailing in the early 1950's—Bs 100 million a year, or less than 2 percent of total export earnings.

Other Sectors of the Economy

Among the most important sectors in this group are those which provide the basic economic overheads of Venezuela—the transport and communications network, power-generating capacity and the construction industry. Then there is the provision of social overheads, especially housing, education and health services. Finally, there are the services supplied by general public administration and by private business engaged in commerce, the professions, etc. Together, these various activities employ almost half the work force and contribute just over half the GDP (see Table 1). The stability of this share in GDP over the last ten years indicates that these sectors have expanded as rapidly as the directly productive sectors combined. But the more rapid increase in their employment indicates a relatively slower growth in output per worker (2-2.5 percent a year, as compared with 6-7 percent in direct production). These sectors demonstrated their role as major employers of new labor by absorbing 70 percent of the increase in employment which occurred in 1950-1959. Their performance as a group is therefore a major determinant of the over-all achievement of the economy in terms of growth in productivity and output and of the use of labor and investment resources.

The *transportation sector* makes but a small (4 percent) direct contribution to output. The investment of some Bs 4 billion, chiefly in highways, has, however, provided the country with an extensive transport network of generally good quality, including a road system of over 11,000 kilometers of which 40 percent is paved. Concurrent with the development of highways has been the decline of traffic on the railroads and a large increase in the number of trucks and automobiles and in the volume of road freight. Vehicle registrations have risen from 34,000 in 1945 to about 300,000 in 1960. In addition, a number of ports and airports have been constructed or expanded, and most of the ports now have substantial excess capacity in terms of cargo handling facilities. Telecommunications facilities have also been increased substantially, the number of phones doubling between 1954 and 1959; but management problems have prevented the full use of the newly installed capacity. In general, the beneficial effect which the improvement in transportation and communications has had on efficiency and output has been lessened by wasteful construction standards and practices and by low levels of management in various enterprises operated by the Government.

Very rapid growth has occurred in the supply of *electric power*. The combined capacity of public and private utilities has risen to 850,000 kw., apart from almost 400,000 kw. of power owned and used by private industrial concerns. This represents a more than eightfold increase since 1948. The private companies have provided the larger part of the increased capacity, but the public sector has grown quickly and now possesses 37 percent of all capacity, including the large hydro station on the Caroni constructed primarily to serve the steel mill. The very speed of the expansion has itself entailed haphazard development and imbalance in the national system. Nevertheless, for an underdeveloped country, Venezuela already has a high standard of achievement in terms of the proportion of potential consumers actually supplied. Over 50 percent of urban families are now served by the electricity network, and an adequate supply of energy is available to industry at reasonable costs.

In the development of power and transportation, as in the expansion of other sectors of the economy, the *construction industry* has of course played an essential role. In 1959, the value of construction activity is estimated at almost Bs 4 billion, or twice the level of 1950. Employment also doubled, reaching 187,000 or 6.5 percent of the total work force. In recent years about half the construction has been for private projects including housing, and much of the Government's construction program has been carried out under contract by private firms. During 1955-57, the industry substantially enlarged its stock of capital equipment and a number of foreign contractors entered business. Since 1958, however, there has come about both a change in the composition of public investment, with greater emphasis on schools and on projects outside Caracas, and a change in the system of paying for contract work. The previous regime paid contractors with notes which had to be discounted in Venezuela or abroad. The new Government has eliminated this haphazard system of contracting credit, but unfortunately has been slow at times in processing payments. The change in financing and in programs placed severe strains on some sectors of the industry, as did the collapse of a private land boom in Caracas which had been going on for several years. The effect on the construction industry is not entirely clear, although it is apparent that large amounts of heavy equipment became idle and contractors have been seeking work abroad. This has made some contribution to exports through the sale of contracting services and of some excess equipment.

Apart from the oil industry, the largest absolute growth in GDP has been in *commerce,* and the rate of growth has exceeded that in most other sectors. Commerce now accounts for 15 percent of the GDP and employs 250,000 or 10 percent of the work force. The growth in employment has been somewhat less than in the value of commercial services, indicating an increase in productivity of almost four percent a year, a rate which is only slightly below the over-all increase in product per worker. This may well reflect the improvement in commercial efficiency which has resulted from the introduction of modern and large-scale merchandising methods.

Finally, there are a large number of *services,* both public and private,

including public administration, defense, health and education services, and a broad range of private activities. Together, these services
form one of the largest sectors of the economy, accounting for more
than 20 percent of employment and 14 percent of GDP. The contrast
in these two percentages may be taken to reflect low average productivity in these industries, output per man rising only one percent a year.
Yet these services represent indispensable contributions to the economy,
especially those rendered by the Government in health, education and
welfare and, as discussed elsewhere in this report, there have been large
deficiencies in government programs in these fields. In addition, public
service salaries until recently were low in relation to other occupations,
and standards of appointment and performance have left much to be
desired.

Foreign Trade and the Pattern of Domestic Demand

The rapid and sustained growth of oil production and exports, the
high rate of investment, rising incomes, and finally the growth in domestic non-oil production, which has made possible the increasing
substitution of domestic output for imports, are reflected in Venezuela's
foreign trade of the past ten years.

A large increase in export receipts—both gross and net—has resulted
from the growth of oil production and a long-run upward trend in oil
prices which reached a peak in 1957 (see Table 9). Despite the suc-
cessively lower levels of gross export receipts in 1958 and 1959, there
was a further increase in net export earnings, as shown in Column 4 of
the table, because of the higher tax rates introduced in 1958. Even with
the rapid increase in iron ore production since 1951, products other
than petroleum have played a minor role in this growth of export
receipts.

From 1950 to 1959, export earnings available for the purchase of imports and for the service of public and private (non-oil) indebtedness
rose more than twofold. Even after allowing for higher import prices,
there was a doubling of Venezuela's purchasing power abroad. Among
underdeveloped countries, this increase in the capacity to import appears to have been matched only by some of the Middle East countries
exporting oil, and the absolute increase in import capacity far exceeds
that of any other underdeveloped country or of the rest of Latin America combined.

Allowing for year-to-year variations, Venezuela's imports of goods
and services have in fact grown in step with the increase in net export

TABLE 9: Growth in Capacity to Import, 1950-59

(in Bs million)

	Net Export Receipts					Import Prices
	Oil		Non-oil[a]	Total	1950 = 100	
	(f.o.b.)	Net	(f.o.b.)			(1950=100)
	(1)	(2)	(3)	(4)	(5)	(6)
1950	3,472	1,903	146	2,049	100	100
1955	5,535	2,973	379	3,352	163	115
1957	7,940	3,211	581	3,792	185	125
1958	7,137	4,032	697	4,729	231	125
1959	6,708	4,361	790	5,151	251	125

[a] Includes iron ore exports which by 1959 amounted to Bs 424 million.

Note: Column 2 equals oil exports minus payments for oil company imports, profits, freight and other services; column 3 equals other exports at f.o.b. prices; column 4 equals the sum of column 2 and column 3.

Source: See Statistical Appendix, Tables S.3 and S.14.

earnings during the 1950's. Within this rapidly increasing volume of imports, there has been a marked change in composition (see Table 10). The proportion of capital goods has risen significantly over the ten-year period, the whole of the increase being in the non-oil sectors. Conversely, the proportion of consumer goods to total imports has fallen during the 1950's. Finally, there has been no change in the relative importance of imports of primary materials and intermediate products, which continue to represent over 40 percent of total imports.

TABLE 10: The Level and Composition of Imports

	Imports (f.o.b.)		Composition of Total Imports in %			
	Exc. Oil Coys.	Total	Capital Goods:		Consumer	Intermediary Goods &
	(in Bs million)		Oil	Non-oil	Goods	Materials
1950	1,809	2,013	10	14	34	42
1955	2,895	3,312	16	15	24	45
1957	4,602	5,827	24	18	17	41
1958	4,261	5,055	17	18	22	43
1959	4,449	4,976	11	20	26	43

Source: Memoria, 1959, Banco Central de Venezuela.

The increased imports of capital goods are a natural concomitant of the high rate and expanding volume of investment in manufactures and other sectors of the economy. The continued importance of inter-mediary products and materials reflects the need of the expanding industrial sector for the raw materials and products which Venezuela cannot or does not yet produce in sufficient quantity or at a cost low enough to compete with imports. Despite high costs and a low level of tariff protection, there has been some success in supplying these needs domestically; production of intermediary goods more than doubled during the 1950's while total industrial output rose more than three-fold. The greatest success in import substitution has occurred in the production of consumer goods, especially non-durable goods (see Table 11). Of course, increased local production did not mean that consumer

TABLE 11: Local Supply as Proportion of Consumer Demand

	Percentage of Market Supplied Locally	
	1950	1958
Foodstuffs (inc. processed)	64	74
Other non-durable consumer goods	47	72
Durable consumer goods	12	25
All consumer goods: Exc. Food	40	63
Inc. Food	52	68

Source: *Memoria, 1959,* Banco Central de Venezuela.

goods imports declined in absolute terms. Total consumer goods imports were Bs 700 million (f.o.b.) in 1950 and almost Bs 1.3 billion in 1959. Reflecting the increasing size and prosperity of the urban middle classes, the rise was most marked in durable consumer goods. Nonetheless, the estimates given in Table 11 imply a substantial increase in volume and variety of industrial production.

FINANCIAL ASPECTS OF THE GROWTH PROCESS IN THE 1950'S

The very rapid growth of the past decade has been achieved with virtually stable prices and a liberal trade and payments system. Until recently, Venezuela has not had to cope with the balance of payments crises which in other countries frequently interrupt growth and which sometimes jeopardize future growth if not properly managed. Only at the end of the decade did there emerge a balance of payments problem.

Venezuela's prices have not risen more than those of its major trading partners, at least until 1959 (see Statistical Appendix, Table S.15). This price stability contributed to the growth of private savings particularly transferable savings which are responsive to the changing pattern of investment opportunities in a dynamic economy. Moreover, profit rates in different sectors have not been distorted by the controls which domestic inflation usually produces. While speculative influences have been operating in the Venezuelan economy, particularly in the Caracas real estate market, these adverse effects have not been compounded by a general urge to invest in goods and property rather than in fixed interest claims, particularly mortgages and savings deposits. As a result of financial stability, entrepreneurial energies have not been unduly diverted from productive activities.

Financial stability, coupled with the rapid growth of foreign exchange earnings, has contributed greatly to the maintenance of a liberal trade and payments system and to the stability of the exchange rate. However, as noted above, because of Venezuela's high cost and price level, some import controls have been applied to foster the development of local industry and agriculture. Exchange rate stability as such reduced the risks facing the private sector and at least until recently encouraged capital inflow. The liberal trade and payments system has permitted the economy to secure imports of goods and services in response to market forces without government intervention in specific transactions in a crucial area of the economy.

Price stability and a relatively free trade and payments system are symptomatic of another important feature of Venezuelan economic development in the past decade: the absence of drastic fluctuations in petroleum production or revenues. The movement of petroleum prices and output did not impose upon the economy the need suddenly to reduce or suddenly to increase its levels of consumption and investment, or its use of imported goods and services. Petroleum's relatively regular, as well as rapid, growth has meant that national product, investment, and consumption could also expand in a fairly regular fashion (see Statistical Appendix, Tables S.2 and S.6).

An exception to this regularity took place however in 1956 and 1957 when the sale of petroleum concessions and the Suez crisis produced an economic boom which was permitted to get out of hand. This led to levels of consumption and investment which could be sustained in

1958 only by increasing the tax burden on the petroleum companies. While the magnitude of the general adjustment problem created by financial and fiscal mismanagement in 1956 and 1957 was not great, its resolution during 1958-60 has been complicated by the subsequent reduction in petroleum prices and petroleum investment, by the budgetary difficulties which arose during the transition to a democratic regime, and by capital flight on a large scale. The restoration of balance of payments and budgetary equilibria had not been achieved by mid-1960.

Balance of Payments and Current Financial Problems

The fact that national income rose more or less regularly and in step with the petroleum sector which provides most of Venezuela's foreign exchange has contributed greatly to the maintenance of balance of payments equilibrium. As a result, imports have not been permitted to get far out of line for any sustained period. As noted above, imports of goods and services increased more or less proportionately to the growth of GNP, except in 1957 when real capital investment (which is import-intensive) and inventory accumulation were particularly heavy.

In 1957, a large deficit in current account was recorded, but capital inflows were almost twice as large as the deficit (see Table 12). It was thus possible to increase gold and foreign exchange reserves by almost US$500 million while increasing the volume of general imports, excluding petroleum company imports, by 50 percent. This increase in imports was produced by a very substantial jump in investment, including additions to inventories.

In both 1956 and 1957 petroleum company payments for concessions contributed to very large capital inflows which in fact were permitted to augment the Government's cash balances. At the same time, however, the Government and its autonomous agencies borrowed on short-term and medium-term to finance investment projects. Although no reliable estimates are available, it is conceivable that the Government's unrecorded indebtedness may have increased by Bs 2 billion in 1956 and 1957, with the largest borrowing concentrated in 1957. An undetermined amount of this debt was owed abroad.

The 50 percent increase in imports in 1957 was also associated with large capital inflows for the non-petroleum private sector and with a record level of petroleum exports. Since 1957, capital inflows for financing non-petroleum imports have declined precipitously, and the value of petroleum exports has also declined. Yet, the 1957 level of imports has been maintained (see Statistical Appendix, Table S.14) as has the level of investment. It has been possible to maintain in 1958 and 1959 the unusually high levels of imports and investment achieved in 1957 while at the same time eliminating the very large deficit on current account even while petroleum exports declined in value. This was primarily because the economy secured, through the increased taxes imposed in 1958, a larger share of petroleum receipts. Thus, petroleum company transactions in 1959 contributed over US$300 million more to the country's balance of payments on current account than in 1957, despite a decline of US$400 million in the value of petroleum exports. As a result, the current account was in approximate balance in 1959 (see Table 12).

TABLE 12: The Balance of Payments, 1950, 1952 & 1954-59

(in US$ million)

	1950	1952	1954	1955	1956	1957	1958	1959
1. Current account receipts	1,165	1,452	1,673	1,903	2,220	2,742	2,516	2,424
2. Net current account payments of which:	1,155	1,411	1,675	1,874	2,293	3,321	2,639	2,405
Imports of goods (exc. oil cos.)	544	602	831	872	932	1,389	1,279	1,331
3. *Current account balance* (1 minus 2)	10	41	—2	29	—73	—579	—123	19
4. Recorded capital flow (net)	9	155	59	46	548	992	34	247ᵃ
5. Unrecorded capital flow (net) ᵇ		—99	—126	—55	—24	—102	82	—301	—633
6. *Over-all surplus or deficit* (3 plus 4 plus 5)	—80	70	—2	51	373	495	—390	—367

ᵃ 1959 includes US$97.7 million of short-term Treasury Notes sold abroad.
ᵇ Corresponds to "Errors and Omissions" items as given by Central Bank.

Source: *Memoria, 1954 and Memoria, 1959,* Banco Central de Venezuela.

Despite the evidence of economic strength displayed by the elimination of the deficit on current account, foreign exchange reserves declined by over US$360 million in both 1958 and 1959 and would have declined even more in 1959 if the Government had not borrowed almost US$100 million abroad on short term. Net international reserves at the end of 1959 totaled US$686 million, down from almost US$1.5 billion at the end of 1957 (see Statistical Appendix, Table S.16). While some of this decline in the two years can be explained either by un-recorded debt payments which were probably heavy in 1958, or by un-recorded immigrant remittances, there must also have occurred a mas-sive exodus of private capital.

Some part of the movement of private capital was a natural response to the ending of the petroleum boom, and this should cause no con-cern, particularly since exchange reserves had been accumulated with which to finance such outflows. Another segment of this outflow may have resulted from the political uncertainties associated with the tran-sition to a democratic regime in 1958 and early 1959. The acceleration of capital flight which occurred in the latter part of 1959 was however the result of vague, and even exaggerated, fears of measures the Gov-ernment might take to control the economy. In particular, there emerged a lack of confidence in the stability of the currency and the maintenance of free convertibility. It was possible for such fears to take hold on a widespread basis because of the apparent inability of the Government to limit budget deficits. These fears could give rise to massive capital flight with little disadvantage to those making trans-fers because the liquidity of the private sector was maintained at an abnormally high level from 1957 to 1959.

Money and Banking

The monetary system of Venezuela has operated reasonably well in supplying the economy with the over-all volume of money and credit necessary to support economic expansion, and inflationary excesses were by and large avoided. Unfortunately, however, during the years 1957-1959, the monetary authorities through inaction permitted the emergence of excess liquidity which, in turn, facilitated capital flight in 1959 and 1960 and endangered the balance of payments.

Venezuela has experienced a large monetary and credit expansion in the past decade. At the end of 1959 the money supply was nearly 2½ times the level at the end of 1950, and it had therefore expanded more than gross national product. Adding savings deposits and time deposits to the money supply, total liquidity was nearly 3½ times the 1950 level. This very large expansion in monetary liquidity was produced largely by commercial bank credit which increased to 6 times the 1950 level (see Statistical Appendix, Table S.17).

The expansion in commercial bank credit occurred without any growth in the Government's direct indebtedness to the banking system.[12] However, in 1956 and 1957, at the same time as the Government increased its deposits in the Central Bank, thereby offsetting the monetary effect of much of the very large increase in the Central Bank's holdings of gold and foreign exchange, it also built up the large floating debt to which we have referred. A considerable portion of this debt had been financed by the commercial banks granting credits to government contractors. In 1957 particularly, when bank credit expanded by 44 percent, this must have been an important factor in the expansion. During that year, primarily as a result of the credit expansion, private liquidity was increased by over Bs 1.5 billion.

The expansion of commercial bank credit which produced this excess liquidity was made possible by the passivity of the Central Bank and the Government in the face of large increases in the reserves of the commercial banks. This passivity reflects the lack of an active bond market and the limited means available to the Central Bank under existing law to engage in open market operations. In the absence of an increase in reserve requirements, which were only 15 percent against demand deposits, excess reserves of the commercial banks grew at a very rapid rate in both 1956 and 1957.

In 1958, the Government drew down its cash balances by over Bs 1.6 billion. The excess reserves of the commercial banks were thereby further augmented. The commercial banks were thus encouraged to expand credit and further increase the liquidity of the private sector, despite the contracting effect of the decline in international reserves. Thus, money and quasi-money together rose by over Bs 700 million in 1958, despite a reduction of Bs 1.2 billion in holdings of foreign exchange.

With the money and quasi-money claims of the private sector totaling at the end of 1958 almost Bs 6 billion, the stage was set for the capital flight which has made management of the balance of payments so difficult. The Government's cash deficit continued in 1959, feeding the commercial banks with the reserves required to offset the decline in international assets. Excess liquidity continued until September 1959 when a genuine confidence crisis appears to have developed. In response to this crisis and despite the excess liquidity, the Central Bank at first took no measures to restrain rediscounts, and rediscounts rose rapidly in the latter part of 1959. In early 1960, recognizing that continued expansion of rediscounts was simply permitting commercial banks to expand credit and to maintain the excess liquidity of the public which

[12] Indeed, by law the Government cannot borrow from the Central Bank, and it may borrow from the commercial banks for a period beyond the fiscal year only with direct authorization by Congress.

was facilitating capital flight, the Central Bank reduced its rediscounts and permitted the decline in international assets to exert its impact on the reserve position of the commercial banks.

Commercial bank credit to the private sector was actually reduced in the first half of 1960. This curtailment, together with the continued reduction in exchange reserves brought about by capital outflow, led to a decline in private liquidity of about Bs 1 billion in the first seven months of the year.

The contraction in bank deposits which took place in the first part of 1960 coupled with the growth of GNP over the last three years, has brought liquidity down to more normal levels (see Statistical Appendix, Table S.17). This should help bring capital flight to a halt, and thereby restore equilibrium to the balance of payments, provided the expansion of bank credit to the private sector can be held in check and budget equilibrium established.

Bank Credit and Economic Development

Just as the over-all volume of credit and liquidity has not been well adjusted in the last three years to the requirements of the economy, so have there appeared certain weaknesses on the qualitative side. The banking system in Venezuela has been prohibited by law from making long-term loans. In practice, a substantial part of commercial bank loans have been made on the understanding that renewals would be arranged. In recent years, commercial banks have tended to grant such longer-term credits to construction companies and to *financiadoras* (affiliates of the commercial banks which developed to help finance government promissory notes and private building). The use of such intermediaries for the channeling of commercial bank credit to longer-term investment permitted looser standards in the granting of credit and added to the difficulties of the monetary authorities in 1960 when commercial bank portfolios had to be reduced.

The restrictions in the present law prohibiting the commercial banks from making a loan with a term of more than two years and from discounting bills with more than a year's maturity have thus led to subterfuges which permit the commercial banks to participate in long-term financing on an unsound basis. At the same time, these restrictions limit the help which the banking system could provide to sound industrial and agricultural enterprises. The Government is currently considering a revision of the banking laws which would remove the rigid limitations in the present law.

Government Finance

Until 1957 the volume of bank-credit expansion which was consistent with financial stability was reserved for the use of the private sector. This is not unhealthy in an economy where the government sector secures through its taxing powers very substantial command over resources. As a result of the rapid rise of tax receipts, the Government budget was generally in balance in the past ten years (see Statistical Appendix, Table S.18). In calendar years 1956 and 1957, petroleum concession receipts permitted government cash balances to rise by over Bs 1 billion a year, despite the fact that expenditures rose sharply. A high level of government expenditures in 1958 and 1959 produced deficits and depleted cash balances. This gave rise to the fear that financial stability would not be maintained.

It is difficult to obtain a clear picture as to the extent of the impact of recent budget deficits on the level of economic activity and the balance of payments because of inadequate and incomplete information available within the Venezuelan Government on expenditures and their financing. The mission has had to piece together the over-all picture, relying in part on guesswork rather than on established fact (see Table 13).

The virtual stabilization of government expenditures since 1957/58 shown in Line 1 of Table 13 gives quite a different picture from that shown in the official statistics which indicate a much lower level of expenditures in 1957/58 (5.44) than in 1958/59 (6.24) and 1959/60 (6.15). The estimates in the above table adjust the official statistics to exclude debt payments from expenditures before arriving at the deficit, and also to include in expenditures an estimate of unrecorded expenditures financed from borrowing. Unfortunately, the estimates of the latter item shown in Line 5 of Table 13 are little better than an informed guess.

If the above picture is correct, the direct expansionary impact of the budget deficit, which reached a peak in 1957/58, had been cut in half by 1959/60. This picture is roughly consistent with the fact that the balance of payments on current account has been brought into virtual equilibrium and that domestic prices had risen but moderately in these two years. If the above picture is incorrect, and if, despite most indications to the contrary, expenditures financed from unrecorded borrowing were smaller in 1957/58 and larger in the two subsequent years, it would be more difficult to reconcile the fiscal outcome with

TABLE 13: National Government: Estimated Receipts and Expenditures, 1957-60

(in Bs billion)

	1957/58	1958/59	1959/60
1. Expenditures, excluding debt payments	5.48	5.57	5.39
2. Tax receipts	4.88[a]	5.31	5.08
3. Budget deficit (1 minus 2)	0.60	0.26	0.31
4. Gross payments on debts	1.46	0.87	0.86
5. Unrecorded gross borrowing (domestic and foreign)	1.50	0.20	0.10
6. Recorded gross borrowing abroad	—	—	0.47
7. Reduction in cash balance (3 plus 4 minus 5 minus 6)	0.56	0.93	0.60

[a] Includes Bs 0.45 billion from sale of petroleum concessions.

Source: Ministry of Finance. For Line 4, see Table 13-13, *Memoria, 1959,* Banco Central de Venezuela, p. 315. The figure for 1959/60 covers only the first six months of the year. There are quite different estimates of debt payments prepared by the Controloria, but these are more limited in coverage. It is clear that many of the payments on "debts" during these 3 fiscal years, particularly in 1957/58, were payments on contracts for construction still in progress. Thus, in 1957/58 we assume that goods and services received by the Government under "debt contracts" were approximately equal to the payments made on such contracts. This figure has been added to the official estimate of expenditures and shown as un-recorded borrowing in Line 5. In 1958/59 and 1959/60, we assume that the receipt of goods and services under contracts entered into before 1958 declined substantially.

the balance of payments results. In that case, a large and increasing deficit in the Government's budget sustained for three years has failed to produce either a large balance of payments deficit on current account or rapidly rising domestic prices. This might be possible if the capital flight of the two years 1958/59-1959/60 had led to a substantial reduction in the level of private investment: but there is no evidence of such a reduction. On the contrary, private investment appears to have held up very well, at least through calendar 1959 (see Statistical Appendix, footnote to Table S.6). Most of the capital flight, as noted above, was associated with a reduction in the domestic liquid assets of the private sector, not with a reduction in real private investment.

Regardless of which interpretation is accepted, both the budget deficit and debt payments have added to the liquidity of the private sector and facilitated capital flight. If the budget is not brought under control in 1960/61, it will be difficult to exercise the even more stringent controls on private credit which would then become necessary.

DISTRIBUTION OF THE BENEFITS OF ECONOMIC PROGRESS

The growth of per capita income which has occurred in the past decade has been so rapid that very large sections of the Venezuelan population must now have a higher standard of living and must enjoy better opportunities for rewarding employment than in the past. This impression is confirmed by the very substantial increase that has taken place in per capita consumption and urban employment, and by the signs of a growing middle class. Yet, it must be recognized that while Venezuela's economic performance in the past decade has been excellent in terms of the rate of growth achieved and while it has been moderately good in terms of creating forces for continuing development, it has been deficient in distributing the fruits of economic progress widely among the people.

The only general quantitative measure of the effectiveness of the Venezuelan economy in conferring its benefits widely is to be found in the 1957 income distribution picture presented by Carl S. Shoup and his associates.[13] According to these estimates, which are admittedly very crude, at the top of the economic scale about one-eighth of the income earners receive one-half of total income. At the other extreme, 45 percent secure only about one-tenth of the income. The poorer half of the population must therefore live close to subsistence levels, with per capita incomes which in real terms are about US$150 a year. While absolute equality of income cannot necessarily be considered a desirable objective from the point of view of savings or productivity, the inequality of income expressed in the Venezuelan data is extreme.

While no data are available which would indicate whether Venezuela's income distribution was more unequal in the 1950's than in

[13] *Op. cit.,* Chapter 1. There is reason to believe that income distribution in 1957 was exceptionally imbalanced. Non-property income, which we can assume is distributed more widely among the population at large than property income, represented 64 percent of total private income in 1957, as compared with 66-67 percent in the previous years of the decade. Since 1957, the distribution of income may have improved, particularly in 1959. According to preliminary and very tentative estimates non-property income in 1959 rose to 71 percent of total private income (see Statistical Appendix, Table S.19).

earlier periods, it is hard to believe that the situation could have been much worse. Indeed, despite the maintenance of a very high rate of growth of income per head for at least 25 years, it may have been somewhat better at an earlier period.

The existence of poverty on a massive scale—particularly in the countryside—is evident to every visitor to Venezuela. The Shoup mission estimated that there were in 1957 around three-quarters of a million *campesinos* and agricultural workers (supporting a population, including themselves of over 2,000,000) with an average income of little more than Bs 1,000 a year. In Venezuela, it is frequently alleged that poverty in agriculture is closely associated with the great inequality in land ownership, since 2½ percent of the "units of exploitation" (namely, those over 500 hectares) account for 82 percent of the total agricultural area in use. The importance of this factor should not be overstated, for per capita income originating in agriculture is so low that even if land were more equitably distributed, poverty in rural Venezuela would be little affected.[14]

More important as factors explaining the great inequality in income are unequal ownership of capital generally, differences in ability and skill, and some special institutional factors, discussed in Chapter 10, which have influenced the determination of wages and salaries. These forces have been ameliorated to only a minor extent by government policies.

The Venezuelan tax structure, even after the 1958 income tax changes, is only slightly progressive. Given very low income and inheritance taxes, inequalities in ownership can be perpetuated with little or no productive effort on the part of the possessor of wealth. Wide differences in the earnings of labor depending on skill have been evident for many years, and the rapid growth of the economy has created new demands which have tended to increase these differentials. Moreover, the pressure of demand for skilled labor has been met in part by intensive use of capital equipment, a practice which has also been promoted by tariff and other government policies. This has tended to maintain the return to capital at a high level.

The premium on skill and the tendency to substitute capital for skilled labor has been accentuated by the unwillingness or inability of the Government to establish, at least until recently, an effective educational and training program. The backwardness of the Venezuelan

[14] According to Shoup's figures for 1957, average income per income earner in agriculture is only Bs 1,700, compared with average income per income earner of Bs 9,300 a year in the non-agricultural sector. Income in agriculture includes returns accruing from rural land ownership.

educational effort is, in the judgment of the mission, one of the major factors limiting a wider distribution of the benefits of economic progress which is correctible by government policy. In the countryside in particular, where the bulk of the farmers manage their own small plots, the fruits of economic progress can be distributed more widely if these farmers are exposed effectively to new ideas and new techniques of production.

While the lag in education and training has seriously impeded a wider distribution of the benefits of progress, other governmental programs have had a mixed record of achievement. Improvements in transportation over the past 20 years have certainly increased the geographical mobility of the low-income farmer and have increased the range of occupational choice, although at the same time exposing many low-income handicraft workers to more effective competition. The very large, and in many ways successful, health program, which has virtually eradicated malaria from the country, has produced immediate tangible benefits in the form of better health and reduced mortality and has provided new areas for settlement on the plains readily accessible to poverty-stricken people living in the Andes. While a larger part of the highway construction program took place initially near the larger cities, more and more employment opportunities created by highway construction were being offered throughout the countryside. On the other hand, construction undertaken under the irrigation and colonization program has been highly concentrated in a few areas (see Chapter 9), and the program itself was not designed to offer settlement opportunities to a large number of families. Similarly, the government housing program has been geared to supplying fairly high-cost housing to a relatively small number of families living in a limited number of cities.

CHAPTER **8**   *THE OUTLOOK FOR PETROLEUM*

The degree to which the Venezuelan economy is dependent upon the production and sale of petroleum has been outlined in Chapter 7. It is clear that government revenues from the petroleum sector will for many years to come largely determine the extent and pace of the country's economic development as well as the extent and pace of improvements in the social well-being of the Venezuelan people. In making recommendations for an investment program and on matters of general economic policy, the mission therefore has found it essential to attempt to evaluate trends in the world petroleum markets and so assess the prospects for Venezuelan oil during the planning period and for some years thereafter. There are many imponderables involved in such an assessment which make certainty of forecasting impossible. However, a consideration of the relevant factors permits estimates of prices and production which, although admittedly subject to substantial variations, nevertheless can serve as reasonable bases for planning purposes.

The World Demand for Oil

In recent years, there have been a large number of studies of trends in energy demand and various estimates have been made concerning the probable demand for oil in the years ahead. Several of the studies have related their forecasts to the years 1959-65, and indicate an increase of from 6 to 8 million barrels per day (b.p.d.) in world demand outside the Communist bloc during that period. While there are differences between estimates on the rate of growth of demand, it would seem that, over the next 5 years or so, U.S. oil demand may increase by some 3 percent to 4 percent a year, European demand by 6 percent to 7 percent, and demand in the remainder of the non-Communist world by some 8 percent to 9 percent. This would imply an over-all average increase in oil demand of about 6 percent a year. While this is not as rapid a growth as occurred between 1945 and 1957 (8 percent a year),[1]

[1] The period 1956-59 was marked by a recession in the U.S. and by a slower growth of output and incomes in Western Europe. Oil demand reflected these adverse market conditions. In this period, U.S. demand grew on average by 2.5 percent a year and elsewhere in the free world the increase was 7 percent a year. These rates compare with postwar growth in oil demand at 6 percent and 12 percent a year respectively.

it would, if continued, entail a doubling of demand and output between 1959 and 1971 from some 17 million to 34 million b.p.d.[2]

There has been general agreement on such broad demand projections, which have taken into consideration, on the one hand, the expected deferment of large-scale use of atomic power and the easing of Europe's balance of payments situation which allows less emphasis on protecting high-cost domestic coal production, and, on the other hand, the increasing availability of U.S. coal and of natural gas in Europe, and the development of gas supplies in North Africa and elsewhere. The differences in demand estimates are of minor significance when compared with the general revision of estimates of the availability of oil and of the possible effects of increased supplies on the price of oil.

World Oil Supplies

The post-World War II period has seen not only a rapid rise in oil demand and production, but also an even greater increase in the quantity of proven oil reserves (see Table 14). In 1959, non-Communist world oil reserves exceeded 260 billion barrels (about 40 years of production at current rates) : in 1948, reserves were about 74 billion barrels, or equivalent to 20 years production at then current rates. Thus in 11 years, output had risen 100 percent, but reserves by 260 percent. Secondly, large-scale investment in oil exploration and exploitation

TABLE 14: World Crude Oil Reserves

(in billion barrels)

Country	1935	1948	1958	1959
U.S.A.	12.2	28.0	33.0	34.0
Middle East	4.0	32.6	174.0	181.4
Venezuela	2.5	9.0	16.5	18.0
Other[a]	2.2	8.7	52.5	60.2
Total	20.9	78.3	276.0	293.6

[a] Includes U.S.S.R. and bloc, except in 1935. Soviet bloc reserves are estimated at 30 billion barrels in 1959.

Sources: *Oil and Gas Journal, Petroleum Press Service,* and *World Petroleum* (various issues).

[2] One million b.p.d. is approximately equal to 50 million tons a year.

came to fruition in 1957-59, at a time when the growth in oil demand was slowing up both in Europe and in the U.S. By 1959, the capacity to produce oil and deliver it to a tanker or long-distance pipeline was about one-third greater than demand. Excess capacity was about 5.5 million b.p.d., of which 3.5 million were in the United States, 1 million in Venezuela, and almost 1 million in the Middle East. So, by 1958/59 a situation of substantial oversupply existed—and there was the prospect of excess supply over demand for a number of years.

At least five sources of supply, aside from Venezuela, may be expected further to increase the availability of oil on world markets and to intensify competition for the anticipated increase of 6 to 8 million b.p.d. in non-Communist world oil demand during 1959-65: Middle East, North Africa, U.S.S.R., U.S.A., Other Areas.

Middle East. The growth in excess capacity has been most marked in the Western Hemisphere, but the growth of capacity actually in use has been most rapid in the Middle East. While production growth in the Middle East was at times interrupted, e.g., by the nationalization crisis in the Iranian oil industry and the Suez Canal troubles, the increase in output between 1945 and 1959 was more than eightfold, from 0.55 million b.p.d. to 4.6 million b.p.d. The 1959 output represented 45 percent of the oil produced in the non-Communist world outside the United States and 54 percent of the oil traded internationally. Moreover, this great postwar rise in production was accompanied by the discovery of some 150 billion barrels of reserves. The Middle East now holds 70 percent of the non-Communist world's reserves, and these reserves are more than 100 times greater than the current level of annual production in the area (see Table 14). Underlying this growth in Middle East output—and the expectation of further substantial increases in supply—is the fact that the major international oil companies have found the Middle East to be the most profitable area of operation and have therefore developed their concessions rapidly. Thus, the world oil situation has been drastically changed by the emergence during the 1950's of the Middle East as the largest source of oil available for international trade (see Table 15), oil with a cost of production which is much below both prevailing world oil prices and costs in other important producing areas.

North Africa. There have been substantial discoveries of oil since 1956 in French North Africa and in Libya. Proven reserves in these areas (which have been estimated at some 6 billion barrels) are but a

TABLE 15: Percentage Shares in World Oil Exports

Country	1938	1948	1958	1959
U.S.A.	30	8	4	3
Middle East	16	36	53	54
Venezuela	26	46	33	33
Others (inc. Soviet bloc)	28	10	10	10
	100	100	100	100

Sources: *Oil and Gas Journal, Petroleum Press Service,* and *World Petroleum* (various issues).

small part of the likely extent of the fields, but at this stage it would seem that French North Africa may be producing some 500,000 to 600,-000 b.p.d. by 1965, and Libya 200,000 to 300,000 b.p.d.

U.S.S.R. The Soviet Union is rapidly expanding its oil output and it is expected that during 1960 it will have equaled or replaced Venezuela as the world's largest producer apart from the United States. Between 1956 and 1960, oil exports to the non-Communist world (principally to Western Europe) rose from 80,000 to 300,000 b.p.d. As in the case of North Africa, there is a wide range of estimates of future exports of the Soviet Union, but it is generally agreed that production will grow more rapidly than demand within the Soviet bloc and that the oil for export will be competitively priced. By 1965, Soviet oil exports may reach 600,000 b.p.d., with Western Europe as the principal market, but with some attempt to penetrate the Latin American market, largely at the expense of Venezuelan production.

U.S.A. Following the failure of the voluntary import restriction program introduced in 1957, mandatory controls on oil imports were instituted by the U.S. Government in March 1959. If continued, this policy will have a major impact on the world oil trade during the next few years. Throughout the postwar years until 1958, the United States had become increasingly dependent on foreign oil supplies. Thus, in 1946, imports of crude oil products supplied 7 percent of U.S. requirements: by 1958 they had risen more than fourfold and contributed 18 percent of supply, or 1.7 million b.p.d. Meanwhile, U.S. production was growing relatively slowly (25 percent during 1948-58, see Table 16) and excess capacity was increasing rapidly. By 1958, "shut-in" capacity was rated as equivalent to Venezuela's daily production of 2.8 million

TABLE 16: Shares in World Crude Oil Production

| | 1938 | | 1948 | | 1958 | | 1959 | |
	Million b.p.d.	%	Million b.p.d.	%	Million b.p.d.	%	Million b.p.d.	%
U.S.A.	3.4	60	5.6	58	6.7	37	7.1	36
Middle East	0.3	6	1.1	11	4.3	24	4.6	24
Venezuela	0.5	9	1.3	13	2.6	14	2.8	14
Soviet bloc	1.0	16	0.9	9	2.5	14	2.9	15
Others	0.5	9	0.9	9	2.0	11	2.1	11
Total	5.7	100	9.8	100	18.1	100	19.5	100

Sources: *Oil and Gas Journal, Petroleum Press Service,* and *World Petroleum* (various issues).

b.p.d.; by 1959 it exceeded 3.5 million b.p.d. The decisions to curb the growth of imports and to restrict supplies of foreign crude oil to a stable percentage of the market entailed a substantial and immediate benefit to U.S. producers; they also implied that in future the increase of domestic oil output would keep pace with the estimated 3-4 percent a year increase in demand, despite the high costs of exploration and development in the United States. Conversely, these decisions implied a slowing down in the rate of growth of foreign oil imports into the United States to 3-4 percent a year as against a growth rate of 10-12 percent a year since 1947.[3] In these circumstances, U.S. imports in 1965 would approach 2.2 million b.p.d., or 1 million less than would have been the case in the absence of quotas and on the assumption of a continued expansion of oil imports at 10 percent a year. However, one must also recognize the possibility that, in view of the high costs of oil development in the United States, imports quotas may be eased, if not abandoned, once the present excess capacity has been absorbed.

Other Areas. A large number of countries have undertaken or intensified exploration and production activities so as to become self-sufficient in oil or to develop export markets. Thus, Argentina—which has been buying more than 110,000 b.p.d. of Venezuelan oil—has contracted for foreign oil companies to help its national oil company develop its resources; and in 1961, after only four years of work, Argen-

[3] Between 1956 and 1958, U.S. imports rose 260,000 b.p.d and production fell 440,000 b.p.d. Between 1958 and 1960, it is expected that imports will rise only 100,000 b.p.d. while domestic output increases by 700,000 b.p.d.

tina is expected to meet its own requirements of some 300,000 b.p.d. Provided a transcontinental pipeline is soon completed, production is expected to grow rapidly in Canada, which now takes 10 percent of Venezuela's oil output. In addition to these Western Hemisphere developments which particularly affect Venezuela, production is increasing in widely dispersed areas of the Eastern Hemisphere.

Likely Trends in Oil Prices

Factors Affecting Oil Prices, 1956-60. There has thus been a great increase in the capacity to supply the world oil market, particularly because of the rapid growth of output and proven reserves in the low-cost fields of the Middle East. With an assumed 6 percent yearly increase in non-Communist world oil demand, the likely behavior of oil prices, particularly during the 1960/61-1963/64 planning period, can only properly be understood against the background of an examination of the chief factors which had previously been affecting the price of oil in world markets.

The world oil market has long been influenced by two principal factors—the predominance of the United States as consumer and producer and the position of the major international companies as producers and distributors of over two-thirds of the non-Communist world's oil. However, the role of both the U.S. market and of the integrated international companies has been modified somewhat during the last few years. Until after World War II, the United States was both the principal oil market and the largest producer and exporter of oil and oil prices throughout the world were based on the Gulf price of Texan oil plus freight charges to the point of consumption. As a result of the great increase in the productive capacity of the Middle East during the 1950's and the shift of the United States from a net export to a net import status, basic changes took place in the price structure. The major international companies producing low-cost Middle East oil sought to widen their markets, first to embrace Western Europe and then to compete in North America with United States and Venezuelan oil. This expansion of markets has been achieved both by absorbing freight charges and by reducing f.o.b. prices relative to those of the Western Hemisphere (see Table 17). During 1946-49, Middle East posted prices (f.o.b.) were 40-70 US cents a barrel less than equivalent U.S. Gulf prices. During 1949-56, the difference was generally about 95 US cents a barrel, and since the Suez crisis Middle East prices have been $1.10 to $1.20 a barrel lower. Finally, with the imposition of quantitative restrictions on U.S. imports of oil, a two-price system has developed—a U.S. oil price and a series of f.o.b. prices for the rest of the non-Communist world reflecting the competition of various producing areas for European and other markets. At the same time, it has to be recognized that the major companies and the governments of oil exporting countries have a vital interest in avoiding competitive price cutting as this would reduce both profits and tax payments.

Two other factors have however recently been working to increase the supply of oil competing in the world market and so to exert a downward pressure on world oil prices. First, independent producers have increased their output significantly.[4] Thus, for national security reasons as well as in response to pressure from domestic independent producers, the U.S. Government has been restricting oil imports, and there has therefore been an increasing supply of oil seeking markets elsewhere. In addition, there has been a large increase in the number of independent concerns—North American, European and Japanese—operating outside the United States, and many of these have pressing contractual or financial reasons for marketing oil below prevailing posted prices.

Secondly, a number of governments have fostered the discovery and production of oil as an import replacement or as a source of export earnings. This has been true, for example, in Canada, Argentina, Libya and French North Africa. It has also been true of established producing nations, as in the Middle East, for example, where governments have entered into agreements with independent firms from Italy, Japan and the United States. Many of these governments may therefore be expected to attempt to pre-empt all or part of certain markets on behalf of particular suppliers. This is likely to hold true of France in relation to North Africa, of Japan in relation to oil produced in the Middle East by Japanese firms, and in Argentina. Finally, the growing amount of Soviet oil being marketed abroad at very competitive prices constitutes one of the most important forms of government intervention in world oil markets. In these circumstances, the large Middle East and Venezuelan producers will inevitably lose some market outlets which have generally been available to them, and pressure on prices will be intensified.

The operation of these various market factors is seen in the movements of oil prices in recent years, but the situation was aggravated by the Suez crisis of 1956/57. With only restricted access to Middle East

[4] For example, the proportion of Venezuelan oil produced by major companies declined from 92 percent in 1957 to 88 percent in 1959 and 86 percent in the first half of 1960.

supplics possible in 1956/57, increased demands on Western Hemisphere producers resulted in substantial increases in price. West Texas prices rose 25 cents per barrel in January 1957, and Venezuelan prices

TABLE 17: Posted Prices for Crude Oil, Principal Export Centers

(US $ per barrel)

Date	West Texas Sour 36° (f.o.b. U.S. Gulf)	Oficina 32° (f.o.b. Puerto la Cruz)	Arabian Crude 36° (f.o.b. Ras Tanura)
January 1, 1946	1.29	1.17	1.05
April 1, 1946	1.39	1.27	—
July 25, 1946	1.64	1.52	—
November 15, 1946	1.74	1.62	—
December 1, 1946	—	—	1.23
March 10, 1947	1.99	1.87	—
October 15, 1947	2.19	2.07	—
December 1, 1947	2.69	2.57	—
March 1, 1948	—	—	2.22
May 18, 1948	—	—	2.03
April 1, 1949	—	—	1.88
July 7, 1949	—	—	1.75
June 15, 1953	2.94	2.82	—
July 21, 1953	—	—	1.97
October 11, 1955	—	2.67	—
January 3, 1957	3.19	—	—
January 21, 1957	—	2.97	—
February 14, 1957	—	2.92	—
June 12, 1957	—	—	2.12
November 22, 1957	—	2.99	—
February 5, 1959	3.08	—	—
February 6, 1959	—	2.84	—
February 13, 1959	—	—	1.94
April 4, 1959	—	2.74	—
January 11, 1960	3.04	—	—
August 8, 1960	—	—	1.80
September 13, 1960	—	—	1.84

Note: — indicates no change in prices.

Sources: *Memoria, 1958,* Banco Central de Venezuela, p. 33, and *Petroleum Press Service.*

rose 25 cents to 30 cents at the same time (see Table 17). In June 1957, with the reopening of the Suez Canal and the continued pressure to replenish oil stocks, Middle East prices rose some 15 cents per barrel. These higher posted prices were maintained despite the rapid increase in U.S. and Venezuelan production in 1957 and in the Middle East in the latter part of 1957 and during 1958. However, with the slowdown in industrial activity which occurred in Western Europe and North America in 1958, coupled with the building-up of oil stocks, substantial discounting of prices below posted levels was noticeable in late 1958, and, early in February 1959, West Texas posted prices were cut 11 cents and Venezuelan prices 15 cents. But, a few weeks later, prices in the Middle East, where output was again expanding rapidly, were reduced 18 cents per barrel, thereby posting the lowest prices for the area since 1953. To help meet this competition, Venezuelan prices were further reduced 5 cents to 10 cents per barrel in April 1959. There was no further change in posted prices in the two areas until August/September 1960, when posted prices in the Middle East (where output had risen 13 percent in twelve months) were reduced by an average of 10 cents (or 5-6 percent) per barrel. Before the Suez crisis, Venezuela's posted prices, f.o.b. Puerto la Cruz, had been 70 cents above Middle East prices: now they were 90 cents higher at a time when narrowing freight differentials were favoring the Middle East. Both the Venezuelan and the Middle East price changes occurred in recognition of the need to readjust prices to the resumption of Suez traffic, the slower economic growth in industrialized areas and the increased marketing of Middle East oil.

Reduction in market prices, which reflect discounts, were even greater than those in posted prices. Even after the reduced postings of 1959 and 1960, major oil companies were on occasion reported to be discounting their prices by 10 cents to 30 cents per barrel and independents were offering crude oil at as much as $1 per barrel below postings. While large discounts have often been cited as a common practice in 1958-60, these do not appear to have applied to the bulk of transactions. Thus, it would seem that during 1959 Venezuelan crude oil was on average sold with a discount of about 15 cents (6 percent) a barrel. Nevertheless, the continued discounting reflects the pressure on the major companies of excess productive capacity, as well as the expanded operation of independent firms and the entry into production of new sources of supply.

Price Trends in 1960/61-1963/64. Judgments on the price effects of the various factors affecting supply and demand during 1960/61-1963/64 must necessarily be arbitrary. There is general agreement that there will be a fairly steady growth of world oil demand (at some 6 percent a year). There is also agreement that there will be a marked increase in the availability of oil from a large number of sources of supply. On the other hand, there are considerable differences of opinion in assessing the effects these changes in supply will have on prices and on the prospects for any one source of supply to the world market. So long as the major firms refrain from extensive competitive price cutting, it will be difficult for independents, with their limited marketing facilities, to have a substantial depressing effect on world oil prices over the next few years. However, in distribution as in production, the number of independents—both private and government—is increasing, and certain areas such as Italy and West Germany are therefore subject to keen price competition in their retail oil markets. Secondly, the chief producing countries have in general refrained from urging the major firms to increase output when this would entail reductions in prices and therefore in revenues. Indeed, efforts are being made—notably by Venezuela and Saudi Arabia—to secure an agreement for the regulation of the supply of oil (e.g., on the basis of a formula related to the percentage of world oil reserves) so as to ensure stable prices and orderly marketing. Late in 1960, the outcome of these efforts was the establishment by Venezuela and the major Middle East producer governments of an Organization of Petroleum Exporting Countries (OPEC). Through OPEC, the member governments hope to persuade the major oil companies to stabilize prices, preferably at levels prevailing prior to August 8, 1960. It is too early to determine whether or not the hopes of the participants in the Organization—looking toward price stabilization and production control—will materialize. Clearly, however, if OPEC is given full support by its member governments, it could become an appreciable price-supporting force.

In the mission's judgment, it is prudent to assume in preparing a basic development program that there will continue to be pressure on prices throughout the planning period, and that this pressure may result in some further reduction in market prices, whether through lower posted prices or increased discounts on present postings. In estimating Venezuela's oil revenues, the mission has assumed that market prices during 1960/61-1963/64 will average some 3 percent below those prevailing in 1959/60.[5] However, the forces making for the orderly marketing of oil (both on the part of the major companies and the

---

[5] The mission has assumed that market prices in 1960/61-1963/64 will average some 10 percent below the level of prices posted in Venezuela in April 1959.

governments of producing countries in the Middle East and Venezuela) are expected to be sufficiently strong to render unlikely any further appreciable reduction in the level of market prices. The increased production from new sources of supply may therefore be expected to have its effect in a slower rate of growth in demand for both Middle East and Venezuelan oil rather than in producing a substantially lower level of prices in world oil markets.[6] If the operation of OPEC should prove successful, it would, of course, contribute to such a result.

Longer-run Price Prospects. In the longer period, the principal factors exerting pressure on prices will continue to be the abundance of Middle East oil reserves, the increase in the number of other sources of oil and the closing of certain national markets to foreign oil, together perhaps with competition from nuclear energy. On the other hand, the mission understands that the oil industry expects a sustained and rapidly growing demand for its products for an indefinite period ahead. And, as for the planning period, so for the longer term, the major producing companies and the governments of the countries where they operate will exert a stabilizing influence on the marketing of oil.

The mission sees no need for a detailed analysis of long-run price prospects. It is sufficient to emphasize the uncertainties of the market situation and to point to the strength of the forces making for increased production and intensified competition in the world oil industry. While no abrupt change in price levels is envisaged, Venezuela must take into account the possibility of somewhat lower prices for its oil over the longer term.

Venezuela's Position in the World Oil Market

For Venezuela, 1957 was in many ways the high point of its oil development—the climax of 15 years of rapid growth, averaging about 10 percent a year. This is true in terms of a varied range of indicators, e.g., total output, average value per barrel of oil sold, net profit in total and as a percentage on sales and on investment, and number of wells drilled. From the point of view of the economy, it was also a

[6] No separate analysis of product prices is given in this chapter. These fluctuate far more than crude oil prices, and often have an important price leading role. Thus, in 1958/59, the cuts in crude oil prices followed pressure on product prices which had risen very sharply in 1956/57. But over a longer period product prices tend to move parallel with crude. It is therefore assumed that the prospects for product prices are akin to those for crude itself.

peak year in revenues paid (including those for new concessions) and
in the oil industry's contribution to export earnings, investment and
national income.

In 1958, there was a marked adverse movement in the various indices
of growth, including a sharp fall in the output and profits of the industry (see Table 18). Only the Government's tax participation showed
any buoyancy, and this was due to the 19 percentage points increase
in tax rates imposed in 1958.[7] A 12 percent drop in actual prices in
1959 more than offset the 6 percent rise in output. The price fall and
the new tax rates resulted in even lower levels and rates of profit,[8] while
investment activity including the drilling of new wells declined by
about one-third—from Bs 1.8 billion in 1957 to Bs 1.2 billion in 1959.
"Shut-in" capacity reached 1.0 million b.p.d., or almost 37 percent of

TABLE 18: Petroleum Industry Operations, 1956-59

Item	Unit	1956	1957	1958	1959
Output	Mill. bbls.	899	1,014	951	1,011
Value of Output	Mill. Bs.	6,830	8,460	7,660	7,260
(inc. refined)	(")	(1,810)	(2,200)	(2,200)	(2,210)
Value Per Barrel of Oil Sold	$	2.33	2.53	2.44	2.20
Value Per Barrel of Royalty Oil	$	n.a.	2.71	2.55	2.47
Full Cost Per Barrel	$	0.85	0.85	1.00	0.96
(inc. wages)	(")	(0.29)	(0.30)	(0.32)	(0.30)
Net Profit—Total	Mill. Bs.	2,115	2,774	1,616	1,321
per bbl.	$	0.72	0.84	0.51	0.41
as % sales	%	31	33	21	18
as % capital	%	29.3	32.3	17	13.4
Taxes Due—Total	Mill. Bs.	2,280	2,950	2,980	3,004
per bbl.	$	0.78	0.88	0.96	0.89
as % sales	%	33	35	39	40
as % of pre-tax profit	%	52	52	65	69
Capital Outlays	Mill. Bs.	1,160	1,822	1,788	1,209
Wells Drilled	no.	1,449	1,746	1,195	707

Source: *Memoria, 1959,* Ministry of Mines and Hydrocarbons.

[7] From 28.5 percent to 47.5 percent of net profits.
[8] However, government tax accruals were sustained at the 1957/58 levels by retroactive claims for Bs 221 million of extra royalty payments.

1959 output, as compared with 620,000 b.p.d., or 24 percent of output in 1958. The high rate of investment in 1956-58 was still bearing fruit in 1959, and capacity rose from 3.2 million b.p.d. at the close of 1958 to 3.8 million b.p.d. at the end of 1959. In the same year, proven reserves increased by 10 percent to a total of 18.0 billion barrels, the equivalent of 18 years' output at current rates. Thus, reserves and excess capacity were at their highest levels. For these reasons—and as a result of the deterioration of confidence discussed below—there was a decline in the number of wells drilled from 1,746 in 1957 to 707 in 1959.

On the demand side, Venezuela had been adversely affected in 1958 and 1959 by the slowdown in the growth of industrial output and national income in her major North American and West European markets. The U.S. quota system introduced in March 1959 checked the growth of Venezuelan exports to the United States; the increase of the U.S. import market was clearly going to be slower in the early 1960's than in the 1950's if the quotas were maintained. However, Venezuela's deteriorating position in the world oil market was not due primarily to demand factors as such, but to increasingly effective competition from other suppliers. This is apparent from the 40 percent expansion of Middle East output in 1955-59 while Venezuelan production rose only 25 percent.

The impact of the Middle East on the world oil market was obscured and even postponed in the 1950's by such factors as the Korean and Suez wars, the Iranian nationalization crisis and the rapid growth in world oil demand. Yet, even by 1956, the more rapid growth of Middle East output and its increasing share in international trade were apparent.[9] Venezuelan output had declined in the recession of 1949 to 1950 and 1953, as well as in that of 1958: Middle East production continued to grow rapidly throughout the postwar period, whatever the state of the market. It was, however, the market conditions in 1958 and 1959 which conclusively demonstrated the competitive superiority of Middle East oil.

Difficulties Facing the Venezuelan Oil Industry

There is a marked difference in costs of production between various producing areas; and particularly between the Middle East and Venezuela. In the first place, the costs of exploration and exploitation are much higher in Venezuela: the number of wells required to produce a

[9] In 1948, the Middle East supplied 36 percent of the oil traded abroad; by 1956 it provided 46 percent.

given daily flow of oil is some twenty times the number in the Middle East, and the volume of proven reserves (secured by a smaller total investment) is ten times greater in the Middle East than in Venezuela. The cost of development has been estimated at less than 5 cents per barrel in the Middle East as against some 25 cents per barrel in Venezuela. Again, it is possible to estimate from published company accounts and government statements that the full cost of production in the Middle East (excluding royalties and other taxes) is less than 40 cents per barrel, while in Venezuela it exceeds 90 cents. In 1959, the Venezuelan wage cost alone approached the full (non-tax) cost of production in the Middle East. Moreover, operating costs are now being increased by the recent wage contract which raises total wages and benefits by some 16 percent. This rise is equivalent to an extra cost of about 6 cents per barrel.

In addition to its operating cost disadvantage, the Venezuelan industry is subject to higher taxes than are the Middle East producers. As a result of the 1958 increase in income tax rates in Venezuela, the combined tax and royalty payments to the Government in 1958 aggregated approximately 65 percent of gross earnings, as compared with about 50 percent in the Middle East. So long as this differential in tax payments exists, the attractiveness of Venezuelan oil operations will be lessened, since the additional tax payment raises costs which, even before taxes, are already much above those of the Middle East.[10] Including all taxes, total cost per barrel may be estimated at $1.00 to $1.10 in the Middle East, and $1.65 to $1.75 in Venezuela. Of this 65 cents margin in favor of the Middle East, some 15 cents may be attributed to the 1958 increase in Venezuelan income taxes.[11]

The post-Suez period has seen one further factor exert a marked

[10] In both 1957 and 1958, the tax paid was about 89 cents per barrel, even though the average realized price had fallen by 29 cents per barrel.

[11] The tax burden on the companies is aggravated by the fact that payments on royalty oil are based on Texas posted prices. In a world oil market in which oil prices outside the United States have become divorced from U.S. prices, there is a marked difference between posted prices in a relatively protected sector and actual prices in a very competitive one. Thus, in 1958, there was an 11 cents per barrel gap between the higher Texas posted prices and Venezuelan market prices, and this gap widened to 27 cents per barrel in 1959. The 1959 royalty payments were some Bs 140 million more than a payment based on actual prices. If royalties were paid on an actual price basis, the net loss of government oil revenues, after allowing for increased income tax payments, would have been some Bs 75 million, and profits would have been correspondingly higher. Thus, with the present royalty price base, Venezuela secures some indirect benefit from the U.S. quota system. Since these restrictions help maintain U.S. oil prices, the royalty base is higher than it would be in free market conditions.

influence on the relative cost situation in the world oil market. As a result of slower growth in oil demand since 1957, and the large-scale construction of tankers, freight rates, both spot rates and long-term charters, have fallen well below pre-Suez levels. A reduction in tanker rates benefits distant producers relatively more than those whose markets are nearby. Reduced tanker rates have therefore improved the competitive position of Middle East oil in both North America and Western Europe. Before 1957, the relative f.o.b. prices of Middle East and Venezuelan oil had been such that the delivered price of Venezuelan oil was well below that of Middle East oil in North America, and was competitive in Europe, especially for certain heavy crudes.[12] By 1959, with posted price differentials somewhat larger than before the Suez crisis,[13] and with the sharp decline in freight rates, the competitive position was reversed. Middle East oil, paying long-term charter rates, could match the posted prices (plus freight) of Venezuelan oil on the East Coast of the United States. At single voyage rates, the Middle East had a margin of as much as 50 cents per barrel (see Table 19). The position of Middle East oil was even more favorable in Western Europe. The further reduction of Middle East posted prices in August/September 1960 made the margin in favor of the Middle East still wider.

One result of the favorable cost and tax situation of the Middle East

TABLE 19: Comparative Prices of Crude Oil Delivered in New York, December 1959

(in US $ per barrel)

	Long-Term Charter Rate		Single Voyage Spot Rate	
	From Kuwait	From Cardon	From Kuwait	From Cardon
Posted Price	1.67	2.55	1.67	2.55
Freight	1.19	0.31	0.46	0.10
Delivered Price	2.86	2.86	2.13	2.65

Sources: *Petroleum Press Service* and *Petroleum Week*.

[12] Before the Suez crisis, Middle East posted prices were some $0.80 per barrel below Venezuelan; but freight to New York was $1.60 per barrel. As the long-term charter rate for freight from Venezuela to New York was $0.50 per barrel, Venezuela had a "freight protection" of $1.10 per barrel in the North American market, so that on the net there was a $0.30 margin in delivered prices in favor of Venezuela.

[13] In 1959, Middle East list prices were on average reduced to 10 cents per barrel below those prevailing in 1956: Venezuelan prices returned only to pre-Suez levels.

oil industry has been a much higher rate of profit for the producing companies than that achieved in Venezuela. With f.o.b. prices of $1.70 to $2.00 per barrel, and under the 50-50 profit-sharing agreements with Middle East governments, the net profit has usually been 70 to 80 cents per barrel. There are no data publicly available concerning the resultant return on capital invested in Middle East oil, but it has been suggested that this may have been as high as 50 percent a year in the decade 1945-55.[14] Only in occasional boom periods has a profit record comparable to the Middle East been achieved in Venezuela. Thus, in 1957, some companies netted 90 cents per barrel and achieved a 40 percent return on capital. But this was not true of earlier postwar years, nor was it sustained in 1958 and 1959 when prices fell and taxes were raised. For 1959, the return after tax was nearer 41 US cents per barrel and 13 percent on capital (see Table 18).[15] That investment in the Middle East is relatively low for the volume of output achieved is indicated by the average daily flow per well: 4,400 b.p.d. as compared with 250 b.p.d. in Venezuela and 13 b.p.d. in the United States. With such a return per well, a very high rate of profit on capital is to be expected. That yields on investment are much higher in the Middle East is also borne out by the fact that Venezuela produces one-third less oil per day, even though the approximately $3 billion capital value of the Venezuelan oil industry is somewhat greater than the total estimated investment in the Middle East area.

An equally significant comparison is that between the profitability of oil operations in Venezuela and in the United States, the principal market for Venezuelan oil. With the protection afforded by transportation costs and tariffs, and more recently by import quotas, the U.S. domestic oil industry (including all operations from exploration to retail marketing) has been earning 10-15 percent on invested capital during the 1950's: meanwhile returns in the Venezuelan oil industry averaged some 20 percent. In 1959, the yields were 10 percent in the United States and 13.4 percent in Venezuela. It is natural that American investors require the attraction of a substantially higher rate of return if they are to invest in the expansion of the Venezuelan, or any other

[14] Sebastian Racite: *The Oil Import Problem*, studies in Industrial Economics, No. 6, Fordham Univ. Press, 1958, p. 54.

[15] During 1947-59, the oil companies in Venezuela averaged a 20.5 percent a year return on capital invested, the years of lower return being associated with recessions abroad. Returns were well below 20 percent in 1949-50 and in 1958-59. In both periods, the 15 percent average return was primarily a result of recessionary factors and tax changes. The 1953 decline to 19.4 percent was related to post-Korea adjustments in the U.S. economy.

foreign, oil industry rather than in domestic oil operations. Other things being equal, then, a narrowing of the margin between rates of profit earned in Venezuela and the United States, as has occurred in recent years, tends to operate to the disadvantage of the Venezuelan oil industry.

While the Venezuelan oil industry suffers from high costs and lower profitability relative to certain other producing areas, notably the Middle East, other important factors are also likely to have adverse effects on the marketing of Venezuelan oil and the growth of the industry in that country. One is the rapid growth in the number of suppliers which may be expected from several newer sources of oil, which are closer to established Venezuelan markets or which will have preferred treatment in such markets.

Another problem tending to hamper the growth of the oil industry is related to the deterioration of confidence which has been evident recently among Venezuelan producers. While the reduction in confidence is partly based on the abrupt reduction in profits resulting from increased rates of taxation, even more important is the uncertainty besetting the industry with respect to its future role in Venezuela. In the first place, there is a natural concern that profits may be still further reduced by the imposition of additional taxes levied to resolve current fiscal problems. Again, the Government's stated policy of granting no new concessions and the creation of the National Petroleum Corporation have been interpreted to mean that private capital will not be permitted to play an active role in the development of Venezuela's extensive reserves not now under concession. The creation of the National Petroleum Corporation in April 1960 and the efforts of the Venezuelan Government to control export prices and to restrict production through international prorationing have created a feeling of pessimism in the oil industry and have given the companies reason to feel that they face the prospects of restricted commercial freedom and lessened profits for some time to come.

Factors Favorable to Venezuela

Running counter to these difficulties which now confront Venezuela, there are factors which may help sustain Venezuela's position in world oil markets. They relate to several aspects of costs and to the desire for diversified sources of oil supply. There are indications that, on the one hand, Venezuela may make some tax and other concessions to the Venezuelan producers, and, on the other hand, that the governments of the Middle East and perhaps of other producing areas may move to increase their share in the revenues of the oil companies. Anxious for greater revenues, these governments may, in present market conditions, prefer to seek a higher tax rate on profits rather than to press for large increases in output as a means to greater revenues. The basis for an increased share in profits has already been provided in recent agreements between several independent companies and the governments of Saudi Arabia, Iran and Kuwait.[16] Conversely, any easing of income tax or royalty provisions on the part of the Venezuelan Government would make Venezuelan oil more competitive and thercfore provide both immediate relief to the industry and an improvement in the business climate.

Secondly, Venezuela's "shut-in" capacity of about 1 million b.p.d. can be brought into production with only a slight increase in total operating costs, and these marginal supplies can be delivered, especially in North America, at prices which are competitive with those of marginal supplies from the Middle East.[17] Thus, Venezuela's comparative cost situation in the short run may not be as unfavorable as it appears over a longer period of time. However, as indicated in Chapter 3, the Venezuelan producers might find themselves in a more difficult position in the long run if their "shut-in" capacity is used as suggested.

Thirdly, freight rates are generally thought to have reached bed-rock, and the coming years should see some rise in spot and charter rates for tankers. This would mean a return toward more customary levels of the freight rate advantages which Venezuela enjoyed prior to the Suez crisis. While it is difficult to foresee a return to conditions in which Venezuela would again enjoy the pre-Suez freight advantage of $1 or more per barrel over Middle East oil delivered in the United States, a firming of the tanker market would necessarily help Venezuela. A change in Middle East taxes or in freight rates would most likely be in a direction favorable to the Venezuelan oil industry. Any such improvement in Venezuela's relative position could be offset by

[16] However, revision of the profit-sharing agreements with the major companies would be somewhat more difficult in the Middle East than in Venezuela. There, only a unilateral change in the income tax law was required: in the Middle East, a contract renegotiation would be necessary. Moreover, the present state of the oil market may be deemed inappropriate for any increase in taxes, unless the action were taken jointly by the governments of the principal producing states.

[17] In comparing these incremental costs and profits with Middle East operations, factors favorable to Venezuela must be taken into account (freight advantages, higher average quality of oil, the tax advantage accruing to U.S. refiners on account of the higher price of Venezuelan oils) and also factors favorable to the Middle East (lower rates of tax and somewhat lower incremental costs of operation).

a price cut which narrowed the relatively large profit margins earned on Middle East oil, unless this move were prevented by OPEC's policy of price stabilization.

Apart from these cost considerations, there is a further factor which is still more likely to help sustain Venezuela's position in the world oil market, particularly in the longer run. This is the desire of the major oil producers and distributors to diversify their sources of supply, even when this entails using relatively expensive oil. Such a policy provides security for the industry as a whole; it also enables more effective bargaining with local governments and provides some degree of independence in the event of unfavorable developments in any particular producing area. This policy is apparent in the maintenance by the major oil companies of large high-cost but profitable capacity in the restricted U.S. market, as well as in their continued activity in Venezuela. For example, in 1957 they derived 37 percent of their oil from the Middle East, 29 percent from Venezuela, 27 percent from the United States and Canada, and 7 percent elsewhere (see Table 20).

There are strong economic and political reasons for a continuation of a policy of diversifying sources of supply. Over-all market strength depends in part on being independent of particular sources of oil, despite the evidence of straight calculations of comparative costs of production. Relative costs and profits are not the sole determining factors in a decision on where to produce oil for the world market. The

TABLE 20: Source of Crude Oil Output for Major Companies, 1957

(in percentages)

	North America	Middle East	Venezuela	Other
Standard Oil (N.J.)	27	20	50	3
Royal Dutch/Shell	18	26	45	11
British Petroleum	1	99	—	—
Gulf	31	53	15	1
Texaco	42	37	14	7
Standard Oil (Cal.)	42	40	10	8
Standard Oil (N.Y.)	40	38	16	6
All companies	27	37	29	7

Note: Combined 1957 output of these firms = 9.6 million b.p.d. In 1957, they produced 93% of Middle East oil and 92% of Venezuela's. In 1959, they produced 92% of Middle East oil and 88% of Venezuela's.

Sources: Corporate Annual Reports.

pertinent questions then relate to the degree of diversification considered desirable and the extent of the premium, in the form of higher costs per barrel and lower profit per dollar invested, which the industry is willing to pay to avoid too high a degree of dependence on Middle East oil.

Prospects for Increasing Production

Because there has been a decline in the competitiveness of Venezuelan oil in world markets during the last few years and therefore in the attractiveness of the industry as a field of operation, oil output failed to increase significantly between 1957 and 1960. In addition, we have expressed the view that during the planning period there may be some further, but slight, fall in market prices relative to those prevailing in fiscal 1959/60. In the light of this analysis, it would seem that Venezuelan output will grow less rapidly than the expected 6 percent a year growth in non-Communist world oil demand, let alone the 8 percent a year growth expected for areas outside the United States. An estimate of how much slower the growth will be depends on an assessment of the factors already outlined and of the likelihood of corrective measures being taken by those most concerned.

The Venezuelan Government has indicated a desire for a 4 percent a year growth rate during the years 1959-64, and the Government's investment plans for the period are based on that estimate. Although it appears to us unlikely that there will be so great an increase in 1960 output over 1959, the mission is inclined to feel that a growth rate of 4 percent a year is possible during the ensuing years, and this increase could probably be ensured if the companies and the Government are prepared to make certain accommodations which we believe could prove to be mutually advantageous.

There would appear to be no reasons why the Government's suggested increase of 4 percent a year in Venezuelan production during 1960-64 should pose any serious marketing problems. Developments in the U.S. import market will have an important bearing on the future of Venezuelan oil, but it is expected that, in view of the U.S. interest in a liberal system of international trade, this market will grow by at least 3-4 percent a year.[18] The mission assumes that arrangements can be made which will enable Venezuela to continue to supply the major part of the increasing import requirements of both the United States

[18] While a more rapid growth of U.S. oil imports may well occur in the longer run, there is even the possibility that this will eventuate before 1964.

and of Canada, whose markets together absorb somewhat more than half of Venezuela's exports. Moreover, Venezuela is particularly favored by the growing U.S. requirements for the low gravity crude which is the principal quality produced in Venezuela. The Latin American and Western European markets, which are growing some 7-8 percent a year, together account for almost all the remaining sales abroad. Here, in particular, Venezuela may expect actual displacement (e.g., Argentina and France) or else slow growth in sales in relation to the increase in oil demand. If one assumes that, for reasons already given, the offtake of Venezuelan oil for sale in these latter areas grows by only half the anticipated rate of growth in demand, then the over-all increase in demand for Venezuelan oil would approach 4 percent a year.[19]

The mission therefore feels that such a projection is not an unreasonable one on which to base an estimate of the operations of the oil industry for the period 1960-64. On the other hand, 1960 output is unlikely to exceed that of 1959 by as much as 4 percent. Specifically, then, for planning purposes, the mission is assuming a growth in output in 1960 of slightly less than 2 percent and an average growth of 4 percent a year in each of the following four years. On these output assumptions, and with the assumption that any further decline in market prices will not exceed 3 percent, the mission has made its estimates of the size and growth of the industry's contributions to exports, national product and, above all, to the government revenues during the planning period (see Annex I). If, however, the mission's assumptions fail to materialize, as indeed they may, substantial adjustments must be made in the Government's development program (see Chapter 6).

To form a longer-run view of Venezuela's oil prospects, we have to take into account the likely trends in both the world markets and in the conditions of operation within Venezuela. On the demand side, it may reasonably be assumed that world oil requirements will continue even beyond the 1960/61-1963/64 planning period to expand quite

[19] On the basis of the analysis in this chapter, non-Communist world oil demand may be assumed to increase by some 7 million b.p.d. in 1959-65. Of this growth, 4.8 million b.p.d. would occur in the non-Communist world excluding the United States. If the United States allows imports to grow in step with domestic demand, there would be an additional market of 400,000 b.p.d. for imported oil. If North Africa produces 800,000 b.p.d., the Soviet Union exports an additional 360,000 b.p.d., and other producing areas (Argentina, Canada, etc.) increase output by 1,000,000 b.p.d., then an extra 3,000,000 b.p.d. would be required from the Middle East and Venezuela in 1965. If Venezuela averaged a 4 percent a year increase in exports (some 600,000 b.p.d.) through 1965, the Middle East would supply the remaining 2.4 million b.p.d. This would still allow a 7.5 percent a year rise in Middle East output, which would appear quite a reasonable assumption for that area.

rapidly, perhaps by 5-7 percent a year. In securing a share of this growing market, Venezuela will continue to be adversely affected by the expansion of output in newer producing areas (Canada, Brazil, Libya, etc.), and by the basic competitive superiority (in terms of costs and reserves) of Middle East oil. On the other hand, the freight and tax rate differentials may become less unfavorable to Venezuelan producers relative to others. Moreover, Venezuela will continue to enjoy a substantial premium for its position as a major source of oil independent of the Middle East. Above all, there is the possibility that the United States may allow imports to meet an increasing, rather than a constant, proportion of demand, and this would particularly assist Venezuela.[20]

In addition to these factors which are largely independent of Venezuelan conditions, there are also factors within Venezuela which affect the longer-run growth prospects of the oil industry. First, there is the question of the continued availability of adequate and economic reserves of oil, and doubts have been expressed on this account.[21] Secondly, as we have already pointed out, there are considerations with a direct bearing on decisions to produce in Venezuela which depend on future government economic policy. These include policies on wage rates and price levels, exchange rates, taxation, new concessions and on the roles of government and private enterprise in the oil industry.

There must inevitably remain a large element of uncertainty concerning the combined effects of these various factors and so concerning the likely rate of growth of Venezuelan oil production in the longer run. The mission believes that, while there are on balance good prospects for the continued growth of oil production, this growth will be much slower than heretofore, and probably slower than in the four-year planning period 1960/61-1963/64. Moreover, in formulating its economic development policies, Venezuela must also take into account the possibility of lower petroleum prices over the long period.

[20] Several recent analyses of the U.S. oil market have concluded that U.S. oil imports may increase by as much as 10 percent a year over the next 10 to 15 years.

[21] However, in contrast to existing proven reserves which are equivalent to 18 years of output at present rates, there may indeed be sufficient oil reserves to allow production to continue at present levels of activity for a much longer period. There is, of course, no clear information on whether (or by how much) the costs of exploration and exploitation would rise. See Anibal, R. Martinez, *Some Techniques of Prediction Applicable to the Oil Industry,* Third Geological Conference of Venezuela, Caracas, November 1959.

PART **III**   *THE SECTOR REPORTS*

CHAPTER 9 *AGRICULTURE*

THE PRESENT SITUATION

Land Resources and Current Use

About 3 percent of the total land area of Venezuela is now under crops, about 3 percent under artificial pasture and about 17 percent is under generally unimproved pasture (see Table 21).[1] Until very recently, cropping has been limited largely to the Andes, the coastal mountains and the Maracaibo basin. The *llanos* (plains) south and east of the mountains have been used for open-range production of cattle, with relatively little capital in relation to land. The area south of the Orinoco River has been, and continues to be, largely unexplored and unsettled.

During the past ten years, the control of malaria, the development of transportation and the rapid economic growth in the petroleum, trade and industrial sectors, have tended to shift cropping down toward the plains with substantial development in the Maracaibo basin and the Portuguesa-Barinas area. Most of the land in these areas is, however, still unexploited and provides substantial possibilities for agricultural development;[2] the soils are alluvial and there is sufficient rainfall for growing two crops a year. The mission estimates that, assuming present prices and costs, up to three million hectares of agricultural land could be developed in the Maracaibo basin and the Barinas-Portuguesa area. This would add more than 50 percent to the existing area under crops and improved pasture.

In the *llanos* proper extending south of the piedmont to the Orinoco, soils are generally poor and inadequately drained. Most of the land is used for extensive grazing on natural grasses. During the dry season there is an acute shortage of water which causes some mortality and heavy weight losses among the cattle. While accurate data on cattle population are not available, meat production is reported to have

---

[1] The mission has been forced to rely on data derived from a 1956 survey, the most recent information on land use available.

[2] The term "agriculture" is used throughout this report to include livestock as well as crops.

139

doubled during the past ten years indicating a more intensive exploitation of these areas in recent years. Production methods are still basically of the extensive type, with a high ratio of land to other input factors.

TABLE 21: Area and Distribution of Land Use in 1950 and 1956

	Land Use According to 1950 Census[a]		Land Use According to 1956 Sample[b]	
	Area (in hectares)	Percent	Area (in hectares)	Percent
Total Land Area	91,205,000	100.0	91,205,000	100.0
Under Census:[c]	22,126,140	24.3	29,590,128	32.5
In permanent use:	1,302,116	1.4	2,924,942[d]	3.2
of which perennial crops[e]	592,919[f]		—	
of which annual crops	709,197[g]		—	
Recent shifting cultivation[h]	1,334,334	1.5	864,001	1.0
Artificial pastures	1,639,424	1.8	2,604,458	2.9
Natural pastures	11,861,538	13.1	15,164,350	16.6
Exploited forests	771,153	0.8		
Non-exploited forests	3,663,828	4.0	7,971,877	8.8
Deforested	239,584	0.3		
Not in use for agriculture	1,314,663	1.4		

[a] Censo Nacional 1950: "Censo Agropecuario" Part I, Ministerio de Fomento, Caracas.

[b] *Encuesta Agropecuaria Nacional, 1956.*

[c] Represents land recorded as in actual or potential use.

[d] Defined as harvested, without any indication about type of use, but possibly counting double-cropped areas twice.

[e] Cacao, coffee, bananas and plantains.

[f] If including cocoas and fruit trees, 647,000 ha. and annual crops 657,000.

[g] Irrigated 237,000 ha., of which 28,600 ha. in farms under 10 ha.

[h] Number of years for 1950 unknown, for 1956 for the four preceding years.

In the Andes proper and in the northern ranges, soils are in general favorable, at least in the bottom lands of the valleys and basins, although sometimes they are saline and badly drained, as is the case in the Valencia Valley. Rainfall varies from valley to valley, depending on the direction of the prevailing winds. The valleys form the centers of permanent cropping in big and in small farms. Where rainfall is favorable, the lower slopes and flats are in cacao, the higher ones in coffee.

Some of the more fertile basins are in improved pasture and sugar cane. In the permanent cropping regions, overpopulation has resulted in diminished farm size; promotion of shifting cultivation on the Andean slopes and, in the drier parts, destruction of the natural cover of forest or shrub has led to the development of poor grasslands, as in Falcon State, with subsequent severe erosion. Especially in the Andes, in the Barlovento area and in Sucre State, overcrowding and partial unemployment are acute problems. (For maps showing rainfall and topography and types of terrain, see Annex V.)

Farm Size and Income Characteristics

As is common in the tropics, the traditional family-sized farm is small (planted area 1-2 ha.) and yields are low, as is productivity per head. This is caused partly by the tropical environment (rapid weed growth, leached poor soils, short days), partly by the traditional farm systems, mostly dependent only on human labor. The consequence of these two factors is a general backwardness in agricultural development, productivity and income. The effect of these factors is strongest in annual field crops, much less in tree crops, pastures and forest.

Of an estimated 400,000 farm families, about two-thirds operated less than 5 ha. in 1956 (see Table 22). Some of these were engaged in small commercial operations such as fruit and vegetable growing. If we assume that population increases have been more or less offset by recent migrations to the cities, there were in 1960 about 200,000 farm families

TABLE 22: Distribution of Farm Sizes in 1956

Size	1956
Under 1 ha.	54,166
1-5 ha.	212,121
5-10 ha.	54,503
10-50 ha.	49,058
50-500 ha.	19,121
500-1,000 ha.	3,095
1,000-2,500 ha.	2,822
Over 2,500	3,937
Total	397,823

Source: *Encuesta Agropecuaria Nacional, 1956.*

living close to the subsistence level. Most of these farmers have had no education and little contact with modern agriculture. They produce primarily for their own consumption and have very little surplus to sell and consequently are unresponsive to market forces and government programs. They mainly work as shifting cultivators using only a machete and a planting stick. They represent the core of the social and political problem in agriculture. The Agrarian Reform Law of 1960 is aimed primarily at meeting their needs.

The remaining 200,000 farm families operate large extensive cattle ranches, large commercial farms, small family-sized mixed farms and small specialized farms producing for the market. These farms are responsive to market factors and have been aided to some extent by government credit, price support and technical assistance. They have been responsible for the increases in production recorded during the past ten years. Where reasonably skilled levels of management have prevailed, these farms have produced acceptable incomes for the farm family.

Land Tenure

As in many Latin American countries, the land ownership pattern in Venezuela is characterized by a number of large, extensively operated estates and a large number of small farmers eking out a living on small plots. At the same time, however, there are vast areas of municipal and state-owned land which are undeveloped and still in virgin forest. The inadequacy of land records makes it difficult to determine the extent and location of these lands, but the Government estimates that there are more than one million hectares of publicly owned land suitable for agriculture available for distribution to cultivators. Some of these lands (250,000 hectares) were confiscated from exiled members of the previous regime on grounds that they were illegally acquired or were not being farmed efficiently. The Government also purchased about 250,000 hectares and has statutory powers to purchase additional land if required.

In the older developed areas, population pressures have resulted in fragmentation of holdings to such an extent that farmers must rely on share cropping arrangements with the larger estates in order to acquire additional workable land. It is in these areas of population pressure that the Government has been purchasing land for distribution. On the other hand, in the relatively underdeveloped areas plenty of land, already publicly owned, is available for colonization.

Prices and Output

Almost all agricultural products are heavily protected and imports are subject to quantitative restrictions in most cases. The result is that internal prices of agricultural products are generally well above world prices. Despite high prices, domestic demand has increased sufficiently to keep ahead of domestic supply in most instances.

Imports of agricultural commodities amounted to over Bs 650 million in 1958. The principal imports were dairy products, wheat and wheat flour, oil and oil seeds, eggs and fruits. The only significant exports were coffee and cacao.

With prospects of a decline in the rate of growth of the petroleum sector, it will become increasingly important to expand domestic agricultural production and to limit imports. This will call for a continuation of protection for some time to come. On the other hand, it should be recognized that Venezuela has certain natural disadvantages in the production of some products and advantages in others. A policy of self-sufficiency at any cost should not be followed if national income is to be maximized. There is however plenty of scope for expanding production of those products for which Venezuela has no natural disadvantages.

Recent Tendencies

Available data indicate that during the past ten years there has been a significant rate of growth in the agricultural sector. The Central Bank estimates that the value of agricultural production has increased by about 5½ percent a year during the period 1950-1959 (see Table 23 for detailed data for 1950-1958; details for 1959 not available). The principal area of growth has been in dairy and livestock production. These account for about one-half of the growth in output. Industrial crops such as sugar cane, cotton, Virginia tobacco and sesame also show rapid growth according to statistics on industrial consumption. Data on other crops are incomplete and subject to a substantial margin of error but indicate a slow rate of growth. Neither coffee nor cacao, the traditional export crops, has shown a consistent upward trend.

Analysis of the growth pattern indicates that the areas of growth have been confined to the commercialized sectors which operate on a relatively large scale. A motivating force has been the rapid rise in demand resulting from the growth in output and income in the petroleum, construction and industrial sectors. The Government has carried out a number

TABLE 23: Value Added of Agricultural Production

(in Bs million at constant prices[a])

	1950	1954	1958
CROPS			
Cereals:			
Corn	63.0	66.3	72.7
Rice	11.9	31.5	5.9
Wheat	2.5	1.1	1.5
Legumes:			
Caraotas	27.6	29.4	36.7
Quinchoncho	3.4	3.6	5.5
Peas	5.6	3.0	2.0
Kidney Beans	14.6	16.5	23.7
Roots and Tubers:			
Yucca	39.9	56.1	54.8
Ocumo	20.1	14.9	27.3
Yams	13.7	18.8	34.4
Sweet Potato	7.5	3.8	8.4
Celery	7.1	4.4	7.6
Mapuey	3.9	2.1	7.4
Potato	17.8	24.5	42.3
Fibers and Oil:			
Sesame	4.0	6.8	14.8
Peanuts	2.2	3.6	1.9
Copra	5.2	13.3	8.2
Cotton (Raw)	8.9	17.2	24.5
Sisal (Fibers)	0.2	0.3	0.5
Others:			
Coffee	114.7	180.6	208.9
Cacao	36.2	32.2	31.7
Sugar Cane	16.1	30.0	50.0
Raw Sugar	60.6	49.4	48.7
Tobacco	64.1	45.7	44.7
Bananas	41.9	53.2	61.4
Fruits and Vegetables:			
Fruits	39.6	44.6	48.4
Vegetables	31.5	36.2	40.9
Total Crops	663.8	789.1	914.8
LIVESTOCK AND MILK			
Cattle	216.1	236.3	340.9
Other livestock	30.7	34.1	42.3
Milk	37.3	83.5	136.2
Total Livestock and Milk	284.1	353.9	519.4
FISH	20.4	18.2	33.1
WOOD PRODUCTS	46.7	52.1	60.8
GRAND TOTAL	1,015.9	1,213.3	1,528.2[b]

Footnotes to Table 23 on page 145.

of commodity programs aimed at meeting this rising internal demand and displacing imports. These programs have applied various mixtures of governmental purchases, price supports, a heavy element of protection either in the form of tariffs or quantitative restrictions on imports, and liberal credits, and, in the case of milk, a cash subsidy. Agricultural growth has been accelerated by the development of improved transportation facilities. Very little emphasis has been placed on basic research, education and extension activities. An important part of the technical and managerial skills in commercial agriculture has been provided by postwar immigrants. Crop yields per hectare are in most cases still low.

The commercialized sector has shown itself to be relatively responsive to market incentives and government programs. It has also gained considerable experience in mechanized operations and some contact with use of fertilizers, improved seeds, pesticides, and other forms of technical improvement. Further increases in agricultural output will come largely in this sector.

In contrast, the bulk of low-income cultivators operate farms of less than five ha. and have received very little benefit from recent economic development. Most of them cultivate less than two ha. and produce very little surplus for the market. Their problem is basically one of lack of know-how. Shortage of land is not generally an immediate limiting factor since they are already cultivating as much land as they can manage under systems of shifting or primitive permanent cultivation and with the non-land resources they have in hand.

The Dual Nature of the Agricultural Problem

The agricultural problem thus has two quite separate aspects: the problem of increasing the production and efficiency of the commercialized sector and the problem of raising the income and living standard of the subsistence farmer. Normally, measures designed to increase output and efficiency will automatically bring about increases in incomes and living standards provided there are no serious institutional obstacles. In Venezuela, however, because of the tremendous gap be-

---

[a] Based on 1957 prices.

[b] Revised estimates given in *Memoria, 1959,* Banco Central de Venezuela show this total at Bs 1,576 million; however, a breakdown of this total by the component agricultural products is not available.

Source: **Banco Central de Venezuela.**

tween the commercialized sector and the subsistence sector, the usual formulas cannot be applied. Production and incomes in the commercialized sector can be increased rapidly through orthodox programs of investment, credits, price supports, subsidies and technical advice. On the other hand, the problem in the subsistence sector is much more complex and the solutions are relatively long-range.

The major handicap for the subsistence farmer is his low productivity, due to a combination of adverse tropical conditions, primitive farming systems, poverty and lack of knowledge. With the primitive techniques known to him, he can manage only one or two hectares. Most subsistence farmers are without animal power, and are obliged to open up and work the soil with machete, hoe and digging stick. Many move their fields from place to place each year or two, since production falls off rapidly after the first year under their primitive system. Being illiterate and unskilled, the only alternatives they now have are to continue as shifting cultivators, get jobs on larger farms or get unskilled jobs outside agriculture. Even when they have permanent fields on good soils they cannot manage more than a few hectares since they generally do not use cattle. However, where cattle are used such as in La Grita in the Andes conditions appear much better.

THE LOW-INCOME FARMER

The Determinants of Policy

The Agrarian Reform Law of 1960 provides the framework for a comprehensive program to deal with both low-income and commercial farmers. The Law calls for establishment of adequate research and extension services, provision of farm credit, improvement of marketing facilities, and also sets forth new regulations controlling land tenure. The total cost of one program designed to fulfill the objectives of the Law was estimated at Bs 23 billion by the *Subcomision Economica* of the *Comision de la Reforma Agraria* of which about one-half would be for preparatory costs such as acquisition of land, irrigation, drainage, electrification and tractor pools and one-half for the resettlement of about 350,000 farm families. Since the Government does not have the resources required to carry out a program of this magnitude in a short period of time, it has not adopted this program. It has instead established an interim program aimed at benefiting the small farmer by such measures as the acquisition, division and distribution of land from estates in crowded areas, expansion of loan operations and initiation of an accelerated colonization program. The Government has not yet taken concrete measures to expand basic research, educational and extension services needed to support these programs. The mission has therefore attempted to determine the relative importance of the various aspects of the agrarian reform program and to suggest a program for agrarian reform consistent with maximum agricultural development.

In the process of assessing priorities, the mission had in mind the following basic considerations:

a. Government colonization or resettlement programs in Venezuela to date do not meet the purposes of the Agrarian Reform Law. They are of a capital-intensive type and are too high-cost and thus provide employment for relatively few people.
b. In some parts of the Andes and in Sucre, population pressures on the land have forced many people to seek new lands elsewhere or employment outside agriculture.
c. The vast majority of the low-income farmers are not sufficiently dissatisfied with their present situation to accept the risks of moving into a completely new situation unless the Government provides various incentives.
d. The large-scale migration into Caracas and other urban centers during the past two years represents a backlog of people who were forcibly kept out of the cities by the previous regime. Most of these people cannot be lured back to the farm.
e. Programs aimed at helping low-income farmers improve their status at their present locations would be relatively inexpensive and a large number of people could be helped by such programs.
f. There is plenty of good agricultural land for those who want to move from their present farms.
g. Most low-income farmers can manage no more than one or two hectares with their present technology.

The mission has thus reached the following conclusions:

a. Since public land is relatively abundant and capital scarce, the Government should be prepared to provide liberal amounts of land with a minimum amount of money expenditures.
b. It will be difficult to establish a large number of efficient farm units within any short period of time, particularly in view of the present state of extension and research activities. However, settlement of farmers on more fertile lands with possibilities for further

expansion should improve incomes and productivity both in the new settlement areas and in the old areas where the remaining farmers could then operate larger units.

c. Provided farmers are established already on reasonably good soils, money spent on assisting them where they are will generally be more productive and bring about quicker results than money spent for colonization or resettlement.

d. Farmers who have the capacity for managing larger units should be given ample opportunity to settle on free land of good quality with the assurance that title will be granted as soon as certain minimum requirements are met. **Government financial assistance should be kept to a minimum.**

e. Research on farm size, cropping systems and various types of management should be carried out on all types of soil.

The basic reasoning behind these conclusions is that since the Government does not have the resources to take care of all farmers on the scale proposed by the Agrarian Reform Commission, it is better, both economically and politically, to benefit a large number of farmers to some extent than to try to provide everything for a few farmers as has been the tendency in the past.

Resettlement of a Capital-Intensive Type

With the exception of spontaneous colonists, resettlement during the past ten years has all been of the capital-intensive type, mainly for commercial farmers. The most extreme case has been the Guarico project where the Government has already invested over Bs 300 million, with an additional Bs 150-200 million required before the area could be brought into full production. In addition to the Guarico project, the Government spent about Bs 260 million for colonization (including Bs 102 million in credits) from 1949 to 1958 and established roughly 1,600 farm units. The sizes of the units varied considerably from about 4 ha. to 250 ha. An important part of the settlement program was the allocation of *microparcelas* (small-plot settlements for low-income farm families). The basic purpose of this aspect of the program was to supply labor for the larger farms.

More recent projects, such as at Aroa, call for a much lower per capita investment and rely to some extent on the colonist carrying out certain operations such as land clearing. Furthermore, beginning in 1958/59, the *Instituto Agrario Nacional* (IAN) changed its policies and tried to put more emphasis on the low-income farmer. The budget for 1958/59 called for establishment of 2,500 farm units at an average cost of about Bs 20,000 per unit. The budget for 1959/60 provides for 4,000 farm units at about the same unit cost.

A number of comprehensive studies have been made of the colonization program. The *Direccion de Planificacion* of the *Ministerio de Agricultura y Cria* (MAC) and the privately operated *Consejo de Bienestar Rural* (CBR) have recently published excellent studies.[3] The consensus of opinion of these studies is that the program to date has benefited relatively few farmers at high cost and that the contributions to national output have not been commensurate with the expenditures involved. Some of the major shortcomings of the program have been:

a. Lack of clear objectives and policies.
b. Lack of realistic planning in terms of selection of area, size of farm, cropping patterns, soil and climatic conditions, capacity of the colonists, etc.
c. A tendency for IAN administration to be too paternalistic, a reluctance to turn over responsibilities to the colonists or other government agencies and delays in giving colonists title to their land.
d. Poor administration due to excessive turnover of personnel, lack of records and over-concentration of activities in the central office.
e. Excessive expenditures on housing, community facilities and land clearing with insufficient attention to the economic productivity of the farms created.
f. Haphazard selection of settlers leading to excessive turnover.

With better planning and execution, resettlement costs could be reduced substantially from past levels. Nevertheless, because of the lack of basic knowledge and experience, heavy capital inputs will tend to yield less-than-normal returns. Past experience in settlement projects has been disappointing in terms of the returns accruing from such heavy capital investment as irrigation works or the provision of farm machinery, and most past capital-intensive settlement projects have been for commercial farming. If commercial farmers have been unable fully to exploit such investment, it is clear that returns would be even lower on settlements for low-income small farmers whose knowledge and experience are even more limited. The mission therefore concludes that resettlement of the capital-intensive type should not be carried out for the low-income farmer.

[3] *La Colonizacion Agraria en Venezuela 1830-1957*, Republica de Venezuela, Ministerio de Agricultura y Cria, Direccion de Planificacion Agropecuaria, Caracas 1959; *Analisis General del Programa y de la Administracion del Instituto Agrario Nacional*, Consejo de Bienestar Rural, Caracas, May 1959.

Furthermore, we recommend that IAN should gradually reduce its administrative responsibilities for existing farm colonies and settlements. Having so far provided these colonies with relatively large amounts of capital, we see no need for continuing day-to-day paternalism. The time has come to encourage individual farmers to stand on their own feet so far as their own individual enterprises are concerned, and to turn over responsibility for community matters to regular local government agencies. The cost to IAN of administering its farm colonics has been nearly Bs 60 million a year; we believe that, with a transfer of administrative responsibility, this cost could be reduced in succeeding years so that IAN's expenditures in this connection should not total more than Bs 115 million during 1960/61-1963/64.

Spontaneous Resettlement

During the past ten years, a substantial number of settlers moved into new areas without any special assistance from public authorities. While there are no accurate estimates of the number of such settlers, a study of spontaneous colonization[4] indicates the following:

a. The system of spontaneous colonization has developed extensive regions in all parts of the country.
b. The largest number of such settlers are found along the base of the Andes in areas recently opened up by roads.
c. The settlers came from the lower areas in the Andes, relatively close by, and knew about the availability of fertile soils.
d. The shortage of good lands under good tenure conditions in the Andes seemed to be the principal reason for leaving their former lands.
e. Most of the settlers engaged, at least part time, in non-agricultural activities (60 percent of the sample group) .
f. The Government did very little for the people other than building the roads.
g. A small proportion of the farmers had more than 50 ha. combining agriculture and livestock and were quite prosperous. Many of these had some capital to begin with, but some worked up from a poor start over a period of some years.

The experience with spontaneous colonization shows that, at least for some people, promise of fertile land accessible to markets is suffi-

[4] *La Colonizacion Agraria en Venezuela 1830-1957*, Republica de Venezuela, Ministerio de Agricultura y Cria, Direccion de Planificacion Agropecuaria, Caracas, 1959, Appendix VII, "La Colonizacion en Venezuela," by Roberto Lizarralda.

cient incentive to move away from their subsistence plots onto new lands. This movement occurs despite the lack of assurance of legal rights on the new land. Furthermore, in the absence of government assistance for housing and land clearing, most settlers have to work hard and live under primitive conditions for some years before the lands can be developed. Most settlers have eventually managed to find a level of living somewhat better than on their original farms, some have managed to find part-time employment outside of agriculture and others have found full-time non-agricultural employment. While some settlers are still not much better off than formerly, they do have possibilities for future development which they could not find in their original homes.

Compared to organized IAN efforts at colonization, the costs to the Government have been practically nothing and the results somewhat better. A significant factor has been the natural selection process associated with spontaneous colonization. In the absence of lavish housing, services and credits, only those willing to undergo hardship and work for prospects of a better life have become spontaneous colonists. Under the IAN programs, many people have been attracted largely by the provision of housing and other facilities, rather than by the prospects of building up a productive farm.

A Proposed Resettlement Program with Emphasis on Land

The mission feels that the pioneering spirit evidenced by the spontaneous settlers is essential for low-cost development of new areas. On the other hand, the haphazard manner in which spontaneous settlers have squatted on lands close to roads will be a detriment to development of any sizeable number of efficient farms. A more orderly approach to spontaneous colonization should be possible. The mission believes that it is feasible to devise settlement programs that represent a realistic compromise between the former capital-intensive IAN policy and a *laissez-faire* approach to spontaneous colonization.

The outlines of the type of resettlement program we recommend are as follows:

  a. The Government should select several large development areas on government- or state-owned land in the Barinas-Portuguesa region, being careful to choose areas of fertile soils, of relative uniformity and with adequate rainfall. After making detailed topographic and leveling survey, the Government should build dirt access roads, into these areas, spaced about 8 km. apart, with necessary drainage facilities. Rights-of-way should be kept for future roads and drainage ditches.

b. The land alongside the access roads should be divided into lots of about 5 ha., with a zone for expansion of 5 ha. behind each lot. A fair degree of flexibility should be allowed to adjust for terrain and soil conditions. This would provide eventually for farms of about 10 ha. This would permit 5 farms per km. on each side of a road or 10 farms per km. of road constructed. Since the estimated cost of roads and drainage is Bs 50,000 per km. for a minimum road with drains and turnouts, the cost would be Bs 5,000 per farm family, if sufficient roads were to be built to give each farmer a plot situated on a road.

c. In order to avoid excessive expenditures for roads per farm family, it would be necessary to locate some farms away from the road. Other things being equal, farmers would prefer lands on the road or close to the road. Hence, to overcome this tendency, farmers who settle away from the roads should be given plots with more land and with proportionately greater land for future expansion. Rights-of-way to provide access to the roads should be reserved, but the Government would not build any of these interior access roads. It should be possible to devise a formula relating size of plots to distance from the road. In this way, the costs per farm family for roads and drainage could be brought down to no more than Bs 2,500.

d. During the first two years, the Government's role would be limited to the initial roads, topographical surveys, major drainage and provision of some housing materials, such as roofing, cement and wells.

e. To assist farmers in the first year before their crops are harvested, the Government should provide a clearing subsidy of Bs 250 per hectare of land cleared (this would mean about Bs 500 per family, assuming clearance of 2 hectares in the first year).

f. Farmers who settle on these lands would be given clear title when they have demonstrated their ability by having cleared half their initial plots, and they would be given the option to buy adjacent land reserved for expansion on long-term credit terms when they have developed a farm plan for the larger unit.

g. Farmers desiring larger holdings should be given an opportunity to buy additional plots adjoining the basic lot which they would receive under the program.

h. The same type of opportunity should also be given to farmers wishing to settle on government-owned land outside of these large development areas. In these cases the Government would not build roads until there were enough settlers. The principal contribution of the Government would be to clarify title. Roofing and cement should be provided to assist settlers in building their homes.

i. An agricultural extension worker should be provided for about every 500 families in the initial year, during which his main task would be to familiarize himself with the area, and distribute housing materials. Cultivators would clear the first two ha. and plant subsistence crops in the traditional manner. In the second and third years, when cultivators will start grubbing and preparing for a permanent-type agriculture, a second extension man should be brought in. Good advice at this stage is extremely important if the cultivator is going to become more than a subsistence farmer.

j. Normal government services such as distribution of subsidized requisites, cattle, and farm credit should be made available beginning in the third year.

k. To the extent that bananas or plantains are either marketable or useable for food or animal feed, cultivators should be encouraged to plant them to reduce the cost of grubbing. If partially cleared land is planted to bananas for about four or five years, the roots will decay and no grubbing is necessary. This would reduce costs substantially.

l. Mechanical grubbing will be required for partially cleared land which is not planted to bananas or plantains. This could be done on a cooperative basis or by individual contract. In either case, government help will be necessary for this purpose beginning in the third year.

The estimated costs per family of the proposed settlement program, over and above the costs of a general program to assist all low-income small farmers irrespective of whether or not they are participants in the specific settlement program, and on the assumption that settlements are located on publicly owned land, are as follows:

Roads and drainage	Bs 2,500
Housing materials	1,000
Grubbing (from third year)	1,000
Implements and cattle (from third year)	2,000
Administration	1,000
Clearing subsidy	500
Total	Bs 8,000

Assuming that 10,000 families are settled in the first year, rising to about 20,000 families by the fourth year, the total cost of a four-year program would amount to about Bs 400 million (see Table 24).

TABLE 24: Mission's Proposed Land Settlement Program, 1960/61-1963/64

	1960/61	1961/62	1962/63	1963/64	Four-year Period
Number of families to be settled	10,000	15,000	15,000	20,000	60,000
Area of land to be settled (in hectares)	60,000	90,000	150,000	210,000	510,000
Costs (in Bs million)					
Roads and drainage	45.0	50.0	50.0	50.0	195.0
Housing materials[a]	10.0	15.0	15.0	20.0	60.0
Grubbing[b]	—	5.0	5.0	5.0	15.0
Implements and cattle	—	—	20.0	30.0	50.0
Administration	10.0	12.5	12.5	15.0	50.0
Clearing subsidy	5.0	7.5	7.5	10.0	30.0
Total	70.0	90.0	110.0	130.0	400.0

[a] Includes wells.

[b] Grubbing program starts in third year, but purchases of equipment start in previous year.

[c] Implements and cattle are provided from third year of settlement only.

Increasing Productivity Without Relocation

While relocation may be the only solution to the problems of the shifting cultivators who are now attempting to work steep, eroded, or otherwise poor, soils, large numbers of other low-income farmers are currently working in locations where there is a potential for improvement in output without relocation. Many low-income farmers are engaged in shifting cultivation in more fertile areas or have small permanent plots in the valleys, and substantial increases in their production are possible through relatively simple measures such as better seed, fertilizers, or changes in cropping and farming patterns which can bring about increases in planted area. A program of agricultural extension, combined with a subsidized distribution of certain farm inputs (seed, fertilizers, etc.), could do much to raise the productivity and incomes of these farmers.

The reasons for the current low productivity of shifting cultivators are numerous and perhaps interrelated. Much labor is required to cut and burn forest or brush each year in order to take advantage of the natural fertility and freedom from weeds of newly cleared land. Since the lands are not cleared of stumps and roots, they cannot be plowed to control weeds. Planting is done with a digging stick between the stumps. There is little control of weeds. Harvesting is by hand. Without fertilization, natural fertility is used up in one or two years, and the farmer must clear new land every year or two, thus limiting the area he can farm. Generally only one crop is grown each year. This pattern of cultivation results in heavy labor requirements for clearing, planting and harvesting, with relatively little labor required during the rest of the year. Measures designed to spread these peak labor requirements would permit the farmer to operate more land and raise the total output. Measures to provide productive employment during slack periods would also raise output, productivity and incomes.

So long as shifting cultivation is continued, substantial increases in productivity will be difficult to achieve. Improved seed has not been developed for use under shifting cultivation. Fertilizer would have limited effect, but might prolong cropping on each plot by one or two seasons.[5] Hence, increases in productivity under conditions of shifting cultivation would be limited largely to measures for providing productive employment during slack seasons. This will call for some diversification of the shifting cultivator's activities. Introduction of small farm animals, cottage industries, and off-farm employment are possibilities along these lines. In this connection, the timing of road maintenance work and public works projects should be fitted into the farmer's slack periods wherever possible.

To the extent that shifting cultivators can be induced to plant at least part of the land as permanent fields, prospects for increasing productivity would become better, since this would open the way for the introduction of improved techniques, better seed, fertilizer and capital investment. Permanent field-cropping would require clearing of stumps and roots, a task which normally requires large amounts of labor or use of tractors, either of which is relatively expensive. The cheapest way of clearing roots and stumps is to plant the roughly

[5] On non-lateritic soils use of fertilizer would prevent rapid exhaustion of soil fertility, but, without grubbing out the roots and stumps, the land cannot be kept free of weeds through cultivation.

cleared land with bananas or plantains and to chop out the subsequent growth twice during the first year. As the bananas or plantains grow, their shade will retard jungle undergrowth and begin to promote decay of the original growth so that, after four or five years, the damp shade so provided will rot out the stumps and roots and leave a clear field. If all land to be cleared were put into bananas or plantains, marketing problems might arise, particularly for the larger-scale farmers. Thus, to the extent that marketing may become a problem, possibilities for using bananas and plantains for feeding hogs should be explored. Furthermore, it may be necessary to provide mechanical grubbing services at a subsidized rate in order to speed up the establishment of permanent fields. The extension service should concentrate initially on advising shifting cultivators how to clear the land, how to establish permanent fields, and what crops to plant.

For farmers with permanent fields, a program for subsidized distribution of fertilizer and improved seed (see below) will bring about the quickest increases in yields and can be carried out on a wide enough scale to affect a significant number of farmers. In addition, programs for increasing farm size by introducing livestock and encouraging high value perennial crops, such as fruit trees, should be started.

Extension Services for the Small Farmer

In 1959/60, the Ministry of Agriculture (MAC) had 42 general extension agencies and 11 coffee extension agencies in various parts of the country. Each agency was headed by an agronomist and had at least two demonstrators. A total of 332 persons were working in the extension service, of whom about 300 were located outside of Caracas. But the extension services are geared to the requirements of the commercial farmer. The mission recommends establishment of a specialized arm of the service designed to take care of the needs of small farmers, both in their present locations and under the proposed resettlement program.

The field staff of the special arm of the extension service should come from the farming communities and be expected to live in the villages. Its principal activities should be to act as liaison between the small farmer and the extension specialists. The field staff should be trained to operate a movie projector, to demonstrate a few techniques, to keep simple accounts, and to distribute fertilizers and seeds. By keeping the training of this staff relatively simple and by limiting its functions, it should be possible quickly to develop a large enough staff to establish contact with the small farmers over a wide area. As more technically trained personnel becomes available, it should then be possible to bring the field workers under closer supervision and direction and to expand the scope of their services. In the meantime, a large group of farmers can be reached with demonstrations of simple techniques.

MAC has been expanding its training program for *peritos* and *practicos*[6] during the past two years and some additional personnel should be available out of the current year's training courses. The proposed reorganization of agricultural agencies and the concentration of all extension activities under MAC (see below) should make additional staff available for organizing the special extension service for small farmers. To get the special service started, about 10 college-level agronomists and administrators should be obtained for planning and directing the program and about 200 field workers, trained as indicated above, should be recruited. In addition, it should be possible to find at least two *peritos* for each of the 42 agencies to work full-time with low-income farmers. Each agency should be provided with two jeeps, movie projector, sound equipment and generators. The program should then be expanded as rapidly as trained personnel becomes available.

The total staff required to operate the program initially would number about 300. Assuming that over the four-year period this staff can be increased to about 800, we calculate that the cost of operating the special service will rise from about Bs 6 million in 1960/61 to about Bs 15 million in 1963/64. We estimate that the cost of the jeeps and other equipment will amount to Bs 10 million over the four-year period.

Agricultural Credit and Subsidies

The introduction of improved technology, such as use of fertilizers, better seed, livestock, drainage and land improvement, would normally call for increased cash expenditures. In most instances, even if the low-income farmer were convinced of the effectiveness of a new technique he would not have the available cash. The mission has considered possibilities of using supervised credits to finance these cash inputs but concludes that the lack of an effective credit organization for small farmers would place severe limitations on the scope of the program.

[6] *Peritos* have completed a three-year vocational course after completion of the 6th grade. *Practicos* have completed a one-year-course.

The Banco Agricola y Pecuario (BAP) already has a special loan program for small farmers. Instituted in 1959, it is essentially a welfare subsidy program. Most of the loans are not effectively supervised, so that a substantial portion of them can be expected to go into non-productive uses and, consequently high percentage of defaults may be expected. Experience throughout the world has shown that this type of high-risk loan requires careful supervision, combined with technical guidance, in order to be successful. A recent expansion in BAP personnel was undoubtedly carried out with this in mind. The mission feels however that the type of personnel recruited and the current methods of issuing loans do not provide for the degree of supervision and guidance necessary to assure productive use of the funds and to prevent excessive defaults.

We therefore recommend a sharp curtailment of the small-loan program to a size which can be managed on a closely supervised basis. The total amount recommended for such loans would be about Bs 50 million for the four years 1960/61-1963/64, starting with a small amount, say about Bs 5-10 million in the first year, and expanding as rapidly as administrative capacity can be strengthened. Since a supervised credit program would make it possible to increase the average size of loans from the Bs 1,000 pertaining until 1959 to Bs 2,000-3,000, the number of loans made in the first year would amount to between 1,500 and 3,000—a range of operations which, in the mission's view, would be well within BAP's present administrative capacity.

Until the supervised credit program for small farmers can be expanded sufficiently to meet most of their needs, we recommend liberal subsidies for input items. Under this proposal, all farmers cultivating 10 ha. or less would be eligible for fertilizer, seed and chemicals to be distributed free, or on a token payment basis, by the extension service; poultry and livestock at subsidized prices; and free assistance for drainage and land improvement works. The advantage of this approach is that the money would be used for productive purposes and that small farmers who are now not benefited by product price subsidies could increase their production and produce some marketable surpluses.

We estimate that the total cost of such a program of input subsidies for small farmers would amount to about Bs 100 million over the four-year period 1960/61-1963/64 (see Table 25). In contrast, a large-scale loan program for small farmers would cost the Government substantially more without assurance that the money would be used for productive purposes.

TABLE 25: Mission's Proposed Input Subsidy Program for Small
Farmers, 1960/61-1963/64

(in Bs million)

	1960/61	1961/62	1962/63	1963/64	Four-year Period
Fertilizers	3.0	5.0	9.0	13.0	30.0
Seed	1.0	1.5	2.5	5.0	10.0
Other chemicals	0.6	1.0	1.4	2.0	5.0
Poultry and livestock	1.0	2.0	4.0	8.0	15.0
Drainage and land improvement	4.0	6.0	12.0	18.0	40.0
Total	9.6	15.5	28.9	46.0	100.0

INCREASING PRODUCTION ON COMMERCIAL FARMS

Technical Research

The rapid growth of the commercialized sector of agriculture during
the past ten years was at relatively high cost and made possible only
because of government programs subsidizing agricultural inputs and
supporting product prices. A major factor in the high cost structure
of Venezuelan commercial agriculture has been the scarcity of proven
production knowledge and lack of experienced management. Despite
these handicaps, a number of technological improvements have been
adapted to Venezuelan conditions. Tractors and agricultural machinery
have been introduced on a fairly extensive scale and some progress has
been made in developing their more efficient use. Fertilizers are being
used in increasing quantities. A number of the more enterprising farmers are trying out insecticides, fungicides, weed-killers and new varieties
of crops and breeds of animals, and are anxious to get information and
advice on how to increase productivity.

Since most recent technical developments in agriculture have taken
place under temperate conditions, they can be used under Venezuelan
conditions only after thorough testing and some modifications. Tropical
conditions with short days, high temperatures and heavy rainfall, poor
lateritic soils, rapid weed growth and prevalence of pests and diseases
often call for special solutions which can be developed only through
long years of competent research. During the past ten years, the Venezuelan Government has devoted very little attention to agricultural

research. Most other tropical countries have also lagged behind in agricultural research and survived in the face of efficient temperate zone production only because labor has been willing to accept low returns and poor living standards. Such conditions cannot continue long and there is an increasing recognition of the need for tropical agricultural research.

In Venezuela, research activities have been centered at the *Centro de Investigaciones Agronomicas* at Maracay, with a few outstations to test results under varying agricultural conditions. The research organization has been understaffed and has been able to do relatively little effective research. Much of the experimentation has been carried out on good soils at Maracay and is not directly applicable to conditions in the more likely development areas. For example, a promising hybrid corn has been developed at Maracay, but farmers in other areas have had poor results with its seed and continue to use their traditional varieties. Systematic experiments on the use of fertilizers for different crops under various soil and climatic conditions have not been carried out. Very little work has been done on animal nutrition and the development of suitable pasture and fodder crops for the main cattle areas.

In addition to the shortage of personnel, the temporary nature of the appointments and the lack of a regular promotion and pension system have led to rapid turnover of personnel, which is particularly serious in research work where continuity of experiments over a period of years is essential for good results. There is also a tendency for available technical personnel to prefer appointments in or near Caracas where opportunities for soliciting pay increases and moving to other jobs are better than in the field offices. This has made it almost impossible to carry out long-range research projects. It has also prevented the development of experienced research scientists.

The mission feels that the effective large-scale use of investment funds in agriculture and acceleration of development will be possible only on the basis of a much larger body of proven knowledge which can only be developed through a greatly expanded research program. The mission therefore recommends the following measures:

a. Make available all funds required to utilize existing supply of qualified research personnel and to increase funds as more personnel becomes available.

b. Arrange for an expanded technical cooperation arrangement with a foundation or a university to supply senior research personnel needed to develop a research organization and establish liaison with tropical agricultural research centers in other countries.

c. Establish additional research stations in major production areas for crop and livestock improvement and develop suitable farming methods for these areas, particularly in the new development areas of Zulia and Barinas-Portuguesa.

d. Expand agricultural training programs at all levels to provide the necessary qualified personnel for research, extension and education (see Chapter 14).

The operating costs of an expanded agricultural research program will rise as more personnel becomes available. We calculate that annual current expenses for this program, which are estimated at Bs 9.8 million in 1959/60, should almost double by 1963/64, during which year they should total Bs 18 million. Over the four-year period 1960/61-1963/64 total current research expenditures should amount to about Bs 64 million, not including university agricultural training (for details on the latter, see Chapter 10). The major capital expenditures in the research field would be devoted to the construction of new stations in Zulia and in the Barinas-Portuguesa area and the strengthening of the existing station at Maracay; we estimate these expenditures at Bs 15 million during the four-year period.

Agricultural Extension

At present, agricultural extension work is being carried out by a number of different agencies, both public and private. On the Government side, MAC and IAN are the principal agencies, but BAP and CVF also carry out some extension activities with reference to special crops. On the private side, *Servicio Shell para el Agricultor*[7] has done substantial work in general extension as well as in popularizing the use of fertilizers, fungicides, insecticides and herbicides. CBR has worked with MAC particularly on the training aspects of extension. Tobacco, sugar, dairy and feed companies have also done some excellent work in their fields. All of these agencies have been concerned with the commercial farmer.

Weaknesses in the Government's extension program have arisen from the shortage of personnel and funds, the lack of sufficient research data and the tendency on the part of extension workers to spend too much time at the desk and not enough time in the field. Excessive demands are made on the MAC extension service for statistical reporting and control functions, which leave little time for constructive extension

[7] Financed by the Shell Oil Company.

work, particularly in view of the large area each agent is expected to cover and the lack of adequate transportation facilities. On the other hand, IAN colonies seem to be well supplied with extension agents, but many of them do not seem to be specifically trained for their particular task and, in any case, they are burdened with many non-extension functions. At Guanare, for example, there are three agents, one for general extension, one for home improvement and one for youth club work, in a community of only 39 farm families. BAP and CVF extension workers are generally concerned with specific crops, but also tend to be saddled with non-extension functions. With several agencies active in extension work, functional duplication has been inevitable; at the same time, large areas are not covered by any service. The Government is now in the process of consolidating the extension services under MAC, and has enlisted the help of CBR in organizing and training expanded services. This should go a long way toward providing a suitable extension service for the commercial farmer. The main problem remaining would then be the shortage of basic research results.

The privately operated *Servicio Shell para el Agricultor* has done excellent work for many years in extension and research, especially on control of diseases and pests and drainage. Although its small staff has had to confine itself to areas relatively close to its research center at Cagua, its experience should be invaluable in reorganizing the government extension services. Similarly the experiences of the private companies, particularly the tobacco companies, in developing raw material supplies should be useful.

A major shortcoming of all of these extension services has been the inadequate attention given to farm management and farm development planning. Here again, however, basic research data on farm management and costs and benefits of development measures have been almost nonexistent. One of the problems in this connection has been the past emphasis on the commodity approach rather than treating the total farm as a unit.

The mission is impressed by the possibilities for effective agricultural extension work among the commercial farmers. Despite the inadequacies of the present system and the scarcity of proven production knowledge, the extension services have been effective in popularizing a number of new crops and techniques. With more research and the reorganization and expansion of the staff, the agricultural extension services can be a key factor in raising production and incomes in the commercialized sector of agriculture.

During 1959/60, MAC has doubled the staff and scope of its extension services. The mission believes that the size of the service is now adequate to meet the requirements of the commercial farming community, given the appropriate measures of reorganization suggested above. Hence, we suggest that the operating costs of the extension services will only modestly increase over the 1959/60 level of Bs 11.4 million. By 1963/64, they may have risen to Bs 13.0 million, and total current expenditures during the four-year period should amount to about Bs 50 million. Some capital expenditures will be required on additional vehicles and demonstration equipment and should total about Bs 10 million during the four years 1960/61-1963/64. Thus, a total of Bs 60 million would be spent on extension services for commercial farmers, in addition to about Bs 50 million which would be spent on the special service for low-income farmers.

Fertilizers

The use of fertilizers in Venezuela is still extremely low, but increased rapidly from 5,000 tons in 1950 to 50,000 tons in 1958. Most of the fertilizer is being used on the cropping land of commercial farms, and would amount to about 17 kg. per ha. if it is assumed that none is used on pastures. The principal exception to this low figure has been for tobacco, grown by farmers on good soils under instructions of the tobacco companies with high amounts of fertilizers averaging 500 kg. per ha., which have resulted in high yields of about 1,500 kg. per ha. Substantial amounts are also being used for sugar cane and potatoes.

A major obstacle to the intensive use of fertilizer has been the lack of knowledge about the requirements of various soils. Systematic field experiments showing optimum applications of nitrogen, phosphorous and potassium under varying conditions in different regions have not been carried out. Only low-concentrate mixtures can be safely used in the absence of such data. Moreover, some soils are lateritic or under-developed and will not give a reasonable response to fertilizers unless first turned into well-drained soils of good structure. In such soils fertilizers are leached out by the rains and disappear rapidly, their effect being greatly reduced. These soils can be improved by adding organic matter or humus to the soil to improve their structure and their water-holding capacity. Unfortunately, cheap reliable methods for doing this on any scale are not yet known for the wet tropics. Hence, one set of studies is necessary for determining the yield responses of various crops on different soils to various fertilizers under varying climatic conditions, their relation to cultural measures and the economics of their use. Another set of studies is required to determine the interaction of soil improvement and fertilizers, especially on the poor soils, and the effect of rotations with pasture, wet rice, green manures, and other crops.

In the good soils, quick responses can be expected. A combination of phosphate and drainage in Turen could bring the yields of maize far above their present low of 1,200 kg. per ha. In the same way, a combination of nitrogenous fertilizers and drainage on alluvial clay soils could increase cotton yields sharply. Coffee and cacao will also react favorably to fertilizers. Even on poorer soils, fertilizers cannot do any serious damage so long as the mixtures are of low concentration, and in most cases higher yields can be expected. The mission feels that the quickest way to increase agricultural production and to raise farm incomes would be to distribute fertilizer on a widespread basis.

The fertilizer plant which is now under construction at Moron will have a capacity of 150,000 tons. The existing demand is only 50,000 tons. Free or subsidized distribution of fertilizers would permit full operation of the plant, and the costs of such a distribution will in part be offset by the cost of idle plant capacity which would otherwise have resulted. Furthermore, the value of the increased production which will result should exceed the cost of the distributed fertilizer.

The mission has already recommended that fertilizer should be distributed free, or with token payments, to the small farmers with less than 10 ha. We now recommend that the rest of the fertilizer produced by the plant should be distributed to larger-scale farmers on a subsidized basis. While it is not possible at this time to work out detailed costs for such a program, our rough estimate assumes that the fertilizer will cost about Bs 300 per ton delivered to the farm and that commercial farmers will be subsidized to the extent of Bs 100 per ton. Deducting the amount of fertilizer required for free distribution, we calculate that about 350,000 tons will be available during the four years, 1960/61-1963/64, about 60,000 tons being available the first year and more than 100,000 tons by the last year of the period. Total cost of the fertilizer subsidy program would thus amount to Bs 35 million during the four-year period.

Control of Weeds, Pests and Diseases

A major factor in increasing production on commercial farms is the control of weeds, pests and diseases. While new chemicals and drugs have enabled farmers throughout the world to reduce related losses and increase yields at relatively little cost, most of these developments are in their infancy in Venezuela.

Weeds are a serious problem in Venezuela, keeping farm-size small and yields low, and weed control, either by effective cultural methods or by a judicious use of weed-killers, should be a major subject of agricultural research and experimentation, the results of which should be widely disseminated by the extension services. *The Servicio Shell para el Agricultor* has carried out substantial research and extension activities, both in the control of weeds and other field-crop pests and diseases, but again the commercial farmers reached have mainly been limited to those in areas accessible to the experiment station. Elsewhere, the use of pesticides, fungicides and weed-killers has been relatively insignificant.

While MAC has done an excellent job of disease control among dairy cattle, very little research and extension work has been done on disease control for poultry and hogs. We would regard the institution of a research program in connection with the latter to be urgent. Much useful work has been done on vaccines and drugs in animal husbandry, particularly for dairy cattle, but availabilities of these vaccines and drugs are very limited. The mission regrets the ban on the import of commercial production of live-virus vaccines, since this has retarded the expansion of poultry-raising and egg output and could also prevent the future development of large-scale hog production.

The mission strongly urges an acceleration of research and experimentation on the various control measures, to be followed by increased extension activity in the field. In order to encourage the use of the appropriate practices, the Government should be prepared to subsidize the distribution of the relevant materials and equipment. Experience in other countries has demonstrated that the costs of control have been negligible in relation to the consequent increases in production.

Mechanization

The trend throughout the world has been to move from human labor to animal power to mechanized equipment. A larger area can be worked with animal power than with human labor alone and, moreover, the work can be done more rapidly. Even larger areas can be handled with mechanization at still more rapid rate. To the extent that animal power or mechanized equipment is used, capital costs per hectare increase while labor costs go down. Mechanized equipment involves an increase in cash costs and requires additional cash incomes, whereas self-supplied labor is traditionally a flexible input which can be sustained at very low subsistence levels if necessary. In Venezuela, most farmers still rely exclusively on human labor. Use of animal power is limited to a few areas in the Andes. On the other hand, a fairly rapid increase in the use of tractors and other mechanized equipment has occurred on the larger commercial type farms as a result of prevailing high wages and the availability of cheap imported machinery.

Costs of mechanized operations have been high due to inexperience, lack of repair and maintenance facilities, purchase of excessive amounts of machinery, the failure to develop a system for fuller utilization of machinery, and lags in other technical developments which normally should accompany mechanization. There is also a lack of knowledge about suitable farm-size and its relationship to the size and number of machines required. The lack of adequate drainage facilities, as at Turen, often limits the time during which machines can be used in the fields, and has particularly prevented the development of mechanical harvesting of corn, with the result that seasonal labor shortages at harvest time have led to higher harvest wages and therefore to higher costs of production.

In spite of these difficulties the mechanization of Venezuelan agriculture has been profitable and will no doubt continue at a rapid rate. This will of itself lead to better repair and maintenance facilities, more efficient use and therefore to lower costs. The mission feels however that the Government could adopt a positive policy of systematic research into the technical problems of mechanization under Venezuelan conditions, including the necessary studies as to optimum sizes of farms under mechanization, together with related extension work to encourage adoption of such measures as the results of research indicate.

Production Credit

Agricultural development, particularly on commercial farms, is dependent on adequate mechanisms for the provision of credit. We have already commented on BAP's loan program for small farmers and recommended its consolidation into a small program of closely supervised credits. On the other hand, BAP has a major role to play in the development of larger-scale farming.

After its establishment in 1943, BAP expanded its activities rapidly reaching a peak in 1948 when it issued 81,903 loans amounting to Bs 116 million. Between 1948 and 1957, there was a sharp decline in the number of loans and a gradual decline in the total amount of money loaned. The average size loan was increasing steadily. During this period, BAP centralized its activities in Caracas and sharply curtailed the functions of its branch and reduced the number of field offices. BAP's credit activities were limited largely to financing the larger commercial farmers who could come to Caracas to negotiate their loans.

In 1958, the new government decided to expand and decentralize BAP's credit activities. Regional credit committees were established to approve loans and supervise the activities of the "branches" and a number of new "agencies" were established. Branches were authorized to issue loans up to Bs 20,000 and agencies up to Bs 10,000. BAP's capital was increased by Bs 85 million and special funds for cattle, coffee, cacao and housing loans were created.

In addition to its credit activities, BAP has had responsibilities for price stabilization, control of agricultural imports, and storage and processing of domestic agricultural products. These activities are not directly related to farm credit operations and yet require a substantial amount of time and energy on the part of the senior bank personnel and also make demands on facilities, and staff and financial resources which would otherwise be available for loans.[8] Managing a credit program is a full-time specialized function. If BAP is to develop a sound credit program it should be freed of these other non-credit responsibilities.

Three other government agencies, IAN, CVF and MAC, have also been concerned with agricultural credit. IAN has been handling the major part of the credit needs of the colonies and settlers under its programs and issued credits amounting to Bs 46 million during the period 1950-58. CVF provides credits in connection with its industrial development programs, and loans under its Rice Plan totaled Bs 135 million between 1947 and 1957, while Bs 44.5 million of loans were issued under its Sugar Plan during the period 1947-55. MAC has provided technical review of loan applications under special credit programs for cattle, coffee and cacao. A number of the lending programs are in process of being brought under BAP and the relationships between BAP and MAC are now undergoing some change.

At present, many loans are related to special credit programs for specific commodities. This means that one farmer may apply for a number of loans for different commodities. Each loan will be processed separately, often by different officials, involving unnecessary administrative

[8] BAP's balance sheet for December 1959 showed inventory holdings of Bs 73 million and agricultural installations of Bs 39 million, as compared with total loans outstanding of Bs 416 million.

burdens and high costs. If each farm were treated as the unit of analysis and the total credit requirements for each farm were worked out at one time, the number of applications processed could be reduced and a more detailed examination of creditworthiness could be made. At the same time, it would be possible to arrange for issuance of loans in installments as required for various farm operations. Repayments could also be geared to periods when the farmer expects to receive income.

Furthermore, the commodity-by-commodity approach has led to an undue emphasis on short-term, seasonal credits for crops. These types of credits should properly be made through commercial channels at commercial rates, so that public credit resources could be devoted to medium- and long-term needs which are unlikely to be met by private commercial institutions. In any case, current BAP interest rates represent in effect a credit subsidy, since BAP's rates are fixed by law at 5 percent, while commercial banks must pay 7 percent on paper discounted with the Central Bank. So long as BAP rates are so low, there is little likelihood of private banks coming into the agricultural financing picture on any substantial scale. It also makes it difficult to avoid leakage of BAP credit into non-farm uses. Given present prices of farm products, the marginal returns on crop credit advanced to commercial farms can be significantly greater than prevailing commercial interest rates. There thus seems to be little justification for the indefinite continuation of subsidized crop credits for the commercial farmer who already benefits from the high prices fostered by the government policy of protection. We therefore recommend the gradual alignment of BAP short-term interest rates with those pertaining commercially.

We further recommend that BAP gradually reduce its own short-term loan activities. We recognize that the amount of short-term crop loans outstanding will continue to increase for some time. To the extent that the large commercial farmers require crop loans, they should be increasingly supplied by the commercial banks at commercial rates of interest, and this would permit BAP to shift to medium-term development financing in both the crop and livestock sectors.

It is difficult for BAP to provide for financing of a medium-term nature such as for purchase of machinery, and execution of minor land improvement works, because, under current banking laws, BAP cannot issue loans other than real estate mortgage loans for a period in excess of a year. As a result, a series of short-term loans has often been used to finance medium-term investments, thus introducing an element of uncertainty and sometimes cutting into requirements for short-term crop financing. The mission feels that adequate provision should be made for medium-term financing at concessional rates in order to facilitate farm development planning on a longer-term basis. The mission would suggest that about Bs 150 million should be allocated for both short- and medium-term loans to commercial farmers during 1960/61-1963/64, and we hope that during this period the emphasis will shift from short-term to medium-term credit.

There is also no provision for long-term, low-interest mortgage credit for land purchase. This hampers the establishment of new commercial farm enterprises and would also limit the purchase of additional land, envisaged as a possibility under our proposed settlement program. The mission therefore recommends that funds derived from liquidation of BAP-held agricultural stocks and BAP facilities for processing and storage be made available for low-interest, long-term mortgage loans for land acquisition. We calculate that about Bs 100 million could be released in this way for this purpose during the four years 1960/61-1963/64.

Credit problems in the livestock sector are distinct from those in crop agriculture and the Venezuelan Government is dealing with them separately. Under a special livestock development program, the *Plan Ganadero,* by far the largest amount of credit under any single loan program is scheduled for allocation during the four years 1960/61-1963/64, with Bs 320 million earmarked for net increases for this purpose. The mission heartily approves of this special effort in the livestock sector, but we doubt whether the present policy emphasis, if continued, would rapidly achieve the declared objectives of the Plan to increase productivity and output.

The majority of credits to date have been devoted to financing the imports of foreign breeds and the construction of fencing, but the mission believes that the provision of fodder and water in the dry season have a higher priority because they would have an immediate effect on the stock already on the hoof in Venezuela. Extra fodder and water would result in lower mortality, the elimination of weight losses, increased reproduction and reduction in the slaughtering age from the present four-five years to three years. This could lead to a doubling of output within a few years.

Since the water and fodder supply problem will vary with each farm, so will technical solutions and therefore the amount of credit needed. In general, fairly detailed surveys will be required to find suitable water sources and areas suitable for fodder crops or irrigated pastures. Credits will also be needed for dams, wells or reservoirs which will provide water for cattle and some of which would also be connected with drainage or irrigation projects for cropping lands and improved pastures. Livestock farmers will also require loans for the storage and silage of fodder crops which could be financed under the Plan.

Thus, while the costs of developing fodder and water sources will vary considerably with different farms, the benefits are such that returns on capital invested should be sufficient to pay off the investment within two or three years, provided there is reasonably competent management and provided technical help is available in drawing up development plans. A program of this type can be carried out under the *Plan Ganadero* by giving priority to applications based on sound farm plans designed to meet the fodder and water problem. While it is still too early to judge on the basis of actual experience with the program whether a net increase of Bs 320 million is an appropriate amount, the mission is convinced that Venezuela has very good prospects in the livestock field and that the Government is fully justified in making substantial resources available for the development of this sector, particularly if the program can be reorientated along the lines indicated above.

To summarize the financial implications of the mission's recommendations in the agricultural and livestock credit field, we calculate that about Bs 504 million should be allocated for these purposes in the capital budgets for the years 1960/61-1963/64, excluding the Bs 50 million we have already suggested for small supervised loans. Of the former total, Bs 320 million would be required for the *Plan Ganadero*, as already noted. The Government is also planning a net addition of a further Bs 34 million for special coffee and cocoa loans. This leaves a final Bs 150 million, much of which we expect will go for crop loans for commercial farmers, but some of which we recommend should be switched in increasing amounts to the provision of medium-term credits for equipment and other farm improvements. About Bs 450 million of loans are currently outstanding and, taking into account some losses on these loans, total outstanding loans at the end of 1963/64 should amount to about Bs 950 million, of which about one-third would be longer-term development loans. In addition, about Bs 100 million should be made available for land acquisition mortgage loans, financed primarily from the liquidation of BAP assets connected with non-credit activity.

Government Activities in the Product Market

As part of its general policy to develop and diversify the economy, the Government has placed high protective tariffs on agricultural products, combined with special exonerations for items considered necessary for development, and quantitative controls on imports. The Government has also instituted a number of domestic price support and price and quantity control programs. Government activities with respect to major products are briefly summarized as follows:

Corn	BAP purchases at price set by MAC and BAP and conducts sales. BAP operates dryers and silos. BAP makes crop loans. Imports prohibited, except for BAP imports to meet shortages.
Rice	BAP purchases paddy at Bs 0.60 per kg. BAP operates dryers and mills. BAP makes crop loans. BAP imports to meet shortages.
Cotton	BAP purchases at Bs 1.30 per kg. for seed cotton. Ministry of Development fixes price for lint cotton (currently Bs 3.70 per kg.). BAP operates one gin. Imports subject to Ministry of Fomento license.
Potatoes	BAP imports and distributes seed (7,400 tons in first ten months 1959) BAP imports to meet shortages. BAP operates cold storage facilities.
Sisal	BAP purchases. Prohibitive tariff.
Onions	BAP purchases. BAP operates cold storage. Imports licensed.
Coffee	BAP purchases. BAP-MAC development loans. Differential exchange rate. Imports prohibited.

Cacao	BAP can purchase.
	BAP-MAC development loans.
	Differential exchange rate.
	Imports subject to prohibitive tariff.
Sugar	Price fixed by MAC and MF.
	Government sugar factories.
	Prohibitive tariff, government imports.
Sardines	Prohibitive tariff.
	Restrictions on fishing methods.
Sesame	Prohibitive tariff.
	Imports free of duty licensed.
Milk	Subsidy.
	Duty exoneration on imports and compulsory purchase of domestic powdered milk.

All these various measures can contribute to developing the agricultural sector if they are properly administered, but their success depends to a great extent on realistic government decisions in relation to production and market trends and on the Government's ability to enforce its decisions. The mission is convinced that, as long as the present exchange rate is maintained, the agricultural sector must continue to be accorded protection at a very high level.

However, the present system of specific duties on agricultural products seems to bear little relationship to the price of the item or the need for protection. It can probably be argued that a tariff of, say, 75 or 100 percent, on agricultural products for which Venezuela has no natural disadvantage might be justified as a diversification premium and as an offset to the temporarily high cost in the period of early development.[9] An industry developed through such a tariff could be expected to survive competitively, once the initial inefficiencies are overcome and economic policies bring Venezuelan prices more in line with external prices. On the other hand, an industry which requires a tariff of, say, 400 or 500 percent will probably never be able to stand on its own feet and should not be encouraged. Yet, when the existing

[9] No such simple rule can be applied to processed products since "effective" protection should be based on value added, not on total cost and must take into account the protection granted to supplying industries.

tariffs are translated into ad valorem rates, there are many specific rates which are much higher than 100 percent (see Table 26) and others which appear to be very low.

The imposition of duties which are either excessively high or unsuitably low has necessitated a complex system of exoneration, import quotas and prohibitions. For example, the tariff on fresh meat is relatively low, but commercial meat imports have been prohibited, although BAP has sometimes temporarily imported meat to relieve specific shortages. On the other hand, duties on sesame and tobacco have been prohibitive, but special exonerations are often arranged so that local industry may be supplied with raw materials. In view of the poor data generally available on production and consumption, it is extremely difficult for the Government to make advance estimates of the level of imports to be permitted. Consequently, industries concerned with special exemptions must allow for the surpluses or deficits which would result if the Government guesses wrongly. Furthermore, a system of licensing makes discriminatory treatment among producers possible. Even if the total deficit for an industry is correctly assessed

TABLE 26: Venezuelan Customs Duties on Selected Commodities, 1958

(in Bs per kg.)

Commodity	International Price[a]	Venezuelan Duty	Domestic Wholesale Price[b]
Coconut oil	1.23 (European ports)	4.00	2.00
Milk powder	0.75 (Netherlands)	0.50	2.23
Sugar	0.21 (f.o.b. Cuba)	16.00	0.90
Corn	0.19 (c.i.f. European ports)	1.20	0.36
Rice	0.40 (f.o.b. Bangkok)	0.23	0.98
Sardines (Canned)	1.40 (c.i.f. New York)	8.00	2.00
Cotton lint	0.95 (c.i.f. Liverpool)	2.00	3.70
Beef	1.80 (c.i.f. London)	0.001	3.13
Tobacco leaf	5.00 (f.o.b. Cuba)	24.00	6.00[c]
Copra	0.86 (European ports)	0.80	n.a.
Sesame	0.75 (c.i.f. La Guaira)	1.20	1.15

[a] Calculated from *FAO Monthly Bulletin of Agricultural Economics and Statistics*, January 1960, and *FAO Yearbook of Production, 1957*.

[b] *Boletin de Precios de Productos Agropecuario 1958* and price data collected in field.

[c] Estimated.

by the Government, an individual plant might still receive inadequate allocation of raw materials and be forced to operate below capacity. All these factors add to costs, since costs are usually closely related to volume of production.

The mission believes that the present system of protective tariffs, exonerations and prohibitions should be thoroughly revised and simplified to provide a more uniform level of protection based on current prices and expectations. Wherever possible, special exemptions should be eliminated. Given present conditions, the level of protection should be set so that internal prices will be no more than double external prices. Such a policy would mean that economic criteria would become more important in determining the allocation of investment funds and political influence in getting favorable tariff treatment or import allocations would become less important. Investments would only occur in those industries capable of producing at less than double the external price, such industries being able to survive in the long run by increasing productivity and the eventual adjustment of Venezuelan prices to external prices.

In addition to foreign trade controls, the Government is also engaged in price support operations for various agricultural commodities produced domestically. From January to October 1959, BAP purchased Bs 25.7 million worth of maize, rice, cotton, coffee, onions and sisal. With the exception of rice, the amounts purchased represented small percentages of production. The development of the price support programs is apparently associated with particular emergencies since the outbreak of World War II. Coffee supports were started as a result of the loss of European markets with the outbreak of war, and rice supports as a result of the wartime and postwar shortages. There seems to be no clear policy as to the criteria to be used for support levels and methods of operations. There is no special financing for price support operations and hence BAP uses some of its general funds for this purpose although they were supposedly originally intended for credit purposes. While there seems to be general agreement that support prices should cover cost of production, it is not clear how cost of production is determined or what methods of production are assumed.

If domestic output of a commodity falls short of domestic demand and imports of that commodity are subject to tariffs or import controls, it is possible to maintain a given level of prices for that commodity by adjusting the level of the tariff and/or the volume of imports. This is the simplest method of price support and requires no investment in facilities and staff for domestic purchase and sale. In fact, the existing tariff walls and restrictions have been the principal price support for all agricultural commodities. BAP nevertheless purchases a number of commodities, the reasons for which vary with the crop and circumstances. In the case of rice, for example, BAP controls most of the drying and milling facilities and hence farmers sell to BAP. If these facilities were in private hands, the farmers would probably get just as much for their rice so long as imports were restricted. BAP's control of dryers and silos probably also plays an important role in its purchase of corn. Another factor is the accessibility to the market. Where BAP has purchasing points in isolated areas, farmers have little alternative but to sell to BAP, since private buyers would not be able to absorb the costs of transporting the grain to the central markets. While it seems clear that BAP operations have thus helped farmers in isolated areas and have tended to reduce seasonal price movements, it seems unlikely that its purchases have in general materially affected the price received by farmers.

In the mission's view, BAP is at present carrying out some price support programs designed to meet particular shortage situations which no longer exist. We feel that no serious problems would result if these operations were discontinued and existing facilities either sold or leased to private operators. In our view, the Government should concentrate on measures to improve the basic structure of markets, on the introduction of basic standards and on the development of necessary production and processing practices which are the bases for efficient marketing.

A special problem is raised by the very large subsidy now being paid to encourage domestic milk output. As explained in Annex IV, the mission sees some justification for this subsidy, but at a lower level than the Bs 30 million currently spent annually. The mission recommends a gradual reduction of subsidies on fluid milk production and elimination of subsidies on raw milk for processing into powdered milk so that increased quantities of low-cost imported powdered milk can be made available to consumers. This recommendation is based on the assumption that agricultural policy should not be designed to achieve self-sufficiency at any cost. Present subsidy arrangements and related controls for milk are leading to an expansion of powdered milk capacity and to the uneconomic expansion of dairying.

For the two export crops, coffee and cacao, there is a provision for BAP purchases and a system of differential exchange rates. At present government purchases have been negligible and the exchange differential has been insignificant at current world prices. Considering the history of price instability for both of these crops, the predominance of small producers and the artificially high domestic prices of other agricultural commodities, the present system for stabilizing coffee and cacao prices seems to be well justified as a standby provision.

Prospects for a sharp expansion in rice output with development of irrigation areas raise the question of whether present price support operations should be continued in the face of possible export surpluses. As indicated in Annex II, the present support price is substantially above recent average import costs and has made rice production extremely profitable. To the extent that rice production does increase, a gradual reduction in support prices should be considered with a view toward increasing domestic consumption of rice and causing some substitution of rice for imported wheat. Surpluses which may develop in the meantime should be exported on a subsidized basis in view of long-run prospects for exporting rice on a competitive basis.

Marketing, Processing, Storage and Distribution

The development of main roads and air transportation during the past ten years has brought farm producers into closer contact with central markets. Nevertheless, prices vary widely between different markets and the gap between prices received by producers and prices paid by consumers is excessive.[10] On the other hand, the marketing of processed agricultural commodities in Venezuela is relatively efficient and the more standardized a product the more closely its marketing conforms to marketing in other developed countries. Hence marketing methods tend to be deficient for such unstandardized and perishable items as livestock, meat, eggs, fruits, vegetables and some dairy products, while fairly regular marketing channels exist for marketing such industrial crops as tobacco, sugar cane, oil seeds and cotton, and some grading has been introduced. Rough standards for marketing corn, rice and beans have also been introduced by BAP.

The majority of agricultural commodities are however unstandardized, ungraded and traded in small lots on the basis of physical inspection. Farmers either bring their produce to small municipal markets or sell to truckers who deliver to the public markets. The latter sell small quantities to small retailers and directly to the consumer. The large number of people engaged in this type of marketing activity have low productivity. Similarly, most retail shops are family-operated enterprises, depending on low volume, slow turnover and high markups with

[10] George L. Mehren, *Agricultural Marketing in Venezuela*, Consejo de Bienestar Rural, Caracas, November 1953.

relatively poor returns to the family labor required. Although some larger self-service type supermarkets have been established and have been fairly successful, the public markets remain the main outlets.

Marketing channels are well developed and relatively efficient for certain commodities such as fluid milk, mixed feeds and tobacco. Where a certain degree of uniformity has been achieved, either through processing or establishment of grades, it has become possible to consolidate products into larger lots and sales are made on the basis of specifications. Where industrial processing facilities have been established, the industries themselves have fostered programs for bringing raw material supplies into closer conformity with specifications. In the case of tobacco, the cigarette companies have provided seed, credits and technical advice, and purchase in accordance with established grades. In the case of milk, the dairy plants have established minimum standards and have assisted farmers in installation of required facilities.

There has been very little development of marketing in the meat industry except for airlifting of slaughtered carcasses to Caracas. There is no organized wholesale market and no grading. An important obstacle to rational meat marketing has been the vested interest of municipalities in revenue from local slaughter. Municipal slaughter houses perpetuate their exclusive local rights through various local restrictions on slaughter and marketing of meat, and have been a factor in preventing the development of a large-scale meat-packing industry. The result is that there are inadequate sanitary standards, waste of by-products, and a lack of systematized grading of meats. The introduction of air transportation for carcasses from the producing centers in the *llanos* to Caracas has resulted in a substantial increase in the total beef output and has reduced seasonal variations in supply prices. The next step toward more efficient marketing should be establishment of large-scale meat-processing plants, turning out standardized products which could be held in cold storage and marketed throughout the country on a volume basis throughout the year. This will require elimination of present municipal restrictions on the private slaughtering and marketing of meat, and we urge the national government to enter into consultations with the various municipal authorities to work out a program of replacing unsanitary and inefficient municipal slaughter houses with privately operated meat-packing facilities.

Storage of agricultural products has been hampered by the same factors which have retarded the development of wholesale markets. So long as large lots cannot be sold on the basis of objective specification large-scale storage operations are not feasible. Facilities are not readily available for small-scale commercial storage. The result is that seasonal gluts and shortages occur, particularly for perishable commodities, and are reflected in sharp seasonal price variations. The only storage program on which the Government has spent significant amounts of money is the corn storage program, under which BAP purchases corn on the basis of a rough grading system and handles a large enough volume to require substantial storage. Present storage is probably inadequate in terms of existing modern type capacity and peak season requirements. The planned expansion of livestock production will call for additional sources of dry-season feed. In this connection, possibilities for on-the-farm storage of corn should be explored by BAP wherever credits are being considered for combined livestock and corn production enterprises.

The mission is convinced that the solutions to the marketing problem do not lie in further expansion of direct government trading or further restrictions on the activities of private traders. The basic problem is one of small-quantity, unstandardized production. To correct this, basic research on varieties and breeds is required, and methods of production should be re-examined with the aim of producing a more standardized product at the farm level. At the same time, the Government should develop standards and grades based on quality and pack, and should also encourage the growth of regular markets reflecting quality differences and changes in national supply and demand.

Access Roads

The rapid development of major trunk roads in the past ten years has not been accompanied by construction of a sufficient number of access roads and this has limited development to those farm lands relatively close to these main roads. We have already mentioned the need for access roads in connection with the major settlement areas. Strategically placed additional access roads could not only encourage additional spontaneous settlements but could also reduce marketing costs in already settled areas. While MAC has in recent years constructed a number of access roads, there has apparently been no systematic program for establishing criteria or priorities and the mission was unable to determine how the needs of different areas are being met. The importance of this program in determining the direction and extent of development makes it essential that a more systematic method be devised for planning road development in coordination with the requirements of land settlement and marketing.

It will undoubtedly be some time before a systematic program for the construction of access roads, based on objective criteria as suggested above, can be devised. As an interim measure, the mission believes that some priority should be given to building access roads where the neighboring landowners who would benefit from such roads are prepared to bear part of the cost. The willingness of landowners to contribute would indicate that they expect economic returns from the road and would be to this extent some indication of an objective need.

Given that systematic planning is undertaken without delay, the mission would concur with proposals now under consideration within the Venezuelan Government to spend an additional Bs 118.2 million on access roads during the four years 1960/61-1963/64.

IRRIGATION AND DRAINAGE

Apart from some small older local works from wells, springs and small reservoirs, mainly in the mountain valleys, and some irrigated coffee gardens, irrigation works in Venezuela date from about 1940. The average initial area of works after 1940 was between 1,000 and 5,000 ha. and they are mainly situated in the central ranges and along the southern side of the western range and of the Andes. By 1950, some 107,000 ha. were irrigated from rivers, 23,000 ha. from reservoirs and about 108,000 ha. from wells and springs, so that a total of 238,000 ha. was under all types of irrigation. Of this total area, less than 30,000 ha. were in farms under 10 ha., so that relatively few small farms were under irrigation and small farmers have had little opportunity to gain experience in irrigated farming.

Some of the irrigation works supplied water to existing permanent cropping lands, as at Valle de Tuy, Cumana, Guataparo, Sarare and Suata-Taiguaiguay. While there have been no studies showing the extent to which irrigation has contributed to higher yields, there is little doubt that increased production and yields have in fact been achieved in many of these areas. On the other hand, the lack of suitable drainage at some of these irrigation works has contributed to declining yields, arising mainly from increased soil salinity, as in the Valencia Lake region.

The remainder of the large irrigation works was intended for opening up new land, as at Guanare, San Carlos, El Cenizo, Guarico and Turen. Not much is known about the resulting yields, and in any case at Guanare, El Cenizo and Turen the systems were not completed. At Turen, for example, the wells were not used, because the farmers judged that the costs of an irrigation system would be too high for the moderate yields obtained.

In 1949, a preliminary study was prepared for a 20-year plan for irrigation to increase agricultural production for the steadily growing population. To keep the costs per ha. low, irrigation areas for individual projects were to be at least 20,000 ha. Gross annual production on new land of one-half capital costs was assumed, simply on the basis of results obtained with sugar cane in Suata from 1947 to 1949. Since no estimates were made for a normal rotation of field crops, the mission has doubts as to the validity of these assumptions.

Under the 20-year plan, works would be carried out on a number of major schemes located on the southern slopes of the Andes and of the western and central range (see map facing page 182). Of six major schemes, none were completed by 1959/60 and construction had only been started on two of them. The status of these major schemes is as follows:

    a. *The Guarico project* is located near Calabozo, on the Guarico River. This project was intended to irrigate 110,000 ha., but is not yet completed. By 1959/60 some Bs 300 million had already been spent on it.

    b. *The Majaguas project,* between the Sarare River and Majaguas Creek, is now under construction, using water from the Rivers Agua Blanca and Cojedes, to irrigate an initial area of 18,500 ha. at a cost of Bs 40 million. It is intended to extend this project as a double-purpose irrigation scheme.

    c. *The Camatagua project,* upstream of Calabozo on the Guarico River, would be a double-purpose scheme for irrigation of 30,000 ha. and the Tiznados scheme for 30,000 ha., on a Guarico tributary. Both schemes are still under study.

    d. *The Bocono-Masparro-Tucupido project,* on rivers of the same names, to serve the region between Guanare and Masparro Rivers. This double-purpose scheme for 220,000 ha. irrigated land is still under study.

    e. *The Camaruco and Tirgua project,* on rivers of the same names, is a double-purpose scheme for irrigation of 60,000 ha., and is still under study.

    f. *The Tinaco and Pao project,* on rivers of the same names, to be designed for 100,000 ha. of irrigated area, is still under study.

Total costs of all these schemes have been estimated at various times between Bs 4 billion and Bs 6 billion and the total area to be brought under irrigation at between 700,000 ha. and 1,100,000 ha. Average costs for the basic construction work, inclusive of canals and roads, have been assessed at between Bs 1,500 and Bs 3,000 per ha. and clearing and settling at between Bs 2,500 and Bs 4,000 per ha.

After 1950, studies were continued on most of the schemes mentioned and were extended with irrigation studies on the Santo Domingo River near Barinas, on the Tocuyo River in Falcon State, on an extension of El Cenizo, on the Limon, Palmar and Apon rivers in northwestern Zulia State, on the Unare River in Anzoatogui State, and on the Cariaco River in Sucre State. Drainage studies were initiated in the very important Zulia region on the Zulia, Catatumbo, Escalante and Chama rivers, in the Barlovento region and in Yaracuy. A study of part of the Orinoco delta was commissioned and San Bonifacio Valley reconnoitered.

Despite the large number of projects under consideration between 1950/51 and 1957/58, the Government actually carried out very little work other than on the Guarico project. Of some Bs 345 million spent on all irrigation works, Bs 247 million was spent on Guarico, not including special expenditures on Guarico by MAC and IAN.

It may thus be said that, although the 20-year planning period is nearly half over, so little of the proposed works has been carried out that it is realistic to reconsider the entire approach to irrigation policy. In fact, the mission questions whether the rapid construction of large-scale irrigation programs can be justified at the present point in Venezuelan development. There are large areas with fertile soils still in reserve, which could be opened up at low-capital cost and which enjoy a climate allowing for two crops a year without irrigation (see Annex V). It would seem to the mission that the development of these areas would have a higher priority than a vast irrigation program. Furthermore, even if the additional costs of opening up new lands in connection with irrigation projects could be kept low enough, and even if irrigation itself were relatively inexpensive, the full benefits of irrigation would not materialize for some years. It will take some time for farmers to overcome other factors, including their own lack of knowledge and experience in modern irrigated agriculture, which are currently holding down productivity.

It is, moreover, the impression of the mission that studies, especially as to the agricultural factors connected with irrigation—soils, crops, yields—have been inadequate and have not been properly used both in planning and execution. In general, the periods of observation of rainfall and river flow have been far too short for forming reliable conclusions. The mission considers that studies should be continued over a longer period to collect more complete long-range data on rainfall, runoff, flow and quantities and qualities of water available in the rivers. At the same time, soil surveys and topographical surveys should be executed for a better knowledge of the soils to be irrigated. It is especially desirable that the soil groups to which the soils belong should be determined, because this gives the best general indication of fertility, content of plant nutrients, water-holding capacity and permeability. Meanwhile, topographical surveys could be used for the development of drainage systems which would be essential for opening up new areas. Studies of small schemes for the densely populated regions with good soils, where some farmers have had experience with irrigation, in the Yaracuy, Sucre, Barlovento and San Bonifacio areas, should be given high priority, since they could be executed in a relatively short time and bring quick returns.

These general considerations make it very doubtful whether large irrigation works should be carried forward in Venezuela at a rapid rate at this stage even if they are well planned and well executed, since maximum returns will not be feasible for some years. As a general principle, irrigation works at an advanced stage of construction should be completed. Even these works will however require improved planning and new research studies, if returns are to be anything more than marginal.

The Guarico Project

Having been the object of the major effort in irrigation works in recent years, an examination of the Guarico project is instructive in indicating the problems that are encountered in developing large-scale irrigation projects in Venezuela. Bs 300 million have been spent on excavating a shallow reservoir with an area of 23,150 ha., on building a colonization center for IAN with houses for its personnel, on constructing the main irrigation canals with their bridges, together with the secondary irrigation system, all of which allows for farm settlement on an area of 10,000 ha., which has been cleared and provided with houses. Development of an additional 10,000 ha. has been involving an expenditure of a further Bs 14 million. The drainage system and the secondary irrigation system for about 90,000 ha. still have to be dug. Further development is being considered in two stages. The first, covering about 60,000 ha., is estimated to cost Bs 120 million, or about Bs 2,000 per hectare. The second stage will probably cost about the same amount per hectare.

The soils are only of moderate quality. They are classified mainly as clays, but most are lateritic. The mission examined the results of a

IRRIGATION

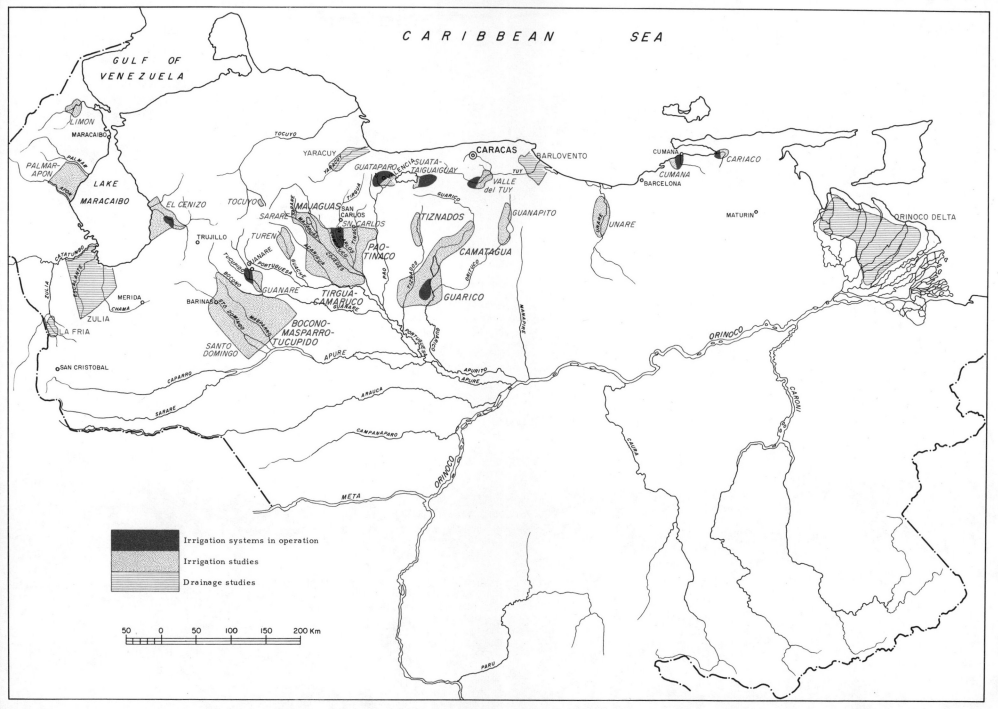

CARIBBEAN SEA

GULF OF VENEZUELA

LIMON
MARACAIBO
PALMAR-APON
PALMAR
APON
LAKE MARACAIBO
EL CENIZO
CATATUMBO
ZULIA
ESCALANTE
LA FRIA
ZULIA
MERIDA
CHAMA
SAN CRISTOBAL

TOCUYO
YARACUY
YARACUY
TOCUYO
SARARE
TRUJILLO
TUREN
BARINAS
SANTO DOMINGO

GUATAPARO VALENCIA SUATA-TAIGUAIGUAY
MAJAGUAS
SAN CARLOS
SN. CARLOS
TIRGUA
COJEDES
PAO-TINACO
GUANARE
PORTUGUESA
GUACHE
ACARIGUA
TUCUPIDO
BOCONO
GUANARE
TIRGUA-CAMARUCO
STO. DOMINGO
MASPARRO
GUANARE
BOCONO-MASPARRO-TUCUPIDO
SANTO DOMINGO

CARACAS
VALLE del TUY
TUY
BARLOVENTO

TIZNADOS
GUARICO
PAO
CAMATAGUA
TIZNADOS
ORITUCO
GUANAPITO
GUARICO
UNARE
UNARE
MANAPIRE
PORTUGUESA
GUARICO

CUMANA
BARCELONA
CUMANA
CARIACO
MATURIN
ORINOCO DELTA

APURE
CAPARRO
APURITO
APURE
ARAUCA
SARARE
CAMPANAPARO
META
ORINOCO
PARU

ORINOCO
CAURA
CARONI

Irrigation systems in operation

Irrigation studies

Drainage studies

50 0 50 100 150 200 Km

45,000 ha. soil survey carried out in connection with the project and
came to the conclusion that, except for some moderately old alluvial
soil of the Cachimbo type which covers only about five percent of the
area, the soils are poor, especially in potassium. They show impermeable layers and are therefore shallow and badly drained. The river
water is high in carbonates, which in the long run will be dangerous
for the calcareous soils, further decreasing their permeability and content of available nutrients. The latter soils would profit from acid
fertilizers (sulphate of ammonia, superphosphate and perhaps some
gypsum), but their extent is not great.

Except for the Cachimbo type, the soils are not suitable for dry arable
crops or for perennial crops, because of the presence of hardpans and
concretions, bad drainage and low waterholding capacity when drained.
Under irrigation, it would be difficult to maintain a good ratio between
water and air in the soil for dry crops, even with excellent drainage,
because the soils are too shallow. They do appear to be suitable in
general for wet rice, if there is sufficient fertilization. The impermeable
layers are of some advantage because they prevent water and fertilizer
losses through leaching to the subsoil. They are also suitable for grassland, if sufficient drainage is provided.

Because of the nature of the majority of soils, a rotation system of
wet rice for some (e.g., four) years, alternating with pasture for a
longer period (e.g., eight years) is indicated. The irrigation system
could be used for both phases of rotation. By damming off the ditches,
the drainage system could be maintained during the growing of wet
rice and then it could be used for evacuating the water from the rice
fields before ploughing or harvesting. Because there would be a tendency for the topsoil to become saturated with water and thus be too
soft for bearing heavy machines, good drainage is of paramount importance. Growing wet rice will tend to conserve organic matter, while
the alternating use of the land for grassland will eliminate noxious
grassy weeds which otherwise tend to multiply under mechanical cultivation when no hand weeding is applied. The system proposed would
only be suitable for mechanical cultivation on farms of at least 100 ha.,
and possibly as much as 200 ha. When irrigated, well drained and fer-
tilized, the pastures would be favorable for livestock fattening. For this
system to work properly, good farm management is obviously necessary.

Assuming that adequate standards of farm management can be attained, it is still not certain that even the suggested wet rice/pasture
rotation system will produce benefits in a high enough ratio to costs to
justify proceeding further with the Guarico project. This uncertainty
arises because insufficient data have been collected on expected yields

of rice and pasture from the particular soils in the Guarico area under irrigated conditions. In the absence of such data, the mission decided to visit a number of farms in the area to obtain some idea of the likely costs and benefits involved. While our conclusions can therefore not be regarded as precise in any degree, they do provide a broad indication as to the likely economic feasibility of a continuation of the project as a whole and, furthermore, they do suggest the lines along which more comprehensive studies should be made by the Venezuelan authorities themselves.

Our investigations indicate that the average yield that can be expected in the Guarico area is about 4,000 kg. of rice per ha. The highest yield observed was 7,000 kg. per ha. from two crops. The mission must emphasize that yields over the whole area may be substantially lower than 4,000 kg. per ha., because even such yields may only be possible on the superior Cachimbo type of alluvial soils which are relatively limited within the project area. Assuming a four-year planting of rice in rotation with an eight-year planting of pasture, in any given year there would be one-third of the total area under rice and two-thirds under pasture. Since about 110,000 ha. of irrigated lands are planned, about 37,000 ha. would be under rice and 74,000 ha. under pasture in any one year. With a yield of 4,000 kg. of rice per ha., the total annual output of rice would amount to 148 million kg. At current Venezuelan prices of Bs 0.60 per kg., the total annual rice crop would be worth about Bs 88 million (see Table 27).

Our investigations also indicate that the income from fattening cattle should be estimated at Bs 200 per ha., on the basis of two animals per ha. If improved suitable grasses were found, average income per ha. could be increased; but, on the basis of present knowledge, the pastures will be of relatively poor grade and consequently not capable of supporting more than the two animals per ha. assumed. Thus, at Bs 200 per ha., that 74,000 ha. under pasture will produce an annual income of about Bs 14.8 million.

Total additional gross income from both rice and cattle-fattening would amount to Bs 102.8 million annually. From this must be deducted operating costs, which we estimate at Bs 35 million, so that net income would amount to about Bs 67.8 million. After allowing for a return to management of Bs 33 million, the net value of additional output would amount to about Bs 34.8 million (see Table 27).

To complete the Guarico project, an additional investment of Bs 150 million would be required for the works themselves, Bs 60 million for farm machinery and equipment, and Bs 20 million to purchase livestock, so that a total additional investment of Bs 230 million would be required. If such an investment would stimulate a maximum additional output valued as we have shown above, at about Bs 34.8 million, a 15 percent return on investment would be achieved. Such a return would justify proceeding with the project.

The mission is not sure that such a rate of return can in fact be assured. First, it is doubtful whether the Venezuelan price for rice, which is more than double the world price, is a proper reflection of the real value of the additional rice to the Venezuelan economy. At the

TABLE 27: Calculation of Potential Return on Further Investment[a] in Guarico Project

(in Bs million)

		At Venezuelan Prices[b]	At World Prices[c]
Value added:			
Rice output[d]		88.0	41.4
Fattened cattle[e]		14.8	14.8
	Total	102.8	56.2
Less Operating Costs[f]		35.0	35.0
	Net Income	67.8	21.2
Less Cost of Management[g]		33.0	33.0
	Net Return on Investment	34.8	−11.8

[a] Of Bs 230 million.
[b] Bs 0.60 per kg.
[c] Bs 0.40 per kg.
[d] 37,000 ha. at 4,000 kg. per ha. equals output of 148 million kg.
[e] 74,000 ha. at Bs 200 per ha.
[f] At Bs 900 per ha. for rice, or a total of Bs 33 million for 37,000 ha., plus Bs 2 million for cattle-raising.
[g] At Bs 30,000 per 100 ha. farmed.

present world market price of Bs 0.40 kg., for husked rice (70 percent extraction) the gross value of the additional rice would be only about Bs 41.4 million and, after allowing for a return to management, would leave a negative return on investment (see Table 27). On the other hand, there are indirect benefits to the Venezuelan economy from an increased rice output in terms of the desirability of economic diversification, so that probably the most appropriate valuation of the additional rice output should be calculated at a rate somewhere between the Venezuelan and the world market price. On the latter basis, the rate of return could probably be reckoned as positive, although perhaps still too small to encourage a continuation of this form of investment.

In any case, it may be optimistic to assume an average yield of 4,000 kg. of rice per ha. If further investigation shows that the high yields observed have only been obtained on superior soils, trials would have to be made on poorer soils to discover whether there is any economic method of ensuring adequate yields throughout the project area. In any case, studies would have to be made to determine whether yields and output can be maintained for the entire four-year rotation period, irrespective of the nature of the soils.

In summary, the mission's view therefore is that the Guarico project should not be continued until the necessary technical studies have been made and the appropriate economic analyses carried out. On the basis of the limited data available to us, we are strongly inclined to believe that further investigation will reveal that the justification for continuing the project is marginal at best. But only such an investigation could confirm or deny this impression.

The Majaguas Project

At the time of the mission's visit, the Government had concentrated its major irrigation construction work on the Majaguas project. The project, as now proposed, calls for eventual control of the Agua Blanca (Sarare) , Cojedes, Camoruco, Tirgua, Tinaco and Pao rivers, with a combined flow of 2,800 million cubic meters of water capable of irrigating 250,000 ha., producing 10,000 kw. of power and controlling the flood waters from these rivers. The Agua Blanca-Cojedes phase would provide irrigation for 90,000 ha. and production of 5,000 kw. of power, the Camoruca-Tirgua, 60,000 ha. and 5,000 kw. and the Tinaco-Pao providing 100,000 ha. of irrigation alone.

During 1959/60, the Majaguas dam and the diversion of the waters of the Agua Blanca were scheduled for completion, permitting the irrigation of 18,000 ha. The Government is also proposing to construct during 1960/61-1963/64 a canal for diverting the Cojedes River into the Majaguas reservoir to irrigate an additional 30,000 ha. Expenditures for this work are estimated at Bs 57 million. From the data made available to the mission, it is not clear whether any of this expenditure is related to the 18,000 ha. scheduled for completion in 1959/60. We were also unable to obtain data on the exact amounts already spent on the project.

In the absence of both detailed cost data and physical data on production possibilities in the area to be irrigated, the mission is nevertheless not favorably impressed by the project. No detailed soil surveys are available, but the region has generally poor soils with hardpans and can be placed roughly in the same class with the Guarico soils. This would mean that, in addition to soil surveys, fairly extensive cropping trials should be carried out before any substantial further investments are made. The mission therefore recommends that the project be temporarily discontinued at the first phase of 18,000 ha. to await the outcome of the investigations suggested above.

The Bocono-Masparro-Tucupido Project

This project was originally called the Bocono-Tucupido project and was designed to irrigate 140,000 ha. and produce 40,000 kw. of power. Total costs were estimated at Bs 605 million of which Bs 60 million was to be allocated for flood control, Bs 238 million for irrigation and Bs 307 million for electric power plant. Plans for the project have since been expanded to include a fourth stage, involving an additional 80,000 ha. and 20,000 kw., and possibly a fifth stage bringing in the Masparro River which would add an additional 40,000 ha. and 5,000 kw. Detailed cost estimates were not available for these expansions.

The Government is considering a proposal to carry out the first stage of the project during 1960/61-1963/64. This would involve irrigation of 21,000 ha. through diversion works and canals from the Bocono and Guanare Rivers, at an estimated cost of Bs 45 million. Detailed plans for this phase were not available. On the basis of earlier studies of the Bocono-Tucupido project and available agroclimatic data, the mission concludes that the project is located on good soils with high agricultural potential and that the costs should be substantially lower than those for the Guarico project. At the same time, it seems clear to us that before the Government makes any large-scale commitment on the project, further studies would be required, particularly with respect to its agricultural implications. It would also be desirable to collect further rainfall and runoff data, as a 1950 consulting engineers' report pointed out.

The Government proposal for a limited irrigation project based on river diversion seems to be a reasonable step, particularly as a means for obtaining additional data on production possibilities and expected returns from irrigation in a promising area. Average costs are not excessive since the lands are situated in a zone of rich alluvial deposits.

The mission therefore recommends that the Government proceed with this pilot river diversion project and continue studies for the over-all development of the area. Capital outlays on river diversion are estimated at Bs 45 million during the four-year period 1960/61-1963/64. We also recommend that Bs 14 million be spent during this period on the necessary studies.

Small Irrigation Projects

The Government proposes to construct relatively small irrigation-drainage projects at Santo Domingo (Barinas), El Cenizo (Trujillo), El Palmar (Zulia) and Guanapito (Guarico). The estimated cost of these constructions is Bs 55 million. The mission believes that such smaller irrigation projects, particularly in areas where there are experienced commercial farmers, can provide relatively quick returns. Furthermore, such projects will provide a basis for developing cropping systems and varieties suitable for irrigated conditions and provide valuable data and experience for future development of larger-scale projects. We therefore recommend that the Government give additional emphasis to this type of development and divert resources from projects such as the Majaguas and Guarico to an expansion of small-scale irrigation works.

Drainage of the Area South of Lake Maracaibo (Zulia)

Preliminary studies have been made of a large-scale flood protection and drainage project to develop an area of 550,000 ha. south of Lake Maracaibo between the Zulia, Catatumbo and Chama rivers, the Pan-American Highway and the Lake. The cost of the total project has been estimated roughly at Bs 100 million. At present about 200,000 ha. is already occupied, with about 20,000 ha. under crops and 180,000 ha. under pasture. The project would permit more intensive use of this area and add an additional 350,000 ha. With the exception of a few marshy areas, the soils in the area are very fertile and suitable for mixed cropping in addition to pastures and tropical fruits. Wherever roads have been built, settlements have developed, usually without any special government assistance. The mission considers this area to be one of the most promising for future low-cost agricultural development and urges that the highest priority be given to this project.

Present plans call for further studies during 1960/61-1963/64, with construction beginning in 1962/63. Expenditures proposed for the four-year period amount to Bs 45 million, of which Bs 10 million would be allocated to studies. About 50,000 ha. would be made available for cultivation and settlement during the period. The mission agrees with the present policy of developing a master plan for development of the area before starting construction. The fact that there are several river systems involved, and that links exist between them, rules out a piece-meal approach of diking off small areas at a time. Control of water in one area could lead to severe flooding in others. On the other hand, for the area east of the Chama River, where the links to the Lake are direct, it should be possible to plan for a more rapid development. Only an extension of the small irrigation system at El Cenizo is presently contemplated for the next four years. The mission urges the immediate study of the drainage possibilities in the area east of the Chama River and their implementation as rapidly as possible. The mission calculates that studies in this area might cost a further Bs 2 million, and that the consequent drainage construction might cost Bs 8 million during 1960/61-1963/64.

Other Drainage

Lack of drainage is a common problem in Venezuelan lowland agriculture and, before large-scale expenditures are made on irrigation, attention should be given to drainage in the new regions in Zulia, as mentioned above, and in Barinas and Portuguesa and also in the old settled regions of Valencia, Barlovento and San Bonifacio. In the densely populated, small-farming regions of Sucre, Miranda, Coro and Falcon, where permanent farmers are accustomed to intensive, efficient cultivation, drainage could increase productivity of land and of labor at relatively low cost. Our general conclusion is that in all those flat cropping regions where drainage is deficient, either because of flooding or too high a soil-water table, the first step toward improved yields would be a good drainage system.

Where bad drainage is due to flooding by rivers, the first task would be to study the possibilities of embanking such rivers. In the Barinas-Portuguesa area, the rich alluvial soils were deposited because of the slowing down and branching of the rivers and hence the areas are susceptible to flooding. Drainage facilities would therefore be essential if the area is to be developed. In Barlovento and San Bonifacio, local studies are necessary since present planning for San Bonifacio leaves out probably the most fertile areas which are now flooded by the river. Studies of embankments and of drainage are recommended here. Topographical surveys are naturally an essential prerequisite for planning a good drainage system. Apart from the prevention of flooding by rivers, surface drainage systems should be introduced on all these good soils.

Drainage is also very important in the Lake Valencia region where a brackish soil-water table reaches too near the surface, and evaporation of the ascending water and of the irrigation water applied cause accumulation of salts in the top soil. Increasing salinization can be perceived in the form of bare spots in the fields. Drain ditches and use of surplus irrigation water for leaching the salts should be applied here, perhaps even the use of tube wells for providing additional water to wash out the soils may be justified.

The Government is currently planning to provide drainage for the Suata-Taiguaiguay (Aragua), Guataparo (Carabobo), and Barlovento (Miranda) areas at an estimated cost of about Bs 15 million. The mission believes that these works should be carried out on a much larger scale. We have provided for drainage facilities in the new development areas under our resettlement program, and also for drainage studies in other areas such as Valencia and San Bonifacio.

Policy and Expenditures

Irrigation and drainage projects normally involve heavy capital outlays, the benefits of which are felt only within a relatively limited area. For this reason, among others, such projects ought to be preceded by detailed cost-benefit analyses, they ought to be compared with alternative projects and they ought to be subject to detailed planning to ensure that suitable farmers, operating with the appropriate techniques, are working within the project area with the correct crops, and that adequate follow-up extension services are provided. It is the mission's impression that there are serious gaps in such basic data in Venezuela, even in connection with irrigation and drainage projects already under construction. Before proceeding further, additional data should be obtained and the projects re-evaluated in the light of such data. The mission feels that these studies will probably indicate that many of these projects are marginal at this stage and that emphasis should be given to drainage rather than irrigation.

Accordingly, the mission has recommended that irrigation works during 1960/61-1963/64 be limited to the completion of the first stage of the Majaguas project, to the diversion of the Bocono and Guanare Rivers, and to the various programed small irrigation works. On the other hand, we not only concur in all the programed drainage works, both south of Lake Maracaibo, including east of the Chama River, and elsewhere, but we recommend additional outlays on drainage and on small irrigation works (see Table 28). These recommendations would entail total capital expenditures on irrigation and drainage of Bs 296 million during 1960/61-1963/64.

TABLE 28: Mission's Proposed Capital Expenditures on Irrigation and Drainage, 1960/61-1963/64

(in Bs million)

	Four-Year Period
Ministry of Public Works:	
Majaguas[a]	12
Bocono and Guanare diversion	45
Small irrigation works (programed)	55
Drainage south of Lake Maracaibo[b]	43
Small drainage works (programed)	15
Recommended additions for small irrigation and drainage works	30
Maintenance & acquisitions	60
Total	260
Ministry of Agriculture and Livestock	36
Grand Total	296

[a] For completion of first-stage 18,000 ha. irrigated area.
[b] Includes area east of Chama River.

Furthermore, we have constantly emphasized the need for preliminary studies, surveys and the collection of data. We calculate that these would entail the expenditure of Bs 54 million during the four-year period. If all this work is to be fully effective, a thorough reorganization of the administrative arrangements in connection with irrigation and drainage works will have to take place. In the process of our investigations, the mission found that the distribution of responsibilities among government agencies concerned with irrigation and drainage projects requires clarification. At present, agricultural aspects are given inadequate attention and, even where there are agricultural studies, they have not been given adequate consideration in the final evaluation of the projects. The mission recommends that the evaluation aspect of irrigation and drainage projects should be assigned to the *Direccion de Plan-ificacion Agropecuaria* of MAC and that several experienced economists be added to the staff to guide these evaluations.

SUMMARY OF PROPOSED EXPENDITURES

The recommendations made in this chapter would entail capital expenditures in the public sector of Bs 1,512.8 million during the four

TABLE 29: Summary of Mission's Proposed Capital Expenditures on Agriculture, 1960/61-1963/64

(in Bs million)

	Four-Year Period
Special Program for Low-Income Farmers:	
Settlement on new lands	400.0
Extension services	10.0
Supervised credit	50.0
Agricultural subsidies[a]	55.0
	515.0
General Program Mainly for Commercial Farms:	
Research[b]	36.0
Extension	10.0
Livestock disease control	4.0
Credit[c]	504.0
Access roads	118.2
Other[d]	29.6
	701.8
Irrigation and Drainage:	296.0
Grand Total	1,512.8

[a] Includes provision of poultry and livestock at subsidized prices and free assistance for drainage and land improvement.

[b] In addition to agricultural and livestock research, provision is made for forestry and fisheries research (see Annexes VI and VII).

[c] Includes Bs 320 million for the *Plan Ganadero*, Bs 34 million for special coffee and cacao credits and Bs 150 million to be divided between short-term crop loans and medium-term farm improvement loans. Not included in Bs 100 million for long-term mortgage loans for land acquisition, which we recommend should be obtained by liquidating BAP's non-credit assets.

[d] Includes soil conservation, afforestation and other special programs already planned.

years 1960/61-63/64 (see Table 29). While some of our estimates are independently derived, particularly with respect to programs which have not been under consideration by the Venezuelan Government, many represent our revision of cost estimates of programs that the Government itself was considering in early 1960, and a few represent our working acceptance of the Government's own cost estimates without revision by the mission.

Arising directly from our recommendations, current expenditures would total Bs 704.3 million during the four-year period (see Table 30).

TABLE 30: Summary of Current Expenditures Arising from Mission's Proposed Agricultural Development Program, 1960/61-1963/64

(in Bs million)

	Four-Year Period
Special Program for Low-Income Farmers:	
Extension services	40.0
Agricultural subsidies[a]	45.0
Cadastral survey	28.0
IAN administration[b]	115.0
	228.0
General Program Mainly for Commercial Farms:	
Research[c]	82.7
Extension[d]	105.0
Livestock disease control	46.0
Fertilizer subsidies	35.0
Fluid milk production subsidy	90.0
Other[e]	63.6
	422.3
Irrigation and Drainage Studies:	54.0
Grand Total	704.3

[a] Includes input subsidies of fertilizer, other chemicals and seed.

[b] To phase out IAN's program of capital-intensive settlement.

[c] As already planned in program under consideration in Venezuela.

[d] Includes Bs 50 million to operate the extension service itself, Bs 50 million to operate schools for extension workers, and Bs 5 million for agricultural fairs and exhibitions.

[e] Includes soil conservation, afforestation and other special programs already planned.

CHAPTER 10 *MANUFACTURING*

PRESENT INDUSTRIAL CONDITIONS

The Record of Recent Growth

Manufacturing in Venezuela has in recent years shown rapid growth, estimated at some 11 percent a year. From 1950 to 1959 output increased from Bs 1,150 million to Bs 3,012 million, rising from almost 9 percent to over 11 percent of the gross domestic product. Even so, manufacturing is still much less developed in Venezuela than in other countries with a similar per capita and aggregate income. Nevertheless, recent expansion has been impressive and has taken place mainly in the private sector, even though private manufacturing enterprise is itself of recent development.

The breadth and depth of recent growth in manufacturing has not been fully appreciated. While growth rates vary widely among industries and some have scarcely expanded at all, growth has not been concentrated in a few enterprises. In 1948 over half of all manufacturing output originated in the food, beverages and textile sectors; ten years later the proportion was reduced to about one-third (see Table 31). This reduction reflects the growth of petroleum refining, which quadrupled its output between 1948 and 1953, and also reflects the very high growth rates in the manufacture of metals, plywood, paints, clay blocks, bricks, cement, tires, auto assembly, batteries, fertilizer. Venezuela's traditional consumer goods industries, despite the direct stimulus provided by the very rapid increase in the market between 1948 and 1958, grew less rapidly than the sectors producing intermediate products. Consumer goods output represented 71 percent of the total in 1948 and 59 percent in 1958. It is thus clear that Venezuelan industrial enterprise has at least emerged from the initial stages of industrial development, even though only 11 percent of the national product originates in the manufacturing sector.

A variety of factors is responsible for the divergent growth rates in the different industrial sectors. Obviously, the considerable public works activity which dominated the economy during the past decade has particularly encouraged the development of building material industries such as structural steel, aluminum (window and door frames) and clay products, cement, plywood and paints. Newly introduced industries, such as rubber tire manufacture, car assembly, battery manufacture and animal feed mixing plants, show high growth rates since they started from a particularly small or even nonexistent production base during the past ten years. Some manufacturing activities such as car assembly, tire- and battery-making, have received a special impetus from the growing highway network in the country which greatly facilitated the growth of motorized transport, while the rather high degree of electrification achieved in recent years has promoted the establishment of electrical installation and repair shops. Further, some industries could grow quickly at the expense of traditional crafts en-

TABLE 31: Composition of Industrial Output by Selected Industries and Major Sectors

(in percentages)

	1948	1953	1958
By Industry:			
Food	24.73	19.05	16.79
Drink	16.64	14.00	12.75
Tobacco	3.76	2.79	2.11
Textiles	9.72	6.94	7.41
Clothing	2.04	3.82	3.49
Timber	2.56	2.10	1.89
Furniture	5.38	3.69	2.16
Paper & paper products	0.93	1.02	1.77
Printing	4.09	5.40	6.08
Hides & skins	1.14	1.03	1.16
Rubber products	1.25	2.46	3.48
Chemical products	6.67	7.32	8.16
Petroleum derivatives	6.57	12.29	12.25
Non-metallic mineral products	6.11	8.38	7.14
Metal products	1.08	2.05	5.50
Repairs to machinery	0.69	0.37	0.34
Construction & assembly of motor vehicles	0.03	0.54	0.46
Repair of motor vehicles	2.11	2.18	1.99
Other	4.39	4.55	5.05
By Sector:			
Consumer goods	71	66	59
Capital goods	2	3	3
Intermediary goods	27	31	38

Source: *Memoria, 1958,* Banco Central de Venezuela.

gaged in the manufacture of similar or substitute products. For example, the ready-made clothing industry can effectively compete with the still numerous small apparel shops of the artisan type because of advanced production and sales techniques. Industrial processing of those foodstuffs previously consumed in a less sophisticated form has expanded rapidly; for example, the crystal sugar processing industry has developed at the expense of *papelon* (unrefined sugar) manufacture.

On the other hand, low growth rates are generally related to such factors as a retarded development of domestic agricultural production and depressed rural incomes, high capital investment requirements per manufacturing establishment, the absence of management and labor skills to sustain a certain production process, and inadequate protection against foreign competition. In a few instances, strong consumer preferences for foreign products together with ineffective tariff protection has been responsible for a slowing down of the growth of some industries, such as tobacco products and cotton textiles. Finally some of the older industries such as cotton weaving and spinning, have been operating with obsolete equipment and working procedures, resulting in higher cost levels than necessary.

The variations both in growth rate and in volume of production of the several manufacturing activities have resulted in a differing degree of import replacement as expressed as a percentage of apparent consumption. From the limited data available, it would appear that significant advances have been made in replacing imports of many consumer goods by domestic production, and that industry has been able to satisfy increasing consumer demands; this holds particularly true for such products as processed foods, beverages, wood products and tires. For other commodities, however, particularly for those belonging to the category of raw and semi-finished materials, domestic production (notwithstanding high growth rates) is still satisfying only a minor part of requirements; this suggests that domestic production has not been able to catch up with increasing demands, and that substantial opportunities for import substitution continue to exist.

The high cost level of Venezuelan manufactures has so far made export virtually impossible; with the exception of petroleum products, minor quantities of cement, and an occasional export of sisal rope, no manufactured products are being exported. Manufacturing is now therefore entirely dependent on the domestic market which is, with a population of only 7 million people, rather small; it is even smaller if the uneven income distribution and the prevalent levels of real income are taken into account. Some 10 percent of all families receive, in aggregate, about half the total private income whereas, by contrast, nearly half the population receive together only one-tenth of total private income. By taking into account such large variations in income, and after making adjustments for differences in purchasing power, it can be calculated that Venezuela would have in effect a consumption market equal to that of a northern European country with a population of less than 2.5 million. Because of the smallness of the domestic market and lack of a foreign market, a wide range of products either cannot be manufactured in the country or can only be produced in manufacturing units of a size which does not permit realization of economies of scale. On the other hand, while the market is small for a majority of commodities, the uneven income distribution does allow for a much larger demand for certain high-priced products than would normally be expected from an over-all market of Venezuela's size.

Since manufacturing is still largely geared towards the supply of non-durable consumer goods and services, industrial location follows the geographical distribution of the population, with modifications according to regional variations of income. Approximately two-thirds of the population live in the Eastern Andes and coastal Cordilleras mountains; this bow-shaped area which crosses the country from southwest to northeast is probably about 1,200 km. long and only 150 km. wide, and it is here that the great majority of the manufacturing establishments are operating. The close incidence between population, income levels and industrial location is especially noticeable in Caracas, where over 24 percent of the total population and 45 percent of the total personal disposable income corresponds with a concentration in the metropolitan area of about 70 percent of industrial production. In recent years, a considerable number of new enterprises have been established in the Lake Valencia area (particularly in and around such cities as Los Teques, Maracay, Valencia and Guigue) where industry finds attractive location advantages such as cheap land as compared with the metropolitan area, easy access to imported materials through Puerto Cabello harbor, a concentrated market in nearby Caracas and the availability of supporting services as provided in the capital. There has been some industrial concentration in a few other major cities, such as Maracaibo, Barquisimeto and in the Puerto La Cruz and Barcelona area, but little elsewhere. No significant industrial development has taken place in the interior. On the contrary, there are indications that the decline in some traditional crafts industries which are predominantly located in and near the Andes States of Trujillo, Merida and Tachira, has further reduced the already small manufacturing labor force in this economically depressed area. The construction of the government-sponsored steel industry in Puerto Ordaz is therefore a first significant shift in the present market-bound location pattern.

Raw Materials as a Cost Factor

As we have already noted in Chapter 9, Venezuelan agriculture tends to be high cost. As a result, those Venezuelan industries which depend on agricultural commodities as raw materials have also tended to be high cost. In general, domestic agricultural raw materials are priced at a multiple of international prices.[1] Venezuelan processing industries are nevertheless forced to use the higher-priced domestic products because the latter are afforded the protection of prohibitive tariffs. When domestic supplies fall short of requirements, imports are allowed but only to the extent of the shortfall, with the Government regulating the permissible ratio of imported to domestic raw materials. Since customs duties are usually very high, when the supply situation warrants imports, a complex system of ad hoc customs duty exonerations is necessary in order to make such imports economically feasible for the processor. In any event, government policy tends to maximize the use of higher-priced domestic raw materials by the processors and at the same time such a policy in itself tends to militate against a lowering in the agricultural cost structure. We have suggested some measures to rationalize government policies with respect to the production of agricultural raw materials (see Chapter 9) and such policies, if adopted, should not only help to expand agricultural output but should also help the processing industries attain a more competitive position.

With some exceptions, the quality of domestic agricultural materials is satisfactory. Home-grown cotton is of a type which enables industry to manufacture cloth of good quality but higher-grade cotton is being imported, and there is little prospect of developing domestic cultivation of such high-quality cotton varieties. Tobacco growing has shifted, in the last twenty years from the darker "negro" variety to the lighter Virginia brand "rubio," and this enables industry to manufacture a milder type of cigarettes as desired by the consumers. The quality of hides and skins being low, substantial quantities of leather are imported, particularly of the better qualities, such as uppers. A general problem handicapping the use of domestic raw material supplies is deficient grading which contributes to inefficient marketing and pricing practices.

In significant contrast to agriculture, the domestic raw material

[1] See Table 26, Chapter 9.

position is most favorable insofar as supplies of mineral origin are concerned. At present the petroleum refining, cement, chemical (caustic soda), clay and glass industries are the main manufacturing activities based on domestic raw materials. The steel mill now being constructed will process domestic iron ore, of which there are huge reserves; coal is available at Naricual, but its suitability for the manufacture of coke to be used by the steel plant is still being tested. Natural gas, which is abundant and cheap, and more readily accessible now that pipelines have been expanded, is being used as a source of fuel in a variety of manufacturing processes, and will be used as a raw material source in some factories now under construction, including the plants for producing ammonia and urea at Moron. Industries based on the country's mineral wealth should have the best development and export potential, even under the present unfavorable domestic cost and price structure. The cement industry is able to enter the export trade and a private firm is planning to start the production, partly for export, of high-quality refractory clay products.

Apart from raw materials, manufacturing is almost entirely dependent on foreign supplies since inter-industry exchange of manufactures within Venezuela is limited to a few commodities such as packing materials and leather products. Dependence on foreign supply sources places Venezuelan industry at some cost disadvantage as compared with manufacturing in industrialized countries since relatively large inventories have to be maintained. The small average size of manufacturing plants tends to inhibit opportunities to economize through bulk purchase and the establishment of composite manufacturing units is likewise inhibited. The strong consumers' preference for well-established foreign brands results, in case of domestic manufacture of such products, in import of selected materials and composite parts from the parent company abroad rather than in the development of domestic manufacture.

Wages, Productivity and Costs

Wage rates in modern factories in Venezuela are high if expressed in foreign currencies and compared with those paid in highly industrialized countries. From data available to the mission[2] it appears that in 1958 unskilled workers received a daily basic wage of about Bs 15 and that wage supplements add 80 percent, which is equivalent to more

[2] *Estudio sobre salarios basicos y prestaciones sociales,* Camara de Industriales de Caracas, Octubre 1959.

than $1 an hour. Skilled workers are paid as much as Bs 35 a day, or over Bs 65 if supplements are included, which is equivalent to more than $2 an hour. Venezuelan wage levels in the modern sector of manufacturing therefore generally exceed those prevailing in Latin American and European countries. Wages paid in manufacturing in general, as opposed to the modern sector, are appreciably lower although still high if compared with wage levels existing in other countries (see Table 32). No data are available on wages paid in all manufacturing on a country-wide basis; however, those contained in Table 32 compare wages in the Federal District with other countries.[3] Venezuelan manufacturing is under an even greater cost handicap with respect to salaried per-

TABLE 32: Basic Wages in Selected Manufacturing Industries in Selected Countries, 1958

(in US$ per hour)

Country	Food	Textiles	Ready-made Clothing	Leather and Products	Metal Products	Printing
India[a]	n.a.	0.12	0.13	0.09	0.11	0.12
Colombia	0.11	0.15	0.10	0.12	0.14	0.16[c]
Brazil	0.18	0.17	0.18	0.20	0.25	0.29
Argentina	0.20	0.18	0.32	0.22	0.22	0.23
Japan	0.25	0.18[b]	0.15	0.25	0.27	0.35
France	0.41	0.37	0.36	0.37	0.49	0.63
U.K.	0.69	0.69	0.72	0.70	0.82	0.89[c]
Venezuela[d]	0.82	0.71	0.62	0.78	0.99	1.48
Sweden	0.97	0.90	0.91	1.00	1.10	1.19
U.S.A.	2.01	1.51	1.51	1.57	2.27	2.59

[a] Rates refer to 1957.
[b] Weaving industry only.
[c] Including the paper industry.
[d] Federal District only.

Note: The wage data, here presented, should be regarded with great caution, particularly since they signify the crude basic wages only, and do not take into account wage supplements which show considerable international variations.

Sources: *Memoria, 1958,* Banco Central de Venezuela; *Yearbook of Labor Statistics, 1959,* ILO, Geneva, 1959.

[3] While data for the Federal District overstates somewhat the wage level in Venezuela, modern factory enterprises wherever located are more likely to have to pay something approximating Federal District wages than the relatively lower average wages paid in all manufacturing outside the Federal District.

sonnel. While many lower level staff in this category receive salaries more or less equal to those pertaining in the United States, the salaries for higher staff positions often exceed those paid in the United States, not to mention remunerations for comparable positions in European industry.[4] It is evident that Venezuela does not share the major advantage that other underdeveloped countries enjoy in competing against products manufactured in advanced countries—a relatively low wage level.

The high wage levels in manufacturing industry can in part be explained in relation to the general problem of the prevailing high cost and price level in the country as expressed in foreign currency (see Chapter 7). But there are also specific factors tending to exert an upward pressure on industrial wages. Convention, law, and trade union pressure have affected factory wages—all of which in turn have been greatly influenced by the petroleum industry. The high wage rates, supplements, and working conditions established in the petroleum industry tend to be applied in other industries even though the petroleum industry provides employment to only two percent of the labor force. The trade union movement and the law are vehicles for the rapid transmission and general application of petroleum industry standards.

The Labor Law, while by no means unique, "is relatively advanced" and "would certainly not be as it is if those who drafted it had not been inspired by the economic possibilities of the petroleum industry."[5] The law establishes minimum standards on working conditions which include a limitation of working hours to eight hours by day and seven by night, and 48 and 42 hours per week respectively; two weeks' holiday with pay and payment of wages during compulsory rest days such as Sundays and public holidays; profit sharing (10 percent of net profits, but not to exceed two months' wages per wage earner[6]); and intensive

[4] University graduates may find employment in the government administration (which pays less than private enterprise) at a starting salary of Bs 2,000 per month plus supplements, or some US$650; by contrast, according to a survey made by Northwestern University, U.S. private enterprise was paying, in 1959, to new entrants with a university degree between $411 (for general business graduates) and $489 (for engineers) per month (see *U.S. News & World Report,* December 21, 1959, p. 48). For a comparison of average earnings in other selected occupations see Statistical Appendix, Table S.22.

[5] *Freedom of Association and Conditions of Work in Venezuela,* ILO, Geneva, 1950, p. 24.

[6] Known as *utilidades,* the Christmas bonus has taken firm roots in the social economy of the country. Even shoeshine boys in Caracas charge twice the ordinary rate during the month of December, whereas enterprises which have been losing money are nevertheless under considerable pressure to pay this bonus.

protection against all forms of unjustified dismissal. With one or two exceptions, these standards refer to all undertakings[7] irrespective of the size of enterprise, and small manufacturing units which are operating with hired labor are therefore governed by the Law; these standards may be raised but not lowered through collective agreements. As a matter of fact, through the machinery of collective bargaining, working conditions in the larger and modern enterprises generally exceed the standards laid down in the Labor Law by a wide margin: many of these undertakings pay more for overtime, for night work and for work on Sunday than legally stipulated. The law itself also contains provisions requiring generous severance payments.

The extensive system of benefits imposed by law and by collective contract exercises a heavy burden on manufacturing industry as compared with other countries, whether industrially advanced or not. While wage supplements may average more than 40 percent of total wages and labor charges in Venezuelan manufacturing industry, similar supplements constitute 17 percent of total wages and charges in United States industry and generally less than 40 percent in some selected West European countries.[8]

Little has been done in the past to improve the quality of the labor force so as to increase its productivity and so reduce labor costs. General education has lagged, as has vocational training (see Chapter 14). In the smaller enterprises, particularly in those located in rural areas, probably not more than half of the workers are literate; in the larger undertakings which are mostly located in or near urban centers, and where frequently the ability to read and write is required for factory employment, probably about 25 percent of the labor force is illiterate. Equally serious has been the lack of vocational training facilities which has resulted in an inadequately trained domestic labor force. In the past ten years only some 500 persons have graduated from vocational training institutions and there is therefore a considerable shortage of such skilled key personnel as electricians, solderers, carpenters and metal workers.[9] Also, no formal apprenticeship training system is in operation

[7] Agricultural labor is governed by special regulations.

[8] Wage supplements in the modern manufacturing sector in Venezuela in 1958 ranged from 67 percent to 93 percent of basic pay or 40 percent to 48 percent if expressed as a percentage of total wages and labor charges. By contrast, wage supplements in selected European manufacturing industries varied between 11 percent in the United Kingdom, 29 percent in France and 46 percent in Yugoslavia.

[9] Such shortages were already reported by an ILO manpower mission in 1954 (see *Informe al Gobierno de Venezuela Sobre la Mision Consultiva de Mano de Obra,* ILO, Geneva, 1956).

with the result that present methods of training new entrants are quite inadequate. Only in the petroleum industry and in a few larger manufacturing enterprises attention is being paid to apprenticeship training as an organized activity.

There are, understandably, great variations in the productivity of Venezuelan labor, including salaried personnel. While there is no comparative data on productivity in Venezuela as compared with other countries, the mission gained the impression from its own observations and discussions with management during visits to a variety of undertakings, that labor productivity in Venezuela averages between 50 to 25 percent lower than that in similar plants operating under similar working conditions in the United States. In general, it would appear that the more output volume is dependent on the initiative and skill of the worker, the greater are productivity differentials. Thus, the productivity record of the majority of the Venezuelan workers in highly mechanized and automatized manufacturing processes compares favorably with that of enterprises in highly industrialized countries, while in the less-mechanized processes, as for instance in material-handling operations, production drops sharply below U.S. and European levels.

We would not like to give the impression that labor is the main determinant in establishing levels of productivity, and that the Venezuelan worker as such is responsible for lower output levels. On the contrary, the Venezuelan worker has as good a performance record as workers elsewhere, if properly trained, motivated and managed, as the mission had occasion to witness in some instances. It should be recognized that the output of the workers depends in large measure upon factors over which labor has no or little control, such as quality of management, applied technology, size of the undertaking and amount of product diversification, labor-management relations and availability and effectiveness of educational facilities. There are also a number of institutional factors which indirectly exert a depressing influence on the quality and quantity of the workers' output. Since manufacturing activities are of rather recent origin, the majority of the workers lacks the industrial background and strong artisan tradition which contribute to the maintenance of certain minimum standards of quality and uniformity. We frequently heard the observation that the Venezuelan worker has an insufficient feeling of responsibility toward the enterprise in which he works; if this is so, then a larger number and a higher quality of supervisors are required in order to obtain satisfactory production results.

Comparative Levels of Manufacturing Costs

It thus seems clear that Venezuelan industry must be operating at higher cost levels (expressed in foreign currency) than industry in the industrially advanced countries. Labor costs are high. The cost of salaried personnel in general and of the managerial staff in particular is even higher. Capital costs, as reflected both in the prevailing interest rates for short-term credit and in the level of profit expectations among potential entrepreneurs, are probably equal to those existing in economies in an early stage of industrial development and are appreciably higher than in the industrially advanced countries. Factory construction costs are not favorable. Lastly, the cost of agricultural materials of domestic origin and of imported supplies is higher than abroad. The only major cost elements favorable to Venezuela are the relative cheapness of domestic materials of mineral origin, and the low transport charges which are equal to or below those in the United States. In addition, electricity costs, which have relatively little weight in total costs in most manufacturing activities, may in the future become favorable to Venezuela.

In summary, depending on specific manufacturing characteristics and the type of product made, manufacturing costs in Venezuelan industry are almost always substantially higher than those abroad, with margins ranging up to 100 percent and even more in some cases.

THE PROTECTIVE SYSTEM

The Encouragement of Domestic Industry

In order to broaden the base of the economy, successive Venezuelan Governments have taken measures to shield high-cost domestic industry from foreign competition. In most underdeveloped countries, some protection is justified in order to promote infant industries. In Venezuela, where it has also been necessary at the prevailing foreign exchange rate to provide extensive protection to agriculture and where wage rates and domestic income levels are generally high when productivity is taken into account, the levels of protection have also had to be exceptionally high. Venezuela has a long history of high import duties which were originally solely designed for revenue purposes but which have been gradually adjusted also to serve the industrialization process. In this respect, customs duties can be broadly grouped in three categories: prohibitive, allowing for some competition, and nominal.

Some duties are so high that they virtually prohibit the import of the commodities so affected; many processed foods and apparel, furniture and soap manufacture are some of the goods which are completely shielded against foreign competition through duty rates (see Table 33). Such prohibitive tariff protection is supplemented by an import licensing system which is used to assure that total domestic output will be absorbed by the market at profitable prices before imports are permitted to enter the country. Such quantitative control is being applied to protect a variety of other food products, leather tanning and manufactures, textiles including sisal packing, tires and tobacco products. Other manufacturing activities receive substantial tariff protection but still have to meet some foreign competition since duty rates allow for imports of similar or substitute products; vegetable lard and beer are some of the commodities which are protected by duty schedules varying between 50 and 100 percent of domestic wholesale prices. Lastly, there is a variety of manufactures such as semi-fabricated products, tools and capital equipment which generally enter the country at nominal or moderate duty rates.

Venezuelan protective policy has in general been successful in creating the basic socio-economic framework within which domestic manufacture could develop and experience be gained in management and skills. Some industries have grown at a high rate, but a number of industries have not responded too well to the incentives provided by tariff protection. For example, the growth of the cotton textile industry has been severely limited by strong competition from the high-quality silk and woolen fabric industries and, because the latter produce relatively high-priced goods, a sharp increase in the tariff schedule for all textiles has been imposed. In the case of cigarette manufacture, strong consumer preference for more expensive foreign brands outweighed tariff protection so that by 1960 domestic production was supplying less than two-thirds of the local market; as a result, the Government then completely prohibited the import of cigarettes. The paper industry has also not responded to tariff manipulation and has lagged behind the over-all average growth rate. This is probably due to the high capital requirements to establish a manufacturing unit and the proportionally higher skills required of management and labor in the manufacture of paper products. Thus, tariff protection alone has not been sufficient to create industrial growth. The success of protection policy depends

TABLE 33: Import Duties and Selected Domestic Manufactures, November 1959

Commodity	Domestic Wholesale Price (in Bs per kg.)	Import Duty (in Bs per kg.)	Duty as % of Domestic Wholesale Price
Beverages			
Beer	1.48	1.10	74.3
Carbonated drinks	0.57	0.40	70.2
Fruit juices[a]	1.58	1.30	82.3
Rum	1.28	5.00	390.6
Food products			
Animal feed	0.30-0.69	0.15	50.0-21.7
Cheese (criollo)	3.45	1.00	29.0
Chocolate	4.60	16.00	347.8
Coconut oil	2.00	4.00	200.0
Cottonseed oil	3.03	4.00	132.0
Margarine	4.26	8.00	187.8
Milk powder[a]	3.67	0.50	13.6
Pasta	0.96	2.00	208.3
Sardines	2.00	8.00	400.0
Sausages	4.00	1.20	30.0
Sesame oil	4.27	4.00	93.7
Sugar	0.90	16.00	1,777.8
Sweets[a]	1.70-3.50	4.50-6.00	204.7-171.4
Vegetable lard	2.58	1.20	46.5
Leather products			
Sole leather	4.25	4.00	94.1
Textile products			
Cotton netting	17.00	20.00	117.6
Cotton yarn	7.75	6.00	77.4
Tobacco products			
Cigarettes (rubios) [a]	27.65[b]	12.00	43.4
Miscellaneous products			
Carbon dioxide	1.14	0.05	4.4
Cement	0.10	0.02	20.0
Gun powder[a]	3.68	2.00	54.3
Insecticide DDT	0.80	free	—
Laundry soap	0.85	2.00	235.3
Nails	1.00	0.45	45.0
Sulphuric acid	7.00	0.001	0.01

[a] Import is under quantitative control.

[b] Based on a reported wholesale price of Bs 7.125 per carton of 12 packages and assuming a carton weight of 9 oz.

Source: *Banco Central de Venezuela.*

in large measure on a favorable disposition of the major factors of production, particularly capital, entrepreneurial interest and the availability of skills.

Industrial Promotion Policy

Venezuela has now reached a stage at which opportunities for industrial expansion are greatest in the manufacture of basic and intermediary goods. Many of these goods have so far been imported at prices well below domestic costs. Accordingly, the replacement of such imports by more heavily protected domestic manufacture would increase the cost burden of the consuming industries and presumably raise prices to the final consumer. It is undoubtedly true that the tariff on some products, particularly on those based on steel, is not providing a level of protection required to assist new manufacturing activities in overcoming initial development obstacles. Since many products included in the commercial treaty with the United States fall in this category, the mission believes this treaty should be modified in order to enable the Government to take some additional protective measures. So long as the bolivar maintains its high value, extension of tariff protection will be necessary if the Government's economic diversification program is to be pursued at an active pace. As tariffs on intermediate products are extended and increased, established consumer goods industries may press for further protection. This should provide an opportunity to examine the protection levels on established industries to see if the time has not come to redistribute the short-term advantages of the existing level of protection on consumer goods in favor of new intermediate product industries. In any event, but particularly if the present exchange rate is maintained, tariff policy will have to be supported by a broad range of additional measures. Before considering some of these measures, many of which have already been initiated, we must consider the direction which industrial promotion policy should take.

The Government has so far pursued an industrialization policy, the major aim of which has been to increase the industrial product over the widest range of manufacturing activities possible, and with little regard for the long-term growth prospects peculiar to particular industrial trades. Factors related to the comparative cost advantages of various manufacturing activities, and such questions as whether industry could in due time be able to dispense with protection against foreign competition or could at a later stage participate in the export trade, have played a negligible role in practical policy decisions to promote indus-try. This has not been too serious a matter to date, since the country has so far been at an early stage in development. As established indus-tries gain experience, there is the danger that they will not be under pressure to use this experience to increase efficiency and reduce costs. If additional protection can always be secured simply for the asking, there will be little incentive to organize production and sales in an efficient manner. Moreover, until recently the Government has been taking a relatively passive role in the promotion of manufacturing. As the Government assumes a more active role with respect to new industries, the possibility of unwisely allocating resources increases as it on its own initiative selects industries whose establishment or expan-sion it wishes to encourage by such measures as protection, credit, tech-nical assistance, and tax incentives. The Government must therefore examine more carefully the economic position of individual industries. The mission was unable to make any detailed analysis of the suitability of different industries in terms of the human and physical resources available in Venezuela, nor was the mission able to assign priorities to specific manufacturing activities. The mission takes the view, how-ever, that in the final analysis industrial growth will be self-sustaining only if a substantial segment of the emerging industrial sector, after it has reached some degree of maturity, is able to hold its own against foreign competition, at home as well as abroad. Even though the export of manufactures may only be possible at some future date when a more favorable cost and price level have been established, the long-term objective of promoting such exports must be given considerable weight in present-day industrial policy. In the very long run no sustained growth can be maintained as long as industry is confined exclusively to the narrow limits of the small domestic market. There is still room for a substantial industrial expansion within the confines of the present market but Venezuela has less internal development opportunities as compared, for instance, with those available to a country like Brazil with its considerably larger market. The Government should thus adopt as its basic long-term policy objective the integration on a selected basis of Venezuelan manufacturing industry into the international economy.

We fully understand that it will take time and considerable effort to reorientate an industrialization policy of long standing. Employers and prospective entrepreneurs have to be reconditioned to a more competitive society and to a pattern of earnings which is based on a sustained and vigorous production and sales effort, rather than relying on the easy returns from operating in a highly protected market; labor for its part should realize that its present earnings are probably inflated as expressed in levels of productivity; and the Government should pursue a more flexible protectionist policy through a selective exposure of industry to more external competition, at the same time providing more protection to promote the establishment of new industries. The Government should carefully consider whether new industry so promoted would have favorable long-term growth prospects so that it may dispense at a later stage with excessive protection. We do not suggest a general lowering of tariffs or an indiscriminate abolition of import embargoes; instead, we recommend that the Government keep a watchful eye on the operation of existing industrial trades and expose to a higher degree of foreign competition those industries which have the potential to improve substantially their operational performance. In creating the highest levels of efficiency in industry, there is no substitute for competition. We do not suggest that the Government should leave it completely to the private sector to meet such increased competition; on the contrary, an extensive program of financial and technical assistance should be initiated to rationalize industry. Nor do we suggest that the suggested shift in basic policy should be an abrupt one; the Government should use its discretion as to the timing of the implementation of the recommended policy. But the mission firmly believes that, unless cost and price levels are adjusted so as to reach a wider market at home as well as abroad, Venezuelan industry will in the not-too-distant future have to slow down its growth rate to such an extent that it will cease to make its contribution to a substantial increase in living standards of the people.

Categories of Industries to be Promoted

In selecting industries for promotion and in considering the type of promotional device to be applied, manufacturing might be divided into three categories. The first category would include those industries which have favorable opportunities to engage in the export trade, either now or after some obstacles have been removed. Candidates for this category would be, prima facie, primary iron and steel products, chemicals and fuels processed from petroleum and from petroleum gases, manufactures based on non-metallic minerals, especially when their production requires a fuel-intensive or power-intensive technology, such as glass and refractory clay products and cement, and probably other products as well, such as aluminum reduction and primary aluminum products. With respect to industries in this category, the Government should pursue an aggressive policy of export promotion. Measures to stimulate exports of mineral-based manufactures might include reduction of the royalty on minerals, when used as a raw material or fuel. New enterprises in this category might further be provided tariff or other protection so as to assure them some protection in the domestic market; such protection should be strictly limited, both in magnitude and duration, possibly to a period of about five years, and should be granted only to enable the industry to overcome the inevitable initial diseconomies associated with the establishment of any new enterprise. Other promotional measures might include preference in government credit assistance, tax facilities above those already granted under the recently revised tax law, special immigration facilities for skilled workers, and similar measures to increase the attractiveness of such manufacturing industries. Government efforts in the case of this first category would be concentrated primarily in helping to overcome whatever obstacles exist in getting the industry established. Since the country has some basic cost advantages in producing items in this category, it is to be expected that private enterprise in this category once established will prosper without any considerable government attention in the way of technical assistance. On the other hand, many of the enterprises in this category must be of fairly large size in order to produce economically, must have considerable expertise and experience. It is to be expected that foreign enterprises, or joint Venezuelan and foreign enterprises, will frequently find it easier to meet the necessary qualifications. It is thus particularly important for the development of these first-category industries that the Government maintain a climate favorable to the entry of foreign investment.[10]

The second category would comprise a variety of manufacturing

[10] In view of recent developments in the transportation of liquefied natural gas (methane) and of programs scheduled for other producing areas, the mission urges the Government to foster the use of flared and unassociated gas as the basis for a methane industry in Venezuela. By virtue of its extensive gas resources and relative ease of transport to North America and Western Europe, Venezuela is well placed to take advantage of this new market. Indeed, as far back as 1957 proposals were made to the Government for the establishment of this industry; but the Government had by 1960 made no positive response. The mission believes the Government should welcome the offers of private companies. The potential benefits to the Venezuelan economy are such that the Government should make a clear statement of policy designed to encourage the development of the industry and should then promptly accept those proposals which offer satisfactory prospects in terms of government revenues and export earnings.

activities for which the country has no obvious comparative advantages, but which might over a period of years reduce their costs so that they could compete with foreign-produced manufactures with only moderate protection. We have in mind industries which are in part dependent, and probably will remain dependent for many years to come, on imported supplies and which are likely to cater for the domestic market only since their cost levels, even under favorable conditions, do not allow them to engage in the export trade. Paper and rubber products and some branches of the textile industry (woolens and synthetic fibers) are among those industries in which competitive strength vis-a-vis foreign producers depends essentially on basic improvements in the industrial structure (such as an increase in the unit-size and the development of a more diversified industrial apparatus), and depends even more so on significant improvements in management practices and labor productivity. While a rather high degree of protection might initially be given to such industries, the Government should aim at developing only those manufacturing activities which eventually should be able to serve the domestic market behind a moderate protective tariff, and perhaps after Venezuelan prices are brought more into line with international prices. In the case of second-category industries it will be particularly important to use all of the Government's promotional and supporting measures to bring about greater efficiency. Credit assistance in particular should be given to those enterprises whose management is alert to the need for improving productive efficiency.

In the third category would be placed those industries or enterprises which have little chance of ever being able to compete, even after more favorable cost and price levels have been established. The Government may feel it should protect some of these industries, at least for a time, simply because they or their agricultural suppliers provide employment opportunities in a region of the country where alternative economic activities are few.

There may also be enterprises unable to compete, not because of some basic or natural disadvantage, but because present management is inefficient. Such situations may arise particularly where single enterprises can supply the whole domestic market behind a high tariff wall. The solution in such cases would appear to be to expose the enterprise in question to more competition from abroad or to deny increasing tariff protection to such single-enterprise industries when greater protection is granted to potential domestic suppliers of intermediate products.

The Latin American Common Market

Some of the problems facing Venezuela in the field of international trade might be in part solved by the formation of a Latin American Common Market and Venezuela's adherence to it. A move in this direction was made in February 1960, when the Latin American Free Trade Association was established under the Treaty of Montevideo, with Argentina, Brazil, Chile, Mexico, Paraguay, Peru and Uruguay as signatory states.

Studies made by the United Nations[11] on the advantages of developing closer economic ties within this area indicate that significant and sustained growth in Latin America as a whole will be difficult to achieve so long as the process of economic development is compartmentalized within twenty separate units. The policy of developing industry through import substitution behind heavy protection has some merit with respect to final consumer goods; but such a policy would run into increasing difficulties if attempts were made to extend such policy to a wide range of intermediary goods requiring a high degree of specialized skills and concentrated capital outlays. On the other hand, an extension of the market to areas abroad would increase the industrial development opportunities for those manufacturing activities which previously could not operate because economies of scale would have required too large a unit of production relative to the size of the internal market. Venezuela finds itself in the stage where the production of intermediary goods, rather than final consumer goods, has the best development prospects, and in this connection Venezuela is fortunate in having considerable comparative advantages in all manufacturing based on its rich mineral resources such as petroleum and petroleum gas, iron ore and, possibly, aluminum. It has been calculated that by 1975, Latin America will have a population of nearly 300 million and that the demand for industrial products may be quadrupled provided that some measure of regional integration can be achieved. It is of special interest to Venezuela that the average annual consumption of steel in the region may increase from 6.6 million ingot-tons in 1955/56 to 37.6 million tons by 1975 of which some 32.3 million tons would be supplied through intra-regional trade; that the demand for chemical products may rise from US$2,300 million to over US$8,000 million

[11] *The Latin American Common Market*, United Nations, 1959 (Doc: E/CR.12/531).

during the corresponding period and that by 1975, 201 million tons of petroleum and petroleum derivatives should be required.[12]

The mission is well aware of the formidable obstacles which have to be overcome before Venezuela would be in a position to join any regional grouping to liberalize trade, established in the form of either a free trade association or a common market. However, should such an economic unit become a working reality without Venezuela's participation, it would be difficult to visualize how the country could share in benefits of such growth in consumption of products for which manufacture she is particularly suited. The mission therefore recommends that the Government continue to study carefully the merits of the project, particularly in the light of the long-term development prospects of the country.

AVAILABILITY OF CAPITAL

Capital for Private Enterprise

During the early stages of industrial development in Venezuela, private enterprise was mainly involved in those manufacturing activities which require relatively little capital investment. For example, in 1953 capital investment per establishment averaged only about Bs 100,000. Although some recent industrial growth has taken place through the establishment of larger enterprises requiring relatively large amounts of capital, capital investment per establishment has probably continued to be low in most fields. In the smaller establishments, the required capital is generally provided by the owner himself, sometimes supplemented by funds contributed by family and friends, in which case a small partnership is formed. The limited liability company *(sociedad anonima),* of which the 1953 census recorded 852 (5 percent of the total number of censused enterprises) against nearly 13,500 individually owned undertakings (84 percent of the total), is nearly always of the closed-corporation type, and only a few companies are listed on the Caracas stock exchange.

The financial problems of smaller enterprises are quite different from those of the larger. Most smaller undertakings have little access to the banking facilities of the country. The backward technology and obsolete managerial practices, found in a large proportion of these

[12] *Ibid.,* pp. 71-78.

enterprises, are in part due to the absence of an industrial credit system geared to their peculiar operational requirements. To fill this gap, the Government has been planning a credit program for craft shops and small industrial enterprises; at the time of the mission's visit this program was not yet in operation. As compared with small industry larger enterprises find themselves in a somewhat more favorable position insofar as they have access to two sources of institutional credit, one maintained by private commercial banks, including the government-sponsored *Banco Industrial de Venezuela,* and the other by the government-owned Corporacion Venezolana de Fomento (CVF).

Foreign capital has played a significant role in the country's recent industrialization. By 1958 foreign investors had invested some Bs 450 million, or approximately 15 percent of total investment in industry. Nearly all these undertakings are modern plants and have been established mostly during the postwar years by internationally known firms mostly from the United States acting as parent companies; manufacturing is confined to established product lines which were previously imported, such as car assembling, tires and food and chemical products.

Apart from this visible foreign capital, an undetermined amount of capital has been accumulated and invested in manufacturing industries by immigrants who entered the country during the 1950's, many of whom are now naturalized citizens. Estimates as to the exact contribution made by the immigrant group to the industrialization vary widely, but the mission has the impression that this group is playing a significant entrepreneurial role in the development of the country's manufacturing industry. There are estimates that not less than one-third of the 400 larger enterprises has been established by, or on the initiative of, and in cooperation with, immigrant groups. Immigrants have also been active in certain small industrial activities such as shoe manufacture, mechanical repair and furniture shops which have received much impetus from the influx of skilled immigrant artisans in recent years. Venezuelan entrepreneurship and capital, traditionally bound to landed property, showed until recently an understandable preference for commerce and the building trade with its high and safe earnings. The catalytic effect of the immigrant groups has done much to channel national initiative, funds and effort into the manufacturing sector.

A major share of the required capital has its origin in the considerable profits made in all economic activities in the country. Accurate data concerning profit levels are not available, but the impression exists that profit rates in manufacturing as elsewhere are high and that a substantial share of these profits is being ploughed back to enlarge and modernize plant and equipment and to establish new undertakings.

Government Financial Support

Until recently, negligible financial assistance has been rendered by the Government to the establishment and expansion of private manufacturing enterprises: from its inception in 1956 to December 1957, the CVF had disbursed a total of some Bs 74.4 million in credits to the private sector,[13] or on an average only Bs 6 million annually. In early 1958, however, the Government, in its desire to stimulate industrial growth, made considerably larger amounts available for lending to the private sector: between March 1958 and November 1959, loans totaling Bs 154.1 million were granted by the CVF to over 219 enterprises;[14] computed on an annual basis, this would amount to about Bs 90 million a year.

From 1953 to 1959, the total capital stock in industry increased from an estimated Bs 2.0 billion to Bs 3.7 billion in all manufacturing enterprises. These figures should be regarded with great caution and are only here presented to indicate the order of magnitude involved. On the basis of these figures, it may be calculated that annual net investment amounted to some Bs 300 million during the period under review. In order to achieve a 10 percent annual rate of growth of manufacturing in the years ahead, an annual net capital investment of at least Bs 400 million, excluding the requirements for government enterprises discussed below, may be required.

It is difficult to determine how much of this Bs 400 million a year should be supplied by the Government. As reflected in the high profit expectations of entrepreneurs, the price of venture capital in Venezuela is extremely high and may amount to an annual return of more than 30 percent of invested equity capital. The provision of credit at concessional rates of interest and on an expanded scale should therefore contribute to a lowering of capital cost in industry. Customary financial arrangements in the private sector do not favor the flow of sizeable amounts of equity capital to manufacturing industry over which the investor has no day-to-day control. Furthermore, the small size of the great majority of the manufacturing units renders the development of an institutional investment pattern extremely difficult. The banking law prohibits the extension of credits for a period exceeding 24 months or discounting and rediscounting for more than one year, and this renders the granting of medium- and long-term credit impossible. More-

[13] *Memoria, 1958-1959,* Corporacion Venezolana de Fomento, p. 70; *Evolucion de los Gastos del Gobierno Nacional, 1954/55-1958/59,* Ministerio de Hacienda, p. 99.
[14] Data supplied by the CVF to the mission.

over, the law does not provide for credit activities with movable property as collateral, such as equipment and inventories (in which a major part of the assets of an industrial undertaking are tied up), and this further restricts the establishment of closer financial ties between the banking system and industry. Although the mission recommends that the banking law be revised in such a way as to facilitate the development of private industrial banking facilities, it will undoubtedly take time before an adequate financial framework will have been developed which can satisfactorily sustain industrial growth. There is thus a noticeable gap in the financial structure of the country, insofar as no institution exists to support deserving industries in their requirements for long-term capital, and it is this gap which the CVF has been trying to close.

In large part as a result of CVF activity, Venezuelan industrial development shows a great dynamism and the mission was, at the time of its visit, much impressed by the considerable activity displayed by established and newly organized manufacturing firms to expand production. An indication of such activity is reflected in the data collected during the manpower survey conducted by the Ministry of Labor in the latter part of 1959: nearly 50 percent of factory owners interviewed (employing over 50 workers per establishment) stated their intention to increase production through the employment of more workers, and a little over 10 percent announced that they were in the actual process of expanding manufacturing capacity through the purchase of new equipment. A government policy which aims at vigorous growth of the manufacturing sector should continue to be supported by a liberal investment policy so that capital will not become a major limiting factor in industrial growth. We have, moreover, suggested a policy whereby private enterprises, in appropriate instances, should be subjected to more competition than is at present the case and such a policy might be implemented by helping manufacturing enterprises so affected to rationalize their operations and to decrease manufacturing costs. Also, the operation of industry under more competitive conditions will undoubtedly reduce the present high profit rates, and as such will decrease the amounts available for reinvestment in industry. Therefore, the mission is inclined to suggest that for the next few years some Bs 110 million should be made available annually by the Government for investment in the private manufacturing sector. This amount is mentioned here as a target figure and should be readjusted up or downwards after periodic assessments as to the actual capital needs to maintain the required growth rate in the private manufacturing sector.

CVF Industrial Credits

The CVF might effectively utilize about Bs 100 million per year, assuming that the CVF continues to apply its funds mainly to medium- and long-term credits.[15] Until recently the funds were utilized mainly to grant long-term credits with a maximum duration of ten years;[16] there has however been a tendency for short-term credits to increase because of the general credit tightness. CVF sets a minimum of Bs 25,000 to its individual loans which carry a concessional rate of interest of 6 percent. CVF credit policy gives preference to enterprises which are receiving special protection through tariffs or otherwise, and to those manufacturing activities which use a high proportion of domestic raw materials and which operate with a labor-intensive, rather than a capital-intensive, technology. Borrowing firms are normally required to match each loan with an equivalent investment of their own, but from information made available to the mission it would appear that this rule has not been stringently applied. CVF has in the main followed in this period of expansion a conservative loan policy: only a little over one-third of the total loan applications amounting to Bs 445.7 million submitted during the period March 1958 to November 1959 was finally approved for disbursement; moreover, much more credit seems to have been provided to finance the expansion of existing enterprises than for the purpose of establishing new undertakings. CVF has a small staff of specialists to process the loan applications and to render technical assistance to the enterprises financed by the corporation. A weak point in its loan arrangements is that all loan applications have to be processed in Caracas, involving delays and expenses for the enterprises located in the interior, particularly for the smaller undertakings.

In the mission's view, perhaps the time has come to strengthen the loan activities of the CVF by organizing these activities in a separate institution, for instance as an industrial development bank. The objective would be to activate private entrepreneurship, savings and skills to profitable investment in private manufacturing. As such, government loan activities should be active rather than passive and seek out invest-

[15] Since the CVF credits revolve, gross lending would exceed Bs 100 million per year.

[16] According to a random sample survey prepared by the CVF, which covered loans to the amount of Bs 16.6 million disbursed during the period of March 1958 to November 1959, about 50 percent of the loans were designed to purchase equipment, one-third to erect factory buildings and approximately 10 percent for the purchase of land.

ment opportunities, attract private funds (for instance, from insurance companies) through the issuance of its own securities properly guaranteed as to repayment of principal and interest by the Government, underwrite long-term loans by private banks (after suitable changes have been made in the banking law), and take other measures to promote the establishment of closer relations between banking and industry in the private sector.

While it would probably be possible to reorient the CVF in the direction visualized, the establishment of a separate institution or the reorganization of the *Banco Industrial de Venezuela* in such a manner might also be actively considered. The International Bank for Reconstruction and Development has considerable experience in the establishment and operation of industrial development banks, and the Government might wish to explore this field further with the Bank.

Small Industry Credit Program

A credit program for craft shops and small industrial enterprises was promulgated by Decree No. 152 in October 1959. At the time of the mission's visit, the program was not yet in operation; the mission, however, understands that the program will be administered, under guidance and supervision of the Ministry of Development, by loan committees appointed for each State in the Republic; further, that it is intended to implement the loan program separately and not in association with the credit scheme for large industrial undertakings, as executed under the auspices of the CVF. An amount of Bs 20 million a year was being considered by the Venezuelan Government for the small industry credit program; credits would be granted to a maximum amount of Bs 25,000 a loan, would bear an interest rate of 6 percent and would have a duration of not more than five years.

There are considerable operational and other differences between the financing of small and larger enterprises, which justify separate institutional arrangements through which loan activities can be channeled. One of the most important relates to the matter of technical assistance. In terms of increasing productivity, the development of small manufacturing industry depends to a large extent on the introduction of better tools and machinery and on the dissemination of skills in handling such equipment effectively. Therefore, any loan program to small enterprises should be supplemented by technical assistance to inform the small plant owner how to use the loan to his best advantage; only in this way can waste in the supply of capital to this sector be avoided. As a matter of fact, a small industrial credit program based on an installment-buying program for equipment, is being successfully implemented in countries, such as India, where the industrial development problem partly relates to the question of how effectively and speedily to modernize the small manufacturing sector.

Since technical assistance and small industrial credit activities should be closely linked together to become really effective, the ability to provide such technical assistance becomes a limiting factor in the amount of loans which can usefully be extended. Specialist personnel trained in small industrial extension work are virtually nonexistent in Venezuela. Even if each specific loan granted were as high as the established credit ceiling of Bs 25,000, a total of 800 loans would nevertheless have to be processed annually if the proposed Bs 20 million were to be fully allocated. In fact, the number of loans to be processed would exceed this figure. We are doubtful as to whether the Government is at this stage equipped to handle such an extensive credit scheme as expressed in number of enterprises to be served, and we therefore suggest a reduction in the amount to be made available for the period 1960/61-1963/64 to about Bs 10 million annually or Bs 40 million for the four-year period. The Government should meanwhile take appropriate action to initiate a training program to build up the required industrial extension service.

While separate administrations of credit schemes for small and for larger enterprises are indicated, care should be taken to maintain close coordination between the two programs. Many small undertakings are expanding, and should be encouraged so to expand, into larger units. Since small manufacturing firms, notwithstanding a high degree of profitability, have little opportunity to turn to the private banking system for credit financing, the small industry loan program should particularly try to identify small industries with favorable growth opportunities and have them transferred for further servicing to the financing agency for larger enterprises.

Industrial Estates

A credit program geared to the particular requirements of small plants might be usefully associated with schemes to establish industrial estates. This is an industrial development device which is increasingly applied in both developed and underdeveloped countries to promote the industrial sector. It can also be used in Venezuela as an aid to the policy of a geographical redistribution of industry. Such estates are meant to provide factory accommodations at reasonable rentals, together with a variety of joint facilities and services (such as for maintenance and repair of equipment, water, power, fuel and sewerage, storage and joint manufacture) which a single small enterprise could not afford to provide. These estates have the additional advantage in that they promote the transfer of existing plants from overcrowded city centers, and experience shows that such transfers are generally accompanied by the installation of new and modern equipment; they create, moreover, conditions which are conducive to the improvement of output and quality, because they provide the small plant manager and his workers with a more suitable working environment.

The mission found ample evidence of the establishment, through private initiative, of land development schemes for the location of larger industrial plants, particularly around the Federal District and in the Lake Valencia area. But no such schemes have so far been established with the special purpose of promoting small plants, and the Government might consider entering this particular field of promotional assistance by initiating industrial estates in, possibly, Barquisimeto, Puerto Ordaz, and the Barcelona/Puerto La Cruz with their favorable growth opportunities for smaller manufacturing firms.

Foreign Capital

Venezuela is fortunate that it has been able to attract the participation of foreign investors in its industrial development process. Foreign capital has an important role to play in the industrial development of the country, both in terms of capital outlays and of technical know-how and operational and managerial skills, and a close cooperation between Venezuela and the advanced industrial nations is important for sound industrial progress. There are so far no signs of a diminishing interest of foreign investors in manufacturing industry, and it would therefore appear that the established policy of maintaining a favorable investment climate which guarantees equal and fair treatment of domestic and foreign investors alike gives the best assurance that foreign capital will continue to be attracted to Venezuela.

The Income Tax Law

In December 1958 the income tax law was amended so as to provide more favorable conditions for the reinvestment of capital in certain types of business firms, including manufacturing enterprises which are meeting certain requirements.[17] Reductions in the income tax schedule are granted to taxpayers in all brackets for income reinvested in manufacturing, and special rate reductions apply to those in the income brackets of Bs 14 million and over. The mission welcomes this effort to facilitate industrial investment, although it should be noted that, with the generally low rate of income tax applicable to most industrial enterprises, reinvestment allowances cannot be expected to have a very significant effect on industrial development.

GOVERNMENT INDUSTRIAL ENTERPRISES

During recent years, the Venezuelan Government has made large investments in nationally owned industrial enterprises. These include iron and steel, chemicals, ship repairing and maintenance, and sugar refining. Expenditures on most of these enterprises have been greater than would normally be anticipated. In some cases substantial further capital investment is required to complete original plants.

Iron and Steel Plant

In 1955 the Government signed a contract with an Italian firm for the construction of an iron and steel plant near Puerto Ordaz, southwest of the junction of the Orinoco and Caroni rivers. The contract, as subsequently amended, calls for a plant of 750,000 metric ingot-tons capacity to provide 600,000 tons of finished products. Nearly 50 percent of production was to be seamless steel tubes, the remaining capacity to provide a variety of products including rails, structural steel, reinforcing bars, and wire. The contract provided for the construction of certain facilities which would enable the plant capacity to be increased at a later date to 1,200,000 ingot-tons at a relatively low additional expenditure. It was also contemplated that a strip mill might be added later on. The control of the plant has been vested in the Iron and Steel Institute which itself is under the general responsibility of the Ministry of Development.

The seamless tube mill was practically complete at the time of the mission's visit, although it was not in operation by mid-1960. Progress

[17] Carl S. Shoup and Assoc., *The Fiscal System of Venezuela*, Baltimore, 1959, pp. 468-471.

in the construction of the rest of the steel plant has been slow: it will not be completed until late 1961 or some time in 1962. This is partially due to the renegotiation of certain contractual matters with the builder and partly to alterations made from time to time in government plans. The Government is now actively considering an increase in the plant's ingot capacity, possible changes in steel-making processes, and also the construction of a strip mill. The timing and exact nature of these possible modifications of plans are yet to be determined.

The mission has not made a detailed analysis of the plant layout nor of the modifications under consideration; neither has it conducted a market survey to determine the range of products appropriate for the plant. It has, however, satisfied itself that the construction of a steel plant in the Puerto Ordaz region is a justified undertaking and, if properly managed, it can be an economically sound one.

Natural Resources. From the viewpoint of raw materials, Venezuela has important natural advantages for establishing and operating an iron and steel industry. Good quality iron ore can be obtained from near the plant site at reasonable prices. Most of the other steel-making components are also available in the country, although it has not as yet been proved that the coal from the Naricual mine is satisfactory for coking purposes. If not, it may be necessary to import coke or else employ one of the new processes based on natural gas, which is plentiful. The mission recommends the Government withhold further action in developing the coal mine until it has obtained the advice of a competent consulting firm, both as to the suitability and cost of the Naricual coal and as to the alternative possibilities of using coal or natural gas for reduction purposes. The new hydroelectric plant at Macagua can provide cheap power to the plant and the latter's situation on the Orinoco River gives it easy access to the needed cooling water, as well as to coastal and ocean shipping. It will be necessary to arrange for the employment of a substantial number of technical personnel from abroad.

Marketing. The import of iron and steel products into Venezuela has grown steadily from a total of 237,000 tons in 1950 to just over 800,000 tons in 1958. The year 1957 was exceptional, for the total in that year was nearly 1.5 million tons. Of the 1958 total, 105,000 tons represented sheet and strip material. The quantity of steel tubes imported in 1958 was 374,000 metric tons, valued at approximately Bs 1,150 per metric ton (f.o.b.). The importation of steel tubes for the petroleum industry in 1958 is estimated at 242,000 metric tons, of which

212,000 metric tons were seamless. There is therefore, particularly in view of the probable decline in the rate of expansion of the petroleum industry (see Chapter 8) , some question as to whether the quantity of seamless tubes needed in Venezuela will be sufficient to keep the plant working at full production, at least during the initial years of operation.

Only one plant exists in Venezuela for manufacture of steel products. This plant, which uses steel scrap, has a reputed capacity of 65,000-70,000 tons of finished products a year, mainly of reinforcing bars. Plans are under way to expand capacity to more than 90,000 tons. During 1959, 150,000 tons of reinforcing bars were imported, and the Institute considers that at this level there will be no conflict between the sale of the output of its plant working to capacity and that of the privately owned company.

The original plans for the mill provided for the production of some 60,000 tons of steel rails and plates and girders for railroads. If the Government accepts the recommendations of the mission not to proceed with railroad expansion, there will be no domestic market for the rails. We understand from officials of the Institute that the rail-making facilities can easily be converted to other products and that the market requirements of Venezuela for all products that can be made in the plant are considerably greater than the originally planned capacity of 600,000 tons of products. The mission has no reason to question this conclusion.

The Institute also estimates that the prices at which the plant can profitably market its products will be no higher than the prices of imported products. The mission believes that Venezuela's natural advantages can make this possible, provided that the investment in the plant is appraised at a realistic figure, that adequate numbers of supervising personnel and skilled workers are employed and that management is first-class. Moreover, under such circumstances, it seems quite possible that Venezuela may eventually be in a favorable position to seek to establish export markets for steel and steel products.

Capital Investment. The amount of capital investment in the plant —made and to be made—is not entirely clear. Certain clauses of the original contract are still being discussed between the Government and the contractor and, in addition, the Government has under consideration the above-mentioned possible plant modifications. However, it appears that the contracted cost of the 750,000 ingot-ton plant was Bs 1,150 million, subject to an escalator clause which could increase that cost by as much as Bs 140 million. The Government expects to bring about some reduction in the cost contemplated in the original contract and it has expressed the hope that, through this reduction, it will be possible to cover the cost of a sheet and strip mill. According to the Government, payments would total Bs 534 million. The Government has also stated that, with an additional investment of about Bs 60 million, it will be possible to introduce new steel-making techniques which would permit a substantial increase in capacity.

The mission does not have sufficient data on which to base a judgment as to the accuracy of the Government's estimates and expectations in this regard. It does believe, however, that the figure for future expenditures is underestimated in terms of total capital requirements yet to be met. Apparently the estimate does not include tools, spare parts, and stores, which, for a plant of this type, might amount to some Bs 100 million, part at least of which should be considered as capital cost. Nor is adequate provision made for working capital and starting-up losses. The Institute apparently did not have in mind any specific amounts for the latter purposes. In the absence of more precise information from the Government as to the dates on which operations will commence, the sales prices to be asked and credit terms likely to be given to purchasers, it is impossible to make more than very rough estimates. On the assumption that the seamless tube plant commences operations at the beginning of 1961 but does not reach full capacity until the end of 1965, and on the assumption that the remainder of the plant goes into operation at the begininng of 1962 and can be brought to full capacity by the end of 1965, some Bs 70 to Bs 100 million may have to be set aside as working capital during the four-year program period.

When a new iron and steel plant is put into operation, the production costs are of necessity higher than they will be when the plant has settled down to work at capacity. If the Government adheres to its intention to sell its products at the point of consumption at prices no higher than those now paid by the consumers, this may lead to considerable losses. Until the Institute establishes its own reckoning for these losses, it would be well to provide cover for Bs 60 to Bs 70 million. The foregoing suggests that the Government may have to provide investment funds for the iron and steel plant of more than Bs 800 million during the four years 1960/61-1963/64.

Management and Labor. The Venezuelan project faces a similar problem to that in most countries undertaking to build and operate an integrated iron and steel plant for the first time. The final planning of such a plant with respect to its market, its raw materials, processes and coordination of operations, as well as the structure of its organiza-

tion, requires the most experienced and capable technical and administrative skill. These requirements are not met by relying on the recommendations of interested supplying contractors. The mission urges
the Government to engage the services of a competent firm, having no
connection with supplying contractors, and to have such a firm review
all phases of the project—from raw materials through to markets—and
make recommendations thereon, including a realistic cash forecast and
projection of working capital requirements during the first five years
of operation. Pending such a review, the mission suggests that no plant
expansion be undertaken.

No important steel operation can be launched satisfactorily if it does
not have the benefit of skilled administration in its early days. The first
operation of any unit of a steel plant is faced with starting-up difficulties with resultant cash losses. Difficulties are magnified when the plant
has to make a variety of products and particularly when the plant is
in a country in which there is no previous operating experience in steel.
For these reasons, the mission recommends further that every effort
be made to contract with the same firm to continue to work with the
Institute in starting up and running the plant, taking full authority
and responsibility for financial control, administration work and mechanical matters.

In addition to arrangements to ensure adequate management, the
mission wishes to stress the importance of providing adequate and efficient supervisory personnel and skilled workers. The magnitude of
this problem cannot be overemphasized. Venezuela, a country without
experience in large-scale steel-making, is almost totally lacking in competent supervisory personnel. This situation is aggravated by the fact
that there is a great scarcity of skilled workers in the country available
for ready training. While the mission is aware of the considerable effort
that is being made by the Institute to have workers trained both at
home and abroad, it is convinced that this will go only a short way
toward finding a solution. It is essential that considerable numbers of
trained personnel be brought in from other countries and that arrangements be made to keep them on the job for periods ranging upwards
from two years, until Venezuelans can be properly trained. At the same
time, increased numbers of Venezuelans should be sent abroad to work
in foreign plants for periods of from one to two years.

The mission recognizes that in all countries establishing an integrated steel plant for the first time there is a tendency to minimize the
difficulties and to feel that local people, even though they may not have
adequate experience, should be able to take care of the operation and
management from the beginning, with only selected assistance from

specialists on certain technical aspects. The mission hopes that Venezuela will judge this problem realistically in this regard. The stakes are very high. Not only will a successful operation reflect itself in national prestige and in the pride of all Venezuelans, but it will have a most important bearing on the national budget.

The Petrochemical Project

The petrochemical project consists of several enterprises, not necessarily related. At its present stage of development, only a small section of the whole can be properly designated as characteristic of the petrochemical industry. Included in the project are an oil refinery, several chemical plants and a system of pipelines for the transmission of natural gas. All have been under the control of the Venezuelan Institute of Petrochemicals (IVP), an autonomous government agency, although the refinery and pipelines are in the process of being transferred to the newly created Venezuelan Petroleum Corporation.

The Government has indicated that it has no intention of undertaking any expansion of the petrochemical project during the four-year period of the Plan. The Government has also expressed the view that the development of the Venezuelan petrochemical industry beyond the range of the Institute's present project should be through the establishment of new plants by private initiative, with or without state participation. The mission strongly supports these views. It considers that Venezuela is in a favorable position for the production of certain selected petrochemicals, but believes that, because of the great amount of research and technical background involved in the industry and because of its high capital costs, efforts should be made to interest private foreign capital.

Venezuela would appear to have many important natural advantages for producing petrochemical products. The plentiful and low-cost supply of heavy oil, refinery by-products and the associated and nonassociated natural gas provide raw materials such as ethylene, butylene and propylene in an abundance unusual in other refinery regions. Since some of these petrochemical raw materials represent as much as 60 percent of the end-product cost, this natural advantage enjoyed by Venezuela should more than offset some of the disadvantages of producing selected petrochemical products in the country. While the mission sees little prospect for the immediate establishment of an integrated petrochemical industry using all by-products of natural gas and oil refining, there are many products requiring relatively small capital investment for which market prospects seem excellent not only in Venezuela but in Latin America as a whole. Some of the chemicals and products which appear to be most promising are urea-formaldehyde, synthetic rubber, polyvinyl-chloride, detergents, and polypropylene. It is reported that a plant for the production of carbon black is being constructed.

The mission is convinced that if the Government adopts an active promotional policy to interest private investors in the petrochemical field, considerable progress could be made in this area in the near future. In the past there has been considerable private interest in the production of petrochemical products, but the Government has been reluctant to define the role of the private sector in this area. Now that the Government has apparently decided to complete the facilities already being established by the IVP, but not to initiate new works, it should be possible to open up this field for private investment. Unless this is done quickly, Venezuela may lose the opportunity to gain a foothold in other Latin American markets.

The Chemical Plants

The chemical plants are now under construction at Moron, situated on the coast near Puerto Cabello about 170 kilometers from Caracas. They are the first stage of what was intended to be a fully integrated chemical plant—to provide caustic soda and chlorine, fertilizers, explosives and insecticides, organic chemicals and particularly the organic chemicals derived from petroleum and natural gas. Their location was decided on several years ago and the construction contract was made before the present Government came into power. What is being presently established at Moron as the first stage are the caustic soda and chlorine plant, a group of fertilizer plants and the associated plants. These are plants for making ammonia, sulphuric acid, nitric acid and phosphoric acid, and a plant for mixing fertilizers. The main fertilizer plants are ammonium nitrate, ammonium sulphate, calcium superphosphate and triple superphosphate and urea.

The caustic soda/chlorine plant has been completed and is in production. It has a capacity for 11,200 metric tons of caustic soda and 10,000 tons of chlorine, but does not yet operate at capacity. The total reputed capacity of the fertilizer factory is around 150,000 metric tons a year. The capacities of the individual plants added together are much higher. The limiting factors are the capacities of the ammonia and sulphuric acid plants. For example, if the ammonium sulphate plant is worked at full capacity, then there will not be enough ammonia to keep the other ammonia-using plants working at full capacity. The plants in the fertilizer group were about two-thirds completed at the end of 1959. The sulphuric acid plant, using pyrites, was scheduled to be ready in mid-1960, and production of phosphoric acid and superphosphate was scheduled to start at the same time. The other plants which require ammonia are expected to be completed and to come into production by the middle of 1961. The plant for mixing fertilizers has been completed and is in production, using imported raw materials pending the completion of the other plant units. It has an annual capacity of about 70,000 tons, and it is estimated that at the beginning of 1960 it was operating at about 22 percent of capacity.

Market. There is a good market within Venezuela for the full 11,200 tons of caustic soda, but there is at present not sufficient demand for the 10,000 tons of chlorine which, from the nature of the process, must be produced at the same time. As a consequence, the chlorine accumulates and plant operations have to be stopped until the disposal of the chlorine is arranged. Strenuous efforts are being made to find markets for the chlorine. The Institute estimates that the plant will be able to operate at 70 percent of capacity before the end of 1960. The mission believes that this can be accomplished if the marketing of chlorine and the associated chlorine products that can be made at Moron is pushed vigorously. The mission also believes that this plant could be run at a profit, taking into account all the usual charges, and could supply caustic soda (on which there is now a high tariff) and chlorine at prices below those at which these products are now sold in Venezuela, provided that the capital spent on the plant and its associated services is written down to a real value and provided also that the plant is well managed.

In 1948, 5,100 tons of natural and synthetic fertilizers were imported into Venezuela. By 1958, the quantity imported was nearly 50,000 tons and the value was Bs 10.4 million. This quantity is about a third of anticipated Moron production. By the time the full range of fertilizer plants is in production, the Institute expects that Venezuelan agriculture will absorb about half of its capacity. In the hope of further increasing usage, the Government is carrying out a program to demonstrate the benefits that follow the use of fertilizers. In addition, it is likely that an added incentive, by way of subsidy, will be needed if the full production is to be used. The best way of applying this incentive should be studied now. At this stage it is difficult to judge what the prospects are of getting Venezuelan farmers to take up the full production of the plant. However, it is the mission's view that, with such a subsidy program as that discussed in Chapter 9, the greater part of the production can be used to the benefit of Venezuelan agriculture. The mission sees little, if any, hope of Venezuela being able to export fertilizer. There is already considerable excess capacity in other parts of the world resulting in sales at very low prices—substantially below those at which Venezuela could compete profitably.

The Institute states that the manufacture of fertilizer and associated products at Moron can be profitable without causing an increase in internal prices. Whether this is so depends on a number of as yet undetermined factors. Among these are: the ability of the domestic market to absorb enough production to allow the plants to run near capacity; the manner in which the subsidy is handled; the extent to which the investment in plant is written down to a realistic value; and the provision of adequate supervisory personnel and management.

Capital Investment. In 1958, the new Venezuelan Government found that there was a great deal of disentangling to be done in the allocation of expenditures among the several parts of the petrochemical project before the exact value of the fixed assets could be established. This work was well under way during the mission's visit. Although it was not possible to state precise amounts by mid-1960, we estimate that, after taking into consideration a fair share of the expenditures on services and facilities used in common with the oil refinery, the investment in the chemical plants (i.e., the caustic soda/chlorine and fertilizer plants) will amount to about Bs 600 million when completed. This amount is far above the expenditure that should be required—probably three or four times higher—to provide plants of their capacity in Venezuela. Now that the allocation of expenditures is well along, the next step for the Government is to revalue the plants and equipment to determine the realistic position. When this is done, the mission assumes that the Institute will put the excess expenditures in a Loss Account so as to enable the organization to proceed with production without being burdened with the excessive initial outlay. Most of the expenditures for plant construction and equipment have already been made, and it is estimated by the Government that the remaining capital payments during the four-year period will not amount to more than about Bs 60 million. However, the mission believes that additional funds will have to be provided for working capital and to cover starting-up losses. The needed working capital will be rather high, as the main product —fertilizers—is seasonal and will probably require holding several months' stock. Making allowances for replacements of certain plant

items and for spares, for current expenses, including stocks of raw
materials and finished products, and for credit, about Bs 50 million will
probably be required (if the plant works at full capacity) spread over
the four years 1960/61-1963/64. Starting-up losses are more difficult
to assess since these depend on the price at which the products are to
be sold. If the Institute adheres to its intention that Moron products
will be supplied at the point of consumption at no higher prices than
the imported products, and if the costs carry the amortization and
interest only on the real value of expenditure at Moron, then considerable losses will be suffered during the starting-up years. Until the
Institute draws up its own projection of these losses, the mission recommends that a sum of Bs 20 million be provided to cover starting-up
losses over the next four years in about equal annual increments. The
mission thus calculates that about Bs 130 million will be needed for
additional investment in the chemical plants during 1960/61-1963/64.

Management and Labor. While the project at Moron is not of the
complexity associated with the integrated range of organic products
that can be made from petroleum, it is nevertheless highly specialized
and requires personnel with much experience in the chemical industry.
The final planning of the plant, the balancing of operations and production, so as to prevent the rather chaotic conditions that can prevail
otherwise, need a high level of technical experience and skill. The
requirements are not met by relying on supply contractors; the need
is for the services of a competent firm who have specialized in the
industry and who have no interest in any firm supplying equipment
and plant. The mission therefore recommends that a firm of the highest
competence be hired as soon as possible to examine all aspects of the
project—raw materials, processes and equipment, specifications for
products, and especially requirements of the market. It should also establish requirements of working capital and the capital needed to cover
starting-up losses.

The mission recommends further that, in selecting the firm, an effort
be made to engage one that can also undertake technical and administrative responsibility when starting up the plant. While the mission
is aware of the efforts that have been made by the Institute to select
and train personnel, it recommends that the firm undertaking the technical and administration contract should provide additional training
at all levels that it considers desirable for running of the plants. The
training needed depends on the arrangements that have been made
with the firm of contractors that are providing the equipment and
plant, regarding the handing over of each completed manufacturing

unit. The mission is not convinced that the responsibilities were clearly defined in the contract. It is partly for this reason that it is desirable that whatever firm is now hired should be employed as soon as possible and thereby have an opportunity of helping in training personnel before the plants are completed. It would be the responsibility of this firm to see that the training of personnel in technical and administrative matters is such that Venezuelans could undertake these functions at an early date. In other words, the measure of the firm's effectiveness and success is the speed with which it does itself out of the job. In achieving these ends, it may be desirable to introduce some key workers; this is a responsibility which should be left in the hands of the firm.

The Refinery

The refinery in operation at Moron, which shares certain facilities and services with the chemical plants, is capable of handling about 2,000 barrels of petroleum a day. This small unit is in the nature of an experimental and pilot plant. The cost of running it has been high and, although its products are saleable, it is difficult to operate such a small unit at a profit. In June 1959, losses were stated to be running at the rate of Bs 270,000 a month. It was the view of the Institute that by the beginning of 1960 it would be possible to operate the refinery without loss. However, it was not clear to the mission what part of the total capital expenditure at Moron had been ascribed to this project. The Government had indicated that it does not plan any further investment in this refinery. The mission strongly supports that decision.

The Gas Pipelines

There are several hundred miles of pipelines for transporting natural gas in Venezuela. A portion of them are privately owned, but the greater part have been constructed and are owned by the Government. The privately owned lines are mainly for supplying gas to refineries and associated requirements of the petroleum industry, although there are exceptions such as the arrangements by which oil companies supply gas for domestic consumption at Maracaibo and for thermal electric plants near Caracas. Gas for cooking is used in many cities, but is distributed in cylinders.

The government-owned gas pipe system is intended to supply gas for both domestic and industrial purposes. The total investment projected for the Government's main line system was Bs 224 million, of which it was expected that about Bs 155 million would have been spent by the end of June 1960. As of that time, lines had been completed from Guacara to Moron, from Anaco to Caracas, and from Caracas to Valencia. Work was well along on completion of a line from Casigua to La Fria. The original plan envisaging a line from Valencia via Barquisimeto to Lagunillas on Lake Maracaibo is being held in abeyance, pending further study.

The benefits to be obtained from the sale of natural gas by means of the pipeline system will depend to a great extent on the success of the distribution network. Apparently, little has been done toward establishing networks for domestic distribution in Venezuela's cities—and it is not yet agreed to whom the franchises will be granted. The mission strongly supports the government action in temporarily postponing further main line construction, and recommends that a market survey be undertaken promptly in each of the large cities to find out the likely number of customers. Whether the distribution systems should be owned and managed by the national government, or by municipal authorities as in the case of Maracaibo, or by private investors, or by a combination of these, is a matter that should be settled by the time the market survey is available.

Dry Dock and Shipyard

For many years there has been a small shipyard at Puerto Cabello where a modest amount of overhaul and repair work was done. In 1955 construction was started on a new dry dock (under the direction of the *Instituto Autonomo Diques y Astilleros Nacional,* Puerto Cabello) as part of an ambitious expansion program. The preliminary work involved an expenditure of Bs 140 million and had been completed at the time of the mission's visit. The Institute next proposes to complete the new dry dock and the needed engineering shops, at a cost estimated by the Institute of an additional Bs 110 million. This would be followed by the construction of a second dry dock for which an expenditure of Bs 110 million is estimated by the Institute. Finally, officials of the Institute believe that by the time the second dry dock has been completed, another dock will be needed capable of overhauling the largest size tankers of 60,000 tons; no estimate of the probable cost of this third dock was put forward.

The Institute claims that, when the first dry dock is completed, the dock and engineering shops can be fully occupied in repairing Venezuelan flag ships of which there are currently 43, distributed as follows:

Gross Tons	Number of Ships
200 to 1,000	11
1,001 to 2,000	—
2,001 to 20,000	26
20,000 and up	6
Total	43

The Institute estimates the yearly earnings of the yard, after completion of the first dry dock, at Bs 39 million. This includes receipts of Bs 17 million, representing the average annual expenditure on the Venezuelan Navy. The annual operating costs are also placed at about Bs 39 million. In making its operating cost estimates, the Institute has put a value of Bs 60 million on the assets already provided, and has allowed 30 years for its amortization and reckoned the capital free of interest. It has assumed the completion of the first dry dock would be financed through a 30-year loan at 5 percent interest. The annual charges for both items were estimated at Bs 8.6 million, leaving about Bs 30 million for other operating costs. The mission does not consider that the operating cost and revenue estimates are very solid. Moreover, it believes that the estimated capital expenditure of Bs 110 million for the completion of the first dry dock is much higher than need be.

The mission suggests that the Government continue its efforts to attract a company experienced in ship repairs and maintenance to take an interest in the enterprise. Some negotiations have been undertaken to this end, and there have been indications that an established company may be prepared to come in and take over part of the investment. In this way, experienced shipyard management could be provided which could bring forward at scheduled intervals Venezuelans who had gained their experience in their own yard. At the same time, the speed at which the yard could be brought to work at full capacity would probably be improved. If the effort to bring about private participation in the enterprise fails, the mission recommends that, before additional funds are invested in this project, the Government employ a firm of consultants experienced in shipyard work to review the entire project and to appraise the need for further investment in the light of prospective use, operating costs and revenues.

Sugar Industry

In 1948, 50,000 tons of sugar were imported into Venezuela. By 1955 this was reduced to 1,700 tons, mainly through the effectiveness of the National Plan for sugar fostered by the *Corporacion Venezolana de Fomento* (CVF). The Corporacion gave credit to sugar cane producers to encourage improvement in cultivation, gave loans to expand existing sugar refining plants, and erected sugar refining plants under its own control. Up to date the total investment made by the Corporacion amounts to about Bs 300 million. At the same time, private enterprise increased its investment in the industry. Capacity is now about 260,000 tons a year, whereas consumption of refined sugar is expected to be about 220,000 tons in 1960. The claim of the industry is that, after a trying period due to lack of coordination between production and consumption, expectations for the future are favorable. Recent studies are reported to show that for a relatively small capital investment, the capacity for production of refined sugar can be brought up to 300,000 tons a year, which should satisfy Venezuela's needs until 1965.

The Corporacion has played its full part in this development. It has helped to establish the *Distribudora Venezolana de Azucares,* which keeps statistical records for the industry and regulates prices of distribution and, to some extent, the quantity which should be produced by each plant. The problems of the industry are now under control. It does not seem necessary for further intervention by the Government other than the granting of credit when needed to the private sector. Having played its role in the development of the sugar industry, the mission recommends that efforts be made to sell the Corporacion's holdings in the industry to private investors and that the revenues gained thereby be devoted to other pressing needs.

Salt Industry

The Government owns a salt works on the Araya peninsula. Its capacity is about 60,000 tons a year. The Government has instituted a program, estimated to cost about Bs 29 million, to mechanize the industry and increase capacity to about 120,000 tons a year. Approximately Bs 19 million had already been spent by 1960. The normal market for salt in Venezuela is only about 60,000 tons a year at present. The demand will increase in the near future by about 15,000 tons to meet the requirements of the caustic soda/chlorine plant at Moron. There is no export market for Venezuelan salt, as its cost is several times the international price. In view of the above facts, the mission recommends that further capital expenditure be limited to the amount necessary to ensure the production of about 80,000 tons of salt a year, which is the likely requirement of the market for some time.

The Role of Government Enterprise

It is not within the competence of the mission to discuss the pros and cons of government ownership of industrial or business enterprises, nor would it serve a useful purpose to do so. However, the mission has expressed the opinion that, in some particular cases, it would appear more in the interests of Venezuela to leave certain activities to the private sector. The mission attaches importance to the need for the Government to make known to the private sector the areas of activity in which the Government does not propose to engage itself. The Government has made some declarations to this end, but, in view of the experiences of the past and of rumors concerning government intentions, the mission urges that this question be further clarified. We do not suggest that the Government tie its hands for all time, but we do believe it important to encourage the private sector to proceed with investments which, because of existing uncertainties, are said to be held in abeyance.

Furthermore, in each case in which the Government does consider it desirable to own and operate an industrial or business enterprise, the mission strongly recommends, first, that such enterprise be placed under the direction of an autonomous authority, with an independent governing board completely divorced from political pressures and influences, and, second, that it be placed as nearly as possible on the same footing as a privately owned concern, subject to the same taxes, regulation and laws.

DEVELOPING AN INDUSTRIAL LABOR FORCE

The high rate of growth since the war of modern industry based on advanced technology has not been associated with a similar modernization of the labor force. The lack of elementary education and of training in specific skills constitutes a serious obstacle to industrial growth. Since the further development of industry will probably increase the proportion of requirements of skilled labor, special measures have to be taken to improve the quality and quantity of the labor force so as to assure a continuation of the industrialization process at a high rate. These measures should distinguish between those designed to improve the quality of currently employed workers and those related to future entrants into a developing industry.

Apprenticeship Training

Expansion and qualitative improvement of the vocational educational facilities in the country, including programs for apprenticeship training, rank first among the measures to improve the quality of the future entrants into industry. The semi-autonomous *Instituto Nacional de Cooperacion Educativa* (INCE) has been recently established and is designed to improve the general educational level, as well as the specific occupational skills, of workers currently employed in establishments operating with five employees or more per unit (but exclusive of government undertakings). To this end, the Institute would organize rather broad programs of educational and training activities with special reference to (a) schemes of a more general nature to eliminate illiteracy among workers, (b) inplant training to improve the operational skills of older workers and (c) programs of apprenticeship training for young workers between 14 and 18 years of age; in the latter case, the Institute may require that manufacturing undertakings employing 20 or more workers should provide special facilities for such training of minors up to a limit of 5 percent of the total employed labor force in the enterprise concerned. To finance this program, all employers covered under the law establishing the Institute are required to contribute 1 percent of wages, salaries and wage supplements paid out to the employees whereas the workers in such undertakings are required to participate by contributing ½ percent of their annual Christmas bonus (*utilidades*) ; the Government, on its part, is expected to supplement the Institute's funds with an amount of at least 20 percent of the monies thus contributed by private parties. In this way, employers alone are expected to raise some Bs 100 million annually to finance the Institute. The Institute, which will operate under the jurisdiction of the Ministry of Education, shall be administered by representatives of the Government (i.e., the Ministries of Education, of Labor and of Development) , of employers' and workers' organizations and of the National Federation of Teachers.

The mission welcomes the effort to improve conditions in this field. We question, however, whether the way in which a solution is being sought is a suitable one. While programs to upgrade skills of the employed labor force, to provide special facilities to train workers in a particular operational activity as required in an enterprise or in a small group of undertakings, and training schemes for apprentices can be legitimately included in the aims of an organization such as INCE, we question whether the funds to be collected would not greatly exceed the cost of any such program to be initiated under the auspices of the Institute. The total cost (fixed and recurrent) of technical education per pupil in Venezuela is at present about Bs 1,800 per year. On this basis, and assuming that the annual contributions by private parties and by the Government would amount to some Bs 125 million, approximately 70,000 workers could annually receive training of the type currently provided within the regular technical school curriculum. It is highly questionable whether the Institute could or should handle such an extensive program. The mission feels that more thought should be given to this program than so far has been possible, and we therefore recommend that, before further action is taken to implement this scheme, a careful survey should be made of the vocational and apprenticeship training programs now in operation in private enterprise and of the facilities which industry could turn to this purpose if appropriate financial and organizational assistance would be made available by INCE, so as to determine more exactly the needs of skilled workers in terms of number of people to be trained, the type of training, and the cost involved. It may be found that a substantial part of the funds now being assigned to INCE could be most effectively employed by the Ministry of Education (see Chapter 14). Because of the high labor costs already prevailing, the mission favors the financing of such programs by general revenues rather than use of a special levy as is provided for INCE.

A National Productivity Program

With the assistance of the United Nations and the International Labour Organization (ILO), the Government is planning to establish a special agency to organize and execute a national productivity program. At the time of the mission's visit, no decision had been taken as to the way in which such agency would be established and operated. The mission warmly supports this project since the scope and speed of the further industrialization process depends essentially on improvement in quantity and quality of management and labor.

A distinction should be made between action to raise productivity in the small enterprises of the craftsman type on the one hand, and those in the larger manufacturing undertakings on the other. Since the main cause of low productivity in small industry is the utilization of an obsolete technology, measures to raise productivity should be directed to providing the small plant owner with facilities to modernize equipment and to train the workers how to handle this equipment in an effective manner; this requires integrated action in the fields of industrial extension, credit and vocational training, and not primarily by the proposed productivity agency. By contrast, higher productivity in the larger enterprises operating with advanced technologies could be achieved mainly by insuring that management possesses the attitudes and skills to organize and utilize the resources at its disposal in the best possible manner, including measures to promote an efficient handling by labor of the equipment and materials with which it works. This requires a development of skills at all levels of the undertaking, including top and middle management, supervisory personnel and the rank and file of the workers, and the establishment of satisfactory labor-management relations. It is of little use to provide better vocational training facilities in the country without training foremen how effectively to organize the work of the operators; in the same way, first-line supervisors can reach higher levels of performance only if middle and top management fully understand the jobs to be done, and are willing and able to assume the necessary responsibilities. The proposed establishment of a national productivity agency is therefore of prime importance, and a necessary complement to other measures to improve the supply position of capital and labor. The promotional effort of the proposed agency would require the full cooperation of all the groups concerned and, to this end, the mission recommends that the agency should be established as a semi-autonomous body, governed by representatives of government, employers and labor.

Selected Immigration

Since it will take time before expanded facilities for vocational training can exert their influence on the qualitative composition of the industrial labor force, additional measures of a temporary nature are required to fill the gap between current needs for skilled workers and the present supply position of such labor in the country. This gap is not negligible and might well become more serious in the future since the further growth of industry is moving in the direction of those manufacturing activities which require a relatively larger proportion of skilled personnel. The high rate of the postwar industrial growth and the rather diversified structure which has been developed would not have been possible without the considerable inflow of immigrants providing the country with a source of skilled workers. Such immigration was suspended in 1959 pending a further examination of the national immigration policy.

For a continuation of the industrialization process it is essential that immigration should be resumed, although possibly on a more selective basis than before. Consideration might be given to an immigration policy whereby skilled workers of certain categories would be allowed unrestricted entrance into the country; the term "skilled workers" might eventually be defined as referring to persons possessing skills which can be acquired only after a vocational training period of more than two years, thereby leaving for the time being the supply of lower skills to the domestic vocational training institutions. The unrestricted immigration of skilled workers should be considered only as a provisional partial solution to the problems involved, pending the establishment of appropriate training facilities within the country, which should be strongly encouraged.

A National Wage Advisory Board

The level of wages and their distribution over the labor force is of great significance in a developing economy. Wage levels contribute in determining levels of income and employment, of productivity and output, the state of labor-management relations and job satisfaction, rates of savings and growth, the country's foreign exchange position and its competitive strength in international markets, and similar determinants of the process of economic development. This interrelationship between wage levels and economic development has received insufficient attention in Venezuela.

The mission therefore recommends the establishment of a high-level National Wage Advisory Board to advise the Government, employers and employees on the role of wages in the process of economic development in general and of industrial growth in particular, and on the consistency of wage levels with over-all objectives of economic and social policy. Such a board, to be established by the Government, should be composed of top representatives of the Government, of employers' organizations and of the trade union movement, together with some independent persons, not associated with management or labor interests, to represent the interest of the general consumer. The board should in its work be guided by three basic principles: the urgent need for a high rate of economic growth and its concomitant of full employment, the realization of a fair and equitable return both to the wage earner and to the employer, and the promotion of the fullest cooperation between management and labor as an indispensable prerequisite for sustained economic growth. The board should formulate practical criteria for adjusting wages, and establish procedures through which such criteria could be applied. The board would also advise on the preparation and administration of labor laws. The board, set up as an advisory body would not be empowered to intervene in labor disputes, but it should stimulate and guide employers and employees alike in conducting their periodic negotiations on wages and conditions of employment by taking into account the broad interest of the country and the need to harmonize the conflicting requirements of social justice and economic expediency instead of, as at present, by basing decisions more on the particular immediate interests of the employed labor force on the one hand, and the current capacity to pay off the undertaking on the other. While it is proper that labor should receive its appropriate share in any increased income from increased productivity, legitimate shares should also accrue to employers and consumers or be set apart to meet capital requirements for further development. Bearing in mind these principles, the board should, as a matter of regular procedure, be consulted by the various arbitration agencies, so as to ensure that, before making awards, arbitrators can take into account any general policy that the board might have developed. The Government, which is already closely cooperating with the International Labour Office in matters concerning the welfare and productivity of labor, might turn to that organization for advice and assistance in the establishment and operation of such a board.

ADMINISTRATIVE IMPLICATIONS

The Role of the Ministry of Development and the CVF

Before 1958, government industrial policy was mainly concentrated on two promotional areas: protection against foreign competition, and participation in the industrialization process through the establishment of government-owned manufacturing undertakings. To implement this policy, the Government established in 1946 the Venezuelan Development Corporation (CVF) which as a semi-autonomous body was to have had the administration flexibility required for financial operations; for the administration of the protectionist policy the Ministry of Development maintained a small staff in the Department of Industry. The shift in industrial policy in early 1958 has resulted in a reorganization and appreciable expansion of the Department of Industry: it has been active in preparing the ground to pursue a more comprehensive policy and is doing commendable work in making industry-wide investigations and development studies, partly with a view to pursue an intelligent protectionist policy. The assumption of new and extended functions by the Department of Industry has, so the mission understands, not been coordinated with the operational activities of the CVF, and this has resulted in duplication of efforts. Now that the Government is intensifying its development activities, it is necessary to streamline the public administration of the industrialization process: Venezuela has limited resources in terms of skilled manpower capable of administering industrial development and it cannot afford a duplication of staff as evident in both the Department of Industry and the CVF. At the time of the mission's visit, no decision had been taken on reorganizing the CVF, although we understand that the Government is considering such a move.

The Ministry of Development should primarily be concerned with the establishment of a favorable investment climate, including the removal of obstacles to growth and the introduction of development incentives. To this end, the preparation of feasibility studies concerning selected industries would assist the private sector in making intelligent investment decisions. Technical assistance of a more technological nature should primarily be geared toward smaller enterprises and should preferably be implemented in conjunction with the small industry loan program. The Department of Industry should further increase its staff and improve its operational efficiency, and to this end should establish special training programs for its officers. It should further take full advantage of the Industrial Advisory Council which should meet regularly so as to advise the Government on all policy matters and which, at the same time, should be the organ through which the Government should reorient the industrial development process in the direction desired; the council should include representatives of the trade unions so as to assure that the labor movement will identify itself with the drive to industrialize the country.

The CVF (or that part of it which eventually becomes an industrial development bank) would continue to channel government funds to the private industrial sector. To operate effectively, it should have a small staff of technical specialists, but it should leave to the Ministry all matters of technical assistance.

Regional Field Offices

In mid-1959, four field extension offices of the Ministry of Development were established. Their main objective is to establish closer contacts between the central government, the state governments and the scattered small industrial enterprises in the interior. The mission applauds this effort at functional decentralization. The vexing problem of industrial overcrowding in Caracas is to some extent the result of the dominant position of the Federal District in matters of government assistance to industry and the Government has been wise to start with some measures of decentralization of its administrative apparatus. These field offices are still in an early stage of development and measures should be taken to establish their precise objectives, and to train personnel accordingly. One of their important functions, as the mission sees it, should be to seek out promising small industries of the sole-proprietor type and to assist such undertakings in their growth toward larger units organized in the modern corporate form with its intrinsic advantages in respect of capital acquisition and formation, and of specialized management. Field offices should further be alert in identifying opportunities for the establishment of larger enterprises. All these activities require specialized training and we therefore suggest that special measures be taken to provide such training.[18] The Government might further consider increasing in due time the number of field offices, for instance, by establishing one in San Cristobal.

SUMMARY OF PROPOSED EXPENDITURES

Many of the recommendations made in this chapter, dealing as they do with measures to stimulate and encourage the growth of industry in the private sector, do not involve capital expenditures on the part of public authorities. However, we do recommend heavy capital outlays for industrial credit programs and for completing certain aspects of the government-owned iron and steel plant and various government-owned chemical plants. In all, we recommend a total capital expenditure during the four years 1960/61-1963/64 of some Bs 1,370 million, an annual average of about Bs 343 million (see Table 34).

[18] Centers which might provide suitable training for industrial extension officers include Stanford University, California, U.S.A. (International Program in Small Industry Management) and the Delft Technological University, Netherlands (International Course on Small-scale Industries).

TABLE 34: Proposed Capital Expenditures in the Manufacturing Sector, 1960/61-1963/64

(in Bs million)

	4-Year Total	Annual Average
Credits:		
CVF	400	100
Small Industry	40	10
State Enterprises:		
Iron and Steel Plant	800	200
Chemical Plants	130	33
Total	1,370	343

CHAPTER 11 *TRANSPORT*

Transport has been an important factor in the past economic development of Venezuela. Although population and economic activity are concentrated in a narrow belt running along the Andes from San Cristobal to the Caribbean and along an equally narrow coastal belt from west to east, most of the developed area is located in relatively mountainous terrain which has made it costly and difficult to move commodities and people. On the other hand, the concentration of the population has meant that only a small number of major heavy duty transport routes were needed. Furthermore, the land transport system is supplemented by waterways along the Caribbean, into Lake Maracaibo and into the great Orinoco basin. These waterways have usually offered cheap transport in Venezuela for heavy bulk goods.

Venezuela's basic inland transport system is centered around a network of good highways most of which are already paved. In August 1959, more than 11,400 km. of highways were being maintained by the Ministry of Public Works. About 4,700 km. of these highways were paved and the remainder graveled (see maps opposite page 254). First-class highways connect all major points in the coastal population belt and also connect these points with San Cristobal in the southwest, San Fernando de Apure in the *llanos,* and Ciudad Bolivar on the Orinoco River. In addition, development roads are being constructed which will connect the potentially rich agricultural areas around Barinas and those south and southwest of Lake Maracaibo with the rest of the country. Deep water is available for ocean-going vessels into the heart of the Lake Maracaibo area and also for approximately 300 km. inland along the Orinoco River. Coastal vessels can travel over 1,000 km. on this great river into the interior of the country throughout the year.

Only a few years ago much of the populated area of Venezuela was joined together by a railroad system almost 1,000 km. in length. In 1946, about 1,400,000 passengers rode these railroads, which also carried approximately 500,000 tons of cargo. However, since then roughly 680 km. have been abandoned, and the main reliance for internal transport in Venezuela is now on highways.

During the five-year period 1954/55-1958/59, capital expenditures on the transport network amounted to more than Bs 3.3 million (see

244

Table 35) . As the result of these large expenditures, the basic transport network is in an advanced stage of completion. Most of the main inland trunk roads are being built to high standards permitting a continued growth of traffic in the future. The one new railroad in the network is almost completed. The airports are, in most instances, large and well-paved. Most of the ports have substantial surplus capacity. For these reasons, the annual public investment program for the transport net under consideration by the Venezuelan Government for the four years 1960/61-1963/64 indicates a decline to below Bs 500 million as compared to the annual average of Bs 661 million during the five years 1954/55-1958/59. While no less than Bs 957.4 million was budgeted

TABLE 35: Summary of Public Investment in Transport Network, 1954/55-1963/64

(in Bs million)

Program Item	Actual Expenditures 1954/55-1958/59		Budgeted for 1959/60[a]	Under Consideration By the Venezuelan Government for 1960/61-1963/64	
	Amount for Period	Annual Average		Annual Average	Amount for Period
Road Construction	1,877.4	375	545.0	254[b]	1,015.8[b]
Bridges	355.3	71	27.6	20	81.4
Road Reconstruction	—	—	87.2⎫	175	699.2
Maintenance of Roads	347.8	69	176.2⎭		
Total Roads & Bridges	2,580.5	515	836.0	449	1,796.4
Railroads	426.0[c]	85[c]	38.0	—	—
Ports	106.3	21	34.0	18	73.7
Airports	202.2[c]	40[c]	49.4	19	76.9
Total Investment[d]	3,315.0	661	957.4[a]	486	1,947.0

[a] Includes debt payments on expenditures previously incurred, amounting to Bs 170.4 million.

[b] Excludes proposed expenditures on Caracas area avenidas, which the mission has considered in connection with a general plan for easing Caracas traffic problems (see Chapter 15) .

[c] These figures are on the basis of budget appropriations; all other figures for 1954/55-1958/59 are on an expenditure basis.

[d] These totals do not include government appropriations for *Linea Aeroportal Venezolana* (LAV) , or appropriations for military construction in the transport field. For details on these appropriations see Chapter 6, Table 3.

for 1959/60, Bs 170.4 million of this amount was allocated to debt payments on expenditures previously incurred and a further large sum
was due to be expended under the emergency program. In any event,
it was impossible when writing this report to estimate how much of
the 1959/60 appropriation was actually spent.

ROADS

Past Benefits

The large investments in highway transport during the past few
years have already resulted in a substantial reduction in the cost of
transport. In fact, there has been a "transportation revolution" in
Venezuela, the magnitude of which is only partially indicated by the
rapid growth in vehicles used and the substantial drop in the rates
charged for transport services. The effect of this transport revolution
on the location of economic activity is just beginning to appear. The
improved highway network now permits industrial and agricultural
growth in parts of Venezuela which have hitherto stagnated. The new
agricultural development areas are being greatly stimulated. The industrially developing areas, around Barquisimeto, Valencia, Barcelona
and San Felix, are the scene of an increasingly large number of prospects for new business projects.

Much of the growth in the road transport system has taken place
so recently that its economic effects are still subject to speculation.
While the number of vehicles registered in Venezuela grew from 34,000
to 275,000 between 1945 and 1958, the number of passengers and amount
of freight carried on the railroads dropped from 1,327,000 passengers
and 531,000 tons of freight to 108,000 passengers and 87,000 tons of
freight over the same period. Rates for carrying goods, which at a
minimum were 22 centimos per ton/km. on the railroads in 1945, had
fallen to between 15 and 18 centimos by truck shortly thereafter. By
1959 further reductions by trucking companies for long-distance transport had brought the average down to about 10 centimos per ton/km.
Rates charged on specific commodities such as wheat transported by
trucks over good roads from Puerto Cabello to San Cristobal, a distance
of over 700 km., fell to as low as 5.5 centimos per ton/km.

In general, the mission found road transport one of the few activities
where Venezuelan prices, even at the present exchange rate, are lower
than those found in many other countries. Of course, fuel is cheap in

Venezuela, the price of gasoline ranging from about 80 centimos (about 24 US cents) a gallon or 21 centimos a liter for extra-grade, and 42 centimos (less than 13 US cents) a gallon or 11 centimos a liter for regular grade. Truckers with whom the mission discussed these problems estimated that fuel accounts for only about 4 percent of the total cost of trucking in Venezuela. The more significant costs are drivers' wages, the cost of tires and the depreciation of vehicles. The cost of tires alone is about three times the cost of gasoline and lubricants. In the course of the mission's discussions, it was clear that the cost of tire renewals and the depreciation of vehicles are being reduced drastically with the improvements of the road network.

The volume of commodities carried on the roads has undoubtedly increased greatly in recent years. Since 1952, the volume of imports carried to the marketing centers has nearly doubled. Manufacturing output has increased 110 percent and agricultural output over 20 percent. The current volume of commodity traffic is estimated by the mission to be nearly 5,000 million ton/km. a year. It is also estimated that some 6,550 million passenger/km. were achieved in 1958. These large volumes were achieved without substantial congestion on most of the main roads in the country and at a relatively modest economic cost.

Establishment of Priorities

Additional funds required to complete this system constitute an important claim on the Government's investment program during the next several years. However, a reasonable economic return on such investment can be maximized only if an order of priorities is established and followed. Priority projects are those which will contribute most to the maintenance and expansion of the Venezuelan economy.

High-Traffic Roads. A high priority should be given to the building and strengthening of those roads which serve the main economic regions of the country. These are roads which interconnect the manufacturing areas of Caracas with those of Valencia and Maracaibo and in turn with the industrially developing areas at Barquisimeto and Puerto La Cruz. They also serve mixed industrial agricultural areas, such as San Cristobal, and such important agricultural areas as Calabozo and Barinas. In most instances, the trunk roads between these various areas, or the leading regional roads within the areas themselves, already carry substantial traffic; for example, 9,000 vehicles per day on the super-highway between Caracas and Valencia, 6,000 vehicles per day on the Valencia-Puerto Cabello road, 4,000 vehicles per day on the San Felipe-Barquisimeto road. On most other roads connecting the manufacturing and industrially developing areas, a traffic rate of 1,500 vehicles per day has already been obtained. (For further details, see map facing this page.)

Output statistics for the various parts of the country also offer some guidance as to current priorities in transport routes between different areas. The major proportion of total output for domestic consumption is concentrated in the areas noted in the previous paragraph. Imports generally enter through the four leading ports, Maracaibo, Puerto Cabello, La Guaira, and Guanta and are then consumed for the most part in the same areas mentioned above.

Some 4 million tons of commodities are carried distances greater than 200 km. in Venezuela. Most of these commodities are transported over the trunk roads indicated on maps opposite page 254. Even if production and movement of commodities were to double in the next decade, it is clear that there are only a relatively few major roads that can achieve traffic volumes above 2,500 vehicles per day considering the output levels of the areas served by the various roads. Practically all the main routes serving the high output areas either are now covered by a high-standard road or such a road is already under construction. Large movements to areas such as Caracas, Maracaibo and Barquisimeto that offer a market for the surplus producing areas often have more than one well-developed route, and in all cases at least one. For this reason, the mission feels that the basic high-traffic network is near completion.

Where there is heavy traffic in Venezuela, high-standard roads, even super-highways, yield a relatively high return on invested capital. For instance, the 19-kilometer super-highway from Caracas to La Guaira costing Bs 270 million, shows a benefit-cost ratio of about 3.6; this means that, on the basis of current traffic levels, the annual total of all road users' savings on operating costs over the new road as compared with their operating costs over the old road are about 3.6 times the annual cost of maintenance, depreciation and interest on the investment in the new road. On a similar basis, the new road between Valencia and Puerto Cabello, which is being built to the high standards of a super-highway, is expected to show a benefit-cost ratio of about 3.0. The existing trunk and primary regional roads in Venezuela in most cases also show high benefit-cost ratios. Where current traffic levels are at least between 1,000 and 1,500 vehicles per day and are expected to increase to between 1,700 and 2,500 vehicles per day within the next

ROAD TRAFFIC FLOW

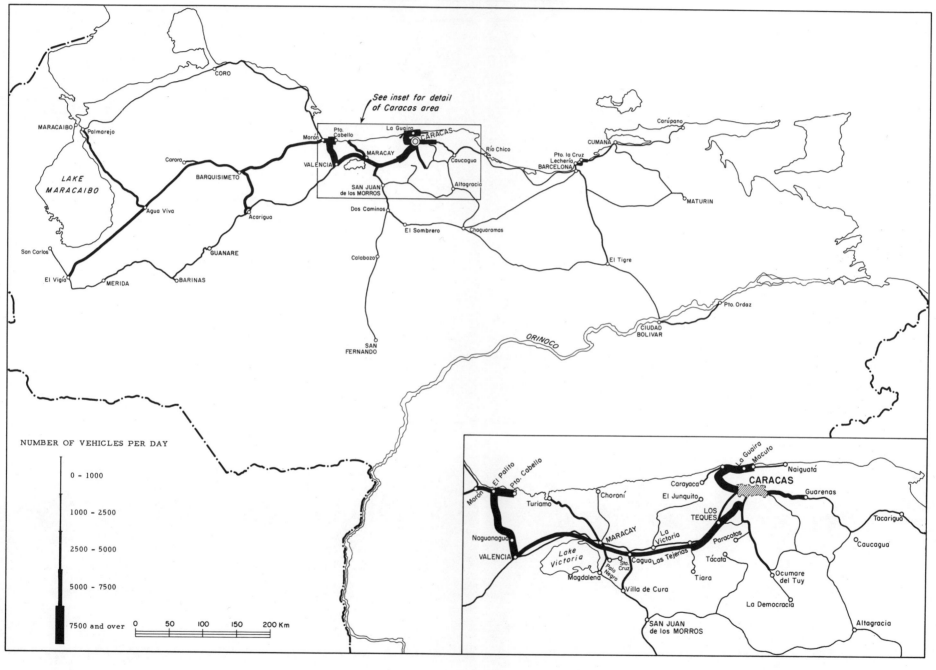

NUMBER OF VEHICLES PER DAY

0 – 1000

1000 – 2500

2500 – 5000

5000 – 7500

7500 and over

0   50   100   150   200 Km

decade, the benefit-cost ratio varies between 2.0 and 3.0 based on the expected traffic levels. (For further details see discussion in Annex VIII).

Low-Traffic Roads. Whether or not a low-traffic road should be accorded investment priority should depend on the potential for development of the area it would serve. Possible development areas are not in all cases now served by satisfactory roads. For example, the Barinas region and the area south and southwest of Lake Maracaibo are potentially rich in agriculture and the Ciudad Bolivar-San Felix area may become the most important industrial part of Venezuela. Roads to and within these areas are especially important even though the possible traffic volumes for the next five years or so will obviously be low. Other developing areas, such as those in the neighborhood of Barquisimeto and Barcelona, have adequate roads now under construction. Roads to all these development, and potential development, areas are considered by the mission to have high priority.

Our determination of priorities in low-traffic road investment necessarily depends to a large extent on our qualitative judgment as to the developmental potential of a particular road. Quantitative cost-benefit analysis has also been used for guidance. The calculated benefit ratios have been based on what traffic volumes, and therefore benefits, can be reasonably expected during the next decade. Where a road is expected to scrve a developmental area, future traffic is uncertain and quantitative analysis difficult. Nevertheless, the benefit from road improvement may be extremely high in some such cases. We have thus considered low-traffic development roads of equally high priority as high-traffic roads. Low-traffic regional roads and local roads where little development is expected are considered to be of low priority.

Since the priority accorded a low-traffic road depends essentially on expectations for the future growth of traffic, a high priority designation should not be given to a low-traffic road without a detailed consideration of the future benefits it will produce.

The mission has made a number of illustrative benefit-cost calculations, on the basis of Venezuelan cost conditions, to show the effect that different traffic levels may have on the economic yield of various roads (see Table 36). These calculations indicate only the minimum economic yield since they simply reflect the operational savings to the road user and do not take into account additional benefits to the economy as a whole. These additional benefits are likely to be most substantial on roads with promise of high-traffic, where the benefit-cost test already indicates a high economic yield. However, if the expected traffic volume

TABLE 36: Benefit-Cost Ratios at Various Traffic Levels Expected in the Future on Different Highways in Venezuela[a]

Highway with Capital Cost of Bs 50,000 per km.		Highway with Capital Cost of Bs 150,000 per km.		Highway with Capital Cost of Bs 290,000 per km.		Highway with Capital Cost of Bs 500,000 per km.	
veh/day	B/C	veh/day	B/C	veh/day	B/C	veh/day	B/C
10	0.3	50	0.4	200	0.7	600	0.8
25	0.7	75	0.6	250	0.9	700	0.9
35	1.0	100	0.8	300	1.1	800	1.0
40	1.1	125	1.0	350	1.2	900	1.1
45	1.2	150	1.2	400	1.4	1,000	1.2
50	1.4	200	1.6	500	1.8	1,200	1.5
75	2.1	250	2.0	600	2.1	1,500	1.9
100	2.7	300	2.8	700	2.5	2,000	2.5

[a] Capital costs of these highways coincide with those of various types of highways as classified in the text below.

is low so that the benefit-cost ratio is well below 1, the investment still might be justified on economic grounds if the traffic generated by building the road develops mainly from the utilization of otherwise unemployed resources. Where potential development is not clearly visible and where therefore traffic may not increase in the coming few years, this benefit-cost analysis properly indicates that the yield on the investment might be extremely low. Similarly, if the traffic increase can be forecast, a reasonably high benefit-cost ratio and an economically viable road are indicated.

The 1960/61-1963/64 Road Program

The 1960/61-1963/64 program under consideration within the Venezuelan Government proposes an annual level of expenditures of Bs 449 million, a slight reduction below the 1954/55-1958/59 level of Bs 515 million. The future road program represents a significant shift in emphasis as compared with the past. Between 1954/55 and 1958/59, 36 percent of the amount spent on highway construction was for superhighways and urban avenues, 23 percent for main trunk roads and 13 percent for primary regional and development roads. Thus, 72 percent of the funds spent during this period were either for main roads with high-traffic volume or for development roads where the traffic volume is expected to increase during the next decade. Similarly, around 80 percent of the Government's current highway construction program for 1959/60 is allocated to high-traffic roads. This pattern is expected to continue during the first two years of the proposed future program while the main traffic roads are being completed. Thereafter, the funds allocated to high-traffic and developmental roads will decline and those for low-traffic local and regional roads will increase from 10 percent of the total in 1960/61 to 28 percent in 1963/64. It is this low-priority low-traffic part of the Government's program which the mission believes should require especially careful analysis.

TABLE 37: Priority Classification by the Mission of the Proposed Road and Bridge Program, 1960/61-1963/64

(in Bs million)

Type of Project and Classification	Amount Proposed for Four-Year Program	Annual Average
High Priority Part of Program		
Road Construction:[a]		
Priority A Super Highways	331.7[b]	
Priority A Trunk Roads	93.7	
Priority B Trunk Roads	44.9	
Priority B Regional Roads	103.2	
Development Roads	133.4	
Total Road Construction	706.9	
Surveys, Land Acquisition, and Inspection	128.7	
Bridges	81.4	
Road Reconstruction	185.0	
Priority Maintenance	400.0	
High Priority Road & Bridge Program	1,502.0	375
Low Priority Part of Program		
Priority C and D Local and Regional Roads	180.2	
Low Priority Reconstruction	51.0	
Low Priority Maintenance	63.2	
Low Priority Works	294.4	74
Total Proposed Road Program	1,796.4	449

[a] For further details of high-priority road construction program see Table 38.

[b] Excludes highways within Caracas, which are treated separately as part of the over-all Caracas traffic easement program in Chapter 15.

The mission has attempted in a very preliminary way to define the high and low priority parts of the proposed highway and bridge program under consideration by the Venezuelan Government. (See maps opposite page 254.) We believe road construction should be re-

TABLE 38: Details of Proposed Road Construction Program, 1960/61-1963/64, Classified by Mission as High Priority

(in Bs million)

	Amount Proposed Over Four-Year Program
Priority A Super-Highways[a]	
Coche-Valle del Tuy	151.6
Valencia-Puerto Cabello	131.9
Access Road to Maracaibo Bridge	48.0
Other Super-Highways	0.2
	331.7
Priority A Trunk Roads	
Maracaibo-Barquisimeto	22.0
Valencia-Barquisimeto	18.6
Barcelona-Caracas	42.1
Valle de la Pascua-Pariaguan	11.0
	93.7
Priority B Trunk Roads	
Moron-Coro-Maracaibo	25.3
Zulia 5-Agua Viva	19.6
	44.9
Priority Regional Roads	
Merida-Pan American	26.6
Bocono-Flor de Patria	5.0
Cumana-Casanay	27.8
Carupano-Caripito	12.6
Valle de la Pascua-Aragua	14.0
Roads in vicinity of Caracas	0.8
Dos Caminos-Calabozo	16.4
	103.2
Development Roads	
San Cristobal-Pedraza-Barinas	58.6
La Flecha-Turen	6.6
La Fria-Encontrados-Machiques	34.7
San Felix-Upata	3.0
Temblador-Los Barrancos	17.6
Guanare-Puerto Nutrias	12.9
	133.4
Total High-Priority Road Construction	706.9

[a] Excludes highways within Caracas, which are treated separately as part of the over-all Caracas traffic easement program in Chapter 15.

stricted to high priority works and therefore that the program could be reduced to an annual level expenditure of about Bs 375 million. Accordingly, total capital outlays on roads and bridges would amount to Bs 1,502.0 million over the four-year period. This would permit the more important works to be carried out by 1963/64, as indicated in Tables 37 and 38, while the remaining low priority works could be delayed a year or two.

The low priority part of the program consists of about Bs 180.2 million for constructing local and regional roads and Bs 114.2 million for low priority reconstruction and maintenance. The low priority roads are for the most part low-traffic roads with a low benefit-cost ratio and an extremely high capital investment per expected vehicle. While new roads are needed to open up new country, we would only designate a low-traffic road of high priority when it opens up a potential development region. For instance, the proposed new road south of Barinas will open up that rich area for agriculture, while a similar new road south and west of Lake Maracaibo will open up that rich area. For this reason, both low-traffic roads are considered of high priority. Similarly, we would designate of high priority the La Flecha-Turen road, because of substantial agricultural activity in the region and the San Felix-Upata and Temblador-Los Barrancos roads because of the expected industrial activity in the area. The Guanare-Puerto Nutrias road may be of high priority because it is intended to give a developing agricultural area access to water transport.

The mission designates as low priority such roads as San Fernando-Achaguas, Carupano-Guiria, San Fernando-San Juan, El Baul-Arismendi, Las Mercedes-Cabruta, Arismendi-Apurito, Puerto Nutrias-Mantecal, Tucupita-Tabasco, San Juan-Puerto Paez and Puerto Ayacucho-Puerto Paez. In the mission's view, potential development in these areas is not such as to justify expensive road building during the next four-year period. The mission feels that this work could be postponed to the years after 1963/64, without any inhibiting effects on the growth of the economy.

Construction Costs

The cost of building roads in Venezuela is extremely high. In the mission's view, administrative deficiencies contribute significantly to such inflated costs. The labor component in Venezuelan highway construction is very large despite the capital-intensive techniques employed. Spot checks made by the mission indicate there are many more field men used by the Ministry of Public Works for maintenance and reconstruction work than would seem to be necessary. Similarly, there are more people employed as clerks, accountants, and in other overhead positions than would seem necessary. Wages are also relatively high. It seems clear that much of the high cost is due to an attempt to carry a large number of people on the public payroll. This practice becomes increasingly more expensive as more and more reconstruction work is now being carried out by the Government's own forces rather than by contract.

Another important factor which is tending to raise the cost of roads in Venezuela is the increasing number of structural failures in relatively new roads caused by the inability of the roads to carry heavy trucks or support the volume of traffic. The mission believes that this problem can be met by proper road design and proper enforcement of established weight restrictions. The maximum legally permissible weight is currently an 8.5-ton axle load. There is, however, no police control of truck weights in the country. The mission found axle loads of 20 tons to be quite common in inter-city transport and recommends that a serious attempt should be made to keep truck weights within reasonable bounds. As a first step, we suggest that a restriction to a 12-ton axle load might be attained and highway construction should be designed for such weights with an additional 25 percent factor of safety. This would materially assist in keeping the roads from breaking up during the next years, while enforcement of weight regulation is being put into effect.

Relating Road Design to Traffic Levels

The mission found serious defects in the present system of road design in Venezuela. The current system is not sufficiently flexible and for practical purposes is limited to two basic road types. One is called Type C road, which costs about Bs 315,000 per km. and is built on a graded width of 10.3 meters with a road surface 6.7 meters wide and with no shoulders; 5 cm. of asphalt concrete surface covering a 30 cm. base foundation. The road most commonly constructed is called a Type B road and is built on a 13.05-meter graded width with a 9.8-meter road surface with two 1.25-meter shoulders; the thickness is similar to that of the Type C road. Type B roads generally cost between Bs 450,000 and Bs 600,000 per km., depending on the terrain. There is also a lower Type D road which is 6 meters wide, without a hard sur-

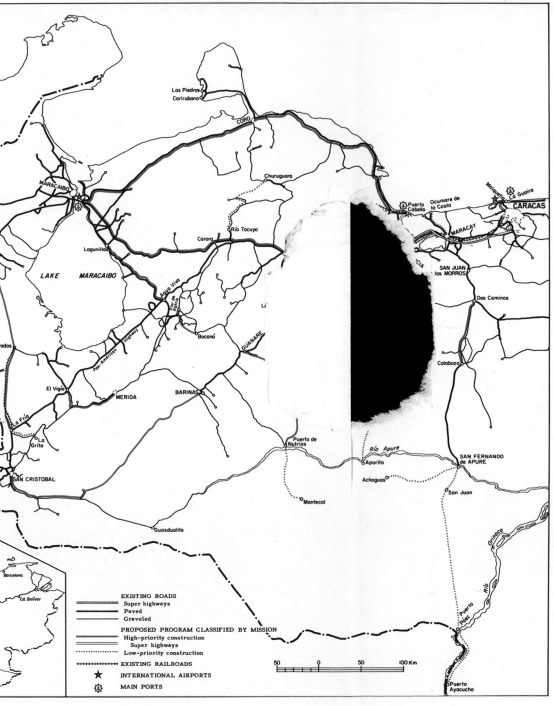

EXISTING ROADS
Super highways
Paved
Graveled
PROPOSED PROGRAM CLASSIFIED BY MISSION
High-priority construction
Super highways
Low-priority construction
EXISTING RAILROADS
★ INTERNATIONAL AIRPORTS
✿ MAIN PORTS

50   0   50   100 Km

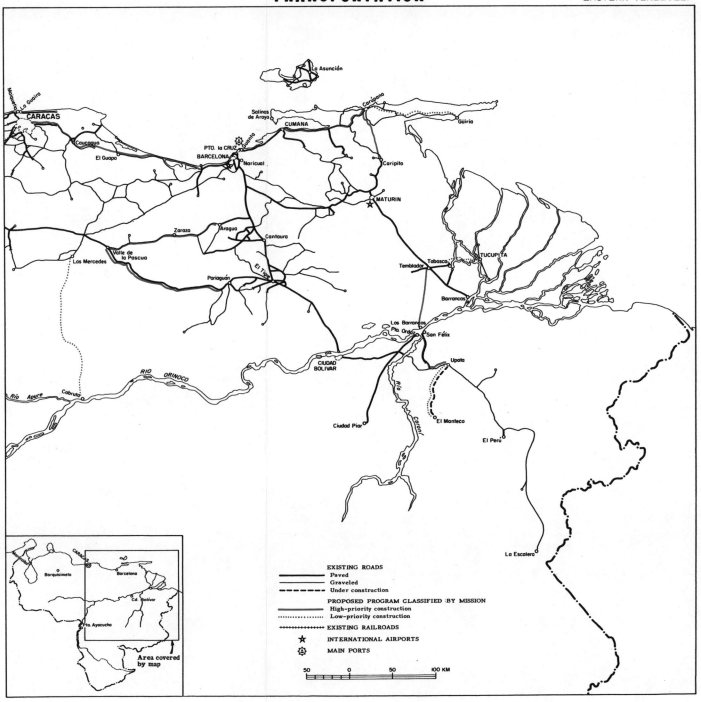

Area covered
by map

EXISTING ROADS
Paved
Graveled
Under construction
PROPOSED PROGRAM CLASSIFIED BY MISSION
High-priority construction
Low-priority construction
+++++++ EXISTING RAILROADS
★ INTERNATIONAL AIRPORTS
✿ MAIN PORTS

50   0   50   100 KM

nearly 2½ times the average of the previous five years. There obviously has been need for some additional funds to maintain increased kilometrage of roads, an increased number of bridges and, particularly, to repair many weak roads built during the past five years; but past expenditures in themselves appear to be much too high partly because they include substantial amounts for the emergency relief program to alleviate unemployment. The need to guard against excessive maintenance costs is recognized by the Venezuelan Government and a maintenance program for 1960/61-1963/64 now being considered would allocate Bs 463.2 million over the period for this purpose. This represents an average annual expenditure of about Bs 118 million, a substantial reduction from current levels.

The mission nevertheless feels that this sum should be cut even further. We suggest that an allocation of Bs 400 million, or an annual average of Bs 100 million, should adequately cover maintenance needs, particularly if efforts are made to build roads stronger so that they can carry heavy traffic and if efforts are also made to strengthen present roads which are failing. In these ways maintenance costs could be reduced. In short, we strongly urge that maintenance be built into highways by more adequate design.

Highway Reconstruction

Given adequacy of original design, not only could maintenance costs be reduced, but also the need for and frequency of reconstruction could be reduced. The mission believes that expenditures on reconstruction programs have been excessive for four reasons. First, inadequate structural designs in relation to truck weights and frequencies have precipitated the need for reconstruction more rapidly than is the practice elsewhere. Second, reconstruction costs on individual projects are high for the same reasons as original construction costs are high. Third, some reconstruction work has been initiated prematurely in order to provide special relief works to alleviate the unemployment problem. Fourth, some recent road failures in Venezuela are due, in part, to ineffective on-the-job supervision which has sometimes led to the use of clay-bearing gravel for the base course, in disregard of present construction specifications.

The mission urges that every effort be made to reduce costs on individual projects and that only reconstruction actually necessary be carried out. So far as structural design is concerned, there is need to build stronger roads at least for the next few years, particularly where there is a large volume of truck traffic. This need arises because, in view of the difficulties in enforcement of the present axle-weight restrictions, the roads are currently required to carry unusually heavy axle loads. The additional capital investment needed to strengthen most of the main trunk and primary roads would amount to about 30 percent above the cost of the roads now being built, but this would be compensated by the elimination of the need for costly reconstruction later. The mission believes that such a program to strengthen roads which are not adequately designed could be carried out within the amounts proposed in the next four-year program by postponing some of the lower priority works.

While the strengthening and reconstruction program is of high priority, a careful evaluation of the size of such a program is needed. As indicated earlier, although about Bs 350 million was spent on maintenance during 1954/55-1958/59, only Bs 4.7 million was spent on reconstruction during the same period. Recent Venezuelan Government plans allocate Bs 236 million for reconstruction purposes during the four-year period, 1960/61-1963/64. If this work is to be done properly, it must be planned and executed to the same high standards as are applied to new construction. The mission strongly suggests that the selection of the roads to be reconstructed should be based on an order of priority established by the traffic carried and the condition of the road. The program now proposed seems to make little attempt at such a selection. The mission believes that it is important to strengthen first those roads which are now carrying heavy traffic.

Much of the repair of broken roads could be performed more efficiently at lower cost by an overlay of from 10 to 15 cm. of asphalt concrete, than by attempting to tear out and replace old foundations with new foundations, as is now the practice of the maintenance division. Sometimes it may be necessary to place from 15 to 30 cm. of new stone base over the broken pavement and under the asphalt concrete. Only in very exceptional cases should it be necessary to remove the old road foundations.

The mission suggests that reconstruction work should be fitted into the new design types which would be related to traffic expectancies. All types of roads would be redesigned in accord with these standards. For instance, low-traffic roads do not need to be paved with 5 cm. of asphalt concrete, as is now customary. Some can be merely graveled surfaces, while others can be made all-weather roads by the placement of 2.5 cm. of asphalt penetration or other type of light asphalt surfacing. Only heavy traffic roads would need the thicker foundations and pavement of the higher type roads.

Having reviewed current reconstruction needs according to these standards, the mission considers that an allocation of some Bs 185 million for this purpose out of the Bs 236 million now under consideration by the Venezuelan Government for the coming four years is the minimum amount needed to accomplish the high priority work needed. This work would have to be carried out with the utmost efficiency if the proposed sum of money is to be sufficient. In the mission's view, the most efficient method of getting specific jobs done would be by contract, letting the work to the lowest responsible bidder. If reconstruction work is also continued as a part of a program to relieve unemployment, additional funds would have to be allocated, and even then it is doubtful whether the job could be carried out to the required high standards.

The mission also believes that some of the new heavy-traffic roads which are included in the Government's program for the next four years should be allocated additional funds for thicker paved surfaces and foundations. For instance, the following roads all will require strengthening on the basis of current estimates of future traffic: the Maracaibo-Agua Viva road, the Carora-Lagunillas section of the Barquisimeto-Maracaibo road, the El Guapo-Barcelona road, and the San Juan-Dos Caminos road. This would indicate that an additional sum of about Bs 30 million should be allocated to build these roads strongly enough to withstand the traffic they will be receiving if the danger of the road failure is to be avoided.

Some adjustments should also be considered in the specifications being contemplated for some of the primary regional highways. The Cumana-Carupano road probably is to be sufficiently strong, but the Dos Caminos-Calabozo and the Araguita-Caucagua-Contada roads will apparently require more strengthening at a cost of about Bs 10 million. With regard to the Guanare-Pan American Highway project, a careful analysis of its traffic should be made before determining whether the road needs strengthening.

In all, the strengthening of roads noted above, which the mission considers are high priority, would cost about Bs 40 million. There is not sufficient traffic information on other roads to make even a superficial analysis. On the assumption that additional traffic information will show the need for strengthening other roads, the mission recommends that a further Bs 60 million be tentatively earmarked for this purpose, so that the total road strengthening program would cost about Bs 100 million over the four-year period. This would raise the priority part of the road program from Bs 1,502 million to more than Bs 1,600 million.

Major Bridge Program

The Venezuelan Government has been considering a total allocation of Bs 81.4 million during the four-year program for the study and construction of major bridges and for general bridge maintenance. The mission considers this allocation reasonable. Of this total, Bs 60 million are committed for supervisory costs and for payments to the contractor for the Maracaibo Straits bridge, construction of which was about 25 percent complete in August 1960. With respect to future major bridge construction in Venezuela, the mission advises against continuing the current common practice of having major bridges designed, built and sometimes financed by construction contractors. We believe that the various aspects of the work should be kept separate, the study and design of the larger and more complicated structures being undertaken preferably by independent consulting engineers of international experience and repute. Whereas alternative designs by contractors might be permitted for comparison with the basic design, such alternatives should be thoroughly checked from all points of view and an upper cost limit should be set and incorporated in the proposals before considering acceptance.

Road Transport Organization and Regulation

The record in truck transport organization has in general been excellent in Venezuela. The existence of competition has been healthy and has resulted in substantial benefits to the economy. The industry has been organized into a large number of very small competing firms, and it appears that some trucking interests would welcome a measure of governmental control. While the mission feels that some regulation, such as limiting truck weights, is reasonable, we also feel that, if highway transport is to continue to grow rapidly, it must not be stifled by unnecessarily rigid laws and regulations. Care should be exercised to avoid undue limitation of competition by means of restricting the establishment of new trucking concerns and by fixing tariffs. The continuance of competition in this field is extremely important to the future economic development of Venezuela.

In addition to a reasonable approach to regulating road transport, the planning of the completion and strengthening of the highway network along the lines we have suggested above, is an essential precondition of a sustained growth in the road transport economy. The

mission feels that the organization of the Highway Division of the
Ministry of Public Works is such as to give promise that planning in
this field would be carried out with considerable efficiency if the present
burden of administrative duplication could be reduced. Like other
sectors of the Venezuelan economy, the planning of road investments
is handicapped by maladministration in government. The overlapping
of public authority and responsibility, the difficulty of securing decisions, the failure to keep accurate records and lack of proper personnel
procedures tend to increase costs and to lower efficiency. Priority steps
should be taken to improve government organization as soon as possible.

Financing Highway Improvement

The cost of highway improvements in Venezuela is mainly financed
by the national budget. There is only one toll road in the country, the
super-highway between La Guaira and Caracas. Tolls on that road
have been sufficient to cover the cost of maintenance, amortization and
interest on total capital invested in the road. Highway-user taxes in
Venezuela are limited to a national tax on the domestic consumption
of petroleum products, a national license fee on vehicles and a tax on
vehicles imposed by the various municipal governments. The general
level of these taxes is low. The tax on gasoline is only slightly over 1
centimo per liter, ranging between 7 percent and 10 percent of the
selling price, depending on the grade of gasoline involved. The federal
motor vehicle license fee is a flat charge of Bs 20 at the time of the
purchase of a vehicle and Bs 15 for renewal of the license each year.
All vehicles, irrespective of whether they are private cars, trucks or
buses, are assessed at the same amount. Municipal licensing fees are
somewhat more substantial.

The yield of these taxes is quite low, amounting to about Bs 25
million a year or only 5 percent of the total annual expenditure on the
road program during the past five years. Gasoline taxes account for
Bs 20 million of the total. The actual consumption of gasoline in 1958
by vehicles was approximately 1,800 million liters. On the basis of this
consumption level, every increase in taxes by one centimo per liter
of gasoline would yield an additional Bs 18 million of revenue. The
mission recommends that serious consideration be given to increasing
the gasoline tax so that at least the maintenance cost of the highway
system is financed from this source during the next four years. We
calculate that this would require that the gasoline tax be increased to

5 centimos a liter. In view of the benefits which road-users are deriving from the completion and improvement of the road network, they should have no difficulty in absorbing such a tax increase.

RAILROADS

Past Performance and Present Situation

There are currently 455 kilometers of government-owned railroads in service in Venezuela, consisting of three sections as follows:

a. *Gran Ferrocarril de Venezuela* (from Caracas to Valencia 177 km.)
b. *Gran Ferrocarril del Tachira* (from La Fria to Encontrados 105 km.)
c. *Ferrocarril Puerto Cabello* (from Puerto Cabello to Barquisimeto 173 km.)

Twenty-seven kilometers of railroad are under construction from the Naricual coal mines to the Port of Guanta and about one-half a kilometer for the extension of the Puerto Cabello-Barquisimeto section to the docks. Funds are also included in the 1959/60 budget for the building of short spurs from the Puerto Cabello-Barquisimeto railroad to the petrochemical works at Moron and to several other plants near the main line.

Since 1945 about 680 km. of railroad have been abandoned in Venezuela. The operating costs of these lines, even without any allowance for depreciation or capital, exceeded the alternative cost of transporting by highway. The Government was faced with the granting of substantial subsidies merely to offset operating losses. As a result, these railroads were not adequately maintained and were ultimately abandoned. With respect to the existing lines, the situation has hardly improved. The Autonomous Institute of Railroads reports that the 1958 revenues of the first two operating railroads named above, were less than one-fourth the expenditures. Computations disclose that the loss was approximately Bs 4.1 million for the year, and that the total loss for the past five years has been Bs 18 million.

The loss during 1958 alone on the *Gran Ferrocarril de Venezuela* (the Caracas-Valencia line), was Bs 3,618,000. Further, the financial situation has been deteriorating rather rapidly. In 1954, the annual income of the Caracas-Valencia line was Bs 1,139,000. By 1958, income had declined to Bs 805,000. Meanwhile, annual operating costs had increased from Bs 3,900,000 to Bs 4,425,000. Freight carried had dropped from 9 million ton/km. to 8 million ton/km. and the number of passenger/km. from 11,260,000 to 5,180,000. The reason for this decline is that the railroads are not competitive. Freight charges for ordinary freight, even at the lowest reported rate from Caracas to Valencia, amount to 17.3 centimos per ton/km., which is substantially higher than the average road transport charges in Venezuela of about 10 to 11 centimos per ton/km. Passenger service is faced with similar rate competition. For example, low-cost bus service is available all the way from Caracas to Barquisimeto, 360 km., at Bs 10-12 per person in much less time than it takes the train to travel the 177 km. to Valencia, and at a much lower charge per passenger/km.

The La Fria-Encontrados line is faced with a similarly discouraging financial situation. In the years since 1954, there has been some increase in rates charged so that the annual operating loss has been reduced from Bs 1,450,000 to Bs 481,000. However, the tonnage of goods carried has been stagnant at 25,000 tons (2,100,000 ton/km.) while the number of passengers carried has declined from 47,000 to 37,400 and the number of passenger/km. from 1,510,000 to 1,210,000.

Since both of these lines face declining demand, are losing money, are narrow-gauge lines and have old and obsolete equipment, the mission suggests that if losses continue to increase it may prove to be economically necessary to abandon them. The Caracas-Valencia railroad must compete with truck competition which can carry all commodities offered between Caracas and Valencia most of the way by super-highway in much less time and at a material saving in costs. It is difficult to see how the deficit on this railway can be eliminated. There is no bulk cargo for which it might be advantageous to use the railroad. Likewise, it is expected that the new highway, now under construction between La Fria and Encontrados, will rapidly take both the freight and passenger traffic away from this railroad.

The problem of the Barquisimeto-Puerto Cabello railroad is quite different. Although the first financial report on this newly completed railroad showed a loss of Bs 1.7 million for the first five months of 1959, it is really not yet completed. The railroad is not connected to the docks and thus handled only 700 tons of freight for the period. Its passenger record was not very encouraging as only 11,700 passengers were carried during the period. However, the Barquisimeto-Puerto Cabello railroad is new and modern, and as soon as it is connected to the dock at Puerto Cabello, and the several short industrial spurs are completed, it should attract substantial traffic. Nevertheless, it is extremely doubtful whether the traffic will be sufficient to make the line an economic success, although every effort should be made toward that objective. The distance covered by this railroad is relatively short. Much of the goods moving in the direction of Barquisimeto are transported beyond that city toward San Cristobal. If the freight is moved by rail from Puerto Cabello, it will have to be transshipped twice which would make it costly. For the shorter-distance direct traffic from the port to Barquisimeto the railroad will certainly remove some of the burden of the heavy traffic of approximately 5,000 vehicles per day on the competing Pan American Highway from Puerto Cabello to Barquisimeto. This should delay the need for enlarging this highway.

The decline of the railroads in Venezuela to their present low level is not a short-term phenomenon. The record shows that during the period, 1920-58 the number of passengers dropped from a high of 2,730,-014 in 1930 to 107,880 in 1958, and the amount of freight carried from a high of 530,544 tons in 1945 to 86,846 in 1958 (see Table 39).

TABLE 39: Transport of Passengers and Freight on Railroads in Venezuela, 1920 to 1958

Year	Number of Passengers	Freight in Metric Tons
1920	1,936,834	366,202
1930	2,730,014	466,871
1940	838,143	426,237
1946	1,392,062	505,948
1950	588,171	305,789
1958	107,880	86,846

Source: Annual Statistics of Venezuela—Ministry of Development, 1954, p. 303. 1958 figures provided by the *Instituto de Ferrocarril*.

The Proposed National Railroad Network

A plan to expand the national railroad system has been under discussion in Venezuela for many years. The new Barquisimeto-Puerto Cabello line was to have been the first link in such a network. The complete plan, as originally conceived, called for the construction of a system totaling approximately 4,250 km. at a total estimated cost of over Bs 5 billion. The system would run the full length of the country from east to west and south to San Cristobal in the west and to the San Felix area in the southeast. There would be a first phase of some 2,400 km. In later discussions, the total program had been reduced to 3,000 km. at an estimated cost of Bs 3 billion. A first stage of 1,400 km. is currently under construction. On the basis of discussions with the Railroad Institute, the mission estimates that this 1,400 km. system would cost about Bs 2.18 billion (see Annex IX).

A very tentative traffic estimate prepared by the staff of Cordiplan indicates a possible volume of 3.1 billion ton/km. for this rail system within the next twenty years. This estimate assumes very little growth in traffic on the road system. The amount compares to the 4.8 billion ton/km. that the mission estimates is now carried on all the roads in the country. The mission believes that the present road network, with some strengthening of various roads, could easily and economically handle all this increased traffic.

The mission's studies cast considerable doubts as to the wisdom of building more railroads. Since the major highway net is nearly complete, new railroads would in effect duplicate an existing transport system. To the extent that there would be any operating savings, they would yield at best a very low return on the additional investment required. In fact, since much of this capital might have to be borrowed, there would certainly be a net loss to the economy. Moreover, the foreign exchange savings or earnings resulting from a more extensive use of railroads do not appear to be substantial in the case of Venezuela. Under the demand conditions for Venezuelan oil, greater domestic consumption would not mean a lower level of oil exports, except possibly in the very long term. On the other hand, a large proportion of the road vehicles, which are now imported, will probably be produced locally as the economy grows and metalworking industries develop.

It should further be noted that in general the movement of goods in Venezuela, both actual and potential, is for distances which are relatively short in terms of economic railroad hauls. In competition with trucks which afford a door-to-door service, the double handling of goods makes railroad haulage over such distances considerably more expensive.

For these reasons, the mission recommends that no more railroads be built in Venezuela during the current planning period. At the end of the period, the railroad situation could be reviewed again.

The Naricual-Matanzas Railroad

Because there seems to be particular interest in Venezuela in building a railroad between Naricual and Matanzas, the mission attempted a special evaluation of this project. The Railroad Institute estimates that this railroad would haul 800,000 tons of coal and limestone a year from near Naricual in the Barcelona area to the steel mill at Matanzas on the Orinoco, as well as 750,000 tons of steel products and other commodities in the opposite direction. The building of this railroad has been formally recommended by several groups of experts in reports submitted to the Railroad Institute. Three fundamental assumptions have been used that the mission considers highly questionable.

The first was the underestimation of the cost of building the railroad and providing the rolling stock. The estimate of cost was about Bs 300 million for the 338 km., including Bs 60 million to build a bridge across the Orinoco near Ciudad Bolivar. This estimate was based upon an assumed cost of about Bs 700,000 per km., whereas the recently completed Barquisimeto-Puerto Cabello railroad cost Bs 1.7 million per km. A more reasonable estimate would be Bs 1.3 million per km., so that including the bridge, the total would be about Bs 500 million.

The second questionable assumption is the use of railroad freight rates substantially below the real economic cost of providing service. A rate of 5 centimos per ton/km. on general freight and 1.7 centimos per ton/km. for coal and limestone was assumed. These rates are much lower than is the charge for such commodities in other countries under similar conditions, and would not cover operating costs and depreciation. According to the mission's estimates, a proper economic analysis of the railroads would entail the use of cost rates, covering both operations and depreciation, of 8.0 centimos per ton/km. for general freight and of 3.5 centimos per ton/km. for coal and limestone (see Annex X).

The third correction necessary in the analysis is to include the cost of drayage and handling incident to rail transport, an addition which is necessary in a comparison with truck transport with its door-to-door service. The mission reckons that an average of Bs 16 a ton should be added to general freight costs to cover drayage costs at one end of the railhaul. This would add about 5 centimos per ton/km. for the haul from Matanzas to the Caribbean end of the line, thus bringing the total cost of 13.1 centimos per ton/km. for the haul of general freight by this proposed railroad.

The alternative means of transporting the freight if the railroad is not built would be via coastal vessel for the 800,000 tons of coal and limestone and via truck for the 750,000 tons of steel and general freight. Some of the steel, particularly piping, would in any case undoubtedly go by water, which would further reduce the advantage of the railroad. Water shipment, including river fees, between Matanzas and Puerto La Cruz would cost about Bs 11 per ton for coal and limestone, according to estimates prepared by the Railroad Institute consultants. This would compare to about Bs 12 per ton if the commodities were carried on the proposed railroad. Water shipment would thus save about Bs 1 per ton or Bs 800,000 per year. For general freight, trucking costs have been estimated at 14 centimos per ton/km. after including the full share of highway maintenance for this traffic. The cost of shipping a ton of steel and general freight by rail between Matanzas and Puerto La Cruz would be about Bs 44 compared to Bs 47 by truck. The annual savings by rail would be about Bs 2,250,000 for general freight. On this basis the net annual savings in operating costs and depreciation by using the railroad would be Bs 1,450,000, indicating a negligible return on the additional capital investment of Bs 400,000,000.

The capital invested in the railroad, as noted above, would amount to Bs 500 million, as compared to the Bs 100 million which the mission estimates might eventually be needed to strengthen the road which follows a parallel route from Matanzas to Puerto La Cruz. However, this work can be scheduled in stages as the traffic actually develops. The excess investment in the railroad compared to the alternative form of transport would thus be Bs 400 million. No additional investment in the waterway or ports would be required for water transport and the costs of vessels is included in the unit cost of shipping assumed. The net annual savings achieved by building and operating the railroad would thus amount to very little return on the additional investment required.

In any event, the traffic on the railroad would probably develop very slowly. It may take some time to get the steel mill operating satisfactorily and other plants are unlikely to be established in the area until much later. Coal traffic is still difficult to forecast. There are some indications that the coal, if used at all, would have to be mixed with at least 50 percent of good-quality foreign coal. There has been discussion of possibly producing coke from petroleum. Any substantial reduction in the estimate of the coal tonnage to be transported by the railroad would indicate an even lower economic yield.

It seems clear that the investment in this railroad would at best yield an extremely low economic return. The mission firmly believes that the building of the Naricual-Matanzas railroad in the current planning period would be a major mistake.

CIVIL AVIATION

Airports

At the end of 1958, there were 122 airports and landing fields in Venezuela. Four of them, at Maiguetia, Maracaibo, Maturin and Barcelona, were international airports. Of the remainder, 41 were national airports, 4 were municipal airports, one was a regional airport, and 72 were private landing fields. In general, these facilities are of a satisfactory standard and in most cases, adequate for the volume of traffic handled. During 1958, there were approximately 102,000 landings on the 43 national and municipal airports. About 1,425,000 passengers, either disembarked or embarked, and 47,000 tons of cargo were transported by air. There were 10,000 landings of aircraft in international traffic at the 4 international airports; 276,000 passengers either disembarked or embarked, and 14,000 tons of cargo were transported.

The investment in these facilities in recent years has been substantial. During the five years, 1954/55-1958/59, more than Bs 200 million was appropriated out of the national budget for airport improvement. About half the national airports now have asphalt landing strips. Twelve national airports have runways capable of handling wheel loads of 25 to 35 tons. Maiquetia can handle the largest jets. Six airports are illuminated for night operations. Eleven national airports have landing strips of 1,500 meters or longer. Maiquetia has one of 2,130 meters and Maracaibo one of 1,905 meters.

The program under consideration by the Government at the time of the mission's visit would have provided about Bs 50 million during 1959/60 and an additional Bs 66 million for the four-year period, 1960/61-1963/64, for airport improvements (see Table 40).

TABLE 40: A Program for Airport Improvement, 1960/61-1963/64, Once Under Consideration by the Venezuelan Government and Amended by the Mission

(in Bs million)

Program Item	Amount	
Studies	2.2	
Construction	26.0	
Paving	7.4	
General Expansion	8.9	
Buildings	3.8	
Land Acquisition	8.0	
Equipment	7.3	
General Maintenance	2.6	
Total Proposed Program		66.2
Less: Proposed Investment at Las Piedras and Barinas		21.0
Mission's Amended Program		45.2

The program included new work at about 20 different airports, including studies, purchases of rights-of-way, extending runways, re-pavement of runways, the building of new airports and purchase and installation of equipment. At many of the smaller airfields, runways need to be lengthened, widened and paved. However, two of the proj-ects incorporated in the four-year program, the expansion of the air-ports at Las Piedras and at Barinas, did not appear to the mission to be of high priority. These airports seemed to us to have sufficient capacity for the traffic levels that can be forecast during the next few years. We therefore suggested that the Bs 66 million program be re-duced by the Bs 21 million under consideration for these two airports. The mission did not have sufficient information to comment in detail on the rest of the program. For this reason, the mission included the residual Bs 45 million in its investment recommendations.

Subsequent to the mission's visit, the Venezuelan Government amended its own plans. The later program would entail a total cost of about Bs 79 million over the four years. Included, however, is some Bs 30 million for extension works at Maracaibo airport, an item not included in the Government's earlier program. It will be noted that, apart from the proposed works at Maracaibo, the Government's later program would cost some Bs 49 million, a figure which does not show a significant variation from the mission's proposed allocation of about Bs 45 million. So far as the project at Maracaibo is concerned, the mission has no doubt that large-scale works there are warranted; we do not, however, have sufficient information to comment in detail on the Government's specific plans in this connection.

Air Transport

Air transport service within Venezuela is generally very satisfactory and rates charged are not excessively high. Most of the domestic passen-ger traffic is carried by two companies, *Linea Aeropostal Venezolana* (LAV) and Aerovias Venezolanas, S.A. (AVENSA). LAV is entirely owned by the Venezuelan Government. AVENSA is a private company, domestic Venezuelan capital controlling the majority of the stock and Pan American World Airways having about a 30 percent minority hold-ing. There are also several privately owned non-scheduled air cargo carriers.

The operations of these lines in the airlift of beef from the southern plains to various points near the coast and thence to Caracas and other cities is one of the most interesting aspects of air transport in Venezuela.

This is becoming a major operation. There are very few roads in that part of the country and the riverboats do not offer a year round service. This airlift costs from 4 to 6 cents per pound from beyond San Fernando to Maiquetia. Carcasses are airlifted shortly after slaughter to higher elevation with lower temperatures, and quickly put in refrigerated trucks upon landing. As a means of opening up central Venezuela, there have been proposals to build a few large airfields specifically intended for the airlift of various commodities. The mission however cautions against sizeable expenditures on such airports until it is quite clear which regions are to be opened up in any case by alternative forms of transport; for example, the construction of a number of roads to these areas is now under consideration.

The regular internal passenger business is subject to rather intensive competition between LAV and AVENSA (see Table 41). For instance, during the first half of 1959, AVENSA offered 53,600 seats on direct flights from Maiquetia to Maracaibo whereas LAV offered 49,500 seats. The entire traffic carried including all intermediate stops was 46,900 for AVENSA and 37,348 for LAV. In flights to many parts of the country the two lines compete directly and provide duplicate service.

TABLE 41: Average Number of Weekly Flights to Various Parts of the Country by AVENSA and LAV during 1959

Routes	LAV	AVENSA
Western Routes	94	80
Eastern Routes	49	99
Llanos	33	—
Gran Sabana	2	—
Average Number of Flights Weekly	178	179

Duplication of service, which extended also to the international part of the business, and inefficiency of LAV have led to a rather low capacity utilization factor. In 1958, LAV carried 372,782 passengers, but only utilized 38.3 percent of the seats available on its flights. The company has been running substantial deficits in its operations for many years. It is estimated that the deficit for 1957 was around Bs 25 million, not including interest on a debt of nearly Bs 66 million. The financial results for 1958 were even worse, with operating losses at nearly twice the 1957 level.

The largest part of LAV's deficit has been in its international operations. LAV has not been able to attract any substantial part of the traffic going to or from Venezuela. For instance, during the last three years, LAV has managed to carry only about 9 percent to 10 percent of all the traffic between New York and Caracas. LAV already has six Super G Constellations and one model 749 Constellation in the international service, but new equipment is needed now if LAV is to stay in the international service and the purchase of this equipment will in all probability still further increase the deficit. New jet planes will cost about Bs 100 million, according to LAV and will probably bring little return.

While the Venezuelan Government feels the need for an international airline for prestige reasons, it is becoming increasingly difficult for countries of Venezuela's size economically to operate such a line, particularly in the new jet age. In an effort to meet this problem, the international operations of LAV and AVENSA were merged in late 1960. The mission has serious doubts as to whether even this will be a profitable arrangement. There already seems to be adequate air service provided to this part of the world by the larger international lines. If the merged operation also incurs a deficit, the possibility should be considered of Venezuelan air interests combining with those of neighboring South American countries to form an even larger merged international airline. In any event, deficits should not be incurred over a protracted period and, if all else fails, international air service operated by Venezuela should be abandoned.

WATER TRANSPORT

Present Limitations

Effective water transportation is being hindered in Venezuela by a combination of poor planning, administrative confusion and unduly restrictive custom regulations. Substantial sums have been spent on port development, much of which has been wasted because of the lack of proper coordination between the agencies involved in the planning. The economic evaluation of port construction work is inadequate and project planning is caught in a maze of conflict among the various agencies responsible for port activities. Both coastal and international shipping are being seriously hampered by outmoded, cumbersome customs procedure.

Coastal and river shipping, except in the petroleum and cement trades, has been brought to a near standstill by a combination of restrictions, customs practices and high charges imposed on this type of shipping by the ports. Purely internal trade between Venezuelan ports must complete nearly all the documentation normally required for international trade. Bureaucratic difficulties and inconvenience cause serious delays. Excessive port charges for loading in one Venezuelan port and unloading in another make it impossible for this trade to compete with truck transport, though in many instances it may be far more economical for the country to use water transport.

The most obvious reason for the high cost of water transport in Venezuela and the delays involved is the poor management of the ports. Ports are now run by at least four or five different agencies. Responsibility and authority are both divided and limited. Reasonably efficient and economical operations of the Venezuelan ports will be impossible so long as divided responsibility exists. We therefore recommend the establishing of an autonomous port authority in each of the large ports. Until this is achieved, major port investment expenditures should be limited to completing the most essential work that has already been started.

It is particularly important at this stage in Venezuelan economic development that efforts be made to stimulate coastal shipping. The chief problem has been the delays in shipping between the Caribbean coastal ports. With the development of the steel industry on the Orinoco River, it will be economically beneficial to utilize the water facilities available for the shipment of steel products, especially from Matanzas to the Maracaibo area, and for the shipment of raw materials for steel production from the Puerto La Cruz area to Matanzas. The mission made a preliminary investigation which indicates that the cost of water transport for the movement of such goods would be less than rail or road transport, and that the savings in foreign exchange would be substantial.

Steps should be taken immediately to promote and encourage coastal trade by a thorough revision of the present customs laws as they affect purely internal traffic. All unnecessary port clearance papers should be eliminated. Port charges for coastal shipping should be reduced to accord with the value of the services rendered, and if possible separate customs facilities should be set aside for the internal trade, as is done at the Venezuelan airports.

Past Port Investment and Current Capacity

The principal ports of Venezuela are at La Guaira, Maracaibo, Puerto Cabello and Puerto La Cruz (Guanta). Each section of the country is well served by one of these ports. In general, the capacity of these ports is adequate to handle the traffic that can be expected during the coming years. Ports are reasonably well maintained and well equipped. Expansion programs now under way can be completed with an expenditure of only Bs 35 million during the next four years, and should result in substantial surplus capacity. Further programs should be very carefully weighed until the whole port situation has been re-evaluated. Although there is congestion and delay in some of the ports, the solution is not to be found in additional new investment. Congestion can be eliminated by an improvement in organization and administration. Once this has been accomplished there will be sufficient time to re-examine thoroughly the future role and requirements of each port.

During the period, 1954/55-1958/59, some Bs 95 million were spent on the improvement of the four major ports of Venezuela. An additional Bs 11.5 million were spent on minor ports. The largest amount, about Bs 52 million was spent on the improvement of the port of La Guaira. Amounts of Bs 20 million were spent in Maracaibo, Bs 13 million in Guanta and Bs 10 million in Puerto Cabello. The largest expenditure for the smaller ports was Bs 2.7 million at Salinas de Araya and Bs 2.1 million at Paraguana (Las Piedras). About Bs 1.9 million was spent at Cumana and Bs 1.5 million at Ciudad Bolivar.

As a result of these improvements, the annual capacity in tons of cargo of most of these ports by 1958 exceeded the peak traffic levels. There was about a 20 percent surplus of total Venezuelan port capacity over the peak load (see Table 42). Over-all, the current rate of operations is substantially below this peak, but some of the ports have been operating near capacity.

The amount of port equipment has expanded substantially in the last few years and seems more than adequate. For example, there were 52 cars, trucks and other vehicles in La Guaira in November 1959, an increase from 28 in June 1957; 105 fork-lift trucks, an increase from 72; 34 mobile cranes ranging from 5 to 30 tons; 16 6-ton quayside cranes and one 30-ton floating crane. The Venezuelan ports are in the main supplied with sufficient mechanical equipment to minimize hand labor. Productivity in the ports is, nevertheless, low. An average of 176 tons of cargo is handled annually per linear foot of quay for all ports and 206 tons in La Guaira even though a daily two-shift operation is in effect. This is hardly a satisfactory performance for ports with a relatively high degree of mechanization. Compared with ports in Western Europe or the United States, Venezuelan port productivity is substantially lower and it is also somewhat lower than that at ports elsewhere in the world, with which the mission has had experience, even though, as compared with some ports in Asia and Africa, Venezuelan ports have sub-

TABLE 42: Capacity in 1959 of Major Venezuelan Ports and Tonnage
Handled in 1957/58-1958/59

Port	Annual Capacity of the Quays as of 1959	Peak Tonnage Handled 1957/58	Estimated Tonnage Handled 1958/59
La Guaira	1,650,000	1,490,000	1,310,000
Maracaibo	800,000	895,000	525,000
Puerto Cabello	940,000	795,000	620,000
Guanta	144,000	265,000	200,000
Cumana	180,000	25,000	25,000
Carupano	150,000	28,000	25,000
Ciudad Bolivar	72,000	20,000	20,000
Las Piedras	154,000	52,000	50,000
	4,090,000	3,570,000	2,775,000

stantially more mechanical equipment and warehouse and open storage space.

Furthermore, even if capacity is calculated at the somewhat modest
annual rate of less than 200 tons per linear foot, the capacity of Venezuelan ports is in many instances greater than the volume of traffic that
could reasonably be expected to develop in the next five years or more.
There are some ports, such as Guanta, where additional capacity had
been required, but expansion programs are under way and excess capacity will soon be available. Traffic actually handled in 1957/58 was
at a peak for recent years and thus may be used as a basis for determining the adequacy of current capacity of the individual ports (see
Table 42).

Future Port Investment

The adequacy of the current capacity level in these ports, including
the effect of current expansion programs, must be considered in the
light of future traffic growth. On the basis of our foreign trade forecasts
(see Chapter 7), we doubt if the traffic through the ports will grow by
more than 2 percent a year during the next five to ten years. Furthermore, the development of the domestic steel industry will undoubtedly
cut somewhat into the traffic of the ports or at least result in some shift
of traffic from international to coastal trade. For these reasons, the mission feels that port capacity in general is adequate to meet the needs of
Venezuela for the next five to ten years and that the future investment
program should be judged in this light.

The various government agencies involved in planning and operating the ports had prepared a program for port expansion which would have involved an expenditure of Bs 337 million during the period, 1959/60-1963/64. This program would have resulted in a substantial expansion in most of the ports as well as the construction of new ports in the south of Lake Maracaibo and at San Felix on the Orinoco. At the time of the mission's visit, a series of meetings between Cordiplan and the Port Department of the Ministry of Public Works resulted in reducing the program to Bs 128 million for the five-year period 1959/60 through 1963/64 (see Table 43).

This program would involve an expenditure of Bs 34 million during the year 1959/60 and an additional Bs 94.2 million during the four years thereafter. Of this latter sum, approximately Bs 35 million is allocated for the completion of projects that are already under way and some Bs 60 million is programed to cover new projects to be initiated after 1959/60. The mission believes that the new project part of the program could be halved to Bs 30 million without preventing the completion of any high priority work. Thus, the mission recommends that capital expenditures during the coming four years, 1960/61-1963/64, be limited to a total of some Bs 65 million.

Table 43 sets out the Venezuelan Government's proposed program for port investment. In order to indicate the types of expenditures which the mission considers may be eliminated from the four-year program, we list below our comments on the proposals for the individual ports.

La Guaira. The capacity of the quays in this port is already about 15 percent in excess of the port's peak year operations and about 25 percent in excess of the 1958/59 rate of operations. Nonetheless, due to poor organization and mismanagement of available facilities, there is serious congestion in the port. An old, partially used quay is being rebuilt and will be equipped with a grain elevator at a cost of Bs 12 million, and when finished will raise the capacity of the quays to 1,920,000 tons, which should be sufficient for many years to come. A new warehouse, which is under construction at a cost of Bs 4 million, will raise the warehousing capacity of the port to 3,140,000 tons, which should also be sufficient for many years. Additional open storage areas are being constructed which seem to the mission to be unnecessary. In general, it may be said that few of the expenditures being made in this port are of the highest priority. The capacity of the port could be raised substantially if necessary without any additional investment merely by improving management.

TABLE 43: Program for Port Improvement under Consideration by the
Venezuelan Government, 1959/60-1963/64

(in Bs million)

Port and Improvement	1959/60	1960/61-1963/64	Total
La Guaira	9.9	10.0	19.9
New quay and grain elevator (1st stage)	3.5	8.5	12.0
Refrigerator plant	0.3	—	0.3
Warehouse	3.5	0.5	4.0
Service buildings	0.3	1.0	1.3
Mechanical equipment	0.2	—	0.2
Other works	0.5	—	0.5
Investigation for expansion	1.6	—	1.6
Maracaibo	0.7	0.1	0.8
Warehouse	0.3	—	0.3
Storage area	0.2	—	0.2
Fire fighting equipment	0.3	0.1	0.4
Puerto Cabello	5.7	3.6	0.3
New quay	2.0	—	2.0
Fire fighting equipment	0.4	—	0.4
Storage area	0.1	—	0.1
Customs building	3.2	3.6	6.8
Guanta	7.0	5.5	12.5
New quay	4.5	1.5	6.0
Storage area	0.1	—	0.1
Coal port	2.4	—	2.4
Administration building	—	4.0	4.0
Other Works	10.7	75.0	85.7
Fishing port at Carirubana	1.8	1.8	3.6
Expansion at Carupano	—	15.0	15.0
Eastern fishing ports	—	4.0	4.0
Central fishing ports	—	8.0	8.0
Port of San Felix	—	10.0	10.0
New quay at Salinas de Araya	1.0	—	1.0
Marine school	4.0	16.0	20.0
Miscellaneous, including studies	3.9	20.2	24.1
Total Port Program	34.0	94.2	128.2

Source: Based on data by the Staff of Cordiplan.

Maracaibo. Facilities at this port appear to be more than adequate
for present traffic. However, when the bridge across the lake is completed, it is possible that some expansion in traffic will result and more

quay capacity will be required. One of the new projects that has been under consideration by the Port Department of the Ministry of Public Works and the Port Services Department of the Ministry of Finance has been the enlargement of this port. The mission feels that port expansion at Maracaibo will be of reasonably high priority for the period after 1963/64 and that the project should be thoroughly investigated during the coming four-year period. It is the mission's understanding that the location of such an expansion will be quite difficult.

Puerto Cabello. The Port Department of the Ministry of Public Works has taken the initial steps toward planning the construction of a new quay. The current capacity of the quays is already 940,000 tons and the port's peak rate of operations has never exceeded 800,000 tons. However, with the improved road connection between Puerto Cabello and Valencia now under construction, this port may well need some additional capacity. The mission therefore agrees that a new quay, to add at least 250,000 tons of capacity to the port, will be useful. The mission has some questions concerning the location of this new quay. We recommend that a very careful study be made of all the factors affecting the most suitable location for a new dock. Clearly the dock should be located to minimize both rail and trucking problems. The funds for the construction of this quay, except Bs 2 million which are to be used to begin developent around the proposed site, have been eliminated from the 1959/60 budget. The mission suggests that the work on this quay, although not urgently required at the moment, may be of higher priority than a new Bs 6.8 million customs office building which is included both in the 1959/60 budget and the 1960/61-1963/64 program. A shift of these funds, if possible, might be very beneficial to the port.

Guanta. This port is one of the few in Venezuela where there has been a definite shortage of berthing capacity. For this reason the mission considers the new quay presently under construction of high priority. The quay will cost Bs 6.0 million to complete and most of the construction is scheduled for 1959/60. This new quay should easily double the capacity of the port and eliminate the existing bottleneck in dock capacity. All of the other related facilities in the port appeared to the mission to be more than adequate. The mission feels that the new administrative building, for which Bs 4 million has been allocated, is of low priority.

Other Port Development. Little of the other port work being considered for the next four years is of the highest priority. Further analysis of the role of each port will be necessary after port management has been improved. A new port on the Orinoco River in the vicinity of San Felix will undoubtedly be necessary if the industrial development of that area proceeds to move rapidly and the mission endorses the plan to establish this port. A thorough investigation of the site of a new port at San Felix has already been completed and Bs 10 million has been allocated for the construction of its first stage. The program under consideration for other ports during the four-year period, 1960/61-1963/64, includes Bs 15 million for an expansion of the port of Carupano. Carupano already has a substantial amount of surplus capacity and the mission thus recommends against this expenditure. The program also proposes that Bs 16 million be spent on a marine school. The mission was unable to obtain any justification for this relatively large expenditure.

Port Administration

The administration of the ports in Venezuela is divided among several governmental agencies. The Port Captaincy of the Ministry of Communications is responsible for operations in the channel and pilotage in each port. The Port Services Department of the Ministry of Finance is responsible for the unloading and loading of cargo; this department also controls port labor and deals directly with the union workers in each port. The Customs Department of the Ministry of Finance is responsible for warehousing. Some maintenance work is shared among these organizations, and the Port Department of the Ministry of Public Works is responsible for all construction and much of the maintenance. Planning of port development is divided among all of these agencies. Port charges are collected by the Port Services Department, warehouse charges by the Department of Customs, and harbor and pilot fees by the Ministry of Communications.

Port charges are generally very high in Venezuelan ports. The average charge by the Port Services Department for all handling of cargo in La Guaira during 1958 was Bs 32.66 per ton of cargo moved which ranks among the highest in the world. Nonetheless, the port's costs were even higher during 1958 at Bs 35.29 per ton and the port reported a substantial loss for the year. One reason for high costs at La Guaira is an even lower productivity rate than that in other Venezuelan ports which, as we have already noted, is in any case generally lower than in comparable ports elsewhere; La Guaira has 30 percent less output per worker than, for example, Guanta. The cause of this poor performance is not to be found in the facilities, but for the most part in labor methods and management. The result is the poor use of existing facilities. Improvement in management and output should be accorded the highest priority in these ports and must precede investment in new facilities.

Coastal Shipping and Waterways

Although Venezuela is blessed with excellent waterways and port facilities, its inland trade is mostly carried by road. The traffic to the minor ports is not substantial. Of 3,449,000 tons of commodities handled by the four major ports in 1957/58, only 140,000 tons originated in or was destined for the coastal trade. Many of the coastal ports on the Caribbean have substantial surplus capacity and are capable of handling large deep-sea vessels. Nevertheless, their trade has either stagnated or declined over the past decade.

The situation in the industrially developing Caroni-Orinoco region may well be greatly influenced by the use of the water facilities available. At present, only about 25,000 tons of general commercial cargo travels the Orinoco each year, despite the fact that the river is dredged to 34 feet all the way up to Puerto Ordaz at a cost of many millions of bolivars a year to the Orinoco Mining Company for super-ore carriers. A sample survey carried out during part of 1958 showed that over three times as much cargo was being carried overland to Ciudad Bolivar as by water. Practically all the cargo carried to most of the ports along the Orinoco and its branches is carried by road, even though coastal vessels can travel at least eight months of the year to San Fernando, Puerto Nutrias and Guasdualito and most of the year all the way to Puerto Paez and Puerto Ayacucho. Most coastal ports on the Caribbean could easily handle these vessels. This is a great resource which should not be ignored in the future development of Venezuela. Serious effort is necessary to eliminate restrictions in coastal shipping. Cumbersome customs practices should be removed and the high charges placed by ports on coastal shipping should be reconsidered. The mission recommends that the present toll of about Bs 2.80 per ton, currently applied to all vessels on the Orinoco, should not be levied on coastal shipping or, at least, should be substantially reduced.

SUMMARY OF MISSION'S PROPOSED EXPENDITURES

The mission's recommendations made in this chapter would entail a capital outlay of Bs 1,710 million during the four years 1960/61-

1963/64 (see Table 44). The mission's investment proposals represent a reduction of Bs 200 million for the four-year period as compared with the program under consideration within the Venezuelan Government. This is brought about by recommending a reduction of some Bs 150 million in the category of roads and bridges, about Bs 20 million for airports and roughly Bs 30 million for ports.

Very little additional recurrent expenditures would be generated by our development program. In fact, the streamlining of all types of transport administration should lead to increased efficiency and so to reductions in operating costs relative to the size of the capital program.

TABLE 44: Summary of Mission's Proposed Capital Expenditures on Transport, 1960/61-1963/64

(in Bs million)

		Four-Year Period	Annual Average
Roads and Bridges			
Roads		707	177
Surveys, land acquisition and inspection		129	32
Reconstruction		185	46
Maintenance		400	100
Special strengthening program		100	25
Bridges		81	20
	Sub-Total	1,602	400
Airports			
New airports		11	3
Improvement of existing airports		14	4
Other construction		4	1
Studies		2	0.5
Land acquisition		8	2
Miscellaneous		6	1.5
	Sub-Total	45	12.0
Ports			
New quays		10	2.5
Buildings		8	2
Equipment		3	1
New Port of San Felix		10	2.5
Expansion of fishing ports		14	3
Miscellaneous, including studies		20	5
	Sub-Total	65	16.0
	Grand Total	1,710	428

CHAPTER 12 *ELECTRIC POWER*

Rapid growth of the Venezuelan economy during the past decade has been accompanied by a substantial development of electric power supply. The production of electric energy has grown over the past ten years at an annual rate of 19 percent or twice the rate of growth of the nation's total output. Very few countries in recent history have matched this rate of growth for as much as a full decade. The rapidity of electric power expansion has left its legacy. Growth has been haphazard. Plants have been badly located in some instances, and distribution facilities neglected. In one case, two companies competed to serve the same area.

Until recently, the government-owned facilities were divided into a large number of individual companies controlled by the CVF, each one separately operated and managed. The management was sometimes very poor. Organizational problems and inefficiency made it necessary to form one centrally-managed company to control all of the government-owned power facilities. While this led to a substantial improvement in the operation of these companies, there is still a serious lack of coordination between the different government regional systems and the private companies that operate in the larger cities of the country. Government development plans often make no allowance for existing facilities owned by private companies.

It is essential for the future development of Venezuelan electric power that there be some form of coordination of future supply plans between the Government and the various private enterprises already serving various cities. There will also have to be agreement as to future long-term plans for supplying the center of the country from either the various Caroni River hydro projects or large modern thermal plants operating on cheap natural gas. Future investment decisions are intimately related to these two issues. The supply situation for the four years, 1960/61-1963/64, will not be greatly affected by these decisions since projects already being carried out should be fully capable of meeting all electricity needs of the country for the next five years, even if the past very rapid growth of the economy continues. The issues must however be settled without delay if development *after* 1963/64 is to take place on a rational basis.

281

The Existing Electric Supply Industry

The existing electric supply industry is large for a developing country such as Venezuela, with approximately 1,250,000 kw. of installed capacity in 1959. About 319,000 kw. of this capacity is owned by the Government, some 536,000 kw. is privately owned in public service, and 394,000 kw. is owned by industrial enterprises for their own use and mainly not in public service. Total electric generating facilities averages 171 watts per capita which is higher than in any other country in Latin America and very close to the level of Japan. Even if the captive facilities of the oil companies are removed from the comparison, Venezuelan electric capacity at 132 watts per capita is only exceeded by Chile in Latin America.

Both the private- and public-owned electric enterprises are among the largest corporations in the country. In mid-1959, *Electricidad de Caracas* had electric properties valued at Bs 435 million, *La Luz Electrica de Venezuela* had fixed assets worth nearly Bs 90 million and the assets of *Energia Electrica de Maracaibo* were valued at Bs 65 million. The public corporation responsible for government power plants had assets estimated to be worth Bs 400 million. Few companies outside the oil industry in Venezuela are this large.

La Compania Anonima de Administracion y Fomento Electrifico (CADAFE) is responsible for the Government's electric facilities and was created by the Development Corporation in November 1958. This company is in charge of planning, executing and administering the National Plan of Electrification and has engaged *Electricite de France* as its consultant. CADAFE took over the administration and control of 15 separate government-owned electric companies with about 200,000 kw. of capacity spread throughout the country and nearly 1,500 km. of transmission lines. It now has 319,000 kw. of capacity and supplies energy to about 150 of Venezuela's nearly 365 towns with populations over 2,500. CADAFE mainly provides service to the smaller cities and towns, with the most important exception being Maracay.

The largest of the private companies are located in Caracas, Maracaibo, Barquisimeto, Valencia, Ciudad Bolivar and Barcelona. The largest private company, *Electricidad de Caracas,* with 340,000 kw. of capacity, is managed and controlled by Venezuelans. *La Luz Electrica de Venezuela,* primarily a distribution company in Caracas, is controlled by the American and Foreign Power Co. with *Electricidad de Caracas* as a minority stockholder. The Maracaibo and Barquisimeto companies, with about 140,000 kw. capacity are controlled by International Power of Canada. The Ciudad Bolivar company with 5,900 kw. of capacity is controlled by private Dutch interests; while the Valencia company, with 16,600 kw. of capacity, is owned and managed by Venezuelans. There are many smaller private electric companies, mostly owned by domestic Venezuelan capital, in nearly 40 other towns in the country.

The Extent of Electrification

Electricity is widely available in Venezuela (see map facing page 284). It has been estimated that about 55 percent of all urban families in Venezuela have electricity in their homes. In the larger cities, the proportion is even higher; for instance, it is estimated that 65 percent of all family units in Caracas and 60 percent in both Maracaibo and Barquisimeto have electricity. In view of the fact that some 40 percent of the families in these cities have extremely low incomes, the proportion of homes supplied with electricity must be considered high. In smaller cities, the extent of electrification is also substantial; it is estimated, for example, that over half the families in the Coro-Punto Fijo area have electricity. In general, it can be said that about 200 towns in Venezuela are supplied with centrally-produced electricity, including nearly all of the towns with populations over 5,000 and about 55 percent of the 365 towns in the country with a population of 2,500 or more.

The Growth of the Electric Supply Industry

The electric supply industry in Venezuela is in the midst of a period of extraordinary growth. Generating capacity devoted to public service has increased from about 100,000 kw. in 1948 to 855,000 kw. in 1959 (see Table 45). To achieve this degree of growth in such a short time, investment in electric facilities during the decade has of necessity been unusually large. Electrical enterprises devoted solely to public service during this period have spent nearly Bs 1½ billion. Approximately 60 percent of this amount, or Bs 850 million, was invested by private utility companies which now own about 65 percent of all capacity in public service. The largest of these private companies have maintained a 20 percent annual growth rate in capacity over the past decade, which has permitted them adequately to meet the needs of some of the fastest growing cities in the world. It has also permitted the construction of substantial reserve capacity to assure adequate electricity supply during the next few years even if rapid growth of the economy continues. Programs already under way will provide an additional 400,000 kw. for the private companies alone by 1964 (see Table 45), which should more than meet the needs of the areas served by these companies.

The growth of the government-owned electric facilities has been equally impressive. Capacity has been increased by more than 30 percent a year during the last decade. The newly-created CADAFE has already made significant improvements in the administration of these facilities. Plans for the future are extensive. According to CADAFE's proposed program, capacity will be increased by about 580,000 kw. by 1964 and at that time the government-owned facilities will probably account for one-half of the electric generating capacity in public service (see Table 45).

The expansion of the government-owned company is, however, burdened with several poorly-located large-capacity generating stations. A 75,000 kw. plant at La Mariposa is short of cooling water during the dry season. A 90,000 kw. thermal plant recently installed at Puerto Cabello has insufficient demand in its immediate vicinity and thus must transmit energy up to 200 kilometers to utilize more fully its intended load. A 300,000 kw. hydro plant on the Caroni, now being readied for operation, will probably not have a substantial load for several years, since its major intended consumer, the government steel plant at Matanzas, is far behind its completion schedule. The utilization of such temporary surplus capacity is one of the more difficult problems in the field of electricity that must be faced by the Venezuelan Government.

Adequacy of Existing Generating Capacity

Most parts of the country already have sufficient electric generating capacity installed or under construction to meet electric energy requirements until the end of 1963/64. The private companies in Caracas, Maracaibo and Barquisimeto have expanded their facilities substantially and should have no difficulty meeting demand. *Electricidad de Caracas* has 340,000 kw. of installed capacity with a peak load of only 240,000 kw. The Maracaibo plants have an installed capacity of 120,000 kw. with a present peak load of only 65,000 kw. Similarly, at Barquisimeto, where installed capacity is 20,000 kw., the peak load is currently only about 12,000 kw. Furthermore, all of these companies are expanding substantially.

The situation in the government-owned sector in most parts of the country is equally ample. CADAFE has recently completed a new

ELECTRIC POWER

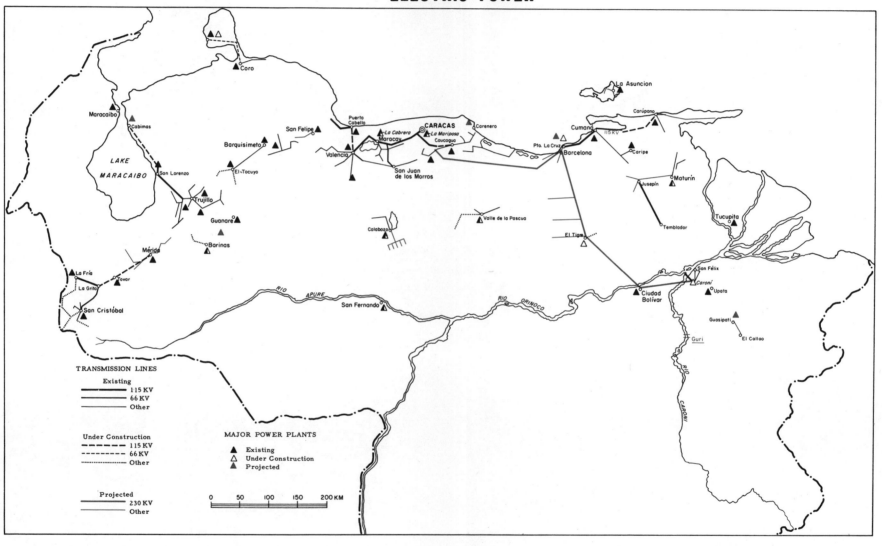

TRANSMISSION LINES

Existing
- 115 KV
- 66 KV
- Other

Under Construction
- 115 KV
- 66 KV
- Other

Projected
- 230 KV
- Other

MAJOR POWER PLANTS
- ▲ Existing
- △ Under Construction
- ▲ Projected

0   50   100   150   200 KM

TABLE 45: Estimated Installed Capacity of Electric Generating Plants in Public Service in Venezuela in 1948 and 1959 and Expected Growth by 1964[a]

(in kw.)

Company	Capacity 1948	Capacity 1959	Capacity 1964
Privately Owned			
C.A. Electricidad de Caracas	40,650	340,000	589,000
C.A. Elec. de Venez. (Maracaibo)	20,000	120,000	252,000
Energia Elec. de Venez. (Barquisimeto)	3,000	20,200	32,000
C.A. Elec. de Valencia	2,000	16,600	16,600
C.A. Luz Elec. de Venez. (San Felipe)	500	6,300	6,300
C.A. Luz Elec. de Barcelona	2,000	7,600	7,600
La Elec. de Ciudad Bolivar	2,000	5,900	5,900
C.A. Luz y Fuerza Elec. de Puerto Cabello	1,000	3,600	3,600
Other private companies	7,850	16,300	20,000
	79,000	536,500	933,000
Government-owned (CADAFE)			
La Mariposa	—	75,000	75,000
La Cabrera	—	30,000	30,000
San Lorenzo	—	20,000	30,000
Cumana	—	9,840	12,000
San Cristobal	—	6,060	6,060
Punto Fijo	—	5,390	17,390
Coro	—	4,500	4,500
Caucagua	—	5,000	5,000
La Fria	—	25,000	25,000
Puerto Cabello	—	90,000	165,000
Caroni	—	—	300,000
Puerto La Cruz	—	—	172,000
Other plants	—	48,210	57,000
	19,876	319,000	899,000
Total capacity in Public Service	98,876	855,500	1,832,450
Public-owned as a percent of the total	20.2	37.2	49.0

[a] As indicated in various company proposed programs and if the mission's recommended changes in the Government's program are carried out.

25,000 kw. thermal plant at La Fria, which should meet the needs of the San Cristobal area for many years, since the current peak load is only about 6,500 kw. A transmission line is under construction to take some of this energy to the Merida area. CADAFE is installing a new 22,500 kw. facility which should meet the normal requirements of the

Puerto La Cruz area. An additional 150,000 kw. plant, which has been included in the 1959/60 budget, is planned to meet the needs of possible extraordinary requirements related to the liquefication of natural gas as well as the future growth expected in the San Felix-Puerto Ordaz area to which it would be connected by a long transmission line. It would also be used to make firm the full installed capacity of the Caroni-Macagua hydro plant. There are also new plants being installed at El Tigre (3,600 kw.) and Cumana (8,000 kw.), as well as a new 20,000 kw. thermal plant at San Lorenzo to serve Cabimas and the rest of the eastern Lake Maracaibo area. In none of these cases is the peak load yet near the capacity level. Furthermore, because the Government's consultants expect the demand to grow rapidly in the area, plans are already under way to expand the San Lorenzo facility.

Potential Shortage Areas

The potential shortage areas in the country during the next few years are mainly concentrated in the central part of the country, outside Caracas. The industrial demand in Valencia and Maracay seems to be outstripping the capability of the existing facilities. Valencia is served by 16,600 kw. of thermal plants belonging to a small private company as well as by a few relatively small CADAFE diesel units. While power demand in the Valencia area has been growing very rapidly, there is no plan to expand either the private or CADAFE facilities during the next few years. Cooperation between the private- and the government-owned companies has made no headway. In some parts of Valencia, the distribution network of the two companies is overlapping. Some additional capacity in this area is obviously necessary and, for this reason, CADAFE is constructing a transmission line to bring energy from its Puerto Cabello plant to Valencia which will then interchange energy with the transmission lines connected to the La Mariposa and Cabrera plants.

The latter are CADAFE thermal plants which provide power for Maracay and for the INOS water-pumping system to Caracas. These plants do not generate sufficient electric power to meet growth requirements if the present demand increases as expected. It has been estimated by the CADAFE planning division that the additional demand during the next five years in Valencia, Maracay and for water pumping to Caracas may run as high as 75,000 kw. above what is now installed. For this reason, CADAFE has planned the installation of a 75,000 kw. addition to the existing 90,000 kw. thermal facilities at Puerto Cabello. It is unfortunate that arrangements could not have been made to utilize some of the excess capacity already planned by the private company now servicing the Caracas area.

The CADAFE facilities at Puerto Cabello are being connected with the rest of the CADAFE central system by a 115 kv. transmission line which will bring energy from Puerto Cabello all the way to the outskirts of Caracas, a distance of nearly 200 km. CADAFE's consultants feel this is a reasonable solution to the needs of this area because facilities at Puerto Cabello will have adequate surplus capacity, can operate on cheap natural gas, and have sufficient cooling water available.

In addition, CADAFE has been concerned not only with the short-term plans to meet the needs of the central region, but also with combining the longer-term plans for this region with those for expansion being considered for the new industrially developing areas around Puerto La Cruz and in the neighborhood of San Felix and the Caroni River. From the point of view of the economy as a whole, it might make sense to plan to meet some of the needs of the central region after 1963/64 by transmitting hydro power from the Caroni area in combination with thermal power from Puerto La Cruz. The latter could be generated by CADAFE and transmitted in bulk to the Caracas area where it would be distributed by the private *Electricidad de Caracas*. However, before such plans could be evaluated, other factors, such as the relative cost of hydro and thermal power and the plans of the private companies, must be considered.

Caroni-Macagua Hydro Power

The Government has nearly completed construction of a 300,000 kw. run-of-river hydro plant at Macagua on the Caroni River near San Felix. (There are also plans under consideration, which we discuss below, for a much larger hydroelectric project to be constructed nearly 100 km. upstream at Guri.) However, the use of such hydro power elsewhere in Venezuela in the coming years would necessitate, in addition to a substantial investment in the hydro-generating facilities themselves, considerable expenditures on transmission lines. A long-distance high-voltage transmission line is being considered to carry power from the Caroni-Macagua plant to the outskirts of Caracas. There would be a double-circuit 230 kv. line, 615 kilometers long, with five sub-stations, estimated to cost Bs 80 million. Preliminary estimates indicate that during the next three or four years scarcely 100,000 kw. would be available for transmission on such a line. Thereafter, considerably less power would be available. The Matanzas steel mill will presumably come into operation during this period and, within a few years, will require up to 220,000 kw. An aluminum plant is also being considered.

Clearly the design and size of the line must be related to the amount of energy available for transmission. The proposed line would have a capability of transmitting perhaps 300,000 kw. and would involve a capital investment of about Bs 265 per kw. If the line is however only used for 100,000 kw., the overhead burden would be Bs 800 per kw. In such a case, the annual cost for transmission alone, assuming a 10 percent capital charge, including depreciation, and a 50 percent load factor, would be about 1.8 centimos per kwh., which would probably result in the cost of hydro power being more expensive than energy produced in a modern 100,000 kw. thermal plant located close to the market.

Hydro power from Caroni-Macagua could be available at the plant's bus bar, under similar assumptions, at a cost of about 1.5 centimos per kwh., a cost far below any other power source in Venezuela today. Assuming however only 100,000 kw. of Caroni-Macagua hydro power were transmitted to the center of the country, the additional transmission cost of about 1.8 centimos per kwh. would mean that the total cost for comparable hydro power at the point of use would amount to about 3.3 centimos per kwh. If less power continued to be available for transmission, the cost would become even higher. On the other hand, a reasonably modern thermal plant, such as CADAFE's 75,000 kw. plant at La Mariposa, operating with natural gas costing 77 centimos per million BTU, generates power at a cost at the bus bar of about 2.1 centimos per kwh. An allowance for the cost of capital would add about 1 centimo, making a total cost for energy of 3.1 centimos per kwh. Furthermore, the cost of thermal power in a new modern plant of 100,000 kw. would be somewhat lower than the cost at the La Mariposa plant. The availability of the plant would probably be 10 percent higher (La Mariposa only had an 84 percent availability in 1958) and it would undoubtedly have a much higher thermal efficiency of about 10,000 BTU per kwh. as compared with La Mariposa's rather poor thermal efficiency of 28 percent or 12,200 BTU per kwh. Therefore, a new modern plant of 100,000 kw. units, as is now contemplated by *Electricidad de Caracas,* might improve on the La Mariposa performance by at least 20 percent. Furthermore, the cost of natural gas in large quantities at Puerto Cabello or Puerto La Cruz is now quoted at 60 centimos per million BTU. Thus, at this cost, such a plant could undoubtedly produce energy at a total cost of considerably less than 3 centimos per kwh. In brief, hydro power in relatively small quantities with high transmission costs would probably not be as cheap for Venezuela as energy generated in new modern thermal plants. It is therefore the mission's view that the transmission of limited amounts of hydro power from Caroni-Macagua to supply the central part of the country would be costly to the point of not being justified.

Caroni-Guri Project

The Government has also been considering a much larger hydro expansion on the Caroni River, upstream at Guri, involving a large dam with perhaps a first-stage installed capacity of 1,000,000 kw. and an ultimate installed capacity of 4,000,000 kw. According to very preliminary recommendations to the Government by its consultants, this hydro plant would also need to be connected by a high-voltage transmission line to the center of the country. This is an additional reason for the consultants' recommending that the transmission line be constructed as soon as possible; energy from the downstream Macagua project would initially be transmitted to the central region until such time as the power from this project is needed in the Caroni area itself and also until such time as the Guri project would be producing energy for transmission. As surplus power from the Caroni-Macagua plant will only be available for a few years, an early start to the Guri project is believed by the mission to be implicit in recommendations to build a transmission line from the Caroni River to the central part of Venezuela. The first stage of the Guri project, without expenditures on transmission, is estimated to cost about Bs 650 million. We have already stated that the transmission line to the center of the country will cost about Bs 80 million if it is to carry 300,000 kw. and the line would cost somewhat more if it were designed as a larger line to carry a greater quantity of energy. Furthermore, much of the central part of the country, particularly in and around Caracas, currently operates on a frequency of 50 cycles, as distinct from the 60 cycles on which Caroni (and much of the remainder of the country) will operate. For the Caracas area to be able to receive Caroni power, it would probably have to be converted from 50 to 60 cycles, a time-consuming process which the government consultants estimate would cost about Bs 100 million.

The construction of a transmission line and frequency conversion in Caracas would only be justified if Caroni hydro power is cheap, say, in the range of Bs 650-670 per kw. According to the preliminary estimates of the consultants, this seems possible. The transmission line and the cycle conversion might then add Bs 330 per kw. and thus the total capital cost delivered near Caracas would be around Bs 1,000 per kw. The cost and trouble of conversion could be minimized by carrying it out over the six- or seven-year period before the first stage of Guri were completed. Energy could then be fed into the private networks in Caracas. Further thermal expansion would be unnecessary. Such a project, even if it should prove economically feasible, would require close cooperation between the Government and the private power companies, particularly since the latter would have to adjust their own plans for expanding thermal generating capacity, as suggested above, and would also have to cooperate in the process of frequency conversion. The mission strongly urges that definitive planning on the long-term expansion of the electricity sector be closely associated with the plans of the private sector. It is difficult to envisage the carrying out of any large electrical expansion in Venezuela without such cooperation.

Implications for Caroni-Guri of Future Market Trends

The market for power will obviously be critical in any economic evaluation of Caroni hydro. The Guri project will require a very sizeable dam and storage reservoir. Given the large overhead which would be involved in the operation of even the first stage of 1,000,000 kw. and in amortizing an investment of about Bs 650 million, the mission found general agreement in the belief that the facilities would have to be reasonably fully utilized. There is general expectation in Venezuela that there will be a substantial number of new developing industries attracted to the steel industry at Matanzas. There is also expectation in government circles that aluminum plants will soon be attracted to the Caroni area.

It should be recognized, however, that if half the power, say 500,000 kw., were absorbed by new industrial projects in the San Felix area during the next decade, that would be a great achievement. For example, this would involve a 200,000- to 250,000-ton aluminum smelter or an electric furnace steel mill twice as large as the one now being built. If general industrial development is to provide the market for the remaining 500,000 kw. of the available power, it would require an increase in national output originating in manufacturing in this area of some Bs 2¼ billion.[1] This is an amount almost as large as the current total manufacturing output in all Venezuela. In brief, the amount of power that is implicit even in the first stage of the Caroni project is so

[1] The calculation assumes a requirement of 1 kwh. for each bolivar of value added, which seems to be the average requirement in Venezuela.

large that it seems clear that it must be absorbed not only by large power-intensive industries in the area but also by large power consumers in other parts of Venezuela, including Caracas. Unless this is feasible, substantial amounts of capacity might go unutilized, the waste of capital would be great and the cost of Guri hydro power high. The project could then hardly be justified.

It is clear that the central area of the country would have to take at least 500,000 kw. of Caroni-Guri power for the latter not to be at a cost disadvantage in comparison with local 100,000 kw. thermal power units. Thus, the critical factor in deciding whether to proceed with the Caroni-Guri project is the size of the future market for electric power, particularly in the central area which currently accounts for 85 percent of all electrical energy consumed.

Electricity consumption has increased at an annual rate of 20 percent during the past ten years. The mission forecasts that consumption will continue to increase in the next ten years, but at a reduced rate of perhaps 10 percent, which is nevertheless still a rapid rate as compared with many other countries. Residential consumption will increase, both because the number of customers will increase and because the average amount of electricity consumed by each residential customer should also rise slightly. In 1959/60 about 60 percent of all urban families were served with electricity. In the next ten years a growth in this saturation rate to 80 percent is not unreasonable. Such a growth would mean that the number of urban residential subscribers might rise from about 450,000 at the present time to 750,000 in ten years, or an average annual increase in the number of customers of 7-8 percent. Average consumption per family probably would not increase substantially, because many of the new subscribers will be low-income families who will avail themselves of the prevailing cheap installation rates in order to be connected with electricity but who will limit their actual consumption. Furthermore, there is the prospect of natural gas being piped into homes which will compete with the use of electricity in some important areas. On the other hand, general economic growth will probably stimulate added electricity consumption among those families which have already been using electricity for some time and among those which will not have the choice of using natural gas. On the net, average consumption per family might rise slightly, say 1-2 percent. Thus, together with the rise in consumption arising from the increase in the number of families connected with electricity supply, total residential consumption should increase by 10 percent annually.

The mission foresees some slowing down in the expansion of the manufacturing sector, but, since there will probably be more power-

intensive industries established than in the past, demand for electricity
from this sector may be expected to continue to expand at about 10 percent a year. Thus, the combined growth of both residential and non-
residential demand for Venezuela as a whole should also be at an annual
rate of about 10 percent, and this also seems to be a reasonable growth
rate for the central region alone.

With a present capacity of 603,500 kw., the central region had an
estimated peak demand of less than 500,000 kw. in 1959/60. On the
basis of a 10 percent growth rate, a maximum demand of 1,000,000 kw.
would be reached by 1967/68. Capacity is expected to amount to 939,300
kw. by 1963/64 (see Table 46) and *Electricidad de Caracas* intends installing an additional 300,000 kw. between 1964/65 and 1967/68. Thus,
total capacity would reach 1,239,300 kw. by 1967/68. If 500,000 kw.
from the Caroni-Guri project is also to be absorbed by this market, it is
clear that there would be substantial excess capacity during the latter
1960's. Therefore the decision as to whether to proceed with the Caroni-
Guri project should be related both to the plans of *Electricidad de
Caracas* for after 1963/64 and to any plans that CADAFE may have for
expanding thermal plant capacity in the central region. Since the units
under the *Electricidad de Caracas* plan would probably be ordered at
the latest by 1961, the mission urges the Government and the private

TABLE 46: Electric Generating Capacity in Public Service in the Central
Region of Venezuela in 1959/60-1963/64

(in installed kw.)

	1959/60	Expected For 1963/64
Private:		
C.A. Electricidad de Caracas	340,000	589,000
Energia Elec. de Venez. (Barquisimeto)	20,200	32,000
C.A. Elec. de Valencia	16,600	16,600
C.A. Luz Elec. de Venez. (San Felipe)	6,300	6,300
C.A. Luz y Fuerza Elec. de Puerto Cabello	3,600	3,600
	386,700	647,500
CADAFE:		
Carabobo	2,430	2,430
Centro	115,920	115,920
Miranda	5,000	5,000
Lara-Yaracuy	3,450	3,450
Puerto Cabello	90,000	165,000
	216,800	291,800
Grand Total	603,500	939,300

company to reach an agreement without delay as to the method under which additional energy should be generated for the central region in the future.

Frequency Conversion and the Caroni-Guri Project

As we have stated above, CADAFE's long-term expansion plans, if they involve the Caroni-Guri project, would require a solution to the frequency problem in the Caracas area. The mission has indicated that, without Caracas and the central market, there is no other market in Venezuela large enough to absorb any substantial quantity of hydro power of the magnitudes that would become available if Caroni-Guri is to be utilized, and the Caracas area can only take the power if its operations are converted to a 60-cycle frequency. The amount of power to be transmitted does not seem large enough for at least the next decade to think in terms of very high tension direct-current transmission, which would eliminate the frequency problem. Furthermore, it is difficult to believe that Caroni hydro could be cheap enough to be transmitted 600 km. and then fed into a cycle-converter for conversion to 50 cycles.

If Caroni hydro is cheap enough relative to thermal power to be brought to the Caracas area, a distance of 600 km., then complete cycle unification and interconnection may be the answer for the future power development of the center of the country. Presumably neither *Electricidad de Caracas* nor *La Luz Electrica* would be willing to absorb the Bs 100 million cost of cycle conversion in the Caracas area, because they can continue developing as a separate system at 50 cycles with thermal power using cheap natural gas. If the cost of this conversion can be justified in terms of the return to the whole economy through gains of interconnection, then we feel that this approach is reasonable because the companies have been operating satisfactorily on the present basis and, from their own point of view, would feel no need for such a conversion.

Tentative Evaluation of Caroni-Guri Project

The approach to the Caroni-Guri project should at this stage be tentative. All cost estimates are preliminary and uncertain. It is a very large project and affects not only the growth of the southeastern part of the country but the direction of the development of electricity supply for the entire country for years to come. A cursory examination of the prospects of the project from the point of view of electricity supply alone seems reasonable only if it is assumed that something like half the first-stage power is absorbed by some local industry such as an aluminum smelter. For calculating purposes it might be assumed that benefit from that part of the project is limited to bearing half of the burden of the overhead. This is undoubtedly a minimum assumption but it makes it possible to examine the possible economic yield of that part of Caroni-Guri hydro power which probably would have to be devoted to central power supply.

A very tentative examination based on these assumptions and on preliminary cost estimates made available by *Electricite de France* indicates only a modest yield on the additional investment in Caroni-Guri hydro power as compared to a thermal alternative. If fuel is assumed to continue to cost over the years the current price charged to the power companies, then the yield on the investment would amount to about 5.1 percent (see Table 47). However, this price probably overstates the real long-term cost of fuel to the economy, since it greatly exceeds the cost of transporting gas and since flare gas is now, and probably will continue to be, produced in quantities much in excess of total alternative uses. If, on the other hand, fuel is said to cost the economy 30 centimos per million BTU, equivalent to 1,000 cubic feet of natural gas, which is the cost of transmission to prospective power sites assuming zero value at the well-head, instead of the going price of 77 centimos per million BTU, the economic yield in the additional investment would be reduced to about 1.2 percent (see Table 47).

The decision as to whether to proceed with this Guri project requires more analysis than is possible with the information available to the mission. For example, there are additional benefits possible for the Venezuelan economy on the 500,000 kw. of power used in industry, if such industries can be developed. The mission therefore recommends that a thorough evaluation of the benefits, which can be expected from the Caroni-Guri project, be undertaken before any further commitments are made.

Investment Priorities

The decision with regard to the Caroni-Guri project will have a very definite effect on the amount of investment in electric power development during the next four years. In the last ten years, the private companies have spent about Bs 75 million a year, while the government-owned companies have invested Bs 45 million annually, together with

TABLE 47: Illustrative Calculation of the Return of the Additional Capital Invested in the Caroni-Guri Hydro for Central Power Supply as Compared to a Thermal Alternative

Assumptions	
1. Installed capacity destined for central supply in kw.	500,000
2. Plant factor assumed (percentage)	50
3. Net annual generation in million kwh.[a]	2,190
4. Estimated cost of Guri hydro plant in Bs per installed kw.	660
Comparative Investment Costs (in Bs million)	
5. Capital investment in Guri allocated to central supply	330
6. Cost of transmission line	80
7. Cost of frequency conversion in central areas	100
8. Total hydro and associated investment (5. plus 6. plus 7.)	510
9. Capital cost of 500,000 kw. of thermal power at Bs 528 per kw.	265
10. Additional investment in hydro (8. minus 9.)	245

Comparative Annual Operating Cost (in Centimos per kwh.)

Thermal		Hydro	
Production expense	0.16	Production expense	0.13
Fuel cost[b]	0.77	Transmission line	0.13
Depreciation[c]	0.40	Depreciation[c]	0.50
	1.33		0.76

11. Annual operating savings on hydro in centimos per kwh.	0.57[b]
12. Total annual operating savings in Bs million (3. times 11.)	12.5[b]
13. Approximate return on additional investment (12. as percentage of 10.)	5.1%[b]

[a] 50 percent of installed capacity (500,000 kw.) times the number of hours in the year (8,760).

[b] On the assumption of thermal fuel costs of 77 centimos per million BTU and 10,000 BTU per kwh. If the cost were only 30 centimos per kwh., fuel costs would only amount to 0.33 centimos per kwh., total thermal costs being thus reduced to 0.89 centimos per kwh., and annual savings on hydro being reduced to 0.13 centimos per kwh., or a total of about Bs 2.8 million a year; in this case, the return on additional investment would only be about 1.2 percent.

[c] A thirty-year straight-line depreciation is calculated for the thermal plant investment of Bs 265 million and a fifty-year straight-line depreciation for the hydro plant investment of Bs 510 million. Sinking fund depreciation would only slightly modify these results.

an additional Bs 20 million per year for the past five on the Caroni-Macagua plant. The 1959/60 budget of the government-owned company alone calls for an expenditure of about Bs 120 million. Approximately Bs 70 million of this amount is to complete works that have been initiated in previous years. Contracts have already been signed and it is doubtful if any change in the program can be considered. However, included in the remaining Bs 50 million are first payments of Bs 20 million on two large thermal plants, a 75,000 kw. expansion in the central region at Puerto Cabello and a new 150,000 kw. plant at Puerto La Cruz in the eastern part of the country. Contracts had not been let for these facilities by the end of 1959.

Although the mission feels that the present surplus capacity available in the Caracas area should be used to meet short-term shortages in the central region as a whole, the Government has apparently already taken the decision not to adopt this solution. In view of this decision, the mission considers that expansion of the Puerto Cabello facilities has reasonably high priority.

The mission believes that the construction of the Puerto La Cruz plant might result in a substantial increase in surplus capacity in eastern Venezuela during the next three or four years. In a sense, it might have been better to wait until the industrial demand from aluminum and gas liquefication plants was more clearly in sight. However, the prospects for the development of these industries—both heavy power users—are bright. The risk of constructing some excess capacity in this form may be worth taking, particularly since it will permit a more considered decision on whether to proceed, and if so at what time, with the Caroni-Guri project, where the amount of capital required is very large.

An interim program of thermal power built around the plants at Puerto Cabello and Puerto La Cruz, plus related transmission lines, would permit delay in proceeding with the Caroni-Guri project without in any way jeopardizing the future electric supply position in possible shortage areas of the country. Even if the growth in the demand for power is as rapid as CADAFE's consultants forecast, these two thermal facilities could still fully handle the requirements of these areas during the next four years or so.

The decision concerning Caroni-Guri would then have its most serious effects on the proposed expenditures in later years, both by the private- and government-owned companies. For the four-year period 1960/61-1963/64, the private companies intend to spend nearly Bs 400 million or somewhat more than they have averaged during the past decade. Cycle conversion in the Caracas area would entail an additional expenditure of Bs 100 million, much of it during the four-year period and probably mainly by the Government. However, since cycle conversion would only be necessary if the Government proceeds with the Caroni-Guri project, we include the cost of this work with that project.

The Government has under consideration plans which involve an expenditure of approximately Bs 900 million during the four years 1960/61-1963/64 if Caroni-Guri is carried out. Bs 260 million is included for the expansion of thermal plants, Bs 130 million for transmission and distribution works and Bs 29 million for other investment. The cost of the Caroni-Guri project for the four years would be slightly over Bs 500 million.

The mission believes that the high-priority part of this program would amount to Bs 255 million (see Table 48). This high-priority program includes expansions at San Lorenzo and Punto Fijo, together with funds for an electrification program for the 165 towns in Venezuela with populations above 2,500 that do not now have central electricity supply. An expansion of 75,000 kw. in the installed capacity of the Puerto Cabello plant is included to assure adequate service for the central part of the country outside of Caracas whether Guri is constructed or not. The cost of converting the CADAFE area from 50 to 60 cycles has been included in the 1959/60 budget and will permit the full utilization of the Puerto Cabello plant.[2]

The mission believes that, before any decision is reached on Caroni-Guri a useful interim program should include the CADAFE proposed 300 km. transmission line from Caroni-Macagua to Puerto La Cruz connecting the hydro power with a new 150,000 kw. thermal plant based on cheap natural gas. Together these two facilities will provide electric service for two of Venezuela's most rapidly industrializing regions. The thermal plant will make firm the full installed capacity of the Macagua hydro plant. The transmission line at 230 kv. should help provide experience in the operation of high-voltage transmission lines and might later be extended to the Caracas area if the Caroni-Guri project is carried out.

Our priority program also includes a substantial sum for improving the distribution network. Since no detailed program was available to the mission, we have assumed that half the Bs 90 million proposed by CADAFE is of high priority. A detailed program should be prepared as soon as possible.

The lower priority part of the CADAFE proposed program for the

[2] Much of the area served by CADAFE, particularly in Valencia and Maracay, currently operates on a frequency of 50 cycles, while the Puerto Cabello plant operates on 60 cycles. The Caracas water-pumping system is also to be converted from 50 to 60 cycles so that it can use Puerto Cabello energy, thus releasing the 50-cycle energy from the La Mariposa and Cabrera plants, the latter to be transmitted back to those parts of Maracay and Valencia which remain on 50 cycles.

TABLE 48: Mission's Estimate of the Priority Part of the Government's Proposed Program of Expenditures on Electric Facilities for the Years 1960/61-1963/64

(in Bs million)

Thermal Investment		
Expansion of 10,000 kw. at San Lorenzo	6	
Expansion of 12,000 kw. at Punto Fijo	6	
Expansion of 75,000 kw. at Puerto Cabello	38	
New 150,000 kw. plant at Puerto La Cruz	75	
Miscellaneous thermal expansion	6	
Thermal units for all towns over 2,500 people without electricity	10	
Total thermal investment		141
Distribution and Transmission Investment		
Transmission line (Macagua-Puerto La Cruz)	40	
Distribution system investment[a]	45	
Total transmission		85
Other Investment		
Final payments on Caroni-Macagua	18	
Miscellaneous projects	11	
Total other investment		29
Total priority program		255

[a] Since no details are available, the mission assigns priority to half CADAFE's proposed program.

next four years includes an additional 150,000 kw. expansion at Puerto La Cruz which seems to the mission to be unnecessary in the foreseeable future. The same reasoning applied to an additional 10,000 kw. expansion proposed for San Lorenzo. As indicated above, half of the amount proposed by CADAFE for distribution has been designated as lower priority. In total, we recommend that works involving expenditures of about Bs 126 million should be delayed until after 1963/64 (see Table 49). So far as the Caroni-Guri project is concerned, it would all depend on when the various studies and evaluations we have recommended are actually carried out, and what results they produce, if and when expenditures on this project should be made. If a positive determination to proceed with this project were made during the four-year period, additional financing beyond our recommended Bs 255 million electricity program would have to be found.

TABLE 49: Expenditures Proposed by CADAFE for 1960/61-1963/64 Which the Mission Suggests Should Be Delayed or Postponed

(in Bs million)

Low Priority Works		
150,000 kw. expansion at Puerto La Cruz	75	
10,000 kw. expansion at San Lorenzo	6	
Distribution improvement	45	
Total low priority works		126
Caroni-Guri Project		
Dam construction and one million kw. at about Bs 600 per kw.	400[a]	
Puerto La Cruz-Caracas transmission and sub-station	40	
Cycle conversion of Caracas area at total cost of Bs 100 million	66[a]	
Total Caroni-Guri Project		506
Total works to be postponed or delayed		632

[a] First four years of six-year program.

Government Regulation

There have been preliminary discussions within the Venezuelan Government toward establishing a law for the regulation and control of the electric industry. Rates are now determined by executive decree and have not been changed for the last several years in most parts of the country. The control of rates by some form of a commission is now being considered. Since the current level of electricity rates is reasonable, the mission sees no pressing need for such control. Development plans of the private companies, although not the subject of review by the Government, are most satisfactory. The private companies on the whole have been progressive and have adequately served the rapidly growing needs of the largest cities in the country. Their expansion should not be stifled by unnecessarily rigid regulation. The scope of their activities should be expanded and coordinated with those of the Government.

The high cost of electricity is cited by those advocating government regulation and control. The mission does not find electricity rates especially high in comparison with rates in other countries. For instance, the price of residential electricity in Caracas for monthly consumption of 40 kwh. is 7.4 US cents per kwh., which is about the same level as in many high-cost areas in the United States and Europe. Industrial rates in Venezuela are only modestly higher than in the U.S. for the fairly large consumer.

The problem in all rate comparisons is to distinguish differences in the utility systems providing the energy, and, in the case of Venezuela, to allow for the special role oil plays in the economy. The price of gas paid by the utilities is surely higher than the real cost of that gas to the economy of the country. Furthermore, until recently, the systems in Venezuela were too small for sizeable modern thermal units to be installed which resulted in very high fuel consumption per kwh. generated. Until 1959/60, *Electricidad de Caracas* had no units larger than 40,000 kw. in operation. No 100,000 kw. units are even contemplated for installation until 1963/64. In fact, as recently as 1957, over 25 percent of all the energy produced in Venezuela was generated in small diesel units. With the price of diesel fuel rather cheap, ranging from 23 centimos to 46 centimos a gallon, the cost of fuel in generating power in small units amounted to $2\frac{1}{2}$ centimos per kwh. in the most efficient units and up to 10 centimos in the less efficient ones, a cost range which would not be substantially lower in other countries operating such small units. Furthermore, the amount of energy delivered to the consumer has been low in Venezuela relative to the theoretical maximum capacity operating level. The over-all average plant utilization factor has been only about 35 percent. This is substantially lower than is found in most of Latin America, because plant, transmission and distribution losses have recently been much higher in Venezuela than elsewhere.

Many of these handicaps could be overcome as the scale of operations increases. It seems reasonable to conclude that both the private and public companies will be able in the future to produce cheap power in Venezuela with low-cost modern thermal units of 100,000 kw. or larger. In the mission's view, what is needed to achieve an electric power system providing the right type and amount of service at the right time and at reasonable cost is not an increase in government regulation of rates or government control over the industry, but rather public encouragement and stimulation of appropriate technological advances combined with adequate consultation between the various interests in order to ensure a rational expansion of facilities.

CHAPTER 13 *TELECOMMUNICATIONS*

The operation of telecommunications in Venezuela, especially the telephone system, is in such a bad state that it is becoming a serious impediment to the economic development of the country. Service in all fields of telecommunication is quite inadequate for the needs of a growing community. In many parts of the country, over 30 percent of telephone calls attempted cannot be completed because of technical limitations. Long-distance calls are extremely difficult to make and costly delays are common. Many large private industrial enterprises have been forced to rely on private radio equipment. Telegrams and radiograms often take several days for delivery.

Poor urban and inter-urban telephone service is without doubt one of the most difficult problems that the Government will have to face in the coming years. The Ministry of Communications has recently proposed that the telecommunications system of Venezuela should soon be brought up to modern standards, and has recommended an investment program of some Bs 700 million. Meanwhile, both inside and outside the Government it has been generally recognized that, without significant improvement in the organization which administers telecommunications, no successful program can be undertaken. There is a great deal of administrative duplication between the government-owned telephone company, *Compania Anonima Nacional Telefonos de Venezuela* (CANTV), and the *Direccion de Telecomunicaciones* of the Ministry of Communications. Furthermore, the organization and management within both these institutions leaves much to be desired. One of the main difficulties is lack of qualified personnel. Many of those in positions of responsibility have not had sufficient experience in the communications field, either to run a system or to carry out an effective expansion program. For this reason, sizeable investments have brought about far less improvement in service than might have been expected. It should be added, however, that the economy has grown so rapidly that even if telecommunications facilities had been properly managed, it would have been difficult to meet the required demand for service, particularly for telephones.

On the basis of data prepared by the telephone company and the Ministry of Communications, the mission estimates that about Bs 375 million have been spent on telecommunications facilities during the five-year period 1954/55-1958/59. As a result, there has been an impressive increase in telecommunication equipment available in the country. There was in June 1959 internal plant capacity, within telephone exchanges, for over 170,000 urban telephone lines and external cable and other facilities, outside telephone exchanges, for over 212,000 lines. About 270 towns in the country are connected with long-distance telephone service, and 141 towns have urban telephone service alone. About 95 percent of all telephone equipment in use is automatic. Telegraph service is available in 573 communities.

URBAN TELEPHONE FACILITIES

Past Growth

The combined investment by CANTV and the Ministry of Communications in urban telephones during the five-year period, 1954/55-1958/59, amounted to Bs 262 million. Internal capacity of approximately 130,000 lines had been installed,[1] far exceeding the most ambitious goals expressed by telephone planners during the early postwar period. About 80,000 lines of internal capacity were installed in the Caracas metropolitan area alone, and about 50,000 in the rest of the country. The magnitude of this increase in capacity, to be appreciated, must be compared to the system as it had existed five years previously, when somewhat under 50,000 lines existed in the whole country.

Until 1954, the telephone system in Venezuela was owned and managed by a private British company. After a long dispute concerning the adequacy of telephone service, the Government then purchased a controlling interest in the company. The Government's complaint had been that 40,000 to 45,000 potential subscribers were unable to obtain telephones. It was, according to the Government, the responsibility of the company to satisfy this demand. The Government had been pressing for a substantial increase in telephone capacity and, as a condition for a loan to the company in 1949, had required the company to agree to the installation of 25,000 new lines in the territory it served. This primarily included the cities of Caracas, Maracaibo, Valencia, La Guaira, Ciudad Bolivar, Maracay, Barquisimeto and Puerto Cabello.

[1] While the greater part of this equipment represented a net addition to the total system, a small proportion was for the purpose of replacing existing out-of-date equipment.

By 1950, the company had in fact installed about 25,000 lines of automatic equipment, including 14,000 lines in Caracas, 2,700 lines in Maracaibo, and 2,400 lines in Valencia.

Meanwhile, the Government had taken steps to install telephones in other cities in the country. A new automatic exchange was installed at Puerto La Cruz. An integrated network was constructed in the State of Tachira. Furthermore, a 1952 commission of foreign experts recommended a program which would involve the installation of 50,000 new lines in Caracas over a five-year period. Since the company indicated that it could not raise sufficient funds to finance such a large program, the Government itself instituted the program for Caracas. Plans were made to install a large number of new lines of Siemens automatic equipment and orders were quickly placed for 62,000 lines of new capacity. The company was not consulted as to how this equipment could be integrated into the existing network. Faced with the threat of a competitive network in Caracas, the company publicly declared against cooperation. The new exchanges at Maderero with 20,000 lines, La Florida with 10,000, La Pastora with 20,000, and Nueva Granada with 10,000 were not even planned in such a way that they could be integrated effectively into the existing cable net. The legacy of this dispute has been badly located facilities, shortage of external plant and, as a direct result, the under-utilization of equipment which has continued to plague the company's operations. While a peak of 95.8 percent utilization of telephone capacity was reached in 1952, utilization dropped to 41.1 percent by 1956 and only rose to 63.0 percent by 1959.

While this equipment was in the process of being installed in 1954, the Government obtained control of the telephone company. The rapid integration of facilities proved impossible. In order to restrict demand in dial offices, a subscription charge was instituted requiring an initial one-time payment of Bs 600 for a business phone and Bs 400 for a residential phone, which permitted a prospective subscriber to apply for telephone service. This charge was quickly effective in reducing the active demand for service, thus giving the company a short breathing spell to meet the most urgent and essential needs for telephones. Without as much pressure on the company, a substantial number of service connections were effectively installed.

The number of principal telephones[2] in service, which had grown from 26,000 to 46,374 between 1946 and 1954, an annual rate of 7½ per-

---

[2] A "principal" telephone is directly connected to the telephone exchange by its own individual line; there may of course be a number of extensions using the same principal line.

cent, increased to 105,060[3] in the five years 1954/55-1958/59, more than doubling the annual growth rate to 18 percent. Compared with 1954, when only 35 cities and towns had telephones, service was brought to an additional 76 towns by 1959, reaching a total of 141 for the country. The growth in the telephone network in effect had been so rapid that even adequate management would have had serious difficulties in coping with consequent organizational problems. As it is, equipment continues to be unutilized while a large number of customers want phones which cannot be supplied. In fact, CANTV has indicated that in Caracas alone, the waiting list is currently between 10,000 and 15,000. Furthermore, it is believed that the removal of the subscription charge would stimulate a further 30,000 requests for telephones.

The Financial Problem

Until 1957, the telephone company had normally made substantial profits, with the company's revenue exceeding expenses in that year by Bs 8 million. In 1958, profits dropped to Bs 700,000 and there has been a deficit in each month since then. The estimated deficit for 1959 is about Bs 3 million, despite an increase in revenue of more than 10 percent. On the other hand, total costs rose by some 25 percent in a single year between 1957/58 and 1958/59, increasing from Bs 62.3 million to Bs 68.2 million. The largest increase took place in wages and salaries paid to employees and accounted for nearly 80 percent of the rise in total costs. Payroll costs have gone up mainly as a result of the general increase in the number of employees, although there have been some salary increases. The number of CANTV employees increased from 2,510 to 4,108 between 1957/58 and 1959/60, while the number of employees in the Department of Communications rose from 3,700 to 5,335 during the same period. This increase in the number of employees has not been accompanied by a similar increase in equipment in service. As the result of the increase in costs, the average cost per principal telephone line in service increased from about Bs 400 per line to Bs 740 between 1954 and 1959, while income had only increased from Bs 500 to Bs 710.

[3] Note that this figure is considerably less than the total internal capacity of over 170,000 in June 1959, as noted above. There is normally somewhat more internal capacity than principal lines, if congestion is to be avoided. The spread in Venezuela is even greater than that often found elsewhere, and we discuss this below.

Utilization of Equipment and Cable Plant

Although there is a large unsatisfied demand for telephone service, there is at the same time a substantial surplus in plant capacity. Both in Caracas and in the remainder of the country, little more than 60 percent of internal plant is in use (see Table 50) .

TABLE 50: Utilization of Internal Telephone Capacity in Venezuela, June 1959

Zone	Capacity of Internal Plant[a] (in No. of Lines)	No. of Principal Lines in Service[a]	Utilization of Capacity (in %)
Metropolitan	102,500	64,500	63
Central	15,500	10,000	67
Eastern	13,500	5,500	40
Western	38,500	24,500	64
Total	170,000	105,000	62

[a] All figures rounded.

Central office internal capacity has been planned for a maximum of 90 percent use (i.e., to have 10 percent more lines than the number of principal telephones installed) , the margin being reserved for load balance within the dial units. The main reasons for the low 60 percent usage in Venezuela are that external cable facilities are not always located in maximum-demand areas while some such cables have been laid in areas where both present and potential demand are limited; furthermore, there are not sufficient external lines in some areas to utilize the available internal plant capacity. Even when this situation is corrected, if it is to be possible to load all offices to the 90 percent maximum, some additional installations will be necessary to increase call-carrying capacity of that part of the equipment which currently has not been engineered for the very high calling-rate per line prevalent in certain sections of Venezuela, particularly during peak hours. In some such exchanges, CANTV is considering the installation of an additional dial unit in the same building with a very high call-carrying capacity to which the lines with the highest calling rates can be transferred; low calling-rate lines only could then be assigned to the existing office, thus permitting full use of the equipment. The mission believes that such a measure could help alleviate the problem and so permit a higher rate of plant utilization.

Once the present difficulties have been overcome and external plant facilities have been installed in appropriate areas and on the basis of a proper balance with internal capacity, maximum utilization of such external plant facilities in the future will depend on adequate forecasts of the growth of new business and residential areas. To this end, appropriate studies of population trends and area development should always be a prelude to contemplated expansions in the telephone network.

Traffic Density and Rate Structure

The imbalance of the existing system not only results in an underutilization of installed internal plant capacity, but also gives rise to high traffic density on a great many principal lines in service. The great shortage of service has caused many subscribers regularly to permit their neighbors to use their lines. Often extensions have been unofficially connected in neighboring apartments and houses. The net effect is that many single lines handle the telephone calls of two or more families. Furthermore, there were no public telephones in Venezuela until two years ago. Merchants permitted their customers and even casual passers-by to use their lines free of charge. Traffic counts at the time showed some lines with 75 to 100 calls per day, a figure for private lines far in excess of other countries. A limited number of public coin telephones have been installed in Caracas, but many more are needed. Until there are sufficient coin telephones to meet the public demand and business users are prevented from offering free service to the public, this source of high traffic density per line may be expected to continue.

When adequate service eventually becomes available, including public coin telephones, the calling rate should drop. In addition, however, the local rate structure also encourages a high call rate, since all telephone service in Venezuela is on a flat rate; i.e., there is a fixed charge per month irrespective of the number of calls made. Changing the rate structure from flat-rate to message-rate might have a more immediate effect, although the mission feels that a message-rate structure would add to the already overloaded administrative burden. Furthermore, the depressing effect of message-rate service on the calling rate is problematical. Most telephone calls during peak hours, for which dial offices are designed, are by business users, and it is unlikely that they will make fewer calls just to save the small charge per call. Residential users might make fewer calls, but, unless there were charges for overtime, they would be inclined to talk longer which would offset the lower calling rates. The introduction of message-rate service in Caracas and Maracaibo, where the high calling rates are most troublesome, would require substantial expenditures to equip the existing dial units with meters. In addition, the cost of preparing customers' monthly bills would increase materially, since thousands of meters would have to be read each month in order to compute each customer's individual charges. Experience elsewhere has been that message-rate service for residential users often results in many complaints and ill-will toward the telephone company, even though the average monthly charge may be somewhat less than is experienced with flat-rate service. This seems to be due to occasional high bills which irritate the customer and make him question the accuracy of the meters. CANTV's public relations are already very bad and it would seem unwise to make them worse by introducing a rate charge which many users will dislike.

There has also been considerable discussion both within the Government and in the press concerning the elimination of the subscription charge. The mission feels that this would be unwise until the telephone company is able to meet all the extra demand for service that would likely develop as a result. First priority should be accorded to an intensive effort to improve service to available customers. Once service has been improved, it should be feasible greatly to expand the capacity of the telephone network, after which the subscription charge might well be eliminated.

Relief of Congestion in the Caracas Area

Congestion in the telephone network is especially costly and time-consuming in Caracas. Its elimination is clearly a high priority activity with a very high economic yield. For this reason, CANTV has proposed the expansion of the internal plant capacity in the Caracas area by some 71,000 lines between 1960 and 1964. On the other hand, a National Coordinating Commission on Telecommunications Services, created by the Ministry of Communications and composed of representatives of the Ministry, the telephone company, the Association of Telecommunications Technicians, has proposed that this expansion be limited during the four-year period to 50,000 lines of internal plant and sufficient related external plant.

These programs compare to an achieved level of installation of 80,000 lines of internal capacity between 1954 and 1959. The capacity installed during these years should not however be used as a basis for projecting the future program. The past expansion has been so large that it was not feasible to expand all the related facilities which would have been needed to increase the number of phones in service by a comparable amount. The limitation on future expansion in this area is not necessarily the absorptive capacity of the market for telephones during the next four years, but rather the ability of the telephone company's management to administer the past investment program and, at the same time, effectively to carry out a new investment program of the size contemplated.

Early in 1960, the telephone company made public its own plans to proceed with a program that would first meet the most urgent telephone needs of Caracas by 1962 and then would further expand the Caracas system in 1963 and 1964. It should be stressed that at the time of the mission's visit the telephone company's program had not been cleared with the Ministry of Communications, nor was it related to the investment program drawn up by the National Commission.

The CANTV program envisages the expenditure of about Bs 47.7 million by 1962 to expand the capacity of internal plant by 28,000 lines. In 1963 and 1964, a further Bs 108.5 million would be spent and a further 43,000 lines would be provided. The total CANTV program in the Caracas area for the four years would thus entail expenditures of Bs 156.2 million and the addition of 71,000 lines. On the other hand, the National Commission's four-year program would involve Bs 73.5 million of expenditures and the addition of 50,000 lines, but with larger expenditures during the earlier years.

The mission believes that the first part of the CANTV program is of high priority and should be carried out as fast as management and personnel can be organized to handle the expanded facilities effectively. However, we believe that, given the present outlook for managerial capabilities, it would be wise to stretch the first-stage CANTV program over the entire four-year period. Thus, we recommend that, instead of the 71,000 lines or the 50,000 lines proposed respectively by CANTV and the National Commission, only 28,000 lines be installed.

In making this recommendation we are not implying that the Caracas telephone market would not be large enough to absorb the full 71,000 additional lines, if the administrative capacity to handle such an expansion were available. We calculate that only 20 percent of the households of Caracas have telephones. This is low considering the average income level of Caracas of about Bs 14,500 a year. It does not seem unreasonable to assume that, if and when the Bs 400 subscription charge is removed, the number of residential families wanting telephones would rise to at least 35 percent of the households in the city, so that the number of residential subscribers would increase from the current level of 54,000 to perhaps 120,000. Allowing for a reasonable increase in commercial and industrial subscribers, a total of 200,000 subscribers would result. If 65 percent of telephones in service continue to be principal telephones (the remainder being extensions), as is now the case, 130,000 principal lines would be required. Assuming a moderate improvement in the utilization factor from 63 percent to 75 percent, internal capacity for 175,000 lines would be needed in order to have 130,000 principal telephones in service. CANTV's total program for the installation of 71,000 additional lines thus would bring internal capacity up to about the required amount and this represents a reasonable target over the longer term *after* 1963/64.

Telephones in the Rest of the Country

Telephones are being installed in the towns and cities outside Caracas at a very rapid rate. Between 1954 and 1959 the total number of towns and cities having a local telephone system rose from 35 to 141. The National Coordinating Commission estimates that 40 percent of all the urban centers in the country with a population of 2,500 or more now have a local telephone system. The Commission, together with the Ministry of Communications, has proposed an extensive program which would bring improved telephone service to those towns that now have telephone service and would install new systems in all of those towns with a population over 2,500 which do not now have telephones. The commission has estimated that this program would cost Bs 133.6 million. Of this amount, Bs 65.0 million would cover the installation of equipment in cities with populations above 35,000; and additional Bs 33.5 million would be for cities with populations above 10,000 to 35,000; and the remaining Bs 35.1 million would be allocated to the smaller towns (see Table 51).

The mission considers that such a program is too ambitious. The capacity for principal lines in all of these towns and cities would be increased according to this program by 88,000 in four years. The principal lines in service during the five years, 1954-1959, increased by less than 30,000 lines from 13,456 to 42,424 lines. Further it is noted that in all of the towns and cities with a population of less than 35,000, the increase over the entire period was only 12,483 lines from 1,895 in 1954 to 14,378 lines in 1959 (see Table 52). This program would increase

TABLE 51: National Coordinating Commission's Proposed Telephone Program Outside Metropolitan Zone, 1960-1964

Cities and Towns	Estimated Population in 1959 (in Thousands)	Present Capacity of Internal plant (in No. of Lines)	Present No. of Principal Lines in Service	Increase Proposed Under Program (in No. of Lines)	Expected Capacity of Internal Plant in 1964 (in No. of Lines)	Estimated Cost in Bs Million
Cities over 35,000	1,595	51,950	28,046	44,000	95,950	65.0
Cities 10,000 —35,000	1,609	9,536	14,378	22,550	32,086	33.5
Towns 5,000 —10,000		3,119		14,680	17,799	21.7
Towns 2,500 — 5,000	669	2,330		9,000	11,330	13.4
Total	3,873	66,935	42,424	88,230	157,165	133.6

capacity in this group of towns and cities by 46,230 or almost four times what had been accomplished during the previous five-year period.

While such an expansion in facilities may ultimately be necessary, the mission feels that, with the present limited capacity to manage an extensive communications system, the approach to expansion should be conservative. Some cities outside Caracas have average levels of income only one-tenth of that in Caracas and probably cannot sustain a much higher saturation level of telephones than currently exists. For example, where there are the most residential phones, as in San Cristobal, Los Teques and Valera, some 9 to 10 percent of households already have telephones, which is probably not low for cities at their income levels. Furthermore, despite the existence of substantial surplus capacity in many of these cities such as in Ciudad Bolivar, Barcelona and Carupano during the past several years, the number of subscribers has increased only slowly (see Table 52).

Out of 88,000 lines proposed in the National Commission's report for installation in the country outside of Caracas by 1964, only 25,000 lines would be installed in the main industrial centers of Maracaibo, Barquisimeto, Valencia and Maracay. The rest would be used to improve the telephone situation within the smaller towns and cities scattered throughout the country. It is the mission's position that a sizeable part of this program should be delayed until the management and organization of the telephone company has been substantially improved. Until such improvement, a greatly increased number of telephones in these smaller towns and cities cannot be regarded as of top priority; economic yields are much higher in the larger cities and, in any case, telephones are not as functionally necessary in the smaller towns.

CANTV has a two-phase program for the country outside Caracas for the years 1960/61-1963/64 which is substantially smaller than that out-

TABLE 52: Principal Telephones in Service Between 1954-59 and Capacity in 1959 in Various Parts of Venezuela

Cities	Number of Principal Telephones in Service[a]						1959 Plant Capacity[b]	
	1954	1955	1956	1957	1958	1959	Internal	External
Maracaibo	4,571	4,579	4,559	5,675	7,823	9,305	14,800	15,800
Barquisimeto	1,632	1,678	1,718	1,743	2,223	2,625	4,000	4,500
Valencia	2,202	2,251	2,412	2,627	2,853	3,009	4,000	4,980
Puerto La Cruz	—	592	579	709	853	1,032	3,000	3,800
Barcelona	—	548	519	523	540	592	2,000	2,400
El Tigre	—	—	—	—	—	—	1,000	1,200
Maracay	1,034	1,065	1,088	1,099	1,593	2,166	3,000	5,400
Ciudad Bolivar	783	784	782	783	817	867	2,000	1,200
Puerto Cabello	807	829	833	847	881	1,008	2,000	2,000
Punto Fijo	—	—	—	—	—	650	1,500	1,800
Coro	—	556	557	563	569	758	1,500	1,800
Los Teques	532	555	567	588	600	600	650	1,200
Maturin	—	—	—	—	—	552	1,500	1,800
Cumana	—	—	665	699	750	866	2,500	3,100
Carupano	—	—	409	464	477	501	1,000	1,200
San Cristobal	—	1,454	1,447	1,463	1,999	2,348	4,000	4,950
Valera	—	568	565	577	752	1,036	2,000	2,600
Cabimas	—	—	—	—	—	731	1,500	1,800
Total Cities Above 35,000 Population	11,561	15,559	16,700	18,327	22,630	28,046	51,950	61,530
Metropolitan Zone	32,918	35,521	41,093	50,750	58,019	62,636	102,663	130,000
Rest of Country[c]	1,895	7,460	10,336	11,794	11,410	14,378	14,985	21,270
Total[c]	46,374	58,540	68,129	80,871	92,059	105,060	169,598	212,800

[a] As of June of each year, except for 1959 when September figures are used.

[b] As of September 1959.

[c] Derived as residuals from the totals, which are annual averages except for 1959 when the September figure is used.

lined by the National Coordinating Commission. During the first stage, 54,300 lines would be installed, mainly in cities with larger populations, but some in smaller towns which already have central automatic exchanges. This part of the program is estimated by the telephone company to cost Bs 68.8 million. It would cover the full needs through 1963/64 of most of the cities in the country with a population over 10,000. An additional 15,000 lines at a cost of about Bs 17.3 million would cover the entire program for most of the towns to which it is feasible to bring telephones in the next few years. CANTV's program would entail total expenditures in 1960/61-1963/64 of Bs 86.1 million (see Table 53) as compared with the National Coordinating Commission's Bs 133.6 million.

TABLE 53: Summary of Proposed CANTV Program for Cities and Towns Outside Caracas, 1960/61-1963/64

	No. of Lines of Internal Plant to be Installed	Estimated Cost (in Bs million)
First Phase:		
Cities with population over 10,000	45,200	56.8
Towns with population under 10,000 but already having automatic exchanges	9,100	12.0
Sub-total	54,300	68.8
Second Phase:		
Towns with population under 10,000 to be converted from magnetic to automatic telephones	10,340	11.5
Towns with population under 10,000 to be provided with telephones for first time	4,670	5.8
Sub-total	15,010	17.3
Grand Total	69,310	86.1

Having examined both the National Coordinating Commission's program and the CANTV program, the mission comes to the conclusion that, in view of present administrative shortcomings, both are too ambitious for the coming four-year period and that telephone investment during this period should be limited to the higher priority parts of both programs in the larger towns and cities. We calculate that the needs of the country outside Caracas should first be met by investment in telephones amounting to a maximum of Bs 50 million, which would cover the largest part of the program in towns with over 10,000 population.

LONG-DISTANCE TELECOMMUNICATIONS

Present Difficulties

Along with the inadequate and poor service, the long-distance telecommunications system of Venezuela is being operated at a heavy loss. Accurate cost and expense data are not available, but we calculate expenditures are about five times higher than receipts. This experience is contrary to that of most other countries where long-distance service is generally the most profitable part of telecommunications operations. The financial results as reported by the Ministry of Communications for 1959 (partly estimated) show an operating loss of Bs 33.6 million (see Table 54). Even though some of the Ministry's reported expenditures probably should have been charged to the telegraph system, the financial situation is quite serious.

TABLE 54: Financial Results for Long-Distance Telecommunications, 1959

(in Bs million)

Expenditures:		
Ministry	29.9	
CANTV	11.4	
Total Expenditures		41.3
Receipts:		7.7
Loss from Operations:		33.6

A major handicap on the long-haul routes, including overseas, has been the shortage and unreliability of the radio channels. Because so few channels are available they have to be shared by several communities so that each has long-distance service for only a few hours. Even the six channels available to New York, which also deal with service to Europe and parts of Latin America, are not operated on a 24-hour basis due to lack of competent manpower.

As a result of inadequate long-distance service, many commercial concerns and some private individuals have set up radio channels and intercommunications systems of their own. Some of these are very elaborate. The oil companies, for example, have local dial systems with hundreds of telephones and interconnecting radio channels between communities over which users can dial. Reports show that over 5,000 licenses have been granted by the Government for private radio channels with the result that the radio spectrum is now overcrowded and there is some interference between stations.

Future Plans

Substantial additions to the radiotelephone network that might improve the shortage of public long-distance facilities are in various stages of completion. A few have been placed in service, others are being built, and many more are planned. A microwave network in the eastern part of the country that will connect Caracas with the Puerto La Cruz-Barcelona area and with Maturin, El Tigre and Ciudad Bolivar is under construction at a cost of Bs 13.6 million. A larger network, costing Bs 61.4 million is being surveyed to service western Venezuela.

The National Coordinating Commission has proposed construction of a country-wide network of nearly 1,000 microwave channels for both telephone and telegraph service to connect all communities of substantial size and also augment the overseas channels. The cost of a five-year program for installing these facilities is estimated at about Bs 119 million (see Table 55). Several foreign technical experts have been working on this program and the Ministry has prepared detailed estimates of the number of channels required between the larger centers of population. These are based on population, telephone call traffic, urban development, business growth, number of urban telephone subscribers, etc. The mission was not able to obtain detailed information on the associated switchboards, toll dial equipment, switching centers and the proposed method of operation of these facilities. On the basis of general impressions, however, it would appear that some of the equipment proposed may be more elaborate and more costly than that used in other countries with advanced telecommunications systems.

The proposed plan is based on the use of radio channels throughout the country. This appears sound for the major network, particularly in view of the rugged terrain of much of Venezuela, but other countries with similar problems have found a combination of radio channels and wire lines the most economical approach. There are some good wire

TABLE 55: Long-Distance Telecommunications Program, 1960/61-1963/64, as Proposed by National Coordinating Commission

(in Bs million)

Item	Equipment	Construction	Total
Western Microwave Network	50.8	10.6	61.4
Eastern Microwave Network	7.3	6.3	13.6
Long-distance Switching	17.0	3.4	20.4
International Network	9.2	0.2	9.4
Teletype System	9.1	0.7	9.8
Trunk Telegraph Network	2.3	2.1	4.4
Total	95.7	23.3	119.0

lines in Venezuela which could offer capacity for a large number of additional channels by the use of carrier systems. The mission questions whether enough consideration has been given to making full use of these available facilities before embarking on such an extensive program of entirely new radio systems. The proposed system would no doubt provide channels enough for a very large increase in telephone and telegraph service but it is not at all clear that the program is the most economical that could be devised or that all the proposed channels would be needed in the reasonably near future. The mission has not been able to obtain information on how the engineering, construction, maintenance and operating personnel for such a large system could be developed in four years.

The high priority of improving long-distance communications facilities in Venezuela at this time cannot be questioned. Some balance must be brought to the existing system and bottlenecks eliminated immediately. For example, although there are now 270 towns and cities with long-distance service, there are still towns, such as El Tigre, which have urban phones but no long-distance service, and, as indicated above, many of the towns only have service during a limited number of hours each day. Heavy traffic areas are not linked with a sufficient number of channels. An indication of this is the fact that the Ministry spends only twice as much to maintain communications between the two major cities of Caracas and Maracaibo, with a population of 450,000, as between Caracas and the relatively small city of Porlamar, the capital of Nueva Esparta, with a population of only 18,000.

The seriousness of the long-distance situation is pointed up by the fact that even though the growth of facilities has been extremely rapid in recent years, the quality of service has not improved. There has been a substantial expansion of the telegraph network, with the number of telegraph offices increasing 50 percent during the last four years, from 438 to 653, and the number of messages sent increasing from 6.3 million to 8.7 million between 1950 and 1957. Nevertheless, several days are often required for the delivery of telegrams and radiograms. The situation in regard to international communications, as noted above, is no more favorable. All communications to Europe and to some countries in Latin America, as noted above, are transmitted through New York, since there are no direct channels with Europe and with most of the Latin American countries.

The mission believes that an effective long-distance system will take far longer to develop than the four years allowed for in the National Coordinating Commission's planning. The usual procedure, which has worked well elsewhere, is first to set up long-range targets outlining basic requirements such as a numbering plan, a switching plan, a method of operation, and types of service to be provided. Having set up the targets, studies can then be made to determine the most economical number and location of switching centers and major routes. This is followed by studies of individual routes, in order of urgency, to determine how many and what kind of channels and terminating equipment should be ordered for a particular location. This step has to be coordinated with consideration of the probable immediate market and the manpower available. Each installation must be designed to fit in with the over-all plan, so that no extensive changes or replacements will be necessary as additions are made. Fortunately, radio and carrier channels, toll switchboard positions, and toll dial equipment, can be added in fairly small increments to minimum installations at little or no cost additional to initial installation expenses and at far less risk of installing the wrong amount and the wrong type of facilities. The mission feels that a step-by-step program along these lines will better provide Venezuela with an adequate long-distance system in minimum time and at minimum cost.

The targets of the proposed program seem reasonable as a longer-term goal. The proposed microwave network would serve 380 towns and cities, as compared to the present 270. Telegraph service would use the same means of transmission. Each microwave channel would allow up to 24 telegraph channels to be used. The Ministry has also noted the possibility of establishing a teletype network using the same channels and is considering the possibility of creating capacity for 1,290 teletype subscribers in 19 of the most important cities in the country. When it would become possible to carry out all parts of this program, an enormous increase in the capacity for long-distance communications will be effected. For instance, Barinas, which currently has only one secondary connection to the main parts of the country available through Merida, would have, after completion of the microwave network, twelve direct channels to Caracas and three to Barquisimeto; Valera will be able to communicate with Maracaibo on 78 channels, compared to the 20 channels that now are available to the entire country.

The mission proposes that more modest targets, than those set for the long run, be established for the next four years in line with what can realistically be done toward improving the management and organization of the communications network. The most important criterion in scheduling an expansion of long-distance communications is not so much in terms of priorities as in terms of what can actually be accomplished effectively. The mission is hampered by a lack of details concerning long-distance planning by the Ministry of Communications. For this reason, the mission's judgment of the actual amount that should be allocated for long-distance facilities during the years, 1960/61-1963/64, must be viewed as being very tentative. A figure of Bs 75 million is used as a working estimate. Such a proposed figure would be based on postponing the teletype system for several years until actual demand is assured, constructing the microwave network by slower stages, and reducing the amount set aside for long-distance switching facilities, which the mission suggests may be out of proportion to the rest of the program.

ORGANIZATION AND PERSONNEL

As indicated above, some of the main reasons for the unsatisfactory state of telecommunications in Venezuela are duplication in organization, inefficient management and the lack of trained personnel. The Ministry of Communications operates the radio system, both overseas and within the country, and CANTV operates the local exchanges and the intercity wire lines between Caracas and nearby cities. The Ministry handles all telegraph service and asserts responsibility for long-range planning of the long-distance network. There is no clear-cut separation of responsibilities, so that neither organization can function effectively.

It is generally recognized within and outside the Venezuelan Government, and the mission agrees, that the whole telecommunications system should be under one management. This is essential to the expansion and improvement of the telephone and telegraph service but, in the opinion of the mission, it is only the first step. It needs to be followed by a reorganization of the company and the recruiting and training of an adequate and competent staff to plan and build new facilities, as well as to operate the existing system efficiently. Without this, the addition of more dial equipment, more urban cable plant and more intercity trunks will provide but little increase or improvement in service.

During the six years that the Venezuelan Government has operated the telephone system there have been repeated disruptions in top management. Each time the officers of the company and the Board of Directors were partially or completely replaced, the plans and policies of the previous administration were largely scrapped. The senior administrators have often had no technical training or experience in telecommunications. The mission suggests that this situation can best be remedied by separating telecommunications completely from political control.

The unification of telecommunication facilities into one organization must be followed by an active campaign to obtain competent staff. One of the most serious shortages in personnel is in the number and the experience of the engineers assigned to planning and designing the expansion and improvement program. CANTV has some engineers with experience in Venezuela and elsewhere, but in the past they have generally been without authority to carry out the improvements they recommended. Recruiting and developing an adequate and competent staff of engineers will be difficult and will probably take many years. A major reason for this shortage is that there are so few engineering graduates of the universities (see Chapter 14) and most of those have been finding more lucrative employment in other fields. To meet the immediate need, it seems necessary to bring in foreign engineers with the appropriate qualifications and to give them a free hand. At the same time, every effort should be made to recruit and train Venezuelan engineers for the telecommunications system of the future.

If the telecommunications system is to function properly, an adequate staff of competent supervisory personnel will also be needed for the efficient operation of the plant. Supervisory staff do not necessarily require an advanced technical background, but at least they should be trained in the work of one department and in the handling of staff and then be assured of some continuity in employment. While some foreign experts in this field will probably be needed if improvement in the present situation is to be realized in the near future, it should also be possible to recruit for this category either by promotion from the ranks or from other large organizations.

There is also the need for improving the work of the rank-and-file in the organization. Available data supplied by the Ministry and by the

CANTV indicates a marked deterioration in productivity per worker in recent years. This undoubtedly is the result of the general inefficiency of the management, the poor methods used in recruiting of new employees, and the promotions system within the organization, often on a basis other than capability, merit and proven fitness. With efficient and conscientious management, free to adopt and execute policies based only on the requirements of the communications system, it should be possible to select enough qualified people to operate the telecommunications system efficiently.

SUMMARY OF MISSION'S PROPOSED EXPENDITURES

The recommendations which we have made in this chapter would entail capital expenditures in the telecommunications field amounting to about Bs 173 million during the four years 1960/61-1963/64 (see Table 56). The mission has derived its recommendations by examining the

TABLE 56: Mission's Proposed Capital Expenditures on Telecommunications, 1960/61-1963/64

(in Bs million)

Program Item	National Commission's Proposals	Mission According to Low Priority	Mission's Recommended Program
Caracas (50,000 telephone lines)	73.5	25.5	48.0
Remainder of country (88,000 telephone lines)	133.6	83.6	50.0
Long-distance Communications	109.0[a]	34.0	75.0
Total Mission Program			173.0

[a] Excludes Bs 10 million spent before 1960/61.

proposals of the National Coordinating Commission on Telecommunications Services, in conjunction with those of CANTV, and coming to conclusions as to the broad division of those proposals as between its high and low priority parts. We then suggest that the proposed program in the main be stretched beyond the four-year period and that only the high priority part be scheduled for completion by 1963/64.

CHAPTER 14 *EDUCATION*

The mission attaches considerable importance to measures designed to improve the Venezuelan educational system. While education is of course desired for its own sake, it is also a necessary precondition for economic development. Many of the programs advocated in this report will be severely handicapped unless shortages of advanced skills can be overcome and unless general educational levels can be raised. Such levels were very low in 1958 at the beginning of the present period of constitutional government. Out of an estimated population of 6.8 million, more than 2 million adults were illiterate. Some 500,000 school-age children, or about 40 percent of the total, were not attending school, and, if past trends were any indication, of those attending school the majority would not even complete the first three grades of primary education.

Since 1958 the Government has made strenuous efforts to make up the backlog. About 400,000 overage children have been taken into the first grade of the primary school system. This has boosted total primary school enrollment by 22 percent and 28 percent respectively in two succeeding years and has placed a serious strain on the primary education system. Lack of suitable buildings and equipment, under-supply of properly trained teachers, inadequacy of curricula offered, and a heavy administrative burden have been some of the results of such a rapid expansion. Furthermore, there have been additional strains at all other points in the educational system—at the intermediate and university levels—where similarly rapid expansions have taken place.

The mission nevertheless applauds these efforts and hopes that even further advances will be possible in the coming years. The sort of "crash program" which has taken place in the last couple of years was probably psychologically necessary in order to make a clear-cut break with the past. But the time has now come, the mission feels, when further educational advance should be phased in terms of ultimate objectives.

In the field of education a four-year program should be regarded as only the first phase in a longer-term plan. Sound educational expansion requires a forward look of at least 20 or 30 years. For example, the quantity and quality of first-year primary education today will have

320

an impact on the type and scope of specialized and higher education possible more than 15 years from now. The proper way to plan educational development is to establish ultimate objectives and then make sure that in the shorter term each phase contributes to attaining those objectives.

We will suggest some very broad aims for educational development, but these need to be worked out in detail, the different parts of the program being carefully coordinated, so that expansion at all levels of the educational pyramid keeps in step. It would be particularly valuable to have a comprehensive survey made of the likely requirements over the next 20 to 30 years for various professional, technical, clerical and manual skills, so that the educational system can be geared to supply them.

Even without a specific survey of manpower requirements, it is possible to discern what Venezuela broadly needs from its education system. First of all, it needs a population, both in urban and rural areas, which is literate and possessing a basic education. Thus, one ultimate objective is that every child should get a primary education. This means that every child under 14 who has not yet been to school should be enrolled with the minimum practicable delay. It also means that in the future every child who becomes seven years old (the legal school age) should be provided the opportunity to start his primary schooling. It further means that every child should have the opportunity, once in primary school, to complete the full six-year course. The mission believes that current low retention rates between the various grades in the primary schools is a serious flaw in Venezuelan education. We believe that it is of little value for a child to enter the first grade, only to drop out in a year or two. In a democracy we believe every child has a right to a basic education and that ultimately a minimum of six years should be regarded as basic.

While Venezuela needs to provide a basic education for a maximum proportion of its population as rapidly as possible, there are other priorities at higher points in the educational pyramid which must be filled at the same time. These priorities are selective. This is to say that, while primary education is a general need which should be met on as broad a base as is possible, the need for further education is defined by the demand-and-supply situation of the various talents involved. Because of previous neglect, the supply of trained personnel in most fields at most levels is likely to trail the demand. Hence the vital importance of settling on an order of priorities.

PRIMARY EDUCATION

Primary schools in Venezuela are intended to provide six years of study for children between the ages of seven and fourteen, which is the compulsory school age as defined by law. Due to many years of neglect, primary education actually falls far short of these intentions. In fact during the school year 1957/58, when the move toward constitutional government took place, only 57 percent of school-age children were actually attending school. Furthermore, retention rates had been so low that relatively few of those who had been in school in previous years had attended for more than a year or two. Thus in 1957/58 more than half of total enrollment was to be found in the first two grades while only some 6 percent were in the sixth grade.

The present Government has done a remarkable job in rapidly enrolling the backlog of school-age children who were without previous education. By the school year 1959/60 it is estimated that some 400,000 of these backlog children had been enrolled while at the same time in each of the two years 1958/59 and 1959/60 more than 200,000 or some 75 percent, of the children reaching seven years of age, had also been enrolled in the first grade. Thus, first-grade enrollment increased from 262,072 in 1957/58 to 434,800 in 1959/60. Total primary school enrollment for all grades went up from 751,561 in 1957/58 to 1,067,900 in 1959/60.[1]

Such a rapid expansion could only have been achieved by adopting a number of makeshift measures, such as increasing the average number of pupils per classroom and per teacher in some schools, by occupying premises which would ideally not be considered adequate, and by employing uncertificated teachers. The mission believes that in the period ahead policy should be aimed at consolidating enrollment gains by improving standards and in particular by taking measures to increase retention rates so that a higher proportion of children who start primary schooling go on to complete the full six-year course.

Future Enrollment

Future enrollment broadly depends on the number of new entrants in each year and the rate at which previous entrants are retained in

---

[1] Figures for 1959/60 are based on provisional estimates available at the time of the mission's visit.

school. So far as new entrants are concerned, it is safe to predict that the backlog of overage children will be eliminated in the coming two years and so will cease to be a source of additional new entrants thereafter. Both federal and state governments have had such success in reducing this problem that we calculate that there are now only 125,000 children between the ages of eight and fourteen who have not yet been enrolled.

Normally, the main source of new entrants in any one year is the group of children who become seven years old during that year. Because of population growth, it can be predicted that this group will grow in each of the coming years. This in itself will boost first-grade enrollment. In the past, however, only about 75 percent of the seven-year-olds have been starting school at that age. Every effort should be made to increase this proportion. We believe that an expansion program will in itself raise the proportion of children seeking an education and furthermore that the economic development programs suggested elsewhere in this report will create the sort of social environment and the economic possibilities that stimulate the desire for education. We thus feel that it is possible that while nearly 80 percent of the 1960/61 seven-year-olds will probably enroll in the first grade, as many as 90 percent of the 1963/64 seven-year-olds will enter school. Thus, the number of seven-year-olds in first grade would rise from less than 190,000 in 1960/61 to more than 230,000 in 1963/64.

There is one further source of first-grade pupils: children repeating this grade from the previous year. This has been a serious problem in Venezuela. In 1957/58, of those enrolled in first grade, 28.7 percent were repeaters. It is thought that the repeater rate has been reduced somewhat but is still about 20 percent. There are a number of factors connected with the repeater rate: poor teaching standards; low pupil aptitude; rigid promotion policies; and, finally, a lack of availability of higher grades which forces some children back into the same grade. The mission believes that each of these factors can be dealt with if the right policies are applied. Given a suitable program of teacher training and an expansion of school facilities, there is no reason why the repeater rate should not be reduced to well below 10 percent at which point it would simply reflect the sort of retardation rate that is expected among any sampling of the population.

Taking into account the backlog of overage children to be eliminated in two years, the increasing proportion of an expanding group of seven-year olds who enter school each year, and a reduced number of repeaters remaining in the first grade, we consider it likely that total first-grade enrollment will amount to about 325,000 in 1960/61 and will fall to about 250,000 in 1963/64 (see Table 57).

TABLE 57: Projected First Grade Enrollment, 1960/61-1963/64

(in thousands)

Year	7-Year-Olds[a]	Repeaters[b]	Backlog[c]	Total
1960/61	186	64	75	325
1961/62	204	44	50	300
1962/63	225	25	—	250
1963/64	232	18	—	250

[a] Assumes that 80 percent of 7-year olds enter in 1960/61, rising to 90 percent in 1963/64.

[b] Assumes that rate of repeaters can be reduced from 20 percent in 1960/61 to 7 percent in 1963/64.

[c] Remaining overage children never before in school.

The other factor contributing to total enrollment is the retention rate. With present enrollment known and new entrant targets established, future enrollments will depend on what proportion of those in school continue with their education. The retention rate is affected by the actual number who continue from one grade to the next, plus those who are repeating that grade for a second year together with any additional pupils returning to their education at that particular grade. In Venezuela the dropout between grades is very large. The retention rate is particularly low between the first and second grades. For some years, total enrollment in the second grade was only half that in the previous year's first grade; even in the last two years this proportion has only been raised to two-thirds. It is true that repeaters, as mentioned above, account for some of this difference. But this can only be a contributory factor. More important is the fact that 26 percent of total primary school enrollment in Venezuela is located in the so-called unitary schools in which usually only one, although sometimes two or more grades are taught. This means that for nearly half the children of Venezuela who do not proceed to the higher grades, there is in fact no education available beyond the first, or at the most the second, grade.

The mission believes that making available the higher primary grades to all who can benefit from them is an urgent task. Higher grades should be added to the unitary schools where practicable or, alternatively, centrally located schools providing the upper primary grades should be established to serve a cluster of nearby unitary schools. While it will obviously be a number of years before all six grades can be made available to all, a start should be made toward this objective without delay.

Thus, first-to-second grade retention rates will only start rising once the effect of making more higher grades available makes itself felt. We feel that while the rate might only rise slightly until, say, 1961/62 after that there could be a sharp increase (see Table 58). Retention rates at the higher grades are already relatively large so that we would forecast a more modest upward trend in these cases. Nevertheless, we expect the over-all retention rate as between the first and sixth grades to rise to 42 percent by 1963/64 as compared with 23 percent in 1959/60.

TABLE 58: Projected Retention Rates, 1960/61-1963/64

Grades	Actual		Projected			
	1958/59	1959/60	1960/61	1961/62	1962/63	1963/64
1st to 2nd	62	63	64	66	70	75
2nd to 3rd	92	93	93	94	94	94
3rd to 4th	86	86	87	88	88	88
4th to 5th	82	83	83	84	84	85
5th to 6th	79	79	80	80	80	80

Even assuming that our expectations as to future first-grade enrollments are roughly fulfilled (see Table 57), and even assuming that retention rates can be raised as we anticipate (see Table 50), we nevertheless believe that total gross enrollment in the primary schools will start declining after 1962/63 and will not turn upwards again until about 1968/69 (see Table 59). While our calculations are necessarily illustrative, they demonstrate that the Venezuelan Government's assumption early in 1960 that primary school enrollment would continue to rise in each successive year of the four-year period 1960/61-1963/64 is likely to be erroneous.[2]

Buildings and Equipment

At the time of the mission's visit to Venezuela, a primary school construction program was being discussed in terms of its relation to

[2] There are indications that total enrollment was in fact higher in 1959/60 than the provisional estimate shown in Table 59. If so, this would suggest that more of the backlog of overage pupils have enrolled than here indicated and that, therefore, the tendency for a decline in total enrollment is likely to be even greater than that illustrated in Table 59.

TABLE 59: Primary School Enrollment

Year	1st	2nd	3rd	4th	5th	6th	Total
				Grades			
Actual							
1953/54	238.9						
54/55	234.7	119.8					
55/56	229.9	125.8	102.6				
56/57	242.2	133.3	111.3	83.9			
57/58	262.1	144.0	119.0	93.2	68.8	48.3	751.6
58/59	371.1	163.6	132.4	102.3	76.7	54.2	900.3
59/60[a]	434.8	210.7	154.3	117.9	87.1	63.1	1,067.9
Mission's Projections							
1960/61	325.0	278.3	195.9	134.4	97.9	69.7	1,105.2
61/62	300.0	213.8	261.6	172.4	112.9	78.3	1,139.0
62/63	250.0	210.0	201.0	230.2	144.8	90.3	1,126.3
63/64	250.0	187.5	197.4	176.9	195.7	115.8	1,123.3
1964/65	255.0	187.5	176.2	173.7	150.4	156.6	1,099.4
65/66	260.0	191.2	176.2	155.1	147.6	120.3	1,050.4
66/67	265.0	195.0	179.7	155.1	131.8	118.1	1,044.7
67/68	270.0	198.7	183.3	158.1	131.8	105.4	1,047.3
68/69	275.0	202.5	186.8	161.3	134.4	105.4	1,065.4
69/70	280.0	206.2	190.3	164.4	137.1	107.5	1,085.5

[a] Based on provisional estimates available at the time of the Mission's visit.

increases in total nation-wide enrollment. We have already indicated that we do not believe that enrollment will increase after 1961/62 and in fact will start declining for a few years. We nevertheless advocate a vigorous primary school construction program for the four years 1960/61-1963/64 to meet a number of needs other than the accommodation of increased total enrollment. In 1959/60, no less than 58 percent of primary school buildings were considered inadequate, 6,883 schools out of a total of 9,121 consisted of only one room, and an undetermined number of areas were without any schools. We estimate that there are now at least 10,000 inadequate classrooms to be replaced. In addition, between 6,000 and 7,000 classrooms are needed to provide higher grades where these are currently lacking. Furthermore, there is a still undetermined number both of new schools required for new areas and for the relocation of existing schools. Thus it is not unreasonable to calculate that in all no less than 20,000 new classrooms will be required.

Against this enormous requirement is the record of about 800 new classrooms built in each of the last two years. We believe that it is administratively and financially possible to step up the annual rate of classroom construction to some 2,000 within a few years, so that total requirements could be met in a ten-year period. (After ten years, further construction will be needed to accommodate an enrollment once again expanding.)

The first ten-year program will require careful planning and a strict adherence to an order of priorities. The first task is to make sure that some sort of school facilities are available in all areas. To this extent, we recommend that during 1960/61-1961/62 emphasis be first laid on building new schools in the more remote areas. This will in effect add to the total existing classroom capacity. Fortunately, the pressure of numbers will in itself be relaxed after a couple of years when total nationwide enrollment will start declining, and this will then afford the opportunity to shift the emphasis to meeting the other needs. The expansion of existing schools to provide the higher grades, on which some start should be made without delay, could after 1961/62 become the top priority in the building program. At the same time, a start should also be made to replace inadequate buildings, to relocate schools and, where necessary to reduce the ratio of pupils to classrooms.

Construction costs have varied widely in the last few years and have in general shown a tendency to increase. We believe that, on the contrary, construction costs should be brought down and that the federal authorities should consult with the states and municipalities with a view to securing such reductions. Clearly, cost conditions vary between localities but the federal authorities should act as a clearing house for the spread of information on low-cost construction so that the experience in such areas as Barinas, where costs in the past few years have been markedly below the national average, can be adapted to the needs of others.

We believe that the target should be to keep average construction costs from rising above Bs 20,000 per classroom in the coming two or three years, in the meantime making determined efforts to reduce this average to Bs 15,000 by 1963/64. It should be remembered that in the primary schools the major emphasis should be on teaching standards and that school buildings, while providing good shelter and adequate sanitary facilities, need not be overlavish.

We would also budget Bs 2,000 per classroom for furniture and other equipment and believe that this is a cost which probably cannot be reduced. Thus, the combined cost for construction and equipment should initially amount to Bs 22,000 per classroom but should be reduced to Bs 17,000 per classroom by 1963/64.

We are not suggesting that it will be possible to boost annual construction from the current level of 800 classrooms to 2,000 classrooms in one year. But we do feel that the target of constructing 8,000 classrooms over the next four years is not unrealistic, assuming an annual construction rate of somewhat less than 2,000 classrooms in the earlier years and somewhat more in the later. If the first 6,000 were built at an average cost for construction and equipment of Bs 22,000 and the last 2,000 for an average cost of Bs 17,000, then the total capital cost over the 1960/61-1963/64 period would amount to Bs 166,000,000.

School Books

Children attending schools in Venezuela have to buy their textbooks and materials. In this sense it cannot be said that the schools are completely without cost to the pupils. This economic burden must act as a disincentive to school attendance and, as the school system attempts to reach out into the more economically backward areas, this disincentive will become increasingly operative. It is true that various community organizations currently pay for books and materials for the more needy children, but the mission feels that access to primary education should not be dependent on local charity.

The mission believes that the public authorities should begin to supply textbooks and materials free of charge to all primary school pupils. We suggest that a system of book loans could be established in the course of the next few years. Children should be obliged to return their books at the end of the school year and there should be some form of financial penalty for failure to return.

The program of free book supply should be phased so that priority is given to the economically backward areas first, together with such other localities where it is believed that low enrollments and high dropout rates might be attributable to economic hardships.

We suggest that about 250,000 pupils be supplied with books in each of the succeeding years. This would mean that some 1.5 million pupils would be supplied with books in the next six years. Since enrollment is not likely to rise much above 1.1 million during this period, this would allow for a surplus of some 0.4 million sets of books or an attrition rate of 30 percent during the period. Attrition will occur because of some losses (although a system of fines should keep this at a minimum), because books depreciate or are destroyed over the years and because books eventually require revision and replacement. The six-year program we suggest will give the education authorities necessary experience in the operation of the program, including some basis to forecast future attrition rates.

We calculate that books and materials will cost an average of Bs 50 a pupil. Allowing for the supply of 250,000 pupils a year, the total program will cost Bs 12.5 million a year, a not inconsiderable sum to be added to annual operating costs. We feel however that such expenditures would be well worthwhile if they stimulate enrollment and particularly if they contribute to increasing retention rates.

Supply of Primary School Teachers

In 1959/60 there were 30,144 teachers in the primary school system. In principle, teachers are supposed to attend a four-year course at a Normal School after which they obtain a primary school teaching certificate. Partly because of the rapid expansion of the last few years, many teachers have not attended a Normal School, do not hold a teaching certificate, and consequently are regarded only as provisional teachers. We calculate that about 57 percent, or some 17,000 teachers, are in the provisional category.[3] Some of these teachers are undergoing special in-service training or attend summer courses, thus improving their professional qualifications. Furthermore, given appropriate aptitudes and sufficient enthusiasm, there is no reason why a lack of formal qualifications should prevent many individuals from being good teachers at the primary level. Nevertheless, the mission feels that the proportion of uncertificated teachers should not be allowed to rise further, particularly as enrollment in the higher primary grades is to be increasingly emphasized. On the contrary, efforts should be made eventually to replace the lower-rated provisional teachers with graduates from the Normal Schools.

We therefore recommend that all new teachers be required to hold the appropriate teaching certificate. In 1959/60 there were 18,800 students enrolled in the Normal Schools, of which some 8,200 were in the first year of study, about 5,400 in the second year, 2,700 in the third and 2,100 in the fourth (see Table 60). Allowing for retention rates of roughly the same order as in recent years, this would indicate graduat-

---

[3] According to the 1958 annual report, there were 9,839 certificated teachers at that time. Some 3,500 graduates of the Normal Schools have been produced since then. There were thus rather over 13,000 certificated teachers in 1959/60.

TABLE 60: Normal School Enrollment

(in thousands)

Year	____ Years of Study ____					Total
	1st	2nd	3rd	4th	5th	
Actual						
1955/56	2.4					6.3
56/57	3.3	1.8				7.7
57/58	3.1	2.4	1.5			8.3
58/59	6.8	3.2	2.8	1.5		14.3
59/60[a]	8.2	5.4	2.7	2.1		18.8
Projected						
1960/61	5.8	7.4	5.1	2.0		20.7
61/62	5.8	4.9	7.0	4.3		22.0
62/63	5.8	4.9	4.4	6.0		21.1
63/64	5.8	4.9	4.4	3.7[b]		18.8
64/65	5.8	4.9	4.4	3.7	3.0	21.8

[a] Based on provisional estimates available at the time of the mission's visit.

[b] Because of the recommended lengthening of the course to five years, this group, and subsequent fourth-year groups, would continue for an additional year of study.

ing classes of about 2,000, 4,300 and 6,000 respectively in the three succeeding years, 1960/61-1962/63.

The projected number of graduates in the following year, 1963/64, would normally depend on how many Normal School students have been enrolled in the first-year course in 1960/61. However, we recommend that, starting with the 1960/61 new entries, the Normal School course of studies be lengthened to five years in order to bring it into line with primary teacher training courses elsewhere in Latin America,[4] and also in order to make the Normal School course the equivalent of other forms of secondary education (see below). Thus, there would be no graduates in 1963/64, but this is compensated by the fact that 6,000 will in any case be graduated the previous year.

We further recommend that about 5,800 new entries be enrolled in 1960/61 and in each year thereafter, so that starting in 1964/65 about 3,000 students will graduate annually from a five-year Normal School course. Given the fact that total primary school enrollments are not projected to rise substantially for some years, this annual output of

[4] See "Informe Final del Seminario Interamericano Sobre Prefecionamiento del Magisterio en Servicio, Montevideo, 1958," *Educacion Rural*, 4, Enero-Marzo, 1959, UNESCO, p. 118.

teachers should be sufficient to meet normal replacement requirements, together with a progressive substitution of certificated for provisional teachers.

During the next four years a total of about 12,300 Normal School graduates will be produced. Assuming an annual replacement requirement of about 3 percent to cover deaths, retirement and earlier voluntary exits from the teaching profession, about 1,000 teachers will be needed annually, or 4,000 over the four-year period, to meet this requirement. A further 8,000 new teachers will thus be available to meet other requirements in the coming four years. Many of them will be required to teach the increased higher-grade enrollments which we have projected above. Others will be needed to replace the lower-rated provisional teachers, as we have also recommended above.

At the time of the mission's visit to Venezuela, a Normal School construction program to replace the current temporary quarters was under consideration. Some of the Normal Schools are housed in buildings which were originally constructed for primary school purposes. New buildings should be designed specifically as training institutions and the current buildings could then be returned to the primary school system. We thus agree with the proposed program of 16 new schools to be built in 1960/61-1963/64 at a cost of Bs 22.2 million. Necessary furniture and equipment for these buildings is estimated at Bs 15.0 million, so that the total capital cost of the Normal School program would amount to Bs 37.2 million during the four-year period.

Rural Schools

We have already noted that much of the future expansion of Venezuela's primary school system is needed in rural areas, some of which are relatively remote and most of which are sparsely populated. In such areas, it is particularly difficult to locate school facilities where they can serve a practically sized enrollment. The Ministry of Education has been considering the possibility of establishing special boarding schools in which children of primary school age can be brought together. We doubt the wisdom of such a policy. Boarding schools are very costly to build and operate and, from the point of view of family economics, it is precisely in the more remote rural areas that parents tend more than elsewhere to count on their children for farm chores.

There are other methods of focusing on this problem. The establishment of a community school-bus system would be one; the itinerant teacher is another; and short intensive courses programed to fit in with the farming seasons is yet another. We recommend that the planning office of the Ministry of Education study this problem and experiment with various solutions before a definite plan is adopted. In any case it will be necessary to accept that in certain rural areas the pupil-teacher ratio will be unavoidably lower than in the more populous areas.

Even where regular primary schools are established in rural areas, it will obviously be some years to come before all of them will be offering the full six-years' course. And it will obviously be even longer before socio-economic attitudes change enough so that all eligible children avail themselves of the opportunity of a complete primary education. Education policy should recognize that there will always be a sizeable group of children who drop out of school earlier. While we believe that all children should be induced to stay in school for at least three grades —anything less is insufficient to make any lasting impact on the child and thus is both a waste for the child and an economic burden on the community—it should be recognized that such a dropout is bound to take place, particularly in rural areas, and at least during a transitional period.

Thus, as an interim measure, a new curriculum should be devised which would meet the needs of such dropouts and so maximize the effectiveness of such education as they do obtain. Essentially such a revision would lead to a study program with a more practical bias related to the agricultural pursuits which the child is likely to follow. A new experimental institution has been established at El Macaro with the express purpose of devising such curriculum revisions. We welcome the new institution and believe that the Bs 3 million budgeted for it in the next four years can be well spent. However, since we recommend that the expansion of primary education into rural areas be accorded a high priority, it will not be possible to await the full results of such experiments. We believe that some revisions of the course of primary school studies could be made without delay, further refinements being instituted once the experiments have yielded results.

INTERMEDIATE EDUCATION

Distribution Between Types

In Venezuela, education after primary school and before university is called intermediate education (*educacion media*). Hitherto there has been a heavy emphasis on academic secondary schools (*liceos*) as against the other forms of intermediate education, which include Normal, vocational (industrial and commercial), agricultural, nursing, social work, plastic arts, music and so forth. In 1959/60, academic secondary school enrollment amounted to some 80,000, or about 73 percent of the 110,000 total enrollment in all forms of intermediate education. In terms of output—the number of students in graduating classes —the academic bias is even more pronounced. There were about 8,200 students in their final year of intermediate studies during 1959/60, but of these no less than 7,600, or 93 percent, were in the graduating classes of the *liceos*. In terms of input—the number of current new entries into intermediate education—it is clear that the academic bias is being reduced. There were more than 60,000 students in their first year of intermediate studies in 1959/60 and 31,847 of these, or 53 percent, were in *liceos*.

We welcome this shift in emphasis and believe that relatively even more stress on various types of vocational training will be needed in the coming years. Until a detailed survey of manpower requirements, as mentioned above, is carried out, it is not possible to quantify the number of skilled manual workers and technicians who will be needed to spur economic development in the coming few years. However, it is clear that the number is far in excess of what the education system can in practice be expected to produce. Accordingly, every effort should be made simply to maximize vocational enrollments, the limiting factors being availability of suitable teachers, capacity to construct schools and administrative capacity. Having determined maximum practicable enrollment, every effort should be made to divert sufficient primary school graduates from the *liceos* to vocational institutions.

We strongly recommend the establishment of a testing program aimed at determining both intellectual attainments and aptitudes, so that students can be selected to follow the type of intermediate education most suited to their potentialities. Furthermore, a guidance and counseling service should be established which would also aim at directing students into the most suitable course of studies.

Every effort should be made to elevate the status of vocational schools. The value and dignity of manual trades should be stressed. Graduation from a vocational school should be accorded the same status as graduation from *liceo*. One way of achieving this would be to have some uniformity of curriculum within the framework of the special studies of each type of school. During the first three years, general studies should be included in the curriculum of all schools in addition to specialized courses, while the specialism, be it academic, Normal, industrial, commercial, agricultural or otherwise, could be followed in greater detail during the final two years. This form of organization would not only tend to accord equal status to the various types of schools, but would also introduce a much needed flexibility into the intermediate system by allowing for transfers between types of schools.

Given this element of transferability, intermediate education should be programed on an over-all basis. It would first be necessary to project total intermediate enrollment for the coming years. The majority of new entries will be the previous year's sixth-grade primary pupils. However, not all these pupils will actually graduate and, of those graduat-

TABLE 61: Projected First-Year Enrollments in All Types of Intermediate Education

Year	6th Grade Primary Enrollment in Previous Year[a] (thousands)	Continuation Rate (percentage)	Projected First-Year Intermediate Enrollment (thousands)
1960/61	63.1	90	56.8
61/62	69.7	85	59.2
62/63	78.3	80	62.6
63/64	90.3	80	72.2

[a] Derived from Table 59.

ing, not all will continue with intermediate education. On the other hand, there is in Venezuela a backlog of overage students who qualified for entry into intermediate education in earlier years but are only now coming forward to enroll. Thus, first-year intermediate enrollments in intermediate education in Venezuela in 1958/59 and 1959/60 were 99.2 and 110.2 percent respectively of previous year's sixth-grade primary enrollment. Clearly much of this enrollment is due to the backlog effect. We assume that this effect will diminish in succeeding years. Furthermore, as primary education spreads, so the proportion continuing with further education will begin to drop. We calculate that the continuation rate in Venezuela might fall from 90 percent in 1960/61 to 80 percent in 1963/64 (see Table 61). This would mean that first-year enrollment in all types of intermediate education would rise from 56,800 in 1960/61 to 72,200 in 1963/64.

Given this total intermediate enrollment, enrollments can be assigned for each year for industrial and commercial schools according to calculations as to the maximum practicable expansion of these types of education in the next four years. Also included are projected Normal School enrollments (see Table 60) and enrollments for other types of schools (see section on agricultural education and health chapter). If these combined enrollments are deducted from the projected total, the remainder represents the maximum number of pupils who will be available in each year for enrollment at academic secondary schools (see Table 62). The mission strongly urges the Venezuelan education au-

TABLE 62: Recommended Distribution of First-Year Enrollment in Intermediate Education

(in thousands)

Year	Projected Total	Normal	Industrial	Commercial	Other[a]	Available for Academic Secondary
1960/61	56.8	5.8	8.6	8.6	2.4	31.4
61/62	59.2	5.8	9.6	9.6	3.4	30.8
62/63	62.6	5.8	10.4	10.4	4.1	31.9
63/64	72.2	5.8	10.4	10.4	4.1	41.5

[a] Includes agricultural, nursing and other schools.

thorities to adopt a policy of initial selection aimed at achieving the sort of distribution of new enrollments as between the various types of intermediate education as suggested here.

Industrial Schools

Industrial education has been comparatively limited in Venezuela. As recently as 1956/57 there were only five industrial schools in the country. Total enrollment was 3,270, of which 1,062 were adult night students following irregular courses, and there were 174 teachers many of whom were part-time. Efforts have been made in the last two or three years to expand this form of education, and the importance attached to it was indicated by the establishment in July 1958 of a special industrial division within the Ministry of Education.

By 1959/60, there were fourteen industrial schools, two in Caracas and one each in Maracay, Valencia, Maracaibo, San Cristobal, Cabimas,

Trujillo, Cumana, Maturin, Merida, Barquisimeto, Punto Fijo and Ciudad Bolivar. Only seven of these were located in buildings designed and constructed specifically for industrial education purposes. Of the remaining seven schools, five were housed in totally inadequate quarters. Furthermore, there has been a scarcity of proper equipment. Machinery and tools, necessary to provide each student with the opportunity to practice the various manual trades, are in extreme short supply. There is also a lack of properly trained teachers.

Despite these limitations, industrial education has registered significant advances, so that by 1959/60 there were about 13,000 students enrolled. The Venezuelan Government now plans to more than double this enrollment by 1963/64, and the mission applauds this intention. If certain handicaps can be overcome, the mission feels that a boost in industrial education of this magnitude would be fully justified. In fact, we calculate that after 1963/64, the Venezuelan economy could easily absorb at least 12,000 skilled workers each year and, since the graduating classes from even the proposed total enrollments will fall far short of this figure, any practicable expansion of industrial training, within the framework of sound education policy, will be well worthwhile.

As with other forms of education in Venezuela, the dropout rate from industrial schools is excessively high. During the past few years, an average of only 62 percent of the first-year enrollment has continued to second-year studies, and only about 40 percent of fourth-year students have proceeded to the fifth year. This is extremely wasteful because a relatively large total enrollment is thus required merely to produce a relatively small number of fully trained students. For example, of the total 1959/60 enrollment of 13,000, only 160 were in the fifth year of studies and only 70 in the special sixth-year course for industrial technicians. As we have stressed before, the proper measure of success for an educational program is not the total enrollment achieved at any given point, but rather the number of trained personnel being turned out by the graduating class each year.

Vigorous efforts along the lines already suggested could do much to increase retention. Guidance, counseling, and testing would introduce an element of selectivity as to which students entered industrial schools in the first place, so that the dropout rate after the first year could be reduced. As far as the dropout in subsequent years is concerned, the curriculum changes we have proposed would do much to reduce the rate. At present, there is an option to drop at the end of the fourth year, an option which past dropout rates would indicate was exercised by the majority of students. The mission is of the firm opinion that a four-year course, if it includes a certain amount of general education, is insufficient to produce a properly trained skilled industrial worker. Thus, we propose that the three-year cycle of combined general and specialized studies be followed by two years of industrial training (with an optional sixth-year for advanced technicians) . Only after five years would a student be able to obtain a recognized qualification. Students who failed to show industrial aptitudes might drop out in the second or third year but, because they would first obtain general intermediate education at the industrial school, there would be a possibility for such students to transfer to other schools.

If the foregoing admissions and curriculum policies were adopted, it should be possible to raise the first-to-second year retention rate from the current 62 percent to about 75 percent by 1963/64. Because of the new possibility of transfer at the end of the third year, the third-to-fourth year retention rate might fall from the current 85 percent to about 75 percent, but this would be more than compensated by increased retention between the fourth and fifth years. Given the incentive to stay until the fifth year in order to obtain a qualification that would otherwise be denied, we see no reason why this retention rate should not rapidly increase.

With an improvement in retention rates and an increase in initial enrollment, the number in the fifth-year class could be increased from 160 in 1959/60 to about 2,400 in 1963/64, a fifteenfold increase (see Table 63) . Assuming the first-year entries indicated in Table 62, these

TABLE 63: Industrial School Enrollment

	Years of Study						
Year	1st	2nd	3rd	4th	5th	6th	Total
Actual							
1955/56	2,294	510	179	133	—	—	3,116
56/57	2,074	781	263	106	46	—	3,270
57/58	2,891	742	467	203	54	36	4,393
58/59	5,305	1,789	685	403	76	50	8,308
59/60[a]	8,120	2,600	1,500	550	160	70	13,000
Mission Projections							
1960/61	8,600	5,000	2,000	1,200	220	120	17,140
61/62	9,600	5,500	4,000	1,500	960	120	21,680
62/63	10,400	6,000	4,400	3,000	1,200	480	25,480
63/64	10,400	7,800	4,800	3,300	2,400	600	29,300

[a] Based on provisional estimates available at the time of the mission's visit.

retention rates would produce a total enrollment which would rise from
13,000 in 1959/60 to about 29,300 in 1963/64. This means that an extra
16,300 places would have to be found during the period and this is precisely what is envisaged in the Venezuelan Government's building
program.

The Government is planning to build twelve entirely new schools

TABLE 64: Program of Industrial School Construction, 1960/61-1963/64,
Under Consideration by Venezuelan Government

(in Bs thousand)

Replacement of Inadequate Buildings:		
Maracay	2,160	
Punto Fijo	2,160	
Maturin	2,160	
Cumana	2,160	
Cabimas[a]	700	9,340
New Schools[b]:		
Puerto La Cruz	2,160	
El Tigre	2,160	
San Fernando/Apure	1,080	
Iron Region (Bolivar State)	2,160	
Puerto Cabello[c]	2,160	
San Juan Morros	2,160	
Guarenas	2,160	
Carenero[d]	700	
Acarigua	2,160	
Carupano	1,080	
Valera[e]	200	
Tucupita	1,440	19,640
Additions to Existing Schools:		
Caracas-Catia[f]	800	
Caracas-Coche	2,160	
Ciudad Bolivar	2,160	
Juan Griego[g]	1,080	6,200
Grand Total		35,180

[a] Bs 800,000 allocated for 1959/60.
[b] Excludes school at Barinas scheduled for completion in 1959/60 at cost of
Bs 1,360,000.
[c] School of naval construction.
[d] Fisheries school.
[e] Bs 1,272,000 allocated for 1959/60.
[f] Bs 3,000,000 allocated for 1959/60.
[g] For conversion from an *artesanal* (primary handicrafts school) to an industrial
school at the intermediate level.

during the four-year period (see Table 64). In addition, it is proposed to convert the *artesanal* (primary handicrafts school) at Juan Griego into an industrial school and expand its size. Furthermore, the existing two schools in Caracas and the Ciudad Bolivar school would be greatly expanded. Finally, five schools would be provided with new buildings to replace the existing inadequate accommodations. Construction alone would cost Bs 35.2 million. The mission fully supports this program and hopes that every effort will be made to accomplish it.

There are however a number of reservations which we believe should be taken into account when planning the implementation of this construction program. First, it is very large, attempting more than to double present capacity in four short years, a task which may well not be achieved, particularly in view of the fact that much construction actually budgeted in the last few years has not been carried out on time by the *Ministerio de Obras Publicas*. Moreover, with the exception of the Puerto Cabello school of naval construction and the Carenero Fisheries School, all other construction work is phased to be completed by 1962/63. In view of possible difficulties in obtaining adequate teaching equipment and suitable teaching staff, both of which we will discuss below, and in view of the not inconsiderable administrative challenge that such a large expansion program will pose, we feel that it might be more realistic to phase some additional parts of the construction program for the last year of the four-year period.

If experience shows that the program could proceed at a faster rate, it would later be possible to speed up construction. Conversely, if the difficulties mentioned prove to be unexpectedly inhibiting, it might be necessary to contemplate part of this program being stretched beyond 1963/64. In any event, it is clear that some order of priority in construction will have to be established. Accordingly, we strongly urge that the replacement of inadequate buildings at existing schools be made the first task of the construction program. This phase would cost Bs 9.3 million.

At the same time, work could be started on new schools, or additions to existing schools, as soon as it was apparent that a potential enrollment of a sufficient size was available at the proposed location and as soon as it was clear that suitable teaching staff could be obtained. Lack of teachers will in fact be a major problem in the field of industrial education.

In 1959/60, there were about 600 teachers at industrial schools, many of whom taught only on a part-time basis and many of whom were not specifically trained for this type of teaching. The *Institutos Pedagogicos* (teachers' colleges) have not hitherto trained teachers to specialize in industrial education. We urge that they do so in the future. In any case, the output of secondary school teachers is limited. Some additional teachers could be obtained directly from the science and engineering faculties of the universities; but again such teachers would not be specifically trained for teaching industrial skills. The best source of teachers would be from industry itself. We recommend that the Government investigate this possibility and that salary differentials be instituted so as to induce both individuals from industry to enter the teaching profession and teachers already in training to specialize in industrial education.

We calculate that the proposed expansion program would entail the recruitment of at least an additional 600 teachers in the coming four years. Even adopting the measures suggested above, we doubt whether this number could be obtained in so short a time. We therefore suggest that the Government consider the temporary employment of foreign instructors. Experience elsewhere has shown that it is easier to integrate such instructors into industrial education than into other forms of education because the need for familiarity with language and custom is at a minimum and the need for facility in mechanical demonstration techniques is at a maximum. While the employment of foreign instructors is costly, it might be worth the price during the interim period of expansion.

Another costly item in industrial education is the provision of suitable teaching equipment. About one-half of all the rooms constructed need to serve as workshops with enough machinery and tools so as to provide the opportunity for each student to have frequent practice in selected manual trades. Foundries, carpentry shops, electronics shops, etc., are expensive and their acquisition in appropriate quantities of the right types requires a good deal of administrative competence. Thus, the construction work proposed above should also be so phased that buildings will not stand empty for want of equipment. We calculate that the necessary equipment costs an amount equivalent to the total cost of constructing the building which houses it. The construction program proposed would therefore also entail a capital outlay for equipment of about Bs 35 million.

Commercial Schools

There is an acute need for trained clerical and commercial personnel in Venezuela. As the economy develops, so the growing complexity of administrative and managerial problems have made increasing demands on the supply of intermediate office help. To meet this demand, commercial education has more than doubled between 1955/56 and 1959/60; student enrollment rose from 6,787 to 13,864 during the period and the teacher force rose from less than 300 to more than 600.

Commercial schools are administered, together with industrial schools, in a separate division as part of over-all vocational education. The mission is not sure that this is the best arrangement, partly because the problems of commercial schools are quite different from those of industrial schools—particularly with respect to the supply of equipment and the recruitment of teachers—and partly because, under certain circumstances which we will discuss below, commercial subjects should preferably be taught in special departments at academic secondary schools.

Commercial schools have suffered from a prevailing attitude that they provide in effect an inferior form of intermediate education and have therefore not in the past attracted their reasonable share of high-quality students. The relatively low level of students enrolled is reflected in the very high dropout rates which have been registered in recent years. For example, of the 4,648 students who enrolled in the first year of commercial schools in 1955/56, only 230 were in the fifth year in 1959/60—a retention rate of under 5 percent. More than 50 percent have been dropping out after the first year alone. Again the guidance and selection procedures we have recommended would help to improve these rates. Curriculum changes, whereby the first three-year cycle would stress general studies in addition to a bias toward commercial subjects, would also help to reduce waste. Efforts should be made to attract a better type of student and to retain the interest of students already enrolled.

In order to increase the output of fully trained commercial personnel who have completed the full five-year course, we recommend, in addition to measures to increase retention rates, an increase in the first-year intake of new students from the 1959/60 level of 8,000 to some 10,400 in 1963/64 (see Table 65). This would mean that total enrollment in all grades would rise from nearly 14,000 to about 25,000 during the same period. Improved retention rates would imply that the fifth-year graduating class, which totaled 230 in 1959/60, could be raised to about 1,200 by 1963/64 with the prospect of proportionately greater increases in subsequent years.

To take care of this expansion, a construction program is under consideration by the Venezuelan Government (see Table 66). The program would entail the expenditure of some Bs 20.5 million on the construction of commercial school buildings during 1960/61-1963/64. Of this

TABLE 65: Commercial School Enrollment[a]

| Year | Years of Study | | | | | Total |
	1st	2nd	3rd	4th	5th	
			Actual			
1955/56	4,648	1,598	399	80	72	6,787
56/57	4,218	1,812	676	189	54	7,949
57/58	5,683	1,963	790	190	117	8,743
58/59	7,624	2,739	1,232	287	153	12,035
59/60[b]	8,000	3,735	1,443	456	230	13,864
			Mission's Projections			
1960/61	8,600	3,800	2,200	500	300	15,400
61/62	9,600	4,300	2,500	1,100	400	17,900
62/63	10,400	5,700	3,000	1,500	900	21,400
63/64	10,400	7,200	4,000	2,100	1,200	24,900

[a] Includes both enrollment at commercial schools and enrollment in commercial departments of academic secondary schools.
[b] Based on provisional estimates available at the time of the mission's visit.

amount, Bs 6.1 million would be spent on building seven entirely new schools, including one at Valencia where most of the work is due to be completed during 1959/60. The remaining Bs 14.4 million would be spent on replacing buildings at eleven existing schools.

Many of the buildings which currently house commercial schools have been reconditioned in the last two years, and the mission is of the opinion that their replacement is of low priority. On the other hand, none of the new schools, except for the one at Valencia, are scheduled under this proposed program for establishment before 1962/63. If the demand for these schools can be verified in terms of potential commercial school enrollments at the specified locations, the mission would urge that new school construction should be accorded a higher priority than the replacement of existing buildings and that therefore the program should be re-phased so that the new schools are built during the earlier part of the four-year program with the replacement program being in the main delayed until the latter part of the period.

If the entire building program were completed, there would then be accommodation for some 17,200 students in buildings designed specifically as commercial schools. This would mean that accommodation would fall short of projected enrollment by some 7,700 by 1963/64.

TABLE 66: Program of Commercial School Construction,[a] 1960/61-1963/64, Under Consideration by the Venezuelan Government

(in Bs thousand)

New Schools:		
El Tigre	1,440	
San Fernando/Apure	720	
Valencia[b]	339	
Punto Fijo	720	
Acarigua	720	
San Felipe	720	
Cabimas	1,440	6,099
Substitution of Buildings at Existing Schools:		
Caracas-Penalver	1,440	
Caracas-Michelelena	1,440	
Barcelona	1,440	
Maracay	1,440	
Ciudad Bolivar	1,440	
San Juan Morros	1,440	
Barquisimeto	1,440	
Merida	720	
Cumana	720	
San Cristobal	1,440	
Maracaibo	1,440	14,400
Grand Total		20,499

[a] Includes furniture and equipment.
[b] Excludes Bs 1,500,000 due to be spent in 1959/60.

However, a large proportion of this excess enrollment would be spread around the country in the smaller towns in such a way that in no single locality would there be a sufficient number of potential commercial school students to warrant the establishment of a separate school for this purpose. In these cases, we recommend that a special commercial education division be established in the local *liceo*. This would not only solve the accommodation problem but would also tend to up-grade the status of commercial schooling in general and also ease the possibilities of transferability between the various types of intermediate education which we have suggested elsewhere. In fact, not only do we suggest the establishment of commercial departments in the *liceos* in the smaller towns, but we also suggest the introduction, on an elective basis, of commercial subjects into the curricula of all *liceos,* irrespective of the size of town.

Academic Secondary Schools

Despite recent, and proposed, shifts in emphasis toward vocational education, academic schools will continue to account for the largest part of intermediate education. This is as it should be. Recognition of the need for an increased supply of skilled workers should not obscure the abiding need for sustaining and enriching the intellectual life of the country. This latter need can only be met by the maintenance and improvement of general educational standards both in the academic secondary schools and, later, in the universities. A broad liberal education is a necessary prelude to the advanced training which must be provided for the growing body of potential administrators, managers, scientists and technicians that a developing economy requires.

There has been a steady increase in academic secondary school enrollment during the last ten years. In 1948/49 there were just over 19,000 pupils in both public secondary schools *(liceos)* and private secondary schools, while similar enrollments in 1959/60 are estimated at about 80,000. Furthermore, since the return to constitutional government, academic secondary school expansion has been almost entirely in the public sector. Whereas from 1948/49 to 1957/58 public secondary school enrollments only rose on an average by 8.5 percent annually, in 1958/59 alone such enrollments rose by 51.7 percent, an increase which in absolute numbers was greater in this single year than the total increase during the preceding nine years. On the other hand, private school enrollments, which had increased by an annual average of 41.7 percent until 1957/58, have now ceased to show any significant expansion. While the 25,000 private secondary school students represented about 45 percent of the 1957/58 total secondary school enrollment of 55,000, about 26,000 such students represented only 33 percent of the 1958/59 total enrollment of 71,000. It would appear that private school enrollment has probably now found a level at which it can serve almost all the pupils who are likely to demand this type of education and that in future virtually all expansion in academic secondary education can be expected to take place in the public *liceos*.

According to plans now under consideration within the Venezuelan Government, an expansion of total public academic secondary school enrollment of nearly 80,000 is programed for the four-year period 1960/61-1963/64. The mission believes that this forecast is much too large. Even allowing for a steady reduction in the dropout rate, the number of pupils available for first-year entry into the academic secondary schools, as indicated in the text and in Tables 61 and 62, is such that

the mission can only project total enrollment rising from about 80,000
in 1959/60 to about 118,000 in 1963/64, or an increase of about 38,000
for the whole period (see Table 67).

TABLE 67: Academic Secondary School Enrollment

(in thousands)

Year	\multicolumn{5}{c}{Years of Study}					Total
	1st	2nd	3rd	4th	5th	
\multicolumn{7}{c}{*Actual*}
1954/55	17.0					38.9
55/56	19.3	10.5				44.4
56/57	21.6	13.2	8.5			52.4
57/58	21.7	13.8	9.9	5.2	4.6	55.2
58/59	27.9	17.2	12.6	8.5	5.1	71.4
59/60[a]	30.7	18.7	13.9	9.1	7.6	80.0
\multicolumn{7}{c}{*Mission's Projections*}
1960/61	31.4	23.0	15.0	11.1	7.7	89.2
61/62	30.8	24.5	18.6	12.1	9.6	95.6
62/63	31.9	24.6	20.1	15.4	10.8	102.8
63/64	41.5	25.5	20.4	17.1	13.8	118.3

[a] Based on provisional estimates available at the time of the mission's visit.

As in all other sectors of Venezuelan education, retention rates are
comparatively low in academic secondary schools. For example, in
1959/60 there were about 7,600 pupils in the fifth and final year of the
academic secondary school course, as compared with a first-year enrollment five years earlier in 1955/56 of 19,381; this represents a retention
rate for the five-year period of only 39 percent. Such a dropout is excessively wasteful: large total enrollments are necessary to produce a relatively small "payoff" in terms of the output of fully trained five-year
graduates. Retention rates have recently been rising and the mission
believes that this favorable trend can be maintained in the coming
years, particularly if the measures for improving the initial selection
of pupils, recommended elsewhere, are vigorously applied. We are assuming that first-to-second year retention can be raised from the current
level of about 68 percent to about 80 percent by 1963/64 and that retention rates between the later years of study, which are already somewhat higher, can be raised to about 85 percent; the five-year survival
rate might eventually rise to above 60 percent. In any case, we believe

that fifth-year enrollment could rise from the current 7,600 level to 13,800 by 1963/64; the subsequent increases in fifth-year enrollments will rise proportionately faster as improved retention rates take effect.

The mission's enrollment forecasts, although derived solely by reference to school population projections and retention rates actually fit more closely to the Venezuelan Government's proposed secondary school construction program than its own enrollment forecasts. While the Government has been forecasting an increase of some 80,000 secondary school pupils by 1963/64, the construction program would provide accommodation for only 42,600 additional pupils, a program which adequately covers the mission projection of a 38,000 increase. We are thus able to endorse the construction program under consideration by the Government (see Table 68) so far as its total size is concerned, although we have some reservations as to its phasing.

TABLE 68: Academic Secondary School Construction, 1959/60 and 1960/61-1963/64, Under Consideration by the Venezuelan Government

Year	No. of Schools	Pupil Places Made Available	Expenditures (Bs million)
1959/60	7	7,200	46.7[a]
1960/61[b]	21	19,800	18.6
61/62	8	8,400	15.3
62/63	9	7,200	13.0
63/64	6	4,800	8.6
Total (1960/61-1963/64)	44	40,200	55.5

[a] Of which Bs 35.8 million is due to be spent in 1959/60 on construction work to be started in 1959/60 but completed in 1960/61.

[b] Includes 19 schools, with 17,400 pupil places available, due to be started in 1959/60 and completed in 1960/61 with expenditures on them amounting to Bs 14.3 million during the latter year. In addition, 2 schools accommodating 2,400 pupils and costing Bs 4.3 million, are scheduled for start and completion during 1960/61.

The program contemplates particularly active construction work in 1959/60 and 1960/61, so that about half the secondary schools due to be constructed by 1963/64 would be completed during this earlier period. While an additional 27,000 pupil places would be made available by 1961/62, we forecast that there will be only some 15,600 additional pupils to be accommodated by that time (see Table 69). Ac-

TABLE 69: Secondary School Construction and Projected Enrollment Increases

Year	Additional Pupil Places Scheduled to be Available[a]	Projected Additional Students to be Accommodated[b]	Excess of Places Over Pupils
1960/61	7,200	9,200	− 2,000
61/62	19,800	6,400	+11,400
62/63	8,400	7,200	+12,600
63/64	7,200	15,500	+ 4,300
	42,000	38,300	

[a] Based on the previous year's completions (see Table 68).
[b] See Table 67.

cordingly, the mission suggests that the Government reconsider the phasing of this construction work in the light of enrollment projections with the objective of making secondary school capacity available only when it is actually required. Much will depend on how much of the 1959/60 construction program has been actually started; those works under way presumably should be completed. In addition, some schools scheduled for construction in areas of special local shortages will in any case have to be built during this earlier period. Others might be delayed until later in the four-year period. Furthermore, we question whether secondary schools should in all cases be planned only on the basis of either a 600-pupil or a 1,200-pupil capacity. It would seem to us that, in certain areas, schools of varying sizes could be built according to current local needs and that they could be flexibly designed so that enlargements would be possible when local population increases warrant them.

In any event, subject to the above qualifications, the mission agrees that a construction program amounting to Bs 55.5 million during 1960/61-1963/64 is of the right order of magnitude. Additional expenditures will be required for equipment and furniture. This equipment is more elaborate than that required for primary schools, and we estimate costs at Bs 150 per additional pupil accommodated. This would amount to Bs 6 million for this purpose during the four-year period.

Another factor affecting academic secondary school expansion is teacher supply. A serious shortage of teachers will develop in the early years of the coming four-year period, although this deficit probably may be almost eliminated by 1963/64.

The main source of teachers for the *liceos* are the *Institutos Pedago-gicos* (teachers' colleges). In 1959/60 there were some 2,000 students enrolled in teachers' training courses. This enrollment included some 1,700 at Caracas and a further 350 at a newly established institute at Barquisimeto. The projected output of trained teachers from the full four-year course is estimated at 75 in 1959/60, who will thus start teaching in 1960/61, and 100, 400 and 800 in the three succeeding years. About 1,375 teachers will be provided from this source during the four-year period. At the same time the Humanities and Education faculties of the universities are expected to graduate 50, 95, 150 and 280 students respectively in the four years for a total of 575, so that 1,950 potential teachers will be available from these two sources com-bined. We estimate that 1,120 additional teachers will be required for the academic secondary schools alone (see Table 70). To this require-

TABLE 70: Intermediate New Teacher Supply and Demand

Year	Requirements by Type[a]				Total No. of Teachers Required	Potential Supply of New Teachers[b]	Cumu-lative Deficit
	Second-ary	Indus-trial	Commer-cial	Normal			
1960/61	270	120	50	65	505	125	−380
61/62	200	125	75	45	445	195	−630
62/63	220	115	100	—	435	550	−515
63/64	430	110	100	—	640	1,080	− 75
Total	1,120	470	325	110	2,025	1,950	

[a] Estimated on the basis of one additional teacher for every 40 additional enroll-ments plus a 2 percent replacement rate for teachers leaving the profession.
[b] Based on projected previous year's output both of the *Institutos Pedagogicos* and the Humanities and Education faculties of the universities.

ment must be added our estimate of more than 900 new teachers required for the other types of intermediate schools during the period. On this basis, there would be a slight deficit in teacher supply for the period as a whole, but this would be compensated in part by the supply of some special teachers for vocational schools from other sources (for example, from industry and abroad). While intermediate teacher supply would be close to meeting demand by 1963/64, it can be seen from Table 70 that a large deficit is in prospect until 1962/63. The mission urges that the scheduling of academic secondary school expansion take into consideration teacher availability.

The Venezuelan authorities managed to double the academic secondary teacher force from 1,022 in 1957/58 to more than 2,000 in 1959/60. The mission notes however that the large majority of teachers at *liceos* are employed on a part-time basis. During a period of rapid expansion such an expedient is probably necessary and the supply situation is such that the part-time teaching system will have to be continued for the next few years. The mission nevertheless urges that a start be made in replacing part-time teachers by full-time professionals wherever possible. Suitable part-time teachers should be given the opportunity for in-service training so that they might qualify for full-time positions. In 1959/60 full-time salaries were raised to Bs 2,200 a month or Bs 26,400 a year, a salary which should make secondary school teaching an attractive profession.

HIGHER EDUCATION

There are seven universities in Venezuela and the two teachers' colleges already noted. Two of the universities were only recently established, the *Universidad de Carabobo* at Valencia in 1958 and the Cumana section of the *Universidad de Oriente* in January 1960. Total enrollment doubled between 1957/58 and 1959/60, rising from 10,270 to 20,618 (see Table 71). Most of this rapid expansion has been in the public universities, enrollments rising from 8,188 to 18,149 in the two years. Private university enrollment seems to have stabilized at about 2,500.

The rapid expansion of the universities has been accompanied by a number of problems. With the return to constitutional government, there was a natural upsurge of the desire to obtain a higher education and an equally natural desire on the part of the authorities to fulfill this desire. As a result, proper standards of selection of students were not always observed. Many of the students were not of the intellectual caliber to warrant such an education. This is reflected by the high dropout and repeater rates. The mission strongly urges that some form of selective admissions policy, based on academic attainment and potential, be instituted. Whatever means is chosen, whether by a general entrance examination or by the use of secondary school grades as an index of academic fitness, specified procedures should be clearly stated in advance and implemented early enough each year so that there is no

TABLE 71: Enrollment by Individual Universities

Institutions	1956/57	1958/59	1959/60
Public:			
Universidad Central (Caracas)	6,159	10,278	12,413
Universidad de los Andes (Merida)	1,352	1,737	2,500
Universidad del Zulia (Maracaibo)	677	998	2,235
Universidad de Carabobo (Valencia)	—	605	801
Universidad de Oriente (Cumana)	—	—	200[a]
	8,188	13,618	18,149
Private:			
Universidad Santa Maria (Caracas)	1,040	1,160	932
Universidad Catolica Andres Bello (Caracas)	1,042	1,348	1,537
	2,082	2,508	2,469
Grand Total	10,270	16,126	20,618

[a] Courses started in January 1960.

delay, as there has been in the past, in starting the following university year.

The lack of selection has also resulted in the growth of faculties without reference to the economic needs of the country. For example, the Economics faculty doubled between 1957/58 and 1959/60 and in the latter year represented 25 percent of the total university enrollment (see Table 72). The Law faculty nearly doubled in the same period and in 1959/60 represented 15 percent of the total enrollment. In both cases, we doubt whether the economic needs of the country are properly reflected by the relative weight given to these two subjects. On the other hand, there were only 348 students in the Agronomy faculty in 1959/60, or about 1½ percent of the total enrollment, and only 174 students, or less than 1 percent, in the Veterinary faculty. About 30-40 qualified agronomists are likely to be graduated annually for the coming few years and about 15-20 veterinary surgeons. As we suggest in our Agriculture chapter, the economy needs many more professionals of these categories than will in fact be produced. The mission feels that an admissions policy should also be directed toward distributing enrollment between the faculties in accordance with estimated future professional manpower needs.

Given some improvement in retention rates, total enrollment will depend largely on the admission of new first-year students. The mission has some difficulty in forecasting first-year enrollment without knowing

TABLE 72: Enrollments by University Faculties

Faculty	1957/58	1958/59	1959/60[a]
Agronomy	144	204	368
Architecture and Urbanism	391	586	689
Commercial Administration	—	—	860
Dentistry	557	652	708
Economics	2,016	3,603	4,097
Engineering, Civil	1,934	2,748	3,537
Engineering, Forestry	42	46	76
Engineering, Industrial	—	86	151
Engineering, Petroleum	103	187	277
Humanities and Education	580	1,153	1,834
Law	1,578	2,588	2,862
Medicine	2,006	2,797	3,241
Pharmacy	619	722	773
Science, General	—	294	394
Science, Bio-analysis	183	311	377
Veterinary	117	149	174
Total	10,270	16,126	20,418

[a] Enrollment by faculties estimated on basis of the distribution of enrollment by faculties at Los Andes University. University of Oriente not included.

what that admissions policy will be in practice. Furthermore, there is no way of knowing exactly how many overage students, not proceeding directly from secondary school, will wish to enroll at university in each of the coming few years. In 1958/59 and 1959/60, some 15,600 students registered for first-year studies at the universities, while, in the years immediately preceding each of these two years, the academic secondary schools had graduated only about 9,700 students. Thus, at least 5,900 first-year university students must have come from the overage backlog; in fact, considerably more than this number must have come from the latter group, because not all the academic secondary school graduates are likely to have continued to university. For purposes of our projections, we have assumed a first-year entry into university in each of the years 1960/61-1963/64 exactly equal to our estimate of the preceding year's number of pupils at the final year of academic secondary school (see Table 73). This number assumes, for working purposes, a non-continuation rate of academic secondary pupils exactly equal to the amount of backlog overage students enrolling in any one year. We believe that the resultant first year enrollment projections will be overestimates, both because a selective admissions policy should eventually reduce the continuation rate and because the passage of time itself will begin to exhaust the potential backlog.

We are nevertheless employing what may well be an overestimate in order to demonstrate that, under any conceivable circumstances, total enrollment will expand at a slower rate than the forecasts currently being used within the Venezuelan Government in programing university education for the four-year period. Our projections indicate that total university enrollment will rise *at the maximum* from 20,418 in 1959/60 to 32,300 in 1963/64, or a total increase of about 12,000. By comparison, the Government's program is based on a forecasted increase in university enrollment of 23,558.

TABLE 73: University Enrollment

Year	Years of Study						Total
	1st	2nd	3rd	4th	5th	6th[a]	
Actual							
1955/56	3,085	1,510	1,106	898	532	194	7,325
56/57	3,958	1,751	1,279	1,115	565	166	8,834
57/58	4,715	2,054	1,424	1,102	771	204	10,270
58/59	7,588	3,744	2,189	1,511	872	222	16,126
59/60[b]	8,000	6,000	3,000	1,800	1,200	350	20,418
Mission's Projections[c]							
1960/61	7,600	6,400	5,100	2,500	1,400	400	23,400
61/62	7,700	6,100	5,400	4,200	2,000	400	25,800
62/63	9,600	6,200	5,200	4,600	3,000	400	29,000
63/64	10,800	7,700	5,300	4,400	3,700	400	32,300

[a] Almost entirely medical students.

[b] Estimated, except for total.

[c] Based on the mission's maximum assumptions as to new entries and anticipated improvements in retention rates. Total enrollments are therefore maximum projections and possibly overestimated.

Part of the proposed university expansion will take place in the new *Universidad de Oriente*. Plans for the development of this University contemplate five campuses, one in each of Sucre, Nueva Esparta, Monagas, Anzoategui and Bolivar States, and each one of which would provide a different selection of faculties. The mission believes that the establishment of a university in eastern Venezuela fulfills a real need, but we doubt whether there will be adequate demand for the proposed student capacity of 10,000 by 1963/64. We have examined academic secondary school enrollments in the five states concerned and calculate that a total of about 4,450 pupils will conclude their intermediate studies during the four-year period. Not all of these students will continue with higher studies. Although some entrants may come from other parts of Venezuela, we doubt that this number, together with the backlog of overage students, justifies the proposed capacity of 10,000. We urge reconsideration of the expansion of Oriente University with a view to stretching the program over a longer period.

In any event, we assume that nation-wide enrollment will increase by the stated 12,000 by 1963/64, including expansion at Oriente University. We calculate that the total capital outlay in buildings and equipment required to accommodate this increased enrollment will amount to about Bs 60 million during the four-year period.

SPECIAL EDUCATIONAL PROGRAMS

There are a number of special educational programs directed toward specific training goals, not all of which are the exclusive responsibility of the Ministry of Education. The major categories dealt with by these programs are agriculture, industry and general literacy, and they are concerned with adult training in addition to some school-age education.

Agriculture

The Ministry of Education currently has broad responsibility for agricultural education at both its lowest and highest levels, while the Ministry of Agriculture deals with agricultural education at the intermediate level.

We have already had occasion to mention the need for more university-trained agronomists and veterinarians. We estimate that the country needs about 1,000 *ingenieros agronomicos* (agronomists) and that there are currently about 380 in the country, of whom about 100 are foreign. Therefore, at least 800 trained agronomists are required as soon as possible. At present, only about 20 are produced annually. Obviously the gap is so large that the deficit cannot be made up in a period as short as four years. But a start should be made.

To increase the number of students entering university agronomic courses, a system of incentives, including differential scholarships which make agronomy relatively more attractive a course of studies, could be instituted. A better initial selection of agronomy students would help in raising retention rates and a larger proportion of total enrollment would eventually graduate fully qualified. Improvement of the conditions of ultimate employment—salaries, promotions, tenure, etc.— would attract more students to agronomy. Thought might also be given to a system of accelerated studies, so that more agronomists could be trained in a shorter time. Capacity and efficiency of existing teaching facilities might in effect be increased by means of a double-shift system of instruction. All these measures would entail the employment of larger agronomic teaching staffs at the universities. It is unlikely that all the additional staff could be found within Venezuela, at least not in the short run. The assistance of FAO and UNESCO should be sought for the interim recruitment of university instructors from abroad. Finally, as a temporary measure, a number of students should be sent abroad to study agronomy.

At the lower level, agricultural courses are provided in the upper grades of a few special rural primary schools, known as *escuelas granjas*. Nation-wide enrollment in this type of school was only about 1,400 in 1959/60 and consequently has so far had limited impact. The mission doubts the need for special schools at this level. On the contrary, *all* primary schools in rural areas should provide rudimentary agricultural education. Efforts should be made to ensure that rural primary school teachers have a background in rural matters, both by upbringing and by special courses at the Normal schools.

At the intermediate level, agricultural education is almost entirely the responsibility of the Ministry of Agriculture and is not necessarily directed only at school-age children. The Ministry operates two types of schools. One trains *peritos* (agricultural technical assistants). The course lasts three years and a previous primary school training is normally required. Two such schools existed until 1959/60, one at Maracay, operated by the Ministry of Agriculture, and one at Valencia, which is privately operated. Three more schools for *peritos* were due to be opened during 1959/60. Output of trained *peritos* should rise as a result of current expansion from about 50 in 1960/61 to about 300 in 1962/63 and in succeeding years. It is estimated that about 1,200 *peritos* are required for the government extension service. Since there were only about 150 *peritos* already in this service in 1959/60, it will take at least until 1964/65 for output to fill this need, and even thereafter some of the annual output of 300 will be required as replacements. Thus the supply of *perito*-trained personnel to practical farming itself will first be negligible for several years and then will be quite limited in relation to potential demand. Since a proper indoctrination in agricultural skills is so important to the future economic development of the rural areas, the mission thus urges consideration of the inclusion of some agricultural courses in the curriculum of academic secondary schools located in rural areas. In this connection, it seems to us that there is room for improvement in the coordination between the education activities of the Ministry of Agriculture and the Ministry of Education.

The Ministry of Agriculture also operates special schools for *practicos* (practical assistants). These provide short courses of practical demonstration in specialized skills, such as coffee-growing, cacao-growing and tractor operation. Since the *practicos* provide direct contact between the extension services and the agricultural population, a large number of *practicos,* trained in a number of special skills according to the region in which they will work, are required. Besides coffee, cacao and tractor-driving, *practicos* should be trained, for example, in dairying, cattle-raising, fruit and vegetable growing and soil survey.

Handicrafts and Industry

In addition to its responsibility for vocational education at the intermediate level, the Ministry of Education has been interested in the promotion of handicrafts instruction at the primary level. Pre-vocational education has been provided at a few selected schools in the upper primary grades. Special *escuelas artesanales* (handicraft schools) provide courses such as sewing for girls and basket-weaving or simple carpentry for boys. Of the 1,246 students enrolled in handicraft schools in 1959/60, 1,173 were girls. As with *escuelas granjas,* the mission doubts the utility of separate and special *escuelas artesanales.* Some form of pre-vocational manual training should be incorporated into the curriculum of *all* primary schools, perhaps with agricultural training being stressed in the rural areas and handicraft training being stressed in the towns.

At a somewhat higher level, the Government has recently established a semi-autonomous National Institute of Educational Cooperation (*Instituto Nacional de Cooperacion Educativa*—INCE) which is to be concerned with various forms of training and education in industry. We discuss the Institute in our chapter on manufacturing (see Chapter 9) and come to the general conclusion that it could be a useful adjunct to the normal educational channels of the country. Care should be taken however that its functions do not overlap with those of the regular education authorities and that it concern itself mainly with apprenticeship training of youths and specific on-the-job training of adults.

SUMMARY OF MISSION'S PROPOSED EXPENDITURES

The recommendations we have made in this chapter would entail public investment expenditures, both for construction and equipment of Bs 415.4 million over the four-year period of 1960/61-1963/64. This figure compares with the amount of investment expenditures under consideration within the Venezuelan Government of Bs 442.4 million for the same period. Table 74 indicates the distribution of these expenditures by type of education.

TABLE 74: Mission's Proposed Capital Expenditures[a] on Education, 1960/61-1963/64

(in Bs million)

Type of Education	Four-Year Total	Annual Average
Primary	166.0	41.5
Normal	37.2	9.3
Industrial	70.2	17.5
Commercial	20.5	5.1
Academic Secondary	61.5	15.4
Universities	60.0	15.0
	415.4	103.8

[a] Includes construction and equipment.

Our recommendations for the development of Venezuelan education will require the allocation each year of additional current expenditures to operate the enlarged educational system. One of the more important items in total operating costs is the payroll of teaching staff and other personnel. Our proposed program would require additions to the teaching staffs of all types of schools. We estimate that there would be about 4,000 more teachers on the primary school payroll in 1963/64 than there were in 1959/60; this would increase the annual payroll by about Bs 44 million by 1963/64. Furthermore, perhaps a further 4,000 certificated teachers would have replaced provisional teachers by 1963/64;

since there is a salary differential of about Bs 2,000 a year for certificated teachers, this replacement would add a further Bs 8 million to the annual payroll. Additional staff for Normal schools would require an increase in annual payroll expenditures of about Bs 3 million; the payroll expenses of the industrial schools would rise by about Bs 11.4 million a year, of commercial schools by about Bs 8.5 million, and of academic secondary schools by about Bs 39.1 million. University teaching expenses (including teachers' colleges) should rise by Bs 21.0 million annually by 1963/64. In all, salaries and wages in the entire education field should rise by about Bs 135 million annually by the end of the four-year period. In addition, we have recommended the provision of books and other teaching materials to primary schools at an annual cost of Bs 12.5 million. Assuming other current expenses, which include costs of administration and maintenance, purchases of consumable goods, and payment for special services, also continue rising at about 5 percent annually, such a rise would entail these costs increasing by about Bs 30 million in 1963/64 over the 1959/60 level.

In all, annual current expenditures in 1963/64 would be about Bs 177 million more than in 1959/60, rising from about Bs 443 million to about Bs 621 million annually during the four-year period. Total current expenditures for the four years 1960/61-1963/64 would amount to approximately Bs 2,217 million, an annual average of Bs 554 million.

We do not express an opinion as to how these capital and additional current expenditures should be divided between the federal, state and municipal authorities. We understand that a good deal of construction work is executed by the states and sometimes by the municipalities, particularly with respect to primary education. It seems likely that the smaller units of construction could often be carried out on the local level more efficiently and less expensively. There is also a case for certain types of education being the operational responsibility of local authorities. We assume that the division of administrative responsibility for our proposed program would be a matter for consultation between the various authorities.

CHAPTER 15 *HOUSING AND URBAN PLANNING*

A Long-Term Policy and Program

Venezuela is today faced with the task of constructing a large amount of housing and certain other community services—such as water and sanitation works (see Chapter 16) —to make up for huge deficits which have accumulated over the past generations. The problem is however more than simply one of quantities: what has also been lacking in the past has been an orderly and rational approach to the planning of such community developments to ensure that they are instituted at such places and times and in such forms as to maximize their efficient use.

Even with an orderly approach to these questions, the development of the physical environment in such a way as best to meet the needs of the people and the country would have had to overcome serious handicaps. The unprecedented growth of the population and the continuous migration within the country, particularly toward urban centers, have complicated the task of providing appropriate housing and related services. Furthermore, the uneven distribution of income, with large sections of the population living on very low incomes indeed, has meant that the provision of housing on the basis of market prices has been well-nigh impossible except with respect to a small part of the population. In addition, the uneven levels of economic and social development as between the various regions and localities around the country have meant that development of local community services has likewise been uneven.

Many of these difficulties can be faced more effectively in the future if a long-term policy and program for community development and interrelated services are drawn up and adhered to. The prelude to such a program would entail the study and forecast of the main lines of economic and social development over the next generation so that physical environment could be shaped to meet the needs of that development. Thus, in the shorter term each construction project and each newly created community service could be measured against the yardstick of the longer-term program.

The importance of having the right kind of organization to implement such a program cannot be overstressed. There is currently in Venezuela a multiplicity of services, ministries, autonomous institutes and other agencies in charge of various sectors of housing and community development activities; for example, the *Direccion de Urbanismo* of the Ministry of Public Works, metropolitan and municipal town planning offices, the *Banco Obrero,* the *Instituto de Vivienda de Maracaibo,* the *Seccion de Vivienda Rural* of the Ministry of Health, the *Instituto Agrario Nacional,* the oil companies, various institutes of the Ministries of Development and Mines, the *Instituto Nacional de Obras Sanitarias,* the *Ingenieria Sanitaria* of the Ministry of Health, the municipal engineering offices, the *Direccion de Edificios* of the Ministry of Public Works, the *Instituto de Deportes,* the *Consejo Nacional de Ninos,* and the technical departments of various other Ministries; there are also a number of private agencies working in the field. Most of these organizations work independently of each other without coordination of their activities and without any over-all program to follow. The net result is that progress in the various fields is inconsistent, depending solely upon the circumstances of the particular agency involved.

What is urgently needed is a specific organization to incorporate and coordinate the efforts presently carried out by the various agencies each of which is currently concerned usually with only one phase of the general community development task. The need for such an organization was emphasized by many Venezuelan officials and private architects and planners during the 1959 *Congreso de Vivienda,* held at Maracaibo. The detailed structure of such an organization would have to be decided by the Government on the basis of discussion between the department concerned, and its final shape and form will be dictated by the experience in the course of operation. The basic role of the organization would be to prepare an over-all housing and community development policy, and to coordinate and implement programs to give expression to such a policy. The organization would perhaps be placed under the Ministry of Public Works and staff could be recruited mainly from the *Banco Obrero,* the *Seccion de Vivienda Rural,* the *Direccion de Urbanismo* and the *Instituto Nacional de Obras Sanitarias.*

While the new organization is being established and while it is proceeding with a nation-wide appraisal of needs, drawing up its policy and its long-term programs, top-priority housing construction must proceed. Even though it may be some time before a general long-term program for community development is established, a housing construction program for 1960/61-1963/64 should get under way forthwith. The latter program could be relatively flexible and subject to modification later in the four-year period if the over-all long-term community development program then so indicates. We therefore address ourselves in the next section to a discussion of a housing program for the immediate future.

HOUSING

Present Housing Conditions

Any precise quantitative evaluation of present housing conditions is impossible because the latest comprehensive information is to be found in the 1950 Census and very great changes have taken place since 1950 in population, its geographical distribution, and the stock of housing. While it is clear that these changes are large, their precise character is not known.

According to the 1950 Census, nearly half the Venezuelan population was living in *ranchos*—below-minimum shelters constructed by the occupant with makeshift materials (see Table 75). Most ranchos

TABLE 75: Status of Housing According to 1950 Census

Type	Number	Percentage of Total
Houses and Families[a]	875,704[b]	100.0
of which:		
Individual houses	428,333	48.9
Apartments	28,048	3.2
Not indicated	10,520	1.2
Ranchos	408,803[c]	46.7
Substandard Dwellings		
with:		
No direct water supply	586,960	67.0
No sanitation	514,410	58.9
Earth floors	456,180	53.1
Matted roofs	377,688	38.6
Overcrowded Dwellings[d]	443,290	50.6

[a] Number of houses is equal to number of families by definition.

[b] Excludes 27,471 collective dwellings such as hotels, hospitals, etc.

[c] Of which 110,205 in urban areas of over 1,000 inhabitants and 298,598 in rural areas.

[d] Dwellings of one or two rooms with average density of over 3.5 persons per room.

have virtually no sanitation facilities, although in urban areas a surprisingly high proportion seems to be provided with electricity. While the rancho is not unsuited to the temperature condition of the country, it does not provide adequate shelter protection and, as normally constructed, leads to very high densities per room. Over 50 percent of all dwellings in 1950 were one- or two-room dwellings with an average of over 3.5 persons per room. In urban areas ranchos are frequently constructed by squatters on land with alternative uses of high value, and their removal constitutes a serious political problem. In rural areas, where three-quarters of the ranchos reported in 1950 were located, they represent less of a social and public health problem, although they provide a very low level of shelter.

Although estimates are based on very slim evidence, it appears that the number of ranchos has increased substantially since 1950, and that much of the increase must have occurred in urban areas. The *Banco Central* mentions an increase in urban areas from 110,000 ranchos in 1950 to almost 250,000 in 1959. Venezuelan experts generally estimate that ranchos now total 500,000 in the country as a whole.

Under severe economic pressure the new urban dweller naturally tends to move into a rancho. Since 1950 the urban population of Venezuela has grown at breakneck speed (see Table 76). With such rapid change in population distribution the pressure on urban housing was acute. With 70 percent of the urban population earning less than Bs 9,600 annually and 80 percent less than Bs 12,000 annually, a large proportion of the urban population has not been able to afford decent

TABLE 76: 1950 and 1959 Population Distribution in Urban Centers and Rural Regions

Category	No. of Settlements		Population		Population as % of Total	
	1950	1959	1950	1959	1950	1959
50,000 and above	7	11	1,099,074	2,656,000	21.0	36.5
10,000 — 49,999	33	50	724,602	1,070,600	14.0	14.5
5,000 — 9,999	43	101	289,704	813,000	6.0	11.0
2,500 — 4,999	88	200	298,431	669,400	6.0	9.0
Less than 2,500	40,292	—	2,623,027	2,090,000	53.0	29.0
Total	40,463	—	5,034,838	7,299,000	100.0	100.0

Sources: 1950 Population Census. 1959 Cordiplan Population Projections.

shelter. In the metropolitan area of Caracas alone, where dwelling units total about 235,000, there were estimated to have been about 40,000-50,000 ranchos in 1959. A substantial percentage of the ranchos in Caracas is rented, the average monthly rental being about Bs 80 per month. Land values, particularly in Caracas, are very high as the result of the very large population increase pressing against the limited land in reasonably level terrain in the Caracas valley. Thus, fairly substantial rents can be placed on even sub-minimum shelter where legal titles are established and respected. High land values and speculative holding of land is encouraged by the absence of an effective system of land taxes and by the fact that capital gains are not taxed.

In addition to the special problems created by rising land values, urban housing construction by the private sector for low- and middle-income groups has been handicapped by government-imposed restrictions. For example, the present Architecture Town Planning and Construction Ordinance of Caracas provides for densities and minima of plots and free-space areas which practically exclude any low-cost housing. Problems for housing have also been created by urban reconstruction in the form of new monumental avenues, creation of parks and other beautification projects in the center of cities. Expropriation for urban reconstruction has increased the number of shelterless families and encouraged land speculation because of expected changes in land use.

Because considerable reconstruction has taken place in the past 15 years in the center of cities, much of the older housing, which would ordinarily become available to lower-income groups as the middle- and upper-income groups construct new housing in the outlying areas, has been destroyed and the land is no longer used for housing. Very little higher-standard housing trickles down from upper-income groups.

Perhaps the major factor limiting the ability of the private sector to provide decent housing to lower- and middle-income groups are the terms on which credit can be secured. Reflecting the high returns which can be secured for credit in other sectors of the economy, interest rates on mortgages generally exceed 12 percent annually, and other charges must be added. Most mortgage credit in Venezuela is medium-term credit. The term of a mortgage rarely exceeds 10 years and most mortgages are considerably shorter. Down payments required are fairly substantial. Some insurance companies, which are willing to offer mortgage money at 8 percent to first-category risks, are unwilling to lend more than 50 percent of the appraised value. Low-income groups as such have virtually no access to mortgage credit.

Housing Construction and Role of Public Sector

While Venezuelan housing conditions constitute a serious social and economic problem and it seems clear that the progress made toward resolving the problem since 1950 has been slow, it is not possible to pinpoint the volume of construction of decent housing that has taken place. The Central Bank recently estimated that the number of urban dwellings other than ranchos rose from about 350,000 in 1950 to almost 750,000 in 1959, an average net increase of 44,000 a year. The basis for this estimate is not known. If one allows for demolition and obsolescence, which this estimate omits, construction would exceed 50,000 dwellings a year. On either basis, the estimate implies a much higher rate of construction than is indicated by the Central Bank's own estimates of housing investment.[1] The latter estimates suggest that no more than 15,000 to 20,000 units have been constructed yearly in urban areas, of which no more than 5,000 were constructed yearly under government programs. On the basis of these estimates, it would appear safe to assume that private residential urban construction, other than ranchos, has rarely exceeded 15,000 units a year. With new urban families being formed at the rate of at least 35,000 per year, private and governmental efforts were probably insufficient to keep up with new family formation, much less correct existing deficiencies.

Governmental housing programs have been carried out primarily by the *Banco Obrero,* founded in 1928, and, to a much lesser extent, in rural areas by the *Instituto Agrario Nacional* (IAN), and the recently established Rural Housing Section of the Ministry of Health. The municipalities have also carried out some programs.

The *Banco Obrero* has constructed more than 40,000 housing units at a total cost of about Bs 1.25 billion or over Bs 30,000 per unit (see Table 77). From 1954 to 1958 emphasis was placed on the construction of almost 20,000 dwelling units in 179 apartment houses, mainly superblocks, in Caracas and La Guaira. These apartments involved a total expenditure of about Bs 700 million, or an average cost per apartment of about Bs 35,000.

The Banco Obrero program has made a contribution to the solution

[1] See *Memoria, 1959,* Banco Central de Venezuela, Table 18-2, in which total housing investment is estimated at some Bs 600 million a year during 1950-59. Assuming an average cost per house of about Bs 30,000 (which is the Banco Obrero's average for 1955-59), the average rate of construction could not have exceeded 20,000 housing units a year.

TABLE 77: Construction and Organization of Houses and Public Services and Community Buildings by the Banco Obrero, 1928-1959

| | | Costs (in Bs thousand) | |
Federal Entities	Houses, Services and Buildings	Total	Average per Dwelling
Federal District	29,615	975,136	33.6
Anzoategui State	1,106	39,617	35.8
Apure State	25	420	16.8
Aragua State	571	10,465	18.3
Barinas State	60	954	15.9
Bolivar State	435	15,920	36.6
Carabobo State	1,861	28,414	15.3
Cojedes State	48	1,038	21.6
Falcon State	203	4,956	24.4
Guarico State	48	1,777	37.0
Lara State	1,467	28,075	19.1
Merida State	50	749	15.0
Miranda State	1,082	50,162	46.4
Monagas State	399	8,672	21.7
Portuguesa State	30	825	27.5
Sucre State	641	11,955	18.6
Tachira State	678	26,682	39.3
Trujillo State	152	2,929	19.3
Yaracuy State	25	535	21.4
Zulia State	2,036	42,826	21.0
Total	40,532	1,252,107	30.9

Source: *Banco Obrero.*

of Venezuela's housing problems but it has generally sought to provide such a high level of housing services that it has failed to reach a significant portion of the people. Plot size, design, and size of dwelling are such as to lead to high cost. Community facilities and buildings have not been designed with an eye to economy. Retention of ownership by the Government in most cases has caused excessive management and maintenance expense; occupants have not had the incentive to maintain and improve their dwellings. Until recently it was not possible to collect rents on apartments and monthly expenditures on maintenance and administration of the superblocks amounted to Bs 2 million, as against only Bs 700,000 in receipts from rents. Attempts have been made since 1959 to remedy this situation. Furthermore, a plan was launched to allow the acquisition of the apartments by the occupants on easy payment terms.

The IAN program—through which 1,950 rural houses were constructed at a cost of Bs 24 million from 1945-1958—is part of IAN agricultural settlement activity. The rural housing program of the Ministry of Health, only recently initiated, is based on the self-help or mutual-help system. Building materials up to Bs 5,000 per family are supplied on credit and technical assistance is made available to families able and willing to provide the necessary labor. Approximately 2,500 rural dwellings were constructed under this program in 1958/59. Costs totaled Bs 18 million, including large sums for training and research looking toward later expansion.

It seems clear that little effort has been made until recently to develop low-cost housing programs capable of meeting any substantial portion of the need. It must be recognized of course that there have been, and will continue to be, severe limitations on the speed with which an increase in housing accommodation can be effected by direct government action. First, funds will become available only relatively gradually because investment in other sectors of the economy must be maintained at a high rate if economic growth is to continue. Second, it will take some time for administrative capacity to be raised to the level required to manage large-scale housing programs. Third, the growth of some of the major cities must be reduced to a somewhat lower rate and speculative influences must be curtailed. Other economic policies can contribute to overcoming these limitations. For example, as economic growth is promoted by government action, individual incomes will be raised so that more people can afford decent housing without government aid. The policies, recommended elsewhere in this report, of raising rural incomes and of discouraging too rapid an influx to the cities will also help solve the housing problem.

Such general policies are not sufficient, however. In the judgment of the mission, the Government must continue to assume direct responsibilities in the housing sector. It is appropriate for the Government, given the level of resources at its command, to distribute the fruits of economic progress more widely by means of a soundly conceived housing program.

At the time of the mission's visit to Venezuela, the Government was giving consideration to a wide variety of proposals and was initiating several new programs. The 1959/60 budget of the *Banco Obrero* included a plot development program under which a large number of families would be supplied with a developed plot with community facilities at low cost. On this plot the owner-occupant would himself erect a modest shelter. In the judgment of the mission, such a program could be expanded with some modification to become the major component of the government program to serve low-income groups in urban areas. The mission would also propose:

    a. A continuation of the self-help rural housing program to supplement outside of settlement areas the rural housing program in settlement areas outlined in Chapter 9.

    b. A credit and guarantee program to mobilize private capital for constructing high-priority housing in selected development areas.

Housing Targets

The first part of the government housing program is viewed primarily as a means of supplying the low-income groups with the opportunity to secure somewhat better housing than they now enjoy. In one sense, there is no limit—except the competing claims on resources in other sectors—on the volume of resources that could be devoted to this objective. In practice, there are many limitations, one of the most important being the planning and administrative capacity the Government can bring to bear upon this task in the next few years.

The program outlined below attempts to take into account this practical limitation and also attempts, on the basis of very sketchy and contradictory information, to achieve certain objectives—the provision of improved housing at a rate sufficient to meet the needs of new families, the gradual reduction in the numbers living in ranchos, and the replacement of existing houses as they become substandard or as they are demolished to permit changes in land use.

Population projections supplied by the Planning Office suggest that the number of families will increase by about 40,000 a year. On the basis of the employment projections cited in Chapter 7, about three-quarters of these new families may be expected to settle in towns with a population of 5,000 or over. Thus, about 120,000 additional urban families must be provided with homes during the four-year period 1960/61-1963/64. Over 40,000 additional families will be settling in small towns and rural settlements.

Simply to take care of additional families it would be necessary to construct about 160,000 new dwellings. It will also be necessary to replace some existing dwellings as they become substandard or as they are demolished to permit changes in land use. Although such replacement is virtually impossible to estimate on the basis of existing information, we assume for the purpose of this analysis that over 25,000 houses must be replaced in the four-year period. Finally, it would be desirable to reduce the number of existing substandard houses, particularly ranchos. It may be possible to replace perhaps as many as 40,000 during the four years.

The four-year target for the private and public sectors combined would thus total about 225,000 dwelling units or over 55,000 a year. On the basis of past experience, it is doubtful that the private sector would construct more than 15,000 units a year, largely for the upper-middle and higher-income groups in urban areas.[2] More might be done under private management and control if government financial assistance were provided.

Role of Government Credit

The mission has carefully considered whether it might not be desirable to place major emphasis on a credit program to the private sector as a means of improving the housing situation. We have concluded that the low-income component of the recommended program could more appropriately be planned and administered by a government agency, including nonprofit instrumentalities of state and local governments. The low-income program, as outlined below, would involve the construction of minimum housing in which the capital employed would in effect be supplied by the Government at subsidized rates of interest to the owner-occupants. Only by offering such rates of interest would it be possible for the lower-income groups to secure such housing. While it would be possible to induce private builders to construct such housing, if the Government offered credit at subsidized rates of interest, the terms and conditions under which the builders would be permitted to sell such housing would have to be strictly regulated. Thus, the scope for private decision-making would in any event be necessarily limited. Under these conditions and in view of the social objectives of the low-income housing program, the mission concludes that the planning, financing, and entrepreneurial function should be performed by the Government. Actual construction of the housing, except in the case of strictly self-help housing, would be carried out

[2] If the estimates of recent rates of housing construction for the private sector are too low—as one of the new series of the Central Bank suggests—the volume of rancho replacement which becomes feasible without undue strain on the government sector is correspondingly increased.

by private contractors, and the houses, when completed, would be sold to occupants on relatively easy terms.

With respect to housing for middle-income groups, the mission feels that government action will need to be severely limited in the next few years at least. The low-income program will probably strain the resources of the housing construction industry, if it is carried out on the scale recommended below. Furthermore, any substantial general program of middle-income housing would require a heavy allocation of resources which the Government can ill afford in view of its other responsibilities. The gradual development of mortgage institutions and other private credit agencies should of course be encouraged, together with other measures to stimulate residential construction by the private sector. The mission recommends that direct government action in the field of upper- and middle-income housing be limited to assuring that housing is available in selected development areas where other government projects are being constructed or where other vital interests would be jeopardized if housing is not made available in accordance with a pre-determined schedule. In such cases—such as housing for the steel workers at Puerto Ordaz—every effort should be made to invite private capital to assume the entrepreneurial and financing function. Housing for middle- and upper-income groups should not generally be subsidized except perhaps to the extent that the Government underwrites certain special risks in new development areas. Where some government finance must be supplied to assure that the necessary housing will be made available for middle- and upper-income groups in selected areas, substantial subsidies in the form of very low interest rates should be avoided.

It is difficult to determine how much the Government will have to provide directly in the form of credit or commit in the form of guarantees to assure that development areas in which the Government has a major interest will not be held back by lack of housing. At the time of the mission's visit, there were discussions of the need for 6,000 dwelling units at Puerto Ordaz to house steel workers and 1,000 houses at Moron for the chemical workers. These two projects alone were estimated to require an investment of almost Bs 150 million. Some of this housing could be provided by the urban low-income program described below, but at least half the workers would belong to the middle- and upper-income groups and could afford better housing. There may be other groups in particular areas—civil servants, for example—who will require special credit assistance. The mission has tentatively earmarked Bs 100 million for government credit or guarantees, on the assumption that the balance required will be made available by private capital.

If private capital is not to be discouraged from venturing into the residential housing field, the profit outlook should not be dimmed by unduly restrictive rent control laws. While there may be some argument in favor of preventing excessive rents in existing structures in areas where speculative conditions exist, rent controls on new housing would either encourage private builders to restrict their activities to building houses for sale only, or to avoid residential construction entirely. In either case, rent controls on new housing would tend to aggravate the shortage. The first task is to provide incentives for the maximum construction effort from all sectors of the economy. As the housing supply increases, rent levels will tend to go down. We therefore recommend against rent controls on new rental construction.

The mission concludes that, with some government credit and guarantees and with a government policy free of restrictions, private housing might supply 60,000 to 65,000 of some 225,000 dwelling units that must be constructed to achieve the target specified above, leaving about 160,000 to be supplied under direct government programs. This government program is divided almost equally in terms of number of dwelling units between rural and urban housing.

Rural Housing

The major government effort in rural housing recommended by the mission has already been discussed in Chapter 9. Credits to about 60,000 families would be made available at a total cost of Bs 60 million in a self-help program for new rural settlements. The mission recommends that a self-help program along the lines already initiated by the Ministry of Health be continued to supplement this in settled areas. The rural self-help program outside new settlements might provide about 22,000 units at a total cost of Bs 36 million, or an average cost of about Bs 1,600 per unit. The rural housing program is of high priority not simply because poor housing conditions exist on a large scale in settled rural areas. In a sense this does not constitute a sufficient rationale for a rural housing program on the scale recommended here so long as housing conditions in more highly concentrated urban areas are not greatly improved. From the point of view of the nation as a whole, the rural housing program is necessary, just as the agricultural program is necessary, in order to provide sufficient opportunities for a better life in rural regions so that the movement of the population to urban areas can be kept to manageable proportions. A rural housing program at relatively low cost, coupled with the provision of related community services, thus reduces the magnitude of the problem with which the urban housing program must deal.

Urban Housing for Low-Income Groups

The government low-cost urban housing program would provide about 80,000 urban dwelling units at a cost of about Bs 424 million, an average cost of about Bs 5,300 per dwelling unit. A program of this magnitude would not result in a substantial reduction in the number of urban ranchos if the population projections and private construction estimates previously cited are correct. However, it does not seem practicable to propose a larger program for the next four years, in view of the time that will be required to organize a housing program.

In order to achieve a unit cost of Bs 5,300 per dwelling, emphasis would be placed on construction of developed plots, "core" and unfinished housing which could be completed later either by self-help or by other means. In all cases, streets would be laid out, and connections to piped water distribution and sewage disposal systems, as well as electricity, would be provided. In some cases, mainly for demonstration and pilot purposes, a very small percentage of complete houses would be constructed. Also it may be necessary in areas where land cost is high to build some apartment buildings, but these should be kept to a minimum. Emphasis should be placed on individual family dwellings, built as a rule in rows to allow for the maximum of economy, to be sold to owner-occupants on terms. We strongly recommend home ownership, even for low-income groups, for a number of reasons. First, home ownership is a deep-felt need. Second, it provides both social and political cohesion. Finally, owners tend to improve their structures and thus preserve community values.

"Core" housing consists of part of a house, for example, two rooms of a house that is designed to have three or four rooms. The two rooms would be completely finished before sale and even these would provide better shelter and community facilities than is now available. The owner-occupant could later add to the house, as envisaged in the original design. An unfinished house differs from a core house in that the main structure is completed at the time of construction. However, only one or two of the individual rooms are ready for occupancy and even these require some additional work by the owner-occupant. Both the core house and the unfinished house would usually be constructed on plots forming part of a planned community development. Plots would vary in size from 100 square meters to 250 square meters and a core house from 25 to 40 square meters. Even with such plot and house sizes, it would only be possible to achieve the average cost of Bs 5,300 per dwelling unit if systematic efforts were made to keep down costs of land development and house construction.

The mission believes that it should be possible to provide a developed plot at an average cost of between Bs 10 and Bs 20 per square meter. For construction of a core house, unit costs of from Bs 140 per square meter to Bs 250 per square meter should be feasible. Such costs are not out of line with recent experience in programs where vigorous efforts have been made to secure economies. The 1959/60 housing program of the *Banco Obrero* provides for the development of plots of 250 square meters at the total cost of Bs 1,500-2,500; the Housing Institute of Maracaibo launched in 1959 a self-help project for the construction of houses at a cost of Bs 0.60 per square meter for land, and Bs 4 per square meter for land and land development; a recent survey in Anaco found that prices of land in the outskirts of the town were as low as Bs 0.3 per square meter, the average being Bs 3-5 per square meter. In 1959 the Popular Housing Institute started a project in Valencia where 45-75 square meter houses were built on 135-200 square meter plots at a cost of Bs 135-140 per square meter for construction. In a recent competition for prefabricated houses organized by the Organization Pro-Venezuela, prices obtained ranged from Bs 90 to Bs 155 per square meter of built area.

It will only be possible to achieve an average unit cost of Bs 5,300 per dwelling unit in urban areas if several principles are adhered to. Construction should be as a rule in rows. Plot frontage should be strictly limited since a substantial part of the total cost of the program will be incurred in the construction of streets, water supply, and sewerage, the costs of which increase rapidly for every additional meter of plot frontage.

The area actually finished in the core or unfinished houses would in itself provide only minimum shelter and housing densities would only be reduced significantly if owner-occupants were able and willing to complete their dwellings. For those ready to complete their dwellings, public authorities could provide elementary training and demonstrations in home-improvement techniques. As far as the core or unfinished houses themselves are concerned, the design should be limited to a few fundamental types which can be adapted to specific conditions. Semi-open and open spaces, such as small patios and courtyards, natural cross ventilation, use of low-cost materials and limiting to the minimum finishing work requiring the use of hired labor should be the main characteristics. The Government should attempt to standardize building materials and other products to be used in the construction and to arrange with private industry to mass produce at the lowest cost under contract such items as doors, windows, roofing materials, etc. Prefabrication should also be considered as a means of keeping costs to the minimum.

The low-income housing program for urban areas, even if as many as 80,000 dwelling units could be constructed, would provide improved housing accommodations to a small percentage of low-income families. Although other low-income families would still benefit later as the program would presumably continue, it would be inequitable if those securing housing during the next four years were not required to pay anything. Moreover, a 100 percent state subsidy of housing on the scale recommended here would impose a severe burden on the state's financial resources in the future. On the other hand, if the beneficiaries of the program had to pay the full cost of the program it is unlikely that it could be geared to meet the needs of the low-income groups on the scale suggested here. The mission therefore recommends that while a subsidy element be placed in the low-income housing program, it be limited.

The program would be geared mainly to those earning less than Bs 12,000 per year. This group, which constitutes 80 percent of the urban population, can afford only minimum housing if the subsidy element is limited. Experience indicates that a reasonable cost for housing corresponds to the equivalent of two to three years' family income. This figure permits amortization within a 20-year period on installments corresponding on a yearly basis to 10-30 percent of income at low interest rates.

We suggest three types of housing for which costs and family income are related (see Table 78). Type A housing, for example, would include a plot of 100-150 square meters and, if a core house were built on it, it would have a floor space of 25 meters; such housing would cost Bs 1,000 for the developed plot alone, and B 4,000 with a core house; given these sizes and therefore these costs, Type A housing would be available to those with annual incomes of less than Bs 4,800, or an average of Bs 2,400 for this income group as a whole. Type B housing, for those with annual incomes ranging from Bs 4,800 to Bs 9,800, or an average of Bs 7,200 for the group, would be somewhat more spacious and therefore somewhat more costly (see Table 78). Finally, Type C housing would be even more spacious and costly (see Table 78) and

TABLE 78: Cost Estimates by Type of Plot and House

| | Area in Sq. M. | | Cost in Bs | | |
	Plot	Core	Plot	Core[a]	Complete House
Type A	100—150	25	1,000	4,000	6,000
Type B	200	35	3,000	7,000	14,000
Type C	250	40	5,000	10,000	21,000

[a] The "core" house and the unfinished house can be designed so that construction costs are approximately the same. These two types are presented together as core housing in order to simplify the exposition.

would be available for those with annual incomes ranging from Bs 9,800 to Bs 12,000, the average annual income for the group being Bs 10,800. It should be noted that complete houses would rarely be supplied; the completion of core and unfinished houses will be dependent on self-help and mutual-help. Thus, actual payments to the Government will be substantially less than 10-30 percent of income, the difference presumably being available to secure some outside financing of materials and labor to permit the owner-occupant to complete the house with his own labor.

The mission has not attempted to work out the details of the financing arrangements that might be offered to beneficiaries. While we would favor at least a small down payment requirement in all cases, the amount of the down payment would have to be determined on the basis of more adequate surveys of the financial assets of low-income groups. Down payments might initially be fixed at 10-20 percent of the value of the housing facility, to be later adjusted on the basis of experience. The amount of the down payment might be set at a lower proportion for developed plots, provided without any structure. Some down payment would seem to be necessary in all cases, particularly at the beginning of the program, in order to guarantee the reliability and serious intentions of the purchaser and thereby to reduce the administrative burden on the Government.

The beneficiaries would be expected fully to repay the total cost over a 20-year period, including the cost of land and land development, cost of construction of the core or unfinished house, and expenses for supervision and collection of installments. The subsidy could conveniently be provided in the form of low interest rates, which could be established on a sliding scale—from, say, 2-6 percent—depending on the income group.

The monthly installments on the purchase and the amount of the down payment would thus be adjusted to the ability to pay. This would follow both from adjusting house types and the corresponding capital investment to the income of the low-income owner and also from varying rates of interest and required down payments. If this program is to be successful, low-income applicants must be screened in accordance with their ability to meet their financial obligations.

Other criteria must also be applied in the selection of beneficiaries. Occupants of existing ranchos in areas that are being cleared should probably be given first priority within any city. In cities, such as Caracas, where the Government is interested in moderating the influx of population a minimum period of past residence should be required of any applicant. The Government will, of course, want to see the program get under way rapidly in, and give priority to, those newly developing areas to which low-income families must be attracted if development of the area is to proceed. Some of the housing at Puerto Ordaz, required not only for the lower-income steel workers but also for other workers in the area, might be provided under this program.

Since the houses would be sold to beneficiaries on subsidized terms, special restrictions should be imposed on resale. The beneficiary should not be allowed to sell the house, say, until at least five years after the date of the contract, except back to the Government or to an approved purchaser on predetermined terms.

For the purpose of arriving at an estimate of the capital investment the Government would make in the low-income urban program, we assume that the 80,000 dwellings needed to reach the targets specified above would be distributed among the three illustrative housing types roughly proportionate to the numbers in the urban population falling in the corresponding income groups, but with slightly more going to the lowest income group (see Table 79). We estimate that the total cost of the program would amount during the four-year period 1960/61-1963/64 to Bs 424 million.

Summary of Proposed Capital Expenditures

The recommendations which we have made in this section would entail capital expenditures by the Government of some Bs 560 million during the four-year period 1960/61-1963/64 (see Table 80). This amount does not include Bs 60 million to be spent on rural housing under the proposed agricultural settlement program (see Chapter 9).

TABLE 79: Cost of Urban Program for Low-Income Housing

Dwelling Type and Income Group	Average Income	Percentage of Low- Income Population	Number of Dwelling Units and Plots	Average Cost per Unit[a] (in Bs)	Total Cost (in Bs million)
A	2,400	50	40,000	3,700	148
B	7,200	40	32,000	6,500	208
C	10,800	10	8,000	8,500	68
		100	80,000	5,300	424

[a] Unit costs are derived from the estimates shown in Table 4, assuming that developed plots alone are assigned to 10 percent, 20 percent, and 30 percent of the beneficiaries in Groups A, B, and C respectively, and that the remainder in each group obtain core or unfinished dwellings.

TABLE 80: Mission's Proposed Housing Expenditures, 1960/61-1963/64
(in Bs million)

	Four-Year Total
Rural self-help program	36
Credit or guarantee program	100
Low-income urban housing	424
Total	560

URBAN PLANNING AND MUNICIPAL PUBLIC WORKS

Regional and Town Planning

In recommending that the proposed not inconsiderable housing program be carried out during the next four years without delay, the mission would not want to diminish the importance it attaches to the necessity for adequate regional and town planning. We believe that the long-run development of the various aspects of the physical environment—housing, public buildings, parks and other recreation facilities, city roads and lighting and the whole range of community facilities—should proceed on the rational basis of proper planning. To this end, we suggest that both regional and town master plans be drawn up without delay. Obviously such plans will take some time to produce, which is both a reason why work should be instituted on them immediately and why the various urgent construction programs we have suggested above will have to proceed concurrently with the work on the master plan. Given sufficient flexibility, however, it should be possible to fit into the later plans the top-priority construction which takes place forthwith.

Master plans for all urban settlements, as well as the most important rural ones, should be prepared; top priority should be given to main urban centers. In each master plan, provision should be made for possible expansions over the next twenty years or more. Integrated communities should be created and provided with all services and buildings.

The planning of the metropolitan area of Caracas requires particular attention. Rapid growth has led to excessive congestion which is beginning to obstruct the efficient operation of city services. Competent authorities have already started building satellite towns to decentralize the industrial activity of the capital. This decentralization process should be continued on the basis of a proper plan, whereby industry and other activities could be shifted to completely autonomous communities independent of Caracas, with their own housing and other community facilities. At the same time, new construction within the city of Caracas itself should only proceed along the lines laid down in its own master plan. In addition, it is clear that, if balanced growth is to take place both within the city and in its outlying areas, a regional plan embracing the entire metropolitan area will be necessary.

Special measures should be taken in those oil areas where the present oil camps have been created as independent units rather than as communities integrated into the social and economic structure of the region, as is already the case in the Paraguana Peninsula. Until regional master plans have been prepared for the major oil areas, remodeling projects at the oil camps should be limited to those of compelling urgency.

Traffic is a serious problem in most Venezuelan cities. The existing road patterns of the old colonial cities, such as San Cristobal, Merida, Barquisimeto, Coro and Old Caracas, were planned for low speeds and should be systematically revised and modified. The difficult case of Caracas is dealt with below. Traffic requirements in other old cities especially at their centers, can no longer be met by existing street patterns which, though admirable for their rational design and their proportions, were conceived long before the advent of the automobile. These street patterns should be reorganized so as to form two separate and independent circulation networks: one for high speeds designed to prevent unnecessary intersections and one for pedestrians.

Caracas Transport

The capital city, like many rapidly growing cities, suffers from extreme traffic congestion. The Government is considering proposals for the construction of a rapid rail transit system to care for the mass transportation of people into and from the central business district as a solution to the problem. The mission suggests that before a rapid rail transit system for Caracas is undertaken efforts first be made to improve the traffic movement on the surface streets. Such action is required in any event, and it is quite possible that this action may defer the need for a subway for a long period of time.

According to estimates prepared by consultants to the Government, an effective conventional-type subway would have to be approximately 30 km. long and would cost about Bs 620 million. A monorail of similar length would cost about Bs 350 million. The proposed transit system would have to be built to handle traffic to and from the east, to the northwest and from the east to the southwest with two additional spurs. Part of the proposed facility would have to be underground, and part elevated. The building of a short section of the system would do little good. On the contrary, it would probably do more harm than good. During its construction in the heart of the city additional traffic jams would develop, probably worse than those experienced to date.

A substantial amount of research has been effected on the general traffic problem by a number of consultants employed by the Venezuelan Government. Origin-and-destination survey data, including present and forecasted "desired" lines of traffic have been presented to the Government. These studies indicate the importance of the completion of the Cota Mil circumferential autopista to the north of the city, the building of an access-controlled autopista along the route of the Avenida Libertador, the completion of the east-west autopista, including the building of an interchange and the prolongation of the autopista Caracas-La Guaira. This work will do much to help the traffic problem in Caracas.

The traffic problem will obviously not be easy to solve. The growth in the number of vehicles in Caracas during recent years as well as the volume of vehicular traffic has been substantial. By 1958, there were 124,232 vehicles registered in Caracas as compared with 36,076 vehicles in 1948, and the average daily two-way traffic volume rose to 441,200 in 1958 as compared with 180,600 ten years previously. Furthermore, the population and the number of vehicles in use are not evenly divided around the city. The eastern section, for instance, has slightly over 25

percent of the population and over 50 percent of the vehicles registered in the city. There are only 6.4 persons per vehicle in the east
compared to 47.2 persons per vehicle in the northeast.

The extent of the problem can be illustrated by indicating the
amount of traffic on the major avenues going into the city. The major
east-west avenues carry large volumes of traffic, especially during the
peak hours. For instance, Avenida Andres Bello carries a peak hourly
traffic of 2,062 vehicles, Avenida Sucre 2,244 vehicles and the autopista
3,799 vehicles. These volumes are large for even the best-designed avenues but they especially create problems in Caracas because they substantially exceed the practical capacity of these avenues to carry traffic.
For instance, the practical capacity on all the major avenues in the east
is 6,080 vehicles per hour, whereas the actual average hourly peak has
been running around 8,500. For this reason, traffic is especially congested.

The Government's consultants have proposed a number of improvements which the mission feels will help ease the congestion. According
to the consultants, as the result of these improvements, it would be
possible to increase the practical capacity of the avenues by 100 percent.
The cost of some of these works will be substantial. The completion
of the Cota Mil circumferential autopista to the north of the city including the purchase of land will probably be about Bs 100 million,
according to preliminary estimates made available to the mission. The
completion of the east-west autopista together with a tunnel at La
Planicie may cost as much as Bs 150 million. However, these improvements are worthwhile because they will permit traffic to go around the
city and avoid the central business district.

On the other hand, a substantial number of other improvements
should cost very little and accomplish a lot. These could include, for
instance, the installation of a well-designed automatic traffic-adjusted
electronic signal-control system for the main streets and avenues; the
proper channelization and signalization of the main intersections;
greater use of one-way streets, particularly in the central business dis-
tricts; and the better control of parking, which may involve its elimination on certain streets, its elimination during peak traffic hours on
others, the installation of short time-period parking meters in certain
areas, as well as the better use of off-street parking in the central business district. All these measures should greatly relieve congestion.

The real issue centers around whether a new mass rapid transit system is needed in addition to these proposed improvements in the main
avenues and the better flow of vehicular traffic. The mission feels
strongly that it would be a major mistake to rush into the construction

of a subway or a monorail. With improved surface transport, a large percentage of the passengers on buses, as well as those traveling in private and commercial cars, who now pass through the center of the city, could go around the city, thus avoiding the most congested area. In fact, 60 percent of all Caracas bus passengers, or 185,300 persons, go into the center of the city each day. The largest share of these passengers comes from the eastern part of the city. However, 84,000 of these passengers go through the center of the city to other parts and could more easily be carried around in buses, if circumferential avenues were available.

Mass transportation of these people could be effectively handled by an improved bus system once the circumferential avenues are completed. The use of fast buses, affording express service from the various areas to and from the central business district or through the center, should be given every chance of success before serious consideration is given to an expensive subway system. The mission recommends that construction of a rapid rail transit system be deferred until improved road transportation has been adequately tested. Road construction permitting such improved surface transportation may cost about Bs 250 million.

National and Local Financial Arrangements

The national government provides very substantial financial support to other urban development investment through general constitutional grants made to states and to the Federal District. In addition, the national government would, in accordance with various recommendations throughout this report, contribute greatly to the public programs having a major impact on urban communities, particularly with respect to housing, sanitation, health, and education. In the past, the national government has given substantial financial assistance to individual cities, particularly Caracas, to support miscellaneous urban investment. The mission is convinced from the fiscal studies presented to the national government and the Federal District Government that substantial taxable capacity exists in the larger cities to finance miscellaneous municipal improvements.

CHAPTER 16 *HEALTH AND ENVIRONMENTAL SANITATION*

HEALTH

Present Health Conditions

Health conditions have improved considerably in Venezuela during the last generation. Death rates, both general and infant, have declined significantly. Malaria has been almost completely wiped out through an intensive and well planned eradication campaign. Deaths from pestilential diseases, such as smallpox, have disappeared through extensive immunization programs and epidemiological surveillance. On the other hand, other preventable diseases, such as gastrointestinal infections, are still major causes of sickness and death (see Table 81). In the mission's view, governmental public health programs have on the whole outpaced public awareness of the importance of proper health standards and we consequently believe relatively more emphasis should be placed in the future on health education in all its forms, both by means of general campaigns among the population and by increased instruction in hygiene and health care in the schools.

The drastic reduction of mortality from malaria and the more gradual one from tuberculosis and syphilis, the growing importance of cancer and of accidents, the appearance of malnutrition among the first causes of death and of consultation (see Tables 81 and 82), and the permanent rank of gastroenteritis as the first cause of death since 1941, are all significant features of the health conditions in Venezuela during the past 18 years. To a great extent they reflect the socio-economic conditions of the population and also indicate the strengths and weaknesses of some of the main public health programs carried out during the period.

The present insignificance of malaria as a cause of sickness and death must be considered a remarkable achievement of the malaria eradication campaign carried out by the Ministry of Health on a country-wide scale. The availability and extended use of facilities for early diagnoses and of modern treatment for tuberculosis and syphilis throughout the

380

TABLE 81: The Ten Main Causes of Death in Venezuela, 1941-1958

(in rates per 100,000)

Diseases and International Code Numbers	1941-45 (Median)	1950	1956	1957	1958
Gastroenteritis (543,571,572)	235	150	164	158	160
Tuberculosis (001-019)	215	124	50	48	41
Heart diseases (410-443)	116	97	116	120	115
Malaria (110-117)	110	(9)	(0.5)	(0.4)	(0.1)
Certain diseases peculiar to early infancy (760-776)	83	109	117	116	110
Pneumonia (490-493)	80	62	72	86	78
Cancer (140-205)	69	78	90	91	88
Nephritis (590-594)	66	35	25	(24)	20
Syphilis (020-029)	33	29	(8)	(7)	(5)
Vascular lesions of CNS (330-334)	29	29	35	37	37
Accidents (E800-E962)	(27)	40	46	49	54
Tetanus (061)	(21)	(20)	(18)	(17)	(15)
Malnutrition (280-286)	(15)	(14)	27	27	22
Influenza (480-483)	(8)	(12)	(10)	30	(17)
Rate, ten leading causes	1,036	753	742	762	725

Note: Rates in parentheses not in ten leading causes for year noted.

country has undoubtedly brought about the considerable reduction in mortality from these diseases. The increasing mortality from cancer may perhaps be taken as a measure of the success in the fight against some of the diseases that attack and kill mainly children and young adults; the same phenomenon has been observed in other countries where the mortality from communicable diseases has been greatly reduced and consequently more persons survive to reach older ages when the risk of having cancer is greater. The Department of Demography of the Ministry of Health has estimated that in Venezuela the expectancy of life at birth has increased from 47 years in 1941 to 59.7 years in 1955.

The dominant role of gastrointestinal infections in mortality and morbidity and the high mortality from tetanus (mainly among the newborn) suggest that programs so far carried out by health units and other departments of the Ministry of Health have not been adequately oriented to meet these particular health problems. In the case of the gastrointestinal infections, whose prevention depends almost entirely on effective environmental sanitation programs, the record is not satisfactory. The majority of the Venezuelan population lives on the peri-

TABLE 82: Ten Most Frequent Causes for Medical Consultation, 1959

Rural Dispensaries	% of Total[a]	Urban Out-Patient Departments	% of Total[b]
Upper respiratory infections	14.7	Diarrheal diseases	11.9
Helminthiasis	8.2	Upper respiratory infections	7.8
Diarrheal diseases	7.0	Anemia	5.0
Anemia	5.4	Acute lower respiratory infections	4.6
Infectious parasitic skin diseases	2.5	Accidents	3.9
Influenza	2.4	Skin diseases	3.3
Asthma	1.5	Tonsilitis	3.1
Severe malnutrition	1.3	Asthma	1.5
Conjunctivitis	1.2	Severe malnutrition	1.3
Acute lower respiratory infections	1.0	Whooping cough	1.0
Total	45.2	Total	43.4

[a] 691,046 consultations, January-April 1959.

[b] 28,058 consultations at four random hospitals (Barquisimeto, Los Andes, San Felipe and Maturin) during February, April, July and September 1959.

phery of the large cities, in small towns and rural areas where adequate water supplies and sanitation systems are not available. Public health services in the field of environmental sanitation have concentrated primarily on routine inspection of food establishments and nuisance control. The enforcement of basic sanitary regulations concerning housing and the environmental sanitation programs in rural areas are responsibilities of various departments in the Ministry of Health. The lack of integration of services at a local level in both urban and rural areas may have been a cause for the relatively little emphasis placed on environmental sanitation by local health officers.

The educational campaigns required to make certain basic sanitary needs felt by large segments of the population have not been as far-reaching as educational campaigns in the field of medical care. In some instances, the technical and financial effort of the Government to provide adequate sanitary facilities has not been complemented by promotion of the use of the facilities available. In Ciudad Bolivar, for example, a modern water system was installed some years ago but more than 40 percent of the houses are not yet connected to it.

Severe malnutrition, which emerged among the first ten causes of death in 1956 (see Table 81), seems to be an even more severe problem than the statistics would indicate. It is believed that malnutrition is also the basic biological factor that underlies the high incidence of anemia (see Table 82) and the high mortality rates from diarrheal diseases and pneumonia and bronchopneumonia (see Table 81). According to the *Instituto Nacional de Nutricion,* malnutrition is conditioned by four main factors: family income, size of community, age and pregnancy. Malnutrition would therefore be more widespread and more severe among children one to four years of age and among women who have borne numerous children and belong to the lower-income groups of rural areas.[1] The main deficiencies of the popular Venezuelan diet are in total protein, animal protein and vitamin B complex. Vitamin C deficiencies are seasonal; vitamin A and iodine deficiencies are seen but much less frequently.

The mission believes that socio-economic conditions and the low level of general education contribute to the unsatisfactory situation concerning nutrition and environmental sanitation in Venezuela. There does not seem to be any doubt that public education has lagged behind general economic development in recent years and that illiteracy and ignorance have contributed to bad diet and so to vitamin deficiency and malnutrition. Furthermore, the economic development of the country as a whole has not been accompanied by a parallel improvement in the distribution of income among the population and large numbers of people, precisely those of lower educational level, still have insufficient income to meet the increasing costs of food and housing. Public health measures cannot by themselves overcome such handicaps, but, with vigorous and concerted effort at the community level, they could improve the situation, particularly among the groups whose unsanitary living conditions depend more on attitudinal than on economic factors.

Doctors

The nation-wide ratio of 1,655 persons per doctor (see Table 83) does not appear unsatisfactory when compared with that of Colombia with 2,940 persons per doctor, or Brazil with 3,288, or Mexico with 2,029 and is not too far above Argentina's 1,378, Uruguay's 1,132 or Cuba's 1,037. However, the geographical distribution of doctors leaves much to be desired. There is a heavy concentration of doctors in urban areas; nearly 65 percent of all doctors practice in the four largest cities —Caracas, Maracaibo, Valencia and Barquisimeto—although their populations represent less than 30 percent of the total for the country.

In general, the states with the larger proportions of rural population have relatively fewer doctors. The scarcity of doctors in rural regions

[1] Liendo Coll, P., *La Alimentacion en Venezuela,* Caracas Radio-TV talk, August 27,1959 (mimeographed).

would be even greater were it not for the intensive program that has been carried out in recent years to establish rural dispensaries and small hospitals in a large number of small towns throughout the country. It is reasonable to assume that many doctors who man these dispensaries (usually in combination with running a part-time private practice) would not otherwise have gone to work in such small communities if they were to be solely dependent on a private practice. The mission thus feels that a further expansion of the rural dispensary program, apart from being desirable in itself, offers the best hope of a further more equitable distribution of doctors' services throughout the country.

TABLE 83: Number and Density of Doctors in Venezuela, 1959

Federal Entity	Population (thousands)	No. of Doctors	No. of Persons per Doctor
Federal District[a]	1,279.3	2,040	627
Anzoategui	349.6	118	2,962
Apure	117.4	29	4,048
Aragua	269.3	124	2,170
Barinas	118.8	34	3,494
Bolivar	195.8	84	2,330
Carabobo	345.3	208	1,660
Cojedes	70.0	32	2,187
Falcon	310.7	103	3,016
Guarico	227.9	63	3,617
Lara	455.8	189	2,410
Merida	248.6	88	2,536
Miranda[a]	433.5	78	5,557
Monagas	220.3	72	3,060
Nueva Esparta	83.9	41	2,046
Portuguesa	170.4	39	4,370
Sucre	378.5	82	4,615
Tachira	344.1	103	3,340
Trujillo	296.8	97	3,060
Yaracuy	160.2	46	3,482
Zulia	866.4	530	1,635
Amazonas Territory	14.0	6	2,333
Delta Amacuro Territory	35.0	9	3,880
Total	6,991.6	4,215	1,655

[a] The number and ratio for the State of Miranda are misleading. The State of Miranda surrounds the Federal District and Caracas so that many of the doctors counted as residents of the Federal District actually belong to Miranda. The Federal District and Miranda together, with a combined population of 1,712,800 and 2,118 doctors, would show a ratio of 808 persons per doctor.

Doctors are also badly distributed as between general practitioners and specialists. Although there are no precise data, it is estimated that only 35-45 percent of all doctors in Venezuela are general practitioners.[2] Since it is widely accepted that about 80 percent of sickness can be treated by a well-trained general practitioner, the low proportion of such doctors in Venezuela has created a relatively greater shortage of doctors' services because more doctors are needed to take care of the various aspects of the health of the population. Specialization in medicine is a natural consequence of medical progress, but the degree of specialization in Venezuela is also due to some extent to the additional incentives which public health agencies have proffered. Positions open to doctors in public hospitals, dispensaries and various other health units are with few exceptions reserved for specialists. Preventive medical care practices also emphasize specialists, so that no one doctor is responsible for the health supervision of the whole family, as is the general practitioner. The mission believes that a number of positions within the public health services should be made available to general practitioners; such a policy would serve the dual purpose of providing doctors for the family unit as a whole and of encouraging more doctors to enter general practice.

Medical education is extremely wasteful of effort and money. Student enrollment is on a non-selective basis and is far in excess of present teaching facilities. The result is that the retention rate is very low and under 25 percent of those starting medical education ever complete the full six-year course (see Chapter 14). The mission believes that some policy of selection of students on the basis of aptitude is essential. Furthermore, we suggest that additional full-time professors be recruited.

We estimate that about 400 new doctors are required annually and that this number can be produced by the existing medical faculties provided there are the appropriate adjustments in admissions and teaching policies. We have calculated that the graduation of 400 additional doctors each year will amply meet likely replacement needs, will allow for expected population growth, and also permit a gradual decrease in the population-per-doctor ratio.

Furthermore, with a better coordination between the various agencies now responsible for public health (see below), duplication could be avoided and even the present supply of doctors would be better equipped to meet the health needs of the country. In any event, the establishment and construction of additional hospitals, dispensaries

[2] In Western Europe about 70 percent and in the U.S. about 61 percent of all doctors are in general practice.

and other health units should not be allowed to outpace the supply of doctors needed to staff them. By 1959/60 official health budgets indicated that there were 6,300 full- and part-time positions open to doctors as compared with 4,225 doctors qualified to practice. Not only is the investment in new buildings wasteful if they are operated below capacity, but the excessive demand on the time of existing doctors, who often carry the responsibility of numerous part-time appointments, leads to a reduction in individual efficiency.

Nurses

The number of graduate nurses was estimated at 2,158 in early 1959. The lack of nurses is one of the main obstacles to the achievement of a better health care organization in Venezuela. Whereas in most countries nurses outnumber doctors, in Venezuela the reverse is true and present educational facilities for nursing training, if not changed, will maintain and aggravate this imbalance. As in the case of doctors, the majority of nurses reside in Caracas and three other main cities, so that in many hospitals and health units there are very few nurses to operate key services. For example, in seven public hospitals and health centers in the northwestern section of the country with a total capacity of 905 beds, 35 percent of the positions for nurses were vacant at the end of 1959. There is only one graduate nurse in the 1,100-bed mental hospital and sanatorium at Barbula and two nurses at the 120-bed TB sanatorium in San Cristobal. A similar deficit exists in hospitals in the eastern and southern regions. As a consequence, important and highly technical responsibilities are entrusted to nurse-aides, most of them poorly trained girls with not more than a primary school education.

Nursing education has been deficient in quality because the standards of admission have been too low and the duration of the studies too short. The number of graduates has also been extremely inadequate. In spite of an average of 380 admissions a year, only an average of 180 nurses have graduated annually during the past eight years after a three-year course at the six nursing schools that were in operation during that period.

In 1959 another school opened with 80 students and one more year was added to the curriculum of all nursing schools, in order that all the students might complete their secondary education in the course of their nursing training. Taking into account the addition of a further year to the nurses' training course and the present enrollment in the seven nursing schools, perhaps not more than 600 nurses might be expected to graduate during the four-year period 1960/61-1963/64.

The mission believes that an emergency program should be instituted without delay for the training of nurses under uniform standards of admission, curriculum and teaching procedures. This will probably require the opening of more schools within hospitals (although it may not be necessary to provide new buildings) , the recruiting of foreign instructors because of the shortage of local teachers and the coordination and technical supervision of the program by an ad hoc national board.

Technical Auxiliary Personnel

There is also a great shortage of qualified technical personnel, such as laboratory technicians, dietitians, physiotherapists and sanitarians. The great demand of ancillary technical personnel, which was created by the opening of new hospitals, health centers and other health services, has not been adequately met by a parallel training program in the various technical fields. Accelerated training courses have helped, but not solved, the problem. A school for laboratory technicians, opened in 1949 at the Central University in Caracas, formerly graduated 60 to 80 students after a two-year course. This school added an additional year to its previous curriculum in 1959. The mission believes that additional training programs for auxiliary technical personnel are urgently necessary. Such programs should preferably be conducted at the main hospitals which are under the supervision of the Ministry of Health, because suitable facilities are available at such hospitals and the standardization of training throughout the country is more likely so to be attained.

The Organization of Health Services

There are a number of agencies that provide health and medical care services for the population:
a. The Ministry of Health conducts nation-wide campaigns against certain specific diseases, establishes norms and standards for foods, drugs and housing and controls the local health work of its own health units, sanatoria, hospitals and other centers, including health-supporting welfare activities.

b. The state governments, through their Departments of Social Assistance, support and control their own hospitals, medical dispensaries and welfare programs. They also provide financial support to some disease-eradication campaigns of the Ministry of Health and to rural medical dispensaries and health centers run by the Ministry of Health.

c. The municipal government of the Federal District operating through the *Junta de Beneficencia* (JB) also is responsible for its own hospitals, dispensaries, blood banks and welfare programs. This organization and the contributions to the support of the hospital in Cabimas and Puerto Cabello by the respective municipal governments are, perhaps, some of the few remaining vestiges of local participation in hospital care that existed during colonial days.

d. The Venezuelan Institute of Social Security (IVSS) administers special programs for industrial workers, including health care. IVSS' growth has been gradual, in accordance with the law that created it and at present covers a relatively small percentage of insurable workers and only in the metropolitan and other industrial areas. Some 315,000 workers and 915,000 dependents were being covered by IVSS against health risks, at the end of 1959. IVSS runs its own dispensaries and hospitals, pays for certain medical services on a unit-cost basis and also rents hospital beds for its patients from the Ministry of Health or JB at predetermined rates per diem in localities where it has no hospital facilities of its own. During the second quarter of 1958, 281,504 workers were insured and 466,787 dependents registered for sickness, maternity, and/or accidents and occupational disease risk coverage by IVSS.

e. In addition to the Armed Forces Medical Services under the Ministry of Defense and the Prisons Medical Service, under the Ministry of Justice, every other ministry and autonomous public institution has either its own medical service or budgetary provision for the care of those of their employees who are not yet insurable by IVSS. Approximately 200,000 people get either full or limited medical care from these various services.

f. The oil and iron companies have their own medical services for employees and their dependents in areas where IVSS has not extended its coverage. Approximately 40,000 workers and 168,000 dependents receive medical care from these enterprises.

g. The Venezuelan Red Cross, which receives subsidies from the federal government, and a few other private charitable institutions, support dispensaries, hospitals and other medical and welfare installations that provide free medical care to needy patients.

h. Private hospitals, infirmaries and group clinics, almost always owned by doctors, are reserved exclusively for paying patients. There is a relatively large number of them and at least one or two are operating in each city of more than 25,000 inhabitants.

The multiplicity of agencies concerned with public health and the lack of coordination between them has hampered the efficient use of funds available. Means should be found for establishing a better working relationship between the various agencies in order to eliminate duplication and to provide common standards and procedures, and to establish uniform salary scales and working conditions for health personnel. At the same time, within each agency effort should be made to decentralize health administration so that the local communities can be drawn into a more active participation in health matters.

Health Service Installations

The various health service installations may be classified as follows:
a. rural medical dispensaries
b. urban medical dispensaries
c. health centers
d. health units
e. general hospitals
f. specialized hospitals
g. sanatoria for mental diseases, tuberculosis and leprosy.

The various agencies mentioned above administer one or more types of such local services. The Ministry of Health runs all types with the exception of urban medical dispensaries, and is the sole administrator of health units and of practically all the sanatoria. Most of the rural medical dispensaries (*medicaturas rurales*) are supported jointly by the Ministry and the various state governments, but the latter also run separate rural posts where emergency nursing care is provided. In 1959 there were budgetary provisions for 410 rural medical dispensaries, but about 4-5 percent of them may not have been in operation because of unavailability of doctors to serve them.

An estimated total of 23,328 beds in 238 hospitals (including 15 health centers) and 33 sanatoria, both public and private, were available in 1959 (see Table 84).

Apart from the special categories of patients for whom services are available in hospitals administered by such agencies as IVSS, the Ministry of Defense, and oil and iron companies, the services of the other public hospitals and sanatoria are free to all people. However, persons wishing to secure special accommodations in these centers may be hospitalized in them through payment of nominal charges. Nevertheless, only 1,541 beds, less than 7 percent of the total, where professional fees and all other expenses are paid directly by the patient, should be classified as strictly private.

The Venezuelan Government has under consideration a program for construction and equipment of hospitals and other health installations during the period 1960/61-1963/64, which involves expenditures totaling Bs 251.6 million. The program would provide for 8,527 new beds, 7,177 in general hospitals and health centers and 1,350 in specialized hospitals for tuberculosis, leprosy and mental cases. Of the 8,527 additional beds, 7,874 would involve actual construction of new buildings; the other 653 are to be made available in installations already built.

TABLE 84: Number and Distribution of Hospitals and Sanatoria, and of Beds, 1959

| | | | Sanatoria | | | | | | | |
| | Hospitals | | TB | | Mental | | Leprosy | | Total | |
Agency	No.	Beds	No.	Beds	No.	Beds	No.	Beds	No.	Beds
Ministry of Health	40	7,220	14	2,772	5	2,548	2	900	61	13,440
States	71	3,156	2	75	2	100	—	—	75	3,331
IVSS	11	1,059	—	—	—	—	—	—	11	1,059
Ministry of Development[a]	1	30	—	—	—	—	—	—	1	30
Ministry of Defense	1	110	—	—	—	—	—	—	1	110
JB	13	2,486	—	—	—	—	—	—	13	2,486
Charitable institutions	8	528	—	—	—	—	—	—	8	528
Oil and Iron-ore companies	17	803	—	—	—	—	—	—	17	803
Private	76	1,173	—	—	8	368	—	—	84	1,541
Total	238	16,565	16	2,847	15	3,016	2	900	271	23,328

[a] A small hospital run by CVF.

The program includes estimates of the federal government contributions to the operation of 195 beds in health centers that have been built by state governments but does not take into account any other hospital construction program that the state governments might have under consideration for the rest of the period. No mention is made either of the new 1,100-bed military hospital in Caracas or of the 600 beds now being added to the mental hospital at Barbula; these 1,700 beds were almost ready for occupancy in mid-1960.

The mission believes that the proposed construction program is far in excess of the facilities which could be properly handled by the personnel likely to be available during, or immediately after, the four-year period 1960/61-1963/64. There is no prospect that there will be sufficient additional doctors to supervise and service the additional capacity. Even more serious perhaps would be the lack of qualified nurses. The ratio of six graduate nurses per hundred beds in general hospitals, as recommended by the Pan American Health Organization, would mean that about 1,200 additional nurses would be required simply to meet the requirements of the programed additional beds in general hospitals. But there are also shortages in existing general hospitals, let alone in mental, TB and other specialized hospitals. We estimate that Venezuela needs nearly 9,000 graduate nurses, as against the 2,200 there were in 1959 and the 600 which are expected to graduate by 1963/64. The gap is just as great in the supply of ancillary technical personnel. It seems to us that it would be a great mistake to add to the demand for medical personnel by further construction until present deficits are made up.

We therefore recommend that hospital construction during 1960/61-1963/64 be limited to that which had already been started by 1960/61. (In addition, we recommend that an 80-bed health center be built during the four-year period in the Anaco-Cantaura area, in place of the proposed 200-bed general hospital. See below.) This would entail a total expenditure during the period of Bs 105.0 million and would add 2,760 beds to the total number available (see Table 85).

Such a construction program would add nearly 12 percent more beds by 1963/64 as compared with 1959/60. Since there will be some 25 percent more doctors practicing by 1963/64 and probably nearly 30 percent more nurses, with increases in ancillary medical personnel of a similar order, there should on this occasion be sufficient available staff to operate the additional facilities and also some opportunity to ease part of the existing shortages as discussed above.

We are not suggesting that most of the new hospital construction under consideration by the Venezuelan Government might not eventually be justifiable. In fact, in most cases only personnel shortages lead

TABLE 85: Proposed Investment Program in the Health Sector, 1960/61-1963/64

Project	Capacity in Beds	Costs (in Bs million)		
		Construction	Equipment	Total
General Hospitals:				
Barcelona	400	20.5	4.0	24.5
Maturin	280	7.0	2.8	9.8
Cumana	400	17.0	4.0	21.0
Maracaibo	600	5.0	5.4	10.4
Cabimas	280	7.0	2.8	9.8
TB Hospital:				
Ciudad Bolivar	300	10.0	3.0	13.0
Health Centers:				
Anaco-Cantaura[a]	80	2.4	0.6	3.0
Tovar	80	2.4	0.6	3.0
Cumanacoa	50	2.4	0.4	2.8
Rio Caribe	50	2.4	0.4	2.8
Colon	50	2.4	0.4	2.8
Additions:				
G.H. Valencia	190	0.5	—	0.5
G.H. Bolivar	—	0.1	—	0.1
Pediatric Center:				
Caracas	—	0.1	—	0.1
Health Unit:				
Barinas	—	1.4	—	1.4
Total	2,760	80.6	24.4	105.0

[a] To replace a 200-bed general hospital under consideration by the Venezuelan Government.

us to recommend against construction during the coming four years. In the mission's view, the recommended delay in construction will not hamper the adequate provision of medical services in the interim. For example, a 200-bed hospital is under consideration at El Tigre; the mission feels that for the next few years the new 50-bed health center already there and the two private clinics could meet local needs if additional staff were available, particularly at the out-patient dispensary, and that it is shortage of personnel, rather than of beds, which is currently the main medical care problem in the El Tigre region. Likewise at Puerto Cabello, where a new 180-bed general hospital is under consideration, we believe that the lack of trained ancillary staff and the limited time available to local doctors—most of whom work at the two existing hospitals—is a more urgent problem than hospital space which is already provided by a 122-bed IVSS hospital and a 152-bed municipal hospital. Rather than any new building at Puerto Cabello, we suggest the reconditioning of the municipal hospital, which is currently in poor repair, and efforts to recruit additional staff. As another example, at Valle de la Pascua there is already an 80-bed public hospital and a 10-bed private hospital which would seem sufficient for the population of the area, but the Venezuelan Government is considering a 200-bed regional medical center to support the smaller medical installations within Guarico State as part of the nation-wide scheme of regionalization of medical services. While the mission supports this latter objective, we believe that, because of personnel shortages, new construction should be deferred. In many of the other cities and towns in which the Venezuelan Government is considering building new hospitals—in San Juan de los Morros, in Acarigua and in San Felipe, for example—personnel shortages, poor training and inadequate administrative arrangements should be rectified first before new facilities are established. In Merida, the case is somewhat different. In this city of 40,000 inhabitants, there are already three public hospitals with 260 beds. It is now proposed to build a new 400-bed hospital. The main rationalization for such a hospital is that it is needed for improved medical education by the University of Los Andes. While the mission agrees that medical education needs improving, we suggest that the first step should be to improve pre-clinical instruction in basic sciences at the University. We therefore suggest that the construction of a teaching hospital be delayed until about 1965/66 by which time improvements in the pre-clinical curriculum should have taken effect.

Thus, we feel that construction should be limited to those buildings which had already been started by 1960/61 (see Table 85). The one exception perhaps would be in the Anaco-Cantaura area where the population is about 40,000 and is growing. There is not a single public hospital in the area, although there are two public dispensaries one of which is now equipped with eight beds for emergency cases. In addition to three private clinics, two of which have hospitalization facilities, there is a private 45-bed hospital operated by the Mobil Oil Company which has a one-day-a-week out-patient dispensary and occasionally hospitalizes emergency cases from the general population. While we believe that such hospital accommodation is inadequate for the population of the area, we also believe that the proposed 200-bed general hospital would be overambitious at this stage and that a new 80-bed health center would suffice. Consideration should be given to whether such a health center might not be accepted as a responsibility by the Anzoategui State Government. Even such a health center should only be established if the shortage of medical staff can be overcome. In 1959/60 the four doctors who worked at the public dispensaries also worked in the private clinics and in private practice and were consequently unable to devote as much time to public service as might be considered necessary.

To summarize, we believe that the more modest program we suggest for the addition of 2,780 beds by 1963/64 will be sufficient to meet the most pressing needs during this period for additional hospital accommodation while at the same time allowing for breathing-space during which staff can be augmented, training improved and administrative capacity increased. Furthermore, we believe that the curative services in Venezuela already compare favorably with those of other Latin American countries and that, in terms of priorities, the major effort in the coming period should be devoted to preventive measures, both in the field of environmental sanitation (see following section) and by means of an augmented public health campaign conducted primarily through the operations of existing health centers.

ENVIRONMENTAL SANITATION

Deficits in the provision of various types of environmental sanitation works are so large that it can only be expected that they will be filled in the longer term. We calculate[3] that in 1959/60 there were nearly 350,000 families in towns of over 1,000 inhabitants for whom no water supply and treatment plant had yet been provided and about 245,000 families in settlements of under 1,000 inhabitants who needed new wells with potable water. Furthermore, about 400,000 families in towns of over 1,000 inhabitants were not served by a piped water distribution

[3] Our calculations are based on the results of a 1956 survey carried out by the *Seccion de Inspeccion de Abastecimiento de Agua* of the Ministry of Health, together with later data provided by the *Instituto Nacional de Obras Sanitarias* (INOS). It must be emphasized that all figures in this section are approximate and used mainly for illustrative purposes. In particular, the special water supply problems in the great urban centers of Caracas and Maracaibo undoubtedly require special measures which should be studied and programed separately; however, for illustrative purposes again, in the following paragraphs we deal with water supply within these two cities as part of a general program.

network. The deficit was even larger in the provision of sewerage facilities. We calculate that systems of sanitary and storm sewers and related disposal treatment plants adequate to serve about 460,000 families, mainly in towns of over 1,000 inhabitants, were lacking, while a program of building latrines for 280,000 families, mainly in settlements of under 1,000 inhabitants, was needed.

In addition to existing deficits there will be needs arising out of population growth and related new family formation, and, in rural areas, out of the special agricultural settlement program[4] (see Chapter 9). We estimate that by 1963/64 there will be an additional 128,000 families living in towns of over 1,000 inhabitants who also will need to be served by water supply and treatment systems, piped water distribution networks and either by a sewage network and disposal system or by latrines. There will also be an additional 60,000 families living in settlements of under 1,000 who will require wells and latrines.

Thus, existing deficits and prospective population growth combined will create a total need by 1963/64 as follows: water supply and treatment systems for 478,000 families; rural wells for 305,000 families; piped water distribution networks for 528,000 families; sewage systems for 588,000 families; and rural latrines for 340,000 families. The mission believes that, from the physical, financial and organizational point of view, this total need cannot be met in its entirety during the four years 1960/61-1963/64. On the other hand, enough additional facilities should be programed to keep up with population growth and new family formation so that the situation does not deteriorate during the four-year period and, in addition, further works should be planned so that at least part of existing deficits can be reduced and the over-all position be so improved by 1963/64. In effect, by suggesting that only part of the existing deficits can be eliminated within the four-year period, we are stating that the total solution to the problem can only be solved in the longer term. Thus, in planning such additional works some order of priority should be established so that the current four-year program can be considered as part of a longer term program.

Environmental sanitation problems are most acute in urban areas where population is most densely concentrated. Furthermore, sanitation works in urban areas tend to be more economic because it is possible to connect a greater number of families to a given length of water or sewage network than it is in rural areas. Finally, because urban

---

[4] Throughout this section the term "new family formation" is used to connote both the results of population growth and the settlement of family units on the land under special schemes.

populations live in closer quarters to one another than do rural populations, the danger of epidemics and the difficulties of disease control are relatively more acute. We therefore suggest that the aim should be to construct enough sanitation works so that the entire deficit in service to cities with more than 50,000 population would be wiped out in twelve years. In the past, INOS has devoted the preponderant part of its program to the Caracas area; in view of the urgency and magnitude of the problems there, this was understandable, but the mission hopes that relatively equal attention can in the future be paid to programs in the other large cities. In the smaller cities, with populations between 5,000 and 50,000, we suggest that the program of eliminating the deficit be stretched to 16 years, while in towns of under 5,000 population and in rural settlements of less than 1,000 inhabitants a program phased over 20 years would seem reasonable. We thus recommend that new environmental sanitation works in cities of over 50,000 inhabitants (including Caracas) should provide service to an additional number of families during the four years 1960/61-1963/64 equivalent to 30 percent of the estimated existing deficit of families not currently so served plus enough such works to service the number of families equal to the forecasted number of new families to be formed during the period. In cities of 5,000 to 50,000 population, we recommend that the amount of new sanitation works should be sufficient to reduce the existing deficit by 25 percent and also keep up with new deficits which would otherwise take place because of population growth and new family formation. In towns of under 5,000 inhabitants and in rural settlements, a four-year program should be equal to 20 percent of the existing deficit plus projected new family formation.

Not all of the proposed works would necessarily be carried out under a special environmental sanitation construction program. We have also outlined a housing program (see Chapter 15) in which the provision of piped water distribution networks and sewage and disposal systems for cities of over 5,000 inhabitants are included. Further, under our proposed land settlement schemes (see Chapter 9), wells and latrines would be provided for 60,000 families in rural areas. Finally, some environmental sanitation works will be carried out in connection with housing projects developed in the private sector (urbanizaciones). We are here suggesting that new works should also be carried out under an independent environmental sanitation construction program in addition to those included in housing or agricultural settlement programs, so that total new works provided by all programs would equal the amounts suggested by the formula outlined in the preceding paragraph.

Water Supply and Treatment Plants and Wells

We estimate that in 1959/60 there were some 605,000 families in Venezuela without any form of potable water supply (see Table 86). Of these, 245,000 families lived in rural settlements of under 1,000 inhabitants in which water supply can normally be expected to be effected by means of wells. If a well construction program to make up this deficit

TABLE 86: Mission's Recommended Program for Construction of Water Supply and Treatment Plants or Wells, 1960/61-1963/64

	Size of City or Town (by population)				
	Above 50,000	5,000 - 50,000	1,000- 5,000	Under 1,000[a]	All
Existing deficit in 1959/60[b]	115	140	95	245	605
Proportion of 1959/60 deficit to be met by 1963/64[b]	30%	25%	20%	20%	23%
Amount of deficit to be met by 1963/64[b]	35	35	19	49	138
New family formation[b]	60	44	24	60	188
Total target for 1960/61 - 1963/64[b]	95	79	43	109	326
To be met by other government programs or in private sector[b]	—	—	—	60	60
Environmental sanitation program[b]	95[e]	79	43	49	266
Cost per family (in Bs)	1,000—1,200[d]	600	400	100	680
Total cost (in Bs million)	102[e]	47	17	5	171

[a] To be supplied with wells.

[b] In thousands of families to be served by additional water supply and treatment plants or wells.

[e] Of which 37,000 families to be served in Caracas and 58,000 in other cities of over 50,000 inhabitants.

[d] Estimated at Bs 1,200 per family in Caracas and at Bs 1,000 per family in other cities of over 50,000 inhabitants.

[e] Of which Bs 44 million to be spent in Caracas and Bs 58 million in other cities of over 50,000 inhabitants.

is to be spread over 20 years, then 20 percent of the deficit, or wells for 49,000 families, would be constructed during the four years 1960/61-1963/64. However, population growth and the agricultural program combined are expected to add another 60,000 families to the rural areas during this period. Thus a well construction program that would both keep up with population growth and reduce part of the existing deficit would involve a total program of wells for 109,000 families. Since 60,000 families would be provided with wells under the agricultural settlement program (see Chapter 9), only 49,000 families would be involved in the independent program. We estimate that wells can be constructed at a nation-wide average cost of about Bs 100 per family, so that the total cost of the program would be about Bs 5 million.

Centers of population with more than 1,000 inhabitants require a central water supply and treatment plant. In 1959/60 there were some 350,000 families living in such areas who were not served by such plants. Assuming that 30 percent of the existing deficit in cities of over 50,000 population is to be made up during the four years, 25 percent in cities of 5,000-50,000 population, and 20 percent in towns of 1,000-5,000 population, then the construction of water supply and treatment plants adequate to serve a total of 89,000 families would be included in the program (see Table 86). Since 128,000 new families will be formed in these areas by 1963/64, a total construction program adequate for 217,000 families will be required. The housing program does not include provision of central water supply plants, so that all construction of central water supply plants would have to be carried out as part of the independent environmental sanitation program.

It is clear that costs will vary according to the location of water sources, topography and other local conditions. However, the mission is convinced that with rational planning and improved administrative efficiency, average costs can be reduced. On the basis of information available to us, we estimate that water supply and treatment plants can be built in the Caracas area at an average cost of about Bs 1,200 per family. In other Venezuelan cities with over 50,000 population, we estimate construction costs at Bs 1,000 per family, while average costs should be about Bs 600 per family in cities of 5,000-50,000 population and about Bs 400 per family in towns of under 5,000 inhabitants. On the basis of these average costs, we estimate that our recommended construction program for water supply and treatment plants would total about Bs 166 million. Together with the rural well construction program, total investment in water supply in the four years 1960/61-1963/64 would thus amount to Bs 171 million (see Table 86).

Piped Water Distribution Networks

To maximize general sanitation, the water from a modern water supply and treatment plant must be piped to the maximum number of families in a given area. We have already noted that in some Venezuelan towns a large proportion of families is not connected to a central water supply although one exists. In some cases this is because individual families are not connected to the main pipe. In other cases, however, the network of main pipes is itself incomplete. As a result, the deficit in piped water distribution networks is somewhat larger than the deficit in central water supply plants. Some 400,000 families were estimated not to be served by piped water distribution networks in 1959/60 (see Table 87), although the deficit in central water supply was estimated to be equivalent only to that required for 350,000 families.

We recommend that piped water distribution networks be built during 1960/61-1963/64 sufficient to connect 231,000 families with central water supply plants. Of this amount, 103,000 families of the existing deficit would be served and the remaining facilities for 128,000 families would be the equivalent of new family formation. Since 124,000 families would be provided with piped water either under the government housing program or in connection with private housing development, the independent environmental sanitation program would involve the construction of piped water distribution networks for 107,000 families.

Again, we estimate that average costs for piped water distribution networks are less in smaller towns than in larger cities, ranging from about Bs 400 per family in towns of under 5,000 inhabitants to about Bs 1,500 per family in Caracas. With a nation-wide average cost of about Bs 680 per family, our suggested program of providing piped water distribution networks adequate for serving 107,000 additional families would cost approximately Bs 73 million during the four years 1960/61-1963/64 (see Table 87).

Sewage and Disposal Systems and Latrines

The existing deficit in environmental sanitation facilities is greatest with respect to sewage and disposal systems in rural areas and latrines in most rural areas. Some 740,000 families were not so served in 1959/60 (see Table 88). We recommend new works equivalent to facilities for 174,000 families be carried out during 1960/61-1963/64 to meet part of this deficit, together with further works equivalent to new family for-

TABLE 87: Mission's Recommended Program for Construction of Piped Water Distribution Network, 1960/61-1963/64

| | Size of City or Town | | | | |
| | (by population) | | | | |
	Above 50,000	5,000 - 50,000	1,000 - 5,000	Under 1,000[a]	All
Existing deficit in 1959/60[b]	165	140	95	—	400
Proportion of 1959/60 deficit to be met by 1963/64[b]	30%	25%	20%	—	26%
Amount of deficit to be met by 1963/64[b]	49	35	19	—	103
New family formation[b]	60	44	24	—	128
Total target for 1960/61 - 1963/64[b]	109	79	43	—	231
To be met by other government programs or in private sector[b]	72	52	—	—	124
Environmental sanitation program[b]	37[c]	27	43	—	107
Cost per family (in Bs)	700-1,500[d]	600	400	—	680
Total cost (in Bs million)	40[e]	16	17	—	73

[a] Not supplied with piped water distribution networks since served with wells.

[b] In thousands of families to be served by additional piped water distribution networks.

[c] Of which 17,500 families to be served in Caracas and 19,500 in other cities of over 50,000 inhabitants.

[d] Estimated at Bs 1,500 per family in Caracas and at Bs 700 per family in other cities of over 50,000 inhabitants.

[e] Of which Bs 26.3 million to be spent in Caracas and Bs 13.7 million in other cities of over 50,000 inhabitants.

mation of 188,000, so that a total of 362,000 additional families would be provided with such facilities during the period. Since 124,000 families would be provided with sewage and disposal systems either under the housing program or in connection with private housing development, and 60,000 families would be provided with latrines under the agricultural settlement scheme, the independent environmental sanitation program would take care of the remaining 178,000 families.

In urban areas, the cost range for sewage and disposal systems is quite wide. The larger the population center the higher is the cost per family. The mission believes that such systems should be costed at an average of

TABLE 88: Mission's Recommended Program for Construction of Sewage and Disposal Systems or Latrines, 1960/61-1963/64

| | Size of City or Town | | | | |
| | (by population) | | | | |
	Above 50,000	5,000 - 50,000	1,000 - 5,000[a]	Under 1,000[b]	All
Existing deficit in 1959/60[c]	175	175	110	280	740
Proportion of 1959/60 deficit to be met by 1963/64[c]	30%	25%	20%	20%	23%
Amount of deficit to be met by 1963/64[c]	52	44	22	56	174
New family formation[c]	60	44	24	60	188
Total target for 1960/61 - 1963/64[c]	112	88	46	116	362
To be met by other government programs or in private sector[c]	72	52	—	60	184
Environmental sanitation program[c]	40[d]	36	46[g]	56	178
Cost per family (in Bs)	2,250-4,500[e]	2,000	100-1,000[h]	100	1,200
Total cost (in Bs million)	122[f]	72	15[i]	6	215

[a] Of which 25 percent to be supplied with sewer and disposal systems and 75 percent to be supplied with latrines.

[b] All to be supplied with latrines.

[c] In thousands of families to be supplied with sewer and disposal systems or latrines.

[d] Of which 14,000 families to be served in Caracas and 26,000 in other cities of over 50,000 inhabitants.

[e] Estimated at Bs 4,500 per family in Caracas and at Bs 2,250 per family in other cities of over 50,000 inhabitants.

[f] Of which Bs 63 million to be spent in Caracas and Bs 59 million in other cities of over 50,000 inhabitants.

[g] Of which 11,500 families to be served by sewer and disposal systems and 34,500 families by latrines.

[h] Estimated at Bs 1,000 per family for sewer and disposal systems and at Bs 100 per family for latrines.

[i] Of which Bs 11.5 million for sewer and disposal systems and Bs 3.5 million for latrines.

Bs 4,500 per family in the Caracas area, at Bs 2,250 per family in other cities of over 50,000 population, and at Bs 2,000 per family in cities of 5,000-50,000 population. Accordingly, we recommend the allocation of Bs 63 million for the construction of storm sewers, sanitary sewers and disposal systems in the Caracas area during 1960/61-1963/64, Bs 59 million in other large cities, and Bs 72 million in cities of 5,000-50,000 population. In towns with a population of 1,000-5,000 rural conditions often exist so that latrines (together with cesspools) are inadequate to meet normal sanitation requirements. We therefore suggest that over-all planning should envisage 25 percent of the sewage requirements of such small towns being met by relatively simple sewage and disposal systems at an average cost of Bs 1,000 per family or a total of Bs 11.5 million over the four-year period.

The remaining 75 percent of the requirements of the small towns, and all of the requirements in rural settlements of under 1,000 inhabitants, can be met by a program of latrine construction. We estimate the average cost over the four-year period would amount to Bs 3.5 million in towns of 1,500-5,000 and about Bs 6 million in rural settlements.

In all, we suggest a four-year construction program of sewage and disposal systems and latrines which would cost about Bs 215 million (see Table 88).

Administrative and Rate Policies

Responsibilities in the field of environmental sanitation are shared between several agencies, although the scale of operations is largest in the *Instituto Nacional de Obras Sanitarias* (INOS) which is in charge of sanitation activities in all urban areas of over 5,000 inhabitants. INOS plans and executes capital works and also operates and maintains existing systems on behalf of municipalities. In towns of under 5,000 population and in rural areas, the *Division de Ingenieria Sanitaria* of the Ministry of Health is responsible for sanitation works. Furthermore, the individual states have carried out small works of their own. In the private sector, many large companies, particularly the oil companies, have constructed their own water and sewer works for their camps and, in some instances, also for adjacent populations. Finally, in a number of private residential housing projects (*urbanizaciones*) adequate sanitation works have been constructed.

Despite some administrative overlap, the system has worked quite well. However, its highly centralized character has dulled feelings of local responsibility. The result is that many municipalities have made little effort to impose economic charges on local consumers. The attitude seems to be that sanitation works and service should be subsidized by the central authorities on a permanent basis. The mission believes that this impression should be dispelled. At present, local charges do not even cover operating costs, let alone capital costs. In a situation of shortage, we believe that INOS should give priority to works in areas where the municipalities have shown some willingness to levy charges to meet costs. We are not suggesting that all costs can be met by 1963/64, but a move in that direction is indicated.

Since the majority of those currently connected are in higher income groups, there is no justification, in terms of social policy, for subsidizing individual water consumers by charging them less than economic rates. Once sanitation works expand to such an extent that large numbers of low-income families are provided with service, it could then be considered whether it would be desirable to establish a system of differential payments which will in effect subsidize such families.

Summary of Proposed Capital Expenditures

The recommendations which we have made in this section would entail capital outlays for various forms of environmental sanitation works which would total about Bs 459 million during the four years 1960/61-1963/64 (see Table 89). These expenditures would be in addition to those made for similar works under the government housing program or by housing in the private sector (see Chapter 15) or under the agricultural settlement scheme (see Chapter 9).

TABLE 89: Summary of Mission's Recommended Capital Program for Environmental Sanitation, 1960/61-1963/64

Program	Thousands of families to be served	Cost (in Bs million)
Water supply and treatment	217.0	166.0
Wells	49.0	5.0
Piped water distribution network	107.0	73.0
Sewage and disposal systems	87.5	205.5
Latrines	90.5	9.5
Total Cost		459.0

ANNEXES

TABLE A.1: Actual and Projected Volume and Value of Oil Output, 1957-1964

Year	Output (mill. b.p.d.)	Value of Output (in Bs million)	
		Exports	Total
Actual			
1957	2,779	7,865	8,463
1958	2,605	7,069	7,660
1959	2,771	6,650	7,260
Projection			
1960	2,823	6,450	7,045
1961	2,938	6,708	7,335
1962	3,058	6,976	7,635
1963	3,182	7,255	7,950
1964	3,312	7,545	8,275

Sources and Notes:

Output. Ministry of Mines data is used for 1957-59. Projection is based on 4 percent a year growth in exports and 6 percent growth in domestic sales in each year from 1958. Hence, 1960 is 1.9 percent above 1959 (which was 6.3 percent above 1958) ; and there are 4.1 percent increments in output in each year after 1960.

Value of Output. Ministry of Mines data is used for 1957 and 1958. The mission has made its own estimate for 1959 on the basis of preliminary series issued by the Central Bank and the Ministry of Mines. The estimates of future value assume that 1960-64 market prices will average 3 percent below the levels prevailing in April-December 1959, following the April 4 reduction in list prices. Taking these increased discounts into account, the 1960-64 market prices are some 5 percent below market prices for the whole of 1959, and this is equivalent to assuming 1960-64 market prices to be 10 percent below the levels posted in April 1959. Domestic prices are assumed to move with export prices. The total value series also includes some Bs 60 million a year miscellaneous receipts. These have been assumed stable at the Bs 60 million level.

TABLE A.2: Estimated and Projected Expenditures and Profits in Oil Company Operations, 1958-1964

(in Bs billion)

Item	Actual		Projection				
	1958	1959	1960	1961	1962	1963	1964
Operating costs	1.61	1.65	1.82	1.85	1.88	2.00	2.03
Administration and other costs	0.73	0.75	0.75	0.75	0.75	0.75	0.75
Depreciation	0.84	0.90	0.93	0.95	0.97	1.00	1.04
Royalties	1.38	1.39	1.38	1.44	1.50	1.56	1.62
Income tax	1.48	1.25	1.03	1.12	1.21	1.26	1.35
Net profit	1.62	1.32	1.14	1.23	1.33	1.38	1.49
Total Receipts	7.66	7.26	7.05	7.34	7.64	7.95	8.28
Gross Investment	1.79	1.21	1.12	1.05	1.10	1.15	1.20

Sources and Notes:

Ministry of Mines data are used for 1958 and 1959, except for mission estimate of 1959 receipts and costs. Projections of *operating costs* reflect 1960 wage contract (16 percent rise in wage and benefit payments) and the assumption that wage payments will continue to rise as production increases. It is assumed that there is no rise in administrative costs, which include several minor taxes. The rise in *depreciation* reflects the assumed *net* investment of some Bs 100-200 million a year. The *royalty payment* assumes 1960-64 Texan posted prices to average 3 percent below 1959.

It is also assumed that there will be no change in the Texas price basis for royalty calculations; and no tax concessions in 1960-64. All tax and royalty statistics are on an *accrued* basis for the relevant year: they do not reflect the 1-year lag in tax payments or increased government income from tax adjustments on previous years (e.g., the 1959 royalty excludes Bs 221 million of charges on the operations of earlier years). The series on gross investment is based on Ministry of Mines information for 1958-1960, and on mission estimates for 1961-1964.

TABLE A.3: Actual and Projected Revenues Derived from Oil, 1957-1964
(in Bs million)

Year	Payments Due for:			Total Direct Revenues	Customs	Exchange Profit	Total Revenues
	Income Tax	Royalty	Other				
Actual							
1957	1,164	1,526	142	2,832	101	225	3,158
1958	1,480	1,380	112	2,972	76	370	3,418
1959	1,245	1,393	108	2,746	49	405	3,200
Projection							
1960	1,030	1,380	96	2,506	50	400	2,956
1961	1,120	1,440	102	2,662	54	320	3,036
1962	1,210	1,500	108	2,818	60	330	3,208
1963	1,260	1,560	111	2,931	67	340	3,338
1964	1,350	1,620	117	3,087	75	350	3,512

Sources and Notes:

For 1957-59 statistics from Ministry of Mines are used, together with data on exchange profits from the Ministry of Finance. For 1960-64, income tax and royalties are based on Table A.2 in this Annex. *Other direct taxes* are changed in accord with income tax, apart from the stable Bs 32 million for land tax. *Customs duty* reflects an arbitrary allowance for lower investment in 1959-64 than in 1957-58, as well as reduction of import duty exemptions during 1960-64. *Exchange profit* declines from 1958-60 levels, reflecting lower demand for foreign exchange after 1958-60 exchange crisis: later, the exchange profit rises with increase in importers' demand for foreign exchange sold by the Central Bank.

TABLE A.4: Actual and Projected Contribution of Oil Sector to Gross National Product, 1957-1964

(in Bs million)

Year	Wages and Salaries	Payments to Government	Depreciation	Total Oil Contribution	GNP (At Market Prices)	Oil as % GNP
			Actual			
1957	988	2,832	812	4,632	20,600	22.5
1958	1,010	2,972	836	4,818	22,500	21.4
1959	998	2,746	900	4,642	23,200	20.0
			Projection			
1960	1,160	2,506	930	4,596		
1961	1,180	2,662	950	4,792		
1962	1,200	2,818	970	4,988		
1963	1,320	2,931	1,000	5,251		
1964	1,340	3,087	1,040	5,467	30,800	17.8

Sources and Notes:

This table is based on Tables A.2 and A.3 of this Annex and on the 1957-59 GNP data in the *Memoria, 1959*, Banco Central de Venezuela. The 1964 GNP estimate represents an assumed increase of about 5.8 percent a year over 1959. The total oil contribution to GNP grows on average by 3.3 percent a year between 1959 and 1964, and therefore represents a declining proportion of GNP.

TABLE A.5: Actual and Projected Balance of Payments, 1959 and 1964

(in US$ billion)

Item	1959[a] Transactions of Oil Companies	Others	1964 Transactions of Oil Companies	Others
Merchandise exports, f.o.b.	2.17	0.22	2.45	0.30
Merchandise imports, f.o.b.	−0.17	−1.33	−0.19	−1.58
	2.00	−1.11	2.26	−1.28
Trade Balance	0.89		0.98	
Transport and insurance (net)	−0.01	−0.16	−0.02	−0.20
Investment income (net)	−0.42	−0.09	−0.48	−0.14
Other services (net)	−0.16	−0.04	−0.19	−0.05
	1.41	−1.40	1.57	−1.67
Current Account Balance	0.02		−0.10	
Direct foreign investment (net)	0.10	0.02	0.06	0.04
Short-term capital in U.S. (net)	—	0.02	—	—
Public capital (net)	—	0.10	—	—
Other capital movement (net)	—	−0.63	—	—
	1.51	−1.89	1.63	−1.63
Surplus or Deficit (minus) in Balance of Payments	−0.37		0.00	

[a] Based on Central Bank's unpublished revised estimates.

Notes to Table A.5:
The bases of the 1964 projections are as follows:

a. *"Transactions of Oil Companies"* is derived from Table A.2 of this Annex, together with an estimate of imports of goods and services. The 20 percent increase in oil production, 1959-64, is assumed to entail a somewhat lower (15 percent) increase in imports by petroleum companies.

b. *"Other Exports"* are based on an assumed 40 percent rise in exports of iron ore between 1959 and 1964, and a 25 percent rise in the value of other exports from US$92 million in 1959 to US$116 million in 1964.

c. *"Investment Income"* is arbitrarily increased to reflect the results of assumed growth in iron ore exports and increased investment by foreigners in manufactures and service industries.

d. *"Direct Foreign Investment"* assumes a higher level of foreign investment than in the past. The US$40 million level for 1964 compares with an average of US$25 million in 1955, 1958 and 1959. This increase is felt to be consistent with the policy of industrialization and encouragement of foreign capital and enterprise.

e. Other items in *"Capital Account."* It is assumed that there will be no capital flight in 1964, and that public borrowing will be offset by amortization payments.

f. *"Other Imports"* are a residual series derived from the above estimated on the basis of the general assumption that the balance of payments will show neither a surplus nor a deficit. Accordingly, *"Other Imports"* would increase by more than one-sixth during 1959-64, or by some 3-3.5 percent a year.

g. *"Transport and Insurance"* are assumed to remain at one-eighth of merchandise imports.

h. *"Other Services"* are increased in rough proportion to the increase in the level of trade.

TABLE A.6: Estimated and Projected Growth of Population and Work Force

(in thousands)

Work Force by Sector	1950	1959	1964	Projected Increase 1959-1964
Oil	43	43	45	2
Agriculture	705	833	913-958	80-125
Mining	6	12	15	3
Manufactures	207	261	321-351	60-90
Power and water	5	12	17	5
Construction	91	187 ⎤		
Transportation	52	86 ⎟		
Commerce	150	249 ⎬	1,495-1,570	200-275
Services	342	522 ⎟		
Unemployed	106	253 ⎦		
Total Work Force	1,706	2,456	2,881	425
Total Population (year-end)	5,049	7,230	8,510	1,280

Sources and Notes:

The 1950 population figure is derived from the Census of that year, while the 1959 estimate is based on Cordiplan studies of birth rates, death rates and net migration during the 1950's.

Work force figures for 1950 and 1959 are those estimated in *Memoria, 1959*, Banco Central de Venezuela; a substantial margin of error may attach to some of the data, especially to that for "unemployed" which is merely a residual series.

While the estimates of total population and work force in 1964 are the mission's own responsibility, considerable reliance has been placed on the work of Cordiplan and ECLA as reported in *Economic Developments in Venezuela in the 1950's*, Economic Bulletin for Latin America, Vol. V., No. 1, March 1960.

The population estimate for 1964 assumes a lower average birth rate than in the 1950's and a much lower rate of net immigration. This is in line with the decline in birth rates which has occurred over the last few years and with a more restrictive immigration policy. Natural increase is estimated at 3.1 percent a year and net migration at 0.2 percent a year, the rate of population growth therefore being 3.3 percent a year as compared with 4.2 percent a year in 1950-59.

On the basis of the Cordiplan and ECLA studies of age composition and participation rates, it is assumed that the work force will grow at about the same rate as the total population—3.3 percent a year.

The estimates of the work force by sector in 1964 are necessarily subject to a large margin of uncertainty. Their chief purpose is to indicate that, under a broad range of assumptions, the direct production sectors can offer only limited opportunities for increased employment.

The estimates for each of the direct production sectors are based on the past record of employment growth, the anticipated growth in output (see Chapter 3, Table 1) and assumptions regarding the increase in output per worker. For *agriculture*, 2-3 percent of the estimated 5.5 percent annual increase in output is attributed to increased employment, and the remainder to rising output per worker. It is also noted that, prior to the move to the cities in 1958, agriculture was absorbing some 20,000 more workers a year. It is expected that government policy, including the agrarian reform program, will foster an increase in rural employment. In *manufactures,* the range allows for an increase in the nonartisan work force of 6-8 percent a year. With growth in output estimated at 11 percent a year (excluding artisan work), this implies a 3-5 percent increase in output per worker each year, a range appreciably below the 7.5 percent a year average achieved in the 1950's. For *mining and oil* the small increases in employment for 1959-64 reflect the capital-intensive nature of the industries.

Similarly, because of their capital-intensive nature, we estimate a small absolute increase in employment in *power and water.*

TABLE A.7: Actual and Projected Government Revenues, 1957/58-1963/64

(in Bs million)

	1957/58	1958/59	Estimated 1959/60	1960/61	Projected 1961/62	1962/63	1963/64	Four-Year Total
1. Oil Sector:								
Income tax	1,013	1,446	1,267	1,100	1,090	1,180	1,240	4,610
Royalty	1,419	1,566	1,461	1,400	1,470	1,530	1,590	5,990
Exchange profit	360	369	412	365	325	335	345	1,370
Total Oil	2,792	3,381	3,140	2,865	2,885	3,045	3,175	11,970
2. Income Tax on Iron Ore Companies	33	159	61	115	145	155	166	581
3. Other Revenues:								
Customs duties	780	751	765	720	810	880	960	3,370
Direct taxes	264	426	494	590	675	730	790	2,785
Indirect taxes	445	440	446	460	540	585	635	2,220
Miscellaneous	111	159	184	200	212	225	240	877
Total Other	1,600	1,776	1,889	1,970	2,237	2,420	2,625	9,252
4. Total Revenues	4,425ª	5,315	5,090	4,950	5,267	5,620	5,966	21,803

ª Excludes Bs 451 million of payments for oil concessions.

Notes: Oil revenue projections for 1960/61-1963/64 are based on Tables A.1-A.3 of this Annex. For our projections of revenues from the iron ore companies we assume a 15 percent output growth for calendar year 1960 and 5 percent a year for calendar years 1961-64. *Direct and indirect taxes* are estimated on the basis of a 5-6 percent a year income growth, together with more effective administration. *Customs duties* are projected on the assumption of a one-sixth increase in f.o.b. value of imports between calendar years 1959 and 1964, together with a 10 percent increase in the average level of duties, raising duty from 15.5 percent to 17 percent of total merchandise imports. The decline in revenues from fiscal 1959/60 to fiscal 1960/61 reflects an assumed 20 percent decline in imports in calendar year 1960. *Income taxes* accrue on a calendar year basis, and these have been converted to a fiscal year basis.

ANNEX II *MAJOR AGRICULTURAL COMMODITIES*

Maize

Maize is the principal crop in Venezuela. More than half the farmers produce maize. A large part of the crop is produced on small subsistence farms, together with other starchy subsistence crops. Yields are extremely low, averaging about 1,200-1,300 kg. per ha. Even on the larger farms yields are low, due to poor drainage, lack of fertilizers (particularly phosphates) and poor varieties. About three-quarters of the production is used for human consumption, generally within a short distance of where it is grown. The price of maize is about Bs 0.35-0.40 per kg., about double the price in the United States.

Ecologically, maize is quite suitable for the plains and the mountains. The research station at Maracay has developed a number of promising varieties, including a hybrid seed which produces good yields at the station itself. Hence, the long-run outlook for maize production in Venezuela could be quite promising.

The problems of the small, low-income farmer have already been treated at some length in Chapter 9. Better seed and fertilizer will help him grow more maize from his small holding, but as long as his other farm enterprises are limited to starchy subsistence crops he will not benefit much. On the other hand, if he can combine his maize production with poultry or hog raising, his prospects for more income will be much better since this would give him year-round employment.

Better seed, fertilizer and on-the-farm-feeding to livestock are also important for the commercial farmer. The mechanization of the harvesting process would also help reduce costs and achieve higher yields. Drainage is also extremely important in improving yields. A very important aspect of a program for increasing yields would be the development of suitable hybrids for use in the major corn producing centers. Hybrid corn has revolutionized the corn industry in the United States, and wherever it has been introduced, because yields can be doubled or tripled over existing levels. The hybrid developed at Maracay shows that Venezuela has the capacity to carry out effective plant breeding work. It will however be necessary to carry out similar work in other stations throughout the country, since corn suitable for one area usually does not produce well under different conditions.

415

The demand for corn as human food is extremely inelastic. In fact, with rising incomes there is usually a negative elasticity. Hence, the long-run future demand for corn in Venezuela must come from the poultry and livestock industries. At present prices, unsubsidized corn is too expensive to be used extensively for fattening cattle and most of the corn not used for human food goes into commercial mixed feed for poultry and dairy cattle.

In the United States, about 85 percent of the corn crop does not enter commercial channels but is fed to poultry and livestock on the farm. This reduces costs of handling and storage and gives the farmer full benefit of the higher prices paid for meat products. In Venezuela also, the demand for meat products can be expected to grow and meat production also has a good future potential for exports. Hence, wherever possible, the combination of corn production and poultry and livestock feeding on the same farm should be encouraged.

Rice

Rice production in Venezuela increased rapidly under government encouragement, reaching a peak in 1954, but has declined since due to a variety of reasons, including appearance of a virus disease on upland rice, reduction of government credits and large stocks on hand. The bulk of the rice is upland rice and production for the market has been concentrated on large mechanized farms. At present prices of Bs 0.60 per kg. for paddy, rice production has been extremely profitable, particularly under wet conditions. On the other hand, the Vergarena Farm south of Ciudad Bolivar found that planting upland rice on newly cleared land did not pay as much as putting the land into improved pasture. In the Barinas-Portuguesa area where soils are better and have higher water-holding capacity farmers found upland rice quite profitable.

Rice is ecologically as suited to Venezuela as to most tropical countries. It can be grown continuously on the same field under irrigation, only however if regularly hand weeded. This is not practical in Venezuela because of high labor costs. Rice growing is suited to mechanization if rotated with dry crops or pasture to control noxious weeds and prevent soil exhaustion. Wet rice is of high value for mechanized farms, because it tends to maintain organic matter in the soil, and hence soil fertility, much better than dry crops. In some areas, such as Guarico and in the Delta Amacuro, it is the only crop which can be grown without danger of soil exhaustion.

Local yields vary around 1,000 kg. paddy per ha., but they include mostly dry or upland rice which is generally a low-yielding and risky crop. Yields of wet rice may range from 2,000-3,000 kg. paddy per ha. per crop. At the present high price of Bs 0.60 per kg. for paddy, this crop presently appears profitable even with very high investments for machinery (Bs 100,000 per 100 ha.). It has even a good chance on moderate soils or soils with a hardpan, in rotation with pasture.

If the Guarico project is completed, about 40,000 hectares could be planted there alone in two crops of rice annually. If reported yields of about 4,000 kg. per ha. for two crops a year can be maintained, this would mean an output of 160,000 tons of rough rice from Guarico alone. This would be in excess of domestic requirements. Substantial increases are also possible in the Delta Amacuro and irrigated tracts in the Portuguesa area. Further expansion of upland rice in the Barinas-Portuguesa area is also likely because of the recent development of disease resistant strains of rice. It is therefore possible that, within the next few years, assuming present prices are maintained, a rapid expansion of rice output could take place.

Such a growth in output would make export surpluses available. At Bs 0.60 per kg. for paddy or rough rice and an ex-mill price of milled rice of approximately Bs 0.90 per kg. compared with an average import price of about Bs 0.35 per kg. in 1958, the present internal price for rice is much too high to permit exports. On the other hand, at present prices, rice production has been extremely profitable to the rice grower. A number of farmers have been able to pay for their machinery in one year. Prices could be substantially cut without discouraging the more efficient producers. Prices will have to be adjusted downward in the long run and lower prices should stimulate domestic demand and perhaps cause some substitution of rice for wheat.

Possibilities for increasing yields through development of better varieties, use of fertilizer, improved cultural practices, and weed killers should be thoroughly explored by the research organization particularly under wet conditions. More efficient use of mechanical equipment will also reduce costs making it possible to consider export possibilities in the long run.

Coffee and Cacao

The production of coffee and cacao has been declining due to neglect and failure to replace deteriorating plants with new higher-yielding varieties. Both crops are suited to Venezuelan conditions and the Government is carrying out a program aimed at putting these industries on a more competitive basis. Prices have been sufficiently favorable so that the Government has had to purchase only a relatively small amount of coffee and no cacao under its price support program. The exchange differential has also been relatively insignificant at present world prices. Export markets should be able to absorb the moderate increases in output envisaged under the coffee and cacao programs in view of the excellent quality of Venezuelan cacao and the fact that Venezuela has not exported the full quota of coffee authorized under the International Coffee Agreement.

The Venezuelan coffee varieties (arabica) are well known for quality. They are suited to the moderately moist slopes of the Andes and the northern ranges at about 500-2,000 meters above sea level with suitable permanent shade. The labor requirements for picking are high, and seasonal labor is usually needed. One family can manage about 2-4 ha. as a farm enterprise. Present yields are about 300 kg. per ha. as compared to normal yields elsewhere of 500-600 kg. per ha. Regeneration and replanting should continue to be encouraged under the Government's special coffee plan. Coffee will then be a valuable enterprise in the hills and lower mountains where slopes impair normal cropping.

The coffee plan aims at rejuvenation and renewal of the coffee plantations and at promoting better processing methods through extension, credits and supply of planting materials. The difficulties in improving the culture are the same as with cacao. The new seedlings from crosses, like Bourbon, should be tried, because they are early maturing, highly productive, and can be planted in rows to reduce the labor in picking. The plan also provides for helping small cultivators to diversify production by introducing fruit trees and other crops. The Ministry of Agriculture estimates that improved varieties can bring about a fivefold increase in yields.

Cacao is suited to the better, well-drained soils of the plains and to the rich soils of the foothills, where rainfall is sufficient for a crop like bananas. Like coffee it has to be grown under shade. Venezuelan cacao is of a high quality and commands a premium in world markets. Yields again are low, about 300 kg., but could easily reach 1,000-1,500 kg. in new plantings after about 7-8 years. Cacao calls for limited but continuous labor. One family without further help for picking can manage about 4 ha. under intensive production and double that under extensive forest culture. It could be an important enterprise in various farm systems, particularly on the low slopes. The Government plan for improvement of the cacao culture aims at gradual renewal of the cacao plantations by increased extension, demonstration plots and supplying better planting material. It is a good plan, but sufficient personnel for research and extension are not available especially for research. More should be done in developing new disease-resistant, high-yielding varieties and crosses. In other countries such varieties have been developed with yields of 3,000 kg. per ha.

One of the problems in replanting existing coffee and cacao areas is that holdings are small and cultivators need the income from existing trees. If programs for resettlement in new areas draw away enough cultivators to permit some increase in farm size in the coffee and cacao areas, the problem could be simplified. However, it is most likely that migration will be slow and that alternative solutions will have to be found. Measures to intensify production of other crops now being grown and introduction of other enterprises such as poultry and hogs will be useful.

Sesame and Other Oil Seeds

Almost 40 percent of the country's edible oil supply was imported in 1958. To supply oil seeds for the domestic edible oil industry, domestic production of sesame has tripled and cotton seed production has more than doubled. This has not kept pace with requirements and imports of sesame and copra have continued at high levels since 1958.

The Government is currently supporting the sesame price at Bs 1 to Bs 1.10 per kg., as compared to about Bs 0.75, c.i.f., paid for imported sesame. Prospects for further expansion of sesame production are good at this price which is not excessively high in Venezuelan terms. The crop is ecologically suitable, especially as a second crop in the dry season. A relatively high degree of mechanization is already apparent. Local experimentation has already produced results and yields could be appreciably increased. Hence, with a stronger extension service and adequate credit, a further rapid expansion is quite feasible.

The increase in cotton seed output will depend largely on the success of the cotton program. As indicated below, prospects for expansion of cotton are good in the long run, but will depend on research findings in the next few years.

Coconuts are not considered promising for Venezuela because of the high cost of picking. Possibilities for expansion of African oil palms should be studied since they produce high yields, require less labor and are ecologically suited especially for the wet parts of Zulia. Experience in other countries indicates that production is most efficient when plantings are on a relatively large scale with a central processing plant for every 2,000 to 6,000 ha. and transportation facilities to ensure rapid transport of fruit from the field. The Malayan small holder projects now being developed in cooperation with the larger estates may be useful techniques for bringing the subsistence farmer into a palm oil development program.

Sugarcane

Although conditions are very favorable for growing sugarcane, yields are rather low (45-60 tons per ha.). Yields could be greatly increased with further research on varieties, fertilization and cultivation methods. Improved drainage and increased use of fertilizers alone could do much to increase yields in a relatively short time. The sugar extraction rate of the cane is presently about 8 percent. This could be increased by at least 25 percent by cutting the cane at the proper time and reducing the time between cutting and crushing. This would involve the development of varieties maturing at different times to prolong the harvesting period as well as the introduction of more efficient transportation and handling methods.

At present sugar is protected by a prohibitive tariff and imports are allowed only to meet shortages. The wholesale price of sugar is more than three times the international price. However, the industry is at present relatively inefficient, particularly in the cane production and cane handling phases. One estimate indicates that one-third of the cost of cane at the mills goes for handling and transportation. This is excessive and indicates that cane production is at present too widely dispersed. In the long run, with further research and more efficient methods, costs could be brought closer to costs in other countries.

Fibers

There has been relatively little development in the production of natural fibers. A small sisal industry has been developed to provide a crop for some of the drier areas and, while the expansion of cotton growing has been rapid, production is still small despite prices 50 percent above the world market. The principal problem has been the low yields and poor quality of the cotton produced. In recent years, the introduction of Coker 100 has resulted in some improvement in yield and quality.

Cotton is ecologically suitable, as a crop ripening in the dry season and thus a good second crop for the better water-holding soils. Present yields are rather low (600-700 kg. per ha. with seeds or about 200-230 kg. of lint) and it is feared that on the moderate soils production will not increase much without irrigation. However, in Central America, on the young volcanic soils of Guatemala, Nicaragua and El Salvador, cotton is grown without irrigation by sowing three to four months before the end of the rainy season with productions of 1,500 kg. (500 kg. of lint). These yields represent a doubling of yield since 1935-40 by better care and fertilization. On the water-holding fertile soils of Barinas-Portuguesa-Zulia, results like these seem also possible but only with good drainage. The plants will need much water after the rainy season and this will be only available if they can root deeply. Trials should be made on earlier plantings such as in Central America. Fertilization up to 500 kg. per ha., especially with nitrogenous fertilizers, proved to be necessary in Central America. Cotton may also be planted as a rotation crop by the smaller farmers in regions with a long rainy season or in irrigated regions where sufficient labor is available for picking. Without well-organized control of diseases and pests, however, cultivation is risky.

Sisal is ecologically possible in the drier regions, but produces much better in a wetter climate or with some irrigation. Yields are around 1,000 kg. per ha. and should at least be doubled for the crop to be worth further consideration. Because the culture is not labor-intensive it makes a good plantation crop in combination with a factory and use of the products at short distance (bags, etc.).

Other Crops

Plantains and bananas, especially the latter, are eminently suitable for the well-drained better soils, particularly in combination with cacao. They are of general significance as supplementary sources of calories in the local diet. The total area under plantains and bananas is second in importance only to maize. Production levels are low and a uniform quality required for export markets has not been developed. However, plantains and bananas are of paramount importance as a means of opening up new land without much capital cost. By cutting the forest open and planting these rather densely to promote shade and a humid atmosphere for rapid decay, the wood and the stumps rot within a few years. Cacao or coffee can be planted in their shade or the land can be made ready for permanent cropping or pasture.

Wheat, barley and oats are grown in the mountains, but are not ecologically suited for the short daylight regions of the tropics, so that yields are very low. As long as high-yielding short-day varieties for the hot or warm tropics have not been found, these crops are not promising.

Beans. The local beans are mostly caraotas or black (kidney) beans (*Phaseolus vulgaris*) and garbansos or chick peas (*Cicer arietinum*), frijoles or cow peas (*Vigna sinensis*), quinchonochos or pigeon peas (*Cajanus cajan*), lima beans (*Phaseolus lunatus*) and arvejas (*Lathyrus satinus*). They form an important and very valuable part of the local diet because they provide the necessary cheap proteins in a manioc, maize and plantain diet. Yields are low (400-500 kg. per ha.) but beans are often interplanted with other crops. Yields could be increased by fertilization but trials are necessary. Caraotas, arvejas and garbansos are ecologically marginal for the low plains; they do better in higher altitudes. The other beans belong in the low plains of the tropics. In both groups selection should be promoted for higher yields and new, better-producing types introduced or short-growing types for trials, like green, gram and mung beans (*Phaseolus radiatus, Ph. aureus, Ph. mungo*). Soy beans should be tried out as a possible rotation crop.

Manioc is one of the main crops of Venezuela, being ecologically very well suited and not requiring much labor. However, the product, with the exception of the protein-rich young leaves, is a poor food, poor in proteins and vitamins, and very cheap. The flour is not very suitable for export purposes and can only be produced profitably in regions with very low living standards.

Potatoes are ecologically suited for regions above 400 meters, but especially for higher altitudes. They are valued in the local market, but their yield is low (6,000 kg. per ha.) and they require too much labor ever to become an export crop. Because they are best suited for higher levels up to 2,000 meters above sea level, produce better and require less labor in these cooler climates, they should be extended there, when not too far from the market, but not on slopes where erosion threatens. The Government program for increasing potato output has been successful in bringing about a sharp reduction in potato imports.

Other tubers are mostly tropical, except apio or arracacha. They are suitable for the low plains: yams (*Dioscorea's, Colocasia*), ocumo (*Xanthosoma*), mapuey (*Dioscorea*) and batatas (*Ipomoea*). They are all locally valuable as a supplementary source of calories, but are rather perishable and have not much commercial possibilities, except in local trade.

Onions are ecologically marginal for the low plains. Only certain varieties are suitable for the short day of the tropical lowlands, but there is some compensation in the cooler climate of the mountains. Very high yields are not probable. They are very exacting as to the soil and require much care and labor. Garlic demands a cool climate. Both are suitable for production for the local market.

Fruits

The variations in climatic conditions, soils and altitude are such that Venezuela is suited to a much larger range of fruit crops than are now being grown. There has been very little research on the types of fruits which could be grown, on methods of propagation, on ecological conditions in various parts of the country, on the effect of fertilizer use and on the control of diseases and pests. Most fruits are still grown in their natural state without grafting and the products are not uniform and generally of poor quality. The demand for fruits can be expected to increase rapidly in the future since the demand for fruits have a high income elasticity.

In order to increase fruit output, extensive experiments should be carried out at all research stations to study the ecology of various fruits, propagation methods, fertilizer response, and marketing methods. Nurseries should be started to provide planting materials and bud wood which should be distributed to low-income farmers by the extension service free of charge to provide them with additional sources of income.

ANNEX III   *LIVESTOCK POLICIES*

Beef Production

Cattle breeding is one of the most promising enterprises in Venezuela. The large tracts of natural grasslands in the llanos led to early development of a cattle industry based on extensive range feeding, and cattle was exported up until about 20 years ago. With the development of oil, domestic meat requirements rose sharply and by 1950 Venezuela was importing beef.

In the longer run there is an urgent need for research on fodder crops, grasses, nutrition and management as well as improvement of breed. To meet this need, the mission considers it essential that an intensive research program be started at the existing station at Calabozo and that arrangements be made with the larger ranches to carry out extensive field trials. In view of the shortage of technicians and the need for their services in carrying out the shorter range aspects of the *Plan Ganadero,* arrangements should be made with a foreign research foundation or university to provide the leadership and technical personnel required for a full-fledged research program. For future breeding purposes the conservation of a non-hybridized *Criollo* stock is advisable.

There is no regular market or market price for cattle. Generally purchased in small lots, cattle are slaughtered on a custom basis at small, unsanitary municipal slaughter houses, and sold without grading within a few hours. No by-products are obtained and there is no systematic grading for quality. We have already discussed these problems in connection with the marketing problems of the commercial farmer (see Chapter 9). However, we would emphasize the need for developing a modern meat-packing industry. CVF and the Ministry of Agriculture have conducted basic studies and prepared outlines of a program for establishment of the industry. Some foreign interest in the program seems to have been developed. The next step would be to modify existing municipal regulations hindering development and to provide municipalities with alternative revenue sources.

424

Hogs

Relatively little is known about hog production in Venezuela and, until recently, there was no special program for promoting its development. Yet hogs provide almost 20 percent of the meat supply and in various parts of the country the mission saw examples of interest in further development of the hog industry. In Turen, for example, one farmer was developing an integrated operation using corn produced on his own farm to mix his own feed. In the Delta Amacuro there are the beginnings of a hog program based on feeding palm nuts. Possibilities of using feeds such as these and bananas and plantains deserve further study, particularly in view of the importance of bananas and plantains in crop rotation and land clearing operations and the high price of commercial mixed feeds.

Rapid development of large-scale hog production does not appear promising in view of the lack of knowledge about disease problems, the undeveloped state of disease control services and the high cost of commercial mixed feeds. On the other hand, prevailing high pork prices should provide incentive for further developmental work to provide a basis for future development. In the meantime, encouragement of small-scale hog production should be given high priority. Hogs can be fitted into the existing system of small-scale farming based on corn and starchy roots and provide a means of transforming surpluses of cheap starchy foods into high value protein. This would provide year-round employment and raise incomes for these small farmers.

Goats

Goats are found chiefly in the semi-arid coastal regions and in the Andes. A program for reducing the goat population was carried out until about 1957, as part of the soil conservation program. However, the program of grazing control was suspended since goat raisers could not find alternative sources of income. Goats are a good source of milk, provide meat and are valuable for their skins. They can subsist on very rough forage and poor pastures, making them particularly valuable in the poorer agricultural regions. Goats do not cause deforestation but will prevent new tree growth. Hence, goats combined with shifting cultivation have created serious erosion problems in some areas. There is need for further studies to determine how goats can be fitted into the existing farming system and perhaps to develop a realistic system of range management to prevent erosion.

Poultry and Eggs

The commercial broiler industry based on imported fertile eggs and using modern techniques has shown rapid growth. Several large-scale egg producers have also started operations. This experience has shown that techniques for poultry and egg production developed abroad can be used in Venezuela with very little change or adaptation. Yet eggs are still supplied mainly from abroad and annual imports run around 17,000 tons costing about Bs 30 million.

Further expansion of commercial poultry and egg production will depend largely on lowering feed costs, on the availability of effective vaccines and drugs and on better government services for control of diseases. A plan which is under consideration to provide up to Bs 150,-000 per family in loans for establishment of commercial egg production seems to be premature in the absence of effective remedies for the problems of feed costs and disease control.

The problem of disease control is more difficult in connection with egg production than with broiler raising. The death of a bird in the broiler industry means loss of one unit of output and does not necessarily involve a prolonged reduction in output. The diseased birds can be destroyed and exposed birds can be marketed before they develop symptoms. With laying hens, however, a disease outbreak can be very serious since egg production will immediately decline and can be restored only after additional laying hens can be raised from fertile eggs or half-grown chicks. This takes about six months. Imports of laying hens to replace diseased birds would be too expensive and yet egg producers have occasionally found it necessary to do so in order to keep their markets. One of the serious problems in this connection has been the ban on the importation and commercial production of live virus vaccines. Until adequate supplies become available from local production this ban should be relaxed to minimize the dangers of serious epidemics.

So long as egg production is on a small scale, the disease problem is not too serious since it can affect only a few birds at a time. Another advantage of small-scale egg production is that feed costs need not be as high since much of the feed can be produced on the farm. However, the problems of collecting eggs from a large number of small producers and shipping them to distant markets require a degree of organization which is presently lacking. Hence, significant increases in commercial supply will have to come initially from large-scale commercial producers. This does not mean that small-scale production should be discouraged. On the contrary, every effort should be made to encourage such production so as to provide supplementary incomes and better diets for the small farmers. Possibilities of distributing chickens or chicks at nominal prices to low income farmers should be given serious consideration. Work should also be started to develop cooperatives for marketing eggs of small producers.

To encourage commercial egg production, the Government should try to take measures to reduce the price of commercial feed. This would involve exploration of possible sales of government-held corn stocks at concessional prices to the feed industry, liberalization of imports of feed possibly under Public Law 480 of the United States, elimination of some of the present restrictions on production of fish meal and research into possibilities for more effective use of other domestically produced feed items such as rice, bran and oil cakes. In addition, of course, research on other aspects of poultry production, particularly disease control should be expanded considerably and a specialized extension service should be developed.

Milk production is reported to have increased from 101 million liters in 1952 to 255 million liters in 1958.[1] At the same time, imports of powdered milk increased from 30,000 tons in 1952 to 46,000 tons in 1958. With the high-income elasticity of demand for milk and prospects of continued high rates of population growth, import requirements can be expected to grow unless domestic production is increased. This has been the basic reasoning for the present policy of protection and subsidies for the dairy industry. This policy has been fairly successful but the costs have been high. Subsidies for the dairy industry currently amount to Bs 30 million annually and are expected to increase to Bs 50 million annually by 1964. In addition to this direct drain on the national treasury, the present policy of requiring importers to buy up local powdered milk production in order to get exoneration of duty on imports, has caused low income consumers to pay excessive prices for powdered milk. The Government has also helped the industry through low-interest loans and subsidized services particularly in connection with disease control.

The basic problem of the dairy industry in any tropical country is that cows give less milk than under temperate zone conditions. Research has been carried out in various countries in an attempt to develop an efficient breed of dairy cow for hot, humid conditions, but so far the best tropical breeds fall far short of temperate zone breeds in milk output. Attempts have also been made to develop cheaper feeds as an alternative way of making the dairy industry more efficient. Some progress has been made in this connection, but there is still relatively little knowledge about tropical grasses and a good tropical legume has yet to be developed.

In addition to the normal handicaps faced by a dairy industry anywhere in the tropics, the Venezuelan industry is too heavily dependent on feeding of high-priced concentrates. Part of this is the result of the high price of land, high corn prices, and restrictions on imports of corn and other feed components. The main problem has however been the failure to develop an integrated operation combining improved pas-

---

[1] Part of this increase may be statistical and reflect a shift from on-the-farm consumption or small-scale cheese production to commercial channels.

428

tures and production of fodder crops with dairy cattle. In the older dairy regions, the scarcity and high price of available land has led to an increasing use of commercial feed and concentrates. The newer areas in the Maracaibo basin are basing their operation on more grass feeding but have the disadvantage of being further removed from the central markets. There has been no significant development or systematic study of possibilities for dairying at higher altitudes where tropical conditions will not limit production. The result is that milk yields per cow are low and feeding costs high.

Including a subsidy of Bs 0.10-0.16 per liter, the farmer receives Bs 0.60-0.85 per liter for milk delivered to the processing plant. This price has been sufficiently high to permit a rapid increase in dairy production despite low yields, high feed costs and inefficient management.

In the case of fluid milk, the purchasers are the higher-income groups and sufficient importance is placed on freshness and quality to provide a market at high prices. Closeness to the market is essential for supplying this market and hence there is always a place for a local dairy industry even under adverse tropical conditions. To the extent that incomes increase, low-income families now using powdered milk can be expected to shift to fluid milk and families now unable to consume any milk will begin using powdered milk. Hence, demand for milk can be expected to increase if current trends of economic growth and broader distribution of income continues. The demand for fluid milk could be met largely through increases in productive efficiency without continuing large-scale expansion of the industry. This will require a gradual reduction and eventual elimination of the milk subsidy since continuation of present prices would probably induce an overexpansion of the fluid milk supply.

Prospects for meeting the expected demand for powdered milk at reasonable prices are not good. Imported supplies are available at very low prices since foreign manufacturers pay prices substantially below fluid milk prices for milk to be processed. At present, the high-cost Venezuelan product must be purchased by importers in order to import foreign powdered milk. The prices of the imported and domestic products are pooled and the consumer pays a much higher price than necessary if the total supply were imported. Thus, in 1959 the f.o.b. cost of imported powdered milk was Bs 2.40 a kilogram, while the f.o.b. plant price of the domestic product was Bs 4.03; however, the retail price of imported powdered milk averaged Bs 5.28 a kilogram, while domestic powdered milk retailed at Bs 4.95.

The powdered milk plant at Santa Barbara in Zulia processed 45 million liters of milk in 1958 and has planned a further expansion of facilities. Taking into account quality and geographical differentials, the plant pays the same price for its raw milk supply and receives the same subsidy per liter as some of the pasteurization plants. However, since importers must buy up this high-priced domestic production to get duty exemption on imported dry milk, the plant is able to make substantial profits in spite of the high cost of raw materials. In most countries where powdered milk is manufactured the prices paid for raw milk vary with the use, and raw milk for manufacture into powdered milk is surplus to the fluid milk market and receives a much lower price than milk going to pasteurization plants.

The domestic price for powdered milk in Venezuela has been fixed sufficiently high to cover the high cost of the domestically-produced powdered milk and hence imposes a heavy burden on the low-income consumer who buys the powdered product. This policy has stimulated the growth of a dairy industry in the area around Santa Barbara but on the basis of high powdered milk prices to the low-income consumer. Whether in the long run such a policy can be justified on social grounds is extremely questionable. From an economic point of view the policy makes little sense since the industry will not become competitive until basic technological problems are solved.

The only reasonable justification for powdered milk production in Venezuela would be to take care of flush season surpluses. The seasonal variation in milk production makes it necessary to dispose of excess production in the flush period, since fresh milk cannot be stored more than a few days. In most areas such surpluses are used for making ice cream, butter, cheeses and powdered milk, which can be stored but which bring a lower return than fluid milk. The Santa Barbara plant performs this function to a limited extent with affiliated plants but the bulk of its milk comes from its own suppliers. The expansion of its plant, with a continuation of present price and import policies, will result only in further subsidy requirements and increased prices to consumers since importers would then be forced to buy a larger proportion of high-cost domestic powdered milk.

The mission recommends, therefore, that subsidies for powdered milk production be reduced and gradually eliminated and that the plant be permitted to pay lower prices for its raw milk supply. This would establish an adequate differential in raw milk prices for different uses which would direct more of the milk supply into the fluid milk plants and discourage expansion of powdered milk facilities. Consideration should also be given to substitution of a moderate protective tariff for the present system of requiring importers to buy from the factory. This would force the factory to reduce prices. Part of this price reduction would be made possible by lower raw material costs and part by lower profits. This would reduce incentives to expand powdered milk capacity until such time as low-cost raw milk supplies become available.

A reduction of subsidies on fluid milk production and elimination of subsidies on raw milk for processing into powdered milk will necessitate readjustments in the operations of existing dairy farms. For the 100 or so relatively efficient large-scale farms, it will mean efforts to reduce costs further to maintain profit rates. However, since their milk is relatively high quality they would have little trouble selling to the fluid milk market which would still be profitable. For the marginal producer it will mean either improving efficiency or shifting resources to other uses in the long run. In the Zulia area, the soils are sufficiently fertile to provide a basis for a mixed type of farming, combining cropping with either dairying (for the fluid milk market) or fattening of beef cattle. Consideration should be given to possibilities for relating subsidy payments to improvements in practices so as to improve productive efficiency and pave the way for future subsidy reductions.

ANNEX V *ASPECTS OF REGIONAL DEVELOPMENT IN AGRICULTURE*

Venezuela can be divided into four distinct regions. The Andes and the northern mountain ranges, the llanos, the Maracaibo Basin and the Guayana. Population and development until recently has been concentrated largely in the Andes and the northern mountain ranges in the montane basins and valleys. The Maracaibo basin has become increasingly important with the development of oil. The llanos and the Guayanas represent the new zones of development, particularly the agricultural regions in the Barinas-Portuguesa area of the llanos and the Caroni development of steel, iron ore and power in the Guayanas. (See maps of rainfall and topography and of types of terrain which are appended at the end of this Annex.)

The Andes

The Andes, or Cordilleras de Merida, form the highest part of the country. The main population centers are in the fertile, intermontane basins and valleys: Valera (500 meters above sea level), Merida (1,600 meters) and the moderately rich depression of Tachira with San Cristobal (800 meters). The northern valleys are rather dry; to the south rainfall increases in two rainy seasons. The western and eastern slopes and the southern regions are rather well forested, but the northern valleys are almost bare, and have no soil-cover protection against erosion in the short, rainy season. If the wet high slopes are not kept under forest, erosion can become a great danger to these slopes and cause increased flooding and deposition of silt on the Andean foothills and the lower plains. The population is largely poor and illiterate. They are generally engaged in permanent cropping on small privately owned plots of land. The pattern of permanent cropping and the rich soils led to a stable food production and a steady increase in population. Settlement started in the basins, terraces and lesser slopes, but population pressures caused gradual splitting up of farms and movement onto the steeper slopes and eventual overflow into the piedmonts on both sides.

This combination of permanent cropping and preponderance of

432

ownership would appear favorable for further development of agriculture. However, out of a total of 53,000 farmers, the 40,000 farm families with less than 10 ha., planted on the average 2.3 ha., whereas the remaining 13,000 families planted an average of 20 ha. The difficult position of the small farmers will become still more evident from the fact that 40,000 small farmers have a total farm area of 150,000 ha. and the other 13,000 farmers have an area of 1,825,000 ha.

Most small farmers own a house and some adjoining land and rent additional land from the big farms. Generally, land is rented on a sharecropping basis and usually keeping of cattle is not allowed. Hence, normal development for these cool mountain regions of mixed farms of about 10 ha. with some pasture has not taken place and an efficient farm system has not been developed.

Evidently an increase in effective farm areas for the small farmers, allowing the development of a mixed type of agriculture by regulating lease of land, would not free enough land to provide all farmers with a farm of sufficient size (10-20 ha.) . Therefore, settlement in other regions will have to be stimulated. Moreover, the steep slopes will have to be closed off and be returned to forest or pasture, depending on soil and climate.

In the drier regions, the possibilities of planting pine forests for pulp wood should be investigated. In the wetter regions, in addition to reafforestation of the steeper slopes, the introduction of mountain dairying could be studied with a view toward developing the use of high-yielding temperate zone breeds such as the Friesian. Studies also should be started on the possibilities for developing mountain pastures.

On the lower slopes (between 500 and 2,000 meters above sea level) around the farmland, in areas not suitable for crops or pasture, fruit trees or new high-yielding varieties of coffee could be planted. The lower well-watered fertile parts would be very useful for horticultural crops such as vegetables, flowers and small fruits. The more level regions and the light slopes could be used for normal crops as maize, wheat, potatoes, tobacco, beans and even sugar cane, rice and plantains, where there is enough water. Cattle, hogs and chickens should be kept. Small dams could be erected for irrigation purposes, especially in the many small valleys. In the drier parts, trees such as carob (*Ceratonia siliqua*) , with fruits containing 10-16 percent protein should be tried. They are suitable for animal feed and varieties developed in Israel are even excellent for human food.

Thus a region could be developed with an intensive mixed farming agriculture in the valleys and basins, occupying the lower slopes with commercial crops and pastures, with forests and pastures on the higher and steeper slopes and a permanent source of employment in the forest environment for part of the population. In this connection, the type of farming of La Grita should be studied, analyzed and, if possible, improved and adapted for other regions. The principal problems of the Andes are overcrowding, small farm size and erosion. Hence, measures designed to move population to other areas and to provide non-agricultural employment are important for further development of a sound agriculture in this area.

Barinas-Portuguesa

The igneous rocks of the Andes, rich in minerals, form the base for the river deposits along their eastern fringe. Below the high, wet slopes partly weathered and therefore only moderately fertile, residual soils are found. These are followed by coarse soil and gravel fans where the many parallel rivers (some very suitable for reservoirs) reach the plains. Here the many rivers lose their velocity and start to meander and to branch, leaving thick layers of young alluvial clay and silt. Toward the plains the climate becomes drier but there are still seven to eight wet months.

Here some of the best soils of Venezuela are found. They are alluvial clays, with the normal streambed variation of more clayey and more sandy layers, built up above the level of the old llanos plains, fanning out according to the wandering courses of the rivers. They are clays and hence have the capacity of keeping available plant nutrients and water for the plant roots; they are rich clays since they contain the reserves in their minerals and in their absorption complexes from the rich parent rocks. They are young enough to be permeable and thus allow a favorable ratio of water and air in the soil for root growth, provided they are not flooded or have too high a water table. Because they have been formed where the rivers tend to branch, they tend to be easily flooded, and usually require drainage.

In Barinas-Portuguesa, a broad stretch of these soils occurs from the neighborhood of Acarigua to the Venezuelan border, east of the road to Barinas and the proposed road from there to San Cristobal. The stretch is perhaps 50 km. wide. Near Barinas it seems to consist of a full cover of alluvium; in the other regions it could be mixed with strips of older and coarser material requiring detailed soil mapping before development. Total area of these soils is in the neighborhood of 2 million ha. Two crops per year can be grown with high yields, if the soils are sufficiently drained. Crops like maize, sesame, cotton, tobacco, plantains, rice, beans, are already grown. Cattle, hogs and chickens would do well on these farms but are relatively rare. Mechanized farms are rather common. The mountain slopes with higher rainfall but somewhat poorer soils are suitable for farms combining some pasture and food crops with cacao, bananas and plantains, while the sandy and gravelly soils between are only suitable for forest and pasture.

In this manner zones could be formed with dairying on the higher plateaus and forest under good erosion control on the higher slopes, to protect the rich alluvial land against too much water and deposits. Pasture, bananas, plantains, fruit trees and cacao could be planted on the lower slopes. Villages, gardens and some local industries could be developed along the main road together with fattening pasture (rain, springs) or forest on the sandy and gravelly soils. A broad belt of good farmland could be developed along the eastern side of the main road followed by cattle farms in the llanos.

Zulia

The area at the southern end of Lake Maracaibo resembles Barinas-Portuguesa in many respects though with some important differences. Rainfall on the western side of this area is much higher while the rainfall pattern in the Eastern part shows two wet and two dry seasons. The higher slopes are again under forest; the lower show some pasture and here protection against erosion is again necessary in the interest of the fertile foreland. The Pan-American Highway which passes here mostly touches the foothills and the sandy levels, comparable with the gravelly region at the east side. Toward the west the sands are covered with clay in layers increasing in thickness.

Again drainage is very important but less simple than in Barinas-Portuguesa. The rivers in the Barinas-Portuguesa area run straight to the unfertile llanos; every improvement in drainage on the fertile soils increases the drainage problems only in the llanos which are infertile. Here only a few rivers between El Vigia and Agua Viva go straight down to Lake Maracaibo; most rivers join the rivers coming from the wedge between the Andes' two ranges and hence improved drainage in one fertile region upstream may mean greater quantities of water in other fertile regions downstream. Hence, a master plan for drainage is needed here for the future development of the whole region.

The fertile soils along the foothills of the Andes are of the same type as in Barinas-Portuguesa, but the central part of the Zulia plain consists of immature tropical bogs, not suitable for reclamation. On the other side of this marsh, in the direction of Machiques, the soils gradually change. Instead of the normal pattern of alluvial soils grading uphill via sand-gravel mixtures into residual mountain soils, an old carapace, remnant of an old terrace, (lateritic hardpan) covers part of the land. Higher on the slopes again residual soils are found. Where the carapace has disappeared by erosion, the soils formerly covered by this hardpan appear to be moderately rich and suitable for reasonable pastures (Machiques), but fertile alluvial soils are scarce and their exact location still has to be determined, as is the case for the whole region south of Lake Maracaibo. Total area is estimated at at least one million ha. A start for the development of this region should be made by building a road from La Fria to Machiques, connected with Santa Barbara-San Carlos. This road connection in the low lands should be an integral part of the necessary drainage projects.

The deep fertile soils in the western part with very high rainfall should be excellent for oilpalm production and for bananas when well drained. Where sufficient drainage would be impossible, for instance near the Lake, good pastures for fattening and dairying could be maintained. The better drained soils can produce much more in cropping plantains, bananas, cacao and normal field crops. The double wet season will provide a dry harvest and could allow the production of higher priced off-season fruits, (mangoes, avocadoes, etc.).

Thus, the whole region could be developed, with forests in the higher Andes and perhaps some dairying on the higher plateaus and slopes of the Eastern Andes, mixed with some pasture of the lesser lower slopes, farms with pasture, coffee, bananas, plantains still lower and farms with cacao instead of coffee in the lower well-drained plains along the road, pasture on the sandy stretches and mixed farms on the clay soils of the Zulia plain. Along the roads small industries, service centers and such, could develop. By settlement of small Andean farmers from Tachira, Merida and Trujillo, mixed with elements from other regions, Barinas-Portuguesa and Zulia, together with the Andes, could become the broad agricultural backbone of the country, supplying both the industrial Maracaibo and Valencia-Caracas regions.

The North Central Ranges and the Dry Forestland

Though the ranges mostly consist of poor parent rocks, the accumulated soils of the basins and valleys mostly are moderately rich since the dry climate has prevented leaching. In the wetter climates they consist of young alluvium of good composition (Barlovento, San Bonifacio). Many of these alluvial soils are however too sandy (Yaracuy, Aroa). The residual soils on the slopes generally are sandy and shallow

(Falcon). In most of these regions drought is the principal enemy, sometimes even resulting in saline soils. Every opportunity should be used to collect water, e.g., in small valleys, for irrigation, but always in combination with drainage. Efficient reafforestation schemes for the steeper slopes could help in water conservation and prevention of silting up of reservoirs. Falcon and Lara are regions especially suitable for many small works, and Sucre also has scope for much more development. The densely populated regions with permanent farming on good soils have excellent possibilities for increasing per capita output through flood control drainage and desalinization combined with irrigation. Replanting of the slopes with high-yielding coffee and cacao varieties is essential. Probably migration or resettlement of a part of the farm population will be necessary in order to permit a gradual orderly replanting of old, overcrowded and unproductive plantations. With the relatively small units now in existence, cultivators are reluctant to undertake replanting in view of the loss of income during the rehabilitation period.

Farm ownership patterns and sizes of farm and of planted area resemble those in the Andes. Farmers mostly own some land worked on a permanent basis, but have to rent additional land on a sharecropping basis and consequently have not been able to build up an efficient farm system. Moreover, much of the share-cropping land is in old neglected and obsolete coffee and cacao plantations. On the other hand, many of the bigger cropping farms in these regions are well managed.

Sucre, Miranda, Aragua, Carabobo, Yaracuy and the south of Lara are mostly in cropping, though on the slopes pastures are to be found everywhere. In Falcon and in the north of Lara, which are very dry, pastures dominate and goats are important. As goats are the only means of livelihood in these regions the possibilities for improvement should be studied.

Some regions, for example, the central part between Carora and Barquisimeto, should be closed in an attempt to stop, and if possible to reverse, the dangerous erosion processes, while in the northern regions along the dry north coast, on the Paraguan Peninsula in the northwest of Zulia, all that is possible should be done to conserve water. There are several wetter regions along the coast, too sandy for agriculture and perhaps even for pasture, but probably suitable for forest exploitation or reafforestation (Lara, Yaracuy, Aroa, Tocuyo). Along the southern margin of the western ranges (Segovia Highlands) the situation is much more favorable and coffee continues from here through the ranges to east in Sucre.

Dairying in the higher parts, sugar cane and fattening in the basins, cacao and coffee, and growing of fruits and field crops dominate along the southern parts of the northern range. Most regions are dry and require irrigation. There is scope for producing market products for the central markets, such as fruits, vegetables, flowers, milk, eggs.

Along the seacoast all that is possible should be done to promote fishing, because the densely populated dry north coast with its neglected coffee plantations and its dependence on goats in Falcon, is sorely in need of other sources of income.

The southern foreland is much less favorable than that of the Andes. From Acarigua to the coast the slopes become drier, the parent rocks poorer and the alluvial fan thinner and of inferior quality. Hardpans tend to occur, either lateritic in the older llanos soils or calcifications probably in the younger soils. This does not look promising for irrigation works. The foreland of the central ranges is rather dry and consists of shallow black soils, resembling black cotton soils or margalites. They could be suitable for reafforestation, for instance with teak, since they are now covered with bad pasture, overgrown with thorny shrubs. More to the east the foreland of the eastern range again has more rainfall and possibilities for pasture and cropping increase, but these depend on a better knowledge of the soils to be found here.

The Llanos

The llanos are the rather low, flat lands reaching from the Atlantic Ocean to the broad base of the Andes between Orinoco River and the base of the northern ranges. They consist of very old residual or sedimentary material and in some areas they are regularly flooded (e.g., between Apure and lower Portuguesa and between lower Apure and Orinoco). The western part consists mostly of lateritic soils with hardpans, here and there (Apure State) interrupted by long parallel higher stretches appearing sandy. The lower parts along the rivers are regularly flooded for long periods; higher up along the rivers the natural draining system is inadequate for rapid removal of rainwater from the impervious soils and hence flooding is a regular occurrence. The middle regions form a dissected plateau and are poor, sandy and very dry; flooding is less serious. To the east, rainfall increases somewhat; the soils appear to improve near Maturin and the delta has a wet climate and some good soils on the natural levees of the many river branches, while the soils between, as far as known, are worthless bogs.

This whole region is in use for pasture and unsuitable for regular cropping. Its principal shortcomings are poor grasses, long inundations in the wet season, and a long dry period without sufficient water and hay, straw or any other fodder. It appears that meat production can be doubled by decreasing mortality and loss of weight during the dry season through providing water and some supplementary fodder (hay, straw, silage, green fodder, grains), but that these operations are costly and require good management on big farms of perhaps over 3,000 ha.

More efficient use of the labor available on the farm should be possible by developing and maintaining better water sources, and growing fodder crops on the alluvial stretches along the rivers. Long-term improvements required include improved grasses and pastures, improved breeds of cattle, fertilizer use, improved methods of fencing, controlling diseases, etc. These call for a substantial increase in research activities and development of better management based on research.

Developing the area with more roads will be a very costly process and hence only the main trunk roads needed for facilitating the transport of cattle to central slaughtering places should be planned at this stage. In Apure, the possibility of using the parallel higher stretches for an alternate use of flooded and drained fields should be studied, while the higher stretches perhaps could facilitate development of transport.

Guayanas

The region south of the Orinoco, mostly forested, is largely unexplored. Besides some flats, which could be alluvial in nature, along the Orinoco River, it is a low plateau, with some older higher plateau remnants (Gran Sabana), with extremely poor residual soils on very old parent rocks, mostly sandy and lateritic and very shallow, on hardpans of kaolin, etc. The climate is wet enough for pastures, especially toward the south where rainfall increases, so that perhaps some remunerative pasture development might be possible. Trials are in progress, for instance, in the large 150,000-hectare farm at Vergarena in the Caroni watershed.

The industrial Caroni development is expected to create some responses in agricultural production in this region. However, conditions for cropping appear poor. There is some shifting cultivation on the slopes of the hills in Upata, where the soils, like in El Palma more to the east, could be somewhat better. It appears that agricultural production for Caroni will be concentrated on the better soils of the levees in the delta and perhaps in its immediate surroundings. For the interior of the Guayanas the only products which appear suitable are high-value, low-weight products of the tropical lowlands such as papain, black or white pepper, vanilla, ginger and ipecacuanha (the source of emetin). The encouragement of these crops could form the basis of the gradual development of the scarce Indian population.

Coordination of Regional Development

In a country like Venezuela with regions strongly differing in conditions and possibilities for agricultural development, the interdependence of the various regions and its effect for the total development of the country should be studied and the direction of regional development decided accordingly. At present, even local coordination of the regional problems is centralized at Caracas. This centralization, however, does not go beyond the agency concerned. The activities of MAC, BAP, IAN, CVF and MOP are not coordinated with each other, with the result that there is duplication in planning, investigation and extension. What is more serious, however, is that all regional projects seem to be handled completely at Caracas level. Much of this planning should take place at the local level where local personnel sufficiently acquainted with local conditions and possibilities are available and can be incorporated, wholetime or part-time, in the detailed planning work. Where this local personnel is not available, such as in frontier regions, or not yet developed, an organization similar to that of Caroni would be a practical solution. It should then be stationed in the region, as indeed is the case for Caroni and not in Caracas.

But regional planning demands also that every part of the activities should be controlled by its own competent counterpart at the highest level. Inadequate investigations and proposals would result if agricultural investigation work were done by MOP instead of MAC, or if credit operations were planned and executed by MAC or IAN instead of BAP. The local team for every specialty should work under the guidance of its own competent organization and report to it, so that full use can be made of the experience and knowledge available at the higher level. In this manner, the branches of various ministries should cooperate at lower level, exchange data and reach adequate decisions in building up integrated projects and development schemes for the central authorities. It should be added that a very promising start already has been made in preparing and publishing some excellent studies on various regions and on developing new farm systems, but these have apparently not been used sufficiently in the actual planning and implementation.

ANNEX VI *FORESTRY*

During the 1950's, the increase in forestry production was comparable with that in agriculture proper. Production of fine wood increased about 25 percent, and that of normal hardwood and softwood about 50 percent. Total production was not much more than 250,000 cubic meters. Most other forest products decreased sharply, production of mangrove bark disappeared and only chicle showed a sharp increase. The total value of forest products was estimated at more than Bs 60 million in 1959.

The area now under forests is estimated at 36.5 million ha. or 40 percent of the total area of Venezuela. As in most tropical countries, the forests are mixed and there are no uniform stands of trees of the same species. This makes exploitation difficult and costly. Since very limited detailed information is available on the extent, location and quality of exploitable timber resources, a forest inventory will be necessary before any large-scale expansion can be envisaged. Failure to do so could lead to rapid exhaustion of forestry resources and create serious problems of erosion and flooding. Reserves of mahogany have already been virtually depleted in the more accessible areas of Barinas and Portuguesa, and serious erosion problems have developed in the Andes and in the central range around Caracas.

Exploitation has been largely private, with the Government issuing permits to fell certain trees or all desirable trees for a fixed fee. Most forests are government-owned, but the exact boundaries of government land are not fixed or even known. A cadastral service of the Forestry Department was founded in 1959 and started with a survey in Barinas. Its first task is to delimit the area of government land (*tierras baldios*). In Aroa, IAN has taken the initiative of combining clearing for agriculture with exploitation of the felled trees in a sawmill. Further experimentation in this direction is advised, because a successful use of the useful trees in clearing operations for agriculture could reduce the costs of agricultural settlement considerably.

The hardwoods and timber woods are of great local importance and their production should be stimulated because wood is still imported into Venezuela. There is an abundance of softwood but up till now there has not been much use for this. It may possibly be used for wood-

441

pulp, but generally it occurs in mixed forests which are not suitable for commercial processing.

There is in general a steadily increasing demand for softwoods for pulp on the world market. As the productivity of pulpwood trees in the tropics can be much higher than in such temperate countries as Canada, Sweden or Finland, study and experimentation in this connection should be particularly encouraged. If part of the softwoods can be used for woodpulp, or if uniform stands of pulpwood could be grown in combination with reforestation, a new industry for diversifying the country's economy could be found. Trials on softwoods and pulping are under way at the University of the Andes at Merida and the eco-logical demands and the suitable sites for various pine varieties for different Andean regions have been established. Furthermore, it is now possible to use mixed softwoods in pulp manufacturing up to 60 per-cent, but the production process is expensive. Study and experiments along these lines should be continued.

For reforestation purposes in the mountains, wattle (*Acacia decur-rems* and other species) could be useful. They produce tanning bark giving a lighter color than mangrove and divi-divi, and they are re-sistant to forest fires so that they could be planted as firebreaks, es-pecially in drier regions where pine forests and related trees susceptible to fire are to be planted.

One zone of the country, up till now of low productivity, could have possibilities for teak, namely, the black cotton soils of the region along the southern slope of the central range from San Juan de los Morros over El Sombrero to Valle de la Pascua, but the llanos with their inun-dations, long dry seasons and hardpans do not appear promising for forest growth.

Services are being organized for fire protection and for a combina-tion of reforestation, soil conservation and protection of hydrologically important watersheds such as in the Andes above Barinas-Portuguesa and Zulia. This important work should be extended.

Besides wood, the various kinds of palm nuts could prove to be useful forest products for local use. In Tucupita (Orinoco delta) for instance, the reasonably soft nuts of the temiche palm *(Manicaria saccifera)* are collected and fed to hogs. It occurs in small stands but never in closed stands of any substantial area. This is the trouble with most palms; they occur in small groups and, moreover, their produc-tions are not high. An FAO report on oil production in Venezuela mentioned the caripa with an estimated oil yield of 85 kg. and 225 kg. per ha. from the kernels and fruit pulp. It also listed the following species:

Corozo *(Acrocomia)*, production of nuts per palm 70 kg. of which pulp 25 percent (30 percent fat) and kernels 10 percent (50 percent fat) ;

Corozo *(Scheelea excelsa)*, per palm 50 kg., fat content 7 percent;

Corozo *(Scheelea macrolepis)*, per palm 20-30 kg., fat content 10 percent;

Cucurito *(Maximiliana regia)*, per palm 20 kg., fat content 10 percent;

Seje *(Jeffenia batana)*, per palm 13 kg., fat content 13 percent;

Temiche *(Manicaria saccifera)*, per palm 6-7 kg., fat content 37 percent;

Yagua *(Scheelea humboldtiana)*, bad flavored, fat content 6 percent. Yields are too low and collection is too difficult in their natural state. Yields appear also too low for exploitation in plantations, but for this conclusion further research will be needed. The same is probably true for the various nuts (Caryocar, Lecythis, Bertholletia) , but they could be helpful as a secondary crop in the Indian shifting cultivation areas south of Orinoco River, since they form products with a high value which perhaps could be transported over the river to the ports. This development could be helpful in opening up this region and contribute as a first step out of the Indian subsistence economy.

Fish production in Venezuela showed an almost fourfold increase between 1942 and 1948. Total fish production subsequently declined somewhat but rose again to a new high in 1957. Within the total, there has been a sharp increase in fresh fish and canned fish production off-set by a decline in salted fish. The sardine catch has increased as a result of the development of the canning industry in the Cumana area and the use of newly discovered specie for the manufacture of fish meal. Japanese fisheries' interests have introduced tuna fishing but at present only two boats are being used because of market limitations. Italian interests have also recently introduced offshore fishing in the western zone out of Maracaibo. Imports of processed fish have been relatively unimportant as a result of high protective tariff amounting to Bs 2 per kg.

Although the Government has assisted fishermen with credits through CVF for motorizing their boats and for modernizing their gear, most fishing is still relatively primitive and the bulk of the maritime fishing is carried on within 10 to 15 miles of the coast. Sardines are caught with beach seines and most fishermen use small hand seines, gill nets, pots and hand lines.

Available data indicate that Venezuela has excellent fishery resources particularly in the coastal waters from British Guiana to Cabo Unare which are rich in sardines, red snapper, spanish mackerel, bluefish and mullet. The western zone from Punta Chichiriviche to the Colombian border is second in importance and produces shrimp, kingfish, drum shark, snapper, small mullet, jack, characin, sawfish and snook. The offshore areas between Blanquilla and Orchila Islands are promising areas for tuna and related varieties.

Despite the rich resources exploitation has been limited largely as a result of marketing problems. During and shortly after the last war, production increased rapidly in response to foreign demand. However, with re-establishment of fishing activities in other countries, Venezuela's high-cost production could not compete in foreign markets and surplus stocks of canned fish began to appear by about 1950. Fresh fish supply was limited by inadequate facilities for landing, transporting and storage. The gradual expansion of fresh fish consumption in recent years reflects improvements in these facilities. However, there are still seasonal shortages and surpluses of fish reflected in fairly sharp seasonal price variations.

With the shortage of protein foods and the high price of meat substantial increases in fish consumption seem likely. Furthermore, the high-income elasticity of demand for protein foods should assure a continuing growth in the demand for fish.

At present the Government's contribution to the development of the fishing industry has been negligible. Aside from a very limited amount of biological and oceanographic research and some credits, the Government's role has been limited largely to certain control measures on type of gear and areas of exploitation. The principal stimulus has come from private investments in canning and marketing enterprises.

The mission believes that further development of the fisheries' industry is likely to continue to depend on private initiative with perhaps some government help in the form of credits. However, the Government should step up its present program of research and study to obtain more facts about the extent of the resources. On the basis of current indications of the extent of resources and the low level of exploitation some of the existing regulations may be unnecessarily stringent and may have hampered higher levels of production. Measures should also be taken to provide better terminal facilities in the ports, particularly adequate refrigerated storage to permit more orderly marketing.

ANNEX VIII *METHODS OF CALCULATING BENEFIT-COST RATIOS IN HIGHWAY CONSTRUCTION*

To obtain the greatest benefits at the lowest cost it is necessary to evaluate alternative roads carefully in order to obtain the maximum yield for the economy. When the benefit-cost ratio is less than 1.0, a road should give rise to other beneficial effects not already reflected in the ratio or it is clearly of very low priority. A low benefit-cost ratio may also indicate the need for lower standards of design. The Planning Department of the Highway Division of the Ministry of Public Works is fully conscious of the need to practice this kind of highway economics and is working to that end. When more basic traffic data are available, a better job will undoubtedly be done. However, in the meantime the mission feels that calculating the benefit-cost ratios of various roads helps indicate the relative priorities of some phases of the road program.

The mission has prepared sample calculations to indicate the benefits to the owners of motor vehicles by using various kinds of roads in Venezuela. These amounts, reduced to a vehicle-kilometer basis, are then used to develop the annual benefits from a kilometer of road in proportion to the annual cost of providing this service. In this manner, an economic yardstick is obtained which can be used to measure the relationship between the traffic the roads are expected to carry and the degree of improvement that seems warranted. It is also possible by this means to gain a fair idea of the economic worth of a program of road improvements.

The economic yield of a road investment is intimately related to the expected traffic level. Not only does it determine specification because of safety and speed consideration, but also once a decision is reached in favor of a certain type of road, the economic yield varies directly with the level of the traffic which materializes. The annual benefits to the road users for each type of road, for the traffic stated, afford a ratio to the annual cost of the road types that is only greater than 1.0 after a certain minimum economic traffic level has been reached. The ratio of around 1.2 indicates a satisfactory benefit-cost ratio and a tentative judgment that the road is a good investment. At a level of 1.0 the return on the investment would only be about 6-7 percent which would barely

446

suffice for Venezuela unless there were other important factors not reflected in the ratio. Where a new road is being built particularly to open up a new area for development, savings to road users may underestimate the benefits to the economy at large.

The benefit-cost analysis indicates the possible benefits that will accrue to the road users and from them to the entire economy by affording better road service at less cost in motor vehicle operation. As the travel increases, this need becomes greater and the improvement will within reason be found to generate new traffic. The relative benefits to traffic of the various road types are determined so as to measure the relation between the increased benefits and the costs on an annual basis.

While operating costs on different kinds of roads should be based on detailed analysis of conditions in Venezuela, rough estimates are illuminating. It is certain that it is less expensive to operate a motor vehicle over a narrow graded road, such as Type 1, than over a rough track (Type 0). Likewise, a change to Type 2 providing a gravel surface will further lower the motor vehicle operating cost, while a change to a Type 3 providing an all-weather oiled road will also reduce cost. Lastly, a change to Type 4, a high-type pavement, will provide a highway that will further reduce cost. Types 5 and 6 (see Chapter 11) permit greater traffic volume with greater safety and time savings, but a different method of analysis is required to evaluate such roads.

No claim is made that the figures in Table A.8 represent an actual statement of motor vehicle-km. operating cost over the various types of roads described. They indicate, however, the relative differences in costs between roads of various types and are useful in the measurement of the approximate benefit factor for the different kinds of roads included in the Venezuelan highway program.

TABLE A.8: Cost Per Vehicle-Kilometer of Operation

(in centimos)

Type of Vehicle	Road				
	Type 4	Type 3	Type 2	Type 1	Type 0
Cars	20	25	33	45	60
Difference		5	8	12	15	
Trucks[a]	80	105	145	195	250
Difference		25	40	50	55	

[a] Weighted average for all trucks based on 1958 registrations (see Table A.2).

The estimates in Table A.8 can be compared to some prepared in the United States a few years ago by the American Association of State Highway Officials. At that time it was found that the cost per car kilometer equivalent on road corresponding approximately to Type 4 was 14 centimos. After allowing for a slight increase in costs during recent years and a 20 percent upward adjustment in costs for Venezuelan conditions, the cost of operating cars in the U.S. study are quite comparable to those that the mission found applicable to Venezuela. Similarly the mission estimates that the operating cost of trucks is on the average four times the average operating cost of cars, which is also in line with what had been found by the American Association of State Highway Officials.

TABLE A.9: Classification of Motor Vehicles in Venezuela in December 1958

Type of Vehicles	Number of Vehicles
Passenger cars	186,000
Buses	5,800
Pick-ups	25,900
Light trucks	19,000
Medium trucks	23,500
Medium-heavy trucks	8,300
Heavy trucks	5,700
Total Motor Vehicles	274,200

With respect to the trucks:

```
 32 percent are pick-ups
 23 percent are light trucks
 28 percent are medium trucks
 10 percent are medium-heavy trucks
  7 percent are heavy trucks
───
100 percent
```

The following calculations illustrate how the benefit-cost ratios are derived, using the operating cost saving shown in Table A.8. The benefits to road users by building a Type 1, narrow, one-way, graded and drained road over a rough track are estimated to be for the average car Bs 0.15 per kilometer and for an average truck Bs 0.55 per kilometer. Traffic is estimated at 50 vehicles per day, of which half are trucks, while estimated road cost is Bs 50,000 per kilometer (see Table A.10 for cost estimates).

The annual benefits will equal:

$$
\begin{aligned}
9{,}125 \ \text{cars} \times 0.15 &= \text{Bs } 1{,}370 \\
9{,}125 \ \text{trucks} \times 0.55 &= \text{Bs } 5{,}020 \\
\hline
\text{Total} \quad\quad\quad\quad\quad &\ \ \text{Bs. } 6{,}390
\end{aligned}
$$

The annual costs are:

$$
\begin{aligned}
\text{Debt service at 6 percent } - \text{ 30 years} &= \text{Bs } 3{,}632 \\
\text{Maintenance} \quad\quad\quad\quad\quad\quad\quad\quad &\ \ \text{Bs } 1{,}000 \\
\hline
\text{Total} \quad\quad\quad\quad\quad\quad\quad\quad\quad\quad &\ \ \text{Bs } 4{,}632
\end{aligned}
$$

The benefit-cost ratio is the annual benefits divided by the annual costs, and equals 1.4.

The benefits to road users by reason of changing from a Type 1, narrow, one-way, graded and drained road, to a Type 2, two-way graveled surface, have been estimated to equal Bs 0.12 per kilometer for an average car, to Bs 0.50 per kilometer for an average truck. The traffic is estimated to be 150 vehicles per day, half of which are trucks. The road is estimated to cost Bs 150,000 per kilometer.

The annual benefits will equal:

$$
\begin{aligned}
23{,}375 \times 0.12 &= \text{Bs } \ \ 3{,}284 \\
23{,}375 \times 0.50 &= \text{Bs } 13{,}687 \\
\hline
\text{Total} \quad\quad\quad\quad &\ \ \text{Bs } 16{,}971
\end{aligned}
$$

The annual costs are:

$$
\begin{aligned}
\text{Debt service at 6 percent } - \text{ 30 years} &= \text{Bs } 10{,}896 \\
\text{Maintenance} \quad\quad\quad\quad\quad\quad\quad\quad &\ \ \text{Bs } \ \ 3{,}000 \\
\hline
\text{Total} \quad\quad\quad\quad\quad\quad\quad\quad\quad\quad &\ \ \text{Bs } 13{,}896
\end{aligned}
$$

Here the benefit-cost ratio would be 1.2.

The benefit to road users by building a Type 3, all-weather surface type road with an oiled macadam top, over a Type 2 graveled road, is estimated to be Bs 0.08 per kilometer for the average car and Bs 0.40 per kilometer for the average truck. The average daily traffic is estimated to be 200 cars and 200 trucks. The cost of Type 3 is estimated to be Bs 290,000 per kilometer.

The annual benefits will be:

$$73,000 \times Bs\ 0.08 = Bs\ \ 5,840$$
$$73,000 \times Bs\ 0.04 = Bs\ 29,200$$

Total   Bs 35,040

The annual costs are:

Debt service at 6 percent — 30 years = Bs 21,064
Maintenance   Bs   3,500

Total   Bs 24,564

Dividing the annual benefit by the annual costs gives a benefit-cost ratio of 1.4.

The benefits to road users by building a Type 4 road, having a high-class paved surface, over Type 3 road, an all-weather oiled macadam road, is estimated to be Bs. 0.05 per kilometer for an average car and Bs 0.30 per kilometer for an average truck. The traffic is estimated to be 525 cars and 525 trucks per day. The cost of the Type 4 road per kilometer is Bs 500,000.

The annual benefits are:

$$191,625 \times Bs\ 0.05 = Bs\ \ 9,581$$
$$191,625 \times Bs\ 0.25 = Bs\ 47,906$$

Total   Bs 57,487

The annual costs are:

Debt service at 6 percent — 30 years = Bs 36,360
Maintenance   Bs   7,000

Total   Bs 43,360

The benefit-cost ratio equals the annual benefits divided by the annual costs or 1.3.

TABLE A.10: Average Highway Construction Costs

(in Bs per km.)

Present Types Used In Venezuela

	Type B		Type C		Type D	
	Level	Mts.	Level	Mts.	Level	Mts.
Paving	150,000	150,000	130,000	130,000	120,000	120,000
Construction	300,000	450,000	170,000	250,000	110,000	160,000
Total	450,000	600,000	300,000	380,000	230,000	280,000
Average cost[a]	480,000		315,000		240,000	

Suggested New Types

	Type 1 (50 Vehicles per day)		Type 2 (50-200 Vehicles per day)		Type 3 (200-600 Vehicles per day)		Type 4 (600-1,500 Vehicles per day)		Type 5 (1,500-5,000 Vehicles per day)		Type 6 (5,000-50,000 Vehicles per day)	
	Level		Level	Mts.	Level	Mts.	Level	Mts.	Level	Mts.	Level	Mts.
Paving	—		20,000	20,000	115,000	115,000	200,000	200,000	225,000	225,000	450,000	450,000
Construction	50,000		120,000	160,000	160,000	235,000	275,000	400,000	375,000	525,000	750,000	1,050,000
Total	50,000		140,000	180,000	275,000	350,000	475,000	600,000	600,000	750,000	1,200,000	1,500,000
Average cost[a]	50,000		150,000		290,000		500,000		625,000		1,250,000	

[a] Assumes 80 percent level terrain and 20 percent mountainous.

ANNEX IX *EVALUATION OF PROPOSED RAILROAD DEVELOPMENT*

A National Railroad Network

On the basis of tentative estimates of traffic prepared by the staff of Cordiplan, the mission is able to analyze the possible economic benefits of a future national railroad network. This analysis is based on a very rough estimate of the tonnage of freight that might be moved between Puerto Ordaz-Barcelona-Caracas-Valencia-Puerto Cabello-Barquisimeto and Barinas within the next twenty years (see Table A.11). The amount of traffic that would be involved is some 3.1 billion ton/km. as compared to an estimated present level of all road traffic of approximately 4.8 billion ton/km. Assuming a 3.5 percent growth per year during the next twenty years, total traffic might reach 9.6 billion ton/km. at the end of the period with one-third of the tonnage being transported by railroad. Therefore, if this railroad system were built, some 65 percent of all the growth in traffic during the next twenty years would be taken over by the railroads, despite the fact that the highways as currently conceived could handle this traffic. This is an ambitious program for the railroads. Furthermore, its economic yield would definitely be low.

After discussions with the Railroad Institute, the cost of building the railroad and providing the rolling stock is estimated by the mission as follows in Bs million:

300 km. through mountain country at Bs 2.5 million per km.	= 750
1,100 km. through level and rolling country at Bs 1.3 million per km.	= 1,430
Total	2,180

The annual cost of operating the railroad (1,400 km.) is estimated as follows, in Bs million:

300,000,000 ton/km. coal and limestone at 1.7 centimos =	5.1
2,800,000,000 ton/km. general freight at 4 centimos	= 112.0
Maintenance and administration cost	8.0
Debt service (excluding 20% salvage), 6 percent — 50 years	110.5
Total	235.6

452

TABLE A.11: Estimated Traffic on the Proposed 1,400 Km. National
Railroad Network in Twenty Years

Destination-Origin	'000 Metric Tons	Kilometers	'000 Ton/Km.
Barcelona-Puerto Ordaz	874.6	380	332,348
Caracas-Puerto Ordaz	4.2	720	3,024
Barinas-Puerto Ordaz	12.1	1,075	13,007
Puerto Ordaz-Barcelona	282.6	380	107,388
Caracas-Barcelona	5.7	525	2,997
Barinas-Barcelona	117.4	790	92,746
Puerto Ordaz-Caracas	447.8	720	322,416
Barcelona-Caracas	166.9	500	83,450
Valencia-Caracas	473.1	750	354,825
Barquisimeto-Caracas	600.9	580	348,522
Barinas-Caracas	1,130.5	690	780,045
Puerto Ordaz-Valencia	110.3	1,150	126,845
Barcelona-Valencia	116.7	950	110,865
Barquisimeto-Valencia	51.5	180	9,270
Barinas-Valencia	95.8	430	41,194
Puerto Ordaz-Barquisimeto	74.3	950	70,585
Barcelona-Barquisimeto	28.3	760	21,508
Barinas-Barquisimeto	48.0	230	11,040
Puerto Ordaz-Barinas	149.4	1,075	160,605
Barcelona-Barinas	36.4	790	28,756
Valencia-Barinas	83.0	450	37,350
Barquisimeto-Barinas	61.5	280	17,220
Total Traffic			3,076,002

Source: Estimates prepared by staff of Cordiplan.

To cover such an annual cost would require freight charges as
follows in Bs million:

300,000,000 ton/km. coal and limestone at 3.5 centimos = 10.5
2,800,000,000 ton/km. general freight at 8.03 centimos = 225.1

Total   235.6

It is assumed that the cost of shipment of coal and limestone by rail
would probably have to be some 3.5 centimos per ton/km. or the
equivalent of the cost of alternative shipment by water. This would
result in a rate of about 8.0 centimos per ton/km. for general freight
to which must be added the cost of drayage and unloading for at least
one end of the railroad trip, to be the equivalent of door-to-door truck

service. This extra cost when spread over an average distance of 623 km. equals 2.6 centimos per ton/km., which would thus result in a total cost for rail of 10.6 centimos per ton/km. At an assumed average long-term trucking cost of 14 centimos per ton/km., there would thus be a saving of some 3.4 centimos per ton/km. by the use of rail instead of trucks. For a total of 2,800,000,000 ton/km. of general freight which is indicated in these tentative estimates, the annual saving by using the railroad would be approximately Bs 95 million or slightly over 4 percent return on the original investment. As there is no saving expected on bulk cargo, these would be the total benefits exclusive of passenger traffic. The case for the 1,400 km. National Railroad Network is, therefore, somewhat doubtful even based upon rather optimistic assumptions of the level of traffic which might be achieved over the next twenty years.

The study of the national railroad problem and the possible future building of more railroads, indicates that on the basis of this quite hypothetical data on possible railroad traffic movement from origin to destination twenty years hence, as tentatively prepared by the staff of the Planning Division of the Venezuelan Government, the justification for the building of more railroads is quite doubtful. The highway network is already well along and before many years the main traffic roads should be strengthened to carry as heavy loads as conceivably will be required. Duplication of transport facilities should be avoided. The economy of Venezuela should not be expected to support both railroads and highways. There is not the slightest justification for the 3,000 km. proposed and even if the distance built is cut over half, as is analyzed in this Annex, there is still little justification on the basis of the most probable developments in Venezuela. Fifteen percent of the cost of building such a 1,400 km. rail system could be spent on strengthening enough to carry the loads without excessive maintenance cost. This is a much more sensible procedure. The mission thus recommends that no plans be made for the construction of more railroads in Venezuela, during at least the current planning period. At the end of this period, the situation can be reviewed again.

The Naricual-Matanzas Railroad

The building of this railroad has been formally recommended by several groups of experts in reports submitted to the Railroad Institute. Three fundamental assumptions used in these reports have been questioned by the mission (see Chapter 11). The adjustments required to make the evaluation of the Naricual-Matanzas more realistic are as follows:

a. The cost of building the railroad and providing the rolling stock is estimated at about Bs 300 million for the 338 km., including Bs 60 million to build a bridge across the Orinoco near Ciudad Bolivar. This estimate was based upon an assumed cost of about Bs 700,000 per km., whereas the recently completed Barquisimeto-Puerto Cabello railroad cost Bs 1.7 million per km. A more reasonable estimate would be Bs 1.3 million per km., so that including the bridge, the total would be about Bs 500 million.

b. The reports assume railroad freight rates substantially below the real economic cost of providing service. A rate of 5 centimos per ton/km. on general freight and 1.7 centimos per ton/km. for coal and limestone was assumed. These rates are much lower than is the charge for such commodities in other countries under similar conditions, and would not cover operating costs and depreciation. A proper economic analysis of the railroads would entail the use of cost rates, covering both operations and depreciation, of 8.0 centimos per ton/km. for general freight and of 3.5 centimos per ton/km. for coal and limestone. Actual operating costs alone should be about 1.7 centimos for bulk cargo and 4 centimos for general freight.

c. For the evaluation to be complete there must be included the cost of drayage and handling incident to rail transport, an addition which is necessary in a comparison with truck transport with its door-to-door service. An average of Bs 16 a ton is reasonable as an addition to general freight costs to cover drayage costs at one end of the rail haul. It is assumed that bulk loading at the Matanzas end would cost very little. This would add about 5 centimos per ton/km. for the haul from Matanzas to the Caribbean end of the line, thus bringing the total cost to 13.1 centimos per ton/km. for the haul of general freight by this proposed railroad.

The calculation below relates railroad costs with the alternative means of transporting freight if this railroad is not built. As is discussed in Chapter 11, 800,000 tons of coal and limestone could be brought via coastal vessel at an annual saving of Bs 800,000. For comparison purposes only, it is assumed that the alternative means of transport for general freight would be by truck; water transport would however be cheaper than road transport. For general freight, trucking costs have been estimated at 14 centimos per ton/km. after including the full share of highway maintenance for this traffic. The cost of shipping a ton of steel and general freight by rail between Matanzas and Puerto La Cruz would be about Bs 44 compared to Bs 47 by truck. The annual saving by rail would be about Bs 2,250,000 for general freight. On this basis the net annual saving in operating costs and depreciation by using the railroad would be Bs 1,400,000 (after making a deduction equivalent to the loss incurred by not using water transport).

The calculation of the return on the additional investment required for the Naricual-Matanzas railroad is as follows:

Additional Investment Required	Bs 400,000,000
Annual Benefits	
750,000 tons general freight at savings of Bs 3 per ton	2,250,000
Annual Losses	
800,000 tons coal and limestone at loss of Bs 1 per ton	800,000
Annual Net Benefits	1,450,000
Benefits at a return on original additional investment	0.4%

Some adjustment would be necessary to establish the return during the full life of the project on the net capital invested. Even so, it seems clear that the investment in this railroad would at best yield an extremely low economic return.

In developing coastal shipping on a large scale, the shipment of bulk
cargo and iron and steel to and from the Matanzas area would be of
major importance. The Iron and Steel Institute is starting the manufacture of seamless steel pipe on the basis of imported ingots. The
Institute expected to produce about 45,000 tons of such pipe during
1960 and, after the plant at Matanzas itself begins making ingots on a
large scale, about 295,000 tons will be produced annually. About 80
percent of this piping will have to be shipped to the Maracaibo area.

The Institute has taken bids from two shipping companies for water
shipment and also from a truck company for highway transport to
various parts of Venezuela, especially Puerto La Salina on Maracaibo
Lake. The price quoted by one for water shipment to Puerto La Salina
was Bs 149.60 per ton and, including Bs 44 per ton port charge, the
total cost would be Bs 193.60 per ton. The other shipping line quoted
Bs 120 per ton or Bs 164 per ton including port charges.

The trucking line's price for carrying the same cargo was Bs 116.11
per ton, or 9 centimos per ton/km., which the mission estimates is
probably below full cost for such a trip. Meanwhile, the Iron and Steel
Institute believes that it would be economic to purchase trucks and
carry the pipe themselves at an estimated cost equivalent to 6 centimos
per ton/km., after allowing Bs 10 a ton for unloading.

It is the mission's belief that the truck cost as estimated by the
Institute is much too low. If the materials are actually to be moved by
truck, it would be much better to consider negotiating contracts with
private trucking concerns, if in fact they are able to charge the advantageous rates quoted above. However, the mission believes that it is
probably much cheaper to ship such cargoes by water. It is our opinion
that the cost of water transport might be as much as 40 percent less
than the cost of the transportation of steel pipe by truck.

The estimate of the cost of trucking made by the Iron and Steel
Institute of 3 centimos per ton/km., which with no return cargo would
amount to 6 centimos per ton/km., is an underestimate for the following reasons:

  a. The total estimate of Bs 580,000 for the purchase and five years

457

of operation of a truck is too low. Based on costs supplied by trucking companies, the mission estimates the cost at about Bs 800,000 for the period.

b. The assumption that each truck could travel 270 days a year is too high. An assumption of 250 days is more realistic, according to the experience of the industry in Venezuela.

c. The assumption that each truck could be driven 650,000 kilometers is also too high. Under Venezuelan conditions, and according to the trucking companies, it is more likely that each truck can be driven about 560,000 kilometers.

d. The assumption of a full load of 30 tons one way each trip is too generous and, for practical reasons, probably should be about 10 percent lower.

When adjustments are made to cover these points, the cost would more likely amount to 10 centimos per ton/km., which is higher than the private truckers' quotation noted above.

For a comparison with water shipment, the mission has conservatively assumed that a 10,000-ton ocean-going ship might be used. The maximum cost of such a ship might be Bs 7,600,000, although undoubtedly, under present market conditions for ships the cost would be much lower. The charge for the annual capital might, for calculating purposes only, be put at about 10 percent of the capital required. This would permit the amortization of the ship in 20 years at 8 percent interest. According to available estimates, operating costs might be about equal to the capital charge, so that annual costs would total at most around Bs 1,600,000. However, the operating costs for Venezuelan ships would be high, perhaps bringing the cost to nearly Bs 3,000,000 a year or, say, Bs 8,000 a day per ship.

The cost of a shipment to Puerto La Salina then, would be as follows:

Distance 1,900 km. equals 1,025 nautical miles at 300 nautical miles per 24 hours, 3.5 days each way required plus 10 days unloading and 8 days loading = 25 days.

25 days x Bs 8,000 divided by 10,000 tons = Bs 20.00 per ton
    plus unloading charge   44.00
    plus Orinoco River toll   2.80
        Total   Bs 66.80 per ton

This is in comparison to the Bs 116 per ton quoted for trucking. The mission believes that in the present world of shipping, if this were let on contract the long-term price might even be reduced to about Bs 40 per ton. Further reductions might also be made by reducing port charges. Each ship would probably make 14 trips a year. Two ships would be required to transport an output of 300,000 tons of steel pipe, including 240,000 tons which would go to Maracaibo; one ship would unload part of its cargo at other Caribbean ports. Four ships in all would be required to handle up to 600,000 tons annual output.

Based on this incomplete analysis of the cost of water transport, including the purchase of special ships to carry steel products, our general conclusion is that a careful investigation of this matter is warranted.

STATISTICAL TABLES

TABLE S.1: Gross Domestic Product at 1957 Market Prices

(in Bs million)

	1950	1955	1957	1958	1959
Agriculture, Livestock and Fishing	1,014	1,352	1,507	1,576	1,642
Mining	20	221	383	379	420
Iron ore	5	187	334	334	377
Gold	3	5	7	6	4
Diamonds	4	10	9	7	6
Other	8	18	33	32	32
Petroleum	3,920	5,777	7,472	7,073	7,500
Crude	3,797	5,514	7,135	6,708	7,154
Refined	123	263	337	365	406
Manufactures	1,150	2,004	2,429	2,607	3,012
Industrial	783	1,663	2,105	2,289	2,703
Artisan	367	341	324	318	309
Construction	827	1,363	1,580	1,618	1,707
Water and Electricity	69	159	238	280	336
Commerce	1,726	2,862	3,933	3,809	4,003
Transport	646	870	828	882	965
Communications	53	81	112	119	125
Rent and Interest	1,161	1,752	2,141	2,398	2,664
Services	2,140	2,884	3,224	3,427	3,632
Government	653	774	754	754	691
Education	173	233	283	335	394
Medical	169	202	239	244	273
Recreation	73	87	94	95	104
Other	1,072	1,588	1,853	2,000	2,171
Total GDP	12,727	19,325	23,848	24,164	26,065

Source: *Memoria, 1959*, Banco Central de Venezuela.

TABLE S.2: Contribution of the Oil Sector to the Gross
National Product

(in Bs million)

Year	Taxes Due	Wages Paid	Depreciation Allowance	GNP From Oil Sector	Total GNP (in Bs billion)	Oil as % of Total
1947	748	550[a]	190	1,488	7.9[b]	18.8
1948	1,202	650[a]	246	2,098	9.5[b]	22.1
1949	964	700[a]	325	1,990	10.6[b]	18.8
1950	972	563	420	1,955	10.6	18.4
1951	1,376	623	495	2,491	11.6	21.5
1952	1,474	686	530	2,690	12.5	21.5
1953	1,436	709	558	2,703	13.3	20.3
1954	1,515	780	613	2,908	14.8	19.7
1955	1,776	743	680	3,198	16.0	20.0
1956	2,209	866	731	3,807	17.9	21.2
1957	2,832	988	812	4,632	20.6	22.5
1958	2,972	1,010	836	4,818	22.5	21.4
1959	2,746[c]	998[d]	900	4,644	23.2	20.0

[a] Mission's estimate based on employment figures.

[b] Mission's estimate derived from ECLA estimate of Gross Domestic Product, prepared for the Ministry of Development.

[c] Excludes retroactive tax payments of Bs 221 million.

[d] Excludes retroactive wage rise payments of Bs 32 million.

Sources: *Memorias* of the Ministry of Mines, 1959 and earlier years.
Memoria, 1959, Banco Central de Venezuela.

TABLE S.3: Venezuela's Terms of Trade, 1950-59

(1957 = 100)

	1950	1951	1952	1953	1954	1955	1956	1957	1958	1959
Export Prices[a]	80	82	82	88	88	93	93	100	96	85
Import Prices[b]	80	96	97	93	91	92	96	100	100	100
Terms of Trade	100	85	84	94	97	101	97	100	96	85

[a] Export prices—average value per barrel of oil sold, as given in *Memorias,* Ministry of Mines.

[b] Import prices—as there is no reliable index of Venezuelan import prices, the United Nations series for manufactures exported from Western Europe and the United States are used (U.N. *Monthly Bulletin of Statistics,* June 1960).

TABLE S.4: Profits, Investment & Taxes of Oil Industry, 1943-59

(in Bs million)

Year	Net Profit (After tax)	Net Value of Investment (year end)	Percentage Yield on Investment	Income Tax Liability	Royalty	All Taxes[a] as % of Pre-Tax Profit	Output (million b.p.d.)
1943	117	1,670	7.3	21	82	58	492
1944	243	1,780	14.1	51	131	51	702
1948	1,060	4,682	25.4	497	524	55	1,339
1949	704	5,586	13.7	277	553	60	1,321
1950	970	5,772	17.1	394	629	51	1,498
1951	1,201	5,922	20.5	518	729	55	1,705
1952	1,263	6,364	20.5	553	758	55	1,804
1953	1,261	6,642	19.4	553	787	54	1,765
1954	1,412	6,787	21.0	564	918	53	1,895
1955	1,710	6,655	25.4	688	1,016	52	2,157
1956	2,115	7,770	29.3	870	1,180[b]	52[b]	2,457
1957	2,773	9,388	32.3	1,163	1,526[b]	52[b]	2,779
1958	1,616	9,603	17.0	1,480	1,380	65	2,605
1959	1,321	10,059	13.4	1,245	1,614[c]	69[c]	2,771

[a] Includes income tax, royalty, surface taxes, import duties and miscellaneous taxes, but excludes concession payments of Bs 54 million in 1943/44, Bs 53 million in 1948/49 and Bs 2,248 million in 1956/57.

[b] Excludes concession payments of Bs 1,046 million in 1956 and Bs 1,202 million in 1957.

[c] Includes payment of Bs 221 million assessed on output of earlier years.

Source: *Memoria, 1959*, Ministry of Mines.

TABLE S.5: Real Income Growth, 1950-59

Year	Non-oil Sector[a] (1)	Oil Sector[b] (2)	Total Real Gross Income (1) plus (2)
	Value (in Bs billion)		
1950	8.81	2.45	11.26
1955	13.55	3.48	17.03
1957	16.38	4.63	21.01
1958	17.10	4.82	21.92
1959	18.50	4.64	23.14
	Average Annual Growth Rates (in percentages)		
1950-57	9.3	9.6	9.4
1957-58	4.4	4.1	4.3
1958-59	8.2	−3.7	5.6
1950-59	8.6	7.3	8.3

[a] Gross Domestic Product originating in these sectors in constant prices (1957).
[b] Represents GNP in current prices originating in oil sector, deflated by import price index given in Statistical Appendix, Table S.3.

Sources: Column (1) from Statistical Appendix, Table S.1 and Column (2) from Statistical Appendix, Table S.2.

TABLE S.6: Gross National Product by Major Expenditure Components[a]

(in Bs million at current market prices)

	1950	1951	1952	1953	1954	1955	1956	1957	1958	1959
Consumption	7,785	8,324	8,141	9,157	9,954	11,494	13,076	16,501	16,901	16,312
Private	6,183	6,584	6,311	7,237	7,831	9,253	10,792	13,945	13,328	12,035
Government	1,602	1,740	1,830	1,920	2,123	2,241	2,284	2,556	3,573	4,277
Gross Fixed Investment	2,756	3,159	4,012	4,282	4,993	4,410	5,098	5,950	5,964	6,721
Inventory Change	118	128	395	34	50	210	229	303	350	406
Net Foreign Investment	−102	17	−31	−125	−226	−127	−473	−2,158	−727	−263
Gross National Product	10,557	11,628	12,527	13,348	14,771	15,987	17,930	20,596	22,488	23,176

Expenditure Components as Proportions of GNP
(in percent)

	1950	1951	1952	1953	1954	1955	1956	1957	1958	1959
Consumption	73	72	65	69	68	72	73	80	75	70
Private	59	57	50	54	53	58	60	68	59	52
Government	14	15	15	15	15	14	13	12	16	18
Gross Fixed Investment	27	27	32	32	34	28	29	29	26	29
Inventory Change	1	1	3			1	1	1	2	2
Net Foreign Investment	−1	0	0	−1	−2	−1	−3	−10	−3	−1

[a] See *Note* on following pages.
Source: *Memoria, 1959*, Banco Central de Venezuela, apart from Net Foreign Investment which is taken from Statistical Appendix Table S. 14. The residual "private consumption" therefore differs from the Central Bank estimate.

Note to Table S.6: This Table is based on the national product series given in Table 19-5 of the *Memoria, 1959*, Banco Central de Venezuela, with the following changes:

1. *"Net Foreign Investment"* represents the surplus or deficit (−) in the balance of payments on current account: all errors and omissions have been attributed to the *capital* account, whereas the Central Bank treats half of these as current items in 1958 and 1959, and the whole as current in previous years.

2. *"Private Consumption"* is a residual item, and the series given in the above table differs from the Central Bank residual item only to the extent that "net foreign investment" has been revised.

3. *Revised data.* In making changes to 1. and 2. above, the mission has used revised balance of payments issued by the Central Bank since the publication of its 1959 *Memoria.*

The mission makes only limited use in Chapter 7 of these estimates of major expenditure components. In the mission's judgment, these estimates are useful for indicating the average level of consumption and investment in the last ten years and for deriving the trend for the period. For the reasons given below they must be interpreted with caution in following year-to-year developments, particularly in the last three years.

Private Consumption. The Central Bank series shows a 4 percent decline in consumption between 1957 and 1959, even in current prices. The mission's revision of the series of net foreign investment, as given in the above Table, results in this residual consumption series showing a 14 percent decline in 1957-59. Either decline is improbable in view of the increase in income, the change in income distribution in favor of non-property income, the rise in prices and population, or the Central Bank's direct estimates of increased consumption in 1957/58. Then, as we have just seen, the mission believes that the national income for 1959 is underestimated, and that investment is overestimated. Adjustment for these two factors would result in an increase in the 1959 consumption estimate as compared with 1957. Moreover, the estimate of government consumption which the Central Bank uses in the national accounts is too high. This is most apparent in the inclusion of the expenditures of government service enterprises for wages, goods and services as government consumption expenditures. Actually, the current expenditures of these enterprises should be treated as purchases of intermediary goods and services and therefore excluded from the national expenditure estimates. For this reason, too, the residual series for private consumption would have to be increased.

Fixed Investment. The series is composed of direct estimates of investment by sector (in constant prices) based primarily on estimates of capital goods imports, annual completions of projects under construction, and in some sectors (oil, roads, power) on direct measures of increases in capacity. To be consistent with the income estimates, the construction estimates should be on a work-in-progress basis, and to be reliable as an indicator of year-to-year changes should probably be based, particularly in 1957-59, on something more sensitive to the actual progress of construction than building permits. The estimates for oil, roads and power should also be converted to a work-in-progress basis. The import component is raised by the use of historically-based fixed margins for installation, etc. Finally, imports going into inventory are included in fixed investment. Although the mission could not obtain the information required to adjust the estimates of the Central Bank, we suspect that the 1957 level of investment is understated compared with previous years and that the 1959 level is overstated as compared with 1958. In any event, the 1959 estimate is a preliminary one.

Inventories. Particularly for 1957, the series does not adequately reflect the large increase in inventories which resulted from the rise in imports Bs 3.8 billion in 1956 to Bs 5.8 billion in 1957. Adjustment for the inventory factor would make the increase in the residual item "private consumption" less than the apparent rise of 30 percent over 1956.

Gross National Product. If the Central Bank's GNP series given in the above Table is deflated by either the cost of living or the wholesale price series, there is a *decline* in real GNP between 1958 and 1959. This would seem to be contrary to the 7.8 percent rise in GDP and the 16 percent fall in profits of the oil sector. The Central Bank estimates the fall in the oil sector's contribution to national income at 7 percent: but this is far too small a decline to account for a fall in over-all GNP when output in other sectors has risen 8.2 percent. It would therefore seem that the Central Bank's 1959 estimate, which is the base figure in arriving at GNP, is too low.

TABLE S.7: Gross Fixed Investment by Sector
(Annual averages for 1950-58 in Bs million at 1957 prices)

Sector	Investment		Government as % Total
	Total	Government	
Agriculture	491	265	54
Mining & Oil	1,210	1	—
Manufactures	427	204	48
Electricity	135	50	37
Transport and Communications	650	610	94
Government, Commerce, Services & Housing	1,993	1,114	56
Total	4,906	2,244	46

Note: This table is a reproduction of Table 18-31 in the *Memoria, 1959,* Banco Central de Venezuela. The mission believes the nine-year averages give an acceptable estimate of the level of total investment. The mission also feels that the sectorial divisions give a generally acceptable guide to the composition of investment, despite the comments made on Table S.6 regarding their limitations when integrated on an annual basis into the national expenditure accounts.

With respect to the above series for government investment, the mission also has reservations concerning the estimated average level. In Chapter 4, Table 3, the mission uses estimates of appropriations for public investment based on material prepared by the Ministry of Finance. There are differences between the two series for the last five years which cannot be explained even after adjusting for known differences in concept, with the Central Bank estimate being higher. As it is impossible to determine the volume of investment financed by credit, considerable uncertainty attaches to any estimate of public investment in Venezuela over the last five years.

No separate series for private investment is given by the Central Bank. One can be derived, however, by deducting from the total investment series the estimates of government investment. The mission is prepared to accept this residual item as a rough guide to the relative role and composition of private investment over the decade, though it is clearly subject to many qualifications. On a year-to-year basis, government expenditure estimates shown in Chapter 7, Table 13, suggest that, in view of the very large increase in current expenditures, capital expenditures financed by the national government have declined by as much as Bs 1 billion over the last three years. If the Central Bank's estimates of total investment in 1957-59 shown in Table S.6 are valid, private investment has in fact increased greatly in both 1958 and 1959.

TABLE S.8: Sources of Financing Investment, 1950 & 1955-59

(in Bs million)

	1950	1955	1956	1957	1958	1959
1. Gross Domestic Investment	2,874	4,620	5,327	6,253	6,314	7,127
2. Less: Net Foreign Capital Inflow	101	29	−294	−1,933	−358	140
3. Equals: Gross Domestic Savings	2,975	4,649	5,033	4,320	5,956	7,267
4. Less: Depreciation Allowances of Oil Companies	420	680	731	812	836	900
5. Equals: Gross National Savings	2,555	3,969	4,302	3,508	5,120	6,367
6. Of which: Public	744	1,544	1,931	2,588	2,023	2,080
7. Private	1,811	2,425	2,371	920	3,097	4,287
8. Of which: Undistributed Profits	641	1,061	1,174	1,389	1,278	1,176
9. Depreciation Allowances (exc. oil)	40	125	200	296	349	403
10. Other	1,130	1,239	997	−765	1,470	2,708
Gross National Product	10,557	15,987	17,930	20,596	22,488	23,176

Source: Based on rearrangement of data in *Memoria, 1959,* Banco Central de Venezuela, with exception of Lines 2, 4 and 6. For source of Line 2, see Statistical Appendix, Table S. 14. The balance of payments on current account as shown in Bs
in that table has been adjusted for purposes of this table by deducting foreign
exchange profits as shown in the government accounts. Otherwise, the contribution
of foreign capital to the financing of investment would have been overstated. Line
4 is based on the oil company accounts submitted to the Department of Mines,
and is somewhat higher than the Central Bank estimate of depreciation. The
residual in line 9 is correspondingly lower. For line 6, see Chapter 7, Table 6.

Note: The Central Bank figures used in constructing this table show a precipitous
fall in private savings in 1957, and then a rise to record levels in 1959 (Line 7). This
strains the imagination. As we have seen, (Statistical Appendix, Table S.6) there
are reasons to believe that, while the investment estimates may be reliable as to
level, they give a distorted picture of the time pattern in the last three years. These
distortions are directly reflected in Line 1 and therefore in the annual estimates of
private savings.

TABLE S.9: Government Revenues, 1956/57-1959/60

(in Bs million)

Fiscal Year	Total Revenues	External Sector							Domestic Sector			
		Total External Sector	Oil Income				Import Duties	Income Tax on Iron Ore Cos.	Total Domestic Sector	Direct Taxes	Indirect Taxes	Other
			Total Oil Income	Royalty	Income Tax	Exchange Profit[b]						
1956/57	3,854	3,145	2,463	1,437[c]	856	170	654	27	709	238	355	116
1957/58	4,425	3,605	2,792	1,419[d]	1,013	360	780	33	820	264	445	111
1958/59	5,315	4,290	3,381	1,566	1,446	369	751	159	1,025	425	440	158
1959/60[a]	5,090	3,966	3,140	1,461	1,267	412	765	61	1,124	494	446	184
1960/61[a]	5,240	3,908	2,967	1,433	1,172	362	763	177	1,332	637	497	198
Percentage of the Total												
1956/57	100	81.6	63.9	37.3	22.2	4.4	17.0	0.7	18.4	6.2	9.2	3.0
1957/58	100	81.5	63.1	32.1	22.9	8.1	17.6	0.8	18.5	6.0	10.0	2.5
1958/59	100	80.7	63.6	29.5	27.2	6.9	14.1	3.0	19.3	8.0	8.3	3.0
1959/60	100	77.9	61.7	28.7	24.9	8.1	15.0	1.2	22.1	9.7	8.8	3.6
1960/61	100	74.6	56.6	27.3	22.4	6.9	14.6	3.4	25.4	12.1	9.5	3.8

[a] Estimated.

[b] Profit on operations of differential exchange rates.

[c] Excludes concession payments of Bs 1,667 million.

[d] Excludes concession payments of Bs 451 million.

Sources: Budget speeches of Minister of Finance, 1959 and 1960.

TABLE S.10: Emigration and Immigration

Years	Arrivals of Foreigners	Departures of Foreigners	Net Gain
1948	71,168	34,169	36,999
1949	72,902	46,498	26,404
1950	79,322	51,901	27,421
1951	74,906	50,895	24,011
1952	84,990	56,042	28,948
1953	102,687	66,607	36,080
1954	113,610	67,749	45,861
1955	137,416	79,874	57,542
1956	136,216	91,436	44,780
1957	150,361	104,305	46,056
1958	138,835	122,970	15,865
1959[a]	141,079	124,133	16,946

[a] Preliminary.

Source: *Memoria, 1959*, Banco Central de Venezuela.

TABLE S.11: Estimated Distribution of Work Force

(in thousands)

Activity	1950	1955	1957	1958	1959	1959 (1950 = 100)
Agriculture	704.7	794.7	827.7	824.4	833.3	118.2
Mining	5.7	9.6	11.2	11.5	11.7	204.3
Petroleum	42.7	42.8	45.5	44.3	43.1	100.9
Manufactures[a]	206.9	243.7	253.0	255.1	261.0	126.1
Food	23.7	30.1	31.5	31.9	35.4	149.2
Drink	5.0	6.7	7.4	8.9	9.0	180.3
Tobacco	3.1	3.5	3.4	3.4	3.5	110.0
Textiles	8.5	11.8	13.0	14.3	14.9	175.5
Clothing and shoes	93.8	97.1	92.4	90.7	88.6	94.4
Timber	2.6	5.6	6.0	5.9	5.6	217.1
Furniture	21.7	30.9	30.9	27.8	27.5	126.8
Paper	0.9	1.1	1.5	1.5	1.8	187.7
Printing	5.8	7.2	8.2	9.9	10.9	187.5
Hides and skins	2.6	3.2	3.1	3.2	3.6	138.2
Rubber products	0.6	1.7	2.0	2.1	2.2	339.2
Chemical	4.0	4.3	4.3	4.4	4.8	121.5
Nonmetallic minerals	8.2	10.1	13.4	12.0	12.6	152.9
Metal products	4.3	5.1	5.6	6.1	6.7	154.4
Repair of machinery and construction and repair of vehicles	18.9	18.2	18.9	20.1	20.6	109.6
Other	3.0	7.1	11.1	12.8	13.3	437.0
Construction	91.1	116.2	183.3	179.6	186.8	205.0
Electricity and Water	5.0	7.9	9.5	10.5	11.9	283.7
Commerce	149.7	199.4	223.6	236.7	249.1	166.4
Transport and Communications	52.3	75.2	78.1	82.5	85.6	163.5
Services	341.8	434.9	475.9	498.4	521.8	152.6
Total Employed	1,599.9	1,924.2	2,107.8	2,142.9	2,204.2	137.7
Unemployment	106.4	171.9	168.0	228.4	252.5	237.2
Total Work Force	1,706.3	2,096.0	2,275.8	2,371.3	2,456.7	143.9

[a] Of which, workers in industrial plants ('000s)

	92.3	137.4	151.9	155.8	164.6	178.0

Source: *Memoria, 1959,* Banco Central de Venezuela.

TABLE S.12: Mineral Production by Volume

Mineral	Unit	1950	1955	1957	1958	1959
Iron Ore	million tons	0.2	8.4	15.3	15.5	17.2
Lime	thousand tons	49.1	42.1	55.4	38.6	45.4
Coal	" "	1.4[a]	30.8	34.6	36.5	33.9
Salt	" "	56.4	62.1	85.7	88.2	77.8
Asbestos	tons	190	1,594	7,611	8,266	4,665
Nickel	"	—	—	1,500	2,000	1,348
Manganese	"	—	—	29,874	8,200	4,060
Gold	million grams	1.07	1.90	2.79	2.36	1.67
Diamonds	thousand carats	60.4	141.1	122.6	89.5	94.9

[a] 27.5 thousand tons in 1951.

Source: *Memoria, 1959,* Banco Central de Venezuela.

TABLE S.13: Production and Import of Selected Agricultural Products, 1950 and 1959

Products	Unit	Output 1950	Output 1959	Imports 1950	Imports 1959	Output as % of Consumption 1950	1959
Milk Products	million liters	174	368	200	404	47	48
Eggs	tons	3,300	9,050	8,600	17,900	28	34
Fruits	index	100	161	100	240	decline	
Sesame	thousand tons	5	16	4	10	55	63
Legumes	" "	62	79	14	24	83	78
Copra	" "	5	5	21	48	20	10
Potatoes	" "	29	93	37	9	44	92

Source: *Memoria, 1959,* Banco Central de Venezuela.

TABLE S.14: The Balance of Payments, 1950-1959

Item	1950 Transactions of		1955 Transactions of	
	Oil Companies	Others	Oil Companies	Others
1. Merchandise Exports, f.o.b.	3,472	146	5,535	379
2. Merchandise Imports, f.o.b.	−204	−1,809	−417	−2,895
2a. 1 plus 2	3,268	−1,663	5,118	−2,516
3. *Trade Balance*	*1,605*		*2,602*	
4. Transport & Insurance (net)	−20	−211	−44	−348
5. Investment Income (net)	−1,154	−63	−1,705	−125
6. Other Services (net)	−191	−68	−396	−111
6a. 2a plus 4 plus 5 plus 6	1,903	−2,005	2,973	−3,100
7. *Current Account Balance*	*−102*		*−127*	
8. Direct Private Investment (net)	−143	210	−61	115
9. Short-term Private Capital in U.S. (net)		−26		118
10. Public Long-term Capital (net) [c]				−11
11. Other Capital Movements (net) [d]		−187		124
11a. 6a plus 8 plus 9 plus 10 plus 11	1,760	−2,008	2,912	−2,754
12. *Surplus* (plus) *or Deficit* (minus) in *Balance of Payments*	*−248*		*+158*	

[a] Central Bank's unpublished revised estimate.
[b] Oil sector includes salary remittances abroad by foreign oil workers.
[c] 1959 item includes Bs 302 million of Treasury Notes issued to oil companies.
[d] Corresponds to "Errors and Omissions" item as given by Central Bank.

Source: *Memoria, 1954 and 1959,* Banco Central de Venezuela.

(in Bs million)

	1956 Transactions of		1957 Transactions of		1958 Transactions of		1959[a] Transactions of	
	Oil Companies	Others	Oil Companies	Others	Oil Companies	Others	Oil Companies	Others
	6,446	459	7,940	581	7,137	697	6,708	790
	−734	−3,099	−1,225	−4,602	−794	−4,261	−527	−4,449
	5,712	−2,640	6,715	−4,021	6,343	−3,564	6,181	−3,659
	3,072		*2,694*		*2,799*		*2,522*	
	−63	−376	−112	−578	−59	−515	−35	−520
	−2,106	−282	−2,740	−414	−1,560	−431	−1,291	−302
	−568	−150	−652	−356	−692	−249	−494	−143
	2,975	−3,448	3,211	−5,369	4,032	−4,759	4,361	−4,624
	−473		*−2,158*		*−727*		*−263*	
	1,189	483	2,481	676	212	58	337	80
		65		−25		−186		51
		−1		−19		10		305
		−69		570		−571		−1,648
	4,164	−2,970	5,692	−4,167	4,244	−5,448	4,698	−5,836
	+1,194		*+1,525*		*−1,204*		*−1,138*	

TABLE S.15: Price Movements in Venezuelan & Major Trading Partners
(1953 = 100)

| Year | Venezuela | | U.S.A. | United Kingdom | Germany |
	Cost of Living	Wholesale (National Products)	Wholesale	Wholesale	Wholesale
1950	94	96	94	85	85
1951	100	102	104	100	101
1952	102	102	101	102	103
1953	100	100	100	100	100
1954	100	102	100	100	98
1955	100	101	101	103	101
1956	101	102	104	107	103
1957	98	101	107	110	105
1958	104	104	108	111	106
1959	109	107	108	112	105

Sources: *International Financial Statistics,* IMF, August 1959 and 1960. *Memoria,* 1957-58-59, Banco Central de Venezuela.

TABLE S.16: Net Official Gold and Foreign Exchange Reserves
(in US $ million)

End of	
1950	374
1955	520
1956	937
1957	1,439
1958	1,040
1959	686
June 1960	584

Source: International Monetary Fund.

TABLE S.17: Liquidity of the Private Sector

Year	Money and Quasi Money[a] (in Bs Billion)	GNP (in Bs Billion)	Ratio of Liquidity to GNP (as percentage)
1950	1.7	10.6	16.5
1955	3.1	16.0	19.2
1956	3.7	17.9	20.6
1957	5.2	20.6	25.0
1958	5.9	22.5	26.1
1959	5.9	23.2	25.5
1960 (July)	4.9	24.0[b]	20.4[b]

[a] Includes notes and coins in circulation, private checking accounts, savings, time and foreign currency deposits.

[b] Estimated.

Sources: *International Financial Statistics,* IMF, September 1960; *Memoria, 1959,* Banco Central de Venezuela.

TABLE S.18: Treasury Receipts, Expenditures & Balances, 1949/50-1959/60

(in Bs million)

Fiscal Year	Receipts	Expenditures[a]	Surplus or Deficit (−)	Year-end Treasury Reserves
1949/50	1,896	1,928	−32	340
1950/51	2,126	2,156	−30	309
1951/52	2,297	2,375	−78	231
1952/53	2,370	2,377	−7	224
1953/54	2,658	2,430	228	452
1954/55	2,826	2,797	29	480
1955/56	3,200	3,054	146	626
1956/57	5,521[b]	3,798	1,723	2,349
1957/58	4,876[c]	5,433	−557	1,792
1958/59	5,315	6,250	−935	857
1959/60	5,040	6,155	−1,065	259[d]

[a] Includes payments on debts, which were particularly large in the last three years, and excludes expenditures financed by unrecorded borrowing, which was particularly large in 1956/57 and 1957/58.

[b] Includes oil concession payments of Bs 1,667 million.

[c] Includes oil concession payments of Bs 451 million.

[d] Decline in Treasury reserves was less than deficit because Bs 467 million were borrowed abroad.

Sources: *Anuario Estadistico, 1954; Memoria,* 1955-59, Banco Central de Venezuela.

TABLE S.19: National Income & Product

(in Bs million at current prices)

	1950	1951	1952	1953	1954	1955	1956	1957	1958	1959
Labor Income	5,147	5,494	5,664	6,317	6,874	7,280	8,129	8,786	9,958	11,219
Property Income	2,387	2,641	3,090	3,145	3,670	3,919	4,305	4,969	5,032	4,596
Total Private Income	7,534	8,135	8,754	9,462	10,544	11,199	12,434	13,755	14,990	15,815
Government Oil Income	1,073	1,412	1,482	1,441	1,610	1,858	2,278	3,027	3,289	2,874
Net National Income (At Factor Cost)	8,607	9,547	10,236	10,903	12,154	13,057	14,712	16,782	18,279	18,689
Depreciation	837	984	1,142	1,259	1,287	1,464	1,693	2,014	2,155	2,370
Indirect Taxes	1,134	1,121	1,178	1,225	1,356	1,489	1,552	1,834	2,090	2,163
Minus Subsidies	21	24	29	39	26	23	27	34	36	46
GNP at Market Prices	10,557	11,628	12,527	13,348	14,771	15,987	17,930	20,596	22,488	23,176
Income Remitted Abroad	1,269	1,379	1,454	1,458	1,606	1,906	2,470	3,251	2,097	1,728
GDP at Market Prices (Income Method)	11,826	13,007	13,981	14,806	16,377	17,893	20,400	23,847	24,585	24,904
GDP in 1957 Prices (Product Method)	12,728	14,212	15,248	16,190	17,749	19,325	21,366	23,848	24,164	26,065

Source: *Memoria, 1959,* Banco Central de Venezuela.

TABLE S.20: Functional Distribution of Government Expenditures as Percentage of Total Appropriations, 1954/55-1959/60

	1954/55	1955/56	1956/57	1957/58	1958/59	1959/60
I—*Political and Administrative*	18.7	18.3	16.2	13.6	15.3	14.8
1. General Administration	1.7	1.6	1.2	0.9	1.9	1.3
2. Police & Justice	4.5	4.4	3.5	2.7	3.0	3.6
3. National Defense	11.6	11.3	10.7	9.4	9.8	9.2
4. Foreign Affairs	0.9	1.0	0.8	0.6	0.6	0.7
II—*Economic and Financial*	43.9	45.4	50.7	55.4	47.9	47.9
1. Financial Administration[a]	8.5	7.6	7.2	6.9	7.1	8.8
2. Mining	1.0	0.9	0.9	0.8	1.0	1.0
3. Agriculture & Irrigation	8.0	9.3	7.9	7.9	6.3	5.9
4. Industry	1.7	3.9	4.9	8.3	5.3	5.8
5. Transport & Communications	21.7	20.6	20.1	23.7	24.1	21.9
6. Electricity	0.0	0.7	0.9	1.1	0.0	1.8
7. Tourism	0.8	1.1	2.5	1.2	1.6	0.6
8. Other	2.2	1.3	6.3	5.5	2.6	2.1
III—*Social and Cultural*	26.5	24.9	23.6	20.7	25.4	26.7
1. Health & Social Assistance	8.0	7.9	7.0	6.0	6.7	8.7
2. Social Security	2.0	2.0	1.7	1.6	1.8	2.3
3. Housing & Urban Development	7.9	7.1	8.1	8.3	8.2	5.4
4. Labor	0.5	0.7	0.6	0.3	0.5	0.7
5. Education & Cultural	8.1	7.2	6.2	4.5	8.2	9.7
IV—*Grants to States and Municipalities*	10.5	11.1	9.2	10.2	11.2	10.4
V—*Public Debt*	0.2	0.2	0.2	0.0	0.0	0.0
VI—*Roman Catholic Church*	0.2	0.1	0.1	0.1	0.2	0.2
Total	100.0	100.0	100.0	100.0	100.0	100.0
(Total Appropriations in Bs billion)	2.9	3.0	3.9	6.1	6.5	6.1

[a] Includes the total contribution to CVF.

Source: Commission for Fiscal Administrative Studies (CEFA), Ministry of Finance, September 1959.

TABLE S.21: Measures of the Importance of Petroleum in the Venezuelan Economy, 1921-1959

Year	Oil Output (Mill. bbls.)	Exports		Government Revenues		Contribution to Gross National Product by Oil Sector (in %)	Employment in Oil Industry ('000s)	Wholesale Prices 1956/57=100
		Oil (Bs Mill.)	Oil as % of Total	Oil (Bs Mill.)	Oil as % of Total			
1921	1	12	9	2	2	1	n.a.	80
1929	137	594	76	50	13	n.a.	n.a.	77
1936	155	684	90	70	30	8[a]	13.8	55
1943	179	786	92	155	45	n.a.	19.0	75
1948	490	3,340	96	1,110	63	22	57.5	101
1950	547	3,472	96	1,010	54	18	42.6	96
1955	787	5,535	94	1,714	57	20	42.8	103
1957	1,014	7,940	93	2,680[b]	63[b]	23	45.5	100
1958	951	7,137	91	2,713	58	21	44.3	102
1959	1,011	6,708	90	3,220	60	20	43.1	104

[a] Tax and wage payments as percentage of *net* national income.
[b] Would be Bs 3,822 million (72 percent) if oil concession payments of Bs 1,202 million were included.

Sources: *Memorias* of the Central Bank and the Mines Department; *Anuario Estadistico* of the Department of Development; *Ingreso Nacional de Venezuela*; Statistical Appendix, Table S.2.

TABLE S.22: Comparable Earnings of Selected Occupations in Venezuela and United States Manufacturing Industry

(in US $)

	VENEZUELA		UNITED STATES	
	Average Basic Wage	Total Earnings Including Supplements	Average Basic Wage	Total Earnings Including Supplements
Skilled Workers and Laborers:	*Average Hourly Earnings*			
Carpenters	1.01	1.83	2.60	3.13
Electricians	1.16	2.10	2.80	3.37
Machinists	1.29	2.32	2.79	3.36
Mechanics	1.10	2.02	2.58	3.10
Helpers	0.64	1.13	2.13	2.56
Guards	0.67	1.22	2.16	2.60
Janitors	0.60	1.10	1.71	2.06
Laborers	0.59	1.10	1.96	2.36
Truck Drivers: Light Vehicle	0.83	1.38	2.16	2.60
Medium Vehicle	0.72	1.39	2.29	2.75
Heavy Vehicle	0.94	1.77	2.48	2.98
Office Workers:	*Average Weekly Earnings*			
Clerks	70.01	105.37	78.91	94.93
Calculating Machine Operators	52.54	74.93	72.20	86.86
Card-Punch Operators	50.75	64.18	70.37	84.66
Secretaries	96.72	130.75	85.68	103.77
Stenographers	62.39	84.48	75.71	91.08
Switchboard Operators	41.79	56.72	70.16	84.40
Draftsmen	95.82	131.04	112.35	135.16
Typists	41.79	56.72	66.27	79.72

Sources: *Wages and Related Benefits,* Department of Labor; Bulletin No. 1240-22, 1958 and 1959; *Fringe Benefits 1957,* Chamber of Commerce of U.S. 1958, p. 10; a flat fringe benefit rate of 20.3 percent of direct wages has been computed; *Estudio sobre Salarios Basicos y Prestaciones Sociales,* Camara de Industriales, Caracas, October 1959.

AVENSA, see Aerovias Venezolanas, S.A.
Acarigua, 393, 434, 438
Accion Democratica, 7
Achaguas, 253
Administration, Public: centralization, 9, 440
  composition, 9
  proposed reforms, 15 n. 1
Aerovias Venezolanas, S.A., 269-71
Africa, North, 117, 121
Agrarian Reform Law (1960), 141, 146
Agriculture: credit, 42, 55, 57-58, 145, 147, 152, 158, 166-70
  education program, 157, 353-55
  exports, 143
  extension services, 55, 98, 142, 153, 154-157, 161-63
  farming methods, 141, 146, 153, 155
  government expenditure: capital, 54, 148-50, 157, 170, 179, 192 *table 29*
  current, 38, 55, 145, 159 *table 25*, 161, 163, 164, 193 *table 30*
  imports, volume of, 98, 143, 475 *table S.13*
  land use and tenure, 5, 113, 139, 140 *table 21*, 141-42
  machinery, 159, 165-66
  marketing, 176-78
  market regulation, 171-72
  output, 143, 144 *table 23*
  pests and pesticides, 159, 162, 164-65
  see also Chemicals
  prices, 143, 145, 171, 174-76
  protection policy, 98, 142, 145, 172
  research, 55, 148, 159-61
  settlement, 48, 56, 98, 147-54 *table 24*
  subsidies, 55, 152, 158
  see also Agrarian Reform Law, *Banco Agricola y Pecuario, Centro de Investigaciones Agronomicas, Corporacion Venezolana de Fomento,* Fertilizers, Housing, agricultural, *Instituto Agrario Nacional,* Irrigation, Livestock, *Plan Ganadero,* Soils, Transport, roads *and* specific crops
Agriculture and Livestock, Ministry of, *see Ministerio de Agricultura y Cria*
Agua Blanca River, 180, 186
Agua Viva, 259, 435

Air transportation, *see* Transport
  see also Aerovias Venezolanas, Linea Aeropostal Venezolana
Aluminum, 51, 62, 195, 212, 296
American and Foreign Power Co., 282
Anaco, 231, 371, 391
Andes, 3, 4, 5, 114, 139, 140, 146, 147, 150, 166, 197, 244, 432-33
Anzoategui State, 181, 352, 384
Apon River, 181
Apure State, 438-39
Apurito, 253
Aragua State, 437
Araguita, 259
Araya Peninsula, 234
Argentina, 119, 121, 135, 212, 383
Arismendi, 253
Aroa, 148, 436
Asbestos, 5, 97
Association of Telecommunications Technicians, 307
Automobile assembly and parts, 194, 195, 196, 214
Autonomous Institute of Railroads, 262-265 *passim*

BAP, *see Banco Agricola y Pecuario*
Balance of payments, 34, 76, 105-106 *table 12*, 111, 411 *table A.5*, 476 *table S.14*
  see also Capital outflow, Exports, Foreign exchange, Imports, Investment, foreign, Terms of trade
Bananas and plantains, 153, 156, 421, 435
Banco Agricola y Pecuario, 40, 58, 158, 161, 166-78 *passim*
Banco Central, see Central Bank
Banco Industrial de Venezuela, 213, 218
Banco Obrero, 39, 359, 363, 365, 371
Barbula, 386, 391
Barcelona, 51, 62, 197, 220, 246, 247, 249, 259, 262, 282, 302, 336
Barinas, 48, 161, 181, 244, 247, 249, 269, 316, 416, 434-35
Barinas State, 57, 139, 151, 189-90, 434
Barloventa, 141, 181, 182, 189-90, 220, 436
Barquisimeto, 62, 197, 231, 246, 247, 249, 259, 262, 282, 302, 336, 348, 376, 383

485

Bauxite, 5, 33
Beans, 97, 176, 422, 435
Betancourt, Romulo, 7
Beverages, 194, 196, 205
Bocono River, 180, 187
Bolivar, Simon, 6
Bolivar State, 96, 352
Brazil, 3, 208, 212, 383
Bridges, *see* Transport
British Guiana, 3
Budget: balance of, 34, 35, 88 *table 6*, 108, 110, 111 *table 13*, 112
  cash balances, 39-40, 72, 105, 108, 110, 111 *table 13*, 479 *table S.18*
  debt service, 11, 39-40, 111 *table 13*
  government borrowing, 36, 40, 70, 71, 73, 74, 105, 107-108, 111 *table 13*
  development stabilization fund, proposed, 70
  projections and prospects, 37, 38 *table 2*, 39-40
  see also Government expenditure, Taxation
Building industry, 100
Building materials, 194, 195, 372
Bus service, *see* Transport
Butter, 430
Butylene, *see* Petrochemicals

CADAFE, *see* Compania Anonima de Administracion y Fomento Electrifico
CANTV, *see* Compania Anonima Nacional Telefonos de Venezuela
CBR, *see* Consejo de Bienestar Rural
CVF, *see* Corporacion Venezolana de Fomento
Cabimas, 286, 335, 388
Cabrera, 286
Cabruta, 253
Cacao: cultivation, 5, 140, 164, 418-19, 438
  credit, 167
  exports 4, 98, 143
  marketing and prices, 171
  protection, 176
  yields, 418
Cagua, 162
Calabozo, 180, 247, 259, 424
Caldera, Rafael, 7
Camatagua, 180
Camoruco River, 180, 186
Canada, 33, 120, 121, 133, 135
Cantaura, 391, 393
Capital inflow, *see* Balance of payments, Budget, government borrowing, Investment, foreign private

Capital outflow, 11, 34-36, 87, 104, 107, 108, 111
Carabobo State, 437
Caracas: as centre of government, 3, 9, 440
  communications, 53, 262, 302, 304, 307-309, 314, 315
  electric power, 231, 282, 293, 296
  health services, 383, 386, 391
  in agricultural development, 147, 167, 177
  in manufacturing development, 5, 62, 197, 217, 220, 242, 247, 248
  schools, 335, 339, 348
  housing and urban planning, 68-9, 71, 85, 362-63, 374, 376, 377-79
  sanitation, 85, 396, 398, 399, 402
Carenero Fisheries School, 339
Cariaco River, 181
Caribbean Sea, 3, 9, 244, 279
Caroni River, 221, 279
  see also Electric power
Carora, 259, 437
Carupano, 253, 259, 278, 310
Casigua, 232
Catatumbo River, 181, 188
Cattle, 4, 5, 139, 146, 167, 184, 424
  see also Plan Ganadero
Caucagua, 259
Caustic soda, *see* Chemicals
Cement, 196, 199, *see also* Building materials
Central Bank, 72, 86, 91, 108, 143, 168, 361
  policy of, 35
Central University (Caracas), 387
Centro de Investigaciones Agronomicas, 160
Chama River, 181, 188
Cheese, 430
Chemicals: government expenditure, 229-230
  manufacture of, 199, 214, 227-31
  see also Fertilizers, Government enterprises, Petrochemicals
Chile, 33, 212, 282
Chlorine, *see* Chemicals
Cigarettes, *see* Tobacco products
Clay, 194, 195, 199
Climate, 141, 159, *see also* Rainfall
Clothing manufacture, 96, 195, 205
Coal and coke, 5, 97, 199, 221, 265
Coffee: cultivation, 5, 140, 156, 164, 418-419, 438
  credit, 167
  exports, 4, 98, 143, 418

Coffee—*Continued*
  International Coffee Agreement, 418
  prices and protection, 171, 174, 176
  yields, 418
Cojedes River, 180, 186
Colombia, 3, 66, 383
Columbus, 6
Comision de la Reforma Agraria, 146, 148
Commerce, 100
Commercial banks: credit, 107, 108, 109, 168, 213
  deposits, 40, 109
  regulation of, 108, 109, 168, 215-16
Commercial Treaty with U.S.A., 207
Commission to study the Fiscal System of Venezuela, 40-41, 93, 113
Commission on Public Administration, 15
Communications, Ministry of, 53
  Direccion de Telecommunicaciones, 301, 303, 308-19 *passim*
  National Co-ordinating Commission on Telecommunications Services, 307-319 *passim*
  Port Captaincy, 278
Compania Anonima de Administracion y Fomenta Electrifico, 282, 284-99 *passim*
Compania Anonima Nacional Telefonos de Venezuela, 52, 301-19
Congreso de Vivienda, 359
Consejo de Bienestar Rural, 149, 161-62
Consejo Nacional de Niños, 359
Contada, 259
Cordilleras Mts., 197
Cordiplan, 265, 275, 452
Corn, *see* Maize
Coro, 189, 283, 376
Corporacion Venezolana de Fomento, 58, 161, 167, 214, 215-18, 234, 240-41, 281
Cotton, 5, 97, 143, 171, 174, 176, 198, 421, 434
  see also Textiles
Cuba, 383
Cuidad Bolivar, 244, 249, 273, 282, 302, 310, 314, 336, 339, 382
Cumana, 179, 259, 273, 286, 336, 444
Currency and credit, *see* Central Bank, Commercial banks, Money supply
  see also Agriculture, credit, Manufacturing, credit

Dairying, 5, 97, 143, 428-31, 438

Dairy products, 143, 176
  milk, 97, 172, 177, 428-31
  milk subsidy, 38, 98, 145, 175, 429, 430
  poultry and eggs, 97, 165, 426-27
Defense, Ministry of, 388, 390
Delta Amacuro, 416-17
Detergents, *see* Petrochemicals
Development, Ministry of, 218, 221, 236, 241
Development program, *see* Government expenditure, proposed
Diamonds, 5, 97
Direccion de Planificacion Agropecuaria, *see* Ministry of Agriculture
Distribudora Venezolana de Azucares, *see* Sugar
Dos Caminos, 259
Dry dock and shipyard, 232-33, *see also* Government enterprises

Ecuador, 66
Education: buildings, 326-28, 331, 338 *table 64*, 340, 341-43 *table 66*, 346 *table 68*
  commercial schools, 340
  enrollments: academic secondary, 345 *table 67*
    commercial, 342 *table 65*
    industrial, 335-36, 337 *table 63*
    normal, 330 *table 60*
    primary, 332, 324 *table 57*
    secondary, 333-36 *tables 61 & 62*, 345 *table 67*
    universities, 350 *table 71*, 352 *table 73*
  government expenditure, 38, 42, 45, 64, 328, 331, 339, 340, 347
  importance and aims of program, 63, 320-321
  industrial schools, 237, 335-40
  Instituto Nacional de Cooperacion Educativa, 236-37, 355
  Institutos pedogogicos, 339, 348
  intermediate, 332-335
  Normal schools, 329-31
  primary, 64, 320, 322-32
  teachers, 329-31
  universities, 349-53
  see also Agriculture, education program, Manufacturing, vocational training
Education, Ministry of, 236-37, 331, 332, 335, 353
El Baul, 253
El Cenizo, 179, 181, 187

Electric power, 99-100, 281-300
  consumption, 283, 291-92
  generating capacity, 51, 99, 282, 283-85
    table 45, 292 table 46
  government expenditure, 43, 51-52, 295,
    298 table 48
  hydro projects: Caroni-Macagua, 51,
    62, 99, 286, 287-89, 295, 297
    Caroni-Guri, 51, 71, 289-95 table 47,
    440
    National Plan of Electrification, 282
    rates, 299
    thermal plants, 52, 284, 286-87, 296,
    297
Electricidad de Caracas, 282, 284, 287,
  292, 293
Electricité de France, 281, 294
El Guapa, 259
El Palmar, 187, 439
El Tigre, 286, 314, 315, 392
El Vigia, 435
Encontrados, 262
Energia Electrica de Maracaibo, 282
Erosion, see Agriculture, soils
Escalante River, 181
Ethylene, see Petrochemicals
Exports: agricultural products, 143
  manufactures, 196
  petroleum, 482 table S.21
  value and volume, 101-2 table 9
  see also Balance of payments, Pe-
  troleum

FAO, see Food and Agriculture Organi-
  zation
Falcon State, 141, 181, 189, 437
Federal District, see Caracas
Fertilizers: in agriculture, 154-56, 159,
  163-64, 228
  imports, 228
  manufacture of, 164, 194, 227-29
  subsidy program, 55, 164, 228
  see also Chemicals
Finance, Ministry of: Customs Depart-
  ment, 278
  Port Services Department, 277, 278
Financial Institutions, see Central Bank,
  Commercial banks
Fisheries, 444
Flood control, see Irrigation and drain-
  age
Food manufacture, 96, 194, 195, 196, 205,
  214
Food and Agriculture Organization, 354

Foreign exchange: controls, 32, 34-36
  exchange rate, 31, 74, 77, 93, 104
  and protection, 31
  for petroleum, 24
  reserves, 34, 72, 101, 105, 106, 478 table
    S.16
  see also Balance of payments
Forests and forestry, 141, 142, 435, 441-
  443
  forest products, 441
  Forestry Department, 441
France, 121, 135
Fruit, 98, 141, 143, 156, 176, 423, 438
Furniture, 205, 214

Gallegos, President, 7
Gasoline: price, 247; tax on, 40, 261
Germany, West, 85, 124
Glass, 199
Goats, 425, 437
Gold, 4, 5, 97
Gomez, Juan Vincente, 7
Government enterprises, 6, 39, 58-61
  chemicals, 61, 96, 227-31
  gas pipelines, 25, 60-61, 231-32
  iron and steel, 58-60, 72, 96, 221-26
  petrochemicals, 60, 226-27
  petroleum refining, 25, 231
  shipyard, 61, 232-33
  salt and sugar, 234-35
  see also Venezuelan Petroleum Corporation
Government expenditure, past, 11, 35,
  37-8, 85, 88, 89, 110, 111 table 13,
  481 table S.20
  see also Budget
Government expenditure, proposed, 38-
  39, 41-44 table 3, 45-6, Ch. 5 passim,
  70-75
  agriculture: capital, 192 table 29
    current, 193 table 30
    education, 356 table 74, 357
    electric power, 298 table 48
    health, 392 table 85
    housing, 375 table 80
    irrigation, 191 table 28
    manufacturing, 243 table 34
    sanitation, 403 table 89
    telecommunications, 319 table 56
    transport, 280 table 44
    see also Budget
Government Planning Office, 18, 366
Government revenue: composition, 89,
  414 table A.7, 472 table S.9

Government revenue—*Continued*
  development of, 11, 88, 111 *table 13,*
    472 *table S.9*
  prospects, 37, 72, 414 *table A.7*
  see also Taxation
Gran Sabana, 439
Gross domestic product, 83 *table 4,* 463
    table S.1
  see also Gross national product
Gross national product: composition, 28
    table 1, 8, 467 *table S.6*
  growth of, 27, 82, 466 *table S.5*
Guacara, 231
Guanapito, 187
Guanare, 162, 179, 253, 259
Guanare River, 180, 187
Guanta, *see* Puerto la Cruz
Guarico, 179
  river, 180
  state, 393
  see also Irrigation, Guarico project
Guasdualito, 279
Guataparo, 179, 190
Guayana Highlands, 4, 5, 62, 439-40
Guigue, 197
Guiria, 253
Guri, *see under* Electric power

Health: doctors and nurses, 383-87, 391
  government expenditure, 45, 67, 392
    table 85
  health services, 387-94
  present conditions, 380-83
Health, Ministry of, 369, 380, 382, 387,
    388
  Department of Demography, 382
  Division de Ingeneria Sanitaria, 359,
    402
  Seccion de Vivienda Rural, 359, 363,
    365
Hides and skins, 198, 205
Hogs, 156, 165, 425
Hotels, 39, 45, 85
Housing: Architecture, Town Planning
    and Construction Ordinance of Cara-
    cas, 362
  agricultural, 152-53, 167, 369
  'core' and unfinished houses, 370-74
  credit, 362, 363, 365, 367-74
  government expenditure, 42, 45, 66,
    363, 369, 370
  ranchos, 66, 360-62, 366, 374
  statistics, 360 *table 75*
  see also Caracas, housing and urban
    planning, Urban planning

IAN, *see Instituto Agrario Nacional*
ILO, *see* International Labor Organiza-
    tion
INCE, *see Instituto Nacional de Co-
    operacion Educativa*
INOS, *see Instituto Nacional de Obras
    Sanitarias*
IVP, *see* Venezuelan Institute of Petro-
    chemicals
IVSS, *see* Venezuelan Institute of Social
    Security
Immigration, 30, 91, 96, 145, 214, 238-39,
    473 *table S.10*
Import substitution, 95, 96, 98, 103, 196,
    212
Imports, 34-5, 90, 92, 102 *table 9,* 248
  composition, 102 *table 10-*103
  growth, 28, 96, 102
  tariff policy, *see* Protection, *see also*
    Balance of payments
Income: distribution, 81, 112-14, 197
  from labor and property, 480 *table
    S.19*
  per capita income, 3, 29, 82, 112, 361
  standard of living, 4, 11, 56, 112
Income tax, *see* Taxation
India, 219
Industrial Advisory Council, 241
Industrial estates, 219-20
Industry, Department of, 241
Instituto Agrario Nacional, 148-51, 161,
    167, 181, 359, 363, 365
*Instituto Autonomo Diques y Astilleros
    Nacional, see* Dry dock and shipyard
Instituto de Deportes, 359
*Instituto Nacional de Cooperacion Edu-
    cativa, see* Education
Instituto Nacional de Nutricion, 383
Instituto Nacional de Obras Sanitarias,
    39, 65, 286, 359, 396, 402-3
Instituto de Vivienda de Maracaibo, 359
International Bank for Reconstruction
    and Development, 218
International Labor Organization, 237
International Power of Canada, 283
Investment: domestic private, 35, 40, 61,
    86, 111, 213, 469 *table S.7*
  foreign private, 40, 55, 85-6, 96, 210,
    214, 471 *table S.8*
  government, *see* Government expendi-
    ture, capital rate of, 85
  see also Capital outflow, Capital inflow
Iran, 117, 127, 132
Ireland, 33

Iron and iron ore, 5, 32-3, 62, 96, 199, 212, 221
Iron and Steel Institute, 60, 221, 223-25, 456
see also Government enterprises
Irrigation and drainage: existing program and expenditure, 161, 180-82
flood control, 187, 188-90
government expenditure, 57, 98, 187, 189, 191 table 28
projects: Bocono—Masparro—Tucupido, 57, 71, 180, 187-88, 190
Guarico, 57, 85, 148, 180, 181, 182-86, 416-17
Majaguas, 57, 180, 186-87, 190
Italy, 121, 124

J. B. see Junta de Beneficencia
Japan, 121, 282
Juan Griego, 339
Junta de Beneficencia, 388
Junta of Government, 7
Justice, Ministry of: Prisons Medical Service, 388

Korean War, 127
Kuwait, 132

LAV see Linea Aeropostal Venezolana
Labor force: 4, 91-2 table 7, 99, 202-3, 235, 236-39, 474 table S.11
growth, 29-30, 91, 412 table A.6
unemployment, 13, 91
see also Trade unions
Labor Law, see Trade unions
Labor, Ministry of 216, 236
La Flecha, 253
La Florida, 303
La Fria, 231, 262, 285, 436
La Grita, 146, 434
La Guaira, 248, 262, 272, 273, 275, 302, 363
Lagunillas, 231, 259
La Mariposa, 52, 284, 286
Land settlement, see Agrarian Reform Law and under Agriculture
La Pastora, 303
Lara State, 437
Larrazabal, Admiral, 7
Las Mercedes, 253
Las Piedras, 269, 273
Latin American Free Trade Association, 212
Leather, see Hides and skins
Libya, 117, 121

Lime, 97
Limestone, 265
Limon River, 181
Linea Aeropostal Venezolana, 39, 50, 269-71
Livestock, 97, 143, 169, 176
see also Plan Ganadero
llanos, 3, 5, 97, 139, 438
Los Barrancos, 253
Los Teques, 197, 310
Luz Electrica de Venezuela, 282, 293

MAC, see Ministerio de Agricultura y Cria
MOP, see Ministerio de Obras Publicas
Macagua, 51, 221
Machiques, 436
Maderero, 303
Maiquetia, 267-68, 270
Maize, 5, 97, 160, 164, 166, 171, 174, 175, 176, 178, 415-16, 434
price, 415
Majaguas Creek, 180
Manganese, 5, 33, 97
Manioc, 422
Mantecal, 253
Manufacturing: costs, 204
credit, 6, 42, 55, 57-8, 96, 213, 215-19
exports, potential, 209
government expenditure: capital, 54, 219, 242
current, 55
growth, 27, 96, 193-96, 216
investment: private domestic, 213-14
foreign, 214, 220
output by category, 195 table 31
raw materials, 198-99, 222
tariffs, 204-06 table 33
technical assistance, 218-19, 242
vocational training, 236-37, 355
wage rates, 199, 200 table 32-202, 239-40, 483 table S.22
see also Import substitution, Labor force, Protection
Maracaibo, 62, 197, 231, 247, 259, 267-69, 272, 273, 275, 282, 302, 315, 335, 383
Basin, 3, 5, 139
Lake, 3, 48, 57, 188, 231, 244, 249, 275
Straits Bridge, 260, 276
Maracay, 62, 160, 197, 282, 286, 302, 335, 354, 415
Masparro River, 180, 187
Matanzas, 265-67, 272
Maturin, 267, 314, 336, 438

Meat production, 97, 139, 173, 176, 177, 424, 439
  air lift, 174, 269-70
Merida, 285, 317, 336, 376, 393, 432
Merida State, 197
Metals, 194
Mexico, 212, 383
Middle East Oil, 117, 120-36 *passim*
Milk *see* Dairy products
Mines, Ministry of, 359
Mining, 6, 32-4, 96-7, 475 *table S.12*
Ministerio de Agricultura y Cria, 156-57, 161-62, 167, 178, 181, 353, 354
  Direccion de Planeficacion Apropecauria, 149, 191
Ministerio de Obras Publicas, 48, 244, 254, 339
  Direccion de Edificios, 359
  Direccion de Urbanismo, 359
  Highway Division (Planning Department), 256, 261
  Port Department, 275, 277, 278
Miranda State, 189, 437
Mobil Oil Company, 393
Monagas State, 352
Money Supply, 36, 479 *table S.17*
  factors influencing, 107-11 *passim*
Moron, 62, 164, 199, 227, 231, 262, 268

Naricual, 199, 221, 262, 265-67
National Federation of Teachers, 236
Natural gas, 51, 199, 231-32, 291, 296
  see also Government enterprises, gas pipelines
New York, 271, 316
Nickel, 5, 97
Norway, 85
Nueva Esparta State, 315, 352
Nueva Granada, 303

OPEC, *see* Organization of Petroleum Exporting Countries
Oil seeds, 143, 176, 419
  sesame, 97, 172, 173, 419, 434
Onions, 171, 174, 422-23
Organization of Petroleum Exporting Countries, 21, 124, 133
Organization Pro-Venezuela, 371
Orinoco Mining Company, 279
Orinoco River, 3, 4, 5, 49, 139, 181, 221-222, 244, 272, 279

POE, *see* Programa de Obras Extraordinarias
Paints, 194

Palmar River, 181
Pan American Health Organization, 391
Pan American Highway, 188, 259
Pan American World Airways, 269
Pao River, 180, 186
Paper, 205, 211
Paraguana Peninsula, 376, 437
Paraguay, 212
Paria Peninsula, 3
Per capita income, *see under* Income,
Perez Jiminez, Marcos, 7, 9
Peritos, 157, 354-55
Peru, 33, 66, 212
Pests and pesticides, *see under* Agriculture
Petrochemicals, 199, 226-27
  see also Chemicals, Government enterprises, Venezuelan Institute of Petrochemicals
Petroleum: concessions, 25, 87, 110
  exchange rate, *see* Foreign exchange
  exports, 11, 21, 82-3, 106, 196, 482 *table S.21*
  foreign exchange receipts, 6, 20-21
  foreign investment, 105
  freight rates, 129, 132
  government investment, 134
  government revenue (royalties and taxation) 11, 23, 83, 126, 128, 409 *table A.3*
  —and G.N.P., 6, 20-21, 26, 82, 84, 410 *table A.4*, 464 *table S.2*
  non-Venezuelan supplies, 22, 116-120 *tables 14-16*
  operating costs, 128, 132
  output, 104, 134, 407 *table A.1*, 482 *table S.21*
  prices, 21, 84, 104, 120-22 *table 17*, 123-124, 135
  profits, 130-31, 408 *table A.2*, 465 *table S.4*
  prospects, 12, 131-36
  see also Balance of payments, Venezuelan Petroleum Corporation
Plan Ganadero, 169-70, 424
  see also Livestock
Plantains, *see* Bananas and plantains
Political parties, 7, 58
Polyprophylene, *see* Petrochemicals
Polyvinyl-chloride, *see* Petrochemicals
Popular Housing Institute, 371
Population: distribution, 4, 361 *table 76*, 366
  growth, 4, 82, 91, 323, 366, 395, 412 *table A.6*

Population—*Continued*
  Indian, 4, 440
  see also Labor force
Porlamar, 315
Ports: administration, 50, 272, 278-79
  capacity, 274 *table 42*
  government expenditure, 38, 49, 273, 275
  see also Transport, shipping
Portuguesa State, 48, 57, 139, 151, 161, 189, 416-17, 434-35
Potatoes, 97, 163, 171, 422
Poultry and eggs, *see* Dairy products
Practicos, 157, 355
Prices: general level, 93, 104, 201, 209, 464 *table S.3,* 478 *table S.15*
  see also Protection
Programa de Obras Extraordinarias, 8, 46, 89, 90
Propylene, *see* Petrochemicals
Protection: tariff policy, 6, 30-31, 94 *table 8,* 95, 207-9
  —in agriculture, 32, 98, 142, 145, 172
  —in manufacturing, 95, 204-11
Public Works, Ministry of, *see Ministerio de Obras Publicas*
Puerto Ayacucho, 253, 279
Puerto Cabello, 51, 62, 197, 227, 231, 246, 248, 262, 272, 273, 277, 284, 286, 302, 388, 392
Puerto La Cruz (with Guanta, its port area), 51, 62, 197, 220, 247, 248, 262, 266, 272, 273, 277, 286, 298, 303
Puerto Nutrias, 253, 279
Puerto Ordaz, 5, 198, 220, 221, 279, 286, 368, 374
Puerto Paez, 253, 279
Punto Fijo, 51, 283, 297, 336
Pyrites, 228

Race tracks, 45, 85
Railroads, *see* Transport
Rainfall, 139-41, 435, 438, 439
Ranchos, see Housing
Rice, 5, 97, 164, 171, 174, 175, 183-86, 416-17, 435
  prices, 176, 417
  Rice Plan, 167
Roads, *see* Transport
Rubber, 211

Salinas de Araya, 273
Salt, 5, 97, 234-5
  see also Government enterprises
San Bonifacio Valley, 181, 182, 189, 436

San Carlos, 179, 436
San Cristobal, 3, 242, 244, 246, 247, 264, 285, 310, 335, 376, 386, 432
Sanitation: government expenditure, 42, 45, 66, 398, 402, 403 *table 89*
  present conditions, 65-6, 394-96
  sewage, 399-402
  water supply, 397-99
  see also Agriculture, resettlement, Housing, *Instituto Nacional de Obras Sanitarias*
San Felipe, 393
San Felix, 48, 49, 50, 51, 246, 249, 253, 264, 275, 278, 286
San Fernando de Apure, 244, 253, 270, 279
San Juan de Los Morros, 253, 259, 393
San Lorenzo, 51, 286, 297
Santa Barbara, 429, 436
Santo Domingo River, 181, 187
Sarare, 179
Sarare River, 180
Sardines, 171, 444
Saudi Arabia, 124, 132
Savings, 86-91, 471 *table S.8*
  public, 88
  private, 87, 90-1, 104
Seed, 154-56
Segovia Highlands, 437
Servicio Shell Para el Agricultor, 161-162, 164
Sesame, *see* Oil seeds
Shipping, *see* Transport
Shipyard, *see* Dry dock and shipyard
Shoup, Carl S., 112
  see also Commission to study the Fiscal System of Venezuela
Silk and wool, *see* Textiles
Sisal, 171, 174, 420, 421
  rope, 196
  packing, 205
Soap, 205
Soils, 5, 57, 98, 139-41, 163-64, 434, 435-436, 438
  soil surveys, 181, 182
Standard of living, *see under* Income
Statistics, 16
Steel: government investment, 223-24
  products, 222-23, 266, 272
  and protection, 207
  see also Government enterprises, Iron and Steel Institute
Suata-Taiguaiguay, 179, 180, 190
Sucre State, 141, 147, 181, 182, 189, 352, 437